W.A.C.

W.A.C. BENNETT and the Rise of British Columbia

With a New Afterword

David J. Mitchell

Douglas & McIntyre
Vancouver/Toronto

To my father

Copyright © 1983 by David J. Mitchell
Afterword copyright © 1995 by David J. Mitchell

95 96 97 98 99   5 4 3 2 1
First paperback edition

All rights reserved. No part of this book may be reproduced, stored in a retrieval system or transmitted in any form or by any means, without the prior written permission of the publisher or, in the case of photocopying or other reprographic copying, a licence from CANCOPY (Canadian Reprography Collective), Toronto, Ontario.

Douglas & McIntyre Ltd.
1615 Venables Street
Vancouver, British Columbia V5L 2H1

Canadian Cataloguing in Publication Data
Mitchell, David J. (David Joseph), 1954-
    W. A. C. Bennett and the rise of British Columbia
    ISBN: 978-1-55365-773-6
    1. Bennett, W. A. C. (William Andrew Cecil), 1900-1979.
2. Prime ministers—British Columbia—Biography. 3. British Columbia—Politics and government—1952-1972* I. Title.
FC3827.1.B45M58 1994   971.1'04'092   C9510033-4
F1088.B45M57 1995

Design by Barbara Hodgson
Cover design by DesignGeist
Cover photograph by Malcolm Parry
Printed and bound in Canada by Best Gagné Book Manufacturers Ltd.
Printed on acid-free paper

The publisher gratefully acknowledges the assistance of the Canada Council and the British Columbia Ministry of Tourism, Small Business, and Culture for its publishing programs.

CONTENTS

	Preface	vi
	Acknowledgements	ix
1	His Father's Son	11
2	"It Couldn't Be Done"	38
3	The Paranoid Style	65
4	A Stab in the Dark	104
5	The Whirl of Circumstance	140
6	An Experiment in Democracy	175
7	Definite Indication of Wrongdoing	211
8	The Rise of British Columbia	255
9	The Politics of Power	296
10	The Power of Politics	333
11	The Good Life	376
12	That Good Night	417
	Afterword	452
	Note on Sources	468
	Chapter References	472
	Index	476

PREFACE

I first met the late W. A. C. Bennett in the spring of 1976. He had surprised me by agreeing to be interviewed. I arrived at his suite in a downtown Vancouver hotel with my notes and tape recorder, half expecting to meet a ten-foot-tall ogre. When I was greeted by a rather short, rotund, smiling grandfatherly man it was the beginning of a long series of collapsing assumptions on my part. The former premier was in fact a very charming man who, in person, belied his stern public image. Why is it that we invariably expect our giants to be mean as well?

I had initiated the interview with the intention of writing a retrospective article on Bennett's political career, but I soon realized that there was a greater opportunity and challenge. With verve, Bennett answered all my questions, often heading off on tangents of his own choosing—clearly he was in control of the interview. At the end of two hours of taping, he said over tea, "Well, my friend, we should do this again." I agreed.

During the course of almost three years, at irregular intervals, I met with Bennett. Taking place in Kelowna, Vancouver and Victoria, the interviews covered the gamut of his public career and often became monologues initiated, of course, by himself; they were lectures on the art and philosophy of Getting Things Done. At first on my own, and later under the auspices of the Provincial Archives of British Columbia, I obtained more than thirty hours of detailed reminiscence from him. It was in that series of archival interviews, which at the request of the Bennett family remains closed to the public until 1989, that this book had its genesis.

The literary equivalent of having a subject sit for a portrait, oral history was an invaluable biographical tool, and the long hours spent alone with Bennett have enriched this book immensely. His own well-considered version of the past often masqueraded as a spate of total recall and, as a historical source, therefore needed to be corroborated in other documentary materials and other interviews. Nonetheless, as is always the case when an interviewer can spend enough time with his subject, the subject revealed more of himself than he knew. And it was usually in the hours spent in candid conversation after the tape recorder had been turned off that I learned the most about my subject.

During this period, for the first time in a quarter of a century, Bennett was free from the concerns and worries of public life. In December 1975 his son Bill had been elected premier, heading a reupholstered version of his father's Social Credit Party. Like a fish out of water, W. A. C. Bennett struggled with retirement, never content to rest, never wanting to retire. Each and every day, out of habit, he dressed impeccably in his somewhat old-fashioned manner: his linen was always spotless beneath a plain dark suit with a dark tie and his shoes well shined. Even in his last years, during successive stages of physical decline, he displayed an undeniable vigour of mind. Speaking in his characteristically convoluted way, his fluency was increased, not impeded, by his stammering—like boulders in a mountain stream which suggest how fast the water is flying. It is not calumny to say that Bennett was not erudite; indeed, he read few literary works and never considered writing his memoirs. He did, however, know political history well, or it might be more precise to say that he knew a great number and variety of stories about politics. He devoured newspapers. He read them all, especially those whose editorial policies he detested. Well into a new age dominated by electronic media, Bennett still thought in newspaper headlines.

A politician who gave no thought to how posterity viewed him would be a rare animal. Moreover, the need to be elusive to contemporaries does not imply an equal need to elude posterity. W. A. C. Bennett, who possessed an ego at least as large as most other leading politicians of his day, was widely misunderstood during the two decades in which he served as premier of British Columbia, and a great deal of fiction naturally grew up around him. This has been difficult to break through, but I believe he was more forthcoming with me during his last years than he had ever been with journalists in his heyday. Only mildly supportive when he first learned of my intention to write his biography, he eventually went so far as to allow me exclusive access to his personal papers and provide introductions to former colleagues and cronies who would not otherwise have spoken candidly with me. However, if he opened doors that ordinarily would have remained closed—perhaps forever—he also attempted to steer me away from other areas. In order to transcend the realms of legend and imagination and move into the hard country of fact it has therefore been necessary to research all available sources, a task that has taken upwards of seven years. This has included lengthy correspondence and interviews with a wide variety of Bennett's contemporaries. The reader should note that dialogue and quotes in the book ascribed to Bennett or other individuals are derived largely from my interviews with them conducted between 1976 and 1981—for details, see the Note on Sources—many years after the events recalled; wherever possible their statements were compared with the available record.

In a sense I feel, as any biographer must, that I have trespassed into prohibited areas, the private domain of a public man's life. But I also feel that the product of this research represents a more complete and truer understanding of Bennett's life, offering more than a fugitive glimpse of his personality and placing it in a clearer historical context.

Of course, writing the history of the very recent past can be audacious. Not only are the himalayas of documentary sources overwhelming; in addition, persons who are part of the events being described are still alive to challenge any version or question any interpretation. Without proceeding further into the contentious and ultimately wearisome controversy over the validity of contemporary history, I would like to suggest, first, that this book is no hasty pudding and, second, that it is perhaps timely to review and evaluate the life and times of W. A. C. Bennett: a man who became premier of B.C. over thirty years ago, whose administration was defeated more than a decade past and, yet, whose legacies still dominate the politics of Canada's Pacific coast province.

A biography of a premier is not necessarily a history of his times, but in the case of Bennett, the story of the rise of British Columbia is coincident with his career. It is simply not possible to recount the province's recent past without continual reference to the man who so boldly shaped it, and I believe this will become obvious to the reader who ventures forth into these pages.

Because W. A. C. Bennett had very definite ideas about the world and his place in it, in order to make sense of his life this book expresses very definite ideas about the recent history of B.C. and Canada. As a biography it attempts to see the world through the eyes of its chief figure—a point of view that became increasingly accessible to me over the years in which I studied Bennett. Perhaps it was an inevitable consequence of spending many hours in conversation with a man of his redoubtable character and great charm; I would prefer to believe that it was a matter of intellectual honesty, but in any event, during the course of my research I developed a sympathy and respect for him. I feel it incumbent to advise the reader of this fact, and to adapt A. J. P. Taylor's statement regarding his life of Lord Beaverbrook: if it is necessary for a biographer of W. A. C. Bennett to regard him as evil, then I am not qualified to be his biographer. This is not to say that the reader will not discover his warts, or criticisms of British Columbia's first Socred government; on the contrary, all of the major points of contention and controversy are addressed. But Bennett's answers to those criticisms are also evident.

The final word on the "W. A. C. Bennett era" will likely never be written: we know too much about it. At the same time, is it not possible that a sympathetic understanding may illumine as well as distort, surely no less than would a purely negative viewpoint? I am confident that this biography presents as real, accurate and complete a portrait as possible at this time. And

I hereby invite the reader to reflect on the life of the largest figure ever to emerge from British Columbia, a man known both affectionately and contemptuously as "Wacky," a man who almost single-handedly moulded a province and thereby cast his shadow over its future.

ACKNOWLEDGEMENTS

After seven years of work on this biography, the persons to whom I am indebted are far too numerous to list, though I would be remiss if I did not thank a select few.

The book could not have been written without the co-operation of its subject, and I would therefore like to recognize W. A. C. Bennett who, in the last years of his life, gave generously of his time and allowed me exclusive access to his personal papers in Kelowna. His daughter, Anita Tozer, who serves unofficially as the Bennett family archivist and historian, greatly assisted by guiding me through the maze of documents and memorabilia that her father collected during the two decades as premier of B.C. A special debt of gratitude is owed to all those who agreed to record their reminiscences of the W. A. C. Bennett years on tape, and to all enterprising oral historians who have helped to ensure that British Columbia's recent past will be more roundly documented than any previous era. The staff of the Provincial Archives of B.C. and the Legislative Library in Victoria were helpful throughout the gestation of this project, often acceding without fuss or objection to unreasonable long-distance requests. I would be negligent if I did not thank the indefatigable Mildred Babey, who typed draft after draft of the manuscript and never once complained. And, finally, I would like to acknowledge the support of my family, in particular my wife Marlene and daughters Madeleine and Jane, who I hope will now want me to become a full-time husband and father.

Regina
February 19, 1983

CHAPTER ONE

HIS FATHER'S SON

*I the Lord thy God am a jealous God,
visiting the iniquity of the fathers
upon the children unto the third and
fourth generation of them that hate me.*
Exodus 20:5

I couldn't have had a better childhood.
W. A. C. Bennett

One of the most remarkable facts about the life of William Andrew Cecil Bennett is that during the course of a long and controversial public career little was revealed of his early years. Even at the time of his death when roving reporters and other researchers were looking for short, easily accessible profiles for obituaries, they had to resort to secondary accounts which, if traced back to their source, undoubtedly came from the horse's mouth.

That it was possible for W. A. C. Bennett to dictate what little would be known about his youth and upbringing is due to a number of factors. His early years were spent in New Brunswick; he later achieved prominence on the other side of the continent in British Columbia. Sheer distance made it difficult to check facts or substantiate legend, and, perhaps naturally, commentators were more interested in contemporary events than in those of days long gone. Bennett's career was followed closely and reported upon daily for over two decades, but the background to his amazing story was never closely examined. Although the news media were generally hostile to Bennett, he was fortunate in their naiveté and seeming inability to dig deeply for facts. The veracity of information he volunteered about his personal background was never seriously questioned.

Obviously it should have been. The early years of a person's life are significant; they sometimes foretell future patterns of behaviour. Obscure as the factors are that form a person's character, we do understand something of their nature. We know, for instance, that they begin to exert their influence at birth—or even earlier—and are strongest during the first years of life. Also, the relationship between a child and parents is considered to be one of the strongest forces in the development of personality. In an effort to understand W. A. C. Bennett—his ambitions, motivations, strengths and weaknesses—it is important to learn about his early years; but Bennett had his own very private reasons for concealing certain aspects of his childhood. This is not to suggest that he lied or deliberately distorted the past when he told his story. It may simply have been too painful for him to recall.

W. A. C. Bennett was born on September 6, 1900, in the small village of Hastings in Albert County, New Brunswick—a Canadian province the twentieth century had forgotten. He was named William for one of his mother's brothers, Andrew after his father, and Cecil for Cecil Rhodes, the renowned British imperialist and business magnate. Many newborn children of British ancestry were named after Rhodes, one of the great men of his era. Apparently Bennett was born with a caul, once believed to be a mark of future greatness.

The hamlet of Hastings no longer exists, having been incorporated into Fundy National Park. However, a tiny lake in the park bears the name of Bennett. The Bennett name is spread widely throughout the eastern seaboard of Canada and the United States. The family has been established in the Canadian maritime provinces ever since 1760 when British colonists from the New England area were brought up to Nova Scotia to take over the lands of the French Acadian settlers who had been forced into exile five years earlier. Zadoc Bennett and his young family were among the so-called Planter settlers who soon spread throughout the region. R. B. Bennett, prime minister of Canada from 1930 to 1935, descended from Zadoc's son, Benjamin, and W. A. C. Bennett's lineage can be traced back to another of his sons, John.

The Planters, a determined and resourceful breed of settler, arrived in the northern colonies sixteen years before the American Revolution. These Yankee newcomers were generally quite poor. They came in search of land—the most basic of all motives—and with some anticipation of official assistance in cultivating it. Many of the United Empire Loyalists, or Tories, who fled to the region during and after the American War of Independence, came because of their loyalty to the British crown: unable to sanction the American colonial rebellion, they courted the possibility of angry reprisals. The Loyalists were closely tied to British power; they were often wealthy merchants, landholders and lawyers whose families could afford the luxury of righteous adherence to monarchy and empire—though many others, of course, were simply attracted by the prospect of free land.

Most secondary sources on W. A. C. Bennett's life state erroneously that he descended from United Empire Loyalists. The basis of this myth lies partly in family controversy, but mostly in W. A. C. Bennett himself, who did his best to perpetuate it. On many occasions throughout his career he trotted out his supposed Loyalist origins as evidence of his conservative credentials and allegiance to the British crown. Of course, his descent from Planters rather than Loyalists does not mean that the blood in his veins was any less conservative nor any less patriotic. But the character of his forebears, their class background and their reasons for migrating northward were clearly different from what Bennett led people to believe—and, indeed, wanted to believe himself. Herein lies the first important clue to an understanding of the man.

W. A. C. Bennett was born in his paternal grandmother's home where in all probability his father, Andrew Havelock Bennett, also came into this world. One of twelve children, Andrew was born on December 31, 1870, and grew into maturity in the poverty of his rural maritime county. His father, John G. Bennett, died in 1892, but his Irish-born mother, Catherine Jane Foster Bennett, lived until 1920, so W. A. C. Bennett knew his grandmother well.

This branch of the Bennett family had suffered great misfortune and hardship. At the beginning of the nineteenth century they settled in the area of Albert County where they were given land grants. From virgin forest they carved out homes and engaged in small-scale logging and lumbering, but were eventually squeezed out of business by large lumber companies. As a result, a deep strain of resentment against big business interests ran through the family. Most of the family left the region; those who stayed were bitter and despondent. Andrew Bennett was one of the few members of his generation to remain at home, living in a very small cottage on a poor, unproductive farm. W. A. C. Bennett was the last of the family to be born there, and after they left, the house was moved and added on to the home of a neighbour to serve as a kitchen.

W. A. C. Bennett's father would be best described as a jack-of-all-trades, except that he was not particularly good at any one of them. Andrew tried his hand at farming, but with little success. He laboured in the New Brunswick sawmills, in Saint John as a longshoreman, and tried working as a carpenter and a wheelwright, but he never kept a job for very long. W. A. C. Bennett, in later years, recalled his father as "a rugged, hard-working person. He wasn't home very much."

His mother, on the other hand, was the backbone of the family. Mary Emma Burns came from the small New Brunswick town of Murray Corner, her family being among the first Scottish settlers in the region. She was born in 1868, one of ten children in a close-knit Presbyterian family. Her father, Henry Burns, was a prosperous farmer. Her mother, Mary Spence Murray Burns, was an educated, deeply religious woman. Mary Emma was trained well by her mother, who had great expectations of all her children.

Through her young adulthood, Mary Emma lived at home and nursed her mother through a long debilitating illness. When her mother died in 1890, she remained at home for a year and a half longer caring for her father and younger siblings. On November 28, 1891, at Port Elgin, New Brunswick, she married Andrew Bennett, a man younger than herself and below her station. In fact, Andrew Bennett was barely out of his teens and had no prospect of secure employment. If it had not been for the recent death of Mary Emma's mother and the subsequent family trauma, the marriage would likely not have been permitted.

It was from these genes and this environment that W. A. C. Bennett emerged. Cecil, as he was called, was the fifth child produced of the marriage, preceded by two sisters and two brothers; two more sisters would follow. However, only five of the seven Bennett children survived infancy. One of Cecil's brothers and a younger sister died of pneumonia in their first year. Mary Emma Bennett stoically ran the household through these and other crises. Cecil said of her: "We knew our mother much, much better than our father because we were with her all the time. You couldn't have a more ideal mother than my mother. She saw that we were brought up very strict Presbyterians." But despite being closer to her, he would find his father's influence stronger and more lasting—and in that sense he was his father's son.

When Cecil was a year old the family left his grandmother's home at Hastings and moved to the town of Hampton in nearby Kings County where they rented a house for three dollars a month. Hampton was a quiet old town with a population of 650 nestled in the valley of the Kennebecasis River. Here Cecil spent his early years and adolescence.

The difficulty in attempting to chronicle the youth of W. A. C. Bennett is that is was unremarkable on the surface and like many North American rural childhoods. The most significant factor affecting his life was his parents' relationship. Great achievers are often the product of an unhappy or ill-balanced marriage, and not only did the marriage of Andrew Bennett and Mary Emma Burns begin inauspiciously but it also followed an inharmonious course. In fact, Cecil and his brother and sisters suffered from the absence of their father who was usually out of work and could not get along with their mother. For years, Andrew and Mary Emma had a tormented "on-again, off-again" relationship. Many years later, Cecil's eldest sister, Cora, sadly remembered: "Regretfully, I must say that my father was not close to his family. Mother brought us up practically alone as father was on a different and lesser wavelength."

What effect did this have upon young Cecil? His domestic situation would not be uncommon today, but in rural turn-of-the-century New Brunswick it was practically scandalous. Cecil grew up knowing that he was quite different from his friends and schoolmates. Not only was his father away for most of his childhood but the family had to struggle to make ends meet. The Bennetts were much less well-to-do than most of their neighbours and relatives. With his father away, Cecil never had the opportunity given to most youths to rebel against parental authority. He might have transferred this natural rebelliousness to his mother but for her stolid, almost saintly character and determined efforts to raise the family by herself, making it difficult for him to openly defy her. Instead, he accepted his mother's authority at home and achieved a kind of independence and maturity beyond his years. His lack of a father did not so much produce a mother-driven boy as a self-motivated young man intent on fulfilling the dreams of his own fertile imagination.

There can be no denying that W. A. C. Bennett harboured fond memories of his years in New Brunswick, but neither can it be denied that he was seriously scarred by his parents' fractiousness. He hid that side of his childhood and never admitted, even to himself, that many of his actions and compulsions as an adult were the direct consequences of that period. He nevertheless acknowledged the importance of childhood in an interview many years later when, with some insight, he commented: "Your mind is clear then, clearer than at any time in your life. And the things that happen then will influence your whole life."

These points are made not to argue that W. A. C. Bennett's future success was achieved in spite of the shortcomings of his childhood, rather to suggest that it was achieved because of them. He seemed to have determined at an early age to lead a life of moral uprightness. He dreamed of performing some great public service. He wanted desperately to transcend the poverty and familial discord of his youth. He decided to strive for and achieve all that he imagined—and more—persuading himself that he had a mission to fulfill. He desired, in his own way, to make up for his father's inadequacies. Where his father had been weak, he would be strong. Where his father had been shiftless, he would be determined. Where his father had wavered, he would be decisive. And yet, always, he would be his father's son.

Young Cecil was a small, thin, sandy-haired boy with deep-set intense eyes. He was bright and undoubtedly clever, but also shy, quiet and introverted. As a youngster, his apparent physical immaturity made its mark on him. For example, in his later years he recalled his first experience at school: "I went to school when I was six. September the sixth was my birthday. I was dressed up with a little peaked cap. Our school was about a mile away, I guess. At first when I walked in I didn't like it a bit. I saw kids put up their hands and snap their fingers, and the teacher would say, 'Yes, John.' 'Yes, Bill.' 'Yes, Helen.' Then they'd go off. I thought that was a pretty good game, so I tried it. 'Yes, Cecil, you may.' I went out to the washroom—and I didn't even wait to get my cap, I just went down those steps and ran for home as fast as I could."

His sister Cora had a somewhat different version of Cecil's introduction to school. She remembered that on his first day he was "doing a good job until recess, when his new cap was thrown up into a tall tree. His dignity insulted, the young student left immediately for home, vowing never to go back to that school."

A series of unanticipated circumstances enabled Cecil to keep his vow. Severe weather and a rash of family illnesses kept him at home for the next few weeks; then a fire destroyed the Bennetts' home. No one was injured, but practically all their clothes and personal possessions were lost. Andrew Bennett was away working in a mill in Saint John at the time, so the family moved to the farm of Mary Emma's brother David, at Hanford Brook, where they stayed for six months. Thus young Cecil helped with the chores on his uncle's farm and enjoyed an extended childhood. After they recovered from their illnesses and their upsetting loss, the Bennetts moved back to Hampton, near a new school.

The following year, 1907, when Cecil attended the new Hampton Consolidated School, he proved to be a bright and serious-minded pupil. Indeed, all of the Bennett children excelled in school. They were referred to as "those smart Bennett youngsters." Cecil's favourite subject by far was mathematics. He seemed to have an innate understanding of arithmetic and developed his own quick system of computation. His school records show that he was usually first in his class in mathematics with an average percentage in the high 90s, often scoring 100. His weakest subjects were spelling, language, writing and composition.

Cecil's older brother, Russell, and sister Cora both continued their educations and eventually became schoolteachers. In fact, Cora returned to Hampton and taught Cecil in grades seven and eight. He did not take advantage of having her as his teacher, rather almost effaced himself in the classroom, and the marks he achieved, especially in mathematics, were the cause of some embarrassment for Cora, for she was warned by the principal: "He must be given the marks he deserves." Russell taught for many years and was a principal when he retired.

The teaching tradition spans several generations in the Bennett family; Cecil eventually married a schoolteacher, and his only daughter spent a career teaching in British Columbia. The number of teachers in the Bennett family suggests more than simply class background; it suggests a desire for service and a need to assume a useful social role, which probably can be traced back to Mary Emma Bennett and the religious convictions she instilled in her children.

Thomas Carlyle wrote, "It is well said, in every sense, that a man's religion is the chief fact with regard to him." About W. A. C. Bennett, especially during his early years and young adulthood, it was the chief fact. What strength his mother derived from her strict regimen was her own secret, but she certainly did her best to transfer her devout Presbyterianism to her children. And Cecil, easily the most sensitive of her offspring, eagerly accepted that devotion.

The Bennett children learned that the Bible was the final authority on all matters and that its teachings should be followed closely. Only by hard work, devotion to Christian principles and helping their fellow man could personal salvation be attained. They were also imbued with a strong notion of predestination. Their mother's influence dominated the household. According to her wishes, on Saturday evening the Bennett children had baths, cut their fingernails, prepared their Sunday clothes and polished their shoes, so that Sunday could be reserved completely for the Lord; even meals for the Sabbath were prepared on Saturday. These household rules were so strictly observed that over half a century later W. A. C. Bennett would feel a painful tug on his conscience if he caught himself clipping his fingernails on Sunday.

On Sunday morning Cecil would go to church; in the afternoon he went to Sunday school to study catechism, and in the evening he attended another church service. His mother was unaware that he sometimes attended the Anglican or Baptist Sunday school classes with friends. On Monday nights he went with an older sister to meetings of the Christian Endeavour group.

This religious regimen was not unusual for the time and place, but Cecil also had the example of his mother who practised her faith with a special intensity, perhaps as a result of her marital problems and the pressure of raising a family on her own. Young Cecil immersed himself in his faith with uncommon eagerness for a boy his age. His great interest in religion, his strides towards "religiosity," and his concentration on living a morally upright life may, in one sense, have been a form of atonement for perceived sins. These sins, however, were not his own; they were his father's.

As a youngster, Cecil was impressionable and somewhat overemotional. His religious devotion could have been a consequence of this side of his character. As an adult he claimed that he had never faltered in his religious faith:

> I learned the Shorter Catechism in the Presbyterian Church and in our home. The Shorter Catechism, of course, I will always remember: "What is the chief end of man?" "The Chief end of man is to glorify God and to enjoy Him forever." Once you learn these basic things they stay with you. I have always believed in a great architect in the universe, and in the great life of Jesus Christ, an amazing life. It amazed me, even as a kid, that after the centuries go by, no critic can find any legitimate

criticism regarding Jesus's morals, his ethical standards. They've stood the test of time better than any person. I never questioned little things. I didn't want to know whether this really happened, or that didn't happen. . . . I looked always at the broad sphere of the universe. And as it unfolded to me and became more wonderful to me, I realized how small this earth was, how great the universe was. This little earth isn't a billionth part of the universe. And I realized as a young boy that man does not stand alone; there is another force.

Of course, young Cecil also enjoyed the secular activities common to most boyhoods. Although he was not athletic, he loved the outdoors—fishing in New Brunswick streams, going to all the church and Sunday school picnics and riding home on the little sternwheeler *Hampton*. He had a passion for strawberries, particularly the variety that grew wild in the Kennebecasis River valley where he sometimes worked picking large flats for a cent-and-a-quarter apiece. In the winters he would skate down the frozen river for miles and in the spring, when grass began to thrust up through the snow, he would run out in it barefoot.

On one occasion at home, while he was helping Russell to saw wood, the bucksaw slipped on a knot and clipped a quarter inch off the end of Cecil's left thumb. The wound healed and the nail grew over the end of the thumb, which Cecil protected by closing his fist over it. Thereafter, he referred to his unique identification mark as his "claw." Strangely, his brother had a similar accident a few years later when he lost part of his right thumb while working in a mill on his summer holidays. Many years later the two brothers prided themselves on their almost identical "badges of industry," but throughout W. A. C. Bennett's many years in public office few if any observers ever noticed his "claw."

Despite his serious strain, Cecil did take part in the usual boyish pranks. At Hallowe'en he helped the other kids in the Hampton area push over all the outdoor privies and take up the wooden walks around neighbours' homes. But, he was quick to point out, "The next day we'd be back there helping to put them back up." At school, though he was a good student, he often allowed his mischievous strain to lead him into trouble, receiving several lickings from the school principal with the butt end of a horsewhip.

It was during his years in Hampton that W. A. C. Bennett first acquired a taste for politics. He wavered between the clergy and politics as possible callings; for young Cecil, both implied a lifetime of duty, dedication and service. Indirectly, his mother's compulsion and his father's deficiencies steered him towards the church; his own fascination with public figures tugged him more towards politics.

The small town of Hampton was hardly a hotbed of political activity, but even as a boy Cecil could not help but be aware of the sharp and longstanding differences between maritime Grits and Tories. As a matter of course, he listened to political discussions among his neighbours and visiting uncles and often overcame his characteristic shyness to contribute to the arguments. At public meetings his hand was often raised to question the speaker of the moment.

Perhaps it is not so remarkable that young Cecil became fascinated with politics, for he grew up in the most exciting period of New Brunswick's political history. Federal politicians often traipsed through the region during election campaigns, but provincial politics were lively all year round. Cecil had the opportunity to hear several great orators, including the doyen of provincial Tories, John Douglas Hazen; Liberal Premier "Walter the Unready" Foster; "the premiers who taught Sunday school," James Kidd Fleming and George Clarke; "Fighting Frank" Carvell; Fielding of Nova Scotia, and a host of others. Some were spellbinding orators and virtually all were impressive by today's standards. These were days of partisanship of a high order in New Brunswick and one learned quickly which side of an issue to stand on.

The enemy was never in doubt. Frank Carvell put it best just after a Liberal election victory: "God damn you," he told a Tory newspaper reporter, "we got you where we want you now, and we intend to keep you there."

Cecil Bennett's extended family were all strong Tories and he followed in that tradition with great fervour. It is not known whether his father was particularly partisan, but during election campaigns Cecil travelled many miles with his uncles to hear politicians speak on the issues of the day. One he remembered was the 1911 federal campaign, the famous "reciprocity election" fought between Liberal Prime Minister Wilfred Laurier and the Tory challenger Robert Borden. Laurier's Grits lost the election and nowhere was there greater jubilation than in the Conservative strongholds of rural New Brunswick. W. A. C. Bennett, who was eleven years old then, recalled: "In our little town of Hampton empty barrels were piled high on election night. The Liberals had a pile and the Conservatives had a pile. On top of the Conservatives' was a picture of Laurier, and the Liberals had a picture of Borden. On election night we knocked down the Liberal pile and soaked ours in oil and burned it. Then we had a torchlight parade." The spectacle and excitement of that political bonfire had a powerful effect on the impressionable Cecil Bennett. The images remained with him and proved useful many years later when he decided to mark a special political watershed with a symbolic public burning of his own.

In the summer of 1915 the Bennett family underwent a change that was common during the early years of the century when people were moving away from their rural backgrounds to live in the cities. In New Brunswick, small towns like Hampton were shrinking, some even disappearing, as larger towns and cities grew rapidly. The Bennetts moved to Saint John, New Brunswick's largest city. The move was essentially an attempt to reunite the family with Andrew Bennett, who had been spending progressively more time in Saint John looking for work; Mary Emma hoped they could live together there.

Life in the city was a different experience for more than just the Bennett family, since World War I was now in its second year and its effect was felt everywhere. Canada, particularly English Canada, had entered into the war wholeheartedly. By the autumn of 1915 Canadian divisions were fighting on the European western front.

Cecil attended high school in Saint John and obtained a part-time job with a hardware firm, Robertson, Foster and Smith's. Jobs were plentiful for lads too young to fight overseas on behalf of the British Empire. Jobs were just as plentiful for men considered too old for service. Andrew Bennett, who had been providing for his family only haphazardly, probably could have landed a steady job in Saint John during this period; there are three reasons why he failed to do so. First, it was not in his nature to hold a steady job. Second, his family's arrival in Saint John made him nervous and edgy. Third, after what seemed a wasted life he strived to do some great thing. Andrew was rapidly approaching his forty-fifth birthday and ran the risk of being refused for military service even though he had served with a nonactive militia unit during the Boer War. But he was desperate. More than anything else he wanted to leave New Brunswick. He knew only too well that he could never find happiness within the confines of family life; these were responsibilities he could not cope with. Yet he was anxious to do something, preferably something great, something heroic.

The 115th Battalion was recruiting for overseas service in Saint John in 1915. A fortnight before his birthday, Andrew Bennett enlisted, having lied about his age. After a few months of training he sailed with the Canadian Expeditionary Force aboard the S.S. *Olympic*. He was stationed in Britain for most of the war, but saw service in France and Belgium as a member of the Canadian Forestry Corps.

Cecil was only fifteen years old. Cora and Russell had completed high school and continued their education with financial assistance from their maternal uncles. A similar offer of assistance was made to Cecil; perhaps he, too, would become a teacher. But he would have none of that, refusing to be a drain on the slim family purse. He dropped out of school after only a few months of grade nine and went to work full time in the hardware store. On a salary of five dollars a week he could pay his own way and help out the family. Never again did he pursue any kind of formal classroom education.

Robertson, Foster and Smith's was a large firm, and because most young men had gone overseas, it could afford to give a serious-minded youngster like Cecil Bennett an opportunity and responsibility that would normally have been out of his reach. He was put to work in practically every department of the hardware business. He kept books and produced balance sheets, applied cost accounting, and learned a great deal about tariffs and customs duties. Mr. Foster, of Robertson, Foster and Smith's, personally supervised young new employees such as Cecil. An elderly gentleman and somewhat deaf, he customarily used an ear trumpet. He was a stern taskmaster and once a week delivered a formal lecture to the employees on the subject of business and economics.

It did not take long for Cecil to decide that he, too, would become a hardware merchant. Asked in the 1970s why the business appealed to him as a young man, he replied that "it was more permanent than anything else. Hardware seemed to me to be *the* substantial business in those days—much more than now." Especially during the war, the hardware business boomed. Tools and fighting equipment were in great demand.

Cecil developed a further interest in politics while living in Saint John. His employer was the brother of Walter Foster, the prominent New Brunswick Liberal who became premier in 1917. The Foster family were Liberal stalwarts and Cecil became well informed of Grit politics while working with the firm. No matter, he still considered himself a staunch Tory. He kept his views to himself, but attended political debates and meetings whenever he could. From this time on, the hardware business and politics seemed a natural combination of interests for Cecil.

Cora described her younger brother in his Saint John years as "in every way an admirable young man." Apparently it was during this time that he adopted an Edgar Guest poem as his motto. The simple poem entitled "It Couldn't Be Done" captured the essence of his developing attitude towards life. He was often heard to recite:

> Somebody said that it couldn't be done
> But he with a chuckle replied
> That "maybe it couldn't," but he would be one
> Who wouldn't say so till he'd tried.
> So he buckled right in with a trace of a grin
> On his face. If he worried he hid it.
> He started to sing as he tackled the thing
> That couldn't be done, and he did it.

Through daily recitation, the verse became carved in his memory. Over half a century later he would regularly recite it without effort.

During this period young Cecil also became a confirmed nondrinker and nonsmoker. His aversion to alcohol might be partly attributed to his deeply religious upbringing. Even in his school days in Hampton he was well aware of the damage that alcohol could do to a person, there being a few well-known "drunks" in the town. It is not known whether there were any drinking problems in his family; he recalled his father as a "social drinker." In any event, from a relatively early age he decided that alcohol would not touch his lips. He became a noted teetotaller, and would often advise, "You only have to make the decision once." His decision not to smoke tobacco seems to have been made during his years in Saint John, according to Cora, "when he and a pal went on a fishing trip each armed with a pipe and a package of tobacco. Cecil's one and only attempt made him deathly sick whereupon pipe and weed were flung into a swamp."

Towards the conclusion of World War I, Cecil entertained the idea of joining the armed forces, but he had promised his mother that he would not join until he turned the legal age of eighteen. Near the end of hostilities the Royal Flying Corps suffered a shortage of airmen and the legal age was lowered to seventeen and a half. The day he turned legal age, in March 1918, he signed up. But he never saw service, nor even wore a uniform. The war ended before the opportunity arose.

"Every man thinks meanly of himself for not having been a soldier," said Dr. Samuel Johnson, and this is especially true of members of W. A. C. Bennett's generation. Not having served in the "War to End All Wars" and later being too old to enlist in the Second World War had a serious effect on Cecil Bennett, who was raised with a set of values that demanded service; he harboured a deep guilt for not having served his country in uniform, saying: "I've always felt I owe something. I can't forget I never fought in either of these wars."

His father, however, did fight. Andrew Bennett returned home in May 1919, but never discussed his military experience with his family. W. A. C. Bennett believed that "the war service had badly affected him." Cora believed her father served as a sergeant in the Military Police, but when discharged he was a private. He had been a staff sergeant when serving with his local militia unit during the Boer War and his military records show that during the First World War he did at various times attain "acting" ranks of corporal and sergeant, but these ranks were never confirmed. The records indicate that he was something of a disciplinary problem. Upon arriving in Britain he stayed in a special hospital for a long period. On at least one occasion he broke out of hospital and forfeited pay as a result of being absent without leave. Towards the end of hostilities, when he was serving in France as a member of the Canadian Forestry Corps, he received several reprimands for a variety of offences, including creating a disturbance, being absent without leave and being drunk on parade—all in the best tradition of the Canadian army of that era; he was not a professional soldier, but a civilian in uniform.

Whatever his experience overseas, the family was hopeful that Andrew would now settle down at home as a father and husband. These hopes were dashed when shortly after his return he announced his intention to head west along with a host of other war-weary veterans. The Soldier Settlement Board, an agency of the federal government, was offering assistance to veterans interested in obtaining and settling land in the Peace River country, and cheap rail passes were offered. According to Cora, their father "had visions of becoming rich in the land of plenty." One thing is certain, Andrew Bennett had no plans whatsoever of either marital reconciliation or remaining in New Brunswick.

His father's return had both excited and upset Cecil. He was doing well at the hardware store and had received a raise to eight dollars a week. From this, the thrifty young man was supporting himself, contributing to his family, making regular church offerings and saving a few dollars a week. He could have easily remained with the hardware firm and, with his few years of experience behind him, would have gradually risen through the ranks. However, his father's return and decision to head west provoked some serious soul-searching on Cecil's part.

Father-son relationships are always complex and difficult to understand. No matter how desperately a son desires to free himself from his father, he will always remain inextricably bound. Cecil's love-hate relationship with his father must have been difficult, but he struggled to understand him and the reasons he preferred to stay aloof rather than reunite with his family. Something else now tugged at Cecil—the romantic notion of travelling into the western hinterland. He asked for and received his father's permission to go with him to the Peace River country.

In July 1919, eighteen-year-old Cecil Bennett boarded a train with his father and headed west. For a young man who had never travelled outside his maritime province, this was an adventure. He carried with him $100 in savings and many unresolved questions. The long journey impressed him; the country's vastness was difficult to comprehend. He and his father slept in their day seats, though regular meal tickets were provided for the dining car. They journeyed across the new prairie provinces, north through Edmonton, and into the great Peace River region which straddles both sides of the northern boundary separating Alberta and British Columbia. Andrew quickly decided to settle a small parcel of land on the Alberta side of the border at a place called Teepee Creek near the town of Sexsmith, northeast of Grande Prairie. The Soldier Settlement Board placed hundreds of veterans in the district during this period.

The Peace River country had a significant impact on Cecil. He was fond of recalling that the only crop you could rely on in New Brunswick was rock, whereas the Peace River area comprised vast amounts of rich farmland with fantastic potential. Its pristine qualities made it seem a world apart from New

Brunswick. The residents of the area, however, were suffering from a lack of railway facilities, badly needed because of their distance from markets. But this did not deter the tide of immigration. Andrew Bennett decided to turn his fertile piece of land—his "ranch," as he called it—into a successful agricultural enterprise. Cecil worked with his father for a short while. "I was just a young kid and had come from an office in New Brunswick. But after a couple of weeks I was hardened up and I enjoyed it."

However, he did not stay with his father long. They could not easily live together, let alone work side by side. Andrew, after all, was running from his past and his family. Young Cecil was ambitious and practical-minded and could have been an asset, were he not a constant and painful reminder of his father's failings. Because he was only eighteen, Cecil was not eligible for any land grants, and he was not prepared to wait around idly until he could apply. He was lonely and missed New Brunswick terribly. He considered returning home, but he persevered, for he was determined to stand on his own: he knew precisely what New Brunswick had to offer him, but in this new country there seemed no limit to what he might achieve.

Cecil left the Peace River in late summer and retraced his tracks to Edmonton. It is not known whether he ever saw his father again. It hurt him deeply to leave him and he never wished to discuss this period of his life. Andrew Bennett remained an enigma to his son. For Cecil, the Peace River country would always serve as a reminder of his father. The two became intertwined in his mind. The great unfulfilled promise of the territory seemed to represent the potential but never realized love between father and son. Years later, W. A. C. Bennett would wistfully remember: "That Peace River country, it was with me all my life, you know."

The province of Alberta was not even as old as Cecil. Edmonton, the capital, was a bustling, disorganized frontier town with a population of 55,000—larger than Saint John and more optimistic about its future. Cecil immediately tried to find work in the hardware business, applying for a job with the large wholesale firm, Marshall-Wells Ltd.

He had only just started his new job at Marshall-Wells when in September 1919 he was surprised by the arrival of his mother, brother Russell, and seventeen-year-old sister, Olivia. Together they rented lodgings.

They had pooled all of their resources to come west. Cora, the eldest, remained in New Brunswick teaching; Bernice, two years older than Cecil, was in the United States studying to be a nurse. But Russell had thought it an adventure to accompany his mother and youngest sister to this new country. He soon acquired a teaching position in Edmonton; Olivia enrolled in high school; Cecil had his new job, and Mary Emma kept house for her children. Everything appeared well, but there was a good deal of tension within the transplanted family. The underlying reason for Mary Emma Bennett's journey across the continent was a last attempt at some form of marital reconciliation. She had come in search of her errant husband.

Shortly after the family was settled in Edmonton, she prepared to visit Andrew at his "ranch." Cecil was extremely apprehensive about her decision; he loved his mother dearly and did not want to see her hurt any more. But she was determined and made the 250-mile journey by herself. It is not known what transpired when she arrived, unannounced, at her husband's homestead. It is only known that she found conditions intolerable and did not remain long; Andrew was not interested in a reunion. With his wife's return to Edmonton, his separation from his family was complete and permanent. None of his children ever expressed further interest in him.

Mary Emma Bennett lived with her children in Edmonton for the next few years, her hopes shattered. Her only consolation was that Cecil, Russell and Olivia drew closer to her than ever before, but she never overcame her deep sense of humiliation in her failed marriage. Cora probably summed up the family's feelings when she said: "For our father we could do nothing. He cut himself off with practically no correspondence. Our standards were not his. The estrangement was his choice, a grief to all of us. Just one of those situations of utter incompatibility." In her letters from New Brunswick Cora pleaded with her mother to return home. Mary Emma was comfortable in Edmonton but lonely for her people in the east, and in April 1924 she returned to New Brunswick where she lived for the rest of her days with Cora. She never saw her husband again. Olivia decided to remain in Edmonton with Cecil, where after completing high school she attended business college. Russell obtained a permanent teaching position in Banff, and stayed there until 1932 when he also returned to New Brunswick.

Meanwhile, Cecil was a very busy young man. These were exciting years to be in western Canada, the fabric of society having been stretched out of shape by the social turmoil left in the wake of the First World War. It was the time of labour radicalism, the One Big Union and the Winnipeg General Strike. Cecil, however, seemed untouched by most of these forces. His family problems and personal ambitions rendered him oblivious to external pressure. He kept his feelings to himself and diverted his energy into his work. When he began with Marshall-Wells in 1919 he was an order clerk. In pursuit of advancement, clerks competed fiercely to see who could fill the most orders in a single day. Ted Evers was an employee of Marshall-Wells who noticed Cecil: "My earliest recollection of young Cecil Bennett was of a youth with a hand truck in the warehouse filling orders and striving daily to exceed the 'items totals' of competing order clerks—and usually succeeding. He had a distinctive gait, springy and bouncy, and always seemed to be in haste, both at work and in his numerous activities after working hours. He was very friendly with everyone but withal there was an unintentional aloofness, very slight, but which seemed to discourage overfamiliarity or uninvited intrusion into his personal or family life."

The hardware business in Edmonton was booming, and Marshall-Wells was the largest wholesaler in a city that supplied the needs of thousands of farmers and settlers in the region. After a year and a half, Cecil became a "pricer"—pricing all the customer invoices. Eventually he was promoted to assistant to the sales manager. He was well known to most of the firm's customers, always looking very businesslike with his freshly pressed linen collar. In fact, he had an obsession for cleanliness and neatness and dressed well above his means. He also developed a penchant for blue serge suits which became one of his trademarks. As he described himself in his Edmonton period: "I was always a suit person—always a white shirt, a white collar and no money." Cecil's fellow employees regarded him as a bit curious. Ted Evers said, "I thought he was a 'comer,' and I must say that this is not hindsight because at that time I thought he was a little crazy. I was even a little afraid of him. He showed great promise, but at times I must admit I felt—uneasy. He seemed to know the answers to questions without the benefit of rationalization. I couldn't tell how he did it, but he certainly did it."

Cecil was obviously bright and unashamedly enthusiastic, anything but a waster. He was very involved in church affairs, having joined the Westminster Presbyterian Church when he moved to Edmonton. He became active in young people's church groups, particularly the Tuxis movement, which was an interchurch organization. Tuxis was an acronym for "Training," U or "You," X or "Christ," "I," "Service," meaning "You and I trained for service centred in Christ." The Tuxis movement, which sponsored secular as well as religious activities, was popular in Alberta during these years. Its effect on Cecil Bennett was profound and he involved himself deeply in all its aspects. He adhered unwaveringly to the Tuxis "Code of Ideals," which included Morning Devotions, Cleanliness and Health, Ideal of Conduct (to smile even though it hurts), Attitude towards the Opposite Sex (to live a life of purest chastity), and Evening Devotions.

One former member of Tuxis, clergyman Dermott McInnes, described the group: "It wasn't too heavily religious. There were sports and social events and all that kind of thing. It didn't impose anything on us except the experience of sharing a lot of things together. It was a fourfold program—physical, social, mental and spiritual. There was a pretty strong emphasis upon service, of being useful in some way or other, making our lives count in the community whatever we were doing. There was always the idea that we had been given gifts and we had privileges and opportunities to share, and we did." Although Cecil Bennett was a younger member and a late addition to the group, McInnes had a clear memory of him: "I remember him as tall and thin and quite active, physically active. He seemed to walk with a little bounce and he had a little hesitancy in his speech, not an impediment, but just hesitancy. I think maybe sometimes it was nervousness, a little cough when he spoke. I can picture him as a happy person . . . he seemed to be smiling quite a bit."

Another member of that Tuxis group, John Tames, who later became a senior business executive, believed it "had a very good influence on people who perhaps didn't have an opportunity at home to have guidance in some things." He described Cecil: "A thin man. He walked just the way he talked, never sauntered. If he was going from A to B, well damn it, get out of the way—he was going. That's the kind of guy he was. He was a pretty fair tennis player, but jerky. He wasn't what you would call a smooth tennis player. And he was just the same in hockey—he'd take a swipe at the puck. It was just his characteristic." He remembered that Cecil would not take a drink when he was out with friends on a Friday or Saturday night, which set him apart from most young men.

This particular Tuxis group met under the watchful eye of R. J. Gillis, their mentor. Gillis was by all accounts a strong individual, deeply concerned about the members of the group. He was a middle-aged man who had had his own share of personal problems; in fact, he was a reformed alcoholic. Through the support of his wife, family and church he overcame his illness and pledged himself to help prevent others from following the wrong path.

It seems clear that R. J. Gillis left a significant imprint on all the young men he worked with. For Cecil he became more than a mentor; he was an idealized father figure. Cecil greatly admired his ability to overcome his bout with alcoholism, while remaining close to his family. In this last respect Gillis had suceeded where Cecil's father had failed. He idolized the man and took his direct and effective personal style as an example to follow. Later, when the group disbanded, Gillis kept in contact with Cecil and the other Tuxis members he shepherded.

In 1919 the Tuxis movement helped to establish the Alberta Older Boys' Parliament whose purpose was to encourage leadership in church youth groups. It met once a year in Edmonton and elections took place in Protestant churches throughout the province. Said John Tames, "That, of course, is where Cec' was in with both his feet. He just loved that. He was in there shaking his head and going after it." In 1921 Cecil was elected premier of the parliament, but before he could take his seat he celebrated his twenty-first birthday and became ineligible for the position.

Cecil enjoyed the parliamentary experience. Although he was a clumsy public speaker, it gave him valuable practice at getting his point of view across within a defined set of procedural rules. During this period he developed a strong belief in nonpartisanship as a way of getting things done. He was frequently heard to say that two people who agreed on ninety-eight or ninety-nine things but disagreed on one or two, such as religion or politics, would be foolish not to discuss the ninety-eight or ninety-nine instead of arguing over the one or two. His belief in nonpartisanship manifested itself in his support for the church union movement, which culminated in the amalgamation of Presbyterians, Methodists and Congregationalists into the United Church of Canada in the mid-1920s. He also joined the interdenominational Church Young People's Movement, serving as president for northern Alberta.

Cecil was doing well at work, but his church-related activities took up a growing number of his nonworking hours. He was a very committed member of his congregation and served on various church boards and committees. When he left R.J. Gillis's Tuxis circle, he did so to lead his own younger group. He delivered devotionals to Sunday school youngsters and taught religious classes. It is worth mentioning that he employed a series of booklets in his classes called *Heroes of the Faith*. He came to know most of their lessons by heart and had his classes study the lives and teachings of prominent Christians from previous ages, including Erasmus, Luther, Savonarola, John Knox and others. He not only believed in the didactic potential of these biographical studies but also became strongly imbued with a "great man" view of history. As well as fostering co-operation and group effort, his classes instilled a firm belief in individualism and the view that a single person can change the world.

During his first five or six years in Edmonton Cecil became so committed to the church that he seriously considered entering the clergy, and it would not have been difficult for his friends to picture him as a minister. However, at some point in the mid-1920s he decided to follow a secular route—first business and ultimately politics; this would be his mission. A factor that contributed to this decision was his strong belief in his own ability to achieve whatever he set out to do, bolstered by the various teachings he studied and courses he completed. He was busy at work and could not afford to return to school for more education but he took a variety of courses by correspondence, including business, business law, economics, commerce and a Roth memory course. He regularly stayed up late at night to study.

Cecil was also tremendously influenced by the self-help literature so widely read in this era. When asked which books had had the most influence on his life, he named two: the Bible and *Pushing to the Front*. *Pushing to the Front* was by an American writer, Orison Swett Marden, who published a magazine called *Success*, popular at the turn of the century. Essentially his message was positive thinking. He wrote several books, all of them containing the basic tenet: "The world makes way for the determined man." *Pushing to the Front* was Marden's best-selling work, going into many editions in several languages. It suggested that by a careful study of history one would discover that the world's great leaders were ordinary people but of extraordinary persistence and perseverance. The book shouted out to Cecil Bennett maxims that echoed in his memory for years to come: "The history of great men shows that there is a disadvantage in having too many advantages." "Knowledge is power only when it can be made available, practical." "Kites rise against, not with the wind." "Weak men wait for opportunities. Seize common occasions and make them great."

These facile messages revealed by Marden had a great impact on him. In general terms, the self-help literature of the day reinforced and gave expression to many of the feelings Cecil had held since childhood. It proved to be a powerful force when combined with his inherited Maritime sense of politics as public service and his deep religious beliefs, particularly his Presbyterian notion of predestination. Of course, there were inconsistencies and contradictions in this ideological mumbo jumbo that was becoming Cecil Bennett's view of the world and his place in it. But Bennett, a self-styled version of Marden's "determined man," would work them out. Years later he left a well-read copy of *Pushing to the Front* in conspicuous places where his young sons might discover it.

In addition to work, church and study, Cecil did allow time for recreational activities during his years in Edmonton. In the summer months he would often get up at dawn and play a vigorous game of tennis before work. One of the people he met on the tennis courts was Einar Gunderson, a young chartered accountant, who would play an important political role with him many years and miles in the future. During the winter Cecil played hockey, eventually becoming coach-manager of the Marshall-Wells hockey team in the Edmonton mercantile league. These were exciting days for hockey in Edmonton. Clarence Campbell, the future president of the National Hockey League, was among the many active participants in the league. It was a rough sport, played on outdoor winter rinks and taken seriously by participants and observers alike. As Ted Evers once said, "Hockey wasn't professional; it was just for blood in those days."

Teams in the mercantile league played most of their games in the city, but occasionally they would take on teams in outlying communities. Dean Colpets, a former resident of Westlock, Alberta, in his description of Cecil Bennett hinted strongly at the future politician:

> It was a midwinter evening, 1926–27. Suddenly, emerging from the shadows of a passageway a young man stepped down onto the empty playing surface of the Westlock rink and started across. Dressed in a long coonskin coat with collar turned up against the cold, he walked briskly and jauntily towards us carrying a bundle of hockey sticks from which trailed the colours of Marshall-Wells. Westlock was having a

particularly good hockey season that winter and, to the partisan crowd packing nearly every seat, this brash young stranger from the big city was a call to battle. We let him get to centre ice and then we let him have it: a chorus of boos and catcalls. Without breaking a stride, he glanced up into the sea of jeering faces and smiled. Such a smile: humour, confidence, delighted appreciation.

The church was a centre of social activity, too. Cecil attended church picnics and other festivities which usually involved the young women's groups. He and two of his friends, Norman Farquharson and John Tames, regularly dated three sisters from the girls' group—the Mulholland sisters. Cecil, who was in his early twenties, went out with the youngest, Ellen, taking her to picnics and occasionally to a show. They also spent much of their time in friendly argument. The relationship came to an end because he refused to take Ellen dancing. She could not understand why he was so adamant in his disapproval of dancing—after all, his sister Olivia went to dances. Years later, he said, "I told her that I had more serious things to do in my life than waste my time around dance halls, that I had a mission. I was planning my life. I didn't smoke; I didn't drink; and I wasn't going to dance around dance halls."

Olivia had been working in an Edmonton office after her graduation from business college. In 1926 she married, leaving Cecil on his own. He moved to a rooming house kept by a Mrs. Robertson, who happened to be the sister of Arthur Meighen, the brainy Conservative leader who served for two very brief terms as prime minister of Canada. Mrs. Robertson was the widow of a missionary who had spent many years in China. Coincidentally through his church, which offered special classes for new Canadians, Cecil became involved in teaching English to Chinese immigrants and giving lessons in general business methods and the operation of Canadian government.

Cecil impressed his classes, and he was frequently embarrassed by their kindness and generosity. They gave him presents of heavy silk from which he had several shirts made. On cold winter days as he walked down the streets of Edmonton, taxis frequently pulled up alongside him. He refused to get in, for he could not afford to pay the fare. Later he discovered that his Chinese friends were sending these taxis when they noticed him walking, trying to show their appreciation for the patience he demonstrated in class. One of the young Chinese was linked with a well-to-do banking family in the Orient and invited Cecil to return to China with him. He was so impressed with Cecil's knowledge of business that he had hopes of persuading him to join the family firm. The offer was politely declined, but years later Bennett wondered what might have happened had he accepted the invitation. He speculated that he would probably have become involved with the Sun Yat Sen group in the middle of the revolution.

While living at Mrs. Robertson's, Cecil had the opportunity to meet Arthur Meighen who stayed with his sister whenever he visited Edmonton. This quickened his interest in politics. Meighen had a fine mind and a witty tongue. He was unfulfilled as Canada's prime minister, but as leader of the opposition in the House of Commons he was Mackenzie King's hated and feared opponent. Said Bennett, "He was a most amazing man. And he won all the arguments against Mackenzie King, but he lost the elections. He was the best Canadian parliamentary speaker that I've heard. King wasn't a very good speaker, but he was good at political manoeuvring."

Cecil had the temerity to ask both the Conservative leader and Mackenzie King to address the same interdenominational young people's conference in Edmonton. "When they found out, well, Mackenzie King, who was prime minister at the time, changed his itinerary. But Meighen came and he impressed us. If he had made the same kind of warm speech he made at our conference politically, he would have served as prime minister longer."

Cecil developed an increasing interest in politics, particularly federal politics. He confided to a friend that a person could have no greater ambition than to serve as a minister in the Canadian government. He frequently attended political meetings and, along with a few friends who considered themselves experts in the art of heckling, took special delight in interrupting Liberal speakers and breaking up their meetings. There could be no denying his Tory persuasion.

He heard an important speech by Prime Minister King in Edmonton in 1924 regarding the Peace River region. "Mackenzie King had this enormous meeting. The great question in western Canada at that time was: would they build a railroad out to Churchill on Hudson Bay, to take the grain out that way? It was frozen most of the year, and there were lots of arguments against it. Or would the federal government money be used to give the great Peace River country a coast outlet? And Mackenzie King—I can see him now—said, 'Not only am I in favour of the Peace River country and its development . . . but I will make the Peace River program the spearhead of my policy.' And he pointed his hands in the shape of a spear." Cecil was particularly interested in this issue as a result of his earlier experience in the Peace River district with his father.

Canadian historian Donald Creighton wrote harshly of King: "His verbal currency was invariably tendered in the highest denominations; but in practical politics he always dealt in very small change." Farmers in the Peace River area at least would have agreed with his assessment. Cecil Bennett shared the disillusionment and cynicism of many in the west when King's

Liberal government refused to act on his promise to provide a Peace River outlet; according to him, "Years later when they attacked King in the House of Commons about it, he said that what he meant by a spearhead was that he would fill up the rest of the country first and deal with the Peace River last. Terrible!" Cecil's objections to Liberal politics were thus reinforced. He held the common view that a railway from the Peace River district to the Pacific coast was the obvious solution to the problem. He dreamed of someday being in a position of power from which he could help the plight of the Peace River settlers.

Like most other young men, Cecil was looking for a potential wife. He had a very well-thought-out notion of the type of woman he was seeking. She would have to be as dedicated and saintly as his own mother and prepared to support him in his "mission." He was always shy with women, so it was fortunate that he did not have to search too far. The first time he met his future wife was in an Edmonton church basement at a meeting of the young people's society. Her name was Annie Elizabeth May Richards, a tall, striking woman almost three years older than him. Like so many members of his own family, she was a schoolteacher. Like Cecil she was a Presbyterian of British stock. May, as she preferred to be called, was born and raised on Vancouver Island where her father worked as a mine surveyor. Later her family moved to Alberta; she completed her schooling and at the age of seventeen, just as the First World War began, she started teaching in a one-room schoolhouse in rural southern Alberta. She boarded a few miles away and rode a horse to and from school. Later she obtained a teaching position in Edmonton, where her father was working for the provincial Department of Mines.

In Edmonton, May became deeply involved with the young people's church groups, serving as president of the interdenominational young people's society the year before Cecil held the post. It did not take him long to notice that he and May Richards shared similar backgrounds, similar interests and a similar view of the world. Indeed, it is difficult to imagine two people more remarkably well suited to one another. They worked together on the boards of their church associations, attended social and recreational functions—and never had a single argument.

Cecil began to visit May at her home and was accepted by her family. When he asked her to be his wife, she did not hesitate in agreeing—although she had been advised not to marry him. "I wouldn't marry Cecil Bennett if I were you," May was told by a friend in her church group. "He's not going to live very long." Cecil was an extremely serious-looking young man, and very slim—at five feet ten and a half inches, he weighed only 132 pounds. Nevertheless, the young couple became engaged.

They decided not to marry immediately. Cecil wanted to go into business for himself first. He was doing well at Marshall-Wells but had little opportunity for the kind of spectacular advancement he dreamed of. He was convinced he had to gain control of his own destiny and become financially independent. Surely that was the first step to a successful political career. He would approach each such step towards the fulfillment of his "mission" in the same calculated, methodical way.

Cecil managed to save $350 and decided to buy a piece of property as an investment, perhaps to build a house on. He went to the Edmonton city hall and scoured their map for land he could afford in an area that was likely to develop. He settled for a good-sized lot being offered for $350 and for paying cash was given a ten-per-cent discount. Not long after, he was approached by a contractor who wanted to purchase the property because it was in the middle of a row of houses he planned to build, but Cecil told him he intended to build his own house on it. Much to Cecil's surprise, the contractor explained that he owned a little bungalow right next door to Mrs. Robertson's and was willing to trade it for the lot if Cecil was prepared to assume the mortgage. He accepted and, since he and May were not yet married, rented the bungalow to two young women—a nurse and a schoolteacher. He then visited various financial institutions to find the highest possible mortgage for his new bungalow. After remortgaging he ended up with $2,000 in cash, in addition to two fine tenants whose monthly rental payments covered his mortgage obligation. It was in this somewhat unorthodox manner that Cecil Bennett began his extremely successful financial career.

Now he could look more seriously for a business of his own. Through his connections at Marshall-Wells and the various salesmen he met, he heard of businesses that were available. In the winter of 1926–27 he learned that Westlock Hardware and Furniture, about fifty miles north of Edmonton, was for sale. It was the largest store in the small town of Westlock, situated on the rail line into the Peace River district. Its previous three owners had gone bankrupt, but Cecil believed he could make the business a success. Westlock may have been a small town, but Cecil recognized that it was the centre of a large farming community with a wide circle of potential customers.

While looking into the Westlock business, he discovered that a man by the name of Joe Renaud was also interested in it. He decided to meet Mr. Renaud to discuss the matter. Joe Renaud was a middle-aged French Canadian originally from Quebec, with no previous experience in the hardware business. In many ways he was Cecil Bennett's antithesis: a strong Liberal and a devout Catholic. Despite these differences, or perhaps because of them, the men took an immediate interest in one another. Renaud had saved a sizeable sum of money and wanted to invest it in a secure business so that he and his family could settle down. Cecil was short of capital and, feeling that he could work with Joe Renaud, proposed a partnership. Ted Evers, his friend at

Marshall-Wells, said: "He had the audacity to go to Renaud and say, 'Look, I'll provide the know-how, you provide the money, and we'll be on an equal basis.' Renaud accepted and it proved to be a marvellous deal. . . . Cecil Bennett may not have contributed financial equality in the partnership but he knew the hardware business from a practical point of view, and his knowledge of supply from his wholesale experience was indeed a valuable asset to their business." They started their partnership on February 19, 1927.

Cecil quit his job at Marshall-Wells and decided to move to Westlock immediately. His fiancée May Richards was in the middle of a school year and could not leave Edmonton, but they planned to marry the following summer. For the next few months Cecil worked extremely long hours, reorganizing the store, ordering new stock, advertising in the area and meeting potential new customers. He maintained his courtship of May by driving down to Edmonton on weekends whenever he could. During the week he wrote to her frequently, sometimes daily, long detailed letters filled with news about the business, predictions of its success, and his hope that their wedding day would soon arrive. These letters were invariably concluded by a long romantic string of Xs and Os.

On July 11, 1927, Cecil and May were married in Edmonton. It was a simple ceremony attended by a few friends and members of the bride's family. Clarence Budd, a friend from Marshall-Wells, was best man. In marrying a woman older than himself, Cecil was following in his father's footsteps. Curiously, it was also a familiar practice in his wife's family, for May's mother was older than her father and her two sisters married younger men.

May was well aware that she was marrying a man and a mission. Cecil firmly believed she could provide a stable home environment from which he could launch out on a successful career; she shared his confidence and never questioned his decisions affecting matters outside the home. Apparently, right from the start, they had an agreement that May would look after the home while Cecil would take care of business. It proved to be a successful division of labour and many years later they both claimed that they never had a single argument that lasted more than a few minutes.

The young couple did not have a honeymoon. After their wedding they boarded a train for Westlock where they were met by half the town and covered with confetti. After dinner at the home of his partner, Cecil and May spent the rest of the evening sorting out their belongings which had been brought to Westlock by truck and dumped unceremoniously in their new rented home. The very next day, Cecil went to work as usual.

After a lot of hard work and perseverance the Westlock hardware store began to be a success. Cecil was not becoming rich—all he drew from the business was a salary of $100 a month, $25 of which went for rent—but the store was becoming a centre of the community. For those who knew Bennett in his later years it is difficult to envisage him labouring in work boots and heavy pants, cutting metal and pipe, delivering oil, and driving around the countryside in the evenings selling farm equipment and radios to the farmers of the area. He became engrossed in all aspects of the business.

The partnership with Joe Renaud seemed an amicable one. They were men of remarkably different temperaments and backgrounds, but they worked harmoniously. One day when Cecil and his partner were busy in the store a blustery fellow came to make a large purchase of farm machinery. He wanted Cecil to have a drink with him before concluding the deal. Cecil politely declined. The potential customer stormed out of the store declaring he would not do business with a man who refused to take a drink with him. Joe Renaud was extremely disappointed at losing the sale. Cecil was not happy either, but he was unwilling to compromise his principles.

A few days later, the same man came back to the store and, to both partners' surprise, apologized for having been so rude and made his purchase. Apparently, when he thought that Bennett simply did not want to drink with him, he had sent in a few friends to use the same approach and they had received identical treatment.

Married life seemed to agree with Cecil and May, even though he was busy at work for more hours of the day than most working men. They were well liked in Westlock and became involved in various community activities. But Cecil had significantly less time for church now that he was in business; attendance at Sunday services was now the extent of his formal religious activity. On May 31, 1928, their first child was born, Mary Anita. Because there was no hospital in Westlock, the baby was born in Edmonton, where May's family could help.

Cecil felt the business was doing well enough that he could think about expansion. Early in 1928 he persuaded his partner of the potential benefit of expanding into the neighbouring town of Clyde. Renaud agreed; all that was necessary was for each partner to come up with $2,000. Cecil immediately left for Edmonton to sell his small house. The mortgage had been diminishing, while property values in Edmonton were rising. The bungalow now had a new tenant who wanted to buy it but could only afford a small down payment of $100. Cecil borrowed from the bank to pay off the existing mortgage and obtained clear title. He sold the house to his tenant and the new owner acquired a new mortgage, with Cecil pocketing the difference between it and the old one. He made an agreement for sale on what was left to pay, discounting the agreement after persuading the purchaser to pay the amount of the discount because he was making such a small down payment. In this manner Cecil Bennett sold his house and took out all his equity in cash. Within three days he had the $2,000 he needed.

Cecil returned to Westlock and finalized the deal for the store in Clyde.

His partner agreed that Cecil should establish the new business, so the young Bennett family moved to the small village and prepared for their next conquest.

Ted Evers was a witness to the birth of the new hardware store:

> My company, Marshall-Wells Alberta Co. Ltd., assigned my services to the opening, on the spot, of the new store, which included the layout of the then completely new idea of self-service in a hardware store, as well as the production of a flyer featuring specials and the promotion of a "Grand Opening" sale. It was wintertime but the sun shone brightly every day and encouraged us to believe in success, until the very afternoon before the Opening Day, and then the sun went into hiding and down came a heavy fall of snow. Next morning, opening day, the roads were almost impassable and not a single customer was in sight. Mrs. Bennett and I were despondent but not Cecil; he was actually enthusiastic. "Don't worry," he said, "they'll come. Curiosity will get the better of them, you'll see." And sure enough, they came.

Life in Clyde was simple but prosperous. Cecil worked harder than ever, and his labours were well rewarded: the store blossomed under his energetic direction. Oddly, his and Joe Renaud's diametrically opposed backgrounds played a part in the success of the respective stores, as Ted Evers described:

> Although the two partners were of different religious and political faiths, and had agreed never to speak of either in their business associations, the fact of it did obtrude itself. The majority of the customers of the Clyde area were Protestant and a few of them might have been slightly anti-Catholic; one or two of them told me of their pleasure in now being able to have a Presbyterian and Conservative atmosphere in the Clyde Hardware Store. On the other hand, the Westlock district had a substantial representation of Catholic and Liberal customers and the two towns were close enough together that for some customers the stores were equidistant if they felt the need of a choice. . . . Although it was a forbidden subject, Mr. Bennett was aware that those very differences of belief were indeed beneficial in the operation of both stores.

In Clyde, May Bennett often helped out in the store while her husband was out selling and making deliveries. Then late in 1929 she travelled back to Edmonton to prepare for the delivery of a new little Bennett. On December 14, Cecil and May's first son was born. He was christened Russell James—Russell after both Cecil's and May's only brothers and James for May's father. There was no disguising the fact that his names were placed in that order for a specific reason: Russell James would always be known by his initials "R. J." in commemoration of Cecil's religious mentor and father figure, R. J. Gillis.

The 1920s were prosperous times on the prairies. Crops were plentiful and prices rose higher every year. Cecil Bennett dreamed of owning a large chain of hardware outlets and began looking for options to buy more stores. But Joe Renaud was neither as young nor as ambitious as Cecil and was not enthusiastic about further expansion. Cecil decided to offer to buy out his partner's share and plunge ahead by himself. Before he did, however, telltale signs of economic disaster began to show. Cecil fancied himself a student of economics, and when the first hints of the Depression of the 1930s emerged he paid notice. In 1929 the stock markets plummeted and wheat prices fell rapidly. Cecil's intuition told him that the prairies, a region almost entirely dependent on the wheat crop, was no place to build a business empire, especially in difficult times. Instead of buying out Joe Renaud, he sold his share of the hardware business to him in June 1930.

Selling out to his partner when he did was a bold, even audacious move on Cecil Bennett's part. He was a young man with a growing family. He felt it was time to look elsewhere for the fulfillment of his mission; though he did not know where, he was confident that success could not elude him wherever he decided to settle. May Bennett had an aunt living in Victoria. The Bennetts decided to go there for a holiday and Cecil would look into business prospects in British Columbia.

So in the summer of 1930 the Bennetts said good-bye to their Alberta friends, uncertain whether they would return and unaware that they were destined to become enduring British Columbians. They left behind relatives, too: May's family was still in Edmonton, as was Cecil's sister Olivia. And there was Cecil's father. Andrew Bennett was no longer in contact with his family, and his vision of becoming rich in the land of plenty had faded. The problem of an outlet for the Peace River district had not been solved and, as a result of overexpansion, the early 1920s were years of stagnation: hundreds of farms were taken out of cultivation and even more were abandoned. The *Peace River Record* of January 24, 1924, noted that: "Given another year such as the past, and there will be a bigger colony of Peace River settlers in California than Alberta." The newspaper correctly predicted Andrew Bennett's course of action. He abandoned his homestead and headed to the coast, eventually ending up in California. However, he was unhappy there and in time returned to the Peace River country where he was known as an interesting and controversial figure. "Andy" Bennett was considered to be a good horseman and was never known to back down from a fight with a younger man at a country dance. Ultimately, though, he was a lonely man. He died of a cancer-related illness at the Veterans' Hospital in Edmonton on Christmas Day 1934.

CHAPTER TWO
"IT COULDN'T BE DONE"

Somebody said that it couldn't be done
But he with a chuckle replied
That "maybe it couldn't," but he would be one
Who wouldn't say no till he'd tried.
So he buckled right in with a trace of a grin
On his face. If he worried he hid it.
He started to sing as he tackled the thing
That couldn't be done, and he did it.
                    Edgar A. Guest

We travelled by car; it was quite a trip. We had friends at different places in Alberta, then we crossed over into the States. You couldn't get from Alberta directly to British Columbia in those days—there were no highways." In the summer of 1930 W. A. C. Bennett journeyed to the coast with his wife and two small children on a belated honeymoon. However, it was an arduous kind of vacation, for the roads were terrible by today's standards.

They stayed at May's aunt's cottage in Victoria, but after a few days Cecil became restless and travelled by ferry to Vancouver to visit his old friend Ted Evers, who was working for Marshall-Wells there. Bennett wanted to scout the province for opportunities in the hardware business. Evers and others suggested several areas to look at and Bennett decided to drive into the southern interior; he did not bother to look in the area of Vancouver, the province's largest city and commercial centre, because if he was going to settle in B.C. it would be in a small but growing community, for he was a firm believer in raising a family in a small town. He had already concluded that if he could not find a promising situation he would return to the prairie. On his way inland he stopped in various towns and chatted with local merchants to gauge the business climate. It took four days of often treacherous driving to reach the Okanagan Valley, and when he arrived he decided to go no farther.

Many people believe there is something about the air in British Columbia's Okanagan region that clears the mind. It seems just as likely that the same air, after clearing the mind, fills it with dreams of future greatness; certainly the Okanagan has produced its fair share of visionaries. When

Bennett drove through the valley in the summer of 1930 he thought it would be a beautiful place to settle: the weather was hot and sunny and people were eating peaches and berries and swimming in the lake.

In Kelowna he discovered a sizeable hardware firm for sale, owned by David Leckie, an elderly Scot and valley pioneer who had established his store in 1904. The business appeared to be much larger than Bennett imagined he could afford, but the Scotsman seemed genuinely interested in making a deal. As Bennett described it: "Twenty people had tried to buy his business before, but nobody could deal with Leckie. He and I drove the countryside and we talked, and he tried to sell me his business. At that time I hadn't decided to go to Kelowna. I had been looking on the way down at Kamloops and Vernon, and I was going to look at Penticton and Princeton before making a decision, but Mr. Leckie kept pressing me and he sent me telegrams and followed me to the coast. He was very anxious to sell, for many reasons, for personal reasons. He had made money and was now anxious to get out." Leckie was also anxious to unload the store because prices were falling and future business conditions looked grim. In fact, the economic depression that would define the next decade had just begun.

After expressing a strong interest in Leckie's business, Bennett returned to Victoria to tell his wife that their future lay in the Okanagan Valley, probably Kelowna. May was delighted, for she had a close friend from Edmonton living there. Then Bennett travelled to Vancouver to negotiate with Leckie. He learned from the business community that the older man had a reputation for driving a hard bargain. For several days the young prairie merchant negotiated with the dour Scotsman. Their marathon discussions took place in hotel lobbies, on Vancouver streets and, chiefly, in the office of Bennett's friend, Ted Evers. There Evers observed the young W. A. C. Bennett's negotiating abilities: "David Leckie found that inexperienced youth against the wisdom and business acumen of maturity was by no means an unequal contest. I cannot speak of Mr. Leckie's reactions to that prolonged session but the experience left me incredulous, somewhat awed, and a little weak—not from the arguments themselves but from the young man's ability to convert dour 'nays' into wavering 'maybes,' and by his competence in keeping the rivers of negotiation flowing freely!"

In the end, Leckie agreed to sell, accepting Bennett's final offer of 68 cents on the dollar for the wholesale stock price of the hardware firm's inventory. In addition, Bennett acquired the large two-storey store which had been erected in 1912. Leckie's acceptance was impulsive and somewhat out of character: he had received other offers for his business but turned them all down, only to accept the proposal of this strangely energetic young businessman from Alberta. As would happen so often in his career, Bennett's timing was fortunate and he seized the opportunity without hesitation. This small business deal would ultimately alter the course of British Columbia history.

Bennett packed up his family and moved to the Okanagan Valley. He authorized the postmaster in Clyde to auction off all their furniture and household effects, for the Bennetts were to start life anew in Kelowna. They rented a home on the main street of town for thirty dollars a month and settled in. Cecil Bennett immediately set to work organizing his new business to face economic conditions that looked ominous.

Kelowna, on Okanagan Lake, had a population of under 5,000 and was growing quite slowly, but since it was situated in the heart of the valley, it had become a hub for the farming, fruit-growing and ranching activities of the region. The Okanagan Valley had gone through several stages of development and even though it had not achieved its early promise, it was still being hailed as the "California of Canada." But when Cecil Bennett arrived in the valley the heady optimism of the early years was evaporating, for the economic depression was becoming increasingly evident. Thousands of unemployed workers were joining the relief lines in Vancouver and small businesses throughout the province were closing their doors. The Okanagan relied heavily on outside markets for the sale of its fruit and other agricultural products, and markets were shrinking. Apple growers were up in arms over the poor prices they were offered for their crops; the slogan "a cent a pound or on the ground" summed up their frustration. Many Kelowna merchants had resorted to bartering their goods for food from farmers who could not afford to pay their bills in cash.

Into this unwelcome business climate strode cheerful, smiling Cecil Bennett. The deal he had struck for the hardware firm with "Old Man" Leckie allowed him a competitive advantage over merchants struggling with falling prices. Bennett's immediate need, after settling his family, was to generate cash flow for his new business, which he did by clearing out some of the store's huge inventory at the grand opening sale. Ted Evers assisted with the promotion and preparation for the sale; he had helped ably with Bennett's first business in Alberta and Bennett was already a firm believer in sticking with a proven formula.

The sale was a huge success, generating $30,000 which helped to put the business on its feet. Not only did Bennett get rid of most of Leckie's old stock but he also met most of the population of Kelowna. His hardware firm dealt largely in heavy equipment for use in local industries, as well as carloads of nails and tons of wire strapping for the wooden boxes in which fruit was shipped.

The store was a substantial structure and well situated on Kelowna's main street. Tony Tozer, a friend of the Bennett children, described the hardware store during its early years of operation: "To a youngster going in there it looked huge—a huge, impressive place. All along the walls it had great side panels filled with little drawers where they kept nuts and bolts. They had ladders that slid along the walls for reaching the top drawers. The boss had an office which was above the store, but he could look out all over it. That was a great man's office." From his perch overlooking the store, W. A. C. Bennett laboured long hours, planning, organizing and building his business.

Bennett believed that the Depression years of the 1930s created an atmosphere conducive to success in business. Almost half a century later he said:

> Oh, yes, they were tough years. But it's easier to finance a business when prices are dropping than when they're rising. When they're dropping it takes less money to replace your inventory. When they're rising, you don't have the money to replace it. The time to start a business is always in a difficult period. Never start in a boom period—your costs and everything would be way out of line. Start it in a difficult period and keep your costs down. Then things get better; you can only go up. The people who go bankrupt are the people who start their business in good times. They think there is no end, that everybody can start a business, which is ridiculous. . . . In the merchandising business there is a difference of six per cent in terms of net profit. If you have three-per-cent loss a year, in a few years you're bankrupt. With three-per-cent, or anything resembling three-per-cent net profit on sales over a period of years, you'll be prosperous. That's the difference—it's very, very narrow.

In retrospect this all seems reasonable, but in fact his early years in the Okanagan were made more difficult by the many local business failures and by severe weather conditions. Historian Margaret Ormsby has written: "The summer of 1931 was the first of a series of long, hot, dry seasons. As the supply of water in the Okanagan Valley became exhausted, the irrigation flumes dried out and cracked, and the leaves hung limply on the trees. Every day now—and for the next three or four summers—the sun, reflecting the flames of forest conflagrations, rose and set as a mammoth ball of fire." The harsh weather was parallelled by the severity of the decline in business, for much of the economy of the region depended on the faltering fruit-growing industry. On at least one occasion Bennett faced a serious crisis:

> Every year we made a little money, but in February of 1933—for the month of February—we took in less money, even with extremely careful management, than our wage bill. So there was no money for rent, there was no money for light, there was no money for operating and mainten-

ance costs, no money for services, no money for replacement of merchandise sold. We were just draining the stock. But I understood that every day was not sunshine in business. In life you're bound to have good days and you have stormy periods. And when you have a stormy period, you do what you'd do when in a bad storm at sea: you get rid of some of your ballast; you sell off your merchandise and you don't replace it. Better to save the ship, better to save the business, than to let it go under.

Of course, Bennett survived the 1930s and his business eventually flourished. The Depression experience gave him a sharp sense of how to manage under the severest conditions. Throughout his first few years in Kelowna, which were clearly the toughest in the valley's history, he kept very little inventory in his store, only stocking items he knew would sell well and quickly. He staggered his employees' hours of work when he could only afford to pay them for a few hours a day, and although some Kelowna merchants felt uneasy about his aggressiveness, his enthusiasm was generally admired. His hardware business ultimately succeeded, for he practised the three principles of business which became his often-repeated motto: "Buy right, sell right and collect your money."

By taking over one of Kelowna's largest stores young Bennett had placed himself in a position of relative prominence in the community. Townspeople were anxious to meet the new owner of the hardware store and were invariably surprised when they did, for Bennett had turned just thirty in the autumn of 1930 and he looked considerably younger. One of the first people to become well acquainted with the town's new merchant was neighbouring grocery store owner, Pasquale "Cap" Capozzi, who described him as: "Just like a kid. He was a skinny little fellow, you know. Why, you would have to put a big rock in his pocket if a strong wind was blowing."

A short while after settling in Kelowna, Cecil Bennett discovered that he was not the only Bennett in town and received in error the mail of "W. Bennett" and a "W. C. Bennett." To avoid any confusion he began to use the initials of his three Christian names and was known henceforth as "W. A. C. Bennett."

May Bennett had settled into life in Kelowna without much difficulty. Her aunt from Victoria moved in with the family in their rented home, and with two small children she was kept busy. During these years, unemployed transient men would often stop at the house to ask for something to eat. May always fed those who were in need, but in keeping with her husband's wishes she showed them to the woodpile first. Those who were simply freeloading walked away; the truly hungry chopped wood and thereby earned a meal.

In the spring of 1932 May was expecting her third child. She hired a young woman, Winnifred Earl, to help with the housework and tend to the young children's needs. Winnie, as she came to be known, soon was an integral part of the Bennett household. She said of meeting W. A. C. Bennett: "I met him the first day I was there. I had seen him before in the store; I knew he was the owner and manager. I remember that first day he came home for his lunch and he was the greatest one.... He was just *so* interested in everyone. He came into the house and the children were there and were clamouring for their dad. And he used to have a great time playing with them, marching around; they used to all go through one room and through the kitchen and the bathroom, the children marching behind him, and they were all singing: 'California here we come, right back where we started from!' "

On April 14, 1932, the third and last Bennett child was born. A tiny, fragile, jaundiced boy, he was named William Richards Bennett. The growing family had moved into a bigger rented house, and a few years later Bennett was offered an astonishing deal on one of the largest, most beautiful homes in the valley, of which he said:

The house was built in 1912 by a great Kelownian, a great Canadian, Frank DeHart. He was a former mayor of the city of Kelowna. The Depression hit him very hard and in due course he passed away—and the home was deeply in debt. I was asked if I would buy it. The DeHart family had surrendered all interest in the house and property, and the first mortgage was held by a company in England that was very anxious to liquidate all their properties—especially in faraway places like British Columbia. I told them I had no money: "Any money I have is more than tied up in my struggling business." "You don't need much money. Make us an offer." Well, I made a ridiculous offer. For the five acres of land and the home I made an offer of $5,500—$500 cash and $500 every six months, with no interest. To my amazement, they accepted it.

So the Bennett family moved into the house and during those lean, depressed years they lived in relatively grand style. It became W. A. C. Bennett's last permanent home, and half a century later it is still one of the finest, most stately residences in the Okanagan Valley.

The hours Bennett spent at home with his family were enjoyable, intensely so, but this is not to say he was a family man. By far the greatest portion of his energies was devoted to his new business and to his developing interests in the community. Shortly after arriving in Kelowna he became involved in the local Board of Trade; he served as vice-president for two years and as president for two years. Perhaps even more important than the Board of Trade was an informal coffee clique that met almost daily at Chapin's Cafe.

Here W. A. C. Bennett, Cap Capozzi and several other local businessmen would meet to talk shop and dream of better days. He joined service groups like the Gyros and the Canadian Red Cross and took part in all kinds of community activities.

Soon after arriving in Kelowna Bennett was also initiated into Freemasonry, the international fraternal order whose secret rituals and teachings its members vow never to divulge. Freemasons believe they should lead by precept and example, so Bennett would view membership as consistent with his religious beliefs and his experiences as a young adult in the Tuxis movement. Socially and politically, Freemasons have played an important part in the development of British Columbia. And Bennett undeniably made many useful acquaintances as a Mason. Within a short time he rose to the rank of Worshipful Master of his lodge. Although he could not discuss his involvement in the order, he did acknowledge that it influenced him greatly. An elderly May Bennett delighted in reciting the old line: "Love to love a Mason, for a Mason never tells."

W. A. C. Bennett worked hard, enjoyed his work and slept well every night. He was, however, practically obsessed with his business and with encouraging the proper conditions for it to flourish in. Of course, all of his community activities can be viewed as self-advertisement, and he was seen by many as a kind of chronic busybody, forever promoting his new home town and the bountiful promise of the Okanagan Valley. In short, he was in the business of making business.

A good example of this aspect of his character was his unlikely involvement in establishing a winery in Kelowna. Shortly after his arrival, Cap Capozzi and a few other Italian settlers had come up with an idea which, if successful, would help to solve the problem of apples rotting on the ground. This enterprising group decided to pool their money and import from Italy machinery that would convert fruit into wine. A crisis occurred when it was discovered that more equipment than they could afford was on its way. Bennett was one of several local businessmen who attended an emergency meeting in the back of Cappozzi's grocery store. The new business venture, Domestic Wine By-Products Ltd., was in dire straits and Cappozzi pleaded for help and financial backing from the assembled merchants. Bennett and one other businessman agreed to sign notes covering the cost of the additional machinery. The winery was now well on its way with Bennett as an active partner.

Initially, the winery progressed slowly. The company, which became Calona Wines Ltd., eventually moved from making apple wine to using imported and locally grown grapes. Bennett spent a great deal of time promoting the product, travelling by car with Capozzi throughout B.C. He also went to Alberta and Saskatchewan where he secured large contracts from the provincial government liquor boards. In time, the product improved and its market expanded. When the worst years of the Depression were over, the wine industry in the Okanagan Valley began to thrive. Not too many years later, Calona Wines was a multimillion-dollar business.

Some have suggested that for Bennett, a noted teetotaller and staunch churchman, to become involved in the winery demonstrates a lack of principle and an element of hypocrisy. But his motives were simple. He was genuinely interested in seeing new industry develop in the valley. He realized that the success of almost any new enterprise would benefit the area and his own business interests. His participation in the scheme also provided another outlet for his boundless promotional abilities. Clearly, he was not interested in wine. In fact, during the years he was involved in the winery he never drank a single glass of the wine it produced. It is also doubtful that he profited much from his efforts to establish the company, for he relinquished his interest well before there was any likelihood of receiving dividends. Nevertheless, Cap Capozzi maintained that the success of the winery was due solely to Bennett's perseverance.

This is the best example of the results of W. A. C. Bennett's particular brand of local boosterism during those years. H. A. Trusswell, a local car dealer and a fellow Mason, said: "Bennett always took a very great interest in anything civic, anything to do with the progress of the city. But, mind you, always as the boss-man; he wanted to direct things to his way of thinking. He used chaps like myself to pass the arguments on to people who were debating the issues." Naturally, because the times were not favourable, many ideas never reached fruition; many plans for creating business opportunities and developing new industries in the Okanagan never went beyond the busy coffee conversation at Chapin's Cafe, but Bennett could almost always be counted on to support the promotion of ventures in and around his home town. Like businessmen everywhere, he was eagerly looking for signs that the economy was moving again, that the long and painful economic depression was waning. Many had lost patience with such hopes, but not Bennett; even during the toughest of times he exuded confidence and wore a perpetual smile on his face.

In many respects the Depression of the 1930s never touched him. His hardware firm might have fared better in more prosperous times, but it did well enough. His young family never went hungry nor suffered any material deprivation. In fact, for a young businessman with a growing family in a new environment, he did exceedingly well.

However, the Depression significantly affected Bennett's ideas and attitudes, especially towards public issues. He was a "child" of the Depression, and like so many thirties people committed his energies to the solution of public problems. The early and mid-1930s became an important watershed in his life. He built his hardware firm, watched over his family, developed social and business relationships, rose to a position of respect and prominence in his community and, all the while, formed opinions and adopted stances on public issues that grew out of economic hardships and the public's cry for security.

As a small "c" conservative, he could easily sympathize with the worries and fears of the great majority of Canadians who wondered if the capitalist system could ever be made to work again. As a Conservative, he had difficulty agreeing with all of the policies advocated by R. B. Bennett, who had the great misfortune to serve as Tory prime minister from 1930 to 1935. Conservatives in Canada subscribed to a party tradition that was not philosophically averse to positive government action. So when the Conservative government nationalized a variety of enterprises and created crown corporations like the Canadian Broadcasting Corporation, party supporters were not necessarily opposed. They did, however, become noticeably uncomfortable when R. B. Bennett's efforts to lift the country out of the Depression seemed so ineffectual, and especially when, in his last year as prime minister, he became so ensnarled in his "New Deal for Canadians."

W. A. C. Bennett felt strongly about the federal government's handling of economic issues. He was opposed to massive intervention in the economy, but believed that the government could and should play an important role in alleviating the suffering of the poor and disadvantaged. He may not have agreed with all of the policies of the Conservative government in Ottawa, but his criticisms were tempered by party loyalty and a firm belief that the depth of the Depression in Canada was attributable to a costly mistake by the ultimate Liberal scapegoat:

> The person responsible for the Depression, really, was not R. B. Bennett, my namesake. The person responsible was Mackenzie King. After the First World War, in 1921, the League of Nations recommended that those countries that didn't have a central bank should set them up. Now in Canada we operated our banking system with the chartered banks on ten-year charters, and they had the sole right of printing all currencies and handling all the credit. And so you couldn't set up a central bank in 1921. But in 1923, when the ten-year charters were up, that was the time to set up a central bank. Well, who was prime minister of Canada in 1923? Mackenzie King. And what did he do? He gave the banks the same old ten-year charter up to 1933. So R. B. Bennett came in with the Depression in 1930 and he had a wheelbarrow to do a bulldozer's job as far as finance was concerned. He just didn't have the machinery. If he

had a central bank, if Mackenzie King had established one in 1923, R. B. Bennett could have financed his way through the Depression. We still would have had difficult times, but we wouldn't have had the times we did.

W. A. C. Bennett always regarded himself as a keen student of finance and banking. Within the Conservative Party he had advocated the establishment of a central Canadian bank, placing himself in the ranks of the progressive, reform elements of the party. He followed closely the Royal Commission on Banking and Currency appointed by the federal government in 1933. And when the proposals of the commission were accepted and the long overdue Bank of Canada was established in 1934, he was so enthusiastic that he decided to try for election to the Bank's first board of directors. However, the period between July 3, 1934, when the federal statute providing for the Bank of Canada was passed into law, and March 11, 1935, when the new central bank began operation, was an extremely difficult time for Bennett. It was during this period that he suffered his first major defeat.

The Conservative government of R. B. Bennett encountered widespread opposition to their proposed method of establishing the Bank, for many Tories were worried about the potential power of a completely government-controlled central institution. The government compromised and announced that it would own half the shares and appoint half the directors, while the general public could buy the other half and elect the rest of the directors. Like most compromises, it turned out to be an unsatisfactory arrangement. In particular, the method of electing directors was one of the obvious weaknesses in the establishment of the Bank of Canada.

W. A. C. Bennett purchased fifteen Bank of Canada shares, at fifty dollars per share, and began his campaign to become a director. His support for the establishment of a central Canadian bank was consistent with his view of capitalism and private enterprise; he felt that certain adjustments were necessary to make the economic system work again. The Depression had seriously eroded the confidence of the Canadian business community and, though not all Conservatives were in favour of a central bank, the move did attest to the need for reform. Besides, the creation of the Bank of Canada, like other important reforms of the 1930s, met real needs, not only of the business community but also of a wide cross-section of the country. The possibility of W. A. C. Bennett being elected to the board of directors must have been remote, considering he was a young store owner from the hinterland of British Columbia. But he was undaunted and seemed confident that he could actually secure election if he approached the task carefully. His approach is worth noting.

Early one summer morning in 1934, Bennett met H. A. Trusswell, fellow businessman and local Tory stalwart. As they walked together towards their respective businesses Bennett began talking about the Bank of Canada, the importance of its establishment, its potential impact on the economy and how British Columbia Conservatives should be represented at the first meeting the following year. Apparently nobody was planning to go from Vancouver, so the Okanagan should send someone. Bennett suggested Trusswell should attend. Years later Trusswell said: "A man would be a jackass to accept a suggestion like that. I didn't know anything about banking. He was the one with the knowledge. He knew this when he was putting the suggestion. So naturally I said he should go and I would be delighted to help him line up proxies and that sort of thing."

In this manner, Bennett enthusiastically began his campaign for election to the board of directors of the Bank of Canada. The act establishing the bank placed in the hands of the shareholders the exceedingly difficult task of selecting seven directors from an unorganized group of over 12,000 shareholders scattered across Canada. Moreover, they were asked to choose directors from diverse occupational backgrounds and representative of the various regions of the country. The election arrangements were extremely haphazard. The government let it be known that it would welcome the sponsorship of candidates by trade and vocational associations; consequently, the Canadian Chamber of Commerce intervened in the election and submitted a slate of nominees.

Bennett did not seek or attain Chamber of Commerce backing but struck out on his own. He campaigned as a representative of the merchandising sector and sent letters to shareholders across Canada making bold policy proposals and inviting support. But in the end, all of his efforts were for naught. At the January 1935 meeting of shareholders in Ottawa, the entire slate of Chamber of Commerce candidates was elected. Bennett never liked discussing this defeat, and yet it may have been one of the most significant events of the Depression years for him. The fact that he seriously sought election to the Bank of Canada's first board of directors says much about his character and self-perception. He was only thirty-four years old and was just getting established in both a business and a family sense. And yet, he was completely sincere in his effort and believed he could be elected. With perspective, it is easy to dismiss this as a misguided, audacious, even presumptuous attempt, but in his later years Bennett would only rationalize his defeat in terms of the loss of an individual pitted against an organized, established faction. In a sense, his defeat presaged a series of such struggles over the next many years and set an antiestablishment pattern for him to follow.

His failure to be elected a director of the Bank was a serious blow to his ego and left a deep scar that never completely healed. In addition, it helped to change his outlook in one important regard. As a youngster in New Brunswick, as a young adult in Alberta, and now with maturing interests in British Columbia, he had always been absorbed by national affairs, his eyes forever focussed on federal politics. It was this interest that compelled him to his Bank of Canada effort. He probably viewed election to the board as a potential steppingstone to a career in federal politics. His defeat, therefore, was a shattering personal experience and more than just a minor setback, for it soured him on national affairs. He began to recognize that a small-businessman from the interior of British Columbia was quite impotent in Ottawa politics and he was prompted to look elsewhere.

He had become involved in local Conservative affairs very shortly after arriving in Kelowna and devoted most of his attention to the federal wing of the party, serving as secretary-treasurer of the Yale Conservative Association and vice-president of the Kelowna and District Conservative Association. Undoubtedly he planned to run sometime for public office, but factors besides his Bank of Canada defeat obliged him to turn away from national politics. First of all, his business and family were young and growing; he could not abandon them for faraway Ottawa until they were both a little older and more established. Secondly, and more important, there was no vacancy. His home riding, the huge federal constituency of Yale, had been represented since 1924 by the venerable Tory warhorse, Grote Stirling. Stirling became minister of national defence in the cabinet of R. B. Bennett, and even during the defeat of the Conservative government in 1935 was easily re-elected; he gave no indication of a willingness to relinquish his hold on the riding.

So Bennett turned his intense interest and energies away from national politics to more provincial concerns and became increasingly involved in the provincial wing of the Conservative Party. In fact, he must have been already well schooled in the peculiarities of B.C. politics, for the structure of the Conservative Party allowed considerable overlap between federal and provincial allegiances. He had acquired a good working knowledge of provincial party politics and made a point of meeting and acquainting himself with several B.C. public figures.

The history of the Conservative Party in British Columbia is a chequered one. When party politics were introduced to Canada's west coast province around the turn of the century, the Tories were strong, even dominant, especially with the popular guidance of Sir Richard McBride who served as premier from 1903 to 1915. When McBride stepped down, his attorney general, W. J. Bowser, succeeded him as premier for about a year, until the 1916 election banished the Conservatives from power. The Liberal Party ruled supreme for the next dozen years, but the provincial election of

1928 gave the Tories another chance in B.C. —perhaps their last for all time. Dr. Simon Fraser Tolmie swept to power with thirty-five of the forty-eight seats in the provincial legislature.

Tolmie's government was in office when Bennett arrived in B.C. and its career served as a valuable lesson in practical politics. In Bennett's opinion:

> You couldn't have found a better person than Simon Tolmie. He was a federal minister in the Conservative government of R. B. Bennett— minister of agriculture. He was then national organizer of the federal Conservatives. As national organizer, he came out to the British Columbia Conservative convention to elect a new leader. They had at the time in their provincial constitution that you had to have sixty per cent of the votes to be elected leader of the party. Well, there were two people involved and neither one could get the percentage, so it was deadlocked. Tolmie was there as an organizer and he came from B.C. and was a popular fellow: they insisted that he take the job. Well, he didn't want the job and he wasn't trained for the job and he wasn't the person for that kind of job. He wasn't tough enough to be premier of a province like British Columbia. And so he got in in 1928, a boom time in British Columbia. Well, he had a "business cabinet" and they were going to do everything. The first couple of years were good years. Money was rolling in and they were spending money and they thought there would be no end to it. And then came 1930 and 1931 and 1932, and they hung on for the full five years. They had a big majority in '28 when they kicked out the Liberals. But do you know how many Conservatives were elected in 1933? Not one Conservative! Not one!

Bennett was right; the 1933 election proved devastating for British Columbia Tories. His memory here, however, reflects a slight problem of definition: one unrepentent Tolmie supporter did gain election to the House in Victoria, as did a couple of other qualified Conservatives; but not a single candidate running under the official Conservative name was elected. Their ignominious rejection by the voters was due to many factors, including the unstable nature of the party, but it was largely a result of the general economic crisis of the period. Indeed, few Canadian governments were able to retain power during the early and most difficult part of the Depression. As a leader, Premier Tolmie proved sadly deficient, and Bennett believed a stronger, more adroit premier could have dealt more effectively with all of the problems Tolmie encountered. Bennett preferred to view the near-ruination of the Conservative Party in British Columbia as a consequence of a crisis in leadership.

The 1933 election campaign and its outcome provided Bennett with a number of important political insights and an invaluable introduction to the politics of his adopted province. If he learned something from Tolmie's crushing defeat, in time he would learn even more from the victor in that election—the new Liberal premier, Thomas Dufferin Pattullo. The 1933 election is considered a watershed in B.C. politics, for it saw the emergence of a new party: the Co-operative Commonwealth Federation. An amalgam of socialist, farmer and labour groups that had coalesced in Regina earlier in the year, the CCF was in large part a political response to the Depression, adopting as its platform the "Regina Manifesto" which called for increased public ownership, new national welfare measures and the abolition of the capitalist system. The B.C. election was the first electoral campaign in the country for which the new party nominated and ran candidates. They elected a handful of their candidates and, because of the dramatic Tory demise, the CCF actually formed the official opposition in the B.C. legislature.

Socialism was not new to British Columbia; it was a force in provincial politics at the turn of the century and a factor in every subsequent political campaign. The particular nature of the B.C. economy, based largely on the primary production of natural resources, had created the situation in which a large labouring population could easily view itself as pitted against and exploited by timber barons and absentee company owners. At a comparatively early date B.C. had become a highly unionized province, characterized by a radical political culture with the dividing lines between classes drawn boldly. It was fertile ground for a new party espousing a socialist philosophy. And now, with the actual rise of an organized socialist party receiving almost a third of the votes cast in the 1933 election, a new pattern was imposed. Seemingly overnight, the CCF became the chief political opposition in British Columbia; only in Saskatchewan would the new socialist party exert a greater influence.

For W. A. C. Bennett, as for most west coast Tories, these must have been dark days. And what must have made them darker than even the emergence of the CCF and the almost complete absence of a Conservative influence in the provincial legislature was the widespread popularity of the new Liberal premier. T. D. (Duff) Pattullo was a flamboyant, pugnacious leader and in many respects B.C.'s first modern premier. Originally from Ontario, he had adopted British Columbia as his own. He had served as provincial minister of lands in the glory days of Liberal rule, prior to Tolmie's premiership. His cabinet experience had given him a solid administrative background, but what proved more significant were his years as opposition leader when he had closely watched the Conservatives and the Depression ravage the province. When he alternately cajoled and lambasted Tolmie and his bumbling administrators, even Tories conceded that he was the most effective opposition leader ever to sit in the B.C. legislature. And now, as premier, he was well prepared for revenge.

The meteoric rise of the CCF demonstrated the depth of the electorate's discontent. Although Patullo considered himself a strong individualist, he now became firmly committed to the notion that the state should play a creative role in the economy to alleviate the collective hardships and fears of the public. Besides, he believed this leftward turn would help to dissipate the popularity of the CCF. Having campaigned on the promise of "Work and Wages," Pattullo ushered in his "Little New Deal" with the help and seeming support of an exceptionally able cabinet, and he pursued his policies with a vigour and gusto never before seen in British Columbia.

When Pattullo became premier in 1933 the Depression was at its nadir and the provincial treasury was virtually empty. Naturally, he was determined to turn this situation around, and his bold efforts to reform the economic system with his "socialized capitalism" not only made a strong impact on both provincial and federal politics but also made him many enemies. He became a self-styled antiestablishment figure, stepping on toes, pricking consciences and challenging loyalties. In so doing, he sowed the seeds of his own eventual defeat and forged a new, if premature, style of western Canadian political leadership—a style that W. A. C. Bennett would one day emulate.

With a Rooseveltian pledge of positive government, Pattullo enthusiastically offered incentives to private industry and poured government money into public works projects. He also tried to promote his vision of northern development for the vast, immeasurable resources of British Columbia's isolated interior. Entwined with this vision was his imperialistic desire to annex the Yukon Territory and thus increase even more the scope and richness of B.C.'s northern prospects.

Although Pattullo firmly held that it was the federal government's duty to chart a national course out of the Depression, he was reluctant to relinquish his grip on areas of provincial jurisdiction and his relations with Ottawa became increasingly strained. For example, he felt that Ottawa should take the initiative and assist the provinces in maintaining an adequate standard of social assistance. In 1935 he called together all western premiers to develop a common strategy in preparation for an upcoming dominion-provincial conference. This bold attempt to forge a special brand of western Canadian statesmanship failed, but foretold the future pattern of federal-provincial relations. Pattullo considered himself a "British Columbia Canadian" but in his first term as premier he was regarded as a narrow provincial rights man, reinforcing B.C.'s historic role as the spoilt child of Confederation. Nonetheless, he undoubtedly expressed a real sense of alienation in the province, and a viewpoint that would be adopted and developed by western Canadian politicians in decades to come.

Only a short while after becoming premier, Pattullo wrote to then Prime Minister R. B. Bennett: "We are an empire in ourselves and our hills and valleys are stored with potential wealth which makes us one of the greatest assets of the Dominion." As the first British Columbia premier to effectively employ the new medium of radio, he told the province in a speech broadcast in 1935: "The Dominion authority is steadily encroaching upon the fields of exclusive jurisdiction without even consulting the provinces." In the same speech he observed: "The truth is that the people of British Columbia understand conditions in eastern Canada much better than eastern Canada understands British Columbia. And the reason for this seems obvious. A very considerable portion of our population originally came from eastern Canada and consequently are familiar with conditions there."

Duff Pattullo fought the Depression, fought the federal government and fought the socialists, too. He consciously moved his government to the left in order to steal some of the CCF's new thunder. In his first term in office he established an industrial relations board and an agricultural marketing board, introduced a bold public works program, improved provincial welfare services, reduced the work week and busied the government in a myriad of other activities and programs. By the end of the term, the first phase of his Little New Deal was almost complete and, while the pains of the Depression had not been relieved, the Liberal machine began to prepare for a provincial election for June 1937.

During this exciting period, where were the Tories? Clearly, after the humiliating defeat of 1933, the provincial wing of the Conservative Party was in a shambles. Surprisingly, however, there were a sufficient number of dedicated old-time party activists to keep the faith alive. Dr. F. P. Patterson, a physician, had become president of the British Columbia Conservative Association. In 1936 he was elected party leader and tried to rally the Tory faithful behind the herculean task of party reconstruction. Although the 1935 national election saw the defeat of R. B. Bennett's administration, B.C. Conservatives showed signs of life, even strength. Many began to talk of a revitalized provincial party as the only practical free enterprise alternative to Pattullo's experiment in "socialized capitalism."

In Kelowna, W. A. C. Bennett became determined to play a part in the reorganization of the provincial party. He met with Dr. Patterson and offered to help organize in the Okanagan Valley. Privately, he had decided to seek the Tory nomination for his home constituency of South Okanagan, and so during the early weeks of 1937 he began to inform friends, fellow businessmen and local Tories of his intention, expressing the hope that unanimity would prevail in order to avoid a painful or embarrassing nomination battle. Bennett was, by this time, a well-known figure in Kelowna and president of the Board of Trade. He appeared a formidable candidate and, until a short time before the nominating convention scheduled for April 7, 1937, it seemed he would not be challenged. However, an unexpected turn of events altered his plans and served to teach him an unpleasant but important lesson.

Like most politicians, Bennett could not remember ever actually seeking election. His memory conjured up visions of his having been asked to run against his will and better judgement. His character and an examination of the facts strongly suggest otherwise. Nevertheless, his recollection of his attempt to win the South Okanagan Conservative nomination in 1937 is interesting: "This was the first time I ever offered myself to run. The Conservative president came up and saw the executive here in Kelowna and they said they wanted me to run. They were unanimous. I didn't want to run; I wasn't ready yet. But the pressure was great and in politics you can't always wait for the ideal moment. So, when they were unanimous, I agreed. But then it got into the papers that Tom Norris, who had been a lawyer in Kelowna and who was very active among Conservatives, wanted the nomination. So he set up an organization. I couldn't withdraw; I had given my word to the executive." But H. A. Trusswell, who along with Bennett served on the South Okanagan executive, said: "I really think Bennett engineered directly or indirectly all of the moves toward any nomination he ever received."

Tom Norris, a Vancouver lawyer, was an establishment figure in the British Columbia Conservative Party and, to W. A. C. Bennett, represented the old-line party machine. His motive in entering the nomination campaign at such a late date is unknown, but it can be seen as an effort by the Vancouver Conservative establishment to exert control over a resurgent provincial party. W. A. C. Bennett was an unknown quantity whereas Tom Norris was a respectable and longtime British Columbia Tory. When he threw his hat into the ring many old-time South Okanagan Conservatives reconsidered their positions. H. A. Trusswell, for example, who had been working for Bennett, moved into the Norris camp because he had known him longer and felt obligated.

Bennett was determined not to let the big city lawyer outsmart the small town merchant. Going into the nominating convention on the night of April 7, Bennett was confident. Simple arithmetic told him he had the support of enough delegates to beat Norris. He described the proceedings:

> I did have the convention won; we had almost eighty per cent of the delegates, and I had a great follower and friend in Cap Capozzi.... A lot of new people had come here—immigrants—and he lined up some of these people as delegates at the convention. One of Norris's people

came up and said, "Instead of going all night, let's just have a standing vote." I said, "That's fine." Over two-thirds were for me and less than a third were for Norris. Then the Norris supporters started to cry, "That's not in the constitution! That's not in the constitution!" After they had suggested it! These chaps, the newcomers, they couldn't spell the names properly when they wrote them in on the ballot. And we lost hundreds. We lost the vote.

No doubt, the nomination fight was a bitter struggle and Bennett did not take defeat easily. H. A. Trusswell said: "The thing went on until three in the morning. It split the Tory party in Kelowna with the group supporting Bennett accusing Norris of being a carpetbagger."

It is interesting that Bennett, who had been in British Columbia for only a few years, could succeed in having Norris, a native British Columbian, branded as a carpetbagger. More important is the fact that Bennett's lack of support for Norris in the election campaign that followed contributed to his defeat. Not even Bennett's smile could disguise his complete lack of affection for Norris; he held himself back from open criticism only out of loyalty to the party. Shortly after his loss at the nominating convention, he wrote to Norris in response to a request for support in what everyone knew would be a closely fought election campaign. With strained politeness, he explained that he could not be counted upon: "Before allowing my name to be put forward as a possible nominee I made my position clear that if I was a candidate in the Provincial Election I would resign as the President of the Kelowna Board of Trade realizing that the Board of Trade is a strictly non-political organization and has to deal from time to time with both Provincial and Federal governments. Now that I am not a candidate I of course will not be resigning as President of the Board of Trade with the result that I will not be in a position to take an active part in your campaign."

The provincial election was held on June 1, 1937. Neither Bennett nor any of his supporters made an effort to see Norris elected. The South Okanagan constituency was won by the Liberal candidate, Capt. Cecil Bull, by a narrow margin of less than 300 votes. Norris, who many years later was appointed to the Supreme Court of British Columbia, would never return to do political battle in Kelowna. W. A. C. Bennett refused any responsibility for the party's defeat: "Where Norris lost out—and this taught me a great lesson—was when he said, 'Look at Bennett, he's got nothing but the bohunks and the wops.' They wouldn't vote for him then and he lost the election. . . . [Norris's supporters] always blamed me for his defeat. His defeat was because he called these people names."

Bennett never reconciled his differences with the establishment Conservatives who controlled the party organization from Vancouver. He was confident that he would have his own day, and learned from his defeat the practicality of political loyalties. He studied strategy and tactics and, most important, resolved to have patience—an indispensable virtue for a politician-in-waiting. In time, he was able to win back the support of most Kelowna Tories—like Trusswell:

> At a meeting after Tom Norris was defeated, I accused Bennett of disloyalty. I got up and said if it hadn't been for the disloyalty of our executive group, Norris would have been elected—notwithstanding that he was a carpetbagger. We had worked hard and the loss was a great disappointment. So, Bennett and I were rather cool for a while. But all the time that I have known Bennett—and he's been very mad at times, mad at me and I've been mad at him—he's always been courteous and always had the courage and the guts to call me up and say he was wrong if he felt he was. And in all those years, even under a lot of tension, I never heard Cecil Bennett swear. I've always admired that about him.

The provincial election of 1937 was a great triumph for Liberal Premier Duff Pattullo. He was returned to power with a majority of thirty-one seats in the forty-eight-seat legislature despite the increased strength of the partially resurrected Conservative Party, which elected eight members. Especially pleasing for the Tories was the fact that they now formed the official opposition since they elected one more member than the socialists.

The CCF had not done as well as expected, their support being partly undercut by Pattullo's move leftward but more crucially by their own internal split. The party was a socialist coalition of groups having different backgrounds, varying principles and strong personalities. In British Columbia it would always suffer from intense internecine warfare; genuine representatives of the working class were constantly at loggerheads with the party's middle-class intelligentsia, and those of a more moderate viewpoint were neither willing nor able to bring the two factions together. In future years, the party was able to force a stern discipline upon its members so that internal battles were no longer fought in public, but prior to the 1937 B.C. election all hell had broken loose. Four of its members who had been elected in 1933, including the CCF leader Rev. Robert Connell, had been excommunicated from the party; they contested the 1937 election without success as "Social Constructives." Pattullo had wisely timed the election to take advantage of the serious divisions within the CCF and, in doing so, was able to withstand the advance made by the resurgent Tories.

Pattullo still possessed a majority in the legislature, but his Liberals had lost four seats. The tone of his second administration was markedly different from his first term in office; he moved more cautiously towards his espoused goal of "socialized capitalism." But as "prime minister" of British Columbia he stood firm as a defender of provincial rights. Pattullo was always an imposing figure and after the 1937 victory he felt secure in his leadership. And yet, over the course of the next few years, he alienated several large and important segments of the populace and eventually lost control of his own party. He liked to see himself as an outsider skirmishing with the establishment, but he fought himself into a corner that left him little room to manoeuvre.

Strangely, W. A. C. Bennett was extremely fond of Duff Pattullo. Party differences aside, they had many traits in common, including background and temperament. Pattullo's personal, aggressive and independent style of politics served as a model for Bennett to follow in future years. In particular, his stewardship of the provincial government taught Bennett how to go about fighting the federal government with one hand and the socialists with the other. On at least one occasion while Pattullo was in office, Bennett demonstrated his admiration for the man:

> After the election of 1937 I was president of the Board of Trade in Kelowna, and all over the province in boards of trade and chambers of commerce they were after Pattullo something awful for all the promises he made which he couldn't fulfill. So he was making a tour and he came to Kelowna and we put on a dinner for him—a very large dinner. My secretary at the Board of Trade was E. W. Barton—a good man, but he didn't like Pattullo. I said to him: "Barton, this meeting with Pattullo is going to be different than any other meeting of the Board of Trade that you've ever attended as secretary, and it must be kept absolutely secret. I want you to buy me—not the Board of Trade, but me personally—the finest gold-headed walking cane you can buy, and I want it fastened under the table where I will be sitting as president. And I want this inscribed on the cane: "For Outstanding Service in a Difficult Period of British Columbia's History." Wherever Pattullo had gone to see chambers of commerce they had all raised cain, so he was ready for attack. But when I stood up to introduce him I traced his history from his early boyhood in Ontario, I traced his history up in the Yukon, I traced his history up in Prince Rupert, and all the things he had in mind for British Columbia, and all the services he had given in public life. I didn't speak long, but when I handed him this cane . . . well, Pattullo had a very ruddy complexion, and he turned white and then turned red and then tears came down.

Bennett's gift to Pattullo, a conspicuous act of nonpartisanship, surprised many of the local Kelowna Tories. But it was not a political act—Bennett was not on the verge of conversion to Liberalism—rather it was a personal gesture of appreciation. There is some evidence to suggest that Premier Pattullo developed a fondness for the young Kelowna hardware merchant, but even if Pattullo were to have offered him a place on his Liberal team, it is unlikely that the offer would have been seriously considered. Politically, Bennett was still two things—a Tory and unproven, while Pattullo, despite Bennett's personal admiration, was a Grit and so the enemy. When Bennett returned his energies to his business interests and his family after the 1937 campaign, he kept one eye fixed firmly on the future—and the next provincial election.

Bennett not only managed his hardware firm but he also expanded to two more locations in the Okanagan Valley. Often he was out of town on hardware buying trips, or promoting his winery interest, or campaigning for the Conservative cause. But although he did not spend a great deal of time at home during this period of his career, he actually gave more hours to his family than he would ever again. His home life provides an interesting insight into his ideals and priorities.

It should be emphasized that Bennett's family was extremely important to him. Because of his own unfortunate childhood, he had resolved to head a unified and harmonious home. He had consciously equipped himself with the twin certitudes of faith and family; these were the cornerstones of his conscience and they sustained him until his death. Clearly, his choice of wife had proved extremely fortunate. May Bennett provided a stable home environment which her husband could depend upon. In so doing, she became a classic example of the woman behind the successful man. The division of labour that Cecil and May Bennett agreed to at the time of their marriage never altered, nor did it ever become a source of conflict. Bennett explained the formula for his marital success: "It is, quite simply, that we agree. We never have any arguments. We had an understanding that she would look after the home and so forth and I would look after the business and politics."

May Bennett organized their home to be convenient to her husband. Consequently, there was never any doubt that while she directed the household, he was its only head. W. A. C. Bennett dominated the home—it was never a child-centred household—so that all familial concerns were secondary to his needs. This was so because May organized the family's regimen in that particular fashion. She never questioned his decisions; he never interfered in her domestic domain. From the beginning, she accepted her husband's word, taking it for granted that he was seriously occupied. She stood by him in silence, without questions, and with constant support.

Not having had a full-time father to model himself after, Bennett simply assumed the role he imagined a good father would fulfill. Essentially, he saw himself as a provider—and, in a material sense, he was undeniably a good provider. But, ironically, he was away from home so much that he was guilty of one of the same sins as his own father, Andrew Bennett. Certainly he could not be accused of being an overbearing parent; rather, the Bennett children learned to cope with the problems associated with an absentee father. However, when Bennett was home he left his work behind and tried to be a good father.

At home, his routine was fixed. Early every morning he woke up the entire household by leaping out of bed and reciting at the top of his lungs the personal motto he had adopted as a youngster in New Brunswick, Edgar Guest's ingenuous poem, "It Couldn't Be Done." He shaved and dressed quickly, ate breakfast while listening to the news on the radio and reading the newspaper, then left for work. Usually, he would arrive back at home only for supper and often left again for evening civic functions; he worked on weekends as well.

His absences were compensated for by the firm control and quiet direction of May Bennett. She ran a well-disciplined and organized household and instilled a sense of responsibility and independence in her children. Every Monday morning they were each given a list of chores which they were responsible for throughout the week. She felt it was important to teach them to work and to know that work was good for them.

The youngest member of the family, Bill, explained: "We were expected to work from the time I can first remember. Everyone had jobs to do in the morning, every morning, and the jobs rotated. Things like making your own bed and tidying your room we took for granted. Dusting the stairs, bringing in the wood, emptying the ashes, doing the furnace, taking out the garbage — these were all chores that were spread out amongst the three of us and we did these as a matter of course every day. Then there were the Saturday chores of either piling wood or extra jobs that were needed around the yard. . . . If anything came out of our upbringing, it's the self-discipline we learned." Bill's sister, Anita, offered this memory: "Our home was well regulated. It wasn't violently strict, I don't think. It was well regulated but it was free. Mother was a very organized person, so we all had chores to do every day. She made up three lists of equal amounts of work. There was nothing about women's work or men's work; you drew your list, you did your work, and when you were finished you could go. You didn't bother procrastinating."

Of course, their parents were devout Christians, so the Bennett children received religious training in the home as well as at church. W. A. C. Bennett did not any longer involve himself directly in church affairs, but May taught Sunday school and saw that her children attended from an early age. But they did not wear religion on their sleeves; it was simply a part of the moral code and training that May in particular desired to instill in her children. They used to have Bible readings on Sunday night, though that practice became sporadic, then ceased.

W. A. C. Bennett was not the stern, strict, authoritarian figure many would imagine him to have been. As a father, he was sympathetic and consistent in dealing with his children. When he was compelled to punish or discipline them, it became a major family trauma. His eldest son, R. J., said: "My father was not a strict person. If he was mad, he was mad, and you'd better toe the line, or else.... There was a woodpile in those days—and if he broke a stick, there was a new supply right there that he could reach for. I only remember two or three times when I was marched down there to meet my mistakes. But, other than that, he was a very understanding person in a lot of respects; you could talk to him about a lot of things."

Considering that the Bennett children grew up during the Depression, they were remarkably well provided for by their hard-working father and completely devoted mother. In a material sense, they probably did not possess much more than their friends and schoolmates, but their father was a prominent businessman and they lived in the largest, most magnificent home in the area. Tony Tozer, perhaps the children's closest friend, said: "The Bennett house was always the beautiful, big house surrounded by a lovely bunch of trees like an orchard or a park. The house was a very special place. I'm sure that everybody thought the Bennetts were a little better off than many of the others living in Kelowna, but if you were friends, you were friends. Bill, R. J. and Anita weren't brought up to show off what they had. It just wasn't important."

The Bennett home was a happy but very busy place according to Anita: "Our home had to be organized because it was always full of people. My great-aunt came and stayed for fifteen years; my mother's younger sister came and lived with us for several years and then she came back several times. My grandfather came and he would stay a few months at a time. This was normal. And in the summer it was worse than that, because the Okanagan is renowned for having lots of summer company—expected or unexpected. The house was always full. I can remember summers when all Bill did was carry suitcases up and down stairs, and all I did was pick flowers and dust and make beds, and all Winnie and Mother did was cook."

On one occasion during Christmas holidays, a visiting relative contracted scarlet fever. The family doctor was brought in and when he announced his intention to quarantine the Bennett household, W. A. C. Bennett quickly packed a supply of clean clothes and rushed out of the house before the doctor could stop him. He booked himself into a downtown Kelowna hotel for the entire six weeks of the quarantine and thereby avoided what would have been an intolerable interruption in his business affairs and political interests.

In all, Bennett was not what might be considered a great family man, neither was he an exemplary father. But he was always loved and honoured by his wife, children and extended family—all referred to him affectionaly as "Pop."

Late in 1938 a Conservative leadership convention was held in Kamloops. Tory leader Dr. F. P. Patterson had died and the two chief contenders for the position were Herb Anscomb, a gruff bulldog of a political infighter and perennial candidate for the party leadership, and Royal Lethington (Pat) Maitland, a soft-spoken, blue-blooded lawyer and classical Conservative. Bennett attended the Kamloops convention and his position in the party and future as a Tory were fixed from that time onwards. He described the occasion:

> A great many people supported Anscomb, but I was a strong supporter of Maitland. I was in the hotel that night in Kamloops and couldn't go to sleep because of the noise next door. There was Anscomb and Tom Norris and a bunch of them in there and they were plotting for the convention—how they'd win it. So-and-so was to make believe he was a friend of Maitland's and get his strategy for the next day. I didn't snoop, but I couldn't help but hear it. So, the next morning, I got in touch with my friend Pat Maitland and I said, "Pat, beware of Greeks bearing gifts. This person is going to come and see you and it's a straight betrayal. Don't trust him at all. He's in their camp." And I told him the story. So, Maitland then changed his strategy. He was warned in time; if not, Anscomb would have won. He came close to winning it anyway.
>
> The reform group within the party was supporting Maitland. He wanted clean government, no machine. He was a great guy and he won. Of course, Anscomb and Norris and these fellows were mad at me forevermore. . . .

Whether or not Bennett's actions actually had any effect on the outcome of that contest, he was now clearly branded as a Maitland man and an open opponent of the machine-style politics practised by Anscomb and other old-line Conservatives. Maitland had won by only 16 votes out of 522 cast, but despite the hard-fought leadership battle—perhaps because of it—the Conservative Party in British Columbia seemed strong. Conservatives were confident in what they believed was a party renaissance and were prepared to challenge Liberal rule in the province. However, the Tories were not the only problem facing Premier Pattullo. In his second term he was confronted with opposition in every direction he turned—ultimately, even within his Liberal ranks.

For instance, he battled with the international oil companies over the rising price of gasoline, thereby alienating a traditional source of Liberal support and raising further doubts in the business community as a whole. When Vancouver's Georgia Hotel, art gallery and post office were occupied by organized unemployed and transient men in May 1938, after the federal government had closed the Depression-era relief camps in the province, it was Pattullo who was ultimately blamed for the violence that erupted in the streets of Vancouver when the sit-downers were roughly removed by police. Clearly, Pattullo's activist approach to government had been severely tested, which when combined with his own sometimes impulsive actions, made his political future questionable. Furthermore, the opposition was more effective in the legislature with the rejuvenated Tories under Pat Maitland and the CCF beginning to solve its organizational problems and broaden its support under a new, colourful provincial leader, Harold Winch.

Perhaps it was lucky for the premier personally that in 1939 war brought a new series of crises—for which he could not be blamed—and a wave of national patriotism that transcended all provincial quarrels. When Canadian troops began leaving for the battlefields of Europe, many of Pattullo's worries marched away with them. Again he found himself somewhere between the Tories, who unquestioningly and vocally supported a united war effort and the defence of Great Britain, and the CCF who eschewed any contribution to imperialist battles. Pattullo gave full support to the principle of Canadian participation in the Second World War and made recommendations for the security and defence of Canada's west coast.

The outbreak of war served to crystallize one of the great concerns in Canadian intergovernmental relations: the distribution of federal and provincial powers. Although Patullo supported the war effort, he was extremely wary that Ottawa might use it as an excuse to further encroach upon provincial areas of authority. He carried this well-cultivated provincial viewpoint into what proved to be his last great battle when, in January 1941, he went to Ottawa to attend a federal-provincial conference which had been called to discuss the recommendations of the Royal Commission on Dominion-Provincial Relations. Known as the Rowell-Sirois Commission, it had been appointed in 1937 to explore all aspects of the relationship between the provincial and federal governments. In large part, the commission was a reaction to the fiscal chaos and national frustration of the 1930s. Its report, presented to Prime Minister Mackenzie King on May 3, 1940, is one of the seminal documents in the history of federal-provincial relations in Canada.

The commission struggled with the concept of Canadian federalism, attempted to define a national interest, and asked broad questions about Canadian identity that are still unanswered. The report made sweeping proposals for redistributing responsibilities in the Canadian federal system. It recommended that key controls over the economy be placed in the hands of the central government as well as responsibility for social services like welfare assistance and unemployment insurance. It proposed to relieve the provinces of their huge accumulated public debts, but also their federal subsidies and control of income tax and succession duties.

Pattullo was unequivocably opposed to the Rowell-Sirois Report, bringing his opposition with him to the Ottawa conference when he objected strenuously to the format of the meeting and, along with Premiers Aberhart of Alberta and Hepburn of Ontario, left when it had barely begun. Back home in British Columbia, Pattullo was severely criticized for his well-publicized performance in Ottawa, and although he staunchly defended his stand for provincial rights, there were grumblings of dissatisfaction within his own cabinet. But although he was subjected to a fierce storm of protest over his stand on federal-provincial matters, the B.C. economy, like other economies, was thriving as war industries seemingly overnight solved the nagging unemployment problem. That summer, Pattullo announced that a provincial election would he held on October 21, 1941.

In the Okanagan Valley, W. A. C. Bennett was watching events closely. In May 1941 the South Okanagan Conservatives had held their nominating convention and this time Bennett was virtually unopposed—Tom Norris was nowhere to be seen. With the nomination locked up, Bennett anticipated the call to the polls and was actively campaigning months before the election announcement. When it came, his organization moved into high gear. He described his first political campaign:

> My attack was all on Pattullo—not on him personally, but on his opposition to the Rowell-Sirois Commission. Not that I wanted him to accept it, but because he walked out of the conference in Ottawa. He and Hepburn and Aberhart, they were the three-man unholy alliance, and they wrecked the conference. Now, mind you, the Rowell-Sirois Commission had no vision of Canada and no vision for British Columbia. It said that British Columbia was a province that could never be successful. All these mountains and everything would mean we would always have chaos here and there was no way we would ever be an affluent province. They were completely wrong. Pattullo knew that they were wrong, but he used the wrong tactics at the time, and he allowed himself to be used by Hepburn and Aberhart. So I ran my campaign on that issue and I condemned him. While Pattullo was a great British Columbian, you must be a Canadian before you are a provincial premier. As a premier, if you don't look after your province, nobody else will, so you're tempted to put your province first, but you must do nothing to wreck your country, ever.

In the electoral district of South Okanagan, Bennett was running against the popular Liberal incumbent, Capt. Cecil Bull. The Conservative Party's provincial organization gave Bennett little help. In fact, they wrote the riding off their list of possible winnings. As a result, Bennett energetically waged his own style of campaign, directed from his hardware store office. He was told it couldn't be done, and like the optimist in the ditty he recited each morning, he rejected the words of the doomsayers; instead he "buckled right in with a trace of a grin" and worked tirelessly. Bennett's campaign literature characterized him as "a man of action who got things done"—an image that would sustain his future career. The Liberals put a concerted effort into holding the seat, even trying to persuade Bennett's strong supporter Cap Capozzi to vote Grit. To the surprise of most political observers, Bennett won. In his first great political triumph, he polled 2,009 votes; Captain Bull received 1,769, the CCF candidate 1,552. Local Tories were jubilant and Bennett was ecstatic; it was a joy he would learn to live for.

However, the provincial results made only confusion. Pattullo's Liberals lost fourteen seats, and by holding on to twenty-one would still form the largest party in the new legislature—but they were four short of achieving a majority government. The Tories increased their support and now had twelve elected. The CCF elected fourteen and, surprisingly, received the largest share of the popular vote, over thirty-three per cent. In addition, a single independent candidate was elected, Tom Uphill from Fernie. It would take some time to sort out the very mixed political bag British Columbia voters sent to the legislature in 1941. But W. A. C. Bennett had moved a large step in the direction of fulfilling his personal mission, and he never looked back from that hard-earned first victory. Among the dozens of letters of congratulations he received in the days following the provincial election of 1941 was one from R. J. Gillis in Edmonton, his former mentor, who wrote: "My Dear Cecil: Congratulations and best wishes. I was sure you would make it. . . ."

CHAPTER
THREE
THE PARANOID STYLE

*There is nothing more devastating
than fear and you cannot run a province
as great as British Columbia on fear.*
T. D. Pattullo, 1941

*We are all sufferers from history,
but the paranoid is a double sufferer
since he is afflicted not only by the real world,
with the rest of us, but by his fantasies as well.*
Richard Hofstadter

W. A. C. Bennett's personal victory in the British Columbia election of 1941 was a dream come true. For many years, as a younger man in Alberta and, even earlier, during his New Brunswick boyhood, he had imagined himself as a representative of the people, and now he was MLA for the electoral district of South Okanagan. But his dream did not die there; this was only the beginning of his mission.

In retrospect, it is apparent that he had joined the House during an uncertain but opportune time. Still elated with victory, Bennett, like most other elected members, searched for indications of how the unstable political weather might settle. Premier Pattullo still led the largest group in the new legislature, but there were signs of discontent within his reduced Liberal caucus of twenty-one. The CCF, headed by Harold Winch, was looking forward to forming the official opposition with fourteen elected members, and the Conservatives, who had increased their strength but elected only twelve members, were acting curiously—as if they had been victorious; after all, they were the obvious losers of the 1941 provincial contest. Despite a strenuous, concerted effort to rebuild the party, they had not only lost the election but also forfeited their status as official opposition. Yet, on the night of the election, after the results were known to all, Tory leader Pat Maitland jubilantly cried: "From now on they'll do as I tell them!"

Perhaps it was the prospect of a minority government that excited the losers. Certainly, both the Conservatives and the CCF would hope to benefit from a weakened Liberal administration in need of support to survive. During the campaign Maitland had been quoted as saying: "We must have the determination to rise above politics and serve our country in this time of war." As the election results became known, visions of a union government in the style of beleaguered and beloved Great Britain danced in his mind. The following day he contacted all members of his new Tory caucus seeking their reactions to a British Columbia coalition government to promote a united war effort. From his hotel suite in Vancouver he jotted down impressions of their various comments. On the whole, his Tory colleagues seemed in favour of the idea. Of the new MLA from South Okanagan, he wrote: "Bennett. Favour of stand to make 3 way government—meant that war must come first. If sincere not interested in personalities. Favours coalition with Liberals." A day later, October 23, 1941, Maitland made a public appeal for the formation of a union government which would include all three parties in the legislature; he forwarded a copy of his proposal to Premier Pattullo.

The first political reaction to Maitland's appeal came from Harold Winch. The CCF leader rejected the idea out of hand, on the basis that: "We were for the complete reformation and overthrow of the capitalist system. How could a party that stood for co-operation go into a government with parties that stood for competition and exploitation?"

Premier Pattullo also curtly dismissed talk of coalition as nonsensical. He believed that there were essential differences among all three provincial parties and was certain that a coalition government was not only unworkable but also unnecessary. He made it clear that he intended to stay on as premier of a minority Liberal administration.

However, the prospect of a minority government did not please many Grits. Still more were displeased with their leader's continuing abrasive style of statesmanship. At both the provincial and federal levels, B.C. Liberals were openly critical of Pattullo's narrow brand of provincialism, and his loss of a clear majority of seats in the provincial legislature significantly weakened his grip on the Liberal Party reins. From the time Maitland first broached the subject there was widespread support for coalition throughout the province. In the weeks following the election several approaches were made to Pattullo urging him to accept some form of coalition as a wartime arrangement. Even Liberal cabinet ministers tried to penetrate his resolve. But the premier did not believe that either the Tories or the CCF would dare defeat a Liberal minority administration in wartime, and if they did, he sincerely believed that the opportunity to go back to the people in another election would win him back his majority.

Pattullo was probably right; the opposition parties would have found it exceedingly difficult not to support the government. But he had overlooked one important fact: as each day passed, the anti-Pattullo forces within his own party were gaining strength. This became apparent to all in mid-

November when his attempt to reorganize a couple of cabinet portfolios following the electoral losses met with disaster. Liberal stalwart George Pearson refused Pattullo's offer of a dual portfolio and announced his support for a coalition government. Publicly and privately other longtime cabinet colleagues informed the premier that they would not accept positions in his administration. The final blow came on November 17 when his finance minister, John Hart, announced that he, too, was in favour of some kind of alliance with the other parties. Pattullo immediately demanded and received Hart's resignation.

John Hart became a rallying point for other disaffected Grits. He was well respected throughout the province and, being a close friend, he had remained a Pattullo loyalist until he realized that the movement for coalition was probably unstoppable. His defection was followed by similar public pronouncements from the remaining members of Pattullo's ministry. The premier was now a lonely, isolated figure. He was convinced that the inspiration for his cabinet's disloyalty as well as the idea of coalition came from the oil companies and business interests he had battled with in years gone by. He said so in a long complaining letter to an unsympathetic Liberal Prime Minister Mackenzie King.

Incredibly, Pattullo still believed he could meet the House as premier, but he was rudely shaken when, without his approval, a Liberal convention was called for December 2 in Vancouver—two days before the new legislature was to meet. He attended the convention and made an eleventh-hour effort to dissuade the party from embracing the coalition principle. He prophesied that a coalition government would spell the demise of the Liberal Party in British Columbia. Many Liberal ears were deaf to his warnings that evening, and when a resolution favouring coalition passed by a vote of 477 to 312, the premier rose and left the hall. He was deeply affected by his loss of respect within the party and was certain that he was the victim of a grand conspiracy. Subsequently, John Hart was nominated and elected as new leader of the B.C. Liberal Party.

Two days later, Pattullo met the legislature for the final time as premier. He announced his resignation as "prime minister" and recommended that the lieutenant governor call on John Hart to form a government. The new Liberal leader then made his case for a union government and appealed for a three-party coalition. Pat Maitland, in a stirring speech, praised the union government of Great Britain and urged the CCF to reconsider their refusal to join with Liberals and Conservatives: "If one party stays, discord is substituted for unity. If one stays, we are going to have controversy, class warfare, party against party, attack and counter-attack, political manoeuvring." In a plea for statesmanship, Maitland declared: "There comes a time when political parties can best serve the people by uniting rather than opposing each other. I have always thought a man who alters his course when properly convinced becomes a greater man." But Harold Winch and the CCF seemed untouched by all appeals. After a single day's sitting, the House adjourned until the new year in order to allow Hart time to form a ministry.

It was in these exciting and tumultuous times that W. A. C. Bennett took his seat as a political freshman. Even though he supported the idea of coalition and therefore had indirectly contributed to Pattullo's forced resignation, he was always sympathetic to the old Liberal leader. In fact, Duff Pattullo was one of his political heroes:

> Coalition came about because of a revolt of Liberal cabinet ministers and Liberal MLAs against Pattullo. Pattullo was a very great leader and within his party a lot of members resented his strong leadership. When he slipped from having a good majority in '41, these people wanted to get rid of him. The very people Pattullo had built up turned on him. All of his colleagues, all of his ministers, all of the people he had built from nothing, turned on him. Personal rivalries are very keen things—and they don't show up in victory, they show up in defeat. The Liberals had twenty-one seats out of forty-eight, and we were in wartime. No other party would dare defeat the provincial government in wartime, it wasn't patriotic, so Pattullo could have carried on easily; but these people— lawyers, newspapermen, Liberals, the strongest Liberals in the party—turned on him. The way to get rid of Pattullo was to form a coalition: that was the Liberal point of view—they wanted new leadership and they united behind John Hart. The Conservative group, which I was in, wanted coalition for the war. We didn't think it was time to make partisan political hay. We wanted to support the war effort one hundred per cent.

On December 4, 1941, the day Pattullo resigned, John Hart wrote to Pat Maitland offering to share the reins of power with the Tories. "You no doubt will agree," he wrote, "that public sentiment is overwhelmingly in favour of a Coalition Government, and your cooperation in forming such an administration is, therefore, cordially invited." A similar formal invitation was extended to Harold Winch and the CCF. Over the course of the next few days, a deal was struck that radically changed the nature of party politics in British Columbia, but the negotiations had some tense moments. First of all, Winch reiterated his unqualified rejection of coalition, saying later that he enjoyed the Liberals' and Conservatives' displeasure: "They were unhappy that they couldn't inveigle myself and my colleagues into it. But we weren't biting on that one. We would have been completely submerged and yet we would have been held accountable for their tactics and their policy, but we weren't biting. . . ." The Tories, on the other hand, were more than simply interested in Hart's offer: they believed coalition was their idea in the first place. Maitland answered Hart's letter with cocky enthusiasm, making many policy stipulations and demanding parity with the Grits in cabinet representation. Subsequently, a great deal of friction developed between Hart and Maitland over the question of how to facilitate the marriage of their political parties.

But Hart was on solid ground, having received Winch's assurance that the CCF would not lightly defeat a Liberal minority government. Winch said of their conversation: "After making it very clear we were still not interested in any coalition involving us, I told Mr. Hart, who had given me the details of the arrangements he had made with Maitland, and what Maitland was still demanding—I told him that I thought he was stupid to be politically blackmailed: 'If Maitland insists on trying to blackmail you, you tell Maitland to go to hell. . . . I will call a special meeting of our caucus and present the idea of holding the Hart minority government in at least long enough to get the major business through and to pass the finances for the coming year.'" About the same time, Herbert Anscomb, the failed but unchastened Tory leadership aspirant, went to Hart and offered his unqualified support for coalition, thus undermining Maitland's bargaining position.

With these high cards in hand, Hart wrote once more to Maitland in a conciliatory but firm tone. Because the Liberals held more seats than the Conservatives, he explained, cabinet portfolios would be apportioned on a pro rata basis. Further, he offered the Tories the deputy speakership of the legislature. Any other policy decisions regarding the prospective coalition government would have to be made after it officially assumed office and not before. He let Maitland know that he was not pleased with the various terms and conditions the Tories were trying to impose: "I feel that this is not the best approach to the formation of the new union which we have in mind."

Hart was never forced to play the big cards he held, for events external to British Columbia and Canada rendered all local concerns insignificant. On the day that Maitland received Hart's letter, December 7, 1941, the Japanese attacked Pearl Harbor. The result was an immediate intensification of the war which now threatened to consume the globe: as a Pacific province, British Columbia was especially vulnerable in the new theatre of war. Maitland quickly accepted Hart's offer.

The new Liberal-Conservative cabinet sworn in before Christmas of 1941 was a talented, experienced administration brought together in a spirit of pragmatism and compromise. Of the eight portfolios, the Liberals filled five. As well as serving as premier, Hart retained the finance portfolio; George Pearson became provincial secretary and minister of labour; Arthur W. Gray was the new minister of lands; K. C. MacDonald was minister of agriculture and Harry Perry received the education portfolio. The Tories ruminated long and hard over which three cabinet posts they should request. Pat Maitland accepted the deputy premiership and also fulfilled a lifelong dream by becoming attorney general. A different type of leader than Maitland would never have allowed a personal adversary an advantage, but, always a gentleman, he nominated Anscomb for the portfolio of mines, trade and industry. The Tories also asked for and received the public works portfolio. Public works was extremely important in an era when patronage was the coinage of power, and the Conservatives had visions of increasing their popularity by building highways, buildings and bridges. But John Hart was well aware of what he was doing when he gave away that plum; he had retained the Finance Department for his own bailiwick. As minister of finance, he believed, he could control public works expenditures very well.

According to W. A. C. Bennett, Pat Maitland offered him the public works post but he turned down the offer with these words of regret: "My business is not in good shape yet, and there's a lot of work to do and also my family is too young. I couldn't do a good job in the government because my mind would be on my family and my business." This point is impossible to corroborate and, though it has become part of the accepted political mythology of British Columbia, it is unlikely on at least two counts. First, Maitland demonstrated his traditionalist approach by bringing Anscomb into the cabinet; most other Conservative MLAs were senior to the novice from South Okanagan in years of service both in the party and in the legislature and therefore would have taken precedence over Bennett. Second, Bennett was openly ambitious and it is extremely difficult to imagine his turning down such an opportunity at this early stage of his political career. If he was, in fact, offered a cabinet position, it was probably made in such a manner that he was obliged to turn it down for the sake of the party and the success of coalition. In that sense, his recollection may have been accurate but his words offered more as an *ex post facto* rationalization. In any event, Rolf Bruhn, a veteran MLA and former minister in the Tolmie government, became minister of public works.

When the legislature was reconvened on January 8, 1942, the sight of Grits and Tories, traditional enemies, sitting and smiling side by side must have been hard for most political observers to believe. After introducing his new cabinet, Premier Hart announced: "We now have, therefore, an entirely different type of Government from those which have pertained in this Province for a good many years, and I believe that the formation of an Administration representing as it does the views of two principal political parties meets with the general approval of the electors of British Columbia. Possible former differences of opinion among the members of which it is composed are unimportant compared with the emergency with which we are faced in connection with the war." Hart was right. The coalition idea was extremely popular and the union of the Liberal and Conservative parties was largely a response to the clamour of public opinion. But many old-time Liberals and Conservatives found coalition difficult to swallow; some would never accept it.

W. A. C. Bennett became a keen supporter of the coalition government, believing in its initial inspiration—nonpartisanship for the duration of the war. His first session as an MLA proved an interesting introduction to the legislative processes he would one day dominate. He always saw himself in progressive terms, as a reformer, and was proud that the first act of the new government—voting a bonus to old-age pensioners—passed through the joint caucus on his motion: "The first reform we got through our coalition caucus was the provincial supplementary payments to old-age pensioners—the first in all Canada. There were many there who wanted to spend money on the civil service, wanted to spend money on other programs, but I said, 'The first thing we're going to show to the people that built the province is that we have a heart.' And I said to Hart, 'You're afraid of those leftists who didn't join the coalition. Mr. Hart, if we do what is right, they'll always be left.'"

Bennett made his maiden speech in the legislature on January 13, 1942. He would never be a great orator: he spoke quickly and jerkily. His words often sputtered out in a curious way as if they were chasing but never quite catching his thought; and yet, he always managed to get his message across. This day, he praised the coalition government as an achievement brought about by the will of the people. He spoke of the wonderful beauty and sunshine of the Okanagan and pressed the need for a plan of road and highway construction in the southern interior. He closed by addressing the CCF, telling them that this was not a time for isolationism; they had been offered a partnership in government and they had rejected the offer. In wartime, he said, everyone had a duty to take a place in the boat and pull an oar. By his comments he made it clear that he was not a friend of the socialists. Reaction to his first legislative performance was generally positive and he was described in the press as "an aggressive, cheerful young businessman from Kelowna. A likeable fellow . . . who is going to be popular with his fellow members."

The former premier, Duff Pattullo, was still an MLA and, though he no longer directed policy, he was an ardent spokesman for his own suddenly out-of-date views. Bennett spoke fondly of sitting in the House with him: "In the legislature, I had the seat farthest from the Speaker, the chair right at the door. Pattullo was given a front row seat, but down from the cabinet. And as his former ministers, who were now in coalition, would speak, he would get up and unmercifully attack them—unmercifully! So, one day when he passed by my desk—and he and I were always good friends—I said, 'Mr. Pattullo, why are you so hard on your former colleagues?' He said, 'Bennett, if they did to you what they did to me, after I built every one of them up from nothing, you would be just as severe.'"

As a Conservative-coalition member, Bennett did not find it difficult to be openly critical of the confrontationist tactics Pattullo had employed in his earlier dealings with the federal government, but during this first session the new Okanagan MLA demonstrated his independence. On February 12, Pattullo moved a resolution calling for opposition to the principle that British Columbia could ever surrender its right to share income tax with the federal government. The Speaker ruled the resolution out of order, but when Pattullo appealed the ruling, Bennett joined with him and the CCF, becoming the only coalition member to break ranks on the recorded vote. This was the first indication of the maverick course that Bennett would pursue.

One personality who always stood out in Bennett's memory was Tom Uphill, the independent labour member from Fernie who later became the longest-serving MLA in B.C. history. The stories that are told of him by more than one generation of MLAs are always humorous, usually ribald and part of the folklore of west coast politics. Bennett's introduction to Uphill occurred during this first session: "In the legislature one night, when I was new, things were awful dull. Tom Uphill sent me a note: 'My friend Cec', will you donate five dollars to the Labour Party?' signed 'Your friend, Tom.' I wrote him back a note: 'My dear friend Tom, glad to enclose attached five dollars. Happy to donate to the Labour Party. But tell me, Tom, who is the Labour Party?' signed 'Your friend, Cec'. Back came a letter: 'Thank you very much, my exceptionally good friend Cec'. Thanks for the donation. I will drink to your health tonight because I am the Labour Party.'"

The 1942 session lasted only five weeks and produced little in the way of controversy; however, the coalition partners, once bitter rivals, were proving that they could work together. The co-operation among members of the hybrid administration was actually greater than that usually found in single-party governments. W. A. C. Bennett was taking his role as an MLA seriously. He served on several standing committees of the House and attended daily sittings with the same diligence that he had attended church as a youth. While in Victoria, he stayed in the stately and convenient Empress Hotel, for seventy-five dollars a month. He became well acquainted with most of his fellow MLAs and laboured long hours trying to learn the intricacies of parliamentary procedure and the organization and operation of the provincial civil service.

One of the major items passed during this session, and the one that had the greatest effect on Bennett, was an act creating a Post-War Rehabilitation Council—the first public body of its kind in Canada. The council, chaired by the minister of education, Harry Perry, was made up of members of all parties in the legislature, including opposition leader Winch and W. A. C. Bennett. Its mandate was to conduct a detailed examination of the needs and wants of all regions of the province in order to prepare for life in the postwar world. The council was to recommend to the legislature how to make B.C. a fit place for war heroes to come home to and start anew.

When Bennett returned to Kelowna at the end of his first session he was satisfied with his performance and looked forward to continuing his new career. At this time, legislative sessions were very short and politicians were only part-time MLAs, most holding regular jobs, practising professions or pursuing private interests over and often above their duties as elected representatives. Bennett, of course, still directed his growing hardware business, but was very serious about his position as an MLA, attending to constituents' problems and busying himself in Okanagan affairs. He was extremely fortunate in his appointment to the Post-War Rehabilitation Council. Not only did it allow him to extend his legislative experience and work closely and regularly with other MLAs but it also allowed him to travel the length and breadth of the province and meet with British Columbians from all walks of life. His work with the council broadened his knowledge of the province; it allowed him to see well beyond the concerns of his home constituency, to assess the potential development of the province. For a new and ambitious politician it was a chance of a lifetime and Bennett approached his work with the council earnestly. Because he had been too young to serve in the armed forces during the Great War and was now too old to fight in World War II, he also viewed this work as a kind of retribution for not serving his country in uniform.

In August 1942 Rolf Bruhn, the minister of public works, died. According to accepted legend, Pat Maitland offered the vacant position to Bennett who turned it down on the grounds that he was still not ready for that kind of responsibility. It is not possible to document this offer either, though it is clear that Bennett privately informed friends he was being invited to consider the position, and in later years he talked of the supposed overture without hesitation. Considering that he had now completed his first legislative session and was enjoying public life immensely, it is extremely unlikely that he would have turned down an opportunity to join the exclusive cabinet ranks—especially now that he had seen first-hand the special status reserved for ministers of the crown. Compounding the unlikelihood is the fact that Bennett's personality was so perfectly suited to the public works portfolio— after all, he saw himself as a builder, a doer, a man who got things done. In any event, Ernie Carson, the Conservative-coalition member from Lillooet, was brought into the cabinet to fill the trade and industry post while the redoubtable Herbert Anscomb switched over to public works.

For Bennett, most of the summer and autumn of 1942 was spent touring the province as a member of the Post-War Rehabilitation Council. He developed a personal friendship with the chairman, Liberal-coalitionist and minister of education, Harry Perry. Bennett informally assumed a kind of co-chairmanship since Perry was often busy and sometimes incapacitated, for according to Bennett: "Harry Perry was my great personal friend, but he had one problem which has plagued too many people in public life: liquor. His Liberal friends would never look after him; but being a teetotaller, I helped him. . . . I helped [him] write the report for the Post-War Rehabilitation Council."

The interim report of the council was completed in January 1943 and tabled in the legislature the following month. It was a massive document which called for major new developments and structural changes in the B.C. economy. Chairman Perry introduced the all-party document with these words: "It is not a capitalistic or socialistic report. It is a report reflecting the collective minds of all members of the Council."

The Interim Report of the Post-War Rehabilitation Council provided a blueprint for the future development of British Columbia. It called for the creation of a steel industry in the province and urged that the Pacific Great Eastern (PGE) railway be extended northwards to the Peace River district. If necessary, it recommended, the government should take the initiative and become directly involved in such projects. The report also recommended the establishment of a publicly owned hydroelectric authority to provide cheap electricity to the entire province. It called for an increased emphasis on developing an agricultural industry with improved production methods and wider access to markets. It strongly urged further development of the province's mining and forest industries, promoted the idea of increased exploitation of natural resources and encouraged the growth of new industries. The scope of the interim report was impressive and, when combined with the council's final report which was completed the following year, it represented a comprehensive portrait of the hopes and aspirations for the next generation of British Columbians.

W. A. C. Bennett, who put so much of his own time and energy into the report, felt strongly about the council's recommendations and he became frustrated and disillusioned when the government did not enthusiastically endorse them in whole or in part. In fact, Premier Hart considered Bennett impetuous and asked him to be patient. Interestingly, years later Bennett himself would have the opportunity to fulfill many of the council's recommendations; the little-known report would become a virtual master plan for the development of Canada's west coast province.

The lack of action on the report of the Post-War Rehabilitation Council was not the only source of frustration for the freshman MLA. Bennett was so impressed with the success of the coalition government and the obvious compatibility of its leadership that he, along with others, declared it was the best government in B.C.'s history. John Hart was playing the role of the honest broker—a role Pattullo could never have pretended to fill. And both Hart and Maitland were well liked in their respective parties. Liberals and Tories had surprised themselves with their easy ability to work together. James K. Nesbitt, a leading political journalist of the day, observed that "the elected members of the two parties act with a single voice in the legislature. There is no fundamental point of policy upon which they disagree. They work as a unit and for all practical purposes are a single and united party." Bennett's experience with the Post-War Rehabilitation Council had further convinced him of the possible benefits and evident practicality of nonpartisanship in politics. He also recognized that the success of the coalition government was beginning to undermine the identities of the Liberal and Conservative parties. Thinking ahead to the potential problems in breaking up the successful political merger, Bennett began to lobby for the creation of a permanent coalition party. The idea proved popular: many ordinary citizens throughout the province supported the notion, as did most of the urban daily newspapers. But Bennett found it hard to get his fellow MLAs to publicly endorse the concept. Privately, several admitted they were sympathetic—but as former Grits or Tories, they were reluctant to commit themselves to something that constituted an offence against their respective party machines.

Nevertheless, W. A. C. Bennett, "the loner from Kelowner," as he was dubbed, forged ahead on his own, championing the cause of a permanent, independent provincial coalition party. He even gave it a name: the United Progressive Party—the UP Party.

Bennett became obsessed with the nonpartisan idea and it is worth describing his early efforts towards establishing a new and permanent political force in B.C. His papers from this period are filled with references to the United Progressive Party and gloomy warnings about the fate of coalition unless the government embraced the concept. In particular, he tried to win the support of his fellow MLAs. He wrote to Mrs. Tilly Rolston, Conservative-coalitionist for Vancouver-Point Grey, a "Personal and Confidential" letter informing her that the United Progressive Party was doing well in the Okanagan and expressing the hope that she was also making headway in her riding. In the summer of 1943, he wrote to his friend, Minister of Education Harry Perry: "I feel as you do that action should not be postponed indefinitely or too long in planning to organize the Coalition forces into a strong united political party as I feel at present that, while we have perhaps the best government the Province has ever had, it is practically without a foundation since it is without a strong and active organization throughout the Province." He put forward a plan for the party's formation and suggested the report of the Post-War Rehabilitation Council as a good basis for its electoral platform. Typical of the response to Bennett's energetic lobbying was Perry's answer: "I am very pleased your ideas, as outlined in your private letter, coincide so closely with my own regarding the political situation. However, I have come to the conclusion that the best place for me is to retire mentally into my own ivory tower. There are so many conflicting ideas . . . perhaps the best thing we can do is let matters ride for the time being."

But Bennett was not a person who "let matters ride"; he believed strongly in his cause and enjoyed the prospect of changing the course of B.C. politics by his own efforts. He tried to win support from Maitland and Hart. The Tory leader was cold and noncommittal on the subject, whereas the premier actually offered some initial encouragement. However, after a trip to Ottawa, where Premier Hart met Mackenzie King, he returned home feeling strongly Liberal and advised Bennett to forget the idea. But Bennett could not forget; he was convinced it was the party machines that stood in the path of his United Progressive Party. In particular, the federal wings of both parties were beginning to indicate that they wanted their provincial counterparts to return to the fold rather than cause any embarrassment or awkward moments during the next round of elections.

In October 1943, Bennett made a public statement calling for the formation of "a non-partisan United Progressive Party" to carry on the government of the province. This event was widely reported by the B.C. press. The *Vancouver Sun*, for instance, hailed it as "the first ever move taken by any British Columbia public man to attempt the untangling of the difficult coil of circumstances into which the present Hart-Maitland Coalition has fallen because of the opposing pulls of Federal and provincial loyalties." Bennett was quoted: "The move, which proposes the crystallization of the present Coalition Government into a united group entirely divorced from federal politics, has the backing of the great majority of coalition members of the legislature." To a degree, Bennett was bluffing — the great majority of MLAs were noncommittal. But he was so convinced of the logic behind the idea of a permanent coalition party that he pursued the cause with evangelistic zeal. He even went so far as to print United Progressive Party posters and UP buttons.

During the 1944 legislative session, Bennett continued to agitate for the UP Party; he also became involved in an issue that would one day dominate B.C. politics — how to provide electricity cheaply and efficiently to the province as a whole. In the Okanagan, the issue of rural electrification was important to his agricultural constituents, and the report of the Post-War Rehabilitation Council had addressed the question squarely. Now, in the spring of 1944, the MLAs were calling for action on this front. After it received some initial discussion in the Throne Speech debate, Bennett pursued it on February 8, urging the government to immediately set up a hydroelectric commission "to give the lowest possible rates to consumers and to spur establishment of industry." In his speech he also advised how to go about purchasing the privately owned company that held command over the province: "The proper way to purchase the company, the B.C. Power Corporation, is to buy the shares of that company at the market value." In keeping with his concern for developing the interior, he also proposed extending the benefits of a new provincially owned entity throughout the province. No immediate action was taken, but many years later Bennett would follow his own advice on the subject.

The following year, 1945, the Speech from the Throne indicated that the government planned to create a hydroelectric commission as a first move towards public regulation of the province's hydroelectric industry. On February 7, 1945, W. A. C. Bennett was given the honour of seconding the Speech from the Throne and took the opportunity to predict that "establishment of a hydro-electric commission in British Columbia will be the most important step taken by any government in the Province in many years, and I wish to prophesy that it will have far-reaching effects throughout the length and breadth of our Province for years to come. . . . After once stepping out on this path there must be no turning back." Of course, he also put in another plug for his United Progressive Party, stressing the "absolute necessity of building an organization throughout the Province to support the Coalition." He recognized the temporary problems his plan would create for longtime Grits and Tories. He told his fellow MLAs: "I know that there are difficulties in the way of setting up a united organization both federally and in some constituencies. . . . But I want to remind every government supporter that he that observeth the wind shall not sow, and he that regardeth the clouds shall not reap." And for perhaps the first time, Bennett presented the spectre of socialism and the possibility of a CCF election victory in B.C. as one of the prime reasons for establishing a permanent coalition party. The coalition government was coming to the end of its term and Bennett, like others, was worried about the next electoral contest.

For all practical purposes, the coalition had been formed originally as an honest attempt at nonpartisan government, but towards the end of its first term the *raison d'être* for the union had noticeably altered. Signs of victory in Europe in 1945 and the anticipation of an end to hostilities in the Pacific rendered the coalition's initial justification obsolete. The war shifted to a domestic one, an ideological battle with socialism, and the threat of a CCF victory in the next provincial election became the glue that would hold the Liberals and Conservatives together.

Government members feared that the primary beneficiary of coalition might prove to be the CCF. Its strong showing in the 1941 election seems to have been largely due to the rapid expansion of the trade union movement during the early war years. By not joining coalition, the CCF maintained its separate identity; as the only opposition party in the legislature, it was the province's sole alternative government. The socialists became *the* political opposition in British Columbia—a status they would be accorded almost permanently in west coast politics.

After the formation of coalition, the popularity of the CCF showed no immediate sign of abatement. The first definite indication of its strength was the Salmon Arm by-election of November 1942, following the death of Rolf Bruhn. Considered a Tory stronghold, the seat was won handily by the CCF. A subsequent by-election in Revelstoke, a Liberal riding, in June 1943 also went to the socialists. These were stunning losses for the coalition. After the CCF victory in Revelstoke, the Vancouver *Province* commented: "The CCF can no longer be ignored as a little party of extremists." The morale of the coalition government began to sink. Premier Hart was severely depressed over the by-election defeats and, for a time, actually considered resigning and applying to the Ottawa Liberals for a Senate appointment. According to Percy Richards, his executive assistant: "All he could see at that time was that he'd been licked; he'd been slapped in the face, and he wanted to get out." The premier persevered, but the by-election losses worried all coalitionists, and events in the rest of the country added to their concern. In Manitoba and Ontario the CCF surged in popularity and became the official opposition in both provincial legislatures. In June 1944, the Saskatchewan CCF formed the first socialist government in North America. In the federal election of June 1945, CCF candidates made strong showings in most parts of British Columbia.

After the federal election, in which B.C. Grits and Tories awkwardly combatted each other in public for the first time in four years, a coalition caucus met to consider the future of their union. It was no surprise that they unanimously agreed to continue the arrangement. A joint resolution issued after the meeting read: "That in view of war conditions and the necessity of united efforts in adequately meeting our postwar problems, it is considered in the best interests of the people and of good government in British Columbia that the Coalition of the Liberal and Progressive Conservative parties should continue."

A formula for the conduct of the next election was devised to ensure Liberal and Conservative co-operation: Liberal-coalition MLAs would not be opposed by Tories and, likewise, Conservative-coalition members would not be challenged by Grits. In ridings not held by either party, joint nominating conventions would select a coalition candidate. This, essentially, became known as the Hart Formula. W. A. C. Bennett was terribly upset over the fact that the joint caucus had not embraced his plan to create a permanent coalition party—a United Progressive Party. After the Hart Formula became public knowledge, Bennett privately expressed grave concern for the survival of coalition beyond that next election. He wrote to Tory leader Attorney General Pat Maitland, protesting that the formula "will make for more opponents to the Coalition cause than existed before." In particular, he was worried about the potential confusion in the minds of voters when faced with three different types of coalition candidates: Conservative-coalitionists, Liberal-coalitionists and straight coalitionists. He bemoaned the lack of a single province-wide organization and was fearful that "as against this loosely-knit and awkward type of campaign, the CCF have every chance of becoming the next government."

On August 30, 1945, the twentieth British Columbia legislature was dissolved and an election was announced for October 25. The campaign that followed was an intense and unusual contest. The nervous coalitionists ran on the promise of postwar expansion and on the track record of their experimental administration—and it was a good record. The Hart-Maitland government had proved very capable and, because it was riding the crest of a wartime boom in revenues, was in a healthy position to ask the electorate for a renewed mandate. Bennett's fear of confusion in the minds of voters was allayed when coalition candidates ran unhyphenated campaigns—the terms "Liberal" and "Conservative" were rarely heard. And in South Okanagan, Bennett established his own impressive Coalition Association.

The potential threat of a socialist victory became a major theme of the campaign. Although the CCF seemed to be making advances during the early years of coalition, its failure to moderate its ideology or rhetoric worked to its detriment. In November 1943 Harold Winch had campaigned for the CCF in the Alberta provincial election, during which he announced: "When we become the government, we will institute socialism immediately." He told his Calgary audience that the CCF brand of socialism would be enforced by the police and military if necessary: "If capitalism says 'no,' then we know the answer—so did Russia."

Winch's infamous statement was widely reported and during the 1945 B.C. election it was frequently alluded to by coalition candidates. During the campaign, Winch responded: "I stand 100 percent behind what I said in Calgary. If big business dares to defy the laws of the people, then they will be jailed by the people's government." No doubt his blunt, extremist style, combined with his perceived belligerency, alienated many voters. But what hurt his party more was the all-out attack on socialism levelled by most coalition candidates—and this was one of the unique features of the 1945 provincial election. Voters were asked to "Vote Coalition" and reminded ad nauseum that it was "the best government B.C. has ever had"; but almost as frequently, they were reminded of the perils of socialism. On Vancouver

Island, Herbert Anscomb was in the crusading style of the coalitionists when he told his constituents that "the two parties had joined to save the province from socialism." Many other candidates played on similar themes suggesting the CCF program would mean a horror greater than that which had been crushed in Nazi Germany. John Farris, a Vancouver Liberal lawyer, told a coalition meeting that the CCF in power "would make Goebbels look like an amateur." Such scare tactics had never before been used so extensively or effectively, and from this time they would be an important feature of politics in B.C. The polarized pattern of left versus right, them versus us, would soon be firmly fixed.

On election night, October 25, 1945, it became apparent that British Columbians were largely satisfied with the government's stewardship of the province. The coalitionists polled almost 56 per cent of the popular vote and increased their seats in the legislature to thirty-six. The CCF received over 37 per cent of the votes but elected only ten members—six less than at dissolution. W. A. C. Bennett was re-elected easily in South Okanagan.

The CCF had lost seats in Vancouver but gained in the north, where casualties included one friend and another mentor of Bennett: Minister of Education Harry Perry lost in Prince George, and former premier Duff Pattullo, running in Prince Rupert as an independent, ended his political career in defeat. Pattullo's ignominious retirement became even more painful when Prime Minister King later refused him a senatorship. He was a sad and disillusioned man before his death in 1956. To the end of his days he was convinced that a conspiracy led by oil interests had been responsible for the debacle of 1941.

Bennett's second electoral victory in 1945 reinforced his ravenous political appetite. He had always enjoyed business but now knew he was made for public life. He thrived on the cut and thrust of politics and believed there was room for considerable personal accomplishment in British Columbia. Tory organizer Russell Walker's early perception of Bennett was that he "didn't know himself where he was going nor by what route, but of one thing he was certain—he was assuredly going a long way in some direction." Bennett's first term as MLA had been a valuable education in practical politics. He suffered minor setbacks and had his knuckles rapped when forced to deal with more experienced politicians, but his memory would later become one of his most valuable weapons: like other politicians, he remembered best the injuries inflicted upon him during his first, insecure years in politics—before his shell hardened.

Although he was now entering middle age, Bennett still maintained a youthful appearance; he had always seemed younger than his actual years. In Victoria, he received a variety of nicknames: "the apple picker," "the apple polisher," and "the apple-cheeked schoolboy from the Okanagan." His slim youthful look had turned into a pudgy kind of maturity, and he was sometimes referred to as "the cherub." Among his personal papers and souvenirs from this era is a poem written by a Victoria acquaintance entitled, "The Cherub from South Okanagan":

> The Cherub is a splendid boy
> Is precious gold without alloy;
> He believes that coalition
> Is the fulfillment of his mission.

Bennett's home life was still very important to him, though it occupied little of his time. May Bennett never attended political meetings with her husband, nor would she stay long in Victoria. She maintained her part of their marital division of labour and put all her energy into raising their growing family. Nevertheless, the Bennetts were significantly moulded by politics. "As far back as one can remember father was always sort of half involved in politics," said R.J., "and this worked for and against us in going through school." Bill agreed: "Sure, we knew we were different. We were in a different atmosphere; we knew we were political and the whole family became political. We were raised in the political environment—the whole conversation around the family was one of enjoyable argument. We knew our father was different because he became a politician in 1941 which meant that he would get on the train every January and go to a place called Victoria and he would be gone for a few months. I used to take some razzing, but politics was serious in small towns and serious among families."

When he returned home from the legislative session, Bennett would put some extra effort into his neglected fatherly duties. According to housekeeper Winnie Earl, upon his return the children would clamber around him while he basked in their attention: "They'd be in there listening, hearing everything he had to say. He'd be describing the parliament when he was first elected. He would come home and tell them how everything took place in the legislature. They were always eager to hear everything; we all were. He would describe where different people sat and what their duties were and how the Speaker would come into the legislature with the Clerk, and the Sergeant-at-Arms would go in first and come back saying, 'Make way for the Speaker!' This used to be a little bit of a byword around the Bennett home. . . . If anyone was coming through, they'd say, 'Make way for the Speaker!'"

The Bennett children were taught to be responsible and independent and they were encouraged to pursue a higher education, although only Anita attended university. R.J. and Bill worked part time in the hardware store from an early age. By the time they reached their early teens they bought their own clothes from the salaries they earned.

As he became increasingly immersed in politics, W.A.C. Bennett was spending less time on his business affairs. He still directed his hardware firms—which were now combination hardware-furniture-appliance stores—and the retail business did very well during this expansionary period. Plainly, Bennett had few monetary worries; if he was not yet a millionaire, he was at least financially independent, and this represented the fulfillment of one of his important goals in life. He had made great efforts to ensure that his businesses were carefully managed and, by his express order, none of his stores was permitted to sell goods to the government. He never wanted his business to be open to political criticism, so he always guarded his back and studiously avoided any potential entanglements. He viewed himself as a progressive politician intent on reforming the old style of political corruption.

An example of the precautions he took against charges of political patronage was the complete disposal of his shares and interest in Calona Wines, the winery he had helped to establish in the Okanagan Valley. Immediately after his election to the legislature in 1941, he resigned as company president. He wrote to his partner, Cap Capozzi: "Now that I am elected a representative in the Provincial Legislature, and as Calona Wines does a considerable proportion of its business with the Provincial Government, I do not think it would be proper for me to retain a financial and directing interest in the Company.... I know that I need not expess to you my regret at having to take this course, but feel that once a person is elected as Member he should represent all industries in his constituency...." Bennett held over 5,000 shares in the winery for which he received about $7,000, making very little in the way of profit from his investment of capital and effort.

For all of his business and political preoccupations, Bennett was also an effective constituency representative. His riding office was above his store in Kelowna, where it remained throughout his political career. His papers from this period demonstrate a multitude of interests and form an impressive catalogue of attempts to deal with his constituents' concerns. A good deal of his time was devoted to agricultural problems, particularly of the B.C. Fruit Growers' Association. He also spearheaded Kelowna fund-raising blitzes for war memorials and a civic centre. One of the more difficult problems he had to deal with in the early postwar period was the possibility of a flood of Japanese settlement into the Okanagan Valley. Thousands of Japanese-Canadians had been herded up and removed from coastal communities during the war for their ostensible security threat, and transferred to isolated internment camps in the interior of the province and on the prairies. At the conclusion of hostilities, the camps were disbanded but the Japanese were restricted from immediately returning to coastal areas. Okanagan residents feared an influx of Japanese settlers to their valley and Bennett was compelled to lobby both the provincial and federal governments to prevent a mass immigration. In the spring of 1946, he assured the legislature: "It is not a question of racial hatred, but of economics." As the war gradually faded into the memory, so did this xenophobic reaction.

Bennett had not forgotten his failed attempt to form a permanent coalition party. Although he no longer bandied about the term "United Progressive Party," his 1945 election victory had further persuaded him of the merits of leaving behind provincial Liberalism and Conservatism for good. He decided to try a new approach and early in 1946 he prepared to organize a permanent coalition organization in his South Okanagan constituency. Planning a large meeting at Kelowna for February 15, 1946, he distributed pamphlets and flyers, broadcast radio announcements and sent dozens of letters of invitation to Okanagan supporters of coalition. Over two hundred people showed up: Tories, Grits and many others of no political persuasion. They enthusiastically endorsed Bennett's plan and founded British Columbia's first permanent coalition organization.

Bennett saw this act as the first positive step on the road to achieving a province-wide organization. The Kelowna *Courier* editorialized: "When more people turn out to an organization meeting of a new political party than turned out to any meeting of any party in the whole riding during the recent provincial election campaign, there must be something behind the idea. . . ." And the Vancouver *Province* commented: "The people of South Okanagan have kindled in the political darkness a promising light that shines a good distance beyond the boundaries of the constituency. . . . As Mr. W. A. C. Bennett told the Kelowna meeting, the life and power of the coalition depends upon the consolidation of coalition support. The Coalition cannot continue to hold office and give the excellent type of administration it has been giving if its supporters continue to live in separate camps and bicker over ancient and musty issues."

Bennett felt he was finally making some headway on the issue and throughout the spring he undertook a variety of activities designed to form a groundswell of opinion favourable to the abandonment of traditional party lines in provincial politics. He was very careful not to interfere in other MLAs' ridings, but let it be known he was available to assist in organizing coalition associations. He went so far as to acquire the assistance of a full-time organizer and fund raiser in Vancouver, F. M. Garland. In May 1946, Bennett wrote to Garland: "The more I study the political situation in the Province, the more I feel that a permanent Coalition Party must be formed. I am enclosing a letter authorizing you to receive donations to assist the setting up of such a party." Bennett wanted assurances that his organizer would not solicit support or funds from questionable or disreputable sources: "It is clearly understood, however, that no promises are to be given to anyone, also that no liquor money is to be accepted either directly or indirectly."

Over the next several weeks, Bennett remained active on several fronts. He kept in close contact with Garland—donations from Vancouver businessmen trickled in along with detailed reports of Vancouver political gossip. Bennett was never a sociable politician who attended receptions, cocktail parties and dinners, feeling ill at ease in those nonbusiness, rather artificial situations; consequently, he relied on others for information and developed an informal network of confidants and informants in order to keep up with the topical and current in the world of west coast politics.

During the spring legislative session of 1946, he continued to agitate for a permanent coalition party. On March 4, during the Throne Speech debate, he clashed with the premier and other cabinet ministers, and was cheered on by the CCF for doing so. He asked: "If the Coalition Government is good, why should it not be made permanent? The government must plan not for two or three years, but must look into the future for 10 or 20 years. This can only be accomplished with a permanent organization." In retrospect, it is amazing that Bennett had kept up his campaign for so long, but a few days after this his stand on permanent coalition and the position of the union itself were seriously shaken. On March 28, 1946, Conservative leader and attorney general, Pat Maitland, died of heart disease. From the struggle to succeed him came stresses that significantly influenced Bennett's political career—stresses that would lead to the eventual disintegration of coalition.

Maitland's death was a serious blow to Bennett's chances of advancement within the hierarchy of British Columbia Conservatism. Although Maitland had never supported the concept of permanent coalition, he was a friend; Bennett, after all, had always been an avowed Maitland man. Bennett's personal papers include correspondence between them which, even when it was official business, always boasted the informal, friendly salutations, "Dear Pat" and "Dear Cece." With the Tory leader's death, he had clearly lost whatever executive support he once possessed. The prospect of Maitland's heir apparent, Herbert Anscomb, succeeding as Conservative leader was not a happy one for Bennett.

Maitland's death also posed problems for the distribution of cabinet portfolios among the coalition partners. Premier Hart was anxious to fill the attorney general's post immediately because of important upcoming federal-provincial negotiations. The Conservative caucus did not contain a single lawyer and Anscomb, who assumed the position of interim party leader, asked the premier to wait until after a Tory leadership contest could be held before filling the cabinet vacancy. Meanwhile, Bennett had ideas of his own. His connections with the federal party were very good and when Maitland died, he sent a telegram to John Bracken, federal leader of the Progressive Conservatives in Ottawa, asking him to release Howard Green from federal politics to be attorney general in the province of British Columbia.

Anscomb did not oppose the idea, and apparently Bracken and Green consented to the proposal which Bennett and a few others felt was crucial if the Conservatives were to retain the attorney generalship. Howard Green, a Vancouver lawyer, was a respected member of parliament who had not played a significant role in provincial politics and whose record was therefore clean enough to allow him to enter into a delicate situation. But Green never had a chance. As Bennett remembered: "The press came to me one day and said, 'Cec', do you know what's happening? Anscomb is up at Government House being sworn in.' A straight double-cross! So there was no room for Green." This was the so-called "double-shuffle": Anscomb was made minister of finance and Gordon Wismer, the old-time Liberal political boss, became attorney general.

The double-shuffle of cabinet portfolios created resentment among both Liberals and Conservatives, since it was worked out in secret without consultation with either party caucus. Anscomb was not popular among all elements of the Conservative Party and he had neither approval nor authority to trade off the attorney generalship for the finance portfolio. On the other side, many Grits were alarmed at the reappearance of Gordon Wismer, especially in the important office of attorney general where it was feared he would dispense party patronage in the grand but embarrassing style he had practised in years gone by as Pattullo's attorney general. Almost unnoticed in the shuffle was the appointment of two new Tory ministers: L. H. Eyres, in railways, trade and industry, and fisheries, and R. C. MacDonald, minister of mines and of municipal affairs. As acting leader, Anscomb decided which Tories were elevated to cabinet rank: both Eyres and MacDonald were Anscomb's strong supporters. Bennett was conspicuously passed over, and could not hope to proceed any farther if Anscomb became *de jure* party leader. Russell Walker correctly observed that Pat Maitland's death "cooked Bennett's goose insofar as chances of becoming a cabinet minister went."

In caucus, Bennett railed against Anscomb for selling out the Conservatives' lot in coalition and he continued his campaign for a permanent coalition party—but with less vigour. His eye became fixed on the Tory provincial leadership contest scheduled for June. He watched closely to see if a candidate would emerge to oppose Anscomb who, as minister of finance and acting party leader, appeared to have the leadership within his grasp. Bennett was also seriously reconsidering his immediate political future. He wrote to fellow MLA Tilly Rolston on May 15: "The question of the Progressive Conservative provincial convention is worrying a lot of people. As it is a straight provincial convention, I do not see how I can attend, as provincially I am a straight coalitionist and as you are aware we have a Coalition Party organized in South Okanagan and I must be fair to it. I don't think now that it will make much difference who is selected leader in British Columbia as he will only have a headache. Mr. Hart without doubt will be leaving the provincial arena before the next election and chaos will be the order of the day." But he concluded on an optimistic note: "Don't worry too much about the situation. It will all come out alright, realizing that the present situation is not permanent and we live in an ever-changing world, especially in a democracy and in British Columbia particularly."

As the date of the leadership convention came nearer and no opponent to Anscomb's candidacy came forth, Bennett not only decided to attend the gathering but also tossed his own hat into the ring. He realized full well that Anscomb's ascension to the head of the party spelled difficult times ahead for himself as an MLA. He also knew that there was a substantial element in the party that felt Anscomb's views were out of date.

Bennett's campaign was low-key. He had the support of only two MLAs, Tilly Rolston and Ernie Carson, but he was backed by the Young Progressive Conservatives as well as most federal Tories, who opposed Anscomb's lack of diplomacy in federal-provincial party matters. Bennett fashioned his campaign in the straightforward style of an interior MLA, a man of the people against the "big city machine," and thereby won the support of many rural delegates. On the opening day of the convention, June 4, 1946, he distributed free cases of Okanagan apples to all delegates—in direct and studied contrast to the forms of persuasion and entertainment offered by Anscomb's organizers.

But Bennett was at a serious disadvantage, compounded by his well-known support for a permanent coalition party. Anscombites played this up and painted Bennett's efforts as a rejection of Conservative principles. Prior to the convention, Anscomb was quoted in the press: "I am a strong Conservative but will back the coalition as long as the menace of communism (CCF) exists"; at the convention, he pointedly directed the following comment at Bennett: "There has been formed in this province a Coalition Party and I want every Conservative to know I will have nothing to do with it." Anscomb was nominated for the leadership by Bennett's old rival, Tom Norris; Bennett was nominated by Tilly Rolston, seconded by Kelowna supporter, H. A. Trusswell. The counted ballots proved that Bennett's quiet approach had made little impact—he was crushed by Anscomb 319 to 188. Gracious in defeat, Bennett moved that the vote be made unanimous.

Anscomb, however, an intensely martial personality, could not force himself to be gracious in victory. He strongly resented Bennett's challenge and never attempted, even for the sake of the party, to accept his ambitious younger rival. Shortly afterwards at a press club party, when the new Tory chieftain was jokingly presented with a portrait of W. A. C. Bennett framed in a toilet seat, he pranced around the stage with the gift and beamed with joy. Vancouver lawyer Les Bewley, then a young Progressive Conservative, was there. "They all thought it was hilariously funny," he said, "but to me it was one of the most disgusting and distasteful exhibitions I have ever encountered. W. A. C. Bennett was sitting alone and I went over to join him. His expression was most extraordinary for a man in his position. He wasn't at all mad or upset. The look in his eyes was one of determination, as though to say 'You may laugh now, but I am going to make it soon!'"

Bennett rebounded from his defeat at Anscomb's hands with more determination than ever. On returning home to Kelowna, he spent no time licking wounds, but wrote thank-you letters to delegates who had supported him. He told backers from the interior: "While we were not successful, yet I think we did bring the Interior more to the attention of the Coast and benefits will be secured by our efforts." He explained to Minister of Public Works Ernie Carson: "It did give me a good chance . . . to show who was the real Conservative." He thanked his friend Tilly Rolston for her support: "It at least showed that we had the courage to fight the machine and I think success will come at a later date, perhaps earlier than we expect." And he wrote his old friend, former coalition cabinet minister Harry Perry, rationalizing his defeat: "I was not over-anxious to secure the leadership at this time, but felt it was the right thing to do because . . . the whole situation is full of possibilities."

Of course, the possibilities were endless. What if Bennett had pulled off an upset and defeated Anscomb? How would that have affected coalition? Or the course of British Columbia history? Alternatively, what if the new Tory leader had been magnanimous and showed Bennett the same politeness and respect Maitland had once displayed for Anscomb? What if he had offered the Kelowna cherub a cabinet post? Percy Richards, Premier Hart's executive assistant, said: "John Hart knew that Bennett was restless and he went to Herb Anscomb and said, 'You know, Herb, if you want to take Bennett into the cabinet, I have no objection. I would even increase the size of the cabinet for you to settle things.' John was a great conciliator. He knew that Anscomb was having difficulties with Bennett and he was anxious to cut off all the recriminations that were going on. But Herb Anscomb wouldn't go for it."

Bennett's optimism had to be carefully guarded, for although B.C. politics seemed to be in a state of flux, there was no immediate issue or cause for him to fight on. Even worse was the strong possibility that he might no longer be taken seriously. In the spring 1947 session of the legislature, he lashed out angrily at his coalition colleagues—his criticism was startling, even for an established maverick, and it was coloured by a tone of desperation. He openly asked the burning political question of the day: "What happens to the Coalition if Premier Hart goes to the Senate? . . . If the present Coalition government is in existence at present only to meet the threat of the CCF then this is a very negative policy and is certainly built on sand. One does not need to be a prophet to see that the government will collapse." He then launched a devastating attack on all aspects of government policy, criticizing in detail what he felt were inadequate economic and social policies. The Vancouver *Province* reported that the member for South Okanagan "uncorked a flood that swept across the cabinet benches leaving desolation in its wake." Bennett made a series of positive recommendations for the government to consider and closed by urging that a new system of voting—the single transferable ballot—be instituted before the next election.

During this session Herbert Anscomb delivered his first provincial budget as minister of finance. The $59-million budget represented a substantial increase in spending over the previous year, predicted a surplus of $8 million, and exhibited concern over the increasing cost of social welfare measures. Bennett criticized it as overly frugal and inappropriate for the needs of a developing province.

As the session progressed, Bennett bolstered his reputation as one of the most outspoken MLAs in Victoria. He repeatedly declared that the coalition government was at the crossroads, but of course this was wishful thinking. Only a significant change in British Columbia's political climate could create conditions conducive to Bennett's advancement. Until this time he had usually been lauded by the press as an independent and outspoken politician, but by the end of the 1947 session it was evident that his honeymoon with the press was coming to an end; the provincial news media would never again support him to the extent they did during his years as a coalition backbencher. The Victoria *Times* went so far as to wonder editorially if perhaps it was W. A. C. Bennett, not the government, who was at the crossroads.

Late in 1947 an event occurred that significantly altered the face of coalition. After much procrastination, sixty-eight-year-old John Hart announced his resignation as premier, citing ill health as his main reason. He stepped down in the belief that national Liberal leader, Prime Minister Mackenzie King, would appoint him to the Senate, but for reasons unknown, King betrayed Hart, as he did so many others; the former B.C. premier never received his hoped-for sinecure in Ottawa's sleepy chamber.

Hart's resignation caused a flurry of political infighting, revealing serious cracks in the foundation of coalition. Herbert Anscomb believed he should succeed Hart as premier, claiming that the coalition leadership ought to rotate between party leaders. Bennett, who disagreed, wrote to Tilly Rolston from Kelowna: "I think the Conservatives are making the mistake of saying that the coalition must be headed by a Conservative. I think that both sides have lost all sense of proportion and are completely out of touch with public opinion, which first of all says they want a good clean non-partisan type of government at Victoria and are not so much interested which side has the premiership as long as it is the best man possible." In any event, the Liberals, who controlled more seats than the Tories in the House, ignored Anscomb's claim and prepared for their December 1947 leadership convention. The struggle for the Liberal leadership was a difficult and complicated affair. Attorney General Gordon Wismer was off and running from the start, but a substantial proportion of provincial Liberals felt he had to be stopped. A compromise candidate was found in the moderate but popular Liberal-coalition backbencher Byron "Boss" Johnson. At the convention he squeezed past Wismer by a mere eight votes out of almost a thousand ballots cast. Johnson was sworn in as B.C.'s new premier on December 29, 1947, while Anscomb and other Tories looked on helplessly.

When the 1948 spring session began nothing seemed amiss; however, the coalition leadership had completely changed since the original political alliance. W. A. C. Bennett had always claimed that the Hart-Maitland administration was the best government the province had ever had, but within a short while he would be loudly proclaiming the Johnson-Wismer-Anscomb government as the worst in B.C.'s history.

The 1948 provincial budget showed another significant increase; Finance Minister Anscomb announced his $77-million budget with some degree of pride but also warned once more against escalating social service costs for British Columbia's growing population, which now exceeded one million. To offset these costs, he introduced a three-per-cent sales tax called the "Social Security and Municipal Aid Tax." Resistance to this new nuisance tax was immense, and Bennett was one of the severest of its many critics. He demanded that Anscomb withdraw his budget and voted with three other government MLAs against the new tax which was creating discontent throughout the province.

The coalition partners were only just discovering the weaknesses inherent in governing by compromise. While many Liberals disagreed with Anscomb's unpopular sales tax, Conservatives were even more firmly opposed to the major social legislation passed in the spring of 1948. This was British Columbia's new compulsory hospital insurance plan, pushed through the joint caucus by "Welfare Liberals" and supported in the legislature by the CCF. The idea of a state-controlled system of health insurance had been discussed and studied for over thirty years in B.C. and Premier Johnson was convinced that hospital insurance would be an important and popular social reform demonstrating the government's commitment to progressive policies. Initial reaction to the plan was positive—all indications were that hospital insurance would be a feather in the coalition's cap. But within a few years, the British Columbia Hospital Insurance Service (BCHIS) would become an extremely unpopular, even hated, program. In principle, most British Columbians were in favour of BCHIS, but the government seriously bungled its implementation and administration. Hospital insurance would soon become the single most controversial issue in B.C. and serve to help permanently change the complexion of west coast politics.

W. A. C. Bennett, the compulsive optimist, was excited about developments in Victoria, but shortly after the 1948 session, much to the surprise of most political observers, he resigned his seat in the provincial legislature to run as the Conservative candidate in a federal by-election. The contest in his home federal riding of Yale resulted from the resignation of Grote Stirling who had represented the constituency for twenty-four years. Stirling had resigned late in 1947 and Bennett, who had actively campaigned for the Tory MP in the previous federal election, had been keeping one eye on the vacant seat.

When the by-election was announced for May 31, 1948, he made his move. Fed up with the frustrations and disappointments of Victoria, he determined to try his hand at federal politics. Many leading federal Conservatives had urged him to run, though close personal friends advised against such a move. But his decision was motivated by a grand vision of eventually rising to the leadership of the national party and becoming prime minister of Canada. In practical terms, his hopes of an easy by-election victory were buoyed by his perception that a political deal had been struck in Ottawa. As he described it: "There was a vacancy in a Liberal seat in Ontario and Howard Green had an understanding with C. D. Howe that if I ran in Yale, the Liberals wouldn't oppose me. And the Conservatives, then, wouldn't oppose the Liberal there. In 1948 the CCF were very strong and there was a fear that a divided vote would give the CCF both seats."

Bennett was unanimously nominated to run and felt he was saying good-bye to Victoria for good. Earlier, while ruminating over the decision, he had written to Tilly Rolston: "Much as I hate to leave the Provincial House, I feel that especially as far as the Okanagan is concerned, Ottawa policies are going to be much more important for the next few years than provincial policies . . . we may be in for a difficult period." His retirement from the provincial scene must have been greeted with a sigh of relief from many Victoria politicians. After his announced resignation, he received a telegram from Herbert Anscomb congratulating him and wishing him luck in his "new field." Bennett did not misconstrue Anscomb's between-the-lines message: "Good Riddance!"

Bennett had received ominous warnings about his decision to try to enter federal politics. Even his wife, who never otherwise interfered in her husband's activities, advised against it. Once the campaign began, Bennett realized that the Conservative stronghold of Yale was not going to be a shoo-in for him, especially as the deal between the Grits and Tories had broken down. Bennett's recollection was that "Howe and Green had one of their battles on the floor of parliament and their gentlemen's agreement was broken. The Liberals then nominated a very fine person—the best person they could possibly get. He was the head of the Fruit Growers' Association, a fellow named Chambers, a great personal friend of mine." Howard Green remembered that Liberal cabinet minister C. D. Howe had said something about a "saw-off," but he did not believe that this was the main reason Bennett had accepted the nomination.

The by-election campaign was short and furious and W. A. C. Bennett waged a different style of battle than he had been accustomed to in provincial contests. The Yale constituency covered a huge area, encompassing almost three provincial ridings, and Bennett travelled it by automobile. Unfortunately, he drove around in a large, brand new Packard which had just the air of luxury to alienate voters in a rural constituency. It was a particularly difficult time in the region, record rainfalls having caused disastrous floods. Many people were critical of the provincial government for not providing adequate flood relief and they felt Bennett would have been more useful applying pressure in Victoria than departing provincial politics for faraway Ottawa. Many Tory heavyweights came to assist him including party leader John Bracken, leadership aspirant and future prime minister John Diefenbaker, Maj.-Gen. George Pearkes, Davie Fulton and Howard Green. But their efforts were all for naught; on election day, May 31, 1948, the popular CCF candidate Owen Jones topped the polls, Bennett came second and the Liberal candidate finished third. As had been feared, the divided Tory and Grit support permitted a socialist victory.

The loss was a hard one for the Tories to take. John Diefenbaker said: "I spent a whole week there, speaking twice a day . . . something I never did for anyone else. I always had great admiration for Bennett and he put up an excellent fight. I went out there on my own to see what I could do for him. The meetings were very well attended; I can never predict the result of an election but if I had, I would have felt that he would win by a small majority." Howard Green said bitterly: "Mr. Bennett put on a good campaign but sometimes you wonder how sane the voters are." Bennett had his own explanation for his first personal election loss: "I put on the wrong kind of campaign; I didn't get down to the ordinary people. That taught me a lesson."

On the other side, the CCF felt its win was a great and portentous victory, though Frank Snowsell, who was campaign manager for the CCF candidate, said: "Of course, Owen Jones was not elected because he was CCF or a socialist; he was elected because he was Owen Jones. He had been an alderman of Kelowna for fourteen years, mayor for four, he was active in the

Legion, he had been internationally known in the Rotary Club—he was an exceptionally fine person. He was known all through the valley as a good businessman and a good citizen. So, you see, he was elected in spite of being a CCFer." But the victory coincided with another CCF by-election triumph in Ontario and had all the earmarks of a socialist sweep. Nevertheless, British Columbia socialists would look back on their by-election win in Yale with mixed emotions. As Snowsell put it: "I remember our rejoicing, but sometimes I think if we'd just let Bennett win that and he'd gone off to Ottawa, he would have lived the rest of his life in obscurity and we wouldn't have been afflicted with him in B.C."

The Yale by-election was a major setback for Bennett—he had gambled and lost and was now in the political wilderness. There was little he could do but wait for another try in the federal general election expected within a year. He wrote letters to all those who had campaigned for him in Yale. To party leader John Bracken, whose only lasting contribution to national politics was the unwieldy prefix "Progressive" attached to the Conservative name, Bennett indicated he was waiting for the general election: "I am hoping the result will be quite different then." To Davie Fulton, a future political opponent, he explained: "The cards were stacked a little against us this time, but tomorrow is another day." To General Pearkes he said: "I guess the apples weren't ready for picking in the Okanagan. . . . However, I think conditions will be a little different in the general election." He also thanked John Diefenbaker and expressed optimism for the future: "Now that the Liberals have had their great chance and come third, they will not be a serious threat in the general election. Also, the CCF swing has caused an awakening in many of our people who are opposed to state socialism. So I believe we have a fair chance of winning this seat back."

Bennett committed himself to try again in Yale at the next opportunity. Some of his friends suggested he should return to the provincial fold and seek renomination in the fall by-election in his former riding of South Okanagan, but he decided against such a move. The South Okanagan Coalition Association, which Bennett had formed, nominated a young, inexperienced war veteran, Bob Browne-Clayton, who had difficulty trying to succeed his controversial predecessor. It has been said that when he appeared in danger of losing to his CCF opponent, Bennett was contacted and drove day and night to return from his California holiday to help with the campaign. But Browne-Clayton denied this, claiming, in fact, that Bennett "would not touch me in my campaign, no assistance whatsoever. He just backed right off, went into a huff, with no help." Nevertheless, the new South Okanagan Coalition candidate won the by-election by a margin of 750 votes.

Early in 1949, it became apparent that a federal general election was imminent. On February 4, the Yale Conservatives met at Penticton to nominate their candidate. Bennett arrived at the meeting fashionably late and found that Theo Adams, the mayor of Vernon, had already been nominated. H. A. Trusswell immediately nominated Bennett and the contest was on. When the votes were counted it was discovered that the ballot boxes had been stuffed—with eighteen more ballots than delegates. Embarrassed riding officials held a second vote and Bennett, much to his surprise, lost the nomination.

He was dejected, but losing the federal nomination was a blessing in disguise and turned out to be one of the luckiest events of his career. If Bennett had won the nomination that evening, he would have been busily occupied later that year when an important provincial general election was called. As it happened, Theo Adams lost in Yale to the popular socialist incumbent, Owen Jones, and there is no evidence to suggest Bennett would have fared better. Bennett rationalized: "Either the forces are with you, which they've been ninety-nine per cent of my life, or they can be against you. You see, basically I'm a Presbyterian, and they believe in predestination. I believe that if you do everything possible that you can do, then things will end right, because I believe God always answers prayers, but sometimes His answer is 'no.' When we complain that our prayers have not been answered, they've been answered but we don't like the answers. I was told very definitely, I think, that my field was not to be federal politics—I was to go back in the provincial field again. I accepted that."

Bennett missed the 1949 session of the B.C. legislature—the only session during a thirty-year period in which he was not an active participant. The annual spring rite in Victoria was obviously the lead-up to an election: the legislative feast offered to the voters included a number of grand economic development proposals. Even though the Liberals and Conservatives had been bickering with one another, the success of their marriage now forced them into maintaining coalition for yet another election. The decision to continue with the coalition formula was less difficult than facing the uncertainties involved in breaking up the partners. With the benefit of hindsight it is easy to see that it was a serious mistake, for both the Liberal and Conservative parties. But rather than addressing the problem of their growing incompatibilities, these consorts took the easy way. Premier Johnson dissolved the twenty-first legislature in April and an election was announced for June 15, 1949.

W. A. C. Bennett was suddenly available to run again in his old bailiwick of South Okanagan and, fortunately for him, Bob Browne-Clayton decided not to seek re-election, a single session as a government backbencher having persuaded him that politics was not all it was cracked up to be. Probably Bennett would have challenged him for the nomination even if he had decided to run. Yet securing the nomination was no easy matter;

government leaders in Victoria tried to persuade Browne-Clayton to run again in order to block Bennett's return. Browne-Clayton recalled that "Anscomb was very upset" and Gordon Wismer had told him he "should stay with it." But his resignation stood and Bennett busily prepared for his return to Victoria.

Under the still used Hart Formula, a Conservative had to be nominated in South Okanagan. Anscomb found some allies among Liberal members of the coalition riding association who resented Bennett's opportunism and they helped to persuade the association president to stand for the nomination. But Bennett was determined not to take anything for granted this time around and his vigorous and skillful local campaign proved that he was the best man available. He won the nomination by a three-to-one margin and presented himself to the South Okanagan voters as their coalition candidate once more.

The provincial election of 1949 was an interesting affair characterized by a high-powered, extremely effective expression of the paranoid style in B.C. politics. Most of the coalition's pitch was for a renewed mandate to encourage investment and development in the province. However, they had needlessly worked themselves into a corner: the hallucination of an impending socialist takeover dominated much of the campaign rhetoric. The threat was more apparent than real, for the CCF proved to be weak and unorganized during this busy period of postwar prosperity. Moreover, the Cold War and anticommunist purges in the United States were having a natural spillover effect across Canada: North American socialism was clearly in retreat.

Nevertheless, the prospect of a CCF victory was still the most important factor in the decision to maintain coalition for at least another term — and the 1949 campaign saw the paranoid style achieve extremes in B.C. Voters were reminded again and again that only the coalition could build the province to the heights of its great economic potential, whereas the CCF could only offer stagnation. Premier Johnson warned that socialism would place a political boss over every person in industry in the province. Herbert Anscomb announced: "Premier Johnson and I have agreed to carry on the coalition for the duration of the emergency — the emergency caused by the spread of the evil cancer of communism and its brother socialism." A widely circulated pamphlet entitled *The Saskatchewan Story* warned of how that prairie province had become an economic wasteland under CCF rule. Socialism was described to B.C. voters as a "foreign old-world theory" that discouraged initiative and enterprise. And in the Okanagan, even W. A. C. Bennett was employing the style with great effect. He frequently told meetings that socialism was the natural precursor of communism, quoting John Stracey, minister of foods in the British Labour government: "Like all socialists, I believe that the Socialist society evolves in time into the Communist society. . . . It is impossible to establish Communism as the immediate successor to Capitalism. Hence Communists work to establish Socialism as a necessary stage on the road to Communism."

It can only be imagined that British Columbians heard more garbled political science during the 1949 campaign than they ever wanted to hear. Herbert Anscomb and Gordon Wismer showed that they had something in common when they told voters that communists had "infiltrated into the ranks of decent, Christian socialists" and that the CCF now sided "with the Kremlin against the free people of the world." All such scare tactics were convincingly reinforced when it was widely reported that at a CCF campaign meeting the marching song "The Red Flag" was substituted for "O Canada." Anscomb, probably the most effective and virulent west coast Cold Warrior, could not refrain from this summation of the contest: "The election could only determine whether free enterprise would win out over totalitarianism."

On election day a large turnout of voters proved that the popularity of the government was still intact. The new hospital insurance program had demonstrated the government's commitment to social policies and the uproar over the introduction of the three-per-cent sales tax had not translated into anticoalition votes. No doubt the strong antileft rhetoric played an important role in what proved to be the coalitionists' most convincing victory ever. They won over 61 per cent of the popular vote and gained thirty-nine seats, while CCF representation was reduced by three, to seven seats. In South Okanagan, Bennett showed he was made for provincial, not federal, politics when he won by an impressive margin of almost 2,000 votes over his socialist opponent.

For the coalition, victory was sweet; but neither Liberals nor Conservatives could have missed the fact that Tory representation had proportionally decreased to the point where Liberal-coalitionists alone could now command a majority in the legislature. Clearly, the political alliance to safeguard the province from socialism was working in favour of the Grits and against the Tories. At the same time, some Liberals began openly to question the worth of the partnership. Further emphasizing the Conservative decline were the results of the federal election that immediately followed the provincial campaign. Under the new leadership of Louis St. Laurent, the Liberals won a national landslide victory. The Progressive Conservative Party won only forty-one seats in parliament and a mere three of those were from British Columbia — their worst showing ever.

W. A. C. Bennett approached his re-entry into provincial politics carefully. He intended to maintain a critical, independent stance in the legislature, and during the election campaign had plainly indicated his intent to continue on a maverick course. In his words, he told the electorate: "Now I want to make it very clear that I'm running under the banner of coalition, but

I reserve the right to be critical on all issues. My first loyalty, of course, will always be to my constituency of South Okanagan and not to the government in Victoria, and I won't hesitate to be critical." Perhaps it goes without saying that over and above Bennett's independent style and political posturing he was still looking for his main chance.

British Columbia's twenty-second legislature opened in February 1950 and before long it was apparent to everyone that coalition was becoming a victim of its own success. Grits and Tories seemed edgy together; increasingly, they met in their separate party caucuses, and their policy differences were now visible to the public. On February 28, 1950, Herbert Anscomb delivered his fourth budget speech as minister of finance; the record budget of $105 million was no cause for cheer, however. He used the occasion of the much-publicized speech to draw critical attention to the growing costs of social services: "I have expressed deep anxiety over the ever-increasing volume of our expenditure and the manner in which our public funds were being applied. I consider it unfortunate that my repeated warnings were not heeded sufficiently to prevent certain trends that, unless checked, soon will have serious consequences."

In particular, Anscomb was referring to the British Columbia Hospital Insurance Service established prior to the 1949 election. He noted that the plan had run up a deficit of $4.5 million in its first fifteen months of operation and he predicted a further loss of $2.5 million in the coming year. The speech was an embarrassment for the government and compounded already adverse reaction to substantial increases in BCHIS premiums. More than causing discomfiture, Anscomb's critical comments underlined the fundamental differences that had always existed between the Conservatives and Liberals and which were now becoming increasingly difficult to conceal beneath the cloak of coalition. In his budgetary appraisal, Anscomb was merely expressing the traditional Conservative approach to government and public finance which had always been wary of increased taxation for the sake of social welfare expenditures. The Liberals, in contrast, insisted on a broad welfare program and saw BCHIS as a centrepiece of government policy.

The BCHIS controversy dominated the 1950 spring session and served to widen the chasm between the coalition partners. The government tried a number of means to bring hospital insurance finances into order, but they only stirred up greater controversy and wider public disenchantment. Several government members joined with the official opposition in denouncing the handling of the plan, and debate on the subject raged on in seemingly endless fashion. In March 1950, W. A. C. Bennett fiercely lambasted the "haphazard approach" in the administration of hospital insurance, and later in the session he let loose a terrific blast on the government's handling of the scheme. He had an intuitive sense that this was an issue the government would never get a firm grip on and he placed himself decidedly on the side of the critics of maladministration in BCHIS.

During the 1950 session Bennett discussed other issues as well: he called for the extension of the PGE railway into the Peace River region so that the northern part of the province could be developed; he made a further appeal for implementation of the single transferable ballot in the next election; in the same breath, he predicted that coalition would not continue for the next trip to the polls.

Bennett always firmly believed in his own prophecies and in the summer of 1950 he travelled around B.C. helping to make them come true. His private and public message was always the same—the coalition, while still popular, was too arrogant and had lost touch with the people—and he discovered that BCHIS was the focal point for popular discontent throughout the province.

Among Conservatives, deep concern for their future in provincial politics began to surface. If the coalition did break up, where would that leave the Tories under the rigid, old-style leadership of Herbert Anscomb? A group of young Tories—the Conservative Action Club—was determined to change things. A young lawyer by the name of Robert Bonner was an important member of the club, which he described as "a self-appointed group of movers and shakers." They worried for the future of the Conservative Party and demanded that the old crowd move aside. The young Conservatives were joined by most federal Tories in their distaste for Anscomb's domineering hold over the party machine. Together, they geared up for a provincial convention to be held October 6, 1950, where they planned to confront Anscomb. Les Bewley, another member of the Conservative Action Club, took six months off from his fledgling law practice to raise the country on the need for a new brand of Conservatism. Such idealistic and enthusiastic young Tories planned a purge of party leadership in order to present a more progressive, dynamic image.

First of all, they needed a person around whom the anti-Anscomb forces could rally. Some speculated that Davie Fulton, federal MP from Kamloops, might be interested—but Fulton refused to commit himself. It soon became apparent that no better or more willing alternative party leader existed than W. A. C. Bennett. Robert Bonner said: "We had canvassed the situation rather carefully to see who might make a leader. And as a result of surveying the scene we decided that W. A. C. had the qualifications to become a provincial leader. Then we subsequently learned that he had the inclination as well. So, at that point, I think he may have been a reluctant nominee—or less reluctant about being a nominee than uncertain about our ability to deliver him. But he had very good credentials and an attractive personality. He was a man who knew his own mind, and of considerable reputation when he spoke. So, he had all the apparent qualifications of leadership."

In September 1950, Bennett announced his intention of challenging Anscomb for the party leadership. The main hurdle that he and his backers faced was garnering enough support for a contest, since an active leader had never before been openly challenged in the B.C. Conservative Party. Anscomb was attacked and villified for his interest in a wine-making firm which did business with the government. Unlike Bennett, who had earlier dissociated himself from the young Okanagan wine industry, Anscomb felt no compunction about his business interests. Bennett, however, never became involved in any mud-slinging; rather, he promoted himself as an energetic alternative to the old-style political leadership that had failed to rejuvenate the party. The Bennett for Leader Committee distributed a pamphlet, "Bennett for Unity," which criticized the government as autocratic and incompetent. It claimed the CCF was gaining ground because there was not an "alternative honest and competent free enterprise party." Bennett promised to rebuild the Conservative Party, and when he was labelled a turncoat for previously rejecting Conservatism in favour of creating a provincial coalition party, he emphasized that the old-line politicians simply would not tolerate a permanent coalition: he was therefore intent on revitalizing his own party. This would not be the last time he was labelled a turncoat.

The second contest between Anscomb and Bennett was a knock-down, drag-out affair. As Russell Walker observed, the two men "entertained the mutual high regard of two cats after the same canary"—though to a surprising degree they held similar views of the world and their place in it. Neither Bennett nor Anscomb had hobbies, being totally consumed by work. Anscomb was more rigid and old-fashioned in his Conservatism, but the main clash between them seemed to be caused by the force of their egos rather than differences in political philosophy. But Anscomb brought out his big guns and demonstrated to all his complete mastery over the party apparatus. There was even talk of his having locked up Tory delegates in hotel rooms so that the Bennett forces could not get to them.

Feelings and temperatures were running high when the convention opened. Bennett spoke to the assembled Tories and urged them to reconsider their losing ways; he also demanded that Anscomb step down as party leader. According to one newspaper report, Bennett "pounded the table until the microphone shook" and exclaimed: "If after four years of leadership there was this much demand for my resignation, no one would have to call a convention; I would ask for one!"

But Anscomb's supporters moved into place on cue and were elected or re-elected to virtually all the party's executive positions. One young Tory,

Waldo Skillings, an alderman from Victoria, was favourably impressed with Bennett: "I could see the way the Conservative Party was going—they were going nowhere with Anscomb—and I thought with a young, virile fellow like Bennett, there was no place to go but up. He was never a great speaker, but he could really impress you with his sincerity and conviction—he had great conviction. So I became a staunch supporter of his." Delegate Skillings became seriously upset when he discovered that Tories from Kelowna, under pressure, had moved over to the Anscomb camp: "There were people down from Kelowna who Bennett thought were his supporters, but they weren't his supporters at all. I used to get around a lot, into the Anscomb headquarters, and I would find these guys in there. I'd say, 'What are you birds doing here?' They had feigned support for Bennett!" In the open convention, Skillings jumped to his feet and shouted: "It is no use meeting here if we are going to stick our heads in the sand without facing our problems. . . . Some of the tactics used here are far from British traditions. What have we to be afraid of?" Delegates responded with shouts of both approval and disapproval; someone yelled that he was out of order. The feisty Victorian shouted: "This is a democracy. I will not sit down until somebody knocks me down!"

As the Tories washed their underwear in public, the convention several times threatened to degenerate into chaos. Anscomb had been reassured of his grip on the party but was so aggravated by the personal attacks on him that he formally stepped down as leader in order to accept Bennett's challenge—in complete confidence of his ability to crush his opponent. In Bennett's final address to the convention, he made an aggressive attack on Anscomb, accusing him of being a "one-man party."

Bennett imagined he had some significant support in his bid for the party leadership, but as the time of balloting approached he began to realize that many supposed backers were eating out of his opponent's hand. He had the support of all the progressive elements in the party, but the Conservative Party machine was very strong. In the end, Tilly Rolston was the only MLA who vocally supported him. Minister of Public Works Ernie Carson, who had been committed to nominate Bennett, at the last moment felt the Anscomb forces turn on the screws. Just before the nominating meeting, Bonner came to Bennett's hotel suite and said: "W. A. C., get yourself set for a shock. Carson is not going to nominate you: he's supporting the other side."

Bennett's bubble burst when Carson appeared before the convention and nominated his cabinet colleague Herbert Anscomb to continue as leader. To make matters worse, H. A. Trusswell from Kelowna, formerly Bennett's friend and supporter who had nominated him in his 1946 leadership challenge, seconded Anscomb's nomination. Tom Norris, Bennett's first political opponent, told the convention: "We need a good dose of old-fashioned loyalty to our leader." Bennett was nominated by Robert Bonner, but could not compete with the party machine's heavy artillery. The vote was more lopsided than anyone had imagined: 450 for Anscomb, 167 for Bennett. The *Vancouver Sun* reported: "W. A. C. Bennett, jut-jawed MLA for South Okanagan, paid [Anscomb] the political courtesy of moving that the election be declared unanimous." Anscomb declared that the victory was "the crowning one of them all." He thanked Tory delegates for the resounding decision, pledged the party to remain in coalition until the end of the present legislature and, aiming a still-burning arrow at Bennett, he advised the convention: "Now we should be looking ahead for a very stable young man who can assume the responsibility [of leadership] I am now taking for the second time."

Anscomb's decisive victory was hugely significant. It split the Conservative Party in B.C. apart—young Conservatives withdrew from any activity in support of the provincial party, and the federal wing of west coast Conservatism would never be reconciled with Anscomb's abrasiveness. By continuing with Anscomb, the provincial Tories had unwittingly doomed themselves to extinction in British Columbia. Robert Bonner summed up the failed *coup d'état*: "I think, looking on it, we were rather remarkably successful—first, in bringing the convention on and, secondly, in rallying as many people as we did, given the fact that the provincial Conservatives in power had a lot of support from adherents and hangers-on who were part of the patronage apparatus of that period. . . . There was a lot of jockeying back and forth and patronage was pretty outrageous. You were either on the team or in the street, that's really what it amounted to."

Clearly, Bennett was now on the street. The door to the top had been closed in his face. He had struggled wholeheartedly to climb the greasy pole of B.C. politics, only to be turned back again and again. His political peers had recognized his ambition but could not see fit to use it. He had been stymied and rejected by the party machine, but he did not look upon its essential mechanisms—the money raising, the compromises, the demands of executive organization, the need to accommodate the grosser needs of a community to its idealistic hopes—as the grounds of his defeat. To the contrary, Bennett knew their value by their sting, and was now convinced that in order to master them he would have to look elsewhere.

He created the opportunity during the next legislative session in the spring of 1951, when it had become evident that coalition was more an inconvenient engagement than a marriage of convenience—Liberals and Conservatives were still together but were visibly unwed. The session was marked by further dissension in coalition ranks, particularly by the heated controversy over hospital insurance. Douglas Turnbull, the new Liberal minister of health and welfare, bore the brunt of the criticism levelled at the administrative monster BCHIS had become. Just prior to the session, he had announced that premium rates would be increased and that patients would be required to pay $3.50 per day "co-insurance" for the first ten days of a hospital visit. This may have been a practical approach to stabilizing the tremendous costs of the scheme but co-insurance became an extremely unpopular feature of an already suspect and controversial program. The session was almost completely devoted to quarrelling over Turnbull's bill. W. A. C. Bennett joined the CCF in battling the proposed premium increases and co-insurance, proclaiming on March 10: "I want to dissociate myself entirely from the government benches on this bill. It's breaking faith with the people of the province." He was one of four coalition members who voted against the government on the issue.

Another indication of the impending breakup of the Liberal-Tory alliance was Herbert Anscomb's delivery of yet another record-breaking provincial budget on March 13. It indicated massive spending increases totalling $154 million, but it also raised grave concern over the growing hospital insurance deficit which had now reached $12.7 million. Obviously, Anscomb did not believe Health and Welfare Minister Turnbull had gone far enough in ensuring that BCHIS would not be a further drain on the public purse. For his budget speech he extrapolated the same themes he had developed in earlier years: "I have no alternative but to warn the Legislature and the people generally that in my opinion far too great an emphasis is being placed upon social assistance." After ruminating over the increasing deficits of the hospital insurance program, he delivered a deliberate affront to his Liberal colleague: "I want to make it quite clear . . . that unless there is a realistic approach by the Minister of Health and Welfare in the administration of the new system he has proposed to the House, I have very grave doubts whether the proposals as submitted will do what they are supposed to do—that is put the scheme in balance. . . . I say quite frankly, that I am not prepared to impose further taxation on our people to cover operating expenses on ordinary account or to finance ventures in socialism."

Traditionally, ministers of finance consult with their premiers before delivering a budget speech. Anscomb had forwarded an advance transcript to Premier Johnson but the sections containing direct criticism were not included in it. Johnson was visibly hot under the collar but did not say a word. Former premier John Hart believed that he should have demanded Anscomb's resignation, and it is possible that the Tory finance minister was deliberately attempting to provoke the breakup of coalition, but Johnson took no action. An automobile accident late in 1950 had seriously affected his health, and many claimed that the premier had never completely recovered—though even if he had, it is far from certain that he had a whip long enough to crack at his defiant minister of finance. Meanwhile, other Liberal-coalitionists, particularly Health and Welfare Minister Turnbull, worried and wondered how long their partnership with Anscomb could last.

Bennett had a keen understanding of where the growing political crisis would end—and wondered about his future. There was little for him in the Conservative Party under Anscomb's stewardship. Bennett had become a well-known MLA, was outspoken, independent and ambitious, but his greatest claim after a decade in politics was that he was a well-worn and remarkable failure. In fact, his career up to this point was a catalogue of defeat: he had failed to get the government to act on the recommendations of the Post-War Rehabilitation Council; he had failed to secure a cabinet post; he had failed in his campaign to establish a permanent coalition party; he had failed to get elected to the federal House; and on two occasions he had failed to wrest the Tory leadership from Herbert Anscomb. Surely, Bennett's mission had gone awry; his dreams had become nightmares. Where could he go next?

Guided by common sense, most other fifty-year-old politicians would have called it a day and thrown in the towel. But Bennett followed his instincts and decided to gamble more boldly—and he decided not to wait. Perhaps he recalled a message in Orison Swett Marden's *Pushing to the Front*: "Don't wait for extraordinary opportunities. Seize common occasions and make them great."

Bennett believed the hospital insurance issue was a good one to stake his political career on and one from which he could launch out in a new direction. On the day the BCHIS bill came up for final reading, March 15, 1951, he rose in his place in the chamber and delivered an hour-long indictment of the coalition. He opposed policies in each and every government department. He told the legislature that the Hart-Maitland administration was the best government B.C. ever had, but the Johnson-Wismer-Anscomb coalition was far and away the worst government the province had endured. He charged that economy was not being practised in public affairs and predicted that another large budgetary surplus would soon demonstrate that the hospital insurance premium increases were unnecessary. After voicing his disgust with the general handling of BCHIS, he concluded his speech with these words: "I now dissociate myself from the present cabinet and the Coalition government both in this House and throughout the province."

Bennett had crossed the floor of the House—a move never before made during a session of the B.C. legislature. He now sat on the other side of the legislative chamber in the opposition benches as the independent member for South Okanagan. Why did he make this dramatic move when he did? His answer: "Timing is everything. I had gone as far as I could; I either did it then or never. I either did it then, or else resigned from public life."

Many MLAs imagined that Bennett had, indeed, resigned from public life, and the widespread belief among political observers was that he had finally gone too far. Attorney General Gordon Wismer was heard to scoff: "Think nothing of it, Bennett has made a fool of himself and he's finished, finished! He'll never get elected again!" In the days to come, however, speculation grew that Bennett was planning to start a new provincial party. Would he attempt to revive the ideas of his long-abandoned United Progressive Party? Nobody knew for certain what he was up to, but he certainly did not appear to be planning for retirement—in fact, he was busier than ever. Amid all the gossip that filtered through the legislative corridors of Victoria in the spring of 1951 was the strange rumour that W. A. C. Bennett was contemplating joining the little-known British Columbia Social Credit League.

CHAPTER
FOUR
A STAB IN THE DARK

He will not go far who knows from the start where he is going.
Napoleon Bonaparte

*As the ancients wisely say
Have a care o' th' main chance,
And look before you ere you leap;
For as you sow y'ere like to reap.*
Samuel Butler

Towards the end of the First World War, a Scottish engineer working at the Royal Aircraft Works in England made a "discovery" that would one day significantly influence people and events in faraway places. He was Maj. Clifford Hugh Douglas, an engineer of repute, who for years had struggled with the accepted beliefs and well-worn explanations about processes explored by the dismal science of economics. Like so many others, he was mystified by the fact that the economy of a nation could be instantly, almost magically transformed from a moribund to a vibrant state by the simple declaration of war against another country. Why could not peaceful, nonmilitary factors supply the same positive economic impetus? The answer to this question came to Major Douglas in the form of a revelation which promised to be the solution to virtually all of the world's economic problems. It certainly changed Douglas's life, the rest of which was devoted to proselytizing and sometimes fierce struggles to keep the faith pure. He called the faith Social Credit.

For a time, his ideas were acclaimed in Britain, and they eventually formed the basis of popular movements and political parties in distant corners of the globe. And yet, it is now customary to dismiss the technical elements of Social Credit theory as fantastic and illogical. Of course, the message was not helped by Douglas's awkward expression or by his throwing in a great deal of extraneous matter which only antagonized most potential converts to the cause. Social Credit did, however, have a sound foundation, for though Douglas was far from brilliant, he had stumbled onto an interesting and credible way of looking at economics. Social Credit theory generated some very useful socio-economic paradigms that helped to focus debate on the future of capitalism. During the period between the two world wars, many people including several prominent thinkers gave tacit support to his Social Credit. Today, Major Douglas is a neglected figure in social, economic and political theory. To a large extent, this is his own fault; he failed to provide effective leadership, was almost hopeless as a theoretician, and guarded his faith with an extreme and peculiar jealousy. Nevertheless, it is worth re-examining his ideas because, even when misunderstood, they have served as the foundation for the various manifestations of Social Credit, and it is impossible to understand Social Credit's appeal without knowing what it pretended to offer.

As developed by Douglas during the 1920s, Social Credit was essentially a repudiation of economic liberalism. Impressed by technology's potential but disgusted with industrial waste and the inefficiency of government bureaucracy, he introduced his theory as a sweeping critique of capitalist industrialization. But it is important to point out that Social Credit was basically reformist; Douglas, a nonsocialist critic of capitalism, wanted to revive the system, not overthrow it. Essentially he believed that the individual in modern industrial society could not be free until he had secured freedom of choice both as a producer and consumer, and a standard of living that was denied to him by the existing systems of production and distribution. Douglas accepted that capitalism had succeeded in raising production to unprecedented levels and had provided goods and services to meet every human need and desire; however, he claimed, it had failed to provide the means for people to consume this production. His theory aimed at the destruction of the mechanism by which economic power was becoming increasingly concentrated in the hands of a few. He argued that the purchasing power of the individual would have to be increased in order to allow the power of consumption to rise to the level of production, and he was convinced that this would solve the paradoxical problem of poverty in the midst of plenty.

Douglas claimed that the existing monetary and credit systems continually drained off vital purchasing power and, consequently, production could not generate income sufficient to buy back the goods. He demonstrated this chronic deficiency of purchasing power with his famous A plus B theorem—an amazingly simple analysis of the industrial process. According to this theorem, every industrial or manufacturing firm has two costs: "A" costs—payments made to individuals for salaries, wages, etc.; and "B" costs—payments made to institutions for materials, machinery and banking charges. In order to recover its costs, the factory must include both in the price of its product—thus the price A plus B. But since individual purchasing power is only A, it obviously cannot command the purchase of A plus B. So the individual consumer could never hope to buy back what he had created as a producer—unless, of course, he went to the banks and asked for credit.

For Douglas, the ultimate solution to this puzzle required government intervention in the economy. The state would have to step in to correct a situation where the amount of money in a community depended on the banking system and not on the actual wealth of the community. In order for the purchasing power of the public to correspond more closely to the production capacity of industry, all goods should be sold at a predetermined "Just Price." Any losses incurred by a retailer for selling at the Just Price would be compensated by the issue of new money. In addition, Douglas advocated that the government distribute a "National Dividend" to every individual as part of the difference between prices and purchasing power. The National Dividend would help to correct that discrepancy and, according to Douglas, would bring all the disparate monetary and economic forces into a new equilibrium. Although he was proposing what amounted to the printing of a new form of paper money, combined with a relatively simple alteration of the accounting procedure of industry, he believed the implementation of his system—Social Credit—would help to usher in a new society in which people would be free to develop their individuality in ways never before possible.

To a large degree, his ideas were original, for he was ignorant of the monetary reformers of his day, but the basic concept behind Social Credit had been around for a long time; it was part of the underconsumptionist tradition of monetary reform which survived on the fringes of intellectual acceptance. With that association in mind, John Maynard Keynes described Social Credit as part of the "underworld" of economic theory. Social Credit economic doctrine was not completely indefensible; its case could be convincingly argued on even the most technical grounds, and its intellectual appeal was such that G. D. H. Cole, Lewis Mumford, T. S. Eliot, Ezra Pound, G. K. Chesterton and a host of other well-known thinkers became associated with the English Social Credit movement. Unfortunately, its founder, Major Douglas, was incapable of fostering widespread support and continually antagonized those who flirted with his ideas. He was an engineer by training, not an economist, and certainly not an intellectual; moreover, he developed Social Credit as more than simply an economic theory.

Ezra Pound once observed: "The surprise on rereading Douglas is that he seems . . . to deal so little with economics and so greatly with the philosophy of politics." In repudiating the existing economic system, Douglas's Social Credit also demanded a rejection of political institutions. This is implicit in most of his rambling writings. After the start of the Depression, which he regarded as proving his theories, he presented Social Credit as a multifaceted doctrine with answers to all of mankind's ills, offering a new "way of life." He believed that the state was an instrument of coercive power controlled by finance and that the political institutions of the modern democratic state were unresponsive to the will of the people. But he never urged direct political action, believing that Social Credit principles could be used by any individual seeking public office and that the role of the movement should be educational not political. He did, however, develop and expound some strange ideas about politics and government which helped to discredit Social Credit in most circles.

Douglas disregarded class, regional and group interests in society and believed in a nearly unanimous "general will." He claimed that all people had the same basic goals: personal freedom and economic security. The role of an elected representative in a Social Credit state would be to give expression to the mass desire of constituents; accordingly, organized political parties were inimical to the interests and real needs of people because they served to frustrate the "general will." Rather than political parties, Douglas would have citizens organize themselves into a Union of Electors through which any individual could make known his wishes to his parliamentary representatives. Under a Social Credit system, voting would take the form of plebiscites, in which people would vote on principles and major objectives, but not on the methods used for implementing these goals. Douglas believed that exceptional ability and intelligence were required to develop and implement government policy—qualities which he felt were foreign to the great majority of both voters and politicians. Under the existing parliamentary system, he considered that it was "quite impossible for the average Member of Parliament to give an intelligent opinion upon more than one half per cent of the things he is asked questions on." He anticipated the need to severely restrict the role of parliamentarians; the formulation and execution of specific government policies in a Social Credit state would be left up to the experts. In short, he proposed that voters should not be confused with the substance of public issues but should simply express their general opinions through their elected representatives who, in turn, would direct a new breed of technocrat to implement policy unimpeded.

It is difficult to assess the plebiscitary democracy that Douglas wrote about, for he rarely dealt in specifics, nor did he define his terms. Perhaps the most important and ironical feature of his scheme is the distinction he drew between the people and the experts. The basis of Social Credit economic theory and its critique of society is directed against the concentration of power; Douglas explicitly denounced such trends and always vociferously attacked authoritarianism in all its forms. And yet, the kind of "democracy" he advocated had obvious totalitarian tendencies. He did not feel, for instance, that the public should be consulted on technical matters, nor should they be told much about the exact nature of government activity. The end would always justify the means. Implicitly, his system contained ominous hints of fascism and suggested the possibility, or even likelihood, of a veiled dictatorship.

In a sense, his political theory can be dismissed as the product of a frustrated engineer's misconception of the nature of society. But his political ideas became an integral part of Social Credit in its British context and, as such, helped to confuse the original thrust of Social Credit as monetary reform.

Although he claimed that his doctrine rejected the pitfalls of the left and right, in Britain whenever there was any positive response to Social Credit, it came from the fringes of those two extremes. Moderates of virtually all political stripes frowned on Social Credit's proposed solutions to the crises of the 1930s. For a while, an unlikely situation arose which saw both Fascists and members of the International Labour Party simultaneously at home under the strained roof of Social Credit. Major Douglas's writings and public utterances were usually vague, probably one of the reasons for Social Credit's diverse appeal, and in some respects the doctrine's contradictory nature was its outstanding feature in Britain.

In an era when economic and political alternatives were being desperately sought, Douglas's theories travelled abroad, sometimes carried by Douglas himself. As early as 1923 he was called to testify before the Canadian House of Commons Banking Committee. At home, he struggled with Social Credit adherents who desired political action and who urged the formation of a political party. As time progressed and no genuine British Social Credit movement emerged, his ideas lost vogue. Perhaps it was inevitable that in attempting to define the real sources of world power he would find a power-seeking conspiracy—his later writings are concerned with "Dark Forces" and identify a deep-laid plot by Jewish financiers to enslave the industrial world. In his final years he was abandoned by all but the most rabid of his followers who, with the somewhat eccentric Major, became mired in antisemitic conspiracy theories.

During the 1930s, Douglas's Social Credit was debated in many countries, including New Zealand, Australia and the United States, but it was in western Canada that it had the most visible effect—in particular, the province of Alberta. Alberta had developed a unique tradition of nonparty politics, provincial governments being consistently formed with huge legislative majorities. Nor were Albertans afraid to experiment with new parties, having long rejected the traditional eastern-dominated Liberal and Conservative machines. Since 1919 they had chosen to be governed by the United Farmers of Alberta (UFA), but the Depression proved a difficult time to stay in public favour and the UFA government took a good deal of the blame for the province's moribund economy. On top of the economic discontent and social dislocation caused by the Depression, Albertans were shocked and outraged when in 1934 their UFA premier, John Brownlee, was involved in a lurid sex scandal. Brownlee's alleged love affair with a young secretary and the subsequent trial was splashed all over a wildly partisan press and helped to sharply focus public dissatisfaction. Voters awaited the next call to the polls so that they could demonstrate their distaste.

Into this swirling political storm came a fundamentalist preacher cum politician, William Aberhart. "Bible Bill" Aberhart, as he became known, was one of the least likely and most unforgettable figures in the history of Canadian politics. From teaching school and Bible classes he had gone on in 1927 to found the Calgary Bible Institute where his forceful, impassioned sermons won him many converts. In the early 1930s he became a pioneer in the art of radio broadcasting, sending his weekly sermons across the air waves into thousands of Alberta homes. His "Sunday Bible Hour" had the highest ratings of any Alberta broadcast and, as a result, his religious mission flourished, though he was soon confronted with competition from other radio evangelists. In 1932 he was introduced to the idea of Social Credit and was struck by what he considered to be the common-sense foundation of Douglas's writings. Partly as an attempt to gain an edge on his competitors, Aberhart began to interject his selective interpretation of Douglas's theory into his sermons and soon discovered that listeners were reacting enthusiastically; they wanted more. In an era when the economic backbone of the country seemed broken, Aberhart appeared to have a solution.

The desperation of the period combined with Aberhart's fiery demagoguery helped to create a tremendous swell of interest in Social Credit. The preacher's religious message was easily translated into an economic panacea. He went on speaking tours throughout Alberta and left a myriad of Social Credit study groups in his wake. Attacks on his teachings forced him into a defensive stance, and then, at the urging of many of his devoted followers, he decided to move Social Credit into the political arena. A young follower of Aberhart, E.C. Manning, described the initiative:

> The Social Credit movement in Alberta did not start as a political movement at all. When Mr. Aberhart started talking about Social Credit theory in 1932 he hadn't the faintest, slightest intention of going into politics. It was purely an educational thing; it was trying to analyze the conditions of the Depression and the possible application Douglas's Social Credit theories would have to the situation. The method that we followed was to have hundreds of study groups scattered all over Alberta. In the summer of '34 and '35 I travelled with Mr. Aberhart all over Alberta; we'd take two meetings a day and just travelled all the

time. These were educational meetings and this was the theory that was advanced: "There are things that can be done, and the thing for you, the people, to do is bring pressure on your elected representative."

According to Manning, Aberhart had tried, without success, to convince each political party in the province to adopt Social Credit, and this failure, combined with the severe criticism he had been subjected to, forced him to take a direct political course. Hence an Alberta Social Credit political movement was formed under the domineering aegis of "Bible Bill" Aberhart. When the faltering UFA government called an election for August 1935, Social Credit candidates offered themselves to disaffected voters.

The election was a curious affair. Under new leadership, the UFA government asked for a renewed mandate on the basis of its record; smelling blood in the aftermath of the Brownlee scandal, the provincial Liberals came on strong; and nobody knew what would be the effect of Aberhart's "Socreds." The campaign was fierce, and the UFA, sensitive to Aberhart's tremendous personal popularity, invited Major Douglas to Alberta in an attempt to forestall Social Credit. Douglas was impressed by the warm reception he was given by members of the noncommittal UFA cabinet and, later, after meeting Aberhart for the first time, he was heard to exclaim, "I have all the damn fools on my side and all the clever men against me!" Nevertheless, he was not about to jeopardize the election chances of a party bearing the name Social Credit and he tried to avoid becoming involved in local politics before returning home to Britain.

Undoubtedly Aberhart's grasp of Douglas's theory was weak, but his ability to convey what he understood was unequalled. If his abilities as a communicator could have been successfully merged with Major Douglas's doctrinal knowledge, Social Credit might have swept the Western world as quickly as it did the Alberta countryside in the spring and summer of 1935. One of Aberhart's main election planks was the promise of a twenty-five-dollar monthly dividend to every man, woman and child in the province. When questioned how it would work, he replied: "The first step would be to engage Major Douglas to come here and organize it and he would do the work." When challenged further, he answered by pointing out that it was not necessary to understand how electricity works in order to use it. His Social Credit message was strongly flavoured with his distinctive evangelical brand of religion; he prayed at campaign meetings, "O Lord, do Thou grant us a foretaste of Thy millenial reign? Organization is not enough, Lord. Our help must come from above." At election rallies supporters sang hymns such as "What a Friend We Have in Jesus" and "O God, Our Help in Ages Past." And when the campaign got rough, Aberhart did not refrain from speaking forcefully, referring to political opponents as "these rats, sons of Satan, liars, fornicators."

On August 22, 1935, voters turned out in record numbers and produced one of the most unexpected electoral upsets in Canadian history. The new, untried and untempered Social Credit Party won fifty-six out of sixty-three seats in the legislature, and Aberhart, the rotund preacher, who was as startled as anyone, prepared to form the world's first Social Credit government. The reaction of observers was generally shock and surprise. In Britain, proto-fascist supporters of Douglas's Social Credit known as Greenshirts marched seven times around the Bank of England beating drums and shouting Aberhart's name. The Very Reverend Hewlett Johnson, the "Red Dean" of Canterbury, who was a friend of Major Douglas, cabled Aberhart and predicted: "Alberta will kindle a world-wide torch." The new Alberta premier wired Major Douglas: "Victorious. When could you come?" Douglas answered: "Congratulations. There will be others but only one first."

Major Douglas never accepted Aberhart's invitation, for he was unsure of the course of events in Alberta and unconvinced of the particular political route Aberhart followed. He also distrusted him and felt uncomfortable with the strong religious flavour he had injected into Social Credit theory. But from afar, Douglas did offer advice, and in an era when European politics headed for disaster, he wanted to believe that Social Credit could provide an alternative. A few years later he wrote: "The adventure to which Western Canada is moving, the forces which are being challenged and the political results of that challenge are greater than anything which is involved in either Russia, Italy or Germany every one of which, whatever its virtues, is an attack on individual liberty."

The reaction in Canada to Alberta's political experiment was astonishment, especially since nobody seemed to know just what Social Credit meant. A few years later, Stephen Leacock used these words to explain events in Alberta: "To this province were imported certain economic profundities of British fog, impossible for most people to understand. . . . The theory is an expansion of the idea of living by taking in one another's washing. It is suggested that if all the people collectively give twenty-five dollars each to all the people separately then each of the separate people can call for work and goods from all the other people, whereby everybody has work and the work supplies everybody with bread." While Leacock was poking fun at Social Credit monetary theory, he, like others, was not sure how to assess seriously Social Credit's impact: "We cannot yet tell whether Social Credit was the end of something just ending or is the beginning of something just beginning."

As premier, Aberhart ran a tough, conservative administration—his government's touch of radicalism was the result of a heavy dose of prairie populism as well as aborted or shot-down attempts at Social Credit legislation. Aberhart actually issued "prosperity certificates"— a version of the proverbial Social Credit dividend—but he ran up against the wall of Canadian federalism; according to the British North America Act, only the federal government controlled banking and currency. When the provincial legislation was disallowed by federal courts, Aberhart was outraged but could only exclaim to his sympathetic fellow Albertans: "You see what we are up against!"

His administration was not able to fulfill its promise of a Social Credit dividend, but he did give Albertans a stable government with strong and popular moral overtones. In 1940 his government was re-elected despite losing twenty seats. Three years later, Aberhart died in office, leading many to believe that Social Credit would also die in Canada. However, his disciple, E. C. Manning, carried on with a staid and very successful conservative administration which never belaboured itself with the ideas of Major Douglas. The Social Credit dividend was never again seriously considered; ideas like the Just Price were rarely discussed, and only a few Albertans could attempt an explanation of the A plus B theorem. Nevertheless, the government flew the Social Credit flag proudly and Albertans came to identify with its symbols. Then in 1947, the dramatic discovery of oil at Leduc, Alberta, helped to keep Manning's version of Social Credit afloat on a black sea of prosperity for many years to come.

Social Credit in Alberta became a strong, well-organized governing party supported by a powerful grassroots movement. Alberta was clearly the homeland of Social Credit in Canada, but concentrated efforts were also made to spread the faith to neighbouring provinces, and Socred candidates contested federal elections as well. Some headway was made in Saskatchewan, but it was the west coast province of British Columbia that would one day challenge Alberta for hegemony within the Canadian Social Credit movement.

Major Douglas's ideas were being studied on Canada's Pacific coast at about the same time that Aberhart discovered them on the other side of Rockies, and the Depression helped to initiate further discussion. In 1932, a reporter working for the *Vancouver Sun*, Henry Torey, stumbled across literary references to Major Douglas. After reading some of Douglas's work he became intrigued with Social Credit theory and, along with a couple of friends, William Tutte and William Rose, engaged a small circle of acquaintances in an informal study group. In the autumn of 1932 they formed the Douglas Social Credit Group, British Columbia Section. They were not connected in any formal way with Social Credit groups elsewhere and made no effort to proselytize or expand. Initially, they simply came together on a regular basis—usually for coffee—to talk about Douglas's ideas and satisfy their own curiosity. It is safe to assume that during the early 1930s Social Credit was never seriously examined by more than a few dozen British Columbians.

This changed almost overnight. In the spring of 1934 Major Douglas was returning home via Canada from a triumphant tour of Australia and New Zealand where he had spoken to huge, enthusiastic crowds and his ideas reached many thousands of listeners. In Vancouver the Social Credit Group assisted the Kiwanis Club in inviting him to address a meeting. Since economic and monetary reform were of great popular interest during this depressed time and the new B.C. premier, Duff Pattullo, enjoyed toying with such ideas, he "wirelessed" Douglas and asked him to address the provincial legislature on his economic proposals. Douglas accepted both invitations.

His reception in Vancouver was greater than could have been expected by the few members of the Douglas Social Credit Group, British Columbia Section: a lively audience of over one thousand turned out to hear the Social Credit prophet who spoke "in the deep intonations of a cultured Briton." A few days later when he made a presentation to an informal session of the legislature, it was reported that his statements on monetary reform "deeply moved the House." In his address, Douglas stressed that his proposed reforms were not political in nature: "Social Credit is not a political reform. It deals solely with the economic system.... It can be administered by any political party.... They can be Liberals, Conservatives, Labor or even a despotic monarchy or dictatorship.... So long as the first thing the administration did was enact the principles of Social Credit they could then go their ways and administer the country as they saw fit, and regardless, poverty would vanish."

Reaction to his visit was mixed but it did serve to arouse a wider local interest in Social Credit. On the one hand, his ideas were heralded as the "New Economic Hope," while on the other, they were criticized as "the picture of a slave economy." Ultimately, little of a practical nature developed from his visit, and Premier Pattullo, as well as other provincial politicians, must have been reassured by Douglas's pronouncement that Social Credit posed no challenge to established political interests.

Perhaps the most reliable indicator of the effect of Douglas's visit was the upsurge of interest and attendance at the weekly Social Credit discussion group in Vancouver, which Henry Torey's brother, Gordon, explained: "The main reason was that an awful lot of people looked around [at the economy] and said 'What went wrong? All the people are still here; all the productive machinery is still here; all the things necessary to produce the kind of living we had before are still here. What's making it so that [the system] doesn't function?' That's where a lot of people started in at, wondering what went wrong. The reason that Douglas's ideas became so attractive was that he supplied the answers. Money was the key—the missing key—the handling of money."

Interest in Social Credit and monetary reform probably would have levelled off over the course of the next year were it not for the activities of William Aberhart in neighbouring Alberta, which culminated in the startling election victory in the summer of 1935 and forced many British Columbians to take notice. The B.C. press expressed a combination of surprise, confusion and skepticism: "Alberta voted for Santa Claus," declared the *Vancouver Sun;* "Albertans are quite willing to leap in the dark," editorialized the Victoria *Colonist;* and the Vancouver *Province* wondered if Social Credit was simply a left-wing variant of Liberalism. Soon Premier Pattullo was again examining Social Credit and, though he indicated that Douglas's ideas warranted reconsideration, it seems clear that he was simply endeavouring to forestall what was now being predicted for his Liberal counterparts in Saskatchewan—a defeat at the hands of Social Credit in the next provincial election.

The informal discussion group now became a regular forum for debating the merit of Douglas's ideas, and increased numbers forced the group to obtain a larger meeting place. Instead of the dozen or so individuals accustomed to meeting in a small office, Social Credit meetings now attracted fifty, sixty and sometimes seventy people on a regular basis. In the autumn of 1935, the group became formally incorporated under the provincial Societies Act as the Social Credit League of British Columbia, whose official aims and objectives were purely educational.

The formation of the League was in part a reaction to the recent growth of interest in Social Credit, but was also indicative of the "old guard's" strong desire to keep the faith pure. The founding members of the Social Credit study group were being inundated with new and enthusiastic converts to Major Douglas's ideas, many of whom wanted political action *à la* Alberta, but original west coast followers did not trust Aberhart; they felt he had confused and perverted the philosophy of Social Credit with his religious posturing and direct political action. These Douglas purists, who controlled the League executive, regarded many of the newer converts as troublemakers. The establishment of the League was an attempt to keep to the spirit of Major Douglas's original concept of the Social Credit movement as an instructional vehicle, *not* a political party.

The Canadian federal election of 1935 was the first national contest for Social Credit candidates. In Alberta, emulating Aberhart's amazing provincial victory, Social Credit sent fifteen MPs to Ottawa, but in British Columbia, the few Social Crediters who offered themselves to the voters finished consistently in last place. It was in the aftermath of the poor showing in the federal contest that many B.C. followers of Major Douglas felt that a province-wide organization was needed if Social Credit was going to have any impact. So although the creation of the League was a deliberate attempt to control the direction of Social Credit by old guard "Douglasites," it was seen by others as a small step towards gaining political strength. These two diametrically opposed urges would be the source of deep division within the B.C. Social Credit movement for many years to come.

The executive of the fledgling League could not stem the tide of those who wanted to prepare for the next provincial election. Alberta Premier Aberhart, who regularly vacationed on the west coast, encouraged political action by the B.C. movement with, as one student of this period said, "himself as its chief helmsman." For a short while, he even sponsored his own British Columbia Social Credit Union—but when it became clear that the League would in fact field candidates in the next provincial contest, he abandoned the Union and joined forces with the League.

During 1936, Social Credit activities in B.C. were regularly covered in the urban press, and the announcement that the League was planning to enter the next provincial election with assistance from Alberta caused considerable anxiety within the established parties. In March, League members appeared before a committee of the legislature and said that a Social Credit dividend in the province could amount to forty dollars per month for every man, woman and child. Later in the spring, the press began to view the prospect of a Social Credit victory as a distinct possibility. In April, under the front-page headline "Aberhart Forces Groomed For B.C.," the Victoria *Times* stated: "Premier William Aberhart of Alberta has both ears cocked for any advance information as to when Premier T. D. Pattullo and his government may go to the country. His forces will be groomed to invade British Columbia. He thinks fifteen good speakers from Alberta would convert the people of the coast province into Social Crediters and provide a government similar to his own."

The first convention of the Social Credit League of British Columbia was held in May 1936, attended primarily by members from the Vancouver and Victoria areas, and despite differences of opinion and wide-ranging debates on Douglas's technical authority, it served as an important consolidation of support for the Social Credit movement. The convention voted to try to field candidates in every provincial riding and produced an election platform which, with the exception of references to Social Credit dividends and price discounts, was little different from the platforms of other political parties.

Throughout the summer and fall of 1936, Social Credit activities were prominent in the press, often made sensational by the pompous pronouncements of a frequent visitor to the province, "Bible Bill" Aberhart. After returning home from a summer sojourn on the coast, he was reported to be excited about the "great activity" in B.C. and he declared that Social Credit groups were "busy sowing the seeds of truth throughout the province." Later that fall, he spoke several times to large audiences in Vancouver and Victoria, where he urged British Columbians to drop "the old line parties which are directed by the unseen hand of international finance." He predicted that a Social Credit government in Victoria was well within sight; he also expounded some curiously imperialistic ideas. He declared, for instance, that he would like to see British Columbia and Alberta become a single political unit and that it would be "a lovely thing" if the two provinces were made "a united people through Social Credit." Close ties between Canada's two westernmost provinces became one of his most popular economic planks, and after returning to Alberta he claimed that Social Credit "is sweeping British Columbia like a prairie fire."

Liberal Premier Duff Pattullo held on until the spring of 1937 before calling an election. During the heated campaign he presented his famous "Work and Wages" program; the Tories meanwhile attacked him for "over-governing" the province; and the CCF desperately tried to dent the armour of both older parties. In this highly charged atmosphere it was difficult for the poorly organized Socreds to make any political headway. They managed to contest only eighteen of the province's forty-eight seats, and most of their candidates were less than serious about getting elected. Peer Paynter, who ran under the Social Credit banner in the riding of Vancouver-Burrard, said: "Actually, we were running candidates without any hope of winning. We didn't have any idea that we might win. But it was one method of getting before the public. And actually our objective at that time was to build up our organization to a point where we could be effective." Surprisingly, the League did achieve a high profile during the first half of the campaign when Social Credit was continually assailed by the press, denounced for being "superficially attractive" to people like the "poor Albertan farmers who have been passing through a period of dire stress."

Even with help from Social Credit MPs and Aberhart's Alberta troops, the B.C. League did not prove to be a factor in the election. In fact, when the results were announced on the evening of June 1, 1937, the only major surprise was Social Credit's almost complete lack of support. Pattullo's Grits were returned to office, with a Tory opposition bolstered by a CCF contingent and two independents. Not only did Social Credit fail to win a single seat but it finished last in virtually every consitutency in which it ran candidates, polling a meagre one per cent of the total votes cast.

Clearly, British Columbia in 1937 was not Alberta in 1935. In this different time and place, the conditions that had made a Social Credit victory possible in Alberta were wholly absent. The potential impact of Social Credit in B.C. had been greatly exaggerated by the urban press. Perhaps it was a kind of apology, but Social Credit would not be considered as seriously by the press until fifteen years later, when it would be too late to engage in idle speculation.

The League's first foray into provincial politics was followed by more than a decade of internecine warfare by struggling splinter groups, but in spite of the infighting and backbiting—perhaps because of it—Social Credit was kept alive in British Columbia. Although it did not achieve the status of a genuine popular movement, it was supported by a core of dedicated workers, thinkers and propagandists. The years immediately following the 1937 election were particularly lean: with the outbreak of the Second World War, interest in monetary reform waned and Social Credit would probably have disappeared were it not for the efforts of a small group of dedicated Douglasites who formed a kind of secret society known but to a few as the Perfect Circle. Peer Paynter was among the members of this select group and described what it was like:

> Patriotism was running pretty high and to advocate any change—well, you were considered a little bit out to the left. So a bunch of the fellows got together and formed what was called the "Perfect Circle." Our badge was a little gold pin with a little gold circle. It was about three-sixteenths of an inch across, I guess. You could hardly see it on your lapel, but it was something that our own fellows would recognize. It was formed like a secret organization and to get in you had to go through an initiation. They had a kind of maze built of about a half dozen different rooms and in each one of these rooms there were three doors. You went into a room through one door and then there were two doors exiting out of the room; one of them led into the next room and the other one put you back in the corridor again. Above the door on one side would be the words "Banks Create Money" and on the other door "Governments Create Money." If you took "Banks Create Money," well, you got into the next room; if you took "Governments Create Money," you were out in the hall again. Each one of the rooms had two doors like that and if you didn't know your basic Social Credit, you'd be out in the hall. But if you did know it, you'd go from one room to the other, you see, right on through. That was your initiation: if you got through all these rooms, then you became a member of the organization. If you got out into the hall, you had to do some more studying.
>
> I don't suppose there were more than thirty members in the organization. It lasted for about two or three years. The idea of the Perfect Circle was that if your money was circulating properly it would keep on circulating—it would make a perfect circle. As your economy grew, you

instilled more money into it so that it would make a perfect circle. That was the idea behind the Perfect Circle. It was carried on at a time when feelings were kind of high as far as any new public ideas were concerned. You were liable to be branded a communist or what have you. After the war was over, the whole thing was dropped.

The Social Credit League of British Columbia remained relatively dormant during the war years. Aberhart was kept busy in his own bailiwick by federal court challenges to his Social Credit legislation and had no time to sally forth to B.C. to tilt at political windmills there. The 1941 B.C. election which precipitated the formation of the coalition government and saw W. A. C. Bennett elected in South Okanagan was not contested by a single Social Credit candidate, but as the war came to a close the movement became more active. Nationally, a concerted effort was made to organize Social Credit across the country and this helped to bring west coast Socreds and other would-be monetary reformers out of the closet as well as encourage new converts to the cause.

Lyle Wicks is an example of the new breed of Social Credit adherent during this period. Wicks was working as a Vancouver streetcar conductor when, in 1942, he was introduced to Social Credit theory. He described this important event in his life: "The nearest thing that I could say is that it was like a spiritual experience that people have when they become saved. . . . I felt very keenly on it because I knew we needed some solutions and we weren't getting any to our problems material." But Wicks found a house divided:

> The first indication I had that there was great divisiveness arose because of the different approaches that people took to Social Credit. In the midst of us we had, first of all, strictly monetary reformers. They pointed out the dangers of the gold standard and the need for a central bank. We had the British Israelites who pointed out certain things about the pyramids and the importance of Britain in world affairs and also subscribed to monetary theories—they were an active group. We also had the Alberta Social Crediters, many of whom didn't know a damn thing about Social Credit. Then we had the pure Social Crediters, those who hung on very tenaciously to the words of Major Douglas, as though he were a prophet and they were the disciples. They were a very small group of intellectuals, but very self-righteous, very much opposed to political action of any kind and always right and very vitriolic if anyone crossed them up.

This description of some of the major subgroupings within the B.C. Social Credit movement of the 1940s is accurate but incomplete. Right from the start there was intense competition among west coast Socreds to prove who represented Major Douglas's "truth." There were, in addition, antisemitic elements who seemed to originate largely from Alberta and who traced the world's economic ills to an international Jewish conspiracy. They were encouraged by the latter-day prejudices of Major Douglas as well as by the overt antisemitism of Premier Aberhart in the years before his death in 1943. In a world of their own were the British Israelites who believed that the British people were one of the lost tribes of Israel and who espoused economic ideas based upon biblical interpretation, like cancelling all debt every seven years. The "B.I.s," as they were known, called for freeing people from economic domination by large banking institutions and connected their ideas, in tentative fashion, with those of Major Douglas. Also prominent at early Vancouver meetings were socialists and proto-socialists who seemed attracted to some of Douglas's ideas and were perhaps marginally confused by the name "Social Credit," somehow associating it with socialism. Persons of left-leaning persuasion, however, caused bitter debates at Socred meetings and were discouraged from attending; by the post-World War II period socialists were no longer flirting with Social Credit.

It is difficult to evaluate the appeal of Social Credit in British Columbia during these years, for it was not a political party but a movement, or a league. The Douglasites chose their official name deliberately to avoid being tainted by partisan politics and it gave the Social Credit movement in B.C. a certain populist appeal which it never lost. The distinction between a "party" and a "movement" was an important one. The early Socreds saw themselves as above the ordinary dirtiness of party politics and believed that their principles should never be sacrificed for political power. As a consequence, people with varying backgrounds and specialized interests, who would have been reluctant to join a political party, became associated with Social Credit—and this helps to explain not only its apolitical thrust but also its largely ineffectual organization.

For a fledgling, ill-organized and disparate movement, Social Credit manifested a curious kind of vitality. Who was attracted to it during these early years in British Columbia? Just as it has been popular to dismiss Major Douglas as a crank, so it has been fashionable to regard adherents of Social Credit as kooks and eccentrics. One student of west coast politics, Martin Robin, has referred to the early Socreds as a "drab collection of monetary fetishists, British Israelites, naturopaths, chiropractors, preachers, pleaders and anti-semites." But it is both inaccurate and unfair to evaluate the movement as a political party. The reform nature of Social Credit appealed to the disaffected, the misfits and even the paranoids—as well as to serious students of monetary reform. It was unfair, too, that Social Credit in B.C. was tarred with the same brush that had been used on Aberhart in Alberta, because the west coast movement evolved separately. Although many ex-Albertans became involved in the B.C. movement and some ties developed between the two organizations, the appeal of Social Credit on the coast did not originate in the religious fundamentalism that had brought Aberhart to power. In fact, religion has never figured as large in B.C. politics as it has in other parts of Canada. In the main, early adherents of the Social Credit cause were workers, union members, small-businessmen, war veterans and a small number of intellectuals. In a collective sense, they were essentially middle class or perhaps lower-middle class. They were serious-minded believers in the basic doctrine of Major Douglas. They viewed themselves as ordinary folk, pitted against large, organized, impersonal forces directing their lives. Their early haphazard efforts gave the movement a kind of populist image which was one of the reasons for its eventual success in British Columbia.

Towards the end of World War II and throughout the 1940s a variety of Social Credit-related organizations were founded: the Democratic Monetary Reform Organization; the United Democrats; the New Democracy movement; the National Dividend Association; the Armed Forces Union, and the Federation of Canadian Voters. None of these groups had a lasting impact but most of them joined forces under the banner of Social Credit for the 1945 provincial election. Much as in the 1937 contest, Social Credit candidates were ill-organized and unconvinced of their chances for victory. The sixteen Social Credit candidates polled 6,627 votes—not much more than one per cent of the total votes cast. The election saw the coalition government safely returned to office.

The Social Credit movement carried on after 1945, but although the poor electoral showing had not seriously disillusioned its members, it became split by internal controversies. The paranoid style that was nurturing the coalition government was also affecting Social Crediters. Peer Paynter was accused of being a Communist Party infiltrator and was openly suspect until an official inquiry by the national Social Credit organization cleared him of the charge. Likewise, Eric Martin, who had worked with the Canadian Youth Congress during the Depression, was suspected of having Communist affiliations. These accusations and suspicions were part and parcel of the Cold War atmosphere but they also demonstrate the intense jealousy and competition within the west coast world of Social Credit.

The controversy that dominated these years was the age-old debate over the grand purpose of Social Credit: education or political action. In 1944 the Social Credit Association of Canada had been formed, and the B.C. wing of the association came under the direction of Maj. A. H. Jukes of Victoria. A former army officer, Jukes was a self-styled intellectual and a firm believer in the teachings of Major Douglas. He was opposed to the principle of running political candiates and, together with a small group of supporters, tried to prevent Social Credit from becoming simply a political party. Major Jukes completely dominated the Social Credit Association, which had succeeded the League as the umbrella organization for the B.C. movement, and ran it as he would a regiment. Obviously, he was worried about the prospect of losing control of the movement to the younger breed of Socreds who viewed direct political action as the only realistic course. Despite mounting pressure, Jukes refused to call a convention, thereby defying the association's constitution. Finally, events came to a head. Eric Martin, a feisty and unusually energetic convert to Social Credit, was one of those at the centre of the conflict:

> Major Jukes was far too dictatorial. He didn't advise his executive or anything. So we called national leader Solon Low to Vancouver to conduct an investigation and recommend what steps should be taken. Well, he couldn't do anything, it was just too far gone. We decided to confront Major Jukes. We laid down what we thought he ought to do, and he promised he would proceed along those lines, but it became very apparent as time went on that he had no intention of carrying out anything that we thought should be done. So, we decided that we'd form another organization. Well, he heard about this and called a group together in Victoria, and we were notified that Lyle Wicks, who was vice-president of the association, was suspended for life. Peer Paynter, myself and two others were suspended for a year, and we were not to attend any Social Credit meetings. Well, I just blew my top and so did the others!

Following this reprimand from Jukes, a group of seventy or eighty Socreds met in Vancouver in 1949 to found the British Columbia Social Credit League. The name was purposely similar to the Social Credit League of British Columbia which had been established in 1935 but had been inactive for many years. The new League was in direct opposition to Major Jukes and his restrained intellectual approach to Social Credit. It elected Lyle Wicks as president and Peer Paynter as first vice-president and immediately set to work preparing for the next provincial election. Major Jukes retaliated by forming the Union of Electors and announced his intention to run candidates as well. Clearly, the Social Credit movement was badly split, and if the Wicks-Paynter faction were the young bright lights who did not hesitate to move in a political direction, older fringe groups refused to be outshone. Later in the spring, when the coalition government decided to go to the people once more, B.C. voters had the confusing opportunity to cast ballots for a variety of Social Credit alternatives. The British Columbia Social Credit League fielded nine candidates; Major Jukes's Union of Electors nominated twelve; and other disaffected Socreds, though sympathetic to the new League, united under the banner of the Social Credit Party and placed seven candidates. The results of the election of June 15, 1949, were no more heartening for Social Crediters than earlier ones. The combined vote of all Socred factions amounted to only about two per cent of the popular vote, and not a single candidate came close to winning a seat—in fact, regardless of the banner they ran under, Socreds finished in last place in virtually every poll of each riding they contested.

Paradoxically, the poor election performance was a victory of sorts for the British Columbia Social Credit League, for in the aftermath it became the dominant organization in the west coast movement. The Douglasites and other fringe groups had expended all their energy on one last fling. The League, on the other hand, survived the electoral debacle and was now generally recognized as *the* British Columbia vehicle for the Social Credit movement. For the first time, Social Credit in B.C. would be devoted primarily to political action. League members were undaunted by the 1949 fiasco and were convinced that they were finally in a position to make significant headway in the political field, especially since they were now devoted to the goal of organization, which west coast Socreds had previously shunned. Indeed, it will always be difficult to pass judgement on the early movement in B.C. on the basis of the truth of its doctrine or the feasibility of its proposed reforms but, judged on its corporate organization and ability to proselytize and win new converts, it must be considered an abysmal failure. The League endeavoured to change all this. It started towards its new objective slowly; in fact, when it registered its charter it took six months to pay the seventy-five-dollar legal fee. But it soon embarked upon the building of a strong province-wide Social Credit movement.

With financial support from Alberta, Peer Paynter became the first paid, full-time organizer for Social Credit in British Columbia. He travelled throughout the province encouraging the formation of constituency organizations. He described his method of organizing:

> I might be away from home for a month or six weeks at a time. I'd go into an area and if I didn't have any contacts, I asked if there was anybody that had moved there from Alberta in the last few years. If I found somebody that had, well about sixty to seventy per cent of the time I'd find a Social Crediter—a fellow who'd supported Social Credit in 1935 and later on. Those ex-Albertans often made the nucleus of our organization in any area. I would set up a public meeting, hire a hall, arrange for advertising. At these meetings I'd give them a talk on the ideas of Social Credit and what we were aiming at in order to form a government. We'd set up, if possible, a small group—maybe eight or ten—with a president and secretary, to form a constituency organiza-

tion, and then we'd have a nucleus to work from. We'd supply them with a certain amount of literature and keep in touch with them from Vancouver.

A new kind of strength arose out of this organizational drive and the Socreds did everything they could to encourage confidence. For the first time, Social Crediters were coming out into the open, selling memberships door-to-door in the cities, organizing house meetings, and talking loudly about an alternative to the existing political parties. One reason the future seemed bright for the B.C. movement was that generous support was now available from the Alberta Socreds. Once the League emerged as the single dominant voice of Social Credit on the coast and declared a desire to move ahead with aggressive organization for the next election, the Albertans were ready to pledge substantial support, with a view to extending their movement. Although this would later become a serious bone of contention, renewed assistance from Alberta became a crucial factor in developments ahead.

The one vital factor sorely missing was leadership. Most if not all of the members of the B.C. League were anonymous, noncharismatic figures, foot soldiers in search of a commander. Sorely needed was a popular, well-known personality to guide the League and give it credibility. It is at this juncture in the history of the British Columbia Social Credit movement that we return to W. A. C. Bennett.

Bennett always gave the appearance of being a devoutly religious man, yet he often surrendered his personal fortune to a pagan god: chance. He was, in fact, a gambler. With friends, he enjoyed placing small, friendly wagers on any kind of contest; but in order to fulfill his self-appointed mission he had to gamble with much larger stakes. For him, gambling was the sublimation of a profound instinct, recognizing that instinct plays an important role in life. Although he always considered his moves carefully and cautiously, at the last moment he was usually willing to trust his intuition and cast his fate to the wind. When he crossed the floor of the B.C. legislature in the spring of 1951 he was simply continuing an amazing series of political gambles. Intuitively, he was convinced he was doing the right thing, but he was uncertain of the course he would now follow.

When on March 15 he became the independent MLA for South Okanagan, he managed to strike a responsive chord. His timing proved extremely effective and the issue—hospital insurance—gave widespread publicity to his demonstration of independence. Former political colleagues may have branded him a traitor, but in other quarters he was hailed for standing up to the Liberal and Conservative machines and for refusing to surrender on a matter of principle. In the days following Bennett's act of political defiance he was inundated with letters and telegrams applauding his courage and integrity. He answered many of them by optimistically predicting, "We are at an important change in the political life of British Columbia." One of the first congratulatory letters was from Lyle Wicks, the president of the British Columbia Social Credit League, who wrote: "It is a rare thing in the political arena to see a man assert his convictions to the extent that he is prepared to leave the Party of his choice rather than stifle his conscience. . . . Please accept our heartiest congratulations and may you continue effectively your campaign to awaken the Government to its responsibility to the people of this Province." Shortly thereafter, Bennett met with him in Vancouver to discuss the future of the Social Credit League in B.C. politics. Apparently Wicks was impressed, but neither man was willing to commit himself to a definite course of action.

Clearly, Bennett was looking for the best possible way to bridge the widening chasm between the old-line parties and the public's trust, and he wanted to capitalize on the favourable reaction to his crossing of the House. From his new seat in the back row of the opposition benches, he exercised his independence by frequently and loudly castigating his former colleagues: his first act as an independent member was to vote against the government on the hospital insurance program premium increase. He no longer spent all his time in the legislature, but his occasional presence enlivened House proceedings and often produced the unlikely duet of himself and the CCF opposition. The socialists could always be counted upon to cheer Bennett on when he rose to lambaste the government he once supported. He often armed his new seat-mate, Leo Nimsick of the CCF, with background information for questions to embarrass his former colleagues—who were becoming increasingly upset. Harold Winch and his troops were beginning to sense that the coalition's days were short, and they hoped Bennett's efforts would contribute to the government's downfall.

When the House adjourned for Easter, Bennett returned to Kelowna and organized a meeting of his constituents, seeking their approval for his abandonment of coalition. The hastily arranged meeting drew over a thousand people and was reportedly the largest political meeting ever held in the Okanagan. Bennett's message to the audience, which obviously supported his performance in Victoria, was direct: "Defeat this government at the earliest opportunity." When asked if he was planning to form a new party, he did not deny the possibility but answered that his first goal was the defeat of the coalition administration.

Bennett had now burnt all his old political bridges. Before making his momentous move in the House he had tried to persuade other dissatisfied coalitionists to join him, and said afterwards: "A number of them were going to, and they said they would, but the pressure on them was too great. I expected at least from four to six to follow, but they didn't." However, with some reluctance, one member did, Tilly Rolston. Bennett's longtime friend and confidante was persuaded to cross the floor shortly after the House resumed sitting following the spring break. Bennett would consider this event as being vital to his own political future:

> Mrs. Rolston and I were reformers within the Conservative Party. And she had supported me in my fight to clean up the Conservative machine. She was a widow, and walking out into the cold from her secure Conservative seat of Vancouver-Point Grey, which was very strong Conservative at that time, was a very difficult decision to make. They promised her everything if she'd stay, because the Liberals and Conservatives in the House both knew that she was a great personal friend of mine. They made all kinds of offers to her. So I said, "Tilly, certainly they can offer you a broken-down old car in the ditch that's not going anywhere. But when they had an opportunity, when they were on the highway with a good car, what did they offer you then? Nothing. They are only talking this way to you because they know that you could be a power. Bennett alone is one, but Bennett with Tilly Rolston is two. It will have tremendous effect throughout the province! They're going to come to see you today, so you've got to make the decision today. It's your decision; you must make it, but I'm going to try to help you make it because I'm your friend." I pointed out all the pitfalls and all the opportunities. She said, "What will I say?" I said, "When the House opens, just say what I said. Just get up right after prayers, before we get into business and say: 'I rise in my seat as the MLA for Vancouver-Point Grey to advise you and members of the legislature and the people of the province that I have lost all confidence in the coalition of Liberals and Conservatives in this House and I now will sit in this House as the independent member for Vancouver-Point Grey.' And then sit down." And that's what she did.

Tilly Rolston's defection, coming a couple of weeks after Bennett's, was significant, for it demonstrated that the coalition was indeed crumbling. Afterwards, a good deal of pressure was exerted to have her return to the fold; even members of her family demanded that Bennett allow her to go back to the Tories. But she had great faith in him and held firm. Her strong stance was remarkable, for she was ill with cancer.

The spring session of 1951 ended in much speculation regarding the future of the coalition government. Bennett's actions provided a focus for public disenchantment, and the government's hospital insurance scheme was the bitter backdrop to the general dissatisfaction. Just prior to prorogation of the session, a petition signed by over 205,000 citizens was presented to the legislature demanding that the premium increases and changes to the hospital insurance plan be withdrawn. A petition of this size was unprecedented, but when Bennett joined the CCF members in calling for a special emergency debate, the government refused. In any event, what proved to be the most important act of the session was Bill 108—an amendment to the provincial Elections Act—which was approved on the final day of sitting, April 18. The amendment provided for a new system of voting, the single transferable ballot, which allowed voters to mark their ballots by listing the candidates in order of preference. If a candidate received a majority of "first choices," he would be elected on the first count. If not, a complex series of recounts would take place in which the candidate receiving the fewest "first choices" would be removed from the competition and his "second choices" distributed among the remaining candidates. This process continued until one candidate received a clear majority of the votes cast.

The new alternative voting system was an ingenious attempt to allow for the expected breakup of the coalition government without forfeiting power to the socialists. Curiously, the idea behind the single transferable ballot had been advocated for some time by W. A. C. Bennett, and when preparing the legislation the government had solicited his advice:

> They knew nothing about the single transferable ballot. They didn't know anything about proportional representation and the different ways you could handle it. But I was a student of politics and I had studied the single transferable ballot and what had happened in different countries with it. So I went to the Conservatives with it and told them that it was their only hope—if not, when they broke up coalition, the socialists were going to beat them and form the government. Anscomb sent me over a note, even though he hated to, and I had about four meetings with him and the Conservatives. At last, I got it through their heads. So Anscomb mentioned this to the Liberals—the single transferable ballot. He came to me and he said, "Will you explain that to the Liberals?"

British Columbia's experiment was inspired largely by the paranoid style of politics which had been practised for a decade. Liberal and Conservative politicians genuinely felt it would be "unfair" to allow a socialist party dedicated to the overthrow of the existing economic system to be elected to government with only 30 or 35 per cent of the popular vote. Of course, they dismissed the fact that parliamentary majorities in multiparty systems are frequently won with less than a majority of votes, for it was felt that the prospective dissolution of their partnership represented a special situation calling for special measures. The single transferable ballot, it was thought, would allow Liberal voters a chance to choose Conservatives as their second choice and vice versa, thereby preventing a socialist victory. The logic was essentially correct. The single transferable ballot would prevent the CCF from attaining power, but it also had other more drastic and unexpected results which W. A. C. Bennett was actively preparing for.

At the conclusion of the session, he busied himself in a frantic effort to consolidate nonsocialist anticoalition forces. When repeatedly asked about his political future, he always sidestepped the question. He railed against the entrenched Liberal and Conservative party machines and often denounced the CCF in the same breath. He called for a "new independent force" to replace the corrupt and undemocratic party system that dominated B.C. politics. He wrote a leading editorial in the *Northwest Digest* in which he stated: "I believe that the time has now arrived in British Columbia when members must be elected to represent constituencies and not to be party rubber stamps and jump through the hoop at the crack of the party whip in Victoria." Clearly, Bennett was still chasing his dream of a new independent provincial party—his long-lost United Progressive Party.

The new independent force Bennett was advocating did not have a name. Some speculated that the name might be Social Credit, but Bennett only smiled at the suggestion. Of course, he had talked with members of the Social Credit League, but President Lyle Wicks publicly dismissed the idea of Bennett becoming one of them, and flatly declared that Social Credit was not interested in any "independents." The Social Crediters were, in fact, divided on the notion of his joining their movement. Many longtime Socreds distrusted the former coalitionist who had recently aspired to the leadership of the Conservative Party. The suggestion that Bennett might lead them to victory was worrisome; if they could not find a leader within the movement, they would have preferred someone innocent of all malodorous political connections. However, another point of view prevailed among a small group of activists within the British Columbia Social Credit League who recognized in Bennett a potential leader to guide them out of the political wilderness. For these Socreds, he was a political paladin. Eric Martin was a member of the latter group; he watched events closely, kept in contact with Bennett and actively courted him—to the chagrin of some of his Socred colleagues.

During the summer of 1951 Martin urged him not to form a new party but to quietly join the Social Credit League. Bennett had an idea of his own. A by-election called for October 1, 1951, in the Vancouver Island constituency of Esquimalt, owing to the death of the sitting coalition member, was precisely the sort of test he had been hoping for. He decided to play a part in the campaign and worked out a plan of action that would make the Esquimalt contest one of the most important in B.C.'s political history.

Many years later, Bennett delighted in recalling his approach to the by-election:

> Frank Barker, who was at that time provincial organizer for the Conservatives, had worked with me very closely when I was trying to reform the party and ran for the leadership of the Tory party. I asked him to go to Victoria to scout the political situation of Greater Victoria regarding Esquimalt—he had friends in the clubs there and in the press gallery, the Legion and different places. I told him to bring me back the names of three people—without approaching them—who would be good independent candidates to support in Esquimalt. I wanted to find out not only their qualities but the reasons they could be elected. So he came back with three names. I've forgotten the other two, but one of them was Commander Wurtele of Esquimalt. He had just retired from the navy and was an alderman in Esquimalt. He was an ideal person, but he knew nothing about politics. So I said, "Fine," and said goodbye to Barker and I phoned Wurtele. I told him I was glad to see his fine record in the armed services and glad to see that now that he was out of the armed services and retired he was still going to serve the people of the province as an alderman in Esquimalt. But I told him that there was a greater calling for him now, a greater opportunity to make a real contribution to the life of this province. He wanted to know what it was, and I said, "To be the new MLA for Esquimalt where you can sound your views on the navy and otherwise. You must have some ideas in your mind that you want to advocate, and this would be a great opportunity to do it in the legislature where you have a good sounding board. You can really do a service to your country." "Well," he said, "I'll have to talk to my wife. I don't think so."
>
> So I left him that way and I sent him a telegram saying that Monday night I'd be in Victoria and invited him and his wife to dinner at eight o'clock at the Empress Hotel. I knew that that was the night of the council meeting, but if he was really interested he'd be there. And as an officer and a gentleman, you know, he'd be there anyway, because he couldn't contact me. He tried to contact me, of course, but I wouldn't answer any phones. So I came over to Victoria and, sure enough, they were there. I'd arranged with a taxi driver beforehand—I gave him the address of the Wurteles and asked him to be there at exactly 10:30 to pick me up. We set our watches. So we had a lovely dinner and, of course, I knew they would invite me to their home afterwards where we

could discuss the situation. He was so sure that he couldn't run. I paid not too much attention to him, but sold his wife on the idea: this was his great opportunity, it comes but once, you've got to grasp it when it's there, thorn or no thorn . . . and at exactly twenty-five minutes after ten he agreed that he'd run. Just then the doorbell rang and there was my taxi driver. I got my coat, said good night and away I went.

I went down to the *Colonist* where they were preparing their morning edition paper and told them about this great candidate who would run as an independent, that he'd be backed by Tilly Rolston and myself, and we'd be running a very strong campaign and we'd welcome people, no matter what political party. We'd welcome them into this new force in British Columbia which was out to abolish patronage, to clean up the mess in this province. They came out with big headlines announcing this. Then my phone started ringing and I paid no attention. I went back to Kelowna and I wouldn't answer any phones. I got telegrams from Wurtele saying that he was very sorry he couldn't accept the nomination. As soon as it was in the paper all devil broke loose for him, because apparently he had been at the nominating convention where the coalition candidate was nominated and they were saying, "You were there, part of choosing their candidate. Now you are a candidate for Bennett. Terrible!" I was looked upon as a very dangerous revolutionary in those days. So I just sent him back a telegram saying that we had made an arrangement. He said he didn't have any money to stand a campaign, and I assured him that he wouldn't have to spend personal money; I'd see the campaign was properly financed. Every point he brought up, I had thought it out and gave him a counterargument. Finally, he said that as an officer and a gentleman, since he was at the coalition convention, he was very sorry, he could not accept the nomination to run as an independent. So I wired him back and said: "Mr. Commander, you and I had a very definite agreement, we shook hands on it. To me a man's word is his bond. I intend to keep my part of the agreement and I expect you, as an officer and a gentleman, to accept your part." So, anyway, he stayed as a candidate.

His reminiscence is interesting in that it demonstrates Bennett's developing fascination with secrecy and manipulation, but why did he put such effort into obtaining a candidate for the Esquimalt by-election? What was his plan? He was endeavouring to show, first, that the coalition was a spent force; second, that the socialists were a real threat; and, third, that there was room for a new, independent B.C. political movement. The Esquimalt by-election proved to be the last time British Columbians were offered a coalition candidate. The governing parties desperately needed to win it as a test and symbol of the government's stability, so rather than divide Grit and Tory support, they opted for one last co-operative effort. Bennett urged the government to try out the new transferable ballot, but it preferred to wait until the next general election as planned. The coalition had chosen the strongest candidate possible in Percy George, who was serving as mayor of Victoria at the time. The CCF, who had never been victorious in Esquimalt, nominated a young local policeman, Frank Mitchell. And, of course, there was Bennett's wild-card independent candidate, Comdr. Alfred Wurtele.

Curiously, in spite of being in the midst of an organizing blitz, the Social Credit League did not nominate a candidate. But from one point of view, perhaps it was not altogether curious. When the Socreds had announced that they would definitely place a candidate, local members nominated W. N. Chant, a former minister in Alberta's original Social Credit government who had left the province over a serious difference of opinion with the then premier, Aberhart. After the nomination, pressure was apparently brought to bear by Albertans who remembered the disagreement. Chant withdrew and the Socreds subsequently decided not to participate. Lyle Wicks explained their thinking: "The Esquimalt by-election in '51 seemed an opportune time for us to put our best foot forward. We had an organization in Esquimalt and we could concentrate our full forces there. That seemed, on the surface, the logical thing to do: had we run a candidate we would have shown some strength. If we lost, that would be discouraging. But if we won it, that would have been even worse—we would be warning the CCF that we now were beginning to be a threat and they would have redoubled their organizational activities. At this time we were waiting in the weeds. Mr. Bennett was most anxious that we not enter it because he had an independent running." Bennett entered into the situation and did a marvellous job of juggling Wurtele and the Socreds. He actually enlisted the enthusiastic backing of Social Credit supporters in Esquimalt for the campaign.

The battle of Esquimalt was an intense and closely watched election. In a time before public opinion polls and electronic media it was difficult to gauge the feeling of the voters, but it was widely assumed that Percy George would win easily for the coalition. However, to George's surprise, it was a tough battle. The CCF candidate worked diligently, aided and abetted by party workers from the mainland. Bennett's independent aspirant waged a strange kind of campaign. After a couple of miserable nonevents that Wurtele had tried to organize, W. A. C. Bennett moved in and took firm control of the campaign. He hired people to take care of advertising and organize meetings; he personally took charge of speech-writing and often delivered them as well. Wurtele later admitted that he did not know what was going on. Bennett and Tilly Rolston spoke at well-attended campaign meetings, lashing out at the coalition government. For part of the campaign Bennett was forced to return home to Kelowna, but he kept in close touch with his Esquimalt helpers. He had hired his Tory friend, Waldo Skillings, to assist with the election and every two or three days Skillings would wire him: "Send me another $1,000." Bennett later estimated that he spent $10,000 out of his own pocket on the Battle of Esquimalt.

On October 1, 1951, the results of the by-election were a shock to most political observers. The CCF candidate, Frank Mitchell, topped the polls with 2,711 votes, Commander Wurtele came in a close second with 2,510, and Percy George polled only 1,693 votes. It was a stunning upset, an unequivocal repudiation of the coalition as well as a warning of the potential strength of the CCF. In a real sense, the by-election was a tremendous victory for Bennett, for it demonstrated the fantastic opportunity for a "new force" in the next general election.

Had Wurtele been elected, the scene in British Columbia might have been different: a win could have encouraged Bennett to form his own party. But he rationalized Wurtele's narrow defeat in Esquimalt as a blessing in disguise: "He would have been looked upon as our spokesman in the House and he didn't have the political background to stand up against the criticism of the Liberals and Conservatives and the CCF in those days. They were great debaters, and he wouldn't have been able to stand up to that. So this was a godsend. But I had to try and see if we could get a new party going." It is probably safe to assume that Bennett received his money's worth from the by-election. It clearly told him what was possible, and he prepared to play a card he had held up his sleeve.

Bennett returned home and wrote letters of thanks to all supporters who had worked in the Esquimalt campaign. He also wrote to the president of the British Columbia Social Credit League, Lyle Wicks:

> I want to hasten to thank you for the cooperation and assistance which you and a number of your members so kindly gave me in the recent by-election. The result of the by-election is very gratifying and our showing was much better than could have been reasonably expected considering we had no organization and Esquimalt was the most difficult constituency in which we could have fought a by-election in the whole Province, being right next to the Government at Victoria. However, if the new system of voting had been in effect, allowing for the preferential or transferable ballot, our candidate would have been elected easily and it shows very clearly what could happen in the general election if we are all working closely together. I believe the provincial general election will take place around June, 1952, which only leaves us about six months to prepare.

Bennett's use of "we" is interesting here, for his relationship with the

Socreds was still ambiguous. In the aftermath of the by-election several members of the League had been in touch with him, urging him to now join Social Credit. Although he was still noncommittal, he confessed a growing interest. He answered one Vancouver Island Socred with these words: "I am genuinely interested in Social Credit and believe that the Alberta Government has been outstanding in its accomplishment. However, I cannot help but feel that there may be different elements within Social Credit and any action taken by me at this time might be misunderstood. All I am interested in as far as public life in British Columbia is concerned is to see that we have a good government which will not represent the monopolies of the Right nor State Socialism of the Left but will give the people in British Columbia a better deal."

Bennett was obviously preparing to join forces with the B.C. Social Credit League. He had convinced himself that it was the only available vehicle on which he could ride to power. For some time, he had been studying Social Credit literature and was keeping in close touch with select members of the League. He felt comfortable with their philosophy, liked their nonparty approach and believed he could change any aspects of their policy or thinking with which he disagreed. He knew the Socreds were finally making some strides in an organizational sense, but they obviously had a long way to go. Bennett approached his task cautiously; he did not want to appear to be in a hurry and, as he was always so fond of saying, "Timing is everything."

A special session of the legislature was called late in October. On his way to Victoria, Bennett stopped in Vancouver to meet with his Social Credit friend and supporter, Eric Martin, who was now a vice-president of the League. Martin described the meeting: "I told him that I would like to see him the leader of our movement, that we were well organized, that we were prepared to run candidates in every constituency, that if he went to Kelowna and took out a membership card the chances were that he would be nominated and elected. But I did advise him not to show any signs of desire for leadership. We did not have a political leader. None of us felt that we were capable of political leadership. But if we ever had to form a government, we'd certainly have to find someone who was capable, and as far as I was concerned, that man was sitting with me." In strictest confidence, Bennett indicated his intention of joining Social Credit, but expressed a need to wait for the correct moment.

The special fall session, called to consider a new pension plan being established with the federal government, lasted for only a few days. W. A. C. Bennett's major contribution was a lengthy speech in which he demanded that the government resign and call an election on the basis of the Esquimalt by-election results. During the course of his harangue, he referred to the provincial government of Alberta in highly favourable terms.

Harold Winch interjected, "Are you the new Social Credit leader?"

"Wouldn't you like to know," replied Bennett. In fact, he was on the verge of receiving an answer to that very question.

During the special session Bennett befriended a small delegation from the north who had journeyed to Victoria to protest the disruption from the Aluminum Company of Canada's massive Kitimat-Kemano project. They were worried about being displaced from their homes and farms without adequate compensation. The construction of the huge aluminum smelter was, at the time, the largest single industrial development in the province's history. Bennett recounted:

> I had messages from Omineca country, from a group up there, they had some problems with the Aluminum Company and they felt that they were being unfairly dealt with. I advised them that they should go to Victoria when the House was in session and make representation to the government, and that while they were in Victoria I'd give them any help I could. So they came—six or seven in the delegation. They were very aroused, very bitter. The cabinet wouldn't see them and they had gone to see Winch and he shoved them aside. So they came to see me for advice and I spent some time with them and did what I could. Finally, they got to see cabinet. It was leaked to me that they got rotten treatment in cabinet—terrible, rough treatment. One of the lady members of their delegation was taking notes and nobody told her she couldn't take notes in cabinet meetings. The premier blew up and grabbed her notes away from her and gave her a tongue-lashing. The poor girl broke out crying. The next night, in the House, I was waiting for the opportunity to get the floor on some subject, any subject. It came, and I got up and steered my discussion along to governments without any feelings towards people, without any heart. "This government is so out of tune with the people, that when a little delegation of country people who had never been in the capital were before cabinet and one of the lady members was taking a few notes, the premier blew up, tore them up and the lady cried—" Johnson got up, and he was so mad in the House that night—so mad! "How did any leak come out of cabinet?" He attacked me personally, bitterly, and I just laughed and smiled.

A short time later when the delegation of northerners was preparing to return home after failing to obtain redress for their grievances, one of them came to thank Bennett for his efforts on their behalf; his name was Cyril

Shelford, an angry young war veteran who would soon spend more time in Victoria than he ever expected. Bennett invited Shelford to accompany him to a meeting that evening in Victoria, a Social Credit function, the first that Bennett ever addressed. Shelford accepted and was impressed by the turnout and by Bennett's fiery speech, essentially an attack on the coalition. After the meeting, Bennett persuaded him to join Social Credit and gave him membership cards to take home to Omineca to sell to his friends. He also encouraged him to seek the Socred nomination in the upcoming election. The enthusiastic pep talk completely sold the young northerner on the merits of the Social Credit movement. Like so many other small, seemingly insignificant events, the encouragement Bennett gave to Cyril Shelford proved crucial to the transformation of west coast politics, which was only six months away.

Plainly, this was an anomalous situation: here was Bennett addressing a Social Credit gathering for the first time, signing up new members, spreading the good word, yet he himself was uncommitted—in fact, he was still a political independent. What was he waiting for? Privately, he had made up his mind: it was now a question of when and how he would officially embrace Social Credit. It seems that the question "how" seriously hampered him. He was not keen on taking Eric Martin's advice to quietly join the League and work from within at the grassroots level towards the next provincial election. Of course, he had much to offer the unfledged Socreds as a practised politician and as a sounding board in the legislature. He realized full well that certain Social Crediters did not look upon him favourably, but he thought there might be enough practical-minded members who would support his being drafted as their first bona fide political leader and spokesman.

When Bennett left Victoria after the special legislative session, it was amid a flurry of rumours about his political future: several "friends" in the press gallery asked to be contacted the minute he made a decision. He travelled to Vancouver where he readied himself for the provincial Social Credit annual convention at New Westminster in the first week of November 1951. He planned to attend as an observer, knowing that several new Social Credit members who supported him would endeavour to broach the subject of leadership. The gathering of over 200 was the largest to that date for Social Credit in British Columbia. It was well run and punctuated by lively debate with no sign of organized machine domination. When the question of leadership arose, a resolution was passed which recommended that a leadership convention be called as soon as possible. This infuriated many Bennett supporters who wanted an immediate draft-Bennett motion.

As the convention drew to a close, preparations were being made for the final banquet. Eric Martin and others urged that Bennett, the only MLA in attendance, be invited to sit as a guest of honour at the head table. This caused a good deal of controversy and the League executive was hurriedly called together to decide the issue. Peer Paynter, a member of the executive, was against Bennett's sitting at the head table since he did not belong to the organization nor had he declared himself; to seat him would have been tantamount to inviting him to come in as Social Credit leader. The seven-man executive was split on the question, with Martin and two others supporting an invitation and Paynter and two others opposed. It was left to League president, Lyle Wicks, to cast the deciding vote—and guess who was *not* coming to dinner.

Bennett, not having been invited as a guest of honour, decided not to attend the banquet at all, but when he left for home the next day, he had learned what he needed to know about the Social Credit organization. From Kelowna, he communicated with several of his confidants and faithful supporters. He received a letter from Ron Worley, a former Liberal and now a leading Victoria Social Crediter and staunch Bennett-booster. (Bennett adopted him as a kind of advance man—in Worley's words, he was "Tonto" to Bennett's "Lone Ranger.") Upset about the outcome of the New Westminster convention, he told Bennett he was "deeply sorry that the affair at that time did not turn out to be a success, although I am satisfied to believe you when you say, 'It was probably for the best.'" Bennett wrote back: "The political situation continues to be very interesting. I have received a number of letters from our friends and have had telephone calls and letters from 'The Victoria Times' very anxious for an announcement, which, of course, is not forthcoming at the present time." He did not appear troubled over the convention's outcome, but Worley found it difficult to understand how leading Socreds could spurn Bennett's friendship and ignore his obvious leadership capability; later in the month he wrote to Bennett again and referred to Lyle Wicks as "the wretched little man." Another friend in Victoria, former Tory Waldo Skillings, who had helped out with the Esquimalt by-election, also wrote to Bennett inquiring about the Social Credit convention. Skillings was a strong personal supporter, but "couldn't see what Bennett could see in those goons." On November 20, 1951, Bennett wrote to Skillings: "The meeting at New Westminster leaves the S.C. situation on the same basis as before. We are still looking into the situation and having talks with some of their officials."

Finally, on December 6, 1951, W.A.C. Bennett announced from Kelowna that he had taken out membership in the local Social Credit association. The voters of South Okanagan had sent him to Victoria as a Conservative-coalitionist; after he crossed the floor of the legislature they supported him as an independent MLA; now, nine months later, the practised gambler made an official statement to his constituents which made front-page headlines in the B.C. urban press:

> When I reported to you . . . during the Easter recess of the British Columbia Legislature I stated in answer to questions as to whether I would form a new Provincial Party, that I was a person who did one thing at a time. . . . During the months since that time I have studied the Provincial Governments of all Canada and the problems and opportunities facing our Province of British Columbia. I have come to the belief that a Social Credit government similar to the one operating in our neighboring province of Alberta would be the best for our Province and our people—a Government based on free enterprise—opposed to monopolies of the Right or Left—a Government of the people. I have therefore decided to join the Social Credit movement.

Reaction to his political conversion was swift and generally critical. In Victoria circles, he became a laughingstock; if his political future was widely dismissed after he had crossed the floor, now his sanity was being questioned. Meanwhile, the press was having a field day castigating him as a turncoat and opportunist. The Victoria *Times* editorialized:

> Mr. Bennett's sudden conversion to Social Credit is one of those phenomena of instant enlightenment, a blinding apocalyptic flash of revelation. . . . After advocating Conservative principles all his life Mr. Bennett wakes up one morning to realize that he has always believed in the very opposite. The veil is torn from his eyes. . . . To those who believe in political miracles, instantaneous conversions and the purging of sin by fire, this is an altogether moving spectacle. . . . Mr. Bennett is still a little dazzled by the fierce spirit of illumination. At least he sees a twisted path which may lead him back to the legislature and a handy weapon to destroy the Conservative party and the policies to which, until yesterday, he had given his life-long devotion.

The Victoria *Colonist* was no less critical. In a leading editorial headlined "Mr. Bennett the Leader," it stated that "in recent years of his political career he has shown a marked resemblance to the boy who demanded his bat back when the team wouldn't make him captain. There will be many who will ask whether he had joined the Socreds because of belief that by doing so he can best represent his riding, or to satisfy an overweening desire to be leader of something, even if only a group with no other representation in the legislature."

Bennett said of the reaction: "The criticism was personal and stiff. But that wasn't the hard criticism. The hard criticism to take was that within the Social Credit movement—those who thought I was a Conservative coming in to take the party over." This attitude was common among the party old guard. According to Peer Paynter:

The attitude towards Bennett was very mixed. There were those who figured that on account of him being an MLA, it would be a great asset to us to have him in the organization. Then there were those who weren't sold on the idea that he was actually a Social Krediter at heart, who thought that maybe he was just taking advantage of the situation to promote himself. There was good argument on both sides and at that point I think most people felt that we just had to tread carefully. I was quite favourably impressed with Bennett, but a person has to realize that we had worked on the Social Credit ideas for a good many years—for almost twenty years then. I felt that we couldn't risk turning over the control of the whole organization to a person we didn't know too much about at that time. I think he was quite conscientious in the things he did, but I felt we were risking the possibility of cancelling out the whole effect of the work that we had done over twenty years and I wanted to be absolutely sure we weren't doing that before I put my support behind him. I didn't think that Bennett had proven himself one way or the other as far as Social Credit was concerned.

Lyle Wicks said:

When Bennett began to show some interest in coming into the movement and particularly following the annual Social Credit convention at New Westminster in 1951, I felt it incumbent on myself to do something. My experience was not as broad as others'—who should I consult? So, I wrote to our national leader, Mr. Solon E. Low, MP, with whom I had a very close and warm relationship. He responded; he had met Mr. Bennett—I believe he had met with Mr. Bennett not only in Ottawa but also in Edmonton—and he spoke of him in most glowing terms as a man of character and principle, a man who could be relied upon and would be a great force in assisting the Social Credit movement. As a result of that particular letter I had no qualms in welcoming Mr. Bennett into the movement, despite the fact that I well realized that others in Alberta, including Ernie Manning, the premier, would not welcome him as it would represent a threat to the Alberta people being able to contain the Social Credit movement to what they thought was best. I think they feared that the Social Credit movement in British Columbia would get out of hand, that the wrong people would get in control of it, and that the movement would be self-destructive and perhaps destroy the movement in Alberta. If that be their motives, they were good motives. But I did have a real friend in Mr. Low and I was able to go forward with great confidence in welcoming Mr. Bennett into the movement when he joined in December of 1951 through his local group in Kelowna.

Of course, not all reaction to his joining Social Credit was adverse or cautious. People like Eric Martin and newcomer Ron Worley were jubilant; at last Social Credit had a potential if not obvious leader in their ranks, and Bennett's move would provide exactly the right spark to ignite Social Credit in B.C. Bennett was quick to point out that he had joined as an ordinary member of the League, but it was widely assumed that he would become the political leader of Social Credit in the province. Bennett took the position: "I'd made certain studies; I absolutely convinced myself that I was on the right track, because I knew there would be no stepping backwards. And the newspapers wrote me right off. They said, 'He's finished!' Later they said, 'He's an opportunist!' Now how could I be both? I had no commitment for nomination in South Okanagan. I had no commitment to be the Social Credit provincial leader—no commitment at all. So if I was an opportunist, I want to know what an opportunist really is. Because I had no assurances. I went out in the very cold north wind."

Why did Bennett take yet another incredible political gamble? On face value, joining Social Credit when he did seemed an illogical act and it certainly took many by surprise. All his life he had been a Conservative. For Bennett, being a Tory politician had meant that he was forever striving for acceptance and respectability in the eyes of the party establishment, and as a coalition MLA with leadership aspirations he was forced to conduct himself in a style that was unnatural for him. During his decade in politics he had travelled throughout B.C. and he discovered that the average voter was suspicious of the fancy politicians in Victoria with their urbanity and false sophistication. Bennett himself was a product of Main Street and felt more at home with small-businessmen and plain-talking country folk than he did with the upper crust of Victoria or the business elite of Vancouver. When he rejected coalition he rejected the old-line parties and all they represented.

It was an uplifting, even liberating experience for him. He had run, pushed and fought for power and thereby developed an outlook on politics and society quite at variance with that of old-line politicians who often had power and responsibility thrust upon them. Bennett was now free to develop his own distinctive political style which inevitably would have strong populist overtones, as indicated by his call, on joining the Social Credit movement, for "a Government of the people." One of the important attractions Social Credit held for him was its appeal to ordinary folk. He was impressed with the fact that in the interior, merchants, farmers, loggers, teachers, small town doctors and hard-rock miners expressed an interest in Social Credit. These were orthodox, middle-class, conservative folk who had been radicalized by disaster (the Depression of the 1930s) as well as the threat of disaster (the Cold War spectre of communism). Instinctively, Bennett knew that the old style of politics was practically dead in B.C. Although he was now labelled a turncoat, he was actually rejecting a political wardrobe that had never properly fit him in favour of a new suit that was almost tailor-made.

He had studied Social Credit theory and as a businessman believed in the merit of some of Major Douglas's ideas; however, he never burdened himself with the intricacies of Social Credit monetary theory, for he knew that fiscal and monetary policy was a federal matter. For him, Social Credit represented a set of ethical simplicities which he incorporated into his life. His faith was direct, unswerving and absolute. Like most converts to any cause his acceptance of the tenets of Social Credit and his anxiety to uphold those beliefs made him more ardent than many old-line members. It is a curious fact of history that the greatest exponents of political principles are usually converts from other parties. In his later years, Bennett was fond of remarking that he was one of the few Socreds in B.C. who could actually explain Social Credit monetary theory and the A plus B theorem. His favourite definition of Social Credit was often quoted in the League's political campaigning: "That which is physically possible, desirable, and morally right, must be made financially possible."

Naturally, Bennett planned to be the political leader of Social Credit in British Columbia: that was the crux of his odds-against gamble. Looking back on his career, it is difficult to know how he acquired his uncanny understanding of what was to come. He seemed to have an eye for the potential for change and new beginnings; but at the same time he had fallen many times in his quest for political success, and there was no compelling reason to believe that this time he would gain it by sheer audacity and perseverance. Certainly, it is no exaggeration to say that by the end of 1951 his political future was considered to be empty. Many observers viewed his antics as a form of mild entertainment; old-guard politicians saw him as a nuisance, nothing more. Up to that time Social Credit had made virtually no political impact on the Canadian west coast, yet strange as it must have seemed, this reputedly ambitious, well-known politician was embracing the immature Social Credit movement. Only time and chance would reveal whether Bennett's move was an act of desperation, the result of incredibly astute analysis, a case of prescience, or a stab in the dark.

CHAPTER
FIVE

THE WHIRL OF CIRCUMSTANCE

Perseverance is the hinge of all virtues.
Thomas Carlyle

*We never understand a thing so well, and make it our own,
as when we have discovered it for ourselves.*
René Descartes

The year 1951 saw W.A.C. Bennett deftly manoeuvring and making brave new political commitments based upon his expectations regarding the faltering coalition administration. Both quietly in private conversation and loudly in public statements he was now making predictions about the fate of coalition and the demise of the Liberal and Conservative parties in British Columbia. In 1952, a momentous year in the province's history, virtually all of his prophesies would come true.

The surest of all Bennett's bets was that the partnership would not survive into the next provincial general election. In retrospect, it is strange that he seemed so alone in his soothsaying. With the advantage of hindsight it is easy to say that the breakup of coalition was inevitable: clearly, it had become the victim of its own success. A host of indicators might have prepared British Columbians for a return to the old days of combat between Grits and Tories. Premier Johnson and Finance Minister Anscomb were increasingly at odds with each other; the federal wings of the Liberal and Conservative parties were campaigning aggressively for a dissolution of the Victoria coalition; and old-time adherents of the party machines were becoming more and more nostalgic for a return to the good old days that had preceded the decade-long experiment in political fusion. As with any marriage in decline, the initial crackup posed the greatest difficulty, but early in 1952 a pretext for separation was found.

Herbert Anscomb was becoming increasingly aggressive in his approach to political problems, and coalition insiders detected in this his preparations for a split. The pot shots he regularly aimed at his Liberal colleagues were certainly ample justification for their taking the Tories to task. Nevertheless, leading members of both coalition parties had made public statements to the effect that—barring unforeseen circumstances—the partnership would continue at least until the next election. However, jockeying for partisan advantage had already begun. Early in January 1952, Anscomb travelled to Ottawa to negotiate new federal-provincial tax agreements, while there enjoying a vigorous round of Liberal-bashing. Upon returning to Vancouver on January 15, he phoned the Victoria press gallery and issued a news release with details of the new tax agreements, thereby making the information public before briefing his coalition colleagues in cabinet.

Compared with many of his previous partisan indiscretions, Anscomb's actions on this occasion seemed relatively innocuous, but they were either the last straw or perhaps the necessary justification for a Liberal move. According to Conservative minister R.C. MacDonald, at the next, and final, meeting of the coalition cabinet on the morning of January 18: "We were all sitting in the cabinet meeting waiting for the premier to enter. He walked in looking a bit edgy and then announced there would be no meeting this morning. He then looked at Mr. Anscomb and said, 'Mr. Anscomb, I want your resignation!' Anscomb hardly changed expression, simply packed up his folders, got up and left the room. Myself and the other three Conservative ministers got up and followed him out."

Premier Johnson used Anscomb's "leaking" news of the Ottawa tax agreement as the reason for the firing. In a statement later that day, he referred to Anscomb's "flagrant and arrogant disregard of the procedure of constitutional government." The premier also made it quite clear that the Tory leader had been severely testing the patience of his coalition colleagues with a "long series of politically reprehensible actions."

For his part, Anscomb appeared more than happy to accommodate the premier; he resigned from cabinet and carried with him the other Tory ministers. Furthermore, he announced that all eleven Conservative coalitionists would leave the government caucus because there was "no other course possible." The Tories then called for an immediate election, arguing that without coalition the Liberals no longer had a mandate to govern. Boss Johnson brooded over the constitutional implications of these arguments but, in the end, decided to carry on. Although he had dismissed Anscomb, the other Tories had left of their own volition; therefore, he declared, his government was still a coalition administration, and he still commanded a slim majority in the legislature. He shuffled his cabinet portfolios and prepared for the upcoming session which, he hoped, would help to re-establish the provincial party's long-lost identity.

The coalition bubble had finally burst and the air in Victoria was filled with acrimony. Public reaction to the dissolved political partnership was mixed but generally resigned; the situation was ably summed up by a Victoria *Colonist* editorial: "Whatever the given pretext for the break-up, and it was a slim one, mutual antipathies both personal and political had made the result inevitable. Not only had the coalition politically outlived its usefulness, but it had fallen progressively into growing disfavor with the public for its latter day blunders, extravagance and dictatorial rule."

While this important act was being played out in Victoria, W.A.C. Bennett was out of the province, having travelled east on family and business matters. Socreds were worried and excited over the turn of events, uncertain of the implications of the coalition breakup, and they missed Bennett's practical and confident input. Ron Worley managed to have an urgent and almost obsequious letter delivered to Bennett in Toronto: "Much has been happening during the past couple of days and my greatest regret is that you are not within reach for consultation. . . . things are going extremely well in our favour . . . although an election too early would catch us somewhat 'short.' . . . Come what may, I am positive that you will be the leader of the movement. No one else will get in unless it is over my dead body. It is felt that you should come back to the province as soon as possible in view of the fact that much is likely to happen, and the Social Credit need your guidance in matters which they are not conversant with owing to lack of experience."

When Bennett returned shortly thereafter, he issued a statement from Vancouver forecasting a "sweeping victory" for Social Credit in the next provincial election. He was getting great mileage from a *Maclean's* magazine leading article by Blair Fraser, "B.C. Coalition Commits Suicide," which suggested doom for the Liberals and Conservatives, referred to Harold Winch and the CCF as tired and caught up in factional squabbles, and observed that "Social Credit is spreading through rural B.C. at a startling rate." Bennett was quoted in the press: "Social Credit is strong in the Kootenays, in the Okanagan, the Cariboo and the Peace River. It is strongest in the Fraser Valley . . . and it is making headway on Vancouver Island. There is great interest in Vancouver."

From Kelowna, Bennett wrote this to his old friend Harry Perry, who had now completely severed his connections with the provincial Liberals and was offering tacit support to the Socreds: "I notice on returning that the political situation is more in flux than ever and that events are proceeding as we had forecast them. Provincial Conservatives and Provincial Liberals for too long have only had a shell organization and now that this shell is collapsing no real substance remains. . . . Even making allowances for my *enthusiam*, I am really amazed at the widespread swing to the Social Credit movement. It is phenomenal and has reached a stage where it can't be checked." And he wrote to a Vancouver friend and supporter:

I believe the Social Credit movement is going along very well and is spreading at a fine rate throughout the province, but there are many constituencies that need to be pulled together in definite organizations to get in fighting form to meet a Provincial election, which no doubt will come in June. The main thing is that we have a real organization to go into battle as our opponents will try to say that we are not a factor and will endeavour to ignore us and try to make out that the election is between the Johnson Liberal Government and the CCF. This we must watch very closely and we must get the best publicity possible to show that we are a real factor in the election so that we will receive thousands of "on the fence" votes, which, after all, are the outstanding factor in any election.

One of the primary reasons people were coming down off their fences on the side of Social Credit in unprecedented numbers was that W.A.C. Bennett had embraced the movement. From the day he announced his conversion there was a flurry of organizational activity, particularly in the interior. Old-time Socreds were bewildered by the drastic surge in memberships, and organizers in Vancouver could not keep up with the pace of activity; nor could they keep up with people in the interior who, independent of the League, were forming Social Credit clubs and lining up new members. Coming when it did, Bennett's own proclamation seemed, almost magically, to create a wave of new support that was wholly unexpected by most observers. Whatever he had to gain by the move, the Social Credit League gained more. In 1950, the League could count on 500 members in British Columbia; by the spring of 1952 membership had mushroomed to over 8,000. As the only practised politician in the movement, Bennett was now in great demand by new constituency associations, and he did his utmost to assist them in setting up sound organizations and electioneering machinery.

He told how he helped to spread the Social Credit faith to virginal areas of the province: "We'd put little ads in the paper saying that we'd like people to know how to join Social Credit. We asked them to fill in the forms and send them in to a box in Vancouver. Then I would go into a town with perhaps eight of these completed forms. Since I'd been in the retail business, I would know a merchant in the town and I'd talk to him and ask about these people. He'd say, 'Well, that guy's no good,' but out of eight, I would find one pretty good guy. So I would see him and start to build around him." Bennett had other, less scientific, methods of promoting Social Credit—for example, he cultivated a network of travelling salesmen who spread the word from hamlet to town in the interior: "I sent these commercial travellers . . . lots of them would call on me, they all knew me. They often said, 'What about this

Social Credit?' I'd tell them, 'It's really growing by leaps and bounds. Leaps and bounds! You've got a job to do to spread it, too.' So they'd go from Kelowna maybe to Vernon, and in the stores in Vernon the traveller would say, 'Oh, Social Credit—' 'There's no Social Credit.' 'Down in Kelowna they're talking nothing else but Social Credit.' " Wesley Black, who helped to organize Social Credit in the southeast interior, confirmed their importance: "It might be amazing to know that the people who kept us in tune with what was going on in the rest of the province weren't the politicians at all, but salesmen. The salesmen who travelled around from this place to that and all over the province—they were the ones who kept us informed and kept us enthusiastic about what was going to happen."

Despite Bennett's popularity and the fierce enthusiasm he cultivated in other Socreds, credit for the success of the underground movement sweeping B.C. in the early months of 1952 was not all his. The Alberta party had provided the funds to make Peer Paynter a full-time organizer and it covered the costs of speaking tours as well as the distribution of Alberta literature. In addition, Orvis Kennedy, the chief organizer and president of the Alberta Social Credit Party, spent virtually all his time in British Columbia. From mid-1951 on, he travelled throughout the province organizing local groups and preaching the Alberta version of Social Credit doctrine. In particular, he set up rudimentary constituency associations and helped to locate prospective candidates, saying of this period: "I always figured if I had a meeting and didn't end up with a committee or a group organized at the end of it, the meeting was a failure—no matter how many people you had, no matter how much fun you had at the meeting. But we were holding two meetings a day, one in the afternoon and one in the evening, and we covered lots of territory—and I don't know of one place in which we didn't leave a Social Credit group."

The influence of Alberta was resented by some west coast members, who sensed that it was trying too hard to control events in B.C. There is evidence to support their suspicion. Shortly after Peer Paynter was made a full-time worker, he received a letter from the president of the Social Credit Association of Canada, Rev. Ernest Hansell, an Alberta MP, informing him that he would be expected to follow directives from Edmonton: "I am afraid that many decisions on minor routine matters will have to be left with myself and Mr. Kennedy." Paynter did not seem overly worried about his prospective lack of independence but others were strongly opposed to the heavy-handedness of their friends over the Rockies.

The biggest issue creating tension between the two unequal partners was W.A.C. Bennett. When the controversial Okanagan MLA joined Social Credit and became touted as the obvious leader of the B.C. movement, Albertans feared they were losing control—and their fear was well founded.

Before Bennett, Albertans clearly dominated the League, but the flood of new memberships following his conversion practically ensured B.C. control. Ernest Manning has said: "I didn't know Mr. Bennett, I hadn't met him, but we'd heard of him. We were made aware by the Social Credit people in British Columbia that this man with legislative experience was showing a very active interest in the Social Credit movement and he had the qualities of leadership. You always get skepticism when anybody goes through a political conversion. You always have a little uneasiness to be sure the conversion is genuine, but I think almost from the beginning Mr. Bennett made it very clear that he was genuine about it and that he was certainly anxious to do something within the framework of the Social Credit movement." Bennett had the reputation of a political rebel and the doubts of the Alberta Socreds were both genuine and natural. It was a parental reaction: as the only Social Credit government in the world, they were inclined to be careful and somewhat overbearing with regard to their progeny.

Lyle Wicks, the president of the British Columbia Social Credit League, had reacted favourably when Bennett joined. He publicly praised his "ability, integrity and public-spiritedness," and made it clear that he felt the Tory renegade was a positive asset to the Social Credit movement. After a couple of private meetings between the two it seems that Wicks had become a Bennett man. Early in 1952, Wicks was summoned to a special meeting in Premier Manning's office in Edmonton with the premier, Orvis Kennedy, Solon Low, Rev. Ernest Hansell and other Alberta Social Credit deans. They expressed concern over the course of events in B.C. and suggested that Reverend Hansell was available to set things straight and lead the League in the next provincial election. Later, many British Columbians viewed this incident as a form of reprimand. Albertans, of course, denied this, preferring to describe it as a simple consultation. Orvis Kennedy, however, did admit that "there were one or two things which we advised quite strongly at the time, but there was no reprimand." Wicks returned home wagging his tail between his legs, and some members of the League executive became more firmly opposed to the Albertans' heavy-handedness; but they were not in a position to forfeit their generous financial support. The single consolation for Wicks was that shortly after he arrived back home he was able to take an extended leave of absence from his job driving streetcars in Vancouver. With Bennett's assistance, enough funds had been raised to provide a full-time salary for the president of the B.C. Social Credit League.

The fourth and last session of British Columbia's twenty-second parliament opened on February 19, 1952. The Speech from the Throne indicated Premier Johnson's view that the province was being governed by a caretaker administration: "Since last you met there have been some changes in the personnel of the government, and in view of the circumstances that have transpired, the only business to be placed before you will be of a nature considered to be essential for the maintenance of the public service. All other matters will be deferred until the people have been afforded an opportunity of clarifying the present situation." The first procedural wrangle arose over the the question of the new status of the displaced Tories. The Speaker of the House, citing the appropriate parliamentary authorities, declared the Conservatives the new official opposition because their number was greater than that of the CCF. Naturally, Harold Winch challenged the ruling but the Conservatives and Liberals combined forces to take away the socialists' privilege. W.A.C. Bennett and Tilly Rolston sided with the CCF on the recorded vote.

The show must have been interesting to behold: in the lulls between harsh words and attempts to gain partisan advantage over each other, the former coalition partners sometimes seemed to forget they were no longer in bed with each other. When Harold Winch moved a nonconfidence motion during the Throne Speech debate, the new leader of the opposition, Herbert Anscomb, announced that the Tories intended to support the government in order to prevent "economic and political chaos." After firing Anscomb, Premier Johnson had assumed the finance portfolio and later in the session he brought in what would be his only provincial budget, which showed an increase in expenditure of 15 per cent to $187.5 million. In a large public meeting in Vancouver, W.A.C. Bennett sneered at the charade of the one-time colleagues: "We are now treated to the spectacle of the former Minister of Finance being paid to criticize the budget he was responsible for preparing."

The 1952 session was clearly a lame-duck affair. The legislature received reports from three special committees of inquiry, including a damning indictment of the government's hospital insurance plan, but the Johnson administration was unprepared to take any action. The single highlight of the session was Bennett's only major speech. The Tory apostate was still referred to as an "independent" but, in fact, he was the first member of the B.C. legislature to espouse Social Credit principles. When he rose to speak on March 7, he was heckled and jeered by virtually all his fellow MLAs. The *Vancouver Sun* reported: "The smiling, fast-talking Bennett experienced one of the roughest rides any member has ever been given by the House. . . . Trouble started when he began referring to Social Credit theories and the record of the Alberta Social Credit party." Apparently, Bennett had to appeal to the Speaker to stop "the shower of barbs and darts." He described the scene in the House:

I didn't speak in the first debate on the Speech from the Throne. I waited. I spoke on the second debate, the budget debate, and I had prepared my remarks. I had difficulty getting an opportunity to deliver my speech, because now that I had joined the Socreds, even the socialists, who were applauding me when I walked across the floor, condemned me just as strongly or stronger than the Conservatives or the Liberals. They were all bitter. I got up in the House and was on my feet for half an hour before I could get one paragraph out—the noise was terrific. I addressed the Speaker: "If the House lasts for an hour or three days, I'm going to make this speech. There are three old parties here and they don't want to hear the truth. They don't want to hear the truth themselves and they don't want the people of the province to hear it either." They kept saying, "What is Social Credit? What is Social Credit?" And I said, "If you'd pause and listen for just one half a minute, I'll tell you what Social Credit is."

Bennett's fellow members never completely let up, but he did manage to sputter out an abbreviated version of his speech which included a pointed definition of Social Credit by way of biblical paraphrase: "While Social Credit may be a stumbling block to the ultra dyed in the wool Tory, and foolishness to the hardened Grit whose first loyalty is to a political machine, it is a new hope to tens of thousands of people throughout British Columbia." Bennett delighted in remembering that this "just made them madder and madder." To the background of howls and taunts, he concluded his speech by predicting that Social Credit would form the next government and that the Grits and Tories would be swept from office "and won't be back for fifty years."

On the penultimate day of the spring session, Bennett took the ferry to Vancouver to address a Social Credit rally. The Socreds, whose newspaper advertisements said simply that "W.A.C. Bennett Is Going to Answer the Machines," had no idea that the meeting would be the largest and most enthusiastic they had ever staged. When Eric Martin arrived to chair the event he had to fight his way through the crowd. After struggling to the stage in bewilderment, he was greeted by a beaming Bennett: "Eric, the province is on fire! Things have changed. People are ready for it. They want it!"

The *Vancouver Sun* reported: "Nearly 1,500 persons jammed Pender Auditorium to stamp their feet, whistle and cheer whenever Mr. Bennett paused for breath." Bennett told the noisy crowd that the first act of a Social Credit government would be "to take the word 'compulsory' out of hospital insurance." But, he warned, "Don't expect us to outpromise the Liberals and Conservatives. We only promise good government. . . . Social Credit is not the dark horse, it is the white hope of B.C." The meeting was clearly a campaign-style performance, which Bennett described:

A lot of people were there as supporters and a lot had come to watch . . . and the other three parties had their hecklers there. Even some of the young Conservatives that had been with me trying to get up in the Conservative Party—now that I'd joined Social Credit I was their enemy. Then the question period came and one of them got up and in a very nice legal style said, "Mr. Chairman, I'm glad to see Mr. Bennett here tonight. I have seven questions I'd like to ask him. I don't want to be unfair to this great meeting but these questions are all in logical order and I think it would be good to hear these questions and the answers at this historic meeting." It sounded as if he was on my side, which he wasn't. Then he said, "Shall I ask these questions all at once, or can I ask them [one at a time]?" So I said to the chairman, "Tell him to ask them [all at once]." As soon as he finished I got up and thanked him and I said, "To the first question, the answer is no; the second question, the answer is yes; third question, I haven't got the information but if you write me in Victoria I'll supply it . . ." I went through the seven questions like that, and he said, "That's no answer! That's no answer!" But nobody knew what the questions were by then.

The Vancouver meeting was a huge success in that it demonstrated a manifest interest in Social Credit in the province's largest city. Bennett, who handled himself in a confident, aggressive manner, made a good impression and was extremely pleased with the popular reaction to his advocacy of Social Credit and his denunciation of the old-line parties. He returned to Victoria for the next day's sitting of the legislature where he was angrily criticized for his performance in Vancouver. He described the scene: "I received an awful personal attack from Anscomb and Johnson. While they were doing the country's business, here last night I was rousing the public up against the government. . . . They were so mad! And Anscomb brought his hand down so hard, I thought he was not only going to break the desk, I thought for sure he was going to break his hand. I thought he was going to have a stroke. Gee, they were mad! I said to my partners, 'My friends, you see—they're scared already.'" On that day, March 26, 1952, the session was prorogued. A couple of weeks later, on April 10, the parliament was dissolved and a general election was announced for June 12.

At the commencement of what would be a long and confusing contest, the Liberals, led by Premier Johnson, seemed cautious but confident in their approach to the voters; the Conservatives, on the other hand, came out swinging wildly with both of Anscomb's pounding fists; and the CCF seemed to believe the demise of coalition was all that was needed for the election of B.C.'s first socialist government. Shortly after the election was called, Tilly

Rolston announced that she had joined Social Credit and would seek nomination for re-election in her riding of Vancouver-Point Grey. This news was a great boost for Social Credit and had a tremendous impact in the Vancouver area. Completely enveloped in his irrepressible optimism, Bennett wrote to one confidant that "all the breaks seem to be coming our way." But the Social Credit League was suffering from a serious problem of identity—it was leaderless. A leadership convention was called for the weekend of April 26 at New Westminster. Bennett was now actively campaigning for the leadership and as the date approached he channelled most of his energy into organizing the convention so that he would win. He was aware that equally determined forces were working against him.

The convention astonished old-time adherents of Major Douglas's philosophy: only a couple of years before, their annual conventions attracted twenty to forty subdued delegates; now over a thousand cheering and excited Socreds were jammed into a New Westminster high school gymnasium, with colourful banners boosting the names of the province's constituencies, bands loudly playing and assorted American-style hoopla. Many attending were actually from Alberta, prompting the press to characterize the meeting as the "Calgary Stampede." The Alberta influence was evident from the start; the convention commenced with the hymn "O God, Our Help in Ages Past." Initially, there was a good deal of procedural confusion. President Lyle Wicks decided to ban the press from the convention, creating some controversy, but the news media finally repaired to the principal's office from where they listened to the proceedings over the public-address system. Before turning to the question of leadership, delegates approved the League's electoral "program"—they studiously avoided using the word "platform" to describe their proposed policies, as it had connotations of the ordinary sort of politics they were attempting to rise above.

Consideration of the leadership issue was preceded by the reading of an "ultimatum" in a letter from the Alberta "parent bodies": "In order to assure the conduct of the campaign in accordance with the fundamental principles of Social Credit it would be in the best interests of the movement for the convention to select a campaign leader from outside who has a solid background of Social Credit knowledge and experience." If the recommendation was agreed to, "the Members of the Alberta government, the Alberta Social Credit League and the National Social Credit Association are prepared to give what support they can to the British Columbia campaign." Many of Bennett's supporters were infuriated by this unexpected stipulation, but the writing was on the wall: the Albertans were dead set against Bennett. Manning later denied that the document read to the convention represented any kind of an ultimatum:

It's quite probable that there were what I would refer to as informal conditions attached. In other words, it may well be that we said, "Now look, we're not going to drum up money in Alberta to send to British Columbia unless we're sure it's being spent effectively to get the story of Social Credit out to your people." That kind of thing might well have been said. But I think it's a pretty gross exaggeration to say that we arbitrarily dictated to them—heavens, they could do what they liked. But you can't ask somebody to pay the bills and give a lot of their time and not be satisfied that what's being done is effective and going to get some results.

Delegates were informed that Rev. Ernest Hansell, an Alberta MP, was available to serve as British Columbia campaign leader. A motion was subsequently passed calling for the election of a campaign leader, the distinction clearly being made between this position and provincial leader, a great disappointment for the pro-Bennett forces who had come to the convention to see him installed as their political spokesman. Bennett, too, was worried, but he helped to engineer the passage of another resolution empowering Social Credit MLAs to elect a full-fledged political leader from among their ranks after the election. Bennett recalled: "I was still new and didn't want to upset things. You don't make a horse go faster by pushing on the reins. And I didn't want the job of campaign manager."

The convention finally arrived at the task of electing a campaign leader. William Chant and Lyle Wicks were nominated. Then predictably, and to loud applause, Reverend Hansell's name was placed before the convention. Oddly, so was that of Solon Low, another Alberta MP and national leader of Social Credit. Convention chairman Eric Martin began to fret; no one was moving to nominate W.A.C. Bennett. He asked another League official to take the chair momentarily and, in a gushing, long-winded speech, himself nominated Bennett.

The leadership nominees were called to the stage. Speaking first, William Chant politely withdrew; Lyle Wicks also declined to stand for the position. Solon Low, pointing out the conflict his nomination posed with his federal responsibilities, also took his name out of the running but noted that there was still "splendid material from which to choose a leader." Now the showdown was between W.A.C. Bennett and Rev. Ernest Hansell—the newly converted west coast upstart versus the genuine, hand-picked son of Alberta. Bennett asked to speak first, and his words surprised many:

Mr. Chairman, distinguished guests, and ladies and gentlemen: I am very glad to be present tonight at this great victory convention here in New Westminster. I want to tell you that we're going to win this next election on June 12th. I want to tell you clearly that no matter what rumour will be going around, at no time was it my intention to be a candidate for this particular office. I want to say clearly, that when I joined the Social Credit movement I joined it hook, line and sinker. I joined it for victory. . . . I want to pledge myself tonight and I want every person at this meeting to pledge themselves . . . one hundred per cent behind our campaign leader who is going to be elected here tonight. Because if we all put our shoulder to the wheel and not just leave it to one man . . . then victory shall be ours. . . ."

He then withdrew his name from the contest letting the Alberta nominee, Hansell, win by acclamation. Eric Martin said of Bennett's speech: "It was like Lincoln at Gettysburg. It has since become known as the 'hook, line and sinker' speech. It was one of the best speeches Bennett ever made in his life." League president, Lyle Wicks, said: "It was totally unexpected to me, and it was a good thing. It saved us, because we had to have some device to keep us from fighting among ourselves. I knew we had a dilemma and it was a stroke of genius, really, on Bennett's part."

Thus, Rev. Ernest Hansell, described by one journalist as "a short, middle-aged man, with a loud tie, a mouth that creased down at the corners and a permanent five o'clock shadow," became the B.C. Social Credit campaign leader. In his acceptance speech to the somewhat bewildered delegates at New Westminster, he pointed out that he had met Bennett for the first time the previous evening and wanted them to know that, after an hour-long conversation, he realized Bennett "stands head and shoulders over what I imagined he stood." By electing Hansell, the League made a decision without precedent in the annals of democratic party politics: they were heading into an election without a *de facto* leader; voters would be asked to mark their ballots for Social Credit without knowing who was their proposed premier. Consequently, the Socreds were subjected to the frequent scorn and ridicule of political opponents who could not imagine they were serious. Herbert Anscomb, for instance, laughed them off as "the headless brigade from over the mountains." But for his part, W.A.C. Bennett did not feel this highly unusual situation would prove an absolute electoral liability and, like other B.C. Socreds, he regarded continued Alberta support as crucial to the outcome of the election. Also, during the campaign, he and other Social Credit candidates could point to the comparative political stability of Alberta as an example of what could be achieved in British Columbia.

As it turned out, Bennett's failure to be crowned king of the Socreds was beneficial to his securing the future support of many old-time members of the League. Shortly after the convention, a former opponent within the movement, L.H. Shantz, wrote to him declaring himself on his side: "I would like to commend you on your stand at the Convention, and feel that it has entrenched you more solidly in our movement than any other action you could have taken." As the campaign progressed, it became clear to many, particularly in the interior of the province, that Bennett was performing as a sort of leader *ex officio*. While Hansell's involvement in the campaign seemed sporadic and low key, Bennett carried on more or less independently, organizing in interior constituencies and speaking tirelessly on behalf of other Socred candidates.

Some of his supporters resented what they felt was only a haphazard effort by Albertans during the campaign's early stages. Eric Martin, still smarting from, as he saw it, bitter defeat at the convention, did not hold back strong criticism of the Albertans' conditional support; he convinced himself that the League had become the victim of a conspiracy hatched in the office of the Alberta premier, saying: "Manning didn't want a Social Credit government in this province.... They [Alberta Socreds] succeeded in getting Ernie Hansell elected as campaign leader and it wasn't long before we knew he was elected to ensure our defeat, not our election. No sooner was he elected than he disappeared for three weeks. We didn't know where he was. He'd gone back to Alberta. Then he showed up in B.C. for a week and disappeared again—this time to Ottawa where he attended a House of Commons session. This was very disconcerting. A lot of people who had backed Hansell woke up. They discovered what was going on."

Martin was probably too harsh on the Albertans, but his opinion was shared by a number of League members. Yet it is impossible to deny the practical assistance rendered by Alberta. Although the Socred campaign was off to a relatively quiet start, it had a solid basis to work from thanks to the background organizational work of people like national organizer Orvis Kennedy, who had been travelling throughout the province for more than a year setting up riding associations and distributing Social Credit literature.

One of the biggest problems confronting the League was to nominate candidates in each of the province's forty-eight electoral districts. Strongly motivated to field a full slate, it came close to its goal largely through Bennett's cultivation of a province-wide network of disaffected former coalition supporters. In many ridings it was simply a case of getting *any* candidate into the field, as it was felt that the chances of other Socred candidates were enhanced by the appearance of a serious and determined effort. Social Credit ended up with forty-seven standard-bearers, failing to nominate only in the isolated far northern constituency of Atlin.

Bennett easily secured his own nomination in South Okanagan. Most other Social Credit stalwarts attained nominations—Lyle Wicks in Dewdney, Eric Martin in a Vancouver riding, Peer Paynter in Revelstoke, William Chant in Esquimalt—but the great majority were newcomers and knew little or nothing about Social Credit theory. And, amazingly, they never pretended to. Tilly Rolston told her nominating convention: "I don't know what it is all about, but I'm all for ya." Some candidates were running because they had had their arms twisted *à la* Commander Wurtele of Esquimalt, and many were in the field because they were simply fed up with present Victoria politics and viewed the Social Credit movement as an honest vehicle of protest. Most candidates were undistinguished, ordinary people who had never before been involved in politics. A good example was Cyril Shelford, the angry young northerner whom Bennett had befriended and talked into seeking the nomination for the vast Omineca constituency. Shelford's only previous claim to fame was that he had been one of the first Canadian casualties of the Second World War (while still in training camp, he was shot in the posterior by another rookie learning how to clean his rifle). He described his nomination:

> We were getting ready to go to the nominating convention in the old Legion hall in Burns Lake. In those days, we were busy on the ranch and when we got to the gate heading out from the ranch, the cattle had knocked the fence down. So I jumped out of the old jeep and chased the cattle out of the field, put the fence back up and my wife and I finally took off for the convention. When we got there everything was just about ready to start. Everyone was there—there must have been two or three hundred people. All I had on were canvas shoes and when I walked into the Legion Hall, everyone noticed. . . . I guess I had stepped into a cow-flop when I was chasing the cows in the field. Someone yelled, "Cyril! You've got manure on your shoes!" I said, "Don't worry at all. I've just come from the Liberal meeting . . ." I think that likely nominated me. I won it on the first ballot.

British Columbia's 1952 election broke the established pattern of pretended unity and socialist-baiting that had been set during the coalition era. To be sure, the Liberals and Conservatives were still painting fearful pictures of the potential consequences of a CCF victory, but in their efforts to gain advantage over each other, their criticisms were sometimes tentative and their campaign strategies ill-focussed. Now, there was more than one enemy—and this confusion made a significant difference. Yet the Social Credit movement was not considered a serious threat by the three established parties. The socialists, for probably the first time, adopted the politics of fear, preaching to potential Social Credit voters, not so much because the Socreds were considered a major factor in the election but because they might eat into possible socialist support. The *CCF News* had earlier dismissed the League as "not of any real significance to the CCF which stands as the only alternative to all capitalist parties." However, once the election campaign was well under way, socialist candidates discovered the Socreds' growing popularity. Harold

Winch denounced them: "I thought Nazism and Fascism had been stamped out with the winning of the last war . . . who would have thought we would see the ugly head of totalitarianism raised in B.C.?" He repeated these kinds of scare statements at several points in the campaign. For their part, Social Credit candidates lacked a unified approach to the election but, generally, directed their attack against the former coalition parties. On a few occasions when Reverend Hansell made appearances in the province, Social Credit too tried to purvey a distinctive kind of paranoia, as when he told an Okanagan audience: "There is a government more powerful than governments—this great monetary power that knows no international boundaries. That is what we are attacking, and everyone who opposes Social Credit is either ignorant of that power or party to it."

Of course, the unique feature of the 1952 election was the new single transferable ballot, one of the most interesting election experiments ever to be conducted in Canada, in which voters were not constrained by the potent argument of the "lost vote." Rather than "wasting" their votes on candidates or parties that, under normal circumstances, would not have a chance of winning, they were allowed the opportunity to cast ballots for favourites, alternate favourites and least favourites. It is surprising that the contesting parties did not develop clear strategies on how to use the balloting to advantage; obviously, the new system was not fully understood. However, some elementary instructions were offered to voters. The Liberals, for example, expected their supporters to vote "1-2 for free enterprise": presumably, this meant give them first preference and the Tories second. But, generally, politicians were reluctant to recommend a second choice for fear of alienating traditional or potential sectors of support. Herbert Anscomb urged Conservative supporters to mark their ballots with only their first choice—in effect, to plump their ballots—as no other party, Liberals included, deserved Tory support. Likewise, Harold Winch asked socialist voters to plump their ballots in order to indicate the essential differences between the bad guys and the good. These were the general guidelines offered by the party leaders; behind the scenes in most constituencies, candidates were lobbying to be the second choice of their rivals' supporters, and it seems clear that most voters were looking forward to the new method of exercising their democratic rights.

The Social Credit League did not develop a unified strategy for alternate ballot choices; rather, a simple effort was made to ensure that their supporters understood the importance of placing the number "1" beside the name of League candidates. Lyle Wicks wrote to all Socred candidates: "Make sure that every possible first choice is given to Social Credit." In South Okanagan, accordingly, W.A.C. Bennett simply asked his constituents to give him their number one choice. Other candidates, like Wesley Black in Nelson-Creston, calculated the potential effect of alternate choices on his chances of victory: "If I came to see you, you might say, 'Wes, I have nothing against you, but I'm really a CCFer, but I'll give you my second choice.' Our people went around door-to-door and kept a list. People in small towns and rural areas are far more apt to tell you what their politics are and how they vote than they are in an urban situation. We kept records of the first choices, second choices and third choices—and our estimate came within 150 votes of being absolutely correct." In a system where the second choices of a defeated candidate's votes could easily determine the outcome of a contest, voting strategy could be all-important—especially in a close race. In some areas of British Columbia, the lobbying, machinations and prognostications were carried on at a frantic pace. One example of the various strategies employed is that of the independent-labour member from Fernie, Tom Uphill, who wrote to W. A. C. Bennett: "Dear friend: If it is in order, I would like to notify the Social Credit Association in Fernie to give me their second choice. . . . a word from you would help considerably."

The Socred "program" was not unlike the platforms of the older parties except that it contained strong reformist overtones. It stressed less government interference in business, an increase in essential health and social services, encouragement of co-operatives, larger old-age pensions and a pay-as-you-go approach to government spending. The advocacy of their programs and the organization of their campaign were notably different from that of the other parties. Although there was talk of the existence of a $100,000 campaign fund raised from individual donations, few Socred candidates derived any financial help from League headquarters. Most campaign literature came from Alberta and was not directly relevant to British Columbia; however, local Socred brochures were produced, usually simple mimeographs, replete with typographical errors, and so unprofessional looking that they stood in stark contrast to the flashy campaign materials of the other parties, which added immensely to the homespun appeal of Social Credit. The unsophisticated approach of the Socred campaign created a great deal of sympathy for this "people's movement."

It is difficult to explain the groundswell of Social Credit support that emerged as election day came nearer. Certainly, it was not immediately perceptible to most observers, largely because political activity in the big urban centres drew the most attention. But Social Credit was making headway throughout the interior, attracting large and enthusiastic crowds. Many commentators referred to the special feeling and excitement of Socred campaign meetings—a sort of "electric current in the atmosphere and a crusading quality in the party hymns." The religious overtones were much the result of the Alberta influence, though the Christian image of Social Credit was never deliberately cultivated by the British Columbia movement. The mixture of Christian fundamentalism and populist politics was certainly no liability. When prominent Alberta Socreds toured the interior B.C. valleys it often resembled old-home week to the host of ex-Albertans who had settled there. Reverend Hansell received a warm welcome everywhere he spoke, and when he told a Vernon audience that "fundamentally, Social Credit is a great crusade for a way of life," he received a loud ovation. Such statements as Tilly Rolston's declared belief "in a return to honest Christian principles in government" were warmly approved by an electorate that had become cynical about politics, politicians and election promises.

Journalists covering the election, as well as latter-day commentators, have poked fun at the "Bible-punching" Social Crediters preaching their fundamentalist philosophy to British Columbia's "Sunday morning people," but the point has been exaggerated by political skeptics searching for an explanation for the huge tide of support that swept behind Social Credit in the spring of 1952. In fact, the Socred candidates—four clergymen among them—rarely wore their religious faith on their sleeves, and the aims of their proposed reforms were blatantly secular. Moreover, they maintained a healthy sense of humour about the issue. When Reverend Hansell spoke to a Kamloops rally, organizers tacked up a sign in the hall advertising, "Haloes checked free." Rev. Harry Francis, Social Credit candidate in Similkameen, campaigned in an automobile with a sign attached to the rear bumper predicting "Eternity Ahead." And in the last week of the campaign, Premier Manning of Alberta, speaking to an audience of 5,000 in Vancouver—the largest campaign rally of the election—apologized for not wearing his halo.

W.A.C. Bennett campaigned mostly in the interior, seldom venturing down to the populous Vancouver area. He sensed that the greatest gains were to be made in the countryside and he travelled tirelessly, stopping at home in Kelowna only long enough to clean up, rest and pick up a freshly packed suitcase prepared by his wife. He drove his own car, travelling alone and usually at night, often sleeping in it on a side road. It was June and the weather was fine. He appeared at well-attended meetings in small towns and interior cities as a man burning to tell the truth, and he would speak with uncontrollable excitement, forever hurrying ahead of his powers of articulation. He rarely combined religion and politics on the public platform, but he admitted that the basis of Socred support was a kind of religious fervour. Always a practical sort, Bennett relied on neither faith nor prayers and did not describe his role, as Reverend Hansell did his, as "missionary work." For Bennett, "Mine was a crusade to win *now*. Missionary work is where you set the foundation for later. We couldn't wait!"

For the largely inexperienced Social Credit candidates, it was a time of learning as they engaged their more experienced and wily old-school political opponents. Cyril Shelford now laughs about his first lesson while running in the riding of Omineca:

I took off in my jeep for Stony Creek, a little Indian village, to talk to the Indians. I grew up with them and they likely knew me better than anyone else. I think everyone in Stony Creek turned out and I told them what I was trying to do—to build new roads and generally make things better. It was a good meeting, and I thought I had all of them on my side, every one of them. Later that day I met the CCF candidate, and told him, "Don't waste your time at Stony Creek; I've got that pretty well sewn up." He said, "Oh, I don't think so. I was up there and they were pretty friendly. I think they're gonna go CCF this time." The next day I ran into the Liberal candidate, in a restaurant, and I told him that I had Stony Creek. He said, "Oh, no, you haven't. I know those fellas; I've known them for years. I ran the movie theatre there and they really like me for taking the cowboy and Indian shows up there." The last day before the election the Conservatives went up there with liquor by the barrelful and they got every vote in Stony Creek. Every single one! So that was my first lesson in politics: you don't count votes before they come out of the ballot box.

In an era before the rise of organized pressure groups and single-issue politics, the 1952 provincial election lacked focus; candidates discussed a hodge-podge of issues and promised a wide array of programs and benefits. But with the advantage of hindsight, it is easy to see that the election marked the start of a new direction in B.C. politics, characterized generally as the "politics of protest." W.A.C. Bennett, for example, after telling his constituents little more than, "It is my conviction that a new, better and honest government is required," received an overwhelmingly positive response. However, if there was one issue that gave substance to the politics of protest, it was the government's hospital insurance program. Because of its controversial nature, many politicians tried to avoid the issue, but the voters could usually be counted upon to voice strong and bitter feelings towards the coalition's great social reform, and Bennett was one of the few politicians to realize its importance. His papers contain dozens of letters from constituents and groups throughout the province expressing contempt and outrage at the manner in which the B.C. Hospital Insurance Service was being administered. Earlier, BCHIS had proved the most important single issue influencing and facilitating his political transformation, and now he was able to capitalize on the issue by following his own dictum: "To win an election you have to get the people aroused and united around one issue. Don't spread your fire. If you're out shooting geese or ducks and the flock is flying over and you just shoot into the flock, you don't get anything. You've got to get your bead on one—a little ahead of it, mind you. Aim for one. And hospital insurance was my issue because I had been fighting for it in the House. It was a great reform and it should have re-elected the government... but it was badly handled."

Why did hospital insurance get off on such slippery footing in British Columbia, and how did BCHIS become so universally unpopular? Ever since its establishment in 1948, hospital insurance had been at the forefront of controversy in the province. The consultant employed by the Johnson administration to devise the plan engaged in a great deal of dialogue with the Saskatchewan government's pioneering health insurance program. The primary problem with BCHIS during its first few years of operation was that, to a large extent, it attempted to copy the Saskatchewan plan whose context was a relatively stable and rural economy; this created many problems which took time to correct. The collection of BCHIS premiums proved extremely difficult and the system of compulsory payroll deductions, which never worked, was bitterly received by west coast workers. In June 1950, a Vancouver woman was sent to jail for refusing to pay her premium; the press exploited the event to the fullest and BCHIS sank to new depths of unpopularity.

The program's well-publicized mounting annual deficit caused fierce political squabbles in Victoria and a general lack of public confidence. When "co-insurance" was introduced in 1951 to improve BCHIS's financial state, reaction was almost violently negative: the $3.50-per-day charge to the patient for the first ten days of a hospital visit became one of the most unpopular nuisance taxes ever levied on B.C. citizens. Organized labour called BCHIS "vicious" and co-insurance generally became a dirty word. Finance Minister Herbert Anscomb's public criticism further undermined BCHIS, for during the time he was still a member of the coalition cabinet he declared that the painful experience with hospital insurance was teaching the province "the cost of socialism." W.A.C. Bennett's grandstanding heightened the ill-feeling towards the plan. Federal MP George Cruickshank, after visiting his Fraser Valley riding, grumbled: "Since I have come home from Ottawa I have heard nothing else but hospital insurance, on the streets, on the dikes, on the fields. Wherever I go I hear complaints. It is too serious to ignore." And few voters ignored it.

It was inevitable that hospital insurance became the predominant issue in the 1952 election. As the Vancouver *Province* editorialized, "The next government may well be elected principally on the basis of the stand the parties take on this one issue." As the campaign rolled along, each party attempted to refine its stance on the question. Only the incumbent Liberals seemed confused. A Liberal policy-making convention favoured the abolition of co-insurance, but Premier Johnson believed that hospital insurance had to be run like a business and that only co-insurance could make it solvent. When Attorney General Gordon Wismer publicly disagreed with his boss, the Liberals were derided as "a horse with two heads." The Conservatives believed that BCHIS required radical surgery and called for a new plan that was neither compulsory nor monopolistic. Anscomb endlessly reminded voters of the Tory promise to abolish co-insurance, with the message regularly carried on radio throughout the province. The CCF did not concentrate on the hospital insurance issue but they, too, promised to eliminate co-insurance and offered to roll back the premiums through higher payments from general government revenue. If elected, the CCF committed themselves to extend BCHIS into "a completely socialized health plan." The Social Credit League pledged to abolish BCHIS and replace it with a voluntary system financed on a pay-as-you-go basis, recommending that "high-cost" co-insurance be modified to a dollar-a-day scheme. Bennett's popularity soared when he planned to cancel all existing premium arrears.

It is ironic that the Liberals, who had fought so hard to establish hospital insurance in British Columbia, were the ones who were hurt the most by the issue. Early in the campaign, the *Vancouver Sun* commented: "Boss Johnson has made hospital insurance the achievement of his political life and he is passionately sure that it is the finest addition to the social services of the province." But as the campaign progressed, his inability to defend its continuing high deficit was helping to erode Liberal support. A couple of weeks before election day an event occurred which, if it had been announced publicly, might have significantly altered the election outcome. BCHIS administrators discovered that they had a large surplus for the 1951–52 fiscal year, co-insurance having turned the system around. Naturally, BCHIS Commissioner Lloyd Detwiller wanted to report the news immediately to the government. Since the minister of health and welfare was busy campaigning in the interior, Detwiller went directly to the premier at his residence on the outskirts of Victoria. Detwiller described Johnson's reaction to the news of the surplus: "He got up . . . and as I watched him I realized what was going on. He was struggling within himself. . . . He walked up and down for a minute or two and he said, 'Det, don't tell a soul. . . . I truly believe that this system has got to be run as an insurance system. If it becomes a welfare state system it will be subsidized and paid for out of the general revenue, and that is not what I want for this province. If I take this to the Liberal caucus, they will force me to drop co-insurance.' "

Commissioner Detwiller kept the news to himself: it does not appear that another soul learned of the surprising surplus until after the election. Boss Johnson had made an important decision, putting principle above pragmatic political considerations. He alone decided not to end the tremendous controversy surrounding hospital insurance, and the voters went to the polls believing BCHIS was running millions of dollars in the red.

Heading into the final week of the campaign all party leaders were predicting victory—and they likely all believed in their predictions. W. A. C.

Bennett exuded extreme confidence: "Walk the floor with me on June 12 and bring good government to the province of B.C.," he told one of his last rallies. His bravado was infectious but not all Socreds shared his optimism. Even a true believer like Ron Worley was becoming sadly disillusioned with the "old dodderers" who were interfering with the League's campaign efforts in Victoria, and he wrote to Bennett. "Honestly... the inexperience and stupidity of some of these characters is most appalling. If the general picture throughout the province is the same you will have a mighty tough job on your hands as Premier." Most old-time Social Crediters refused to believe Bennett's confident predictions of victory. When Harold Winch, speaking in a riding on the Alberta border about ten days before the election, said that Social Credit would elect not more than three candidates, Peer Paynter was surprised that Winch thought they could elect even three. The Alberta Socreds were cautious in their forecasts, though Manning "was pretty convinced, after sensing the enthusiasm of the people there, that they were going to elect... a healthy bloc of Social Credit members in the B.C. legislature."

As the other parties entered the final days of the campaign, they feared that the Socreds might play the spoiler. The Liberals took out full-page newspaper advertisements over Premier Johnson's signature which read: "Voting for leaderless individuals could result in hopeless chaos such as this province has never before experienced.... One party must be given a mandate. All parties concede the Liberals will have the largest group.... Anything else is bound to result in confusion, confiscation and frustration." Herbert Anscomb expressed similar apprehensions: "The Social Credit Party is so bold to presume that British Columbians are prepared to entrust their future to a leaderless group whose philosophies are beyond all comprehension." And the Vancouver *Province* sounded its editorial alarm: "British Columbia needs good, sensible, experienced government to meet the needs of the times.... This is hardly the time to dabble in questionable experiments."

All day long Thursday, June 12, 1952, British Columbians trooped to the polls; some wrestled with their consciences, while all wrestled with the confusing ballot forms. But there were neither victory celebrations nor losers' wakes on that night. The single transferable ballot proved too difficult to tabulate and no one went to bed with any certainty about the election outcome. The electoral machinery practically broke down in the attempt to count the votes for 212 candidates in 48 ridings.

The following day, Friday the thirteenth, proved unlucky for many as the results finally started to be made known. Only five candidates were elected on the first count by virtue of receiving over 50 per cent of their constituents' first choices. These were: W.A.C. Bennett in South Okanagan; Kenneth Kiernan, Socred candidate in Chilliwack; Ralph Chetwynd for

Social Credit in Cariboo; CCF leader Harold Winch in Vancouver-East; and Frank Calder of the CCF in Atlin. Most astonishing was the overall picture: the CCF were leading in a total of twenty-one ridings; the Socreds were ahead in fourteen; Johnson's Liberals were in front in only nine; the Tories led in a lowly three; and, of course, Tom Uphill was at the head of his class in Fernie. If the single transferable ballot had not been in effect, these results would have meant a CCF minority government and a Social Credit official opposition. The percentage breakdown of the province's popular vote on the first count is another measure of the dramatic consequences of the politics of protest: CCF, 30.78 per cent; Social Credit, 27.2 per cent; Liberals, 23.46 per cent; Progressive Conservatives, 16.84 per cent.

Ron Worley phoned Bennett to congratulate him after the first count was known. "That was a good show, next time we should make government."

Bennett scoffed, "What do you mean, next time? We're going to make it this time! And with one or two seats more than any other party."

The political climate in British Columbia was confusion. One commentator declared: "I don't know what government we got. I don't know what government we didn't get. I don't know what government we are going to get." The rejected Liberals and Conservatives could only hope for better results from the count of the voters' second choices. The socialists, however, were prepared to march over to Victoria and take hold of the reins of office. They were clearly in the lead, thanks to the Socreds undercutting Liberal and Conservative support; a final decision in their favour seemed inevitable and they were sure that Harold Winch would form the next government.

British Columbians sat back in suspense and waited for the himalayas of votes to be counted and recounted. They had to wait three weeks for the second choices from last-place finishers to be distributed among the remaining candidates. The results of this next count were announced on July 3, and they compounded the initial shock of June 12. Liberal cabinet ministers were going down to defeat in the interior where the Socreds were increasing their meteoric gains. It was becoming clear that Social Credit was a popular second choice among supporters of all other parties. Bennett could not sit back in silence. On July 4, he issued a brave news release from Kelowna: "The political revolt which has been building up in British Columbia for the last year and a half showed itself clearly in the June 12th Provincial election. . . . I am confident that when the final election results are in, Social Credit will form the new Government of British Columbia and will open a new era of stability and progress for our Province."

His statement seemed premature but over the next few days, as the results of further counts came in, his optimism appeared almost justified. By July 5, both Social Credit and CCF had elected fourteen members; four days later, each had sixteen. It was the results of the third count that demonstrated conclusively that the one-time coalition partners had outsmarted themselves with the new form of balloting: Premier Johnson went down in defeat to his little-known CCF opponent in "impregnable" New Westminster; and in Oak Bay, the Tory bull would roar no longer—Herbert Anscomb was also declared a loser. A full month after election day, Social Credit had elected sixteen new MLAs and were leading in three ridings; the CCF had elected sixteen and were leading in two; the Liberals won six seats; the Conservatives had two and were leading in two others; and the independent had Fernie. The number of contests won by a margin of only a few dozen votes was astonishing and unprecedented. In the two-member constituency of Vancouver-Burrard, for example, the Socreds and the CCF played a close game of seesaw each time a new count was taken. Eric Martin was finally elected on the fifth count and his Social Credit running mate, Bert Price, also made it by a handful of votes. When the CCF requested a judicial recount, its application was tossed out of court on a technicality.

A few dozen well-placed votes could easily have changed the outcome of the election and the course of B.C. history. Nevertheless, nothing could have changed the electorate's flat rejection of the Liberals and Conservatives. The rebellion against the old-line parties was far more severe than was first realized. They were ruined, probably for all time in British Columbia. The CCF and the new Social Credit League presented themselves to the voters as "people's movements." Henceforth, political parties would be successful in the province only by demonstrating a broad-based populist appeal. The 1952 election was actually tailor-made for a decisive socialist victory, but the upstart Socreds had moved into place and frustrated it. The election clearly demonstrated how, by dramatically exploiting latent dissatisfaction with existing parties, a fresh new political force can crystallize a wide base of popular support almost overnight.

The final electoral count gave Social Credit nineteen seats (six short of a majority), the CCF eighteen, Liberals six, Conservatives four and one independent. The Socreds had forged their small plurality on the basis of strength in the interior mainland; they elected only three members in Vancouver and none on Vancouver Island. An amazing combination of factors had put Social Credit on top, including the decline of coalition, the assistance of Alberta Socreds and Bennett's great individual effort. But the vital and decisive factor that enabled the Socreds to snatch what now looked like victory from the jaws of the CCF was the single transferable ballot. In that sense, at least, the new form of balloting served its purpose. Ironically, the Socreds had cause to celebrate because they were a popular second choice. Perhaps because they were not considered a serious contender, and perhaps in a kind of sympathy vote, Liberals, Conservatives and CCFers placed a "2" beside Social Credit candidates more often than not. Antipathies, jealousies and ancient fears all played a part in the apparent strategies of B.C. voters. The Socreds were new and therefore the least-hated alternative for supporters of the older parties. Even CCF voters, ignoring their leader's direction to "plump," tended to choose Social Credit as their favourite second choice. As one student of the era has remarked, "It was abundantly clear that a large number of socialist supporters did not see Social Credit in the Marxist light of Harold Winch." The net effect of the transfer of votes, as prescribed by the single transferable ballot, gave the Socreds an additional five seats, gave one to the CCF but denied them four others, gave one to the Tories, and took three away from the Grits.

The pattern repeated in various parts of the province is not difficult to understand. The northern riding of Omineca stands as a useful illustration of the way the single transferable ballot worked. On the first ballot, Cyril Shelford was leading his nearest opponent, a Liberal, by a mere thirty-eight votes. But he had nowhere near 50 per cent of the votes cast. On the second count, the Tory candidate's second choices were distributed and the largest proportion went to the Liberal, placing him now sixty-nine votes ahead of Shelford, but still shy of an overall majority. On the third count, eliminating the CCF candidate, his second choices overwhelmingly favoured Social Credit, giving Shelford the necessary plurality. In this case, the Liberals and Conservatives seemed to be giving each other their second choices, but CCF voters were giving theirs to Social Credit instead of the old coalition parities. Thus, the CCF helped to send young Cyril Shelford and Social Credit to Victoria.

The question that had somewhat focussed the politics of protest—hospital insurance—was widely cited as the most important single issue contributing to the humiliating defeat of the two old parties. By July 11, 1952, although the final outcome of the election was still in doubt, Premier Johnson was willing to face the fact that he and the Liberals were ruined. In his last official news conference he announced, to the bewilderment of many, that BCHIS had a "surprise surplus" of over $3 million. A press release from his office stated: "The Premier, in making the announcement, said that he thought it was only fit and proper that he do so before his departure from office in order that the people should know the success of the policies laid down in connection with the Hospital Insurance Service." It was generally assumed that the surplus had only been discovered since the election. But the beleaguered BCHIS commissioner, Lloyd Detwiller, could only shake his head in silence. Years later, he reminisced: "Boss Johnson was saying, 'You see, I was right.' And the cartoon that I'll never forget was one that showed a stage with a magician pulling the rabbit out of the hat—and the rabbit was BCHIS with a $3-million surplus tag on him. [Johnson] was dressed in a magician's clothes and there was the audience, but the seats were all empty. The caption was, 'Boss, it was a wonderful trick. Why didn't you pull it off while the audience was still there?' And that tells the whole story."

Under normal conditions, the Liberal government would have been easily re-elected. The B.C. economy was beginning to boom. The provincial budget was up 15 per cent over the previous year. West coast wages were the highest in Canada and unemployment seemed all but stamped out. Yet, the voters were sadly disillusioned with the bickering and cynical brand of politics practised by the former coalition parties. Some were downright angry. As one woman voter told a reporter, "I didn't know anything about Social Credit before the campaign, and I still don't. But I wanted to give a slap in the nose to the government."

Uncertainty still lingered over who would form the next administration. Rumours began to circulate about the possibility of a new coalition—after all, no party alone could command a majority in the legislature. One such rumour suggested the Liberals were willing to coalesce with the CCF. Meanwhile, the Socreds, who had declared they were above dealing with anyone for power, were still leaderless. But when the final electoral count was in, a Social Credit leadership convention was called for July 15 at the Hotel Vancouver.

The convention took on great importance now because the new leader would in all likelihood become the next premier of British Columbia. W.A.C. Bennett was the obvious front-runner in the group of Socred MLAs-elect who, according to the decision of the April convention, would choose a leader from among themselves. As the day of the convention approached, a stop-Bennett lobby was attempting to subvert the earlier decision. Worley wrote to Bennett just before the meeting: "It appears that the defeated candidates are trying to procure a vote in the leadership decision. This I think is utterly out of order in view of the fact that such action would be contrary to the resolution passed at the April convention. . . . There are so many inexperienced and some most unintelligent persons in the organization. . . . You will have to use a firm hand to stop the Social Credit from falling into the same ways as the old line parties." It seems that the pressure to stop Bennett originated from Alberta, and that, incredibly, the good Reverend Hansell, a nonresident of the province and a federal MP from an Alberta riding, fancied the idea of becoming premier of British Columbia. Alberta organizer Orvis Kennedy would admit as much: "I think perhaps Hansell had an idea they might choose him."

But the stop-Bennett movement was too late; in fact, the Alberta influence on the B.C. Social Credit League was clearly diminishing. When all of the successful and some of the unsuccessful Socred candidates gathered in a large salon of the Hotel Vancouver, they were on the verge of surrendering their future to one man's fate. The meeting behind closed doors began with a quavering rendition of "O Canada"; no religious hymns attended this very special occasion which would formalize the secularization of Social Credit in British Columbia. President Lyle Wicks, who convened the meeting, quickly established that only the elected MLAs would be entitled to vote for the purpose of selecting a leader. This was opposed by the old-timers who could see that power was passing from them to W.A.C. Bennett, the new force, not yet considered by many to be a Social Crediter but obviously the only giant among them.

The meeting got off to a slow start because of procedural difficulties. It was confirmed that unsuccessful candidates could not vote for the new political leader, but in a conciliatory though impractical move, it was agreed that unsuccessful candidates could be nominated for the position. Lyle Wicks announced that he would not allow his name to be nominated. Eric Martin and a few others were nominated but withdrew. J.A. Reid, a logger and successful candidate from Salmon Arm, allowed his name to stand; so did Thomas Irwin, the pro-Alberta MLA-elect from Delta; Rev. Philip Gaglardi had been elected in Kamloops and was certainly not too shy to let his name stand; W.A.C. Bennett was nominated by Eric Martin; and Peer Paynter, who despite several efforts could never secure the confidence of voters, became the only nonelected leadership aspirant. Before the voting took place, it was agreed that the winner would require 50 per cent plus one vote, but scrutineer Claude Powell needed only a few minutes to count the votes and announce W.A.C. Bennett the winner on the first ballot. Once the count was made known the ballots were destroyed; because of a later controversy arising from the ramblings of Phil Gaglardi, who claimed he lost by a single vote, it was revealed then that of the nineteen ballots cast, Bennett received fourteen, Paynter two, Irwin one, Reid one and Gaglardi one.

At long last, the moment was Bennett's—and now it looked like the future was his as well. Eric Martin described the occasion:

> Bennett moved up to the side of the green cloth table and it was a dramatic moment. I'll never forget it. Here we were putting in as leader a man who had been a member of the movement only a few months; a man who'd had a very chequered career in the legislature, had been a thorn in the side of the coalition government for its entire ten years, had run twice against Anscomb for the leadership of the Conservative Party. . . . We were placing our entire future in the hands of this man. He stood there before us, very compact looking and neat, always well turned out and always in dark clothing. And he could hardly speak. He had the greatest difficulty in commencing to talk. Well, he dealt with each of the issues and had other matters to speak of and he dealt with those in a manner entirely satisfactory to every one of us. He was very proper in his manner, in what he said. But on two occasions he almost

broke down. I knew what was going on in his mind. He had lived for this. Ever since he was a small boy he was going to be the big shot in some political puddle. And there he was within a short step of reaching the premiership of the province, and I think that on these two occasions the thought caught up with him. Finally he concluded his remarks and I'm quite sure if you took out a knife you could have cut a square out of the air it was so thick. . . . Apart from being born, I suppose it was the outstanding event of my life—certainly the most dramatic.

After Bennett concluded his remarks, he wanted a chance to acquaint himself with what would become the first-ever B.C. Social Credit legislative caucus. Reminding his listeners of the press and crowds outside, he said the meeting would appear too cut and dried if they announced the outcome so quickly; he asked all elected members to speak. This was to help him in choosing his cabinet. Outside, the press thought that a great fight was going on inside. Finally, the meeting was adjourned and the media were given a conference with the new Social Credit leader—presumably the premier-elect. Bennett handled the press with confidence and ease, impressing his colleagues with his ability to switch gears and perform under pressure. After some initial baiting and badgering by the reporters, he stated that "Social Credit is the opposite of funny money; it is just common sense. . . . Our main policy is to bring stability and confidence to British Columbia. With God's help, we will do our best." The new Socred chief was acting as though he were already in charge of the province. When pressed further, he concluded the news conference, "Go easy on the monetary stuff. Remember, it doesn't concern us now. The main problem is to bring confidence throughout the province—the press can help a lot in that."

As Bennett now waited for the final electoral formalities to be completed, he faced a daunting task: moulding a cabinet from the ranks of elected Socred members. They were a sincere but inexperienced and motley crew: railway workers, garage mechanics, restaurant owners, bus drivers, teachers, farmers, loggers and clergymen—not much administrative depth from which to form a government. But in the very best of democratic traditions, these elected representatives were *the people*. Aside from Bennett, Tilly Rolston was the only other elected Socred with legislative experience, and he was determined to fulfill an earlier promise by making her British Columbia's first female cabinet minister. He also wanted to make a cabinet minister out of his staunch supporter Eric Martin. The day after the leadership contest he asked Martin to be the new minister of health and welfare. "I automatically accepted," said Martin, "and I was on cloud nine as I walked away. Then suddenly I realized that this included hospital insurance."

During the last two weeks of July, Bennett worked intensely. He appeared to stand apart from the great whirl of circumstance that had thrown the door to the province's future wide open. If he was to have control over events and his own destiny, then it was best that he isolate himself from the schemes and rumours filling political conversation and newspaper gossip. The situation was extremely unsettled and talk of some new form of coalition still abounded. Boss Johnson had not yet formally tendered his resignation; constitutionally, he was still adviser to the lieutenant governor and therefore responsible for recommending a course of action. Earlier, he had indicated his intention to recommend that the largest group in the House form the government; but to some, the word "group" connoted any possible combination of members. The CCF had pooh-poohed the idea of joining forces with the Liberals, who now had a Social Credit leader to negotiate with. Immediately after the convention, Bennett received a confidential handwritten letter from Liberal Attorney General Gordon Wismer congratulating him on the Socreds' dynamic campaign and his selection as leader. Said Wismer, "If I can give you any information or advice as the result of my long experience, I shall be only too pleased to do so." Shortly thereafter, Bennett was contacted by prominent Liberals urging him to invite Wismer to retain the attorney generalship in the event that Social Credit formed the new government, but Bennett flatly rejected the proposal, not wanting anything to do with old-style politics or old-line politicians: the people had spoken. And, naturally, he had ideas of his own.

Bennett often said that for a government to be successful, it requires a strong premier, a capable attorney general and a good minister of finance. What was he to do in 1952 about these two key cabinet portfolios? Among elected Socreds there was not a single lawyer, nor was there an experienced financial person. Because Bennett believed the success of a Social Credit minority government would depend upon these important cabinet cornerstones, he decided on an unorthodox and daring course of action. Without confiding in any of his colleagues, he decided to draft two potential ministers from outside the ranks of the Social Credit movement and even outside the ranks of elected MLAs.

The morning after Bennett had been made Social Credit leader, Robert Bonner was on his way to work at the courthouse adjacent to the Hotel Vancouver. The young lawyer, who had earlier backed Bennett as a Tory leadership candidate, decided to stop by the hotel to offer his congratulations. Bonner recounted what took place: "I picked up the house phone to see if he was in, just to wish him well. And when he heard my voice on the phone, he said, 'You're just the man I want to see; come right up.' So I went up and he said, 'I want you to become attorney general.' I was quite astonished and I said I'd give it some thought." Why Bonner? Bennett felt it was absolutely necessary to have a lawyer for the attorney generalship, but his options were limited. There was not a Socred lawyer in sight who was suited for the responsibility. Bonner was a noted Conservative; he had spoken on behalf of a Tory candidate during the election campaign. But he was young, too young to be considered an establishment figure. Best of all, he had shown support and loyalty for Bennett in battles long past.

Bennett was a very shrewd psychologist and said to Bonner: "You know, I'm a Conservative, I'm from the Conservative Party. It's very simple—you just go from A to B and never look back." Bennett was obviously not too bothered about past political affiliations. Bonner did not require much time to make a decision, for the government of the day was shattered and dispersed. He consulted with his father who thought it was a good idea and claimed that the Conservatives and Liberals were finished in the province for thirty or forty years. Bonner said he would accept.

For the important portfolio of finance, Bennett had long considered a trusted favourite, Einar Gunderson, whom he had known as a young man in Edmonton and who had served as a tax consultant to the Alberta government prior to the Aberhart era. He had since moved to British Columbia where he was now a partner in one of the province's largest and most respected firms of chartered accountants. Gunderson handled the account of Bennett's small hardware empire and, over the years, had spent many long hours discussing with him the potential for economic growth and development in B.C. When in Vancouver, Bennett would sometimes accept Gunderson's invitation to lunch at the exclusive Vancouver Club, on which occasions some businessmen and scions of the west coast establishment would shun their table, acting as though Gunderson had contracted a rare disease. The two men were friends and Gunderson may have been the only person in the province to whom Bennett would defer on matters of finance and economics.

Gunderson was a supporter of the Liberal Party, but Bennett assured him this would pose no problem—for Bennett, there was no deed greater than converting from an old-line party. Gunderson had other hesitations, especially about the technicalities of becoming finance minister and who his colleagues would be. When he asked, "Who have you got for attorney general?" Bennett said, "I'll tell you what we'll do. We'll meet you in Manning Park for dinner, and I'll introduce you to the fellow I want to be attorney general."

The secret meeting at Pinewoods Lodge in Manning Park, halfway between Vancouver and Kelowna, was an important event. Neither Bonner nor Gunderson knew that the other was going to be there and they were amazed to see each other. They were acquainted, for they worked in the same office building in Vancouver, though they were not personal friends. Over dinner, Bennett told them the direction he wanted to take in government and why he wanted them to be ministers. Gunderson had done some soul-searching before this special meeting and he had asked a few of his leading corporate clients in confidence for their opinion of such a move. Their reactions had been enthusiastically in favour of Gunderson accepting the offer and giving the untried, untrained Socreds some solid financial expertise and respectability. He was still apprehensive about Social Credit and its reputation for far-out doctrine and practices. Bennett, as usual, was prepared to engage in a little salesmanship. He pulled out a piece of paper and handed it to his old friend, explaining that it outlined the four aims of Social Credit: (1) The individual is the most important factor in organized society; (2) The major function of democratic government is to give the people the results they want in the management of their affairs; (3) The individual must be guaranteed economic security without the sacrifice of his personal freedom; (4) That which is physically possible, and desirable, and morally right can and should be made financially possible. Neither Gunderson nor Bonner could disagree with these philosophical simplicities, and a pact was made. Bennett would greatly depend on both these men in the months and years ahead. Their private dinner that evening represented the first-ever cabinet meeting of the imminent Social Credit government. They spent the rest of the evening discussing the problems that faced them: Bennett assured his new colleagues that when the time arrived, he would take care of the fact that neither of them held seats in the legislature.

All of these discussions and audacious machinations were carried on in the strictest privacy. In years to come, Bennett was often criticized for an excessive fascination with secrecy and manipulation. Power, of course, holds it own fascination, and Bennett wanted it on his own terms. He had taken great pains to work out a plan of action that he felt was next to foolproof. As he headed into the last days of July 1952, his enormous problem, selecting a credible cabinet, required complete confidentiality, for he had to keep his options open until the last moment. He was always a practical politician and his bold moves were precisely calculated, but on this occasion the man was much more than simply a politician—he was a genius. If word had leaked out about his arrangements with Bonner and Gunderson, Social Crediters would have been outraged. All the old fears about Bennett taking over the Social Credit League for his own purposes would seem justified. An internal revolt against his leadership would have been impossible to contain and the chances of the Socreds being called upon to form a government probably destroyed. But Bennett kept his cards close to his chest and at the end of July put the final stages of his plan into effect. He sent his cabinet nominees confidential telegrams instructing them to come to Victoria, call him at his room in the Empress Hotel but not to stay at the hotel themselves, and on no account to tell anyone of their visit to Victoria.

Bennett wanted to ensure that all was ready for a bloodless coup.

Stationing himself in a suite at the Empress, he prepared to accelerate the pace of events. One by one, his nominees for cabinet filtered into Victoria; some of them had never before visited the capital and many had difficulty getting there. Lyle Wicks had to borrow $100 from the bank, which he found easier to do now that he was an MLA. Few of them could afford hotel-living, but their leader did not intend any of them to stay there long. He called each of his proposed ministers to his suite individually, told them which portfolio he had in mind for them and instructed: "Under no circumstances make yourself conspicuous, and don't talk to anyone, not even other Social Crediters, until I contact you again." So, for a couple of warm summer days a strange dance was performed around Victoria's inner harbour. Wicks passed Martin, Martin strolled by Black, Socred encountered Socred without a tip of the hat or a hint of recognition.

What was Bennett waiting for? Lieutenant Governor Clarence Wallace must ask him to form a government. A wealthy shipbuilder by calling, Wallace's forte was not statecraft nor constitutional law—he was having trouble making the weighty decision of whom to call on. He was also the recipient of conflicting advice. When he went east and asked Prime Minister St. Laurent for an opinion, he was curtly told he was on his own. B.C.'s chief justice, Gordon Sloan, recommended to Wallace that he *not* call on Bennett; apparently he advised: "If you let those Socreds in there, you'll never get them out." Harold Winch visited Wallace a few times and argued forcefully that the CCF should be asked to form an administration. Winch was of the view that the lieutenant governor had a constitutional responsibility to give the socialists a chance. He pointed out that although the CCF had one less seat than Social Credit, his members were experienced legislators and therefore capable of handling a minority government position. He also pointed to the final election results which showed the CCF with a bigger percentage of the popular vote. When Wallace remonstrated that he was nevertheless one seat short, Winch argued that Tom Uphill, the re-elected independent-labour member, would be inclined to support a socialist government. But Wallace remained noncommittal; in truth, he was confused. Never before in British Columbia's history, and only rarely in modern parliamentary democracy, has a representative of the crown been obliged to make such an important decision.

Bennett, nonetheless, was confident, for it was in his character to be so. He ignored all the plotting and political gossip circulating through Victoria in this hot summer of 1952. For the cabinet apparent, the few days in the capital must have seemed like months, but they followed Bennett's instructions, and the wait would be worth their while. Rev. Phil Gaglardi, one of his prospects for the executive team, has said: "There was an awful lot of gandy-dancing and a lot of sparring at that time; W. A. C. Bennett's greatest feat was his ability to convince the lieutenant governor to swear us in as government. Even a greater accomplishment than the election was to get to be government, and he engineered that on his own."

On Friday, August 1, Bennett met Tilly Rolston for breakfast in the coffee shop of the Empress Hotel, having told the press that they would be there. Sure enough, their morning meal was interrupted by inquiries about why they were in town at this time of year. Was Social Credit going to form the next government? Bennett just smiled and said it was a nice time of year to visit. The afternoon newspapers reported on the curious number of MLAs "on holiday" in the capital, which had the effect that Bennett planned. Boss Johnson offered his resignation to the lieutenant governor. Wallace refused to accept it, but he did phone Bennett, saying, "I just want to talk to you, Mr. Bennett. I'm going on the midnight boat tonight to Vancouver and on to the interior, and I want to talk to you before I leave. Can you see me at four o'clock?" Bennett replied, "Yes, because there are some things I'd like to talk to you about as well, Lieutenant Governor." Then Bennett called in Ron Worley—he needed an obedient assistant to carry out small details and matters of protocol—who arrived at Bennett's suite and was introduced to Bonner for the first time.

Bennett told Worley, "You're my executive assistant."

"I'm honoured," he answered, "but I've never been an executive assistant."

"That's fine, Ronald, my boy, I've never been a premier."

Bennett gave his executive assistant his first official chore, sending him over to the Parliament Buildings to obtain from the deputy provincial secretary the blank forms necessary for swearing in a new cabinet. When he returned with them, as Worley recounted, he was given his next task: "I want you to put these names to the portfolios," said Bennett. He handed him the list. "Whatever you do, this is top secret; don't let anyone see it. Guard it with your life, and make three copies."

Robert Bonner closed the door behind him, but quickly opened it again and said, "You'd better bring the carbon paper with you!"

Bennett arrived at Government House to see Lieutenant Governor Wallace at precisely four o'clock. He came well prepared, in a sense having readied himself for this meeting his whole life. When Wallace told him that he had refused Boss Johnson's resignation and that a decision was still several days away, Bennett said, "This is a terrible situation, this lame-duck period. It's very bad for the province; there's chaos everywhere. Now the final votes have been counted, everybody knows where the parties stand in numbers. There must be quick action now, Your Honour. It must come now; it must come today."

"Oh, no. Not today. I've got to think things over."

Bennett replied, "Your Honour, this responsibility is yours, but I've a responsibility too, to the people who voted for me. Our party came from nowhere. Why? Because the people of British Columbia want us to be government. It's very clear and we must be called today."

"How can we call it today?"

"My prospective ministers are here, the forms are all ready. We can be sworn in in half an hour, and you can catch the midnight boat." Bennett went on, "I've been very quiet, but if we're not called today, I've a responsibility to the people of British Columbia. I'm not threatening, I'm just telling you—it's my duty then to tell the people of the province that this instability is not my fault, that I was ready."

Wallace was stubborn; he continued to protest, so Bennett brought out other ammunition. Earlier in the day he had been secretly informed by Boss Johnson's executive assistant, Percy Richards, that the Liberal premier had recommended the Socreds be called to form a government. Bennett, therefore, fired his next volley at Wallace: "Your Honour, the Queen's representative can only have but one adviser at a time. Your adviser now is Premier Boss Johnson, and I have reason to believe that he has advised you to call on me. Therefore, you have no alternative."

The lieutenant governor still hesitated; he told Bennett that the CCF, with the support of Tom Uphill, had as many seats as the Socreds and, therefore, a decision simply required further consideration. With this opening, Bennett fired his final round. From an inside pocket he pulled out positive proof of the weakness of the CCF's position. Tom Uphill had written to Bennett several times during the election campaign and its aftermath; apparently, he hoped to become minister of mines if Social Credit did squeeze its way into power. Bennett showed the lieutenant governor one of these letters, a handwritten note on Legislative Assembly stationery, written when the final electoral outcome was not yet certain. Uphill offered Bennett the best of wishes and expressed the hope that the Socreds would form the government. He referred to Bennett as "the next Premier of this Province" and went on to say: "I am praying you will have the most Members when the final count is made, I sure hope you beat out the CCF in numbers."

So now, Bennett said, "Here's the letter. Is he an enemy of ours? Even he expected me to be called." This last shot seemed finally to shatter the lieutenant governor's resolve. He made no promises but concluded the meeting by telling Bennett he would call him within an hour.

Bennett returned to his hotel suite to wait for the call. There he found Bonner with the Victoria *Times* in his hands pacing the floor. The newspaper headline read, "The new government is not being called at the present time. Resignation of Johnson refused." Bonner was worried and said he would have to return to his Vancouver law office.

"Bob, you've studied a lot at the universities and you've been in the Conservative Party and been studying law. You've got a very keen mind. But this is your first practical lesson in politics—don't believe the press. Things are not always as they seem. Sometimes they are the exact opposite."

Bonner asked, "Were you called to be premier?"

"No," Bennett said, "but before this night is over you will be attorney general of this province. Don't go far away. That phone will ring."

Within forty-five minutes of Bennett's leaving Government House, the telephone rang. It was Wallace. Bennett assured the lieutenant governor he could have his cabinet assembled and delivered for nine o'clock. Bonner was as excited and incredulous as Bennett was cool and calm. The Social Credit leader contacted Worley, gave him a list of names and phone numbers and told him to gather the soon-to-be ministers in his suite.

In the meantime, poor Clarence Wallace now had another problem on his hands. He called Chief Justice Gordon Sloan to tell him the news and invite him, as required, to the swearing-in, but Sloan said he would not attend. That night when Wallace and his wife sat down to dinner, he could not eat for fretting that Sloan would not come. "I was so damned worried... I couldn't even take a drink," Wallace said. Halfway through dinner, the butler announced that the chief justice was on the phone. Sloan had reconsidered; he and his wife would come to the ceremony. Relieved, Wallace "had a couple of good slugs and ate a real dinner."

Back at Bennett's suite in the Empress Hotel, members of the future Social Credit cabinet were nervously mingling. The excitement was tremendous and the prospective ministers were behaving like schoolboys, asking each other: "What portfolio are you getting? What are you getting?" Most of them knew each other, but Bennett had to introduce Bonner and Gunderson to their new colleagues, some of whom were surprised and bewildered at meeting two nonelected cabinet ministers. But all questions were laid aside for the present. Bennett invited the press into the suite for a hastily called news conference before he and his team departed for Government House. Taxis deposited them at precisely nine o'clock and, awestruck by the occasion, most of them walked slowly into the stately green-draped drawing room where the ceremony was conducted. W.A.C. Bennett was sworn in as premier and president of the Executive Council. The executive members were then sworn in as follows:

Wesley Black, provincial secretary and minister of municipal affairs
Robert Bonner, attorney general
Robert Sommers, minister of lands and forests; mines
Einar Gunderson, minister of finance
Kenneth Kiernan, minister of agriculture

Rev. Philip Gaglardi, minister of public works
Ralph Chetwynd, minister of railways; trade and industry; fisheries
Lyle Wicks, minister of labour
Eric Martin, minister of health and welfare
Tilly Rolston, minister of education

This was an emotional moment for Bennett. During the ceremony, as he watched his ministers take their oaths of office, he was choking back tears. Afterwards, he spoke briefly to the press: "It will be the policy of our government to give fair treatment to all and special privileges to none. . . . In this task I ask the support of all citizens of British Columbia. I want to make it clear that our government will not be a government of the right or of the left. A Social Credit government will be a middle-of-the-road government." He then thanked the lieutenant governor and shared a few kind words with Chief Justice Sloan. Many years before, Sloan had attended a similar ceremony in which he was sworn in as attorney general at the young age of thirty-four. The chief justice now offered his congratulations to Robert Bonner who, at thirty-two, was the youngest attorney general ever. Following a brief reception and skirmish with news hounds, the new government retreated to Bennett's hotel suite for refreshments. The waiter took orders for martinis and scotch and sodas, but when it was Bennett's turn, he said, "Anybody can drink what they like tonight — as long as it's tea, coffee or Ovaltine." They all complied, becoming the first government ever to be sworn in on Ovaltine.

Bennett's assault on British Columbia's fortress of power had finally succeeded. For a long time — to him it must have seemed an eternity — he had been preparing for this moment; now he had arrived. According to some commentators, Bennett was simply the right man, in the right place, at the right time — the last accident in a series. But this ignores his integral role in the events that culminated in the evening of August 1, 1952, when he became the twenty-fourth premier. Indeed, his career up to this point is a persuasive argument in favour of the role of the individual in history. Anyone wanting to understand Bennett or the nature of his obsession need only study the methods by which he attained power. At a time when doubt was thick in the air, Bennett was certain, his vision fixed on a single goal. He subsequently said: "There was never any doubt in my mind. I was sure when I walked across the floor of the legislature that I was going to be premier. Once I joined Social Credit, I was sure." Of course, he was always sure. Pit a man of this tremendous "sureness," relentless will, organizational genius and sympathetic understanding of the needs and wants of ordinary people, and the chances are that he will be called to power.

CHAPTER
SIX
AN EXPERIMENT IN DEMOCRACY

*Democracy is based upon the conviction that there are
extraordinary possibilities in ordinary people.*
Harry Emerson Fosdick

*If you have embraced a creed which appears to be free
from the ordinary dirtiness of politics . . .
surely that proves that you are in the right?
And the more you are in the right,
the more natural that everyone else
should be bullied into thinking likewise.*
George Orwell

One wonders if members of British Columbia's first-ever Social Credit cabinet managed to sleep on the night of Friday, August 1, 1952, after being sworn into office. W.A.C. Bennett claimed to have slept the sweet sleep of a babe, such was his temperament—or the effect of Ovaltine. At any rate, the following morning after an early breakfast, they met in the premier's hotel suite where each was greeted formally, "Good morning, Mr. Minister." Bennett addressed even his longtime friend Tilly Rolston as "Madam Minister." Once assembled, the eleven cabinet colleagues marched in twos and threes up the scenic walkway to the Parliament Buildings and into the premier's office where Bennett quickly dismissed the press corps: "I have enjoyed seeing you and I think highly of newsmen and am looking forward to a long and friendly association with you all in the legislative press gallery." Then, in the premier's chair, behind the premier's desk, he spoke to his cabinet: "Now you will be shown to your offices and introduced to your staff. I want you to study your departments so that you know more about your departments than your deputy ministers do, because you'll have to make the decisions. I don't want you ever blaming your deputy ministers or staff, because I'm going to hold you responsible, and the people of the province are going to hold you responsible, for the operation of your department. . . . You learn to operate your departments within announced government policy. If you run into problems, you make your decisions and come to me with solutions. But don't bring trivial matters to me." The premier's executive assistant, Ron Worley, then showed the new ministers to their offices.

Who were these virgin members of the B.C. Executive Council? Virtually unknown to their fellow citizens, they were the "new men" of west coast politics who had stumbled into the most important and powerful offices in the province. It is worth taking a closer look at them.

Hon. Tilly Jean Rolston was sixty-five years old, a grandmother of nine, and a staunch believer in W.A.C. Bennett. She had taught school for two years before her marriage and now, in becoming minister of education, was Canada's first female cabinet minister with portfolio. Elected to the legislature in 1941, she was the only Socred other than Bennett to have sat in the House. One of her few successes during those years was winning the battle to legalize coloured margarine in B.C. In the cabinet, only Bennett knew that she was dying of cancer.

Hon. Eric Charles Fitzgerald Martin, forty-six, was born in Winnipeg but came to British Columbia at an early age. He received a private education in England and in Victoria, where he ranked consistently at the bottom of his class. Martin rode the rails during the depths of the Depression before taking a job with a South American construction firm. His adventures in South America included a two-year stint in Chile during a time of chaos and rebellion; he became actively involved in a popular uprising against the government in Santiago which was eventually overthrown. Upon returning to British Columbia, he embraced Social Credit and briefly served as a sergeant-instructor in the Canadian Army during the Second World War. In 1945 he was the ringleader of a gang of rebel war veterans who occupied the Hotel Vancouver and converted it into a hostel. Prior to 1952, Martin had run unsuccessfully as a Socred candidate in provincial and federal campaigns, and in 1951 he became the first Social Crediter to actively court and encourage W.A.C. Bennett. Before becoming minister of health and welfare, Martin was employed as a junior accountant in a Vancouver firm. A feisty pepperpot of a man, he would soon earn a new nickname from his cabinet colleagues—"Crisis Martin."

Hon. Lyle Wicks, thirty-nine, longtime president of the British Columbia Social Credit League, was the new minister of labour—perhaps by virtue of his being a Vancouver streetcar conductor and bus driver and therefore a trade union member. Wicks had visited the legislature only once before, in 1929 when he was a member of a church parliamentary group for boys.

Hon. William Kenneth Kiernan, thirty-six, was born in Alberta's Peace River country and had settled in Chilliwack where he owned and operated a service station. The new agriculture minister was a quiet-spoken, sincere and methodical man who belied the stories circulating about "wild-eyed" Social Crediters.

Hon. Wesley Drewett Black, forty-one, was the new provincial secretary and minister of municipal affairs. Born and educated in Vancouver, he had worked in logging camps, shipyards and on road crews before graduating from the University of British Columbia and becoming a teacher; he had attained the rank of vice-principal at Creston Elementary School in the Kootenays.

Hon. Robert Edward Sommers, forty-one, was born in Alberta of German immigrant stock. A schoolteacher by profession, he had taught in B.C.'s Peace River district before moving to Castlegar where he was an elementary school principal. Sommers spent his holidays working for the B.C. Forest Service in charge of fire suppression crews, his only obvious qualification for his dual post, minister of lands and forests and of mines. His hobbies included playing the trumpet and gambling.

Hon. William Ralph Talbot Chetwynd, sixty-two, the son of an English baronet, had emigrated to Canada in his teens and became involved in a variety of adventures in the province's Cariboo country. He had worked as a public relations officer for the PGE railway and, later, as a self-employed rancher. Bennett gave him the multiple cabinet portfolio of railways, trade and industry, and fisheries. Chetwynd had co-authored a novel, *Heifer Dust Inn*, published in 1951, which had as its lead character a provincial cabinet minister whose experiences at a Cariboo roadside inn enlightened him on the "real" problems of British Columbia. The novel is a morality tale about communism versus capitalism and, in a sense, anticipated the rise of Social Credit in B.C. W.A.C. Bennett claimed never to have heard of the book and speculated that perhaps Chetwynd, the only novelist to become a Social Credit cabinet minister, was too embarrassed to bring it to his attention.

Hon. the Reverend Philip Arthur Gaglardi, thirty-nine, the new minister of public works, was one of eleven children born to poor Italian immigrants who had settled at Mission in the Fraser Valley. An elder sister's efforts helped to convert the entire Catholic family to the Pentecostal faith; Gaglardi married his local pastor and pursued an intense missionizing career. Settling in Kamloops, he and his wife served as pastors of the Calvary Temple and spread the word of their God through their distinctive brand of radio and eventually television evangelism.

Hon. Einar Maynard Gunderson, fifty-three, Bennett's old friend, was born in North Dakota of Norwegian parentage and as a boy moved to Saskatchewan where he received his education. In Edmonton in the early 1920s he met young Cecil Bennett on the tennis courts and, though not close friends, the two men kept in touch. Gunderson joined the audit department of the Alberta government in 1928 where he helped to set up the provincial taxation system. He fled from the civil service in 1935 when Aberhart's Socreds came to power, and went into private practice in Edmonton as a chartered accountant, eventually becoming comptroller of Marshall-Wells's Canadian companies. At the conclusion of the Second World War, he settled in Vancouver and became a partner in the largest local accounting firm, Gunderson, Stokes, Peers, Walton & Company, which, coincidentally, looked after the accounts of Bennett's hardware firms. Described by one of his new Socred colleagues as "a teddy-bear type of man," Gunderson was actually very distinguished looking with his silver-white hair and cultured manner; as a young man he seriously considered a career as an opera singer. A Liberal by conviction, he was different from his Social Credit partners. Clearly, he was the new minister of finance because Bennett had talked him into the job.

Last, but by no means least was Hon. Robert William Bonner, thirty-two, the youngest and perhaps brightest member of the new government. Formerly a Conservative supporter of Bennett, he now became the premier's closest confidant. Born and educated in Vancouver, Bonner graduated from the University of British Columbia in 1942 in economics and political science. Serving in the war with great distinction in the Seaforth Highlanders, he became the first officer wounded during the invasion of Italy. After returning from overseas, he was a charter student at UBC's new law school and graduated in 1948; between Tory politics and articling he did not gain much in the way of practical legal experience before becoming B.C.'s chief law officer in 1952. In his later years, Bonner was always regarded as a brilliant legal thinker, which is ironic for his ability lay more in administration and organization than in law. In 1952 he was obviously one of the brightest young Tories on the west coast and his decision to accept Bennett's invitation helped to sound the death knell of British Columbia Conservatism. Shortly after becoming the new Social Credit attorney general, he was asked to address a meeting of the Canadian Bar Association in Vancouver, attended by another Tory lawyer, John Diefenbaker, who said to Bonner, "Nothing since Saul was on the way to Damascus has ever equalled such an instantaneous change of viewpoint." Bonner laughed and said, "If you can tell me how a person could become a Queen's counsel and attorney general any faster way, it's your move!"

In many ways this was the most interesting and diverse group yet to serve as Executive Council of B.C. They represented a new people's party with no past obligations, no political debts to a hulking party machine—only a straight commitment to public service. Compared with other provincial cabinets, they were inexperienced, nonprofessional, idealistic and naive— refreshing qualities for politicians. Their election represented an exciting experiment in democracy, one of those historic convulsions which all too rarely serve to redistribute the coalition of established political forces.

If the government was formed by an almost entirely new party, it was moulded and directed by a not entirely new man. For most British Columbians, Bennett was a fresh leader emerging from the husk of an ordinary politician; but he had been training and preparing for leadership all his life. His first priority after assuming office was to sort out his personal, family and business affairs. On the evening the new government was sworn in, a newspaper reporter called Mrs. Bennett in Kelowna: "How does it feel to be the wife of our new premier?" She replied: "I didn't know I was, thank you for letting me know! I was beginning to wonder if it ever would happen. Now we're all proud of him. He's been so busy lately, I've hardly had a chance to catch up on all his activities."

Attaining the premiership forced Bennett to sacrifice his first love, business. If he was not quite a millionaire at the time, he certainly owned a flourishing business in his chain of five hardware stores. He phoned his family in Kelowna and told his sons R.J. and Bill, who were working in the stores, "I've got a new job. Now you're in complete control. . . . You'll make mistakes; I don't want to hear about them, only your victories. I trust you." When they asked if they could take their problems to him, he said, "No, I've got a thousand problems down here compared to yours. You handle your own."

W.A.C. Bennett and his wife considered moving their home to Victoria, but decided to keep their lovely house in the Okanagan and rent a modest but comfortable waterfront apartment in Oak Bay for their Victoria headquarters. This was not because Bennett thought his stay in the capital would be short, rather it emphasized that his home would always be in Kelowna, in the province's hinterland—or, as he preferred to call it, "the heartland." At the first formal state banquet, where Lieutenant Governor Clarence Wallace learned that May Bennett was still in her apartment, he said: "Mrs. Bennett, you're going to be here for twenty years, so you might as well get properly prepared for it."

Bennett, an optimist and idealist, was never known to suffer from what Winston Churchill once referred to as "the black dog of depression," but during the first months of the new Social Credit government the number and variety of problems he tackled and the hectic pace he set for himself and his colleagues was unbelievably gruelling. He worked compulsively and, although his colleagues never knew it, for the first six months he was afflicted with a constant, painful migraine headache. There was labour unrest throughout the province and the hospital insurance plan was in chaos; on the whole, it was not an easy time to come to power. The CCF, Liberals and Conservatives demanded that the premier call the legislature into session to deal with the problems of the day, but he explained that he and his ministers needed time to study their departments, prepare legislation and rework government spending estimates. Critics cried that the Socreds were afraid to meet parliament; however, Bennett was in no hurry to subject his green minority administration to the rancorous opposition parties which were vastly more experienced in the legislative processes and therefore eager to get the Socreds in the House. The premier advised members of his cabinet to ignore the taunts being levelled at them and urged them, by his own example, to immerse themselves in the day-to-day operation of government.

From the start, Bennett directed his administration with the confidence of a veteran political satrap. He shunned all advice on how to handle his new position, though he undoubtedly took note of a memorandum prepared for him on the subject of his constitutional responsibilities in which one authority was quoted: the premier is "a sun around which the planets revolve." Certainly it proved to be an accurate description of Bennett's relationship with his cabinet. To an incredible degree, the making of policy was centralized in the person of the premier during those early months of power. Bennett assumed the two equally demanding roles of chief administrator and chief communicator for the new government, and yet his ministers were satisfied with his ability to delegate authority. He was tough on his cabinet but also knew how to flatter them and obtain solidarity and a special kind of loyalty. Bennett stated publicly that he was convinced he headed the best cabinet in Canada—and later confided that "they were a great team because they were all new and so they took advice well."

On August 6, 1952, the first formal Social Credit cabinet meeting was convened and from that point onwards the planets learned to revolve around their sun. Robert Bonner described the situation: "I think we all recognized our relative inexperience and the necessity for getting on top of the job quickly and for consolidating our position. If you have those fundamental recognitions, the notion that there should be for the most part a single spokesman is a very practical one. That was the course we adopted. The understanding that we reached rather freely and quickly was that we should restrain individual utterances in deference to the premier's position, who would be for all practical purposes the spokesman for the government for the first few months while everybody got his feet under the desk." Even so, it must have been exceedingly difficult for the novice ministers to keep up with their obsessed leader. At the end of the first week, the premier came bustling in to cabinet, took his chair at the head of the table, looked around and said, "My goodness, look at yourselves! You're grey, and your faces are lined. You're heavy with fatigue. You'll go under if you go on like this!" He advised them to get more rest and not to work so late; only now did he realize he was setting too fast a pace.

Despite the theory of collegiality in modern cabinet, W.A.C. Bennett took few of his ministers into his close confidence. Nevertheless, he inspired a happy but disciplined camaraderie which helped the cabinet to operate in an informal but efficient manner. A pattern was quickly established: cabinet was where decisions were made and policy was formulated; ministers brought solutions to cabinet meetings, not messy unresolved difficulties. However, consultation and much of the real problem-solving work of government took place between the premier and individual ministers prior to cabinet ratification and approval. The premier explained that his ministers had to conduct themselves in a manner befitting their office and that it was their prerogative and responsibility to be accountable for the actions of their office. Whereas civil servants were to give advice necessary for decision making, it was they who must make the decisions. The premier was fundamentally a manager and ran his Executive Council like the board of directors of a company.

Being green to government worked decidedly to the Socreds' advantage, both in terms of public perception and their ability to work together as a team. They were people who did not have too many notions of self-importance, and they found that government was a twenty-four-hour a day job, not an exercise for dilettantes. They had no executive assistants then. Ministers worked closely with their departments, answered their own mail, in some cases even answered their own telephones. They were not helped by the previous administration which had emptied their filing cabinets leaving no records to consult. They started from scratch.

One of the initial problems confronting the Social Credit administration was the establishment of a good working relationship with the provincial civil service. Bennett attempted to foster a friendly, family atmosphere in government-employee relations and presented himself as a kindly father figure. Although the executive of the British Columbia Government Employees' Association looked upon the Socred administration warily and would soon find itself in open disagreement, employee relations did not become a major issue during the early part of Bennett's premiership. Even though the bureaucracy was riddled with patronage appointments, he preferred to close his eyes to it in the hope of gaining the trust and co-operation of civil servants. When the apprehensive employees' association sent a group of representatives to ask where they stood with the new government, according to Bennett, he said, "These are fair questions. But before I answer them, will you tell me, in turn, how you were each appointed?" When they had all admitted they were appointed by political preferment, he said, "Now you're in, you want me to throw away the ladder." They were embarrassed, and he continued, "Certainly I'm going to throw away the ladder. And I expect you to be good citizens, but I don't expect you to be actively attacking the government when you work for us. We're in a period of adjustment, getting ready for a great period of development. There are going to be many opportunities in the civil service in our province. Nobody's going to be fired without real cause—not political cause—unless you're just completely stupid, which I'm sure you're not going to be."

From the perspective of current political practice, one could say that the most remarkable aspect of Social Credit's early impact in Victoria was that not a single deputy minister resigned or was fired. But Bennett made it plain that the deputies and the bureaucracy would not run the government; his ministers would. British Columbia had given birth to a different style of government. The new premier did his best to foster a reformist approach to governing. Shortly after assuming office, he pledged Social Credit to be an open government and promised no more secret orders-in-council. Describing orders-in-council as simply the minutes of cabinet meetings, he declared that all such minutes would now be public documents, and thereby further tarnished the already soiled image of the previous administration for what had been an accepted practice. One of Bennett's proudest accomplishments of this early exuberant period of power was his abolition of political patronage: "Patronage is the cancer that destroys the democratic system of government. The very first day, I phoned down to the purchasing agent and told him to destroy all the special lists that he had to buy supplies, and to let everybody tender. I phoned down to the Department of Public Works, 'Cancel all those preferred lists. Let everybody tender.' 'Everybody?' 'Yes everybody.' 'They might not be able to do the job.' 'You get the deposit; you have the holdback. Give them a chance. Everybody!' "

Of course, because Social Credit was new, the government was in a position to avoid the evils of party patronage. Few ministers had any political obligations and their support was in the street, not in the board rooms and yet not in the trade union halls either. This is not to suggest that Bennett had no problems with the B.C. Social Credit League. Almost immediately upon occupying the premier's office, he received a letter from a Vancouver Social Crediter protesting the appointment of non-Socreds like Bonner and Gunderson: "It is felt that persons receiving S.C. appointments, particularly important ones . . . should have been 100% Social Crediters." The letter also noted: "In this serious and critical view I am joined by no small number of S.C.s." But Bennett had anticipated adverse reaction and met the criticism head on, declaring that the political arm was not going to run the legislative or administrative arm. One can almost hear him repeating a favourite theme—*The elected must govern*—to a group of Socred lobbyists who travelled to Victoria demanding jobs and special considerations, for he had appointed his cabinet, including two nonelected non-Socreds, entirely in secret, taking the Social Credit League, as well as the province, completely by surprise.

Social Credit in British Columbia had now reached a new stage in its evolution: the 1952 election victory marked the end of the Social Credit "movement." Indeed, when a movement begins to attract individuals pursuing their own interests and careers it ceases to be a movement; when W.A.C. Bennett embraced Social Credit and took command, it became a "party" in the strictest political sense. Yet Bennett realized the vitality of the movement and attempted to preserve and enhance its grassroots base in order to keep his party growing. His signature on official correspondence now appeared over the title "Premier and Leader of the Social Credit Movement."

The saddest figures in the history of Social Credit in B.C. were the movement's founders, the intellectuals who had paved the way for a success they had not anticipated. Their ideals were now tossed aside in favour of practical democratic politics. Peer Paynter was one such casualty who, because of his opposition to Bennett, was said to have no political future. At the first party convention following the election Paynter contested the presidency of the Social Credit League but was easily defeated by John Perdue, believed to be backed by the premier. As time progressed, Bennett actually developed a healthy relationship with the League; he encouraged its growth and independence, promoted its interests, but would brook no interference in the development of policy or the operation of government. Symbolically, it is worth noting that 1952 also saw the death of Maj. C.H. Douglas in Britain. Thus, the ideological founder gave way to the pragmatic politician who defined Social Credit in his own idiosyncratic way. In this sense, and much more than was ever the case in Alberta, W.A.C. Bennett played Stalin to Major Douglas's Lenin.

The priorities of Bennett's early administration could not have encompassed all the initiatives promised by Social Credit candidates during the election campaign. Nevertheless, the premier had already fixed his sights on winning a legislative majority someday and knew this depended on an early show of strength, confidence and action. British Columbians could hardly have been disappointed, for after less than a month in office, the Socred administration was moving, said one west coast newspaper, "with a speed that is almost breath-taking." Clearly, Bennett's team was not performing in the meek manner of a minority government. The new administration's style can be seen in its handling of the controversial hospital insurance issue. Before the election, Bennett had pledged to abolish the B.C. Hospital Insurance Service's compulsory plan and to alter its much-reviled co-insurance feature. Now, his novice minister of health and welfare, Eric Martin, described by a Liberal critic as "a mild inoffensive man who was out of his depth in the hospital field," was forced to grasp this thorny problem. The premier wanted to make good his campaign promises, but his cabinet was split on the issue. Martin did not believe BCHIS could operate on a voluntary basis and he argued this position in cabinet. But the premier's point of view prevailed. A pattern was already emerging: when he decided to steer his government on a specific course, his ministers resigned themselves to the fact that the premier alone steered the ship of state.

Bennett cancelled all arrears and made participation in the hospital insurance plan voluntary so that nobody would ever again go to jail for not paying premiums. He rolled back BCHIS premiums, encouraged all British Columbians to take part in the plan, and retained co-insurance—but on a "dollar-a-day" basis. Almost magically, these innovations seemed to nullify the previous widespread protests against BCHIS, and economically they provided a great boost to a system that had been struggling under the expensive, time-consuming burden of enforcing premium collections. The changes, however, hardly improved the quality or lowered the costs of the hospital services provided. And with dollar-a-day co-insurance, patients requiring lengthy hospital stays could conceivably pay more than they would have under the former system which charged $3.50 for only the first ten days of hospitalization. But Bennett's changes proved to be politically astute and, besides, "dollar-a-day" was an agreeable slogan. The ex-hardware merchant had once more come up with an effective sales pitch, and the new hospital insurance plan was, on the whole, widely accepted.

Of course, one of Bennett's advantages in dealing with the hospital insurance issue was inheriting a system that was in surprisingly good financial shape. The previous administration's weakness was that it did not have a firm grip on provincial revenues, leaving itself open to political embarrassment. Bennett was determined to change all that, and perhaps his greatest innovation during this early period was his transformation of government revenue and expenditure policy. The 1952 budget had been the responsibility of the former government and Bennett had no intention of meeting the legislature to introduce a new one, so he continued to administer the Liberals' deficit budget—in his own special way.

He was convinced that the previous administration knew nothing about finance, and that to make proper financial judgements, just as in business, he had to have up-to-date information. He asked the deputy minister of finance, J. V. Fisher, for a financial statement that was accurate to the day. To Fisher's "Impossible!" Bennett said, "I want one tomorrow morning at eleven o'clock, and from now on it's pay-as-you-go all the way."

Fisher argued that the province, being young, had so much to do and insufficient revenues to do it. It needed to borrow money.

Bennett replied, "Mr. Deputy Minister, I'll make the policies and you'll carry them out. We're going to stop borrowing money immediately, and we're going to plan for a surplus this very year. And we're going to start reducing the debt."

Fisher expostulated, "Impossible! Just impossible!"

"Jack, I don't want you to think about it again. I'm just telling you what the chart is. Don't worry about it; that's my job."

During this early grace period Bennett was fortunate in having his friend Einar Gunderson for minister of finance. The concept behind the restructuring of the province's finances and implementation of a pay-as-you-go approach to government expenditure was the result of long discussions which had taken place between them even before Bennett had embraced Social Credit. Pay-as-you-go was basically Gunderson's idea; he had seen it work for one of the eastern States, and his thinking was: "If you spend a million dollars on building roads, and you borrow the money for it, before you get it paid for it has cost over two million. You have a debt to carry which comes right off the top of your taxation. If you can keep expenditure down to your cash flow, you're building cheaper roads." The Socreds were therefore guided by Cicero's dictum, "Economy is of itself a great revenue." Bennett reflected on this new unorthodoxy: "In all the years up to 1952, no matter what type of government was in British Columbia, they had unbalanced budgets and borrowed lots of money on ordinary account. So we introduced a policy of no debt, paying off the old debt and having balanced budgets. We were able to build up great confidence in the public's mind—and when you build up confidence, you've got expansion. When you get expansion in a private enterprise system, you get more confidence, more spending and more jobs. The government gets more total revenue in taxes."

With Gunderson's assistance, Bennett was able to work within the budget he had inherited from the Johnson administration. No department could spend money without Gunderson's approval, and Bennett insisted on costs being kept down and no more borrowing. The ministers did not like it, nor did their deputy ministers, but Bennett got his way.

Using his hardware store training, Bennett tackled the government's overhead expenses. The previous administration had hired a private consulting firm to conduct a study on efficiency in government but he tossed out their report and pronounced what would become one of his favourite anti-intellectual maxims: "An expert is only an ordinary person three miles from home and lost." Instead, to ensure against the buildup of bureaucracy, he instituted his own simple but effective efficiencies. He instructed his ministers to cut down staff, not by firing but by not replacing those who resigned or retired and encouraging transfers within the civil service. Using this approach to personnel management and similar economies, the new Social Credit government completed the 1952–53 fiscal year with an $8-million surplus, instead of the projected deficit.

In those early months of power, Bennett concentrated on governing with ferocious single-mindedness and, to a great extent, he worked on his own. He once stated: "To be a successful premier one must forgo the privilege of having many close friends." Only two cabinet ministers, Bonner and Gunderson, had the premier's unlisted home telephone number, and these men were his closest confidants, lunching with him virtually every day when they were in Victoria. In the autumn of 1952, these three were making the important decisions about the future of British Columbia. Bonner has said of this period:

> In any group of people there tends to be an inner group. I was fortunate in finding myself very close to the premier. He was a very positive-thinking man, a prime example of conventional-unconventional thinking. We would sometimes see problems differently, but in the end we saw them together. Training as a lawyer is not the most useful training for public life; you tend to think too logically. I learned with W.A.C. to be a little more plastic in my thinking, to look at things from more points of view. In the beginning, at least, I would have to deliberately exercise my mind in unconventional ways to see my way around problems. But we got to the point where the premier would start a sentence and I could finish it, or the other way around. We could discuss problems rather freely and easily.

The method by which Bennett had brought Bonner and Gunderson into government, compounded by their recognized status as his most trusted colleagues, naturally caused friction among Social Crediters, who referred to them as the Three Musketeers or the Triumvirate. Bonner and Gunderson were pretty much accepted by their cabinet colleagues but not by the other Socred MLAs. For instance, Tom Irwin, the member for Delta, thought he should have been included in the cabinet before either of them; he went to Edmonton to see Ernest Manning and asked him to intervene. According to Bennett, Manning nearly kicked him out, saying, "No, Premier Bennett has full power. You just go back and behave youself." Irwin confessed his indiscretion to Bennett, but there were half a dozen others who complained in those early days.

A more vexing problem facing Bennett in his first months as premier was how to acquire legislative seats for his two nonelected ministers. Both Bonner and Gunderson had accepted their posts with the assurance that Bennett would look after their elections. They threw themselves into the work of their portfolios while their leader boldly moved to secure two seats, in accordance with parliamentary tradition, before the start of the session. For an inexperienced government, the problem must have seemed insurmountable—after all, among elected Socreds there were virtually no "safe" seats. The premier held a press conference in which he appealed for the resignations of two Vancouver Island opposition MLAs in order to make way for his ministers, thereby affording Vancouver Island representation in cabinet. This audacious suggestion, made with a straight face and in an earnest tone of voice, was received with incredulity. Members of the other parties scoffed and jeered at the premier's request and the press fired a barrage of criticism. The Victoria *Times* editorialized that the remarkable plea "must be regarded in charity as a jest. Mr. Bennett surely did not expect his proposal to be taken seriously, as if the politics of British Columbia was a sporting event." Bennett would claim that he was completely serious, arguing: "Vancouver Island was the original crown colony. And we didn't have one member elected on the Island—not one. I thought the original crown colony should have cabinet representation." But Robert Bonner said of the incident: "Oh, he had a great sense of fun, you know. If you could pick up two seats in that fashion, why not?"

Naturally, opposition resignations were not forthcoming and Bennett began to work within the ranks of elected Social Credit, asking quite a number of MLAs to resign and make way for his attorney general and minister of finance, but caucus opposition to his scheme was formidable. Eventually, Reverend Francis in Similkameen and Orr Newton in Columbia gave up their seats but only after some of Bennett's super salesmanship, and even then they tried to withdraw their resignations after giving them to the premier.

By-elections in the two interior ridings of Similkameen and Columbia were announced for November 24, 1952, and Bennett absorbed himself completely in the task of getting his key ministers elected. The first hurdle was obtaining nominations for Bonner and Gunderson against tremendous local opposition. Bennett craftily drafted a double-barrelled resolution that said: "This meeting of the Similkameen constituency wants to thank the Reverend Francis for the services he has rendered this constituency and the province so far, and thanks him for making a personal, temporary sacrifice for the good of the province and the good of Canada; and that Einar M. Gunderson be nominated in his place." The resolution was carried and the ploy was repeated successfully in Columbia.

With his two hand-picked cabinet ministers now nominated, Bennett prepared to parachute them into the legislature. It was an enormous gamble with everything at stake. If he lost either of the by-elections, Harold Winch would be the new premier: with even one more seat, Winch would then have nineteen seats and Social Credit eighteen. Bennett took all the risks.

The by-election campaigns dominated the news. Bonner and Gunderson did little actual campaigning, other than speaking at some meetings arranged for them by Bennett's campaign team. To impress the importance of the contests upon the locals, the entire Social Credit cabinet traipsed through the two interior ridings. In Columbia, Bonner was opposed by CCF and Liberal candidates, while Gunderson was challenged in Similkameen by the CCF and a fringe labour candidate. Bennett's confidence and his air of having a mission may, at this point, have been somewhat contrived, but it won a determined and inspired effort by Socred campaigners. Even political opponents admitted the boldness of his gamble, as Randolph Harding, CCF member for Kaslo-Slocan, did: "One would have to be impressed. Bennett had taken a chance on a minority government and he was trying to get good men in as finance minister and attorney general. A minority government can get into a tremendous amount of trouble if they don't have capable individuals in their two key portfolios. I think Bennett recognized this right at the start and this is why the move was made. You've got to give him all the credit in the world for gambling his government on this move."

The by-election campaigns are each a study in political curiosa. A big city financier was offering himself to the farmers and ranchers of Similkameen, while an ambitious young city lawyer was asking for the support of residents of the quiet mountain valley riding of Columbia. At one meeting, Bonner advocated cheaper long-distance telephone rates only to discover later that the community he was addressing had only one old-fashioned crank-handle telephone, which rarely worked. But the fact that they were out of place did not seem to hamper the willingness of voters to support them. These were by-elections of convenience in which the constituencies were being asked to assist the new government taking office. Change was in the air and people seemed anxious to see that change come about. Because the single transferable ballot was still in use, the by-election results were waited upon with even more trepidation. But, no matter, on the night of November 24, both Bonner and Gunderson won handily on the first counts. The victories were decisive, even though both ridings had been extremely narrow Social Credit victories in the general election, Similkameen having been decided by a judicial recount. Bennett must have slept wonderfully well that night; an extremely large incubus had been lifted from his shoulders.

The by-election hurdles behind him, Bennett now carried on with the task of governing and planning for the first legislative session. A week after the by-elections, on December 1, 1952, he delivered his first province-wide radio address as premier in which he introduced his cabinet, talked of the various fronts the Social Credit administration was moving on, and brought in several themes and catch phrases which he would use again and again in years to come: "Your Social Credit government does not believe in representing any one economic group, but will give fair treatment to all, with special favours to none. . . . Your Social Credit government believes in genuine competitive free enterprise and is opposed to monopoly. Your government believes in social reform but is opposed to state socialism. . . . Having only nineteen Members out of a total Legislature of 48 Members, makes the task of government not an easy one. However, we will do our best."

On December 20, 1952, the premier, accompanied by Bonner and Gunderson, travelled to Edmonton for a summit meeting with Premier Ernest Manning and his cabinet. The meeting, which took place at Manning's invitation, was an historic occasion—the first time that two heads of Social Credit governments had ever conferred. It was a useful exchange of information and dispelled, once and for all, any hint of Alberta dominance over B.C. Socreds. One of the most interesting outcomes was the joint declaration of the desirability of extending their respective provincial boundaries northward. Bennett's brand of west coast imperialism was couched in terms of a "northern vision"—and perhaps it was not all that new, for the proposal was only a slight variation on former premier Duff Pattullo's plan to annex Yukon Territory. Another declaration emanating from the Edmonton summit meeting is worth mentioning: Premier Bennett persuaded Premier Manning to support a joint submission to Ottawa urging construction of a rail link giving the Peace River region a direct outlet to the Pacific coast. After little more than four months in office, Bennett was already drawing on his experience as a young man in Alberta and his father's failure in Peace River.

Bennett was now looking towards the day when he would have a majority government. He had come to power with a bulging agenda, his mind full of ideas of what he might accomplish as premier, but most of his plans would have to be deferred until he consolidated his power. It is impossible to determine whether he ever seriously considered trying to avoid a session of the legislature in favour of asking the lieutenant governor to grant an early dissolution so that he could go to the electorate for a decisive democratic judgement. Of course, such a request would have been out of order but, just as certainly, a minority government in B.C.'s volatile political climate did not stand much chance of surviving a session. Shortly after becoming premier, Bennett met privately with W.C. Woodward, president of Woodward Stores of Vancouver and a former lieutenant governor of the province who served in the early 1940s. Not long after their meeting, Woodward wrote to Bennett offering "unsolicited advice" on the basis of his own personal experience as representative of the crown during the tumultuous days when Pattullo was ousted from office and the coalition was formed: "I am sure you know there is practically very little written law regarding the powers of Her Majesty or her representatives, and, to the best of my knowledge, what was done in the past constitutionally, is more or less precedent when Mr. Pattullo wished a dissolution . . . before the forming of the Coalition Party. I refused on the best advice I could get, to allow him to go to the country before he met the Legislature, and although I am not in a position to say so, most probably this is the attitude His Honour will take at the present time." Speaking for the Vancouver business community, Woodward concluded his letter: "Anyway, we all would very much dislike His Honour to be obliged to call in the alternative party and ask them if they could form a Government. Most likely you are fully aware of these circumstances, and would not leave yourself in the position where an alternative Government might be called in before an election."

Bennett was not only aware of the circumstances but was completely preoccupied by them. He believed that political leaders forge their own majorities and, despite his nerve-wrenching by-election gambles, had not the slightest intention of losing power. He realized he would eventually have to test the dark, dangerous political waters by meeting the legislature. All of his efforts and strategies, therefore, were sharply focussed on using his minority position in the House to Social Credit's advantage. With this specific goal in mind, he announced that the first session of British Columbia's twenty-third parliament would open on February 3, 1953.

Calling the session provided the opportunity for all Socred MLAs to meet in Victoria for the first time as a government caucus. If members of cabinet were green when they first arrived in the provincial capital, the remainder of elected Social Crediters were even more so. This was an era when newly elected representatives had virtually no support staff or services and were offered very little in the way of formal orientation to the legislative process or parliamentary procedures. Bennett put great effort into preparing his caucus for what he described as "the stormiest session ever."

The premier's strategy was to be prepared for defeat at any time, but, assuming that defeat would come later rather than sooner, he devised a plan to frustrate the more experienced parliamentarians sitting on the opposite side of the House. He recalled telling the caucus:

> This session is our first test. We're either going to make or break this Social Credit movement in government. You've all made political speeches and you've attacked the CCF and those other old parties and torn them to pieces, but you've been addressing sympathetic crowds where nobody was answering you. You're now in a debating hall of experts. The CCF have been here for years and their best people have great claims as political speakers—the same with the Liberals and Conservatives. They'll make mincemeat out of you, but you've got to go in there and have your bumps the same as anybody else. My advice is to do what I'm going to do. I'm not going to enter the first debate. I'm going to be taunted and heckled and called names, but I'm not going to yield—because temptation is not sin; yielding is sin. I'd really like to tell

these people off now that I'm premier of this province, but I won't yield and neither must you.

After the Speech from the Throne it is my duty to select two members to move and to second the reply to the speech; they'll be Tilly Rolston and Ken Kiernan. There will be no heckling there. They'll prepare their speeches well and short. Then we'll go through the whole debate and none of us will speak. In the end, the speaker to wind it up will be Attorney General Bonner, who's a polished speaker. He'll tear these people to pieces. I'm confident he'll do a great job, not only for me, but for you and everybody else. I want you to agree or disagree right here. I don't want anybody to have second thoughts later. They're going to say Bennett's got you by the nose and you're all just his yes-men, but if you're going to last, you've got to keep your heads down and let those bullets whiz over. Bonner will give the answers and you'll be proud of him.

The Socred troops agreed to their commander's battle plan, and on February 3 they took their seats in the legislative chamber. The first official business of the new parliament was selecting a member to serve as Speaker of the House. Bennett decided upon a gambit that would force the combined opposition forces to show their hands early, which he described:

I wanted Tom Irwin to be our Speaker—he was a very great critic of mine originally, but he had good qualifications; of all our group, I thought, he was the right person. So, I nominated Tom Irwin and instead of asking Harold Winch as leader of the opposition to second the nomination, I had Bonner second it. I wanted to make the opposition a little mad, to challenge them on the first day. The combined opposition could have defeated my choice of Speaker, but by voting for us they confirmed to everybody that I was in control, that Social Credit was in control of the legislature. I could then report to the lieutenant governor that we had the right to govern. By refusing to challenge it, the opposition surrendered to our administration. They should have challenged it; they should have nominated somebody else in Irwin's place. Of course, I was prepared for that. If they had nominated somebody else, I would have withdrawn my nomination and would have joined with them to make it unanimous. Then I wouldn't have had to tie up one of my own members as Speaker.

Tom Irwin took the Speaker's chair and introduced Lieutenant Governor Clarence Wallace who read the Speech from the Throne. Prepared personally by the premier, the speech was vague but optimistic, promising "measures of considerable importance." In the ensuing Throne Speech debate, which lasted several days, the novice Socreds demonstrated remarkable discipline and an ability to stick closely to Bennett's strategy. The greenhorn members' closed mouths and smiling faces stunned the opposition. After Tilly Rolston and Ken Kiernan moved and seconded the Address in Reply to the Speech from the Throne, not a single Social Credit MLA entered the debate. Time and time again, opposition members rose to lambaste the government; they criticized the Socreds' silence, called them Bennett's puppets, and teased and ridiculed endlessly. And though many of the Social Credit members were restless and fidgety, the premier sat comfortably in his seat smirking. Arthur Turner of the CCF, clearly riled by the government's refusal to enter the fray, said: "Their laughter and chatter and grinning can only be described as simian behavior." Liberal Nancy Hodges, a former Speaker, snorted: "There must be a miraculous power of thought transference or mental telepathy over there—Social Credit minds but a single thought, eighteen Social Credit hearts beating as one." Referring to the premier, who studiously ignored her words, she exclaimed: "Oh, I wish he'd heckle me. . . . Why doesn't he? He used to be the talkingest man in the House." After several days of this intriguing, unprecedented legislative behaviour in which the Socreds silently bore a sustained attack of verbal abuse, the premier was satisfied with the frustrating effect of his tactics, telling his party, "Don't worry. Give thanks for those attacks because neither a kite not a great plane can rise unless it rises against the wind."

Finally, when all twenty-eight of the smouldering opposition members had spoken, Robert Bonner stood in his place next to the premier and delivered his first and what would probably be his best speech in the legislature. Bennett beamed like a proud father as his "bright young attorney general" provided a masterful climax to the debate on Social Credit's inaugural Speech from the Throne. Bonner had prepared very carefully, and by now he had lots of ammunition. He had checked the newspapers for some of the foolish things that were said before the election and had noted some of the even more foolish things said in the House. He had great sport for about two hours, exposing, member by member, their inconsistencies. In the end, they were hopping up and down, hardly able to contain themselves. Bonner finished with: "Now look, Mr. Speaker, it's very clear. We've listened here for ten days to these wonderful speeches, all critical of this new government which has hardly been in office. Yet we've been accused of committing every sin on the calendar. If one hundred per cent of it is correct, this government should be defeated today. If fifty percent of it is correct, we should be defeated today. If ten per cent is correct, we should be defeated today." And he sat down. Everybody voted for the Address in Reply to the Speech from the Throne—there was not a single dissenting vote. Bonner reflected: "Of course they supported us. It didn't matter whether they did or not, but it would have been preferable from our point of view to have been defeated at that point. But, now, there was an awful lot of rioting on the other side, because they had prepared their own meat-hook and they were hanging from it for the rest of the session."

The next major event of the session was the introduction of British Columbia's first Social Credit budget delivered by Minister of Finance Einar Gunderson on February 18. The budget proved to be a popular and optimistic accounting of the province's needs and it offered a variety of new tax exemptions which were roundly applauded. In his budget speech, Gunderson pointed out the innovative approach of Social Credit, featuring: "administrative economies that not only will ensure the provision of adequate current services in an efficient yet thrifty manner, but economies that will enable the greatest possible division of current income to the provision of capital works in order to eliminate, or at least to reduce, Provincial borrowings to a negligible amount." How many modern governments can brag about spending *less* than was spent the previous year? But that is exactly what the Socreds did, while emphasizing debt reduction and a pay-as-you-go policy of public finance. In addition, they were determined to create a less onerous revenue and taxation structure for the province. Gunderson's budget featured such popular items as raising the exemption on the five-per-cent tax on restaurant meals from fifty cents to one dollar, broadening the tax exemption on the purchase of irrigation equipment for farmers, and a ten-per-cent reduction on automobile licence fees. Also announced was the creation of a new provincial crown corporation, the Toll Highways and Bridges Authority, to establish and operate these capital projects. And, of course, in keeping with Social Credit's populist image, tax increases for industry were introduced including a ten-per-cent tax on net income from logging operations, but exemption for small operators; a further tax affecting the logging industry on tracts of land held for speculative purposes; and an increase from four to ten per cent in the provincial tax levied on income from mining operations.

So the budget offered a few tax reductions for the common man, increased the level of taxation for big business, and predicted "a solid floor of prosperity ahead." And lest anyone doubted the philosophical leanings of the new Social Credit regime, Gunderson concluded his speech with a ringing endorsation of capitalist principles:

> Individual initiative under a free enterprise system has come nearer to providing an abundant life by producing the highest standard of living and the least poverty the world has ever known. If British Columbia is to take advantage of the future, it is necessary that an economic climate be maintained to encourage more people to work for themselves, more

small businesses and small industries, more large businesses and large industries. The building of such an economy is a progressive task and an enormous responsibility, requiring constant effort and vigilance, and demands financial measures, and an economy based on the surest foundations in order to yield worthwhile returns for the common good.

This was the Social Credit manifesto for British Columbia, the product of long conversation and private debate between Bennett and Gunderson. Now it was the blueprint for the province's future economic development.

In the next few weeks, as the budget debate took up most of the legislature's time, the House began to hear from some of the new Socred members—and there were surprises. Many of the Social Credit "outbackers" made sincere and useful contributions in debate and, if less formal and erudite than opposition members, generally made a good impression. On February 24, the Reverend Phil Gaglardi, minister of public works, made his maiden speech in the legislature, a speech filled with blustering inanities and his own unique phraseology. One press report noted:

> The bitter personal feelings surging through SCers and CCFers against each other came to the fore more strongly than ever before in the legislature when Public Works Minister Gaglardi spoke. During such exhibitions of this bitter feeling, Liberals and Conservatives sit quietly observing, almost as if glad that at last, they're more or less at rest. Mr. Gaglardi has a loud but not unpleasant voice which he used with dramatic effect. . . . There were times when he thundered and dropped his voice; he grew angry, then calm, a very good actor you see. . . . He started his speech by saying that he'd probably feel more at home if someone with a wastepaper basket took up a collection. He said that he's not only a Minister of the Crown, of the Queen, but also a Minister of the King of Kings. He said, "In this little fella, you'll find lots of faults and I'll make lots of mistakes but, with the help of God, I'll do my level best for British Columbia."

A little later, when an opponent accused him of lying, he responded with what would become a typical Gaglardi-ism: "Mr. Speaker, if I'm telling a lie, it's only because I'm telling the truth."

Probably the most significant feature of the session was the incessant feuding between Bennett and the aspiring, perspiring leader of the opposition, Harold Winch. The CCF leader was a past master of House procedure and each day's sitting began with a challenge on a technical matter such as the time the legislature would commence or some other point of order. For his part, Bennett usually sat smiling his infuriating smile, only entering the dogfight when he was on very sure ground. On February 26, the premier and the leader of the opposition were very testy, their duelling becoming more aggressive. Bennett called for debate on a motion Winch had placed on the Order Paper asking the government to table a special report of a committee of deputy ministers on education costs. Winch's intent was to embarrass the raw Socreds, for he was certain the government had ignored the report's recommendations. After Winch stated the reasons he wanted the House to see the report, Finance Minister Gunderson rose and bluntly called for adjournment of the debate. The Vancouver *Province* reported on the subsequent proceedings:

> The voice vote came and there were some "no's" from the opposition side. "What is it? (the vote)," the Premier called to Mr. Speaker. Mr. Speaker wasn't sure. The Premier rose to call for a recorded vote and as the division bell rang he declared: "I want to say that this is a vote of confidence or non-confidence in the government." That started an uproar of shouts and taunts from the opposition: "Shame," "Out of order," "Intimidation, eh?" . . . In the midst of the uproar, House Liberal Leader E.T. Kenney snapped: "There shouldn't be any threats to this." Retorted the Premier: "This is no threat. It's a statement of fact."

The premier had effectively called the divided opposition's bluff. On the recorded vote, the Tories joined with the CCF in voting against adjournment of the motion, but the Liberals supported the government. By a vote of twenty-three to nineteen, therefore, Winch's motion was adjourned; the Social Credit government had survived what Bennett defined as a vote of confidence, and the procedural gamble served to momentarily clear the supercharged air of the legislature.

The combative relationship between Bennett and Winch was interesting in itself. They were seasoned veterans of the political fray and could often read each other like well-thumbed books. Winch was clearly the stronger of the two in terms of powers of oratory and knowledge of parliamentary procedure, but Bennett grew more mighty with each successive challenge to the Socreds' right to govern. Bennett, who never cared to believe he had an enemy on this earth, described Winch fondly: "He and I were great personal friends. But political rivalry—oh, terrible! We were bitter political rivals, but personal friends. He was a peculiar mixture: a revolutionary and a patriot. To my way of thinking, Harold Winch was the best leader of the opposition British Columbia has ever had. He was a good oppositionist. The socialists are good oppositionists, but they're not good administrators because they don't believe in the system. They don't believe in the personal initiative of people. They believe in Karl Marx, which I studied and rejected." Harold

Winch's assessment of Bennett showed quite a different sentiment: "I had no use for Bennett at all, because I knew he was completely unprincipled. I knew him first of all as a Conservative. I knew him as a coalitionist. I knew him as an independent. Then I knew him as a Social Crediter. Now, a man who switches politics like that is completely unprincipled. I had no use for him; I never had." Despite the bitterness of these feelings, Winch gave Bennett something that would survive well beyond their relationship: in the heat of debate, he once said of the premier, "He's W.A.C., and W. A. C. is Wacky." This rather obvious acronym would become the single most popular nickname for Premier Bennett, a term of scorn or endearment, depending on how it was used and by whom. From now on, Bennett became widely known as "Wacky" and if he had to endure this sobriquet he also, at times, indirectly encouraged it.

The 1953 spring session dragged on longer than many had expected. This was certainly no fault of the Socreds, who provided ample opportunity for defeat in the House, but the opposition parties were wary of bringing down the government without good reason. The Socreds did not behave with the customary timidity of a minority government and, in fact, courted defeat on their own terms. Each day as the members entered the House they joked about whether or not it would be their last. On several occasions the tension in the Assembly built to a high peak but, at the last moment, one or another of the opposition parties would back down: the government continued to hang by a thread. Many speculated that the Socreds' budget was the obviously important measure on which the opposition parties could combine to defeat the government. On March 9, Robert Sommers, minister of lands and forests, wound up the budget debate with a call to arms: "The citizens of British Columbia are waiting to see whether the Members of this House are going to vote in favour of the Motion, thereby encouraging the Government to go forward, or to vote against the Motion and thereby keep these benefits from the people of British Columbia. The issue is clear, the Government rests its case." But the recorded vote on the budget motion showed the Liberals willing to prop up the Social Credit administration which survived the vote twenty-four to twenty-one.

The session carried on for two more weeks amid veiled threats and unfulfilled promises. Finally, it was left up to the premier to choose the issue upon which the government would be defeated. He chose Bill 79, "An Act to Amend the Public Schools Act." More commonly referred to as the Rolston Formula, after the minister of education who introduced it in the legislature, it was an extremely complex piece of legislation which proposed to restructure the financing of education in favour of rural areas at the expense of urban school districts. Bennett informed the caucus of his intentions and while they marvelled at his strategy, many Socreds were depressed, some were terrified.

They had not passed any legislation during the session, bringing various bills no further than second reading stage where they were debated in principle. Bennett held back from sending any bills to committee stage where the opposition could have amended them. He kept in close touch with Lieutenant Governor Wallace during the session, apparently receiving assurances that if his minority government were defeated, the House would be dissolved for a general election. In fact, Bennett stopped by Government House to see His Honour on the evening of March 24, 1953, before returning to the legislature for an evening sitting. Harold Winch was waiting in his office to see what business would be called that night, and when the premier indicated that Bill 79, the Rolston Formula, was on the agenda, the opposition leader pleaded with Bennett not to bring it forward. When Winch realized that there would be no backing down, he left the office in anger, shouting, "Tonight is your night!"

On this unavoidable evening the session was destined to reach its climax. Bennett made his first speech of the session on second reading of Bill 79, and the CCF, Liberal and Conservative members railed against it; for the first time they seemed equally determined to back up their words. Arthur Turner of the CCF attempted to adjourn debate on the bill, but his motion was defeated. Harold Winch explained: "Bennett was not content to stay on as a minority government, but he knew that we weren't going to give him an opportunity; he knew that he'd have to force it by bringing in something that neither we nor the five Liberals nor three Conservatives in the House could possibly support.... And that's when they brought in the Rolston Formula for education finances. It was just brought in for the very purpose of bringing about dissolution of the House."

The government was defeated on the Rolston Formula by a vote of twenty-eight to seventeen—the first administration defeated on the floor of the B.C. legislature in over half a century. Bennett recalled the moment when he rose and said, "Now the government's been defeated, we can't propose any new legislation. But we should have order and not chaos; because what must follow now is an election. If it's a Liberal premier that comes back, or if it's a Conservative premier that comes back, or if it's a CCF premier that comes back, or a Socred comes back, we want stability, to be able to carry on. So we've got to have some estimates approved, certain things done—I suggest that tomorrow at ten o'clock the leaders of the parties meet in the premier's office so we can have an open discussion on what we should do for now." The House was adjourned and the party leaders met the next day in the premier's office. The canny Bennett apparently outlined to them:

> Here are all the bills. We can't have any more debate, and we've lost the right to be government because we've been defeated on a major issue.

But you have the right to say—because you've got the majority—whether you want any of these bills to be passed. If you want some passed, because you may be the next government, you pick them out, by four o'clock this afternoon please. As far as the estimates are concerned, if you so rule, there'll be no estimates. But if a new government comes in and has to deal with special warrants, with no continuing policy on anything, no department will know what to do. Remember, you think you're going to be elected—we all think we're going to be elected to government; so you're not only deciding what the Social Credit position is going to be after the election, you're going to decide what your position will be. We'll appoint a committee to meet with the deputy minister of finance, to go over the estimates and break them down to the essentials—not for the full twelve months, but the essential estimates. And we'll have to agree on that, because when they come to the House there can be no debate.

The next day the House, continually reminded of their leaders' agreement, passed vote after vote without debate—an incredible performance. With the rules of the legislature suspended, fifty-six noncontroversial bills were passed through second and third reading, and a special Appropriation Bill, granting $94 million in interim supply, was approved. Roy Brown, one of the leading B.C. political columnists, credited W. A. C. Bennett with the "smartest political coup" ever. Writing in the *Vancouver Sun*, Brown declared: "No such proceedings have ever been seen before in a Canadian legislature. The rigamarole of the legislative machine grinding out so many votes per hour . . . presents one of the queerest phenomena of our times." The following day, March 27, Lieutenant Governor Wallace was summoned to give royal assent to the hastily approved legislation; he then prorogued the session. Shortly thereafter, British Columbia's twenty-third parliament was dissolved. There were no MLAs, no opposition, but there was a cabinet.

On the last day of the session, Harold Winch said, "Mr. Premier, you think you're smart. . . . I'll be up to see His Honour before you. I'll be the new premier."

Bennett said, "Mr. Leader, nobody can blame you for thinking that."

Harold Winch's position was:

We were entitled to form a government by nearly all precedents. When you have a minority government that is defeated the first session after an election, when you have the closeness of electoral support that we had at that time, then it is the precedent throughout the world, over the centuries, that the leader of the opposition should be invited to form a government. In addition, something generally not understood now is that had we formed a government, we would have had more support on the floor of the legislature than Mr. Bennett had. That may seem rather strange, but it's a fact, because the only voting support that W.A.C. Bennett had were the nineteen Social Credit members. We had eighteen members. I had the support of the independent labour member, Mr. Uphill, which made it nineteen. But, in addition, the three Conservative members said they would support me as a minority government. Therefore, I had more support than Premier Bennett had had when he was government. So, from both angles of precedent and ability to carry on, we were entitled to be called upon to form a government. But the lieutenant governor refused to do that.

Bennett described Harold Winch's sad last moments in provincial politics:

Winch went to see the lieutenant governor and, of course, I had already seen him. I was at a cabinet meeting getting ready for the election, and Harold arrived at my office where Worley told him I was not in. I don't think Harold was feeling too much pain. His Honour was a first-rate entertainer and he had bad news to give him, and Harold loved painkiller, so he was feeling no pain. Then he heard the bell ring—the one that rang whenever I came into my office by my private entrance—and he said, "He's in there now." He burst into my office and said, "Mr. Premier, you win, I lose!" He had tears in his eyes, poor guy. We chatted, but he was heartbroken. Heartbroken.

Harold Winch became one of the tragic figures in British Columbia political history. So near to leading his party to power, he was doomed to ignominy. After his unsuccessful consultation with Lieutenant Governor Wallace and his pathetic tête-à-tête with Premier Bennett, he returned to his own office where he became embroiled in a quarrel and fistfight with fellow CCF members who felt he had betrayed their socialist-egalitarian principles by prostrating himself at the feet of the Queen's representative.

Winch resigned his post as leader of the provincial party and, though he would eventually serve as a federal MP, he would never again measure up to the politician he once was, and could have been. He reflected on his personal agony and frustration:

I figured that with the situation of another election and myself having been leader for so long . . . that there was time for a change—let somebody else have a try. Also, I was on the verge, and did have, a nervous breakdown. You've got to realize that being leader of the opposition in those days was not like being leader of the opposition today. Today you have permanent staff, you have research help; we didn't—we had no help. I was on the go not only all hours of the day, but seven days a week and twelve months of the year. When the House wasn't sitting, I was on the road covering the province. I had to do all my own research: when the budget speech came down, or when the government came in with a new policy, I had to be on my feet the next day on those policies, understanding them and accepting them or rebuffing them. I just gave up.

A general election was announced for June 9, 1953. The Social Credit government had been in office less than a year, but longer than most observers had predicted. During that time west coast politics had undergone a transformation which was not yet generally appreciated. In the June 1952 election, a strong Liberal Party headed by an incumbent premier had been challenged by the cocky and aggressive Tories led by the veteran Herbert Anscomb and by the seemingly omnipresent CCF under the experienced leadership of Harold Winch; the Socreds were leaderless and not considered to be a factor. Now, heading into the 1953 election, Social Credit alone could boast experienced leadership in its strong and popular incumbent premier; the opposition parties were discredited and demoralized. The CCF elected a new provincial leader, Arnold Webster, a mild, gentlemanly school principal with little political experience. The Conservatives' ruination had been exacerbated by the deaths of two of their three MLAs, and they had elected a new leader, the unknown Deane Finlayson, a thirty-three-year-old Nanaimo insurance agent. The Liberals also had to scramble about for a new leader when E. T. Kenney, the former coalition minister who had served as Grit House leader, announced his retirement from politics; they elected federal MP Arthur Laing to lead them into battle. The political tables had turned completely. As the 1953 campaign got off to a brisk start, it became evident that Bennett and the Social Credit Party had a decisive edge over all oppponents.

Since the government had been defeated in the House over the Rolston Formula, all parties were forced to defend their actions, and they were hard pressed to explain the issue. Randolph Harding, CCF member for Kaslo-Slocan, said: "The Rolston Formula was a gimmick for the government to get defeated upon. It was very detailed and complex and so difficult to explain that none of the Socreds knew what it was about and I'm quite sure our people didn't know too much about it either. I'm convinced that the Social Credit government never had any intention of bringing it in. They threw a dead duck into the ring and let the opposition parties tear it apart."

The Rolston Formula and even less complex issues became lost in a sea of electioneering verbiage, emotion and clever clichés. While the opposition parties and their new leaders flailed away at the Socreds, Bennett was able to dictate the tone and style of the campaign, which he did with a simple, straightforward flair that became one of his trademarks. Two slogans dominated his campaign, one attempting to paint the large overview, the need for stability—"Social Credit or Chaos"—and another trying to exemplify Bennett's new approach to government—"Economy with Efficiency." These two catch phrases were surprisingly effective in focussing the campaign on Social Credit; the opposition parties were on the defensive from the start. Of course, as the party of government, the Socreds were on completely different ground than they had been during the electoral fiasco a year earlier, and their campaign was easier to finance—for governments will always have resources that are otherwise unavailable to parties.

Bennett actually ran a nonpartisan election, recognizing the constraint of the transferable ballot. He appealed to disgruntled Liberals, disgruntled Tories and to those CCF voters who were not real socialists but who wanted social reform. He began his campaign in the central interior city of Prince George (where in an intense nomination battle a local schoolteacher, Ray Williston, had defeated the Social Credit incumbent, Lew King; Bennett had been asked to intervene on behalf of his MLA but refused to do so after finding no irregularities in the riding association's democratic decision). Bennett used the same election campaign speech at meeting after meeting and, invariably, he used the same approach. At one rally, he was heckled as a traitor to the coalition. He quickly shot back: "Traitor if you will, but traitor to a false government." Said one Socred candidate: "He never really enjoyed a political meeting unless he got it well disrupted and had the fire going both ways. That was a matter he really worked on. I don't know whether people ever realized that, but the premier never got going in a political meeting unless there was repartee between the audience and himself. He never really performed unless he had hecklers."

The other parties' campaigns were ill-focussed attempts to discredit the Socreds and undercut their populist appeal. The CCF promised the voters a "return to sanity." Arnold Webster, their mild-mannered leader, avoided doctrinaire invocations and instead emphasized the "Christian origins" of socialism. The CCF seemed to be attempting a left-wing replication of what they perceived to be the Socreds' religious appeal. However, in presenting the CCF as "a great Christian movement" they were actually emulating an Alberta feature of Social Credit that Bennett's party had practically abandoned. Christian or not, all three opposition parties castigated the Socreds without mercy; it was an all-out attack employing the worst aspects of B.C.'s paranoid style. The new Liberal leader, Arthur Laing, was especially irresponsible in his near-hysterical denunciation of Social Credit. He referred to them as a gang of "radical McCarthyites" masquerading as free enterprisers, and as fascists opposed to the United Nations, Jews, Liberals, labour, education, social security, free enterprise and parliament. Laing desperately tried to paint a picture of his party as the only reasonable alternative to the evils of fascism under Social Credit or the even worse horrors of socialism under the CCF. The Conservatives and their new leader Deane Finlayson had the most difficult time of all in a campaign that was stacked against them before it started. In the months since Social Credit had taken power Tories throughout B.C. were joining Bennett's movement. As a result, the Conservative Party could not attract high-calibre candidates and ended up eight short of a full slate. Finlayson tried to undercut right-of-centre support for Social Credit by branding it "socialistic," "dictatorial" and alien to the Canadian way of life. When Bennett predicted that Social Credit might rule in B.C. for fifty years, Finlayson compared it to Hitler's boast of a thousand-year Reich.

Premier Bennett, declaring the election "the most important ever to be held in British Columbia," appealed to voters on the basis of his administration's short record: "In the eight months of office we have been subjected to the worst tirade of abuse by politicians of the parties who we defeated in the election of June 12th last; and political writers, who oppose us and the rising tide of a people's movement, have endeavoured to misinterpret, in every way possible, our actions which were for the good of the people as a whole and not for any special group of people, class or lobbyists." Bennett presented an honest and sincere face to the electorate and implored all candidates to "keep the campaign a clean one." His goal was a majority government for Social Credit: "I believe that British Columbia is entering its greatest period of expansion and stable government is urgently required."

Because the single transferable ballot was still in effect, it was difficult to immediately determine the exact outcome of the election, but Bennett and three other Socreds were declared victorious on the first count, as were two CCF candidates; Social Credit was leading in thirty ridings, the CCF in seventeen and Tom Uphill was ahead in Fernie. The premier's prayers were answered, his majority seemed assured, and although the final count was still four weeks away, he set September 15 as the opening day of the new legislature and departed for eastern Canada and a national Social Credit strategy conference.

A majority government was a great achievement, and all the more remarkable because of the use of the single transferable ballot—a system of voting which Bennett would later describe as patently designed to defeat any government that allowed it to be used. Perhaps it is not surprising, then, that he would have to qualify his election-night expectations. If the first-count results had obtained, the Liberals and Conservatives would have been wiped off the electoral map. But the net effect of the transferable ballot was to take two seats away from Social Credit, leaving them with twenty-eight; it stole three from the CCF, leaving them fourteen; it gave four seats to the Liberals and one to the Tories; and it left Tom Uphill secure in Fernie. An analysis of the election results shows that the Socreds were no longer the voters' popular second choice. A single year's experience with a Social Credit government had dispelled widespread ignorance of the movement and even caused hard-core supporters of the old-line parties to redirect their alternate ballot choices. At the same time, the Socreds had achieved a comfortable majority government; the percentage breakdown of the popular vote after the final count showed Social Credit with a resounding 45.5 per cent, the CCF with 29.4 per cent, Liberals 23.3 per cent, and the Conservatives a shameful 1.1 per cent.

Despite the convincing victory, Bennett was deeply hurt by the two seats denied to Social Credit incumbents by the transferable ballot. Both candidates were dear friends and close cabinet colleagues: Tilly Rolston and Einar Gunderson. Minister of Education Rolston had run again in the three-member riding of Vancouver-Point Grey and at the end of the first count she was 1,649 votes ahead of her nearest rival, Liberal leader Arthur Laing, but short of the required 50 per cent. After five long and painful counts in which other candidates' second choices favoured Laing over Rolston, the Liberal leader was declared victorious. Bennett sincerely grieved over the defeat of his old confidante who had been through so many battles with him in what now seemed like ancient times. Rolston had hardly been a shining success during her short stint as cabinet minister for she remained aloof, fiercely loyal to Bennett but unable to work closely with other Socred ministers. For the premier, however, her loss was an emotional one, especially since she was rapidly losing on another front, her battle with cancer.

Einar Gunderson's defeat at the polls had an emotional side as well; but from an administrative point of view it was a very serious loss. Neither Gunderson nor Bonner ran again in the interior constituencies they had won in such spectacular fashion in the November by-elections. By earlier agreement they left those seats and contested urban ridings. Bonner was successful, ironically, as a running mate of Rolston in Vancouver-Point Grey. Gunderson ran in the suburban Victoria constituency of Oak Bay. On the first count, he was ahead of his Liberal opponent, Archie Gibbs, by ninety-eight votes, with Conservative leader Deane Finalyson running a distant third. However, in the same fatal pattern as Point Grey, both the CCF candidate's and the Tory leader's second choices favoured the Liberal over Gunderson, who was declared defeated after the third count.

Bennett looked at questions of practical politics differently than most politicians: personal loyalty, for instance, came before all other considerations. Einar Gunderson was one of his personally selected cabinet ministers and, unlike Bonner, was of his own generation with ties going back to their days in Edmonton. Bennett had trusted his minister of finance to the extent that during the Socreds' first year in office as a raw minority administration Gunderson often served as acting premier at official functions. Consequently, Bennett could not accept the defeat of his old friend and he persuaded him to stay on as finance minister. Meanwhile, he researched the constitutional implications of a minister remaining in cabinet after an electoral defeat, and looked around for a sacrificial lamb so that a door to the legislature could once more be opened for Gunderson.

The three-member Victoria riding had gone solidly Social Credit and the premier persuaded one of the winners, Percy Wright, to resign his seat "for the good of the province." The by-election date was November 24, 1953, exactly one year after the original by-election gamble that had ratified Bennett's confidence in Gunderson. The Victoria race became an all-out attack on the now secure Social Credit administration by the humiliated old-line parties. Because Conservative leader Deane Finalyson was still searching for a seat, he entered the fight along with Liberal and CCF candidates. During the fall 1953 legislative session, the premier was able to do away with the unpredictable transferable ballot, and so the by-election represented a return to normalcy for the B.C. electoral system. But Bennett's manipulation reached a little too far. Gunderson had always been a reluctant politician at best, and now, with Bennett's pushing, the issue was forced. Gunderson was an administrator and freely admitted that he was not a campaigner, saying: "It's not me." So, though Gunderson entered into Bennett's scheme, he did so with only half his heart. He lost the Victoria by-election to Liberal George Gregory by a mere ninety votes.

Even a persistent man like the premier had to recognize that this was the end of Gunderson's political career. Disappointed and disheartened, Gunderson wanted to leave Victoria and return to his private practice in Vancouver as a chartered accountant, but Bennett persuaded him to stay on as a special financial adviser to the government, a kind of "dollar-a-year man." Gunderson played an important role in provincial affairs for years to come. Robert Bonner claimed that "Gunderson was never properly recognized for the contribution he made to public life. He had a good grasp of financial matters, he knew where to look in the books, and he knew how to put budgets together. He certainly didn't have to be in government, and he wasn't really a political animal. It's really a pity he was not re-elected. The task of government—and the task of the premier, for that matter—would have been much simpler if he had been able to play a fuller role. As it was, Gunderson served very effectively in an advisory capacity for a long time." Rather than appoint someone else as minister of finance and have to convey his philosophy of balanced budgets and debt repayment, Bennett, for the rest of the time he was premier, was also minister of finance.

With the 1953 general election behind him, he had now consolidated his position of power. Social Credit was no longer a rural-based mainland party: of the nine new seats it won in 1953, all were in the province's two largest urban areas, Vancouver and Victoria. Under Bennett's direction, Social Credit had become an omnibus party representing voters from all classes and regions of British Columbia. The achievement was astounding. Only a few years previously, in 1949, Socred candidates had mustered a mere 1.5 per cent of voters' support. Now, in 1953, they were the party of power with a solid majority of legislative seats and nearly half the popular vote. Bennett's leadership was the obvious key factor; in particular, his organizational strategy of "drawing the circle ever larger" was instrumental in practically annihilating the provincial Grits and Tories and blocking the CCF's chances of power. Yet, British Columbia voters would rarely admit to supporting Social Credit.

No sooner did Bennett achieve his longed-for majority than he demonstrated how he intended to use unbridled power. In his first province-wide address after the election he declared:

> We in British Columbia . . . share the undoubted belief in the tremendous future of our province. Here in British Columbia are to be seen the wealth of mineral, forest, oil and natural gas and potential hydroelectric resources which constitute perhaps the last economic frontier of North America. . . . To the virtually limitless resources of British Columbia there must be added as a matter of deliberate policy the additional resources of population and of capital if this province is to develop as it should. . . . I trust that with the election over and a very great job at hand, we shall achieve in British Columbia a unity of purpose and outlook and a firm resolve to get on with the business of the province.

For Bennett, the primary objective of politics was to capture the public imagination by conjuring visions of future greatness which he himself firmly believed in. Coming out of the coma of the coalition years, west coast politics revived its dormant curiosity. It was one of those times in history when by general agreement a new era was dawning. As a leader, Bennett engendered an idealism and optimism that almost instantly quickened the province's sensation of life—surely one of the greatest gifts of a leader to a people. Power, of course, can do strange and unpredictable things to those who wield it, yet some leaders can tolerate large quantities and still retain mental and moral faculties: Bennett had trained for the task and now proved that he could handle this large dose of power.

The twenty-fourth parliament was opened in Victoria in the fall of 1953 during a happy time: the young new monarch, Elizabeth II, had taken the throne in Great Britain, and Bennett now sat comfortably on his in loyal British Columbia. The month-long session was necessary to complete the unfinished budgetary and legislative business that had precipitated the general election. Supply was approved for the remainder of the fiscal year, as were forty-seven additional pieces of legislation. The short session was a useful exercise for the Social Credit government, unaccustomed to the security of a strong legislative majority and the relative certainty of getting its own way on most issues. One of the ironies of the session was the passage of a new Liquor Act which made sweeping liberal changes in the province's archaic liquor laws: no longer would people be forced to conceal bottles at dances, dinners and in hotel rooms; in keeping with the recommendations of a Socred-appointed royal commission, restaurants and dining lounges could now sell liquor, wine and beer with meals; and music and entertainment would be allowed in the province's grim beer parlours. These enlightened regulations were cheered by the public, and the irony was that the government implementing them was headed by an old-fashioned teetotaller whose first task upon assuming office in 1952 had been to clear out all the liquor cabinets in the offices of the Parliament Buildings. The new liquor laws demonstrated that Bennett was, first of all, tolerant in his personal beliefs, and secondly, cognizant of what was going on in the main streets of the province.

The years following the 1953 election were prosperous and heady. Wages were rising and provincial revenues were rapidly increasing; all the most optimistic predictions of postwar expansion seemed justified. The Social Credit government, with a secure mandate, found itself in office at a time when no problem appeared insoluble and all goals seemed within reach. The spring 1954 session saw the government increasing its popular base by reducing or eliminating several small nuisance taxes. The psychological impact of these reforms was undoubtedly more impressive than the economic. For example, it exempted sales tax on children's clothing, eliminated a ten-per-cent liquor tax, sharply reduced the registration fee for automobiles from ten dollars to one dollar. At the same time, it increased social assistance allowances and the bonuses paid to old-age pensioners. The coalition's albatross, hospital insurance, once again appeared; increasing costs combined with the newly reduced rates suggested there might be future funding shortfalls. Bennett responded in typically unorthodox fashion by abolishing premiums altogether and raising the provincial sales tax from three to five per cent, saying afterwards that the two-per-cent increase was "not to be earmarked for hospital insurance but to supplement the general revenue of the province so that the province could take care of hospital expenses without raising premiums." The "hidden tax" proved more than adequate to cover the needs of hospital insurance and therefore generated extra government revenues. (When the sales tax had been first introduced by the coalition administration in 1948, Bennett severely criticized it as a "brick around the government's neck.") The supposedly "voluntary" nature of hospital insurance was a farce since now everyone, even visitors to the province, would be subsidizing the plan through payment of sales tax. But the new financing formula was also less regressive, so that hospital insurance costs were now less a direct burden on lower income families. Of course, the government was criticized for the way it handled the conversion. The Victoria *Times*, for example, editorialized: "Mr. Bennett who came to office as the champion of free enterprise and the only reliable opponent of Socialism has swallowed a socialist theory whole. All hospital insurance is to be socialized. The CCF is entitled to credit for its largest victory in British Columbia."

The controversy over hospital insurance was a problem inherited from the previous government. Bennett dealt with it and other such issues quickly and with verve, but his Social Credit administration was also launching out into new areas of activity. The premier's approach to government was strongly shaped by the Depression experience of the 1930s as well as by the high level of government spending and intervention in the economy that Canadians had become accustomed to during World War II. He firmly believed in private enterprise as an agent of economic development, but he also cultivated an activist approach to government. Hardly a believer in laissez-faire, he saw the role of government as being central to providing social security and protecting the economic well-being of the populace, as well as creating the proper conditions under which a spectacular kind of economic development could occur. In his first budget speech as minister of finance, on March 8, 1954, Bennett allowed for a substantial increase in government expenditure, with a total provincial budget of over $204 million. He told the legislature that his budget reflected the government's "boundless faith in a splendid economic future" and he promised to "spare no effort toward the attainment of British Columbia's manifest destiny." He described his government's goal: "to secure for every citizen an unfettered opportunity to obtain, through his own initiative and enterprise, a share of the material abundance of our vast resources." Amazingly, on March 19 when the legislature concluded debate on Bennett's first budget, not a single opposition MLA voted against it. Recovering from momentary shock the premier requested that the unanimity and obvious good sense of the House be recorded for posterity in the *Journal* of the Assembly.

Bennett was quickly emerging as one of the canniest politicians ever to wield power in B.C. His government was spending more money than any other in the province's history yet was preaching thrift. Social Credit was providing increased social services, taxing big business at unprecedented levels, and yet was spouting platitudes about the power of capitalism and individual initiative. Bennett had all but vanquished the Liberal and Conservative parties in the province and was significantly undercutting support for the CCF. He fondly predicted a return to a two-party system, but he almost seemed to be striving towards a new kind of one-party state. Criticism of the Social Credit administration was stiff but largely ineffectual—or perhaps Bennett was right when he later said that the tremendous popularity of his government was owing to the ill winds of castigation steadily blowing from die-hard supporters of the old-line parties: the socialists tried to brand him as a friend of big business, desperate Liberals called him a "phony" and a "fascist," and the moribund Tories' vitriol was barely heard. However, writing in *Saturday Night*, Stuart Keate asked the salient question: "If this is a right-wing, businessmen's government, how does the Premier rationalize the new tax burdens on industry and his extraordinary socialization of the health plan?"

Perhaps the most important front the Socreds were advancing on was transportation. After creating the Toll Highways and Bridges Authority, which provided a controversial financing formula for road and bridge construction, the government rapidly undertook an ambitious program of infrastructure development, required for economic development and integration. Recognizing the desperate need for highway construction, particularly in the interior, Bennett created a new Department of Highways in 1955 and placed it under the direction of flamboyant Phil Gaglardi who declared his intention to "take the wraps off British Columbia." The year 1955 became the so-called "Year of Bridges" with local dignitaries and Social Credit ministers eagerly lining up to attend major bridge openings in Vancouver, the Fraser Valley and in the interior. But by far the most controversial aspect of the government's transportation policy concerned the Pacific Great Eastern Railway. The provincial government had been in the railway business ever since 1912 when a group of private entrepreneurs conceived of a railroad linking Vancouver with B.C.'s vast interior, and then went broke. A political football for almost forty years, the PGE was an embarrassing drain on the provincial treasury and was widely ridiculed as a railway which started nowhere (Squamish) and ended nowhere (Quesnel). Among the popular meanings for the acronym PGE were: "Please Go Easy," "Province's Greatest Expense," "Prince George Eventually," and "Past God's Endurance."

A group of Social Crediters advocated selling the PGE for one dollar to any private group who would agree to take over its debt and attempt to make it work, but Bennett had other ideas. He negotiated with Canadian National Railways to see if the PGE could be incorporated into the national system, but he was not encouraged. He travelled to Ottawa to ask for federal assistance to extend the railway; but his request was flatly turned down. Still he was confident that the railway could be used as a development tool and a symbol of action—the kind of symbol he wanted his government to be associated with. In the fall of 1953, by an act of the legislature, he cancelled over $90 million of the PGE's accumulated public debt and issued provincial bonds for the remainder of its $60-million indebtedness. The business community was horrified at this move, but Bennett argued that the debt was uncollectable and that the PGE needed a fresh start. He appointed himself president of the railway and reorganized its entire administration, with a new board of directors including former finance minister Einar Gunderson. Bennett told the legislature: "Of all the interests I have in public life, none is a greater challenge. No money in this province could pay me for the satisfaction I would feel if this railway were changed from a joke and put on a sound financial basis."

In the most optimistic terms, Bennett spoke of extending the PGE from Vancouver not just to Prince George, which had been achieved in 1952, but all the way north to the Peace River country. In his budget speech of 1954 he declared: "If there is any one thing of basic importance to the further development of British Columbia, it is the development of the rich resources of the northern and central interior regions of the Province. The Peace River particularly is one of the areas in Canada most ripe for development." When he pointed out that an extended PGE was the obvious agent of development for the planned exploitation of those northern riches, he was playing on a theme from his earlier years in Alberta. The PGE, according to him, would become the Peace River region's long-sought outlet to the west coast. In addition to being a wise economic and political move, building the railway through to the Peace River would be a kind of personal vindication for Bennett; undoubtedly the vigour with which he pursued the policy was at least partially motivated by memories of his enigmatic father. Bennett's attitude to questions associated with the north would always be irrationally influenced by his bitter though secret recollections. His government's railway policy and a host of other grandiose northern development projects constitute a striking example of how private turmoils can shape public policy.

In the months following the 1953 election the Social Credit government was as popular as any administration in B.C. history. For a new party with a fresh mandate and a strong legislative majority, an extended honeymoon with the public seemed not only justified but widely desired. The Socred government was moving quickly and boldly in many areas, and despite continuous criticism from the urban press and opposition parties, its actions were generally applauded. British Columbia was booming; in fact, the province was only just beginning a period of remarkable industrial growth in which its economy would become integrated in a manner dictated largely by one man, W. A. C. Bennett. He was proud of these early accomplishments and of his team of Socred colleagues, who were perceived as fresh new faces and, like their leader, sincere, idealistic and honest. The Bennett dream was becoming a reality.

Heading into 1955, "Wacky" Bennett appeared in full control of the province's destiny. On February 4, 1955, as minister of finance, he delivered his second budget speech in which he spoke of "caution" but demonstrated optimism in a budget of over $211 million. However, the spring session was seriously marred by a controversy that raised its head almost simultaneously with the presentation of the record-breaking budget. A blustery Liberal MLA, Gordon Gibson, accused the premier of fraudulent handling of forest management licences, the means by which the government administered the province's largest, most important industry. Accustomed to criticism, especially from old-line partisans, the Socreds sat back and carried on with their legislative program, in spite of vague speculation that money had changed hands in return for an unspecified favour to the forest industry. Perhaps the exuberance of the period justified a certain complacence, but the Socreds were remiss in having let down their guard. On February 15, Gordon Gibson, the self-proclaimed "Bull of the Woods," rose again in the House and bellowed: "I firmly believe that money talks and has talked." It was at this specific moment that Bennett's dream threatened to become a nightmare. The charges, countercharges and various sordid consequences of Gibson's famous "money talks" speech were the beginning of the end of B.C.'s experiment in democracy.

CHAPTER
SEVEN
DEFINITE INDICATION OF WRONGDOING

> . . . he that filches from me my good name
> robs me of that which not enriches him,
> and makes me poor indeed.
> William Shakespeare, *Othello*

> The task of the politician is to climb the tree
> and shake down the acorns to the pigs below.
> Sir John A. Macdonald

Upon assuming the office of premier, W.A.C. Bennett was concerned about the possible forms of retaliation that the previously entrenched and still influential establishment forces in B.C. might bring against the Socreds. Perhaps it was because he was schooled in the paranoid style of west coast politics that the new premier was extremely cautious about his own behaviour and urged his cabinet ministers to follow an equally ascetic path. As it turned out, his caution was well founded.

During the first week of his government in August 1952, Bennett had warned his colleagues to be on their guard at all times. Being honest was not enough; the Socreds had to be seen to be honest. He admonished: "THEY are watching our every move in an endeavour to discredit the government." It seems he had reason to believe THEY were watching his own movements from the moment he left for work in the morning until he went home at night. Bennett had many "friends" during this politically fluid period; one such Liberal acquaintance informed him that both he and his ministers were being followed and observed constantly. He managed to obtain a copy of a purportedly secret RCMP report which stated that British Columbia's new premier leads a life "quieter than a Baptist minister's."

Bennett was always on the alert for potential scandal and he frequently tested his ministers with unexpected references to their extracurricular activities. One night Ron Worley had a drink with Eric Martin and Wes Black at the Pacific Club, where the two ministers were temporarily residing. The next morning the premier told Worley that someone had complained to him that his boys were seen drinking too much in the Pacific Club, and used the occasion to drive home his early warning about having to appear "honest." Other ministers received more serious warnings. Phil Gaglardi, who later became embroiled in a long string of messy controversies, in his early years as a cabinet minister was informed that he was being watched day and night, and that one of the parties had studied his background from A to Z. The office of the registrar of companies was being checked two and three times a week to see if he was involved with any companies. Many times he received threatening phone calls.

Bennett warned his neophyte ministers that they would suddenly have a host of new friends eager to help in the cause of good government, and he was fond of remonstrating: "Don't tell me about my enemies, but guard me against my friends." He was especially wary of one potential source of scandal: women. He once cautioned each member of his cabinet that if he were out walking at night with a woman, to make sure it was his wife—and to walk under the street lamps so that everyone could see she was his wife. His precautionary advice was not the result of a wild imagination, nor was it completely rooted in a political persecution complex. He had reason to believe that there were people out to destroy him and the Social Credit government. During one of his first official trips to Ottawa as premier, a woman phoned his hotel room claiming to be from British Columbia and said she urgently needed to see him. Bennett told the unidentified female caller that he was sorry, but he was too busy to see her. A short time later, the same woman came to his hotel room door; however, Bennett would not let her in, and he held the door firmly when she tried to force her way into the room. Bennett suspected that the Liberals were trying to set him up and he had a sneaking feeling that there was a photographer waiting around the corner. After this incident, he warned his fellow cabinet ministers to *stay away from women*.

It was not a sex scandal that would cause the first great controversy of B.C.'s Social Credit administration; rather, it was the indiscretion and naiveté of one particularly vulnerable cabinet minister: Robert Sommers. Prior to 1952, Sommers was unknown outside his home territory around Castlegar in the southern interior. He was an accomplished musician and a thoroughgoing community man. A teacher by profession, he worked his way up to the principalship of three elementary schools in the Kootenays. His first wife, whom he married in 1930, died after bearing a child. Sommers remarried in 1940 and had two more children. His family life appeared happy; his teaching career was successful; and his musical and community affairs seemed fulfilling. In 1934, he joined Social Credit and became the first president of the Castlegar Socred group; but he did not become serious about politics until shortly before the 1952 provincial election when he was nominated as the Social Credit candidate in his constituency of Rossland-Trail. That election dramatically changed his life, sending him suddenly into the world of politics and power, industry and intrigue. In retrospect, it is easy to see that Sommers was inadequately prepared for his responsibilities as a minister of the crown, but, for that matter, so were most of his Socred colleagues. For Sommers, however, the cost of his moment of political glory was an infamous future. Kipling's description of politics as "a dog's life without a dog's decencies" is apt here.

When Bennett was confronted with the problem of forming a cabinet he did not have a pool of proven talent to draw upon. He interviewed each prospective minister and made a characteristically intuitive judgement. Of Sommers he said: "He was a brilliant young man. I interviewed him and said, 'Tell me now, what bad habits have you? Do you drink? Do you take drugs? Do you chase women? I want to know now.' He said, 'I don't chase women; I'm happily married. I don't take drugs. I did play cards and I did drink, but I promise you that those days are gone. I went through a difficult period; those days are over. I have only one idea and that is to serve the people of Rossland-Trail and the people of British Columbia.'" Shortly after this interview, Sommers wrote to Bennett and lobbied for the portfolios of either forests or education in the prospective Social Credit cabinet. He concluded his letter with the words: "you may depend on my loyalty." A few weeks later, Robert Sommers was sworn into office and given the multiple resource portfolios of lands and forests, and mines. With hindsight, it is possible to argue that it was the nature of his new responsibilities, rather than any personal weaknesses, that proved his undoing.

It seems surprising that Bennett would assign the resource portfolios to Sommers, who had a somewhat unsavoury reputation: on face value, he was an exemplary citizen, but he was known as a sometimes heavy drinker and a gambler—and a not very good one at that. This was well known by many Socreds: certainly by Gaglardi, Kiernan, Chant and Williston, each of whom later admitted knowledge of Sommers's "hobbies." His victory in the 1952 election was remarkable in that he won over the popular incumbent, Douglas Turnbull, minister of health and welfare. Naturally, the coalition minister was dejected by his surprising defeat at the hands of the voters of Rossland-Trail. Later that year, Turnbull's wife angrily diarized: "Instead they prefer a school teacher of poor standing, doubtful character and little integrity."

All of this suggests that Bennett had possibly made a mistake in giving Sommers the important and extremely sensitive resource portfolios. After all, the premier was a firm believer in Saville's dictum: "A man who cannot mind his own business is not to be trusted with the king's." But he was either too busy to worry about concerns over Sommers's character or was hopeful that the "brilliant young man" would prove the rumourmongers wrong. Moreover, Sommers had given his word that his difficult days were over and had made a pledge of loyalty. For Bennett, a man's word was always his bond.

A couple of years after Sommers assumed his cabinet responsibilities, stories began to circulate in the B.C. forest industry which were cause for serious concern. When Sommers had moved to Victoria he discovered that the expenses he was incurring greatly exceeded his ability to pay. He received a stipend of $3,000 per year as an MLA, plus a ministerial salary of $7,500—not enough, it seems, to meet his expectations of the life of a powerful cabinet minister. In fact, when he arrived in the provincial capital his bank account was $900 overdrawn. A forest company executive had warned the novice minister to beware of the "bandits" populating the industry, but Sommers treated the warning lightly. At the time, he considered H. Wilson (Wick) Gray to be his only friend on the coast. Gray was president of a small logging operation, Pacific Coast Services Ltd., and had once hired Sommers and his six-piece dance band to play for a company party. Wick Gray soon became a frequent visitor at the home Sommers had bought in Victoria. The house cost $9,500, of which Sommers had borrowed $3,500 from a bank for the down payment. With renovations and new furnishings, costs quickly accumulated. Within nine months of becoming minister, Sommers had borrowed more than $7,000 from the obliging Gray. Then his daughter announced plans to be married; Sommers again asked his friend to help him. These were wholly private transactions between Sommers and Gray, but reports soon began to filter through the cocktail circuit that a certain forest company could guarantee a highly coveted forest management licence for a large cash payment.

When this information inevitably reached W.A.C. Bennett's ears, he decided to have it quietly checked out. As he described it, he privately hired the best detective in Vancouver who came back with a report that there was nothing to the charges: the rumours were all partisan, all political. Bennett had no reason to doubt the veracity of his private investigator's report. As premier, he knew that the granting of forest management licences was not a routine administrative matter but a major government decision requiring the approval of cabinet. But he was unaware that Sommers had placed himself in a situation that made him susceptible to political embarrassment. In so making himself vulnerable, he made Bennett vulnerable, because the premier's single greatest weakness was his unswerving loyalty.

The forest industry was the most important economic activity in British Columbia. As the mainstay of the coastal economy, it generated millions of dollars in taxation revenues and was the source of growing riches for the powerful, expanding companies that dominated it. Historically, most of the forest resources in the province have been owned by the public and leased out to companies for logging on a conditional basis. In 1945, a royal commission headed by Justice Gordon Sloan proposed a new system whereby B.C. forest resources would be managed through the issue of a limited number of forest management licences (FMLs). These licences were intended to improve management and conservation of the forest resource while providing companies with the long-term secure timber supply required for large-scale capital expansion. The Sloan Commission advocated the principle of sustained yield—which has been interpreted to mean a constant yield of timber every year, forever. The concept of sustained yield, it was hoped, would ensure that the coastal forests would never be depleted; through careful management (including the restriction of harvests to the sustained yield capacity of the land), fire protection, reforestation and adoption of modern logging methods, forestry would be British Columbia's perpetual industrial backbone. The first FML was granted in 1948, and a new pattern was established in the economic life of the province. Now, virtually all coastal timber would be either under reserve for FMLs or in public working circles—forest lands set aside for small logging operators.

By 1952, when the Socreds arrived on the scene in Victoria, twelve FMLs had already been approved covering 2.3 million acres of prime forest; twenty-three other applications were under study. Holders of licences obtained the rights to specified areas of forest on a sustained yield basis. Under government regulation, licence-holders logged the tracts and developed the resource as they saw fit; the government was paid for each tree cut. The system did not precisely follow the recommendations of the Sloan Commission; however, it did provide an answer to the difficult problem of managing B.C.'s most important resource. Bennett was in favour of FMLs and continued with the system when he became premier.

Nevertheless, no matter how rational or inspired, opposition to it was rampant. Small loggers complained that the FMLs created even larger companies and that they would soon be squeezed out of business. The general public was also upset, for in that period forest management was a new concept. Perhaps its most contentious aspect was the tendency of companies to exclude the public from forest management areas because of their liability for accidents on their roads and their responsibility for fire protection. In the early stages, most companies took the simple measure of putting gates across these roads. It was also argued that the government was becoming too involved in regulating the industry and that it should abandon the "socialistic" FMLs in favour of a return to free enterprise in the forest industry. But even dedicated capitalists like the Socreds favoured and defended the new system. As minister of lands and forests, Robert Sommers met the criticism head on: "There is a great deal of talk about 'free enterprisers' in the forest industry. . . . Unfortunately, the term is used at times where 'freebooter' would be more appropriate. . . . The free enterprise system is justifiable only as long as it serves the public interest." Partly in an attempt to assuage criticism, and also to reassess the impact of the system, in January 1955 the government appointed Chief Justice Sloan to reinvestigate its forest policy.

By far the greatest problem associated with FMLs was the manner in which they were granted. The very fact that there was choosing from among the many applicant companies generated charges of discrimination and foul play. The minister of lands and forests was placed in the extremely delicate position of having to recommend to cabinet, on the basis of various submissions placed before him, whether a particular company should be awarded an FML. A yes or no could mean the difference between survival and extinction for many forest companies. Essentially, the minister controlled the resource base upon which the entire industry depended. This kind of subjective system of FML allocation, therefore, was bound to create difficulties. It was widely believed that the coalition government had used the awarding of FMLs as a means of raising party funds; but as C. D. Orchard, chief forester and deputy minister of lands and forests, said: "Doubtless, party funds profited substantially from time to time; but I never had reason to think that the minister profited more than a meal, a bottle, a souvenir, prestige, and the like." However, Robert Sommers's tenure as minister of lands and forests would come to an end because of the problem, and the issue that brought it to a head was the consideration of FML no. 22.

British Columbia Forest Products Ltd. was a large and growing forest company owned by Toronto industrialist E. P. Taylor and his Argus Corporation. B.C. Forest Products had first applied for an FML in 1947 but had been unsuccessful so far. In 1953, Taylor came to Victoria and met with Premier Bennett to discuss the company's plans for expansion on Vancouver Island and the necessity of obtaining an FML. The meeting, which took place in the Empress Hotel, was also attended by Taylor's right-hand man Wallace McCutcheon, Robert Sommers, Einar Gunderson and a few others. Bennett described the meeting: "We wanted that licence to go ahead, provided there were no special concessions given in any way. We wanted to get development; we wanted jobs; we wanted work — but no special treatment for them in any way. I'm sure that Sommers didn't give them any special treatment, and I didn't ask him to. He dealt with it the same as any other forestry licence." Sommers recalled the meeting: "I can remember Taylor saying, 'Why are we being penalized in this licence?' The licence said the company had to put in access roads to communities in the region at a cost of about $800,000. Bennett told him it was because the previous governments had not looked after the interests of the people; in future, licences would do this. Bennett said it was a licence he would be pleased to show the public. It had the highest stumpage rates, the roads, and provision for small contractors to work in the forests." Sommers also remembered that at this meeting the premier and E. P. Taylor agreed between themselves that the FML would eventually be issued;

Bennett promised that his minister would have his departmental officials work out the necessary details.

Was any undue influence brought to bear in the consideration of what would become FML no. 22? On the surface, this licence was simply an example of the informal but straightforward approach that Bennett's government took to large questions of economic development and industrial growth. But the controversial aspect of FML no. 22 was the inclusion of forest lands previously earmarked as part of a public working circle for small loggers. At least one person suspected that all was not well: J. Gordon Gibson, the logger-millionaire MLA. Gibson had been an early opponent of FMLs, claiming that they favoured large forest companies and forced out small independent loggers. His criticism was not always taken seriously; many felt that he and his family had benefited more than anyone from the new system of management licences. He and his brothers, who had been successful in a variety of business ventures, owned a logging operation on the west coast of Vancouver Island and received an FML in 1954. They soon sold out their logging interests to a larger firm, making a sizeable fortune in the process. The Gibsons were well-known B.C. millionaires, Liberal in affiliation and independent in temperament; Gordon Gibson was elected to the legislature in June 1953 as the gritty Grit member for Lillooet. As an opposition MLA he became a loud critic of the government's forest policy, reiterating his complaint that FMLs were discriminatory. Through his contacts in the industry, he seems to have caught wind of B.C. Forest Products' application and the government's intention to grant the company FML no. 22. This licence became the undeclared target of his vociferous attacks, and it seems clear that he objected to it primarily because it would take land away from a public working circle, which he viewed as a giveaway to a large corporation at the expense of independent logging firms who were increasingly engaged in a fight for survival.

In the legislature Gibson was possibly the most boisterous and bombastic MLA; outside the House he could be a charming man, a friendly giant. His vague criticisms, usually conveyed in raving speeches, were tolerated but never accepted nor fully digested by the Social Credit government. However, Gibson was serious about his concerns and early in 1955 decided to approach the minister of lands and forests personally.

One evening he had dinner with Sommers and they got onto the subject of FMLs. According to Gibson, he said to Sommers: "They're wrong. I wish that you would put your foot down firmly and not issue one more until you know more about them...." Sommers replied: "That's one thing I won't do. ... They [FMLs] are pretty well all committed, and I know where they're going." "Bob, is there any money in it?" Gibson asked. "If you're just short a lousy five or ten thousand dollars, I'll lend it to you; but don't put your neck out here or you'll be ruined. I'm just the man who will do it. I know what you make and I know all about your poker games in the Empress, the men who are playing there, and that they are losing intentionally, and you know that they are. So just quit now." Apparently, Sommers told him to mind his own business; Gibson warned him that he meant to see Bennett in the morning, and Sommers got very drunk.

The following morning, February 2, 1955, the cigar-chomping MLA for Lillooet was admitted to see Premier Bennett and told him the same story he had related to Sommers. According to Gibson, Bennett "would not listen either" and after a hard half hour of talking said: "You had better mind your own business, Gordon. You Liberals started this. We're no worse than you are." Gibson was hardly a man to mind his own business—especially when ordered to do so. Later that day in the legislature, in "a voice that would have shamed a moose," he accused the government of fraudulent handling of FMLs. He claimed that forest companies were making huge profits by selling shares at tremendously inflated prices after they had received a licence but before they had cut a single tree. He demanded an investigation into the method of awarding FMLs. But his speech was received with only faint interest among the government benches and, as the days passed, it was clear that he could not expect any response from the Socreds. On February 15, the "Bull of the Woods" rose again in the House and this time grabbed the attention of all MLAs with a purposely provocative attack. He reiterated his concern over the method in which FMLs were granted and then bellowed: "I firmly believe that money talks and that money has talked in this." He demanded that the matter be referred to the legislature's forestry committee so that an all-party investigation could study his charges. The House was momentarily stunned by the seriousness of Gibson's accusations. Then there was pandemonium, with members from all sides yelling at one another until the Speaker called for adjournment.

Perhaps no one could fully appreciate the import of Gibson's charges until they appeared in boldface headlines in the morning press. As Gibson said: "The Socreds were caught where the hair is short by the public outcry which followed publication in the newspapers." The government was knocked off balance and was forced to scramble for an appropriate reaction to what is now regarded as one of the most memorable speeches ever made in the B.C. legislature.

When the House convened that day, Attorney General Bonner demanded that Gibson withdraw the "implication of false motives." Gibson refused to retract his unparliamentary remarks and Speaker Irwin therefore "named" the member for Lillooet, ordering him from the House until members decided how to deal with him. Gibson stormed straight up to the public gallery which was off limits to members while the House was in session. One member yelled, "Mr. Speaker, there is a stranger in the House," which meant that the business of the House had to stop until the offending member was removed from the gallery, though anybody else may sit there. Gibson roared down to the premier from the gallery: "I'm either a member on the floor of this House, or a private citizen up here in the gallery." There was much shouting on the floor as the members argued what should be done. Gibson appreciated the predicament he had created: "It was like calling a man a 'bastard' when he doesn't know who his father is. He's apt to be a bit touchy."

The members of the Legislative Assembly decided not to expel Gibson, but asked him to return to the chamber and "reconsider" his situation. He was present the following day, February 17, when Attorney General Bonner rose to announce the appointment of a one-man commission of inquiry to investigate Gibson's "money talks" charges. Judge Arthur Lord, a justice of the county court in Vancouver, was appointed to look into the accusations as they related to the government's handling of FMLs. He was empowered to hire staff, hear testimony from interested parties, and was requested to report "with the utmost dispatch consistent with the holding of a thorough inquiry." Gordon Gibson hailed the appointment of the Lord Commission as a "great victory." The *Vancouver Sun* commended the government for its decision to hold an investigation into "loose allegations of corruption in the granting of forest management licences," while the *Province* editorialized that it "belatedly retrieves a bad blunder." W.A.C. Bennett, wondering what kind of scent the "Bull of the Woods" was onto, had a confidential personal and corporate history prepared on Gordon Gibson.

All eyes became focussed on the Lord Commission, which sat in Vancouver on the 7th, 8th and 9th of March 1955. The Liberal Party offered Gordon Wismer, the former attorney general, as Gibson's counsel, but Wismer believed that involving Liberals from previous administrations would be awkward, and wanted the issue quickly quashed. Gibson eventually acquired his own counsel and through him told the commission that his allegations did not refer to any one individual but simply to the way in which FMLs favoured the big operator over the small. Since he was now outside the legislature, Gibson had lost his special privilege of parliamentary immunity, and was therefore frustrated from making any direct or specific charges to the commission for fear of being sued for slander by any of the forest companies he might mention while trying to substantiate his earlier claims. As it turned out, the only witness to appear before the Lord Commission was the deputy minister of lands and forests, C.D. Orchard. He told the hearing that he knew of no dishonesty in the handling of FMLs. However, Orchard was very nervous—and with good reason.

There was never any love lost between himself and his minister; he later referred to his boss as "the infamous, treacherous R.E. Sommers." Departmental officials had apparently raised serious objections to the B.C. Forest Products application for FML no. 22, and Orchard refused to approve it. After he left government service, he recorded his account of the incident:

> In March '55 the futile Lord Commission sat in Vancouver. Gibson had suspicions and perhaps some inside information, but nothing that would stand the test as evidence in court. The proposed BCFP licence was the undeclared target. Prior to the hearings Sommers had me in his office for what proved to be an acrimonious review of what my evidence should be. He demanded a written statement from me to the effect that I approved the award of the licence — which I refused to give. He told me that the premier says I did approve the licence and that he, the premier, was going to hold me to that approval. I said in that case the premier is an unqualified liar and asked to be taken to the premier, but Sommers didn't take me up on the challenge. The minister [Sommers] said that Bonner wanted my OK on every file dealing with management licence applications. I had approved all the others but objected to going back at this date and "doctoring" closed files. The government, or Sommers at least, was suffering from a bad case of the jitters.

Orchard did not volunteer any of this information to the Lord Commission. At the time, he was fearful for his job. Although he later said that "the government devised the Lord Commission as a brush to give its monstrosity a coat of obscuring paint," his own mild-mannered and evasive testimony to the commission suggests that he was one of those wielding the brush. Judge Lord found no evidence of outright bribery and the case was closed on March 9. Gibson said of the commission: "Only one-tenth of the evidence had been presented and as far as I was concerned the proceedings had been a government mop-up job." Nevertheless, he had had his day in court and failed to substantiate his claim that "money talks."

Judge Lord reported to the government: "On the evidence and on statements of counsel on behalf of Mr. Gibson, I find that there has been no impropriety on the part of any person in connection with the issuance of any forest management licences." The nervous Socreds had survived the test of a royal commission and proved Gordon Gibson false. Attorney General Bonner said his view was "that if anyone had had anything in mind, that would have been the opporunity and indeed the public obligation . . . to come forward. We were anxious as an administration to assure ourselves that matters were correct, and when Gibson had made the charges we were quite mystified; we were taken completely by surprise. I think our general reaction was one of disbelief and indignation — which was reinforced by the findings of the Lord Commission." Subsequently, on May 18, 1955, the government awarded FML no. 22 to B.C. Forest Products.

Gibson found it difficult to carry on with the weight of his well-publicized failure hanging about him. In an ambiguous statement, he announced his resignation to his fellow MLAs: "On February 15th, in the House, I expressed my convictions concerning the principle of the granting of forest management licences. Because I consider this denial of justice of such vital importance to all the people of this Province, it is my intention to take the issue to the people, and I therefore advise you that I am resigning my seat and will seek re-election." Gibson's action, on this occasion at least, seems peculiar; it is difficult to imagine how a by-election would prove either the truth or falsity of his charges or, for that matter, offer any kind of personal vindication. The premier eventually announced a by-election for the constituency of Lillooet for September 12, 1955. Meanwhile, Gibson continued his uncertain crusade from outside the legislature. He appeared before the Sloan Commission studying forestry matters and charged that large companies like B.C. Forest Products had threatened Vancouver Island residents with unemployment, loss of a paper mill and no new access roads unless they supported the company's application for an FML. Gibson believed he had an understanding with the leaders of the CCF and the Conservative Party that they would not field candidates in the Lillooet by-election, leaving it a straight two-way fight between him and the Socreds. But since neither party could contain its local riding association, they both nominated candidates. The new leader of the CCF, Arnold Webster, was simply unable to live up to his spoken agreement because he did not have enough influence in the party. Gibson had been elected to the legislature in 1953 on an extremely thin edge; those were the days of the single transferable ballot and he had beaten out the CCF candidate on the third count — ironically, by virtue of the transfer of Social Credit support. Now, in a four-way race, Gibson's gamble was enormous. On August 20, 1955, he appealed to the voters of Lillooet, explaining the by-election as a fight on behalf of small independent loggers who were being forced into receivership by increasingly large companies in collusion with the government: "The issue in this by-election is simply this — will you join with me in fighting for the fundamental right of every citizen to buy our timber resources at open competition? . . . Do you favour forest management licences which guarantee timber forever to the few government-selected operators or do you favour equal opportunity for all? . . . No more vital issue was ever considered by electors anywhere. The big operators and the government will spend money like water to defeat me."

The Liberals campaigned with all their dying might. Provincial leader Arthur Laing declared: "The issue in the by-election should be the policy of this money-mad government, tumbling over itself to make grants of our crown resources in perpetuity for the short-term return of immediate investment, against a policy of insisting on a plan for participation by the small operator, and the retention of our resources for future generations." The "money-mad" Social Credit government poured tremendous energy into the by-election battle. Gordon Gibson expressed the Socreds' strategy in these terms: "Who is apt to steal from the public—a poor little cabinet minister, or a man who has made a million out of timber? And how did he make it? He must have made it out of you poor working people, by graft." Bennett undoubtedly took the by-election seriously, and a number of cabinet ministers went to Lillooet to support their candidate. This was their second electoral test since the 1953 election giving Bennett his majority; the first had been Einar Gunderson's final fling in Victoria, and they did not want to take any chances of losing this time, nor did they want Gordon Gibson back in the House. Gibson claimed that the government promised the constituents "all kinds of schemes that could never be carried out," and that "every baby within the radius of twenty-five miles was kissed at both ends."

Premier Bennett teamed up with Robert Sommers to speak to several large meetings during the last week of the Lillooet campaign. Bennett described one of them:

> We had a candidate up there, Donald Robinson, who had never entered public life. But we had some great meetings. Sommers was a great campaigner—a great schoolteacher. He'd take a blackboard and pointer and he'd show the problems and analyze them. He was tremendous, the best member I had in my party for that. We had a big meeting on the Saturday night before the Monday election, and the town was crowded with people. All parties were there, but it was our meeting. As Sommers and I walked up to the front, for every cheer, we got at least ten boos against us. That didn't bother us. . . . The CCF had their people challenge us to let them on the platform. I said, "Certainly, you can have the platform any day that you hire it. But you can't get a meeting like this. You just want to tune in and lay an egg in some other nest. What kind of bird are you, my friend?" . . .
>
> Our [former riding] president was there supporting the Liberals, so I told him to stand up. I told the meeting about the telegrams I had sent to him when he was Social Credit [riding] president, [rejecting] special favours he wanted from the government. I repeated that as long as I was premier, no special favours to anybody—none, none, none! The people cheered at that. . . .
>
> We were in the question period, toward the end of the meeting; I looked up at the clock and it was about twelve minutes to twelve o'clock—midnight hour, Saturday night. So the chairman got up and thanked everybody for attending, and said, "I think perhaps we can close it now." They shouted, "No, no, no, we've got lots of questions.

Mr. Premier, don't dodge the questions." So I got up and said, "I agree with the audience. We came here to speak. We came here to answer questions. We'll answer questions right up to the Sabbath. We do not have any political meetings on the Sabbath, so I will not make a speech or answer questions after midnight; but up to midnight we'll answer questions." They asked some questions of me, then they had a question for Sommers—there were about five or seven minutes to go. I said [to Sommers], "Now Mr. Minister, just keep going, no matter what they say, just keep going, going, going. Tell your story. Keep going, going, going." After a while they said, "We've had enough of that! We have other questions!" But Sommers just kept going. Right at the midnight hour, the pianist hit the chord on the piano and I stood, we all stood for "The Queen." The feeling there was terribly bitter: one fellow just about hit one of my friends—he had his fist up—but he was saved by "The Queen." After the meeting was over, one very nice lady came up to me and said, "Mr. Premier, I'm the head of the women's organization of the Liberal Party of this riding. Gibson might have your president in his pocket, but all day Monday I'm going to phone all my Liberal friends everywhere in this riding—and I'll promise you that for every vote your president gives to Gibson, I'll get three Liberals to vote for your candidate." She kept her word. We won, and won well.

September 12, 1955, was a great by-election celebration for W.A.C. Bennett and Social Credit. The votes on that crisp day in Lillooet were 1,709 for the Socred candidate, 1,282 for second-place Gordon Gibson, 844 for the CCF, and 201 for the Conservatives. Robinson, the victor, a PGE railway engineer, was heard to exclaim: "Rome was not built in a day, but it might have been if our premier had been in charge." It appeared that, once and for all, Gordon Gibson and his upsetting accusations would be laid to rest.

However, any such assumption underestimated the stubborn pride of the "Bull of the Woods." The election defeat made him more determined to see the issue through and to clear up his name, for he felt that he had become a laughingstock. He let it be known that he would like to see anyone who had any information to offer regarding irregularities in the forest industry. The Social Credit government was aware that he was up to something, for Sommers later recalled that Attorney General Bonner phoned him one day and commented that one of Gibson's "henchmen" had been found beaten up behind the Devonshire Hotel in Vancouver. Bonner wondered if Sommers had anything to do with it, and Sommers assured him he knew nothing about the incident. The Socreds were cautiously optimistic that although Gibson was looking for dirt, they were clean. But Robert Sommers had not told his colleagues about his relationship with Wick Gray and the various loans he had received from his facilitating friend in the forest industry. This proved to be Social Credit's Achilles' heel.

During the spring of 1955 when the Lord Commission was looking into Gibson's original "money-talks" charges, Wick Gray had visited Sommers's home in Victoria. He brought with him notes to cover the loans made to Sommers and urged the minister to sign them. The notes were signed, but neither he nor Gray noticed that secret identification marks had been affixed to the reverse side of each document. They had been placed there by Gray's bookkeeper, Charles W. Eversfield, an extremely cautious and worried man. When the threat of a forestry scandal had emerged, along with the many rumours circulating in Vancouver business circles, Eversfield began to panic; he was frantically concerned about his employer's relationship with Robert Sommers and the monies being passed between them. As Gray's accountant, Eversfield feared that he would be implicated in any scandal. Naturally, he did not want to end up in jail, but in addition, some animosity had built up between him and his boss. He looked out for himself by copying all the confidential business files and documents he felt were relevant to Gray's friendship with Sommers. A short while after the Lillooet by-election in September, Eversfield approached Vancouver lawyer David Sturdy requesting his opinion as to whether it was legal to carry the documents in his possession out of the country. Eversfield subsequently moved to Los Angeles where he was employed by a small firm as a chartered accountant.

In the meantime, Gordon Gibson's feelers into the forest industry were producing some limited results. A secretary in Charles Schultz and Co., a firm working closely with Wick Gray's company, offered to give Gibson some valuable information in exchange for money. Gibson talked to her and for "the first time . . . got wind of which tree to look up. I didn't make a deal with her." He feared to become involved in money exchanges, but he did make a deal with another person he had been told about: David Sturdy. The Vancouver lawyer met with Gibson and related Eversfield's confidential story to him. Gibson supplied Sturdy with the money necessary to fly down to Los Angeles, take a sworn deposition from Eversfield and to gather up the documents. After looking over the material, the Gibson brothers and a small circle of Liberal friends — including Don Cromie, publisher of the *Vancouver Sun*, Stuart Keate, publisher of the Victoria *Daily Times*, and a few Vancouver lawyers — sat down to hammer out a plan of action; they felt certain that the Eversfield documents were sufficient to blow the lid off the Social Credit government. They decided that the best thing to do was to keep everything out of the newspapers and not to let anyone speak until they had sufficient evidence. Gibson, as he later admitted, personally put up almost $5,000 to finance Sturdy's sleuthing, and he was no longer acting alone. The Socreds suspected that someone was masterminding Gibson's moves, and it now appears that he was in fact part of a coterie of Liberal interests dedicated to the destruction of Social Credit in B.C.

They decided to present their material to the Sloan Commission, but Chief Justice Gordon Sloan gave an opinion to the effect that such evidence might not be within his commission's order of reference. Gibson and his friends wired Eversfield and brought him to B.C. where they compensated him for the salary he was losing in the U.S. On December 7, 1955, Sturdy and Eversfield walked into the attorney general's office with a sworn affidavit and 198 documents. They claimed to possess proof of a criminal conspiracy by the directors of several companies to obtain FMLs by means of bribery and corruption. During the course of a two-hour meeting, Bonner examined the affidavit that Sturdy had obtained from Eversfield, but was denied the accompanying documentation. Sturdy rejected Bonner's suggestion of a confidential police investigation, preferring a public royal commission of inquiry. Bonner decided to take the charges lightly, apparently saying: "This whole thing sounds to me like a political racket and I'm taking no action."

The attorney general's attitude should be placed in perspective. He knew that Sommers could not have issued an FML on his own—such cabinet business was always thoroughly aired before approval; and earlier, the Lord Commission had failed to produce any evidence of irregularities in the granting of FMLs. Also, there was at the time another by-election campaign in progress in Vancouver-Centre: Bonner suspected that Sturdy's accusations might simply be an attempt to influence the outcome of that contest. Only the day before, he had received an anonymous telephone call warning him to expect a forestry scandal disclosure by political opponents. There were other factors contributing to his incredulity: Eversfield had disappeared and could not be found for questioning; and Sturdy had only a week or two earlier met with the attorney general seeking an appointment as a magistrate and had not raised the subject then. Nevertheless, Bonner reported the accusations to the premier and confronted Sommers with them. Sommers told him that there was absolutely no truth to the allegations, but for the first time he confided that he had borrowed some money privately and had written notes covering the debts. Bonner ordered him to get the notes back because "the situation might be misunderstood if it became public knowledge." Sommers immediately took out a bank loan for $8,000 and paid back $7,100 to Gray, thereby redeeming his *ex post facto* promissory notes.

The day following his meeting with Sturdy and Eversfield, Bonner wired Sturdy:

HAD NO PRIOR KNOWLEDGE OF PURPOSE OF YOUR VISIT YESTERDAY BUT ANONYMOUS PHONE CALL TO EXPECT ATTACK UPON A GOVERNMENT MINISTER MADE SENSE BY THE TIME YOU LEFT. YOUR MYSTERI-

OUS BEHAVIOUR, INCLUDING REFUSAL TO DISCUSS SUBJECT MATTER OF INTERVIEW IN ARRANGING APPOINTMENTS, DESIRE TO CONCEAL WHEREABOUTS OF YOUR INFORMANT, YOUR ADVICE THAT YOUR INFORMANT HAD IN HAND ALL SORTS OF MATERIAL SUPPOSEDLY SUPPORTING ALLEGATIONS MADE FOR TWO YEARS BUT NOT PRESENTED TO LORD COMMISSION AND THAT YOU ARE ADVISED OF SUCH MATERIAL AS LONG AGO AS SEPTEMBER, TOGETHER WITH CONTENTS OF TODAY'S WIRE, ALL NOW COINCIDING WITH A BY-ELECTION CAMPAIGN, FILLS ME WITH A PROFOUND SCEPTICISM TOWARDS THE ENTIRE MATTER, PARTICULARLY IN VIEW OF THE MINISTER'S REACTION THERETO. IN THE CIRCUMSTANCES, YOUR SUPPORTED DOCUMENT AND YOUR SUGGESTION OF CRIMINAL CONSPIRACY OF ACTIVITY BY THE DIRECTORS AND MANAGEMENT OF SEVEN COMPANIES SEEMS FAR-FETCHED.

Sturdy sent a telegram back to Bonner indicating that he was not satisfied and planned further action. Bonner replied suggesting an appointment for the following week. However, there was to be no further meetings. On Friday, December 16, 1955, Sturdy appeared before the Sloan Commission stating that he possessed a "certain body of evidence that, if proved true, could form the basis for an inference that the Minister of Lands and Forests had received considerations for the issuance of forest management licences." The commission refused to hear his "body of evidence." But now, for the first time since Gibson's "money talks" speech, the cat was out of the bag—charges against Sommers had been made in public. In Victoria, the minister was coaxed out of a cabinet meeting by excited reporters. When he was told about Sturdy's statement, his face whitened and he blurted out a quick denial. When the premier was asked about the charges and informed of what the minister had said, he replied, "That's it. That's it, then."

Social Crediters were genuinely concerned about the potential impact of Sturdy's claims. But Sommers vehemently denied the accusations and promised that there was nothing to them. Because there had already been an initial inquiry at which Gordon Gibson failed to present any evidence, the government was critical of submitting to another. Several of Sommers's fellow ministers were concerned and felt that "where there's smoke, there's fire," but they also felt obliged to accept Sommers's word. Attorney General Bonner, however, wanted more than simply the minister's word, for he knew that if there had in fact been any wrongdoing the onus would be on his department to prosecute. Through senior officials, he initiated inquiries into the Department of Lands and Forests and received no indication that ministerial influence had been brought to bear on the issuance of forest management licences. He later said: "Having ascertained that the internal administration of the department had not been violated, we took the position that whatever Sommers's difficulties were, they were a matter for his personal honour."

On the Monday following the Friday on which Sturdy had made his charges to the Sloan Commission, Sommers launched a civil suit against Sturdy for libel and slander. Sommers said that he took the action on Bonner's recommendation, his sole objective being to clear his name. As time progressed, political opponents charged that the civil suit had been filed only to block further discussion of Sturdy's allegations. For almost two years, Bonner would stick firmly to the position that he could not speculate upon the subject nor launch any action until the civil suit was settled. If there was any immediate political consequence of Sturdy's charges against the government it certainly was not evident: on January 9, 1956, Social Credit was easily victorious in the Vancouver-Centre by-election which sent a young lawyer, Leslie Peterson, to strengthen its legislative ranks.

The first real sustained attack levelled against the Socreds on the basis of the Sturdy charges occurred during the spring legislative session, which opened January 27, 1956. Opposition leader Arnold Webster suggested that the attorney general should inform the House of the action he had taken in a case where either someone was guilty of bribery or someone else was guilty of perjury. CCF member Tony Gargrave urged Sommers to drop the civil suit against Sturdy so that a royal commission could be appointed to study the matter, and he criticized Bonner for delaying the case, predicting that he had "forfeited any chance he might have had to become known as a great Attorney General." In his driest legal manner, Bonner replied that he could not accept "assertions, however set forth, when such assertions appear, and are said to be inferred from a 'body of evidence' which, if it exists at all, has not been presented to me. Under these circumstances, neither the action of an inquiry nor the machinery of criminal law is to be set in motion. This is the principle I feel governs the matter whether it is popular or not." Premier Bennett dismissed the opposition criticisms as "fluff, fluff and bluff," "carping criticism," "smear," "propaganda," "politics"; and he defended Bonner: "Our Attorney General is one of B.C.'s finest." However, the attacks went on; the government was pummelled endlessly by an opposition which finally seemed in possession of an issue capable of inflicting significant creases in the Socred armour.

It soon became evident that the Sturdy charges would be the dominant issue of the 1956 legislative session. George Gregory, the Liberal MLA who had defeated Einar Gunderson, was Sturdy's legal counsel and therefore took no part in debate on the subject. On February 7, Bonner wrote to Gregory and asked that his client hand over all the evidence he had obtained from Eversfield so that it could in turn be given to the RCMP for a confidential police investigation. Gregory obtained the material from Sturdy and on February 9 transferred it to Inspector W.J. Butler of the RCMP. That day in the legislature, Gregory's Liberal seat-mate, Bruce Brown, referred to the forthcoming Butler Report: "We now have the sorry spectacle of the chief law officer of B.C. referring allegations made against a brother cabinet minister to the RCMP for investigation." This was the first public mention of the RCMP report, and it drew a new storm of debate, chiefly demands for Sommers's resignation. Bruce Brown urged Premier Bennett to suspend the minister of lands and forests until the police inquiry was completed. Randolph Harding of the CCF made a similar demand and stated: "If there was neither ineptitude nor bungling, then we are witnesses to an extremely shrewd and clever piece of political manoeuvring and covering up by the Attorney General." Within the government ranks there was also agitation: members of cabinet were ill at ease over the lingering charges and the caucus was not comfortable with the attorney general's course of action—some believed that Bonner and the premier were not on a clear-cut course.

After a couple of weeks of continuous controversy, the premier regretfully decided to end the indecision. On February 27, when the House had adjourned for supper and was due to return for a night sitting, Bennett brought Bonner and Sommers to his office and said, "Mr. Sommers, until this matter is cleared up, you will not be minister."

Shaken, Sommers asked, "When do you want my resignation?"

"Within the half hour, Mr. Minister. And I want you to come to the night sitting: I'll be appointing two new ministers. I'll take this opportunity to expand my cabinet."

With his new ministers—Ray Williston and Ken Kiernan—Bennett went to Government House. The press knew nothing about it. Williston was sworn in as the minister of lands and forests and Kiernan as minister of mines.

That night, before the House assembled, Bennett went to caucus. There was normally a caucus meeting before night sittings but the premier did not often attend; this night, he explained the situation, and when the legislature sat, only the Socreds were aware that Sommers had been stripped of his responsibilities and that his cabinet portfolios were now divided between Williston and Kiernan. Therefore, when Sommers rose in his place to finally answer his critics, the House was not fully prepared for the drama of the moment. While Bennett leaned back and watched with "a stone-grey face," Sommers, one of the best Social Credit orators ever to hold forth in the legislature, gave his most virtuous performance:

> The time has come to break my silence on a matter which has been bruited about in this House in a most irresponsible and reprehensible

manner, and which has been the subject of the most dirty and slanted news coverage in the history of B.C., conducted principally by Mr. Stuart Keate, publisher of the Victoria *Daily Times*. Ever since I took office as Minster of Lands and Forests, my department and myself personally have been subjected to a continuous and increasingly bitter attack. The stakes are large enough to warrant the expenditure of the hundreds and thousands of dollars that have been invested in this campaign of destruction in the past three and a half years. The ultimate objective, I can assure you, is to wipe out all legislation that provides for government control in the cutting of our forests. It would be much more profitable to these operators if they were allowed to continue the "cut-and-get-out" variety of logging.

He accused Gibson and the Liberals of resorting to a

campaign of distortion, falsehoods, and vilification that is without parallel in the political annals of this great province. They have spread across the length and breadth of B.C. a blanket of propaganda that has not one iota in fact.... Never at any time have I used my ministerial office for personal gain either directly or indirectly, either morally or technically.... About a year ago an individual named Eversfield fled to California.... With him this man, who had been a trusted employee, took photostatic copies of a large number of documents belonging to his employer. These documents, it is claimed, are the evidence that shows that the Minister of Lands and Forests accepted bribes. Let me tell you that this charge is as phony as the man who makes it. In December this trusted employee sneaked back into Canada and swore to an affidavit before his only friend, Sturdy. He stayed in this country long enough to appear before the Attorney General, then he hurried back to Los Angeles, where he would be safe from any prosecution except for extraditable crimes.

Referring to the civil suit he had filed against Sturdy, Sommers said: "I don't have to point out what my fate will be if I am unable to justify the action that has been launched. I don't believe there is any question about the ends of justice being met through the course that is being followed."

And then, to the surprise of his listeners in the opposition benches, who were probably anticipating more pleas of innocence, Sommers announced his resignation as a minister of the crown. Opposition critics seemed stunned by the move; they had been angrily demanding Sommers's head for weeks, but hardly expected it to fall. For their part, members of the government appeared relieved. The torrent of abuse and vilification would now, they hoped, be stopped. Robert Bonner had privately concluded that if Sommers would not resign, he would do so himself, so untenable had the situation become.

But the Sommers affair was far from over for the Socreds. A few days after the minister's resignation, the estimates of his former departments were recalled for consideration in the House. "Estimates" is generally a free-for-all period when opposition MLAs question the details of each minister's proposed departmental spendings for the coming fiscal year. Fulfilling the important parliamentary principle of "grievance before supply," members can examine all aspects of policy and administration before agreeing to the proposed expenditures. In this particular case, the two ministers who had only just assumed Sommers's portfolios were up at bat without much practice. Ray Williston was first up as minister of lands and forests; the time was 8:30 P.M., March 1, 1956. The questions came in a steady flow and the opposition was hammering hard on the issue of forest management licences and the reasons for the resignation of Robert Sommers, who was now seated three or four seats down from the cabinet benches. It was an angry night in the House; tempers flared and blood pressures rose as the new minister repeatedly demonstrated an inability to answer questions concerning matters with which he was unfamiliar. Bonner's resignation was demanded; some members asked for Sommers to resign as an MLA. "This rotten display of deceit and cover-up," one member called it. "The government has perverted democracy in not telling the people the truth," said another. The heckling and chatter back and forth across the floor was especially heated—members were called "liars" and "idiots" and "crooks." Liberal George Gregory produced some new allegations, charging that "the bucket shop that exists for the purpose of securing forest management licences" had paid for airline tickets to eastern Canada for Sommers and his family in 1953 and covered their expensive hotel bills in Ottawa, Toronto and Detroit.

From the riotous mood of the legislature, it became apparent that the lands and forests estimates would be delayed by an opposition only too happy to filibuster. Premier Bennett decided that the honourable members would not be interrupted. In fact, if they wished, they could talk all night. This was not the first time, nor would it be the last, that he used this tactic to satiate an opposition's hunger for debate. The hours rolled by amidst threats, warnings and black predictions. A CCF member shouted: "You seem to think people have short memories. But the people will not tolerate deceit or cover-up. You are going to find out what I mean." But the opposition forces were ill prepared to maintain their momentum and the marathon sitting soon degenerated into a series of almost irrelevant monologues punctuated by rude, monosyllabic name-calling. As the sun rose over Victoria and the early daylight hours came on, the opposition had either made its point or run completely out of steam.

The House finally agreed to the estimates of the Department of Lands and Forests, and in about ten more minutes approved those of the Department of Mines. The record-breaking sitting of the B.C. legislature adjourned at 7:36 A.M. Bennett's strategy had apparently fulfilled members' appetites for debate, for the following day all remaining legislative business was completed and the session was prorogued.

Not long after the fourth and final session of the twenty-fourth parliament passed into history, the Department of the Attorney General received the first part of the RCMP investigation into the Sturdy charges—the Butler Report. The report had been keenly anticipated and some Socreds were nervous about what it might contain; they wondered whether the contents would remain confidential. One expects that when it was conveyed to the ministry on March 14, it would have been given immediate attention. Strangely, that apparently was not the case. Robert Bonner could not recall having ever actually seen the report, though one journalist wrote that "for him not to have read a report on which the fate of the government might have depended—and which was the talk of the province even though its contents were secret—would have been like Long John Silver refusing to take a peek at the treasure map of Treasure Island." Nevertheless, Bonner has consistently maintained this stance and there is no way of proving otherwise. One of the difficulties of chronicling the way the Butler Report was handled is that the attorney general's department was in a period of transition. The report had been forwarded to the deputy attorney general, H. A. MacLean, who shortly thereafter received an appointment to the provincial supreme court. It seems, therefore, that a senior department official dealt with it. The new deputy attorney general appointed in the spring of 1957 was Gilbert Kennedy, who said that there were no instructions for him regarding the report. He said that he never even saw it until five or six months into his job, and he remembers it as saying little. He also said that the senior official who had handled the report wrote a memo to the attorney general saying that there was nothing in it to warrant a prosecution.

All of this is astonishing when one considers the actual contents of the Butler Report: a fairly detailed examination of the charges made against Robert Sommers. Inspector Butler examined C. W. Eversfield's documentation, interviewed Eversfield, and examined and re-examined several forest industry executives before preparing his report which describes fictitious invoices, fictitious names, and "the setting up of alibis." The crucial portion, however, is paragraph 13 which states: "that there is definite indication of wrongdoing" on the part of Robert Sommers, Wick Gray's company, Pacific Coast Services Ltd., C. D. Schultz, and B. C. Forest Products Ltd. The covering letter to the attorney general's department said: "Your attention is particularly directed to the contents of paragraph 13."

"*Definite indication of wrongdoing.*" Yet the attorney general's department did not seem inclined to pursue the matter. Certainly, the report alone did not prove that the Sturdy charges were true, but neither did it clear Sommers *et al.* of his accusations. Inspector Butler suggested that further steps be taken — but his recommendations fell on deaf ears. Robert Sommers remembered asking Bonner to show him the Butler Report, but Bonner refused — and rightly so, since it was a confidential police investigation. Sommers also remembered Bonner visiting him at his home on a Saturday afternoon and assuring him that he had nothing to worry about. When Bonner was questioned about the Butler Report years later, in particular about paragraph 13, the former attorney general said:

> Indications of wrongdoing, however, are not the basis of a prosecution. I've never seen the Butler Report. I removed myself from direct involvement so that the officials in the department could bring forward recommendations untrammelled by any point of view that I might have. . . . In any event, the net effect of the Butler Report, as it was conveyed to me, did not justify a prosecution. It simply was inconclusive as to guilt or innocence. I think we were all of a view that in the presence of an inconclusive report calling for official action, the matter would be canvassed in any event in a civil action which was then pending. We decided that the appropriate course would be to reserve our further view until the evidence, which would be part of the civil action, came forward.

So, definite indication of wrongdoing or not, Bonner decided on a course of action which he considered logical: Sommers's civil suit against Sturdy should be pursued. However, the logic was questioned by many, including Robert Sommers himself. During the summer of 1956, he and his lawyer, Alfred Bull, met Bonner in the Hotel Vancouver and requested that a criminal charge be laid against Sommers. They also asked that he be charged alone — supposedly, this would have placed a limit on the kinds of evidence that could be admitted in court, making conspiracy difficult to prove. The attorney general refused, saying that prosecutions were not held for that purpose and that, on the information he had received, prosecution would undoubtedly result in acquittal because the evidence was insufficient; the proceeding would therefore be viewed as a whitewash. Bonner's view on the subject was plain: criminal prosecutions were for the purpose of pursuing law, not clearing reputations; Sommers's civil case was the proper vehicle for clearing his name. Sommers began to suspect that the attorney general was not completely on his side.

For Bonner and the government, the Sommers case had taken new twists; the former minister had sworn that there was nothing to the Sturdy allegations, yet now he was strongly interested in dropping his civil suit so that criminal charges could be laid against himself alone. Fortunately for the Socreds, the entire matter could not be publicly discussed while the civil suit was before the courts. On August 13, 1956, W. A. C. Bennett caught many by surprise when he requested the lieutenant governor to dissolve the legislature and ordered the writs for a provincial general election for September 19. The election came with only three years expired of his five-year term.

It must be understood that little of this drama was known to the general public, which was aware only that a lawyer named Sturdy had made vague charges that Sommers was guilty of unspecified irregularities in the granting of FMLs and that, under pressure from the opposition in the legislature, the minister had resigned his cabinet post until his name could be cleared in a civil court action which he had launched against Sturdy. The Sommers affair, while interesting, was hardly a major public concern when Bennett announced the 1956 general election.

The practical achievements of the Social Credit government and the feeling of progress engendered by bold predictions of even greater economic growth easily dwarfed the apparent mud-slinging of frustrated political opponents. As minister of finance, Bennett had described his 1956 budget as a "great prosperity budget," a "share the wealth" budget; it provided for increased aid to pensioners and other social assistance recipients, boosted the salaries of civil servants, reduced the provincial amusement tax, offered additional grants to municipalities and launched a gigantic new road construction program. Bulldozers and construction crews could be seen at work virtually everywhere in the province; B.C. was a booming frontier, teeming with new activity, relishing the growing pains. In little more than a year new capital investment had more than doubled to $1.3 billion. Announcing the election in a province-wide radio broadcast, Bennett referred to the Social Credit credo: "Anything which is physically possible and desirable can and must be made financially possible." Few listeners could argue with their premier when he concluded: "Never before in British Columbia's history has such rapid or such orderly progress taken place as in the past four years. Never before has the prospect for continued economic advance and material well-being appeared so promising." Few British Columbians wanted to hear about unsubstantiated government scandal, which sounded suspiciouly like the muckraking skullduggery of jealous politicians. So, although it had arrived sooner than expected, now appeared a good occasion for the Socreds to seek a renewed mandate to let the good times continue.

During the election campaign of 1956 Social Credit faced the remnants of the old-line parties and the CCF, which had once more changed leaders. Squabbling socialist factions had forced Arnold Webster to relinquish his tenuous hold on the leadership; in his stead came Robert Strachan, a

Nanaimo carpenter with a "brogue as heavy as an oak plank." The young Scotsman mounted an aggressive campaign in an effort to reassure free enterprise that it had nothing to fear from the election of a CCF government. However, Strachan's efforts were hampered by the bitter infighting of his colleagues, and he was effectively dismissed by his opponents. Robert Bonner, for example, laughingly referred to Strachan as "the breeze from the Hebrides." The Liberals tried again with Arthur Laing as leader, and the Tories went once more with Deane Finlayson. The campaign lacked focus; it was as if the now mighty Socreds were fighting against unarmed opponents. The Sommers affair was potentially the government's most vulnerable spot, but his civil action still precluded public discussion.

Was Sommers's libel suit purposely drawn out so that Sturdy's charges could not be transformed into a major election issue? This was the claim made by opponents of Social Credit and believed by many political observers. The process of the law can be tediously slow at the best of times, but in this instance the pace was especially frustrating. In June 1956 the provincial appeal court had refused Sommers's request for more particulars from Sturdy. On June 30 Sturdy demanded action on the case. He wanted an early decision so that the facts could be known before the election; but Sommers stalled and won. On August 16 the court registrar indicated that the court list was full and the case could not be heard until November—well after the election on September 19. Bennett had denied that the suit had anything to do with his timing of the election, but Sommers understood that the strategy of continuing his suit was deliberately to nullify the possibility of the charges being aired. In the end, the civil suit did not hamper open discussion of the allegations against Sommers, and political opponents hammered the government on the issue to the extent that Bonner would say: "In point of fact, it was discussed freely by everybody. So what the critics say and what was done seem to be quite unrelated."

Some people believed that Sommers should not seek re-election until he was absolved of the accusations against him, but he felt that not to run would have been to acknowledge some liability. He steadfastly assured his fellow Socreds that all was well, and in his interior riding of Rossland-Trail he was received like a homecoming hero. Surprisingly, the allegations of wrongdoing appeared only to strengthen his local popularity; the Social Credit troops gathered round him in this worrisome time. In February, when Sommers resigned from cabinet, Premier Bennett had received several votes of confidence from Sommers's constituents. For example, the Castlegar Social Credit group telegrammed: "WE WISH TO EXPRESS OUR ABSOLUTE CONFIDENCE IN OUR MLA MR. SOMMERS IN HIS HANDLING OF HIS TWO PORTFOLIOS WE REGRET HIS RESIGNATION AND WOULD LIKE TO SEE HIM REINSTATED AT THE MOST PROPITIOUS MOMENT." Now, his supporters mobilized for the election, and the Rossland-Trail nominating convention on August 21 became a Robert Sommers love-in. Only a single "no" was heard from the back of the steamy, crowded Trail hall when his name was put forward; the vote was recorded as unanimous. Sommers's nominator referred to him as "a small school teacher who has emerged to prominence . . . a first class asset to the province." Liberal leader Arthur Laing and Gordon Gibson were referred to as "a couple of professional hatchetmen." In his acceptance speech, Sommers alluded to the "great smear." He promised: "When the facts are in there will be great sorrow in the enemy's camp." At the conclusion of his remarks, the crowd cheered, hoisted him on their shoulders, and stamped their feet while the pianist played "For He's a Jolly Good Fellow." From his perch above the wild crowd, Sommers beamed: "Let the cold winds blow. I am terribly happy in this vote of confidence." From that night, voters in Rossland-Trail were urged to support "Honest Bob."

Of course, the party faithful did not know very much about the Sturdy charges and probably did not want to know. But the Socreds' opponents were making unruly demands and Sommers worried that they might begin to comment on the case. A letter from his lawyer, Alfred Bull, went out to the opposition parties threatening action for contempt of court should they dare to broach the subject during the campaign. Tory chieftain Deane Finlayson, clearly the most desperate of the opposition leaders, decided to risk a jail sentence for the possibility of media attention. On August 20, in a jam-packed North Vancouver church hall, Finlayson claimed that the issue of the election was not the guilt or innocence of Robert Sommers, but the complete dereliction of duty by the premier. He then slowly read a detailed list of specific payments made by Wick Gray to Sommers—these were the Sturdy charges, which until now had not been spelled out to the public. Two Vancouver newspapers published Finlayson's speech; Sommers immediately cited them for contempt of court. Interestingly, Sommers claimed that Bennett was extremely upset by the decision to press contempt charges because it was simply adding to an already dangerous campaign issue. The premier was not the only one who saw no wisdom in the move; on August 28, Justice J. O. Wilson dismissed the action for contempt and ordered Sommers to pay all costs. Not only did he throw the charge out but he did so with rather unnecessary flair. The judge called Sommers's earlier cabinet resignation speech a diatribe and hyperbolic virtuosity. He concluded: "He has wielded both the whitewash brush and the tar brush, and it ill becomes him to complain of the bare recital of a set of charges already known to the public." Thanks to the good judge, the Sturdy allegations were now on the record and, for the opposition parties, the Sommers case became the dominant issue of the campaign.

While the government opponents appeared to be chasing after one man's reputation, the Socreds were campaigning on an impressive collective record. Their slogan in 1956 was "Progress not Politics"—and that seemed to neatly sum up the latent urge of most British Columbians. Bennett's campaign began with a well-publicized opening ceremony for the PGE southern extension to North Vancouver. He then travelled to the far north where he spoke of the province's vast natural resources and painted his "northern vision" of development which would bring increased prosperity for all. He had already pushed through a redistribution of the legislative seats in 1955, increasing the Assembly from forty-eight to fifty-two members. Three Vancouver area ridings were made two-member constituencies and the northerly Peace River riding was split into two electoral districts. Opposition members screamed with indignation, since the population of the Peace River region did not justify one, let alone two, MLAs; and the incumbent was a Social Crediter. However, the premier rattled on about the great developments that were bound to open up the north. His new theory of democratic representation was totally unorthodox, based as it was on hoped-for population growth; and of course he was anticipating the allegiance of future generations. This episode provides another striking example of Bennett's irrational behaviour over matters related to the Peace River country.

In his chase after a majority of the fifty-two seats in the legislature, Bennett ran a brilliant, fast-paced campaign; he emphasized that tremendous progress had been made in B.C. since Social Credit came to power in 1952—roads, highways, bridges and rail lines. It was progress people could see. To demonstrate Social Credit's regard for the "little man," the premier came out with an innovative benefit: he promised to institute an annual grant to every homeowner in the province, and referred to this novel form of tax relief in pure Social Credit terminology as a "first dividend"—"Social Credit in action."

"Progress not Politics": Bennett was the first B.C. politician to successfully seek office by censuring the essence of his trade. Of course, in the populist tradition, what he meant by the slogan was a criticism of the kind of carping politics that he felt the opposition parties were using against his former minister. On the few occasions when he did refer to the Sommers case, he promised to stand by the decision of the highest court in the land—the voting public. In Kelowna, he bemoaned: "What poor Sommers is trying to do is first to clear himself in his home constituency. No one has charged him; no one is suing him. He knows he must clear himself first with the people in the local constituency, which is the highest court of the land in our democracy." In Vancouver, a crowd of 2,500 jammed an auditorium and was so thick with hecklers that the premier could not be heard. Bennett accused some of the rowdies of being communists, others of being paid. Fistfights broke out. On another occasion, Bennett promised that Sommers would return to cabinet when cleared of all the charges, and in an uncommon literary burst, he quoted from *Othello:* ". . . he that filches from me my good name robs me of that which not enriches him, and makes me poor indeed."

As the election campaign approached its conclusion, the opposition parties—and the urban press—flayed away at the Sommers issue. Strachan, Laing and Finlayson each demanded that Bonner release the Butler Report; he refused. Socred opponents claimed that Bennett and Bonner were part of a diabolical cover-up and argued that the people should defeat the government so that the facts of the matter could be made known. But the opposition parties seemed to go too far, and their denunciations produced a rebounding effect. Robert Strachan tried to prevent the Sommers affair from becoming the predominant point of attack, but his efforts were in vain. He explained: "With three opposition parties attacking the government on this one issue, it looked like this poor little government was being attacked by these terrible opposition parties." The Liberal *Vancouver Sun* published a screaming front-page editorial denouncing the government's "deceits and slick political trickeries." Bennett responded by denouncing the old-line press and claimed there was a sinister conspiracy of the big city establishment against his people's government. He cried: "I call upon all citizens of our province to rise up and support Social Credit government candidates against this newspaper baron's [Don Cromie's] dictatorship."

British Columbians responded to their premier's plea in record numbers and on September 19, 1956, elected thirty-nine Social Credit members to the fifty-two-seat legislature. The CCF finished second with ten seats; the Liberals maintained two; and Tom Uphill was again successful in Fernie. Not only had the Socreds significantly increased their majority but they had also fashioned one of the most lopsided electoral victories in B.C.'s history. They received 45.84 per cent of the popular vote; the CCF mustered 22.32 per cent; Liberals, 21.77 per cent; Conservatives, once more shut out, took 3.11 per cent. In Rossland-Trail, "Honest Bob" Sommers was easily re-elected by the "highest court in the land," winning almost twice as many votes as his nearest rival. On election night, Minister of Health Eric Martin remarked that although the government required currycombs to scrape off the campaign mud, "the people have made us pure as the driven snow." Plainly, it was a remarkable victory, especially considering the hysterics of the campaign. Bennett boasted that the Socreds had beaten not just the combined forces of the opposition parties, "but the Canadian Broadcasting Corporation and the majority of the metropolitan press." He hailed the Social Credit sweep as the "greatest victory for the ordinary people since the Magna Carta."

The staggering victory allowed Bennett and his government to bask for a while in the glory of representative democracy. The election results seemed to momentarily clear the highly charged, partisan atmosphere; attacks on

Sommers were, for the moment, infrequent, but if the "highest court" had been willing to exonerate the former Social Credit minister, the civil courts were having a more difficult time of it. In October 1956, a judge agreed to allow Sturdy to examine Sommers's bank records. This was appealed in the Supreme Court of Canada, which did not reject the appeal until the following March. Sommers's civil suit was destined to drag on and on. During the spring legislative session of 1957 the weakened opposition forces once more took up the fight. They demanded that Bonner, once and for all, release the Butler Report. The attorney general was if nothing else consistent—he again refused to release the document. He would argue:

> Police reports are not released because they are intended to bring all points of view together into some sort of summary and, in themselves, are not evidence. They are a narrative or they contain speculations or they contain suggestions. But for further lines of inquiry they are documents of the most confidential nature; otherwise, there would be no reputation safe in the country, because I'm sure that people are mentioned, much to their surprise, in a great variety of police reports and in ways which are totally innocent. So the presence of a police report is to be viewed as a confidential document and is not to be released for the benefit of one person or the salvation of a government or anything else.

The opposition had difficulty accepting Bonner's position; they asked for a proper judicial inquiry and demanded the attorney general's resignation for perceived delays in the determination of justice. For the third consecutive year, the Sommers case highlighted the legislative session. Liberal MLA George Gregory reported on the contents of the secret Butler Report, without explaining where he had received the information. He declared that Sommers had received money from Wick Gray, one of whose firms "existed for no purpose other than to assist its clients to obtain forest management licences." Gregory stated that it was as great an offence in law to accept loans as to accept gifts, or bribes, if the purpose was corrupt. "A crime was committed," he said, "whether it be accepting bribes or committing perjury. It is such a serious crime that it shocks the comprehension of people interested in the administration of justice that the Attorney General should do nothing about it." From Bonner's perspective, however, the matter was being handled in a legal and proper way. He well knew that the matter would have to be resolved, but was determined to maintain an arm's length position, for to do otherwise would have been to court personal and political disaster.

Through all of this Sommers kept quiet. He participated in the 1957 session as a government backbencher and buckled down to the job of ordinary MLA. Some of his old confidence seems to have returned, but he appeared oblivious to the legal skirmishing of his civil suit. On September 8, 1957, he failed to show up for the annual meeting of his Rossland-Trail constituency association; a wire from Victoria said he was ill. He was reported seen in Castelgar on September 14, but afterwards dropped out of sight. Sommers was ordered to appear for a pretrial hearing on September 23, but did not attend. His lawyer produced a medical certificate saying his client had "paroxysmal tachycardia"—at times, his heart beat too fast. He was ordered to appear for a medical examination three days later or else have his civil suit against Sturdy dismissed. Once again, Sommers was nowhere to be found. On October 28 his suit against Sturdy was tossed out of court after twenty-two months of futile manoeuvring. Where was Sommers? All that was known was that he had mysteriously dropped from sight. Later, however, it was disclosed that he had fled the country—Sommers's heart was beating too rapidly in the United States.

This is one of the most curious episodes in the entire controversy surrounding Robert Sommers. The former lands and forests minister had been growing increasingly apprehensive about his future and, in particular, feared that a powerful conspiracy was out to get him. He became anxious about his chances of clearing himself before the B.C. courts. Apparently he was advised that if he left the country nothing could be done to him; and so, in the autumn of 1957, he "skipped." He took this action impulsively, it seems, and informed neither Bennett nor Bonner beforehand. But Waldo Skillings, with whom Sommers had served as a teaching intern thirty years earlier, became directly involved with Sommers in exile. The recollections of Sommers and Skillings conflict on many details. According to Skillings: "Sommers phoned me from Seattle and he said, 'Waldo, I'm at a motor court on the highway and I'm broke. I need some money.' I said, 'Look, Bob, I don't know why you're coming to me.' 'Well,' he said, 'you get hold of Gordon Wismer; he'll tell you that there are friends of mine up there who don't want to see me starve to death.'" Skillings decided on impulse to see what he could do; he would stress that he acted alone, advising no one of his actions. Wismer, former attorney general and aging Liberal machine boss, apparently put Skillings in touch with a prominent member of the Vancouver business community. Skillings refused to name the person and would say only that he was the spokesman for a consortium of business interests, "possibly" a number of large forest companies, who were prepared to help keep Sommers in exile. Skillings was told: "We business people have come to the conclusion that Sommers is a bad apple and we want to keep him out of the country." Skillings related:

> There were more negotiations. I never mentioned it to Bennett; I never mentioned it to Bonner. I thought at that time that I was doing a service

to my country, because Sommers was a liability to this government that was doing such a fantastic job. So they said, "Here, Waldo, we've got $25,000 in American money"—because he wanted it in American money—"We want you to make the delivery and get him to sign this piece of paper." "Well," I said, "suppose he won't sign it." And they said, "Don't deliver it; it's as simple as that." I said, "Alright." So I took the money in a moneybelt and went to Seattle and saw [Sommers]. He said, "There's no way I'm signing that thing. I'd be signing my life away. No way." I said, "Well, that's that."

Skillings flew back to British Columbia and returned the money.

In his meeting with Skillings, Sommers recalled being told that "there is a group of people who were interested in keeping the Social Credit Party from destruction, who were prepared to finance me if I left the country." Sommers said Skillings offered him $600 a month for life and refused to reveal the source. "The proposition was made to me that now that I'd resigned, maybe it would cool everything down completely if I stayed in the United States. [Skillings] said he could arrange to pick up my family and sell my house." Later, Sommers said he was "hazy" on the details regarding the $600 a month for life.

In any event, Sommers and Skillings were destined to have one more rendezvous in Seattle. A week later, Skillings recalled, Sommers phoned him and said, "Waldo, I haven't eaten for three days. I've reconsidered that idea. . . ." So Skillings got in touch with the consortium again and this time they worked out a plan to offer Sommers $5,000 a year for five years. Skillings went to Seattle and offered him $5,000, saying, "In one year, if you do what you say you'll do, you get $5,000. After that, another $5,000, and another—until it comes out to $25,000." Sommers, according to Skillings, agreed to the plan and accepted the $5,000.

Skillings returned to Victoria and told Bennett about the strange affair he had become embroiled in. He said the premier was furious: "Waldo, what did you get mixed up in this thing for?" Skillings probably thought he had helped to lay the Sommers case to rest, but within a few weeks, in November 1957, Robert Sommers quietly arrived back in Victoria. It seems that his wife and family could not be persuaded to run and hide, and he somehow had renewed hope that he might win his case in court. Skillings had kept in touch with the business interests wanting to keep the former cabinet minister out of the country. By returning to Canada, Sommers had broken his word and the deal was off. Apparently, Skillings was told: "He's back now and there's no more money. We wash our hands of the whole thing. You just keep your mouth shut and as far as we're concerned it never happened."

But for Skillings, this was not the end of his involvement in the bizarre drama. Sommers, on his lawyer's advice, wanted to be charged alone in order to avoid a broad inquiry into the allegations surrounding him. He avoided contact with the government but went to Waldo Skillings's house and said, according to Sommers, "Waldo, I feel the only way to settle this whole thing is to have charges laid against me and me alone. I'm prepared to defend myself alone because I know what I did and I don't know what anyone else has done. But I'm beginning to feel that maybe they did do something." Sommers pleaded with Skillings to pass on this request to the premier and to ask him to instruct Bonner to act accordingly.

Skillings nervously told Bennett of Sommers's request but did not receive any assurance as to how charges would be laid. It seems the premier was upset and said, "Waldo, what are you meeting with him for? Didn't I tell you to keep away? You're stupider than I thought you were."

"I was doing what I thought was the right thing. Should I tell Bonner?"

Bennett apparently replied, "Tell Bonner nothing and don't tell anybody that you spoke to me. I'm not supposed to know anything. And I don't want to know."

Sommers desired yet another meeting with Skillings who was now extremely worried and said, "Bob, you're being watched and I know damn well that I'm being watched. I'm not going to your house and you're not going to my house." But they met in Mount Douglas Park on the outskirts of Victoria two or three times over the next few days. Sommers believed that Skillings was acting as an intermediary between himself and the premier, and that the necessary arrangements were being made for him to be charged alone. Skillings denied that this was the case and claimed to be meeting with Sommers on his own volition out of compassion for him. Sommers said that at their final meeting they reviewed the situation and Skillings informed him of the day and hour that he would be arrested. Aside from the fact that these meetings did take place, there is no way of corroborating either man's story; neither Bennett nor Bonner offered any enlightenment on these clandestine events.

Meanwhile, the process of justice was taking definite direction. When Sommers's civil suit had been dismissed, Sturdy filed Eversfield's documents in the Vancouver court registry; now, for the first time, the full details of Sturdy's charges were public. The call for action and the clamour of the agitated political opposition had reached new heights. Attorney General Bonner was on a trade mission in Europe at the time and the trans-Atlantic wires began to buzz; Bennett wanted Bonner's opinion. The attorney general issued the statement to the press that there would be no judicial inquiry, nor for that matter would he release the Butler Report; but after consulting with the premier Bonner changed his mind and stated that an inquiry was not ruled out. On November 1, 1947, a tired-looking Bennett announced that

Chief Justice Sloan had been appointed as a one-man royal commission to probe the long-standing Sturdy allegations. He went out of his way to stress that the investigation was launched on Bonner's recommendation, though Gilbert Kennedy, the deputy attorney general, commented: "The attorney general was not too happy about it. But I think it is fair to say that it was the premier who felt it should be done." Upon announcing the commission, Bennett was asked if he now considered the attorney general had erred in not acting sooner. Normally, the premier would have smiled and said. "Mr. Bonner is the finest . . ." but on that night, with his chin sunk into his chest, his only comment was: "My friend the attorney general is the attorney general." This happened while Sommers was still in exile and in a curiously impulsive act, he recorded a message that was broadcast on several B.C. radio stations: he admitted to receiving loans from Wick Grey, claimed he possessed sufficient evidence to prove his innocence, and would "genuinely welcome criminal prosecution."

The Sloan Commission met for the first, and what would be only time on November 12, 1957. In fact, it sat for only half an hour. Alfred Bull, now acting on behalf of Charles Schultz's company, said that the government had no constitutional right to set up a royal commission to investigate criminal charges. This abruptly threw the meeting into confusion, then immediate adjournment. The Sloan Commission was quashed and, as a result, the Sturdy charges were for the first time formally in the hands of the Department of the Attorney General. Bonner was now in a position that demanded him to act, and he was far from comfortable. He ordered routine criminal proceedings against his former cabinet teammate, although his department had the gravest doubts that they would secure a conviction.

At 8:00 A.M. on November 21, 1957, the RCMP knocked on the front door of Robert Sommers's home in Victoria and presented a warrant for his arrest. They came with a matron for Mrs. Sommers should she break down, but the family were waiting for them and offered them coffee. When Sommers read the charges, however, he became ill. He was not being charged alone—he was accused of being part of a conspiracy involving B.C. Forest Products, Pacific Coast Services, C. D. Schultz and Co., and Evergreen Lumber Sales. That same morning, the RCMP arrested Wick Gray and Charles Schultz. On the direct orders of his one-time colleague, the attorney general, Sommers was flown in a police aircraft to Vancouver where he was formally charged with conspiracy and bribery. According to Sommers, this was "the big double-cross"—he believed that he had made a deal with Bonner and Bennett, but events were not proceeding according to his imagined plan. Responding to Sommers's charge that he was double-crossed in the laying of charges, Bonner said that that was "a lot of baloney." Sommers's arrest came an incredible 707 days after Attorney General Bonner had first heard the allegations of Sturdy and Eversfield. Sommers made arrangements for bail and the preliminary hearing was set for February 12, 1958.

The second session of British Columbia's twenty-fifth parliament was opened on January 23, 1958, and it was clear from the start that the Sommers case—even though before the courts—would again be the foremost topic of discussion. Sommers attended the session, which in itself became a point of controversy. He had been unsure whether he should attend the session as the duly elected member for Rossland-Trail or be present at the preliminary hearing for his trial which was being held that day in Vancouver. He said he went to Bennett for advice and he told him to be in the House; Sommers applied for and received permission to be absent from the hearing. It was subsequently appealed by the attorney general's department. Sommers was furious. He stormed down to the Parliament Buildings and demanded to see the premier. Ron Worley informed him that Bennett was in the middle of a meeting with national Social Credit leader Solon Low. No matter, Sommers barged into the premier's inner sanctum and, in an angry and no doubt embarrassing exchange, demanded to know who was running the government, the premier or the attorney general? Bennett immediately phoned Bonner who apparently did not know of his department's attempt to force Sommers to attend the preliminary hearing. In any event, the appeal against Sommers's request for permission to be absent from the hearing was unsuccessful and he was allowed to take his seat in the House alongside his uncomfortable Socred brethren.

Far and away the most uncomfortable member of the overwhelming Social Credit majority was Attorney General Robert Bonner. Opposition leader Robert Strachan denounced him for placing political considerations before his public duty: "He has clouded the issue with the jargon of his voice—worn phrases and the ingenuities of legal verbiage." Other opposition MLAs criticized him for not laying criminal charges against his former cabinet colleague at an earlier date. Bonner could easily deflect these routine partisan attacks, but he was not as well prepared for an assault from within. Several Socreds, including Cyril Shelford, Hugh Shantz, Stan Carnell and Irvine Corbett publicly expressed dissatisfaction with the manner in which the attorney general had dealt with Sommers. However, the major troublemaker was Mel Bryan, Social Credit member for North Vancouver. On January 29, 1958, Bryan rose in the House and denounced Bonner, demanding that he resign his post of attorney general. A quiet, little-known MLA, Bryan electrified the legislature with his speech; as he read a lengthy statement of criticism, Bonner blushed beet red. Bryan told the excited House that in 1952 Social Credit had brought a new concept of government to the province: "something new, clean and sincere.... I believe generally the people charged with governing our province today have shown a realization of this different concept of government, have shown it with a vigour and progressiveness that is reflected in the great strides forward taken in our economy. But I insist that the manner in which the attorney general failed significantly to deal with an issue involving a cabinet minister and the government itself has placed a serious strain on the respect and support that this government has generally deserved. . . ." The attorney general, who was asked by the press for a reaction, offered a single terse comment: "I've never walked away from a tough job in my life and I don't intend to now." Bennett was in Vancouver at the time attending a banquet for a special visitor: Queen Mother Elizabeth. Contacted for a response to Bryan's demand for Bonner's resignation, the premier, who was in a royal mood, quipped that Bonner "is the most outstanding Attorney General this province or any other province has ever had."

Bryan's speech produced a new crop of anti-Social Credit newspaper headlines. The member for North Vancouver was invited to cross the floor of the House and join the opposition forces. He met privately with other disaffected Socred MLAs in an effort to consolidate what seemed a possible Social Credit revolt over the issue. But Bennett, Bonner and the vast ranks of loyal Socreds held firm. Outspoken government backbencher John Tisdalle, for instance, pleaded in the House for Bonner: "I am not admitting the Attorney General erred, but if he did, he should be treated with understanding and forgiveness." Bryan had virtually burnt his Social Credit bridges; on February 4, he rose white-faced in the legislature and announced that he was indeed crossing the floor to sit as an independent member in opposition to the government. Bennett, who had made a similar trek to that side of the House not too many years earlier, was visibly agitated. In a rare burst of uncontrolled anger, he denounced Bryan as a traitor. He went so far as to accuse him of packing the convention that had nominated him as a Socred candidate in 1956. Above a chorus of catcalls and opposition heckling, Bennett shouted: "He was warned, and he was warned again, but he packed the convention and he got the nomination." Bryan's defection seemed to hit a raw nerve and Bennett reacted in a manner almost completely foreign to his character. Even years later, he would ask rhetorically: "Was Bryan a Social Crediter or was he a Liberal plant?"

The government survived Mel Bryan's heroics over the handling of the Sommers case, and it survived the 1958 legislative session—although not without a few additional bruises. On March 3, during the review of the attorney general's estimates, opposition leader Strachan moved a motion of nonconfidence because of "almost two years of deliberate evasion and failure to act." Just before the vote was taken on the motion, three government MLAs slipped out of the House: Cyril Shelford, Irvine Corbett and Fred Sharpe absented themselves from the proceedings in order to avoid embarrassing the government any further, for their consciences prevented them from supporting Bonner's handling of the case. Needless to say, the government won the vote; Strachan's motion was defeated twenty-nine to fourteen. The Socreds once more demonstrated a united front in public, but privately were severely split over the issue. It is difficult to determine exactly what forms of discipline, if any, were applied to the Social Credit caucus on this occasion. Bonner explained to government members and to the public that the reason criminal charges were not originally filed against Sommers was due to the advice he had received from senior civil servants in his department. It was felt that Sommers's civil action for slander would clear the air, but when the civil suit was dismissed because of Sommers's mysterious absence, and when the subsequent royal commission was disbanded, the government was compelled to get to the root of the matter. Therefore, the case was now before the criminal courts and should not have been the subject of uninformed discussion. Although Bonner seemed rattled at the time by the criticisms of fellow Socreds, his view throughout was: "It's really of no consequence what any MLA thinks about the way a case is handled—or any member of the public for that matter. The way a case is handled has to be to the satisfaction of the court and is not a subject which is susceptible of influence from the streetcorner, even if it is the streetcorner in the legislature. So, what MLAs may have thought is of no consequence. And once the prosecution is launched, it's in the hands of the crown prosecutor, and the progress of the trial is in the hands of the trial judge, and comment from the legislature or anywhere else has no incidence whatsoever."

On March 20, 1958, the legislative session in Victoria was prorogued. Persistent criticism over the Sommers affair had produced visible scars on the government's hide, but the Socreds remained intact as B.C.'s governing party. During the session the term "forest mangement licence" had been scrapped—having become a certifiably dirty word—and replaced by a new term, but similar concept: "tree farm licence." Also, former Chief Justice Sloan was appointed as a special adviser to the provincial government on forestry-related matters. Meanwhile, Sommers's preliminary hearing was concluded and the long-awaited trial date was set for May 1. The eye of the storm shifted to the courts of Vancouver.

Before discussing the actual trial, it is worth making a few observations about this very important court case. Sommers and the other defendants involved opted for trial by judge and jury. Justice J. O. Wilson was chosen as the trial judge, and this seems a decidedly strange choice. Wilson, who had a reputation for handing down harsh sentences, was the same judge who had heard and dismissed Sommers's contempt charge against Deane Finlayson in the 1956 election campaign. Even Wilson was surprised when he was chosen. Another puzzle concerns Sommers's legal counsel. Ten leading lawyers argued before judge and jury; on Sommers's behalf was the well-known Vancouver "gladiator of the courts," Angelo Branca. No one seems clear on how Branca received the assignment. Apparently, he was defending the former cabinet minister on the instructions of a leading Vancouver law firm. Branca never discovered who paid for his legal services, but was well aware that Sommers was not a moneyed man. Branca's biographer later noted: "Inadvertently he did learn that the money came from a man not known at all in politics but known in industry. He never heard his name." Among the other unanswered questions relating to this case was the sudden death of one of the prime witnesses: Hector Munro, head of B.C. Forest Products, the main forest company mentioned in the suit. As president of the company, he would have been able to answer many unresolved questions, especially in the fuzzy areas of political campaign donations and FML negotiations. Munro's death practically coincided with the commencement of the trial; apparently it was a suicide. One other mystery relates to Sommers's bank loan of $8,000 taken out to redeem his notes from Wick Gray after Sturdy and Eversfield had made their unsubstantiated allegations to Bonner. A few days prior to the start of the trial, Sommers dropped into the bank to ascertain the amount of the loan outstanding. The bank manager informed him that the loan had been paid off in full, but would not say by whom. Sommers's lawyer could not find out either. One writer, Paddy Sherman, later speculated that the loan was repaid by Social Credit Party funds.

It was in this atmosphere of intrigue and suspense that the court battle was fought. It was a bewildering and complicated case: the court heard over a million words of testimony and received 1,060 exhibits which were wheeled in and out of the courtroom in a hand truck. The trial lasted through six adjournments and eighty-two days of testimony, becoming one of the longest criminal trials in Canadian history. Throughout, the public and especially the partisan press feasted on the details of an embarrassing, extremely convoluted story. There was the weaseling of Wick Gray and his shady relationship with Sommers, the machinations of B.C. Forest Products in an effort to procure a much-coveted FML and, most important, the money and other fringe benefits received by Sommers—were they loans or bribes? B.C. Forest Products paraded a steady stream of witnesses testifying to the company's integrity and virtue. Lawyers for all companies attempted to show that the monies were simply contributions to political party funds. Branca defended Sommers by arguing that the funds that passed from Gray to his client "were personal loans from an old friend to enable him to live in a style befitting a cabinet minister, and were being repaid." Other defence lawyers suggested the existence of a sinister and nefarious plot to destroy Social Credit. Wick Gray decided not to take the stand but on August 6, the fifty-fifth day of the trial, Sommers opted to testify. He described his activities as a minister of the crown and pleaded innocent of any wrongdoing in the awarding of FML no. 22 to B.C. Forest Products. Several times he was forced to respond to the pointed questions of crown prosecutor Victor Dryer by claiming cabinet confidentiality or suggesting that only the premier could answer. However, Bennett was not called upon to testify. C. W. Eversfield, who was flown in from California for the trial, survived several days of cross-examination; he remained calm, composed and never once cracked. As he stepped out of the witness box for the last time, an experienced court reporter was heard to remark: "There goes the ball game." Many years later, Robert Sommers revealed that for $5,000 "someone" had offered to bump off Eversfield so that he would never show up at the trial.

Throughout the trial, Judge Wilson attempted to clarify the legal points and nuances of testimony for the benefit of the jury. Much of the evidence admitted consisted of detailed accountancy records and it is difficult to imagine how the lay jury of nine men and three women could serve justice under its weight. On one occasion, while the jury was excluded from the courtroom, Judge Wilson ruled a certain matter irrelevant and therefore inadmissible. "And," he added, "it would only confuse the jury." Defence counsel Alfred Bull immediately shot back: "Your lordship would not want to take from us the last refuge of defence counsel—the right to confuse the jury?" This was a rare moment of levity in an otherwise painfully serious trial. The jury retired on October 30, 1958, after living with the case for six months. It stayed out for more than fifty-two hours, grappling to arrive at a just verdict. At 4:10 P.M. on November 1, the seventy-sixth day of sitting, the jury made up its collective mind. That night, Robert Sommers and the other principals in the case walked into the Vancouver Courthouse from the cold evening rain. Sommers chewed on an imaginary piece of gum while the verdict was delivered—a strained, defeated look quickly spread over his face. He was found guilty of being part of a criminal conspiracy to accept bribes; also guilty was Wick Gray. B.C. Forest Products was found not guilty of three charges and proceedings were stayed on a fourth charge. The jury disagreed about the others involved. As Sommers left the courtroom and walked slowly down the steps to the cells, he managed a strained, painful smile.

Robert Sommers and Wick Gray were remanded in custody until the conclusion of the assize for sentence. On November 3, Judge Wilson advised the jury that since Sommers had been found guilty of conspiracy, it would not be inconsistent to acquit him on the bribery charges. In effect, proof was required that money had changed hands for corrupt purposes; Sommers would need to have known that he was taking money in exchange for awarding licences. On November 5, the jury found Sommers guilty of five of the seven charges against him, including: receiving rugs worth $607; bonds worth $3,000; $1,000 mailed in cash, and $2,500 sent by telegraph. Gray was convicted of eight charges involving $13,107. It was a strange finding in a long, drawn out case. The jury decided that B.C. Forest Products was not part of a bribery plot in connection with the FML it had received; yet Sommers was guilty of receiving bribes in connection with the licence. On November 14, Sommers and Wick Gray prepared to receive sentencing. With his head bent at the rail of the prisoner's dock in Vancouver assize court, Sommers stared dully. Judge Wilson, as might be expected, had a few words to say:

> I do not enjoy hitting men when they are down, as both you men are, but this is an exceptional case, and requires comment. The jury, not I, has found that you are both scoundrels. The evidence on which that finding must be based reveals that both of you have befouled the political and moral atmosphere of this province over a period of many years, resorting to every sort of shabby device to conceal your iniquities. The harm you, Sommers, have done to our traditional respect for government will I hope be slight, because, thank God, the sort of behaviour of which you have been convicted is not just exceptional but unique in our political history.

Wilson then sentenced both Sommers and Gray to five years in jail and fined Gray's companies almost $20,000. This final act took up eighteen minutes of the eighty-third and final sitting day of the trial. The ordeal was over—almost.

Although the direction of the trial must have psychologically prepared him for conviction, Sommers was in a sorry state of shock over the sentence he received. Indeed, most observers were surprised by the harshness of the sentence. "Honest Bob" Sommers was about to become the first minister of the crown in the British Commonwealth to serve a prison term. Sommers was extremely bitter, saying that if he was not a "fall guy" for "some other people," then he was at least "used as a vehicle for their self-betterment. And yet the situation was unknown to me that I was being used in this way." Robert Bonner was "a little surprised about the convictions in view of what crown counsel had told me. The indications I had received were that they had a very thin case. And I knew it to be thin . . . the chief counsel for the crown was very doubtful that he could get a conviction; if Sommers had not taken the stand in his own defence, I don't think he ever would have." Many Social Crediters felt hard done by; it was commonly held that B.C. Forest Products had escaped scot-free, while Sommers paid a disastrous personal and political price. As Bonner noted: "That was one of the difficulties in the whole case, and one of the difficulties we had in the matter of considering a prosecution. . . . Nobody received any preferential treatment on any subject whatever; and so one element of the bribery aspect seemed to be missing."

During the final days of the trial Bennett vacationed in Phoenix,

Arizona. Upon his return at the Vancouver airport, he was swamped by news media enquiring about the damaging political fallout resulting from the conviction of his former minister. Tanned and in good cheer, Bennett informed the incredulous reporters that Sommers's conviction had actually strengthened the Social Credit government, that the people now realized British Columbia's government operated without fear of favour: "Once they thought there was a law for cabinet ministers and a law for people who sweep streets. Now they know that Mr. Bonner, the most brilliant Attorney General who ever went through law school, has done his duty."

According to Robert Sommers, however, the attorney general was doing more than his simple duty. Before receiving his sentence, Sommers had resigned his seat in the legislature and, while awaiting the results of an appeal that he had launched, was freed on bail raised by Socred MLA Irvine Corbett. Unaccountably, the crown also decided to appeal, seeking a longer sentence. The RCMP arrived unannounced at Sommers's home at 1:00 A.M. with notice of the appeal. In a fit of anger, Sommers phoned Bonner, getting him out of bed, and shouted: "What in the hell are your trying to do to me now? Aren't you satisfied with five years?" Bonner claimed that the decision to appeal for a harsher sentence would have been made purely at the discretion of crown counsel. But Sommers felt that Bonner was personally determined to persecute him and he threatened to retaliate by fighting against the government in the forthcoming by-election in his former riding of Rossland-Trail. He also threatened to release some potentially embarrassing details about the inner workings of the Social Credit Party. No matter, the appeal was not withdrawn, though it did fail. During the period of the appeal procedure, when Sommers was making angry noises behind the scenes, several former Socred colleagues contacted him in an effort to dissuade him from causing any trouble. Eric Martin, Wes Black and Ken Kiernan were among those who tried to soothe his defeated spirit. Phil Gaglardi telephoned: "Bob, I'm praying for you . . . and I'll be praying for you until I see you." More than two decades later, Sommers said that he still had not seen Gaglardi, "so it has to be the longest prayer in history."

Sommers did not participate in the by-election campaign to fill the vacancy in his former bailiwick. The contest was scheduled for December 15, 1958, and it became an all-out test of confidence in Social Credit, W. A. C. Bennett, Robert Bonner and the legacy of "Honest Bob" Sommers. Donald Brothers, Sommers's former campaign manager, was nominated to try to hold the Social Credit seat, and he described the campaign: "I realize that it was a critical by-election for Social Credit; the government viewed it as critical, so did the opposition. . . . W. A. C. Bennett says that politics is war. It *was* war; it was real, active, hand-to-hand combat. He came up and he addressed the largest political campaign meeting ever held in Trail. It was the final rally of the campaign, and it was difficult for him to get there, he was up all night coming through a snowstorm. He made a very good speech, and promised that the government would build a bridge across the Columbia River." Brothers won a close decision in an extremely tight battle among Social Credit, CCF, Liberal and Tory candidates. Following the victory, Robert Sommers snidely commented that his criminal conviction was "the best thing that ever happened" to his former constituency, since the government offered the electors almost everything and delivered on all of their promises, including the bridge over the Columbia. "To think that for three years I was beating my gums for those things," said Sommers, "and never dreamed that the way to get them was to go to jail."

After an unsuccessful appeal, Sommers was sent to prison in the spring of 1959, eventually serving two years and four months of his sentence before being paroled in July 1961. Ironically, while he was in jail his wife supported the family with a manual labour job at B.C. Forest Products. With much bitterness, Sommers later recalled that she worked "damn hard." For its part, B.C. Forest Products remained untouched by the entire episode, getting FML no. 22, which became a successful and profitable addition to its business as well as to the economy of Vancouver Island.

The Sommers affair cast a long shadow over B.C. politics, the repercussions being felt long after the former minister was removed from the scene. During the spring session of 1959 the legislature once more debated the case—for the fifth consecutive year. Opposition members castigated the government for the protracted delay in the achievement of justice. Once again, they challenged Robert Bonner to release the Butler Report, which three years earlier had referred to "definite indications of wrongdoing" on the part of Sommers *et al.* They endeavoured to use the Butler Report recommendations to prove that Bonner had perpetuated a kind of cover-up to protect a fellow cabinet minister. For a time, demands for the attorney general's resignation were rampant: CCFer Randolph Harding asserted that the tragedy was not that a crime had been committed but that Bonner had failed to act decisively. Bonner defended himself by stating his belief in the principle that a man should not be placed under investigation or assumed guilty when his accusers refuse to put forth their evidence:

> The failure of Eversfield to bring his material to the Lord Commission; his silence on the subject for two years; the fact that Mr. Sturdy should keep such a matter to himself for three months, and deliberately fail to place his evidence in official channels . . . are inexcusable. Secondly, even in the midst of such charges as these, if a man believes his reputation is in issue in respect of allegations which might be criminal in

import, the crown is nevertheless not justified in setting aside his civil remedy by issuing an indictment except upon the clearest of evidence consistent with the guilt of the accused, and inconsistent with any other reasonable interpretation.

In retrospect, it must be admitted that Bonner's position does not seem unreasonable—and certainly he maintained it firmly and consistently. However, in the heat and subjectivity of the day, his defence was unconvincing, even to some members of his own party. On March 3, 1959, during the legislature's annual review of the attorney general's estimates, Cyril Shelford and Irvine Corbett joined with twelve opposition MLAs in a vote of nonconfidence against Bonner. The attorney general survived the vote and the Socred government survived the Sommers scandal, but the scars would never completely heal.

One aspect of the Sommers affair is that, both at the time and even more so after he was convicted, most Socreds were unable to believe that Sommers was actually guilty of any wrongdoing. Of course, he consistently claimed that he had been railroaded—and many took his word. Ray Williston, who succeeded Sommers as lands and forests minister, could say: "I can't remember the time when we were willing to admit, even to ourselves, that some substantial wrong had been committed. . . . I *still* think that on the basis of wrongdoing which has taken place, likely Sommers suffered more at the hands of the court than any public official on the Canadian political scene." When Williston had taken over the lands and forests portfolio in the spring of 1956, he went through departmental files with a fine-tooth comb in an effort to determine whether or not any ministerial pressure had been brought to bear on the awarding of FMLs and conluded that: "The only thing which I think might have happened was that in the large number of applications which were received for licences, Sommers may have shuffled the deck, and he may—and I just say *may*—have given attention to certain applications and he may *not* have given attention to other applications. That is the only one thing I could discover in the examination of the files: the fact that there seemed to be no rhyme nor reason to the manner in which the various applications were given attention."

W. A. C. Bennett could never agree with the court's verdict: "History will show that Sommers was an honest man—stupid and foolish perhaps, but honest . . . foolish to surround himself with certain people and to borrow money from them. But you tell me one person who in one period of their life, somewhere, did not do something that was stupid and foolish—that person can still be a good and honest man. Sommers made some bad decisions, but he gave no special concessions to anybody, anywhere. That's the reason the courts never proceeded against these companies about any special concessions—because there were none. I think history will vindicate Sommers."

One of the most intriguing aspects of the Sommers incident remains the multilayered web of conspiracy argued from a variety of viewpoints. Robert Sommers's view was that: "The whole exercise, of course, was to destroy the government, not to destroy me. I was just the vehicle, the caboose on the train." But Robert Bonner did not entirely agree with that position and commented:

> I don't doubt that from the political point of view people were arguing that the government should have been defeated because of the Sommers affair. But that's not to say that the Sommers affair represented an attack on the government. It was an excuse for an attack on the government. If there is some perceived or imagined weakness and you are in the opposition, you play upon it. I think the importance of the events in which Sommers found himself were unduly publicized with a view to try and bring down the government. But, that's not to say that Sommers did not bring the difficulty on himself. I think that has to be the inescapable conclusion: Sommers placed himself in difficulty and jeopardy. The fact that he had done so was made much of against the government but, in the end, he was not put upon—he was the author of his own difficulty.

Bonner's sober summation is probably an accurate assessment of the nature and cause of the entire sordid affair. Yet many years later most Social Crediters still preferred the "fall guy" theory. In particular, there exists a strong and bitter feeling among Socreds that Sommers was the victim of a Liberal conspiracy. No longer the dominant force in B.C. politics, the Liberals still controlled the federal government for most of the period in which W. A. C. Bennett served as premier. The ubiquitous Liberal influence was perceived to be at fierce odds with Social Credit in British Columbia. If not as powerful in terms of representational politics, Liberalism was certainly still potent in the spheres of the media, business and, according to Socreds, the judiciary—where seeming legions of defeated Grit candidates regularly received appointments to the federally administered courts. Bennett expressed a commonly held view when he said: "If Sommers had been a Liberal, I don't think he would have gone to jail." On another occasion he referred to the Sommers affair as "a Liberal-machine railroading job." Waldo Skillings, an important player in a mysterious part of the Sommers imbroglio, believed that "if Sommers had been a Liberal, he would have been exonerated and made a senator or something." Bonner is credited with saying of the Liberals: "Beat 'em at the polls and meet 'em at the bench."

W. A. C. Bennett managed to remain personally aloof, almost untouched by these events. In spite of all the accusations, counteraccusations and fierce partisan battles, few ever suggested that the premier was involved directly or indirectly in any wrongdoing. It seems almost incredible that, while presiding over a government rocked by one of the most serious political scandals in Canadian history, Bennett could have survived with his personal reputation intact. In retrospect, it is easy to see that he did so by deflecting any criticism over the manner in which the case was handled in the direction of the attorney general. Of course, as chief law officer for the province, it was Bonner's responsibility to deal with the messy matter that has since been described as "Our Very Own Watergate," and it was he who bore the burden in the Socred government. He never complained of this fact. He simply explained in his characteristically dry manner that justice had been done. Few critics or colleagues ever seemed to take into account that, as attorney general, Bonner was in an extremely difficult position, since the fair prosecution of a political partner has to be considered a most unenviable task, constituting a no-win situation. If there were to be any more political casualties of the Sommers case, surely Bonner would be one, and yet he survived—though opposition leader Robert Strachan correctly predicted that the Sommers affair would haunt him for the rest of his life.

One revealing sidelight of the Sommers case was the way it emphasized the important place of personal loyalty in W. A. C. Bennett's make-up; and in this context, it seemed a weakness. Bennett chose his colleagues intuitively and he defended them with tremendous faith and tenacity. He would often say: "If you expect loyalty, you must give loyalty." Even when his faith in a colleague was betrayed, he was usually prepared to look the other way, and held his loyalty as a strength, rather than a potential weakness. Perhaps he was right. If he had swiftly demanded Sommers's resignation at the first sign of trouble, much agony would have been spared, but Sommers had given the premier his word, and Bennett reciprocated the only way he knew how—with dogged loyalty.

Although the Social Credit government survived the Sommers debacle, it was an issue that would be revived time and time again in the years to come, a battle never completely won nor lost. It helped to shape the public perception of the new emerging political stereotypes on Canada's west coast. From its beginnings as a political force in 1952 and its attainment of a majority government in 1953, Social Credit had represented a fresh start for British Columbians. The Socreds were perceived to be an honest, sincere group of ordinary folk interested in good government. The Sommers affair altered that image. As Gordon Gibson has said, the Sommers incident was "the first really sleazy act of the old Bennett government." Whether this is true or false is certainly open to debate. However, that the Sommers affair *seemed* like a sleazy act and *seemed* directly linked with the internal workings of the Bennett government could not be disputed and consequently helped to transform the public attitude towards Social Credit.

When Bennett referred to the Sommers affair as the "dark spot" on the history of his government, he was alluding to the fact that it was a thankfully rare moment in his premiership when he had little control over events. But more than just a blot on the Socred escutcheon, the scandal marked the end of the government's honeymoon. The Socreds were humbled and brought down to earth, and they were fortunate to survive. The legacy of the Sommers case was a vague but lingering suspicion that Social Credit had somehow abandoned its small town, populist roots in favour of some ill-defined and possibly corrupt relationship with big business interests. This new political alignment was neither manifest nor declared—especially if one studies the political rhetoric of the period—but the giddy excesses of the Socreds' first few years of power now appeared to give way to a fierce new form of populism, expressed in a hard but positively exuberant fashion. The Sommers affair had definitely weakened Social Credit's base as a people's movement but, ironically, it made it a stronger, more combative party. One thing was certain: British Columbia's unique and idealistic experiment in democracy was over.

CECIL BENNETT (*middle, second row from back*) at Hampton Consolidated School, New Brunswick. His teacher in grades 7 and 8 was his eldest sister, Cora (*right*).

CECIL BENNETT, age late teens.

HARDWARE MERCHANT W. A. C. Bennett (*centre*) with Joe Renaud (*right*), his partner in the Westlock and Clyde, Alberta, stores from 1927 to 1930.

W. A. C. BENNETT with his children, R.J., Anita and baby Bill, at home in Kelowna, mid-1930s.

KELOWNA GROCER Pasquale "Cap" Capozzi, who went into the apple wine business with teetotaller W. A. C. Bennett in the early 1930s; the winery eventually became Calona Wines Ltd.

MAY BENNETT (née Richards)

CAMPAIGN LITERATURE for 1948 Yale federal by-election. Conservative Bennett was defeated.

Who Is this Man BENNETT?

- He is a Native Son, born in Hastings, N.B., Sept. 6th, 1900.
- For the last 18 years he has been a successful hardware merchant in the Okanagan Valley.
- He has been a Member of the Legislative Assembly of British Columbia, representing South Okanagan, since 1941.
- He is your Progressive Conservative Candidate for Yale.

Why You Should Vote for BENNETT

- Bennett knows the FARMERS' problems.
- Bennett knows the WORKERS' problems.
- Bennett knows the BUSINESS MEN'S problems.
- Bennett has Parliamentary experience.
- He is a young man.

Canada Needs a New National Policy

VOTE FOR

W. A. C. BENNETT

ON MAY 31st

Published by the Yale Progressive Conservative Association
Printed by The Vernon News Ltd., Vernon, B.C.

Courtesy Diefenbaker Centre, University of Saskatchewan

FREEMASON BENNETT in regalia, 1945.

PABC

PREMIER BENNETT'S predecessors: (*top left*) Conservative Dr. Simon Fraser Tolmie, (*top right*) Liberal T.D. "Duff" Pattullo, (*bottom left*) Liberal-coalitionist John Hart, (*bottom right*) Liberal-coalitionist Byron "Boss" Johnson

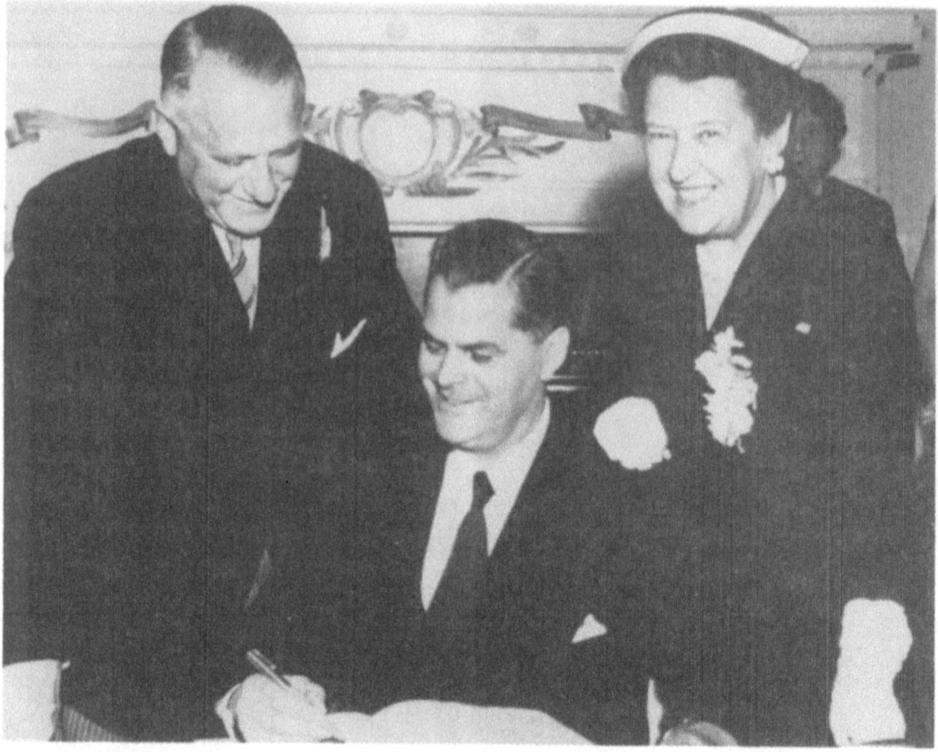

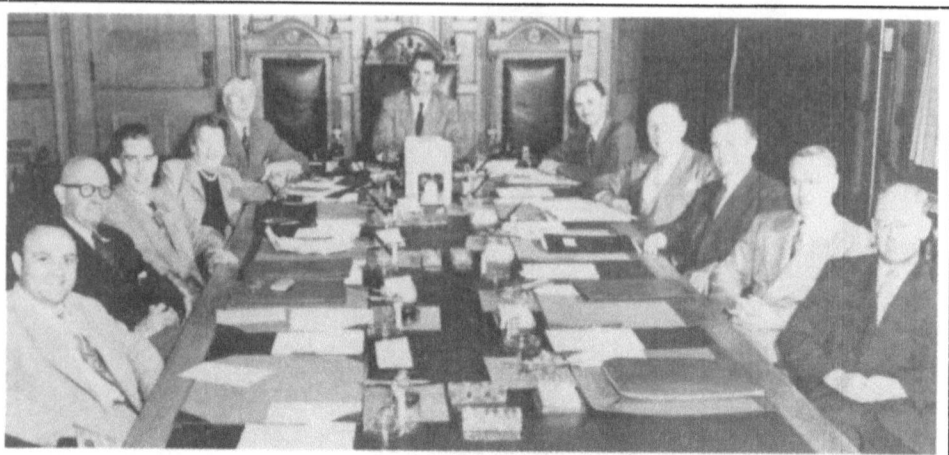

LIEUTENANT GOVERNOR Clarence Wallace attends as Bennett and Tilly Rolston, the only experienced MLAs in the new Social Credit government, are signed into office in August 1952.

Ryan Collection, PABC

THE ORIGINAL 1952 Social Credit cabinet: (*from front left*) Phil Gaglardi, Ralph Chetwynd, Ken Kiernan, Tilly Rolston, Einar Gunderson, Bennett, Robert Bonner, Wesley Black, Robert Sommers, Lyle Wicks, Eric Martin.

PABC

BENNETT WITH Einar Gunderson after his final defeat at the polls. When he lost in the 1953 general election, Bennett's minister of finance ran unsuccessfully in the Victoria by-election arranged for him.

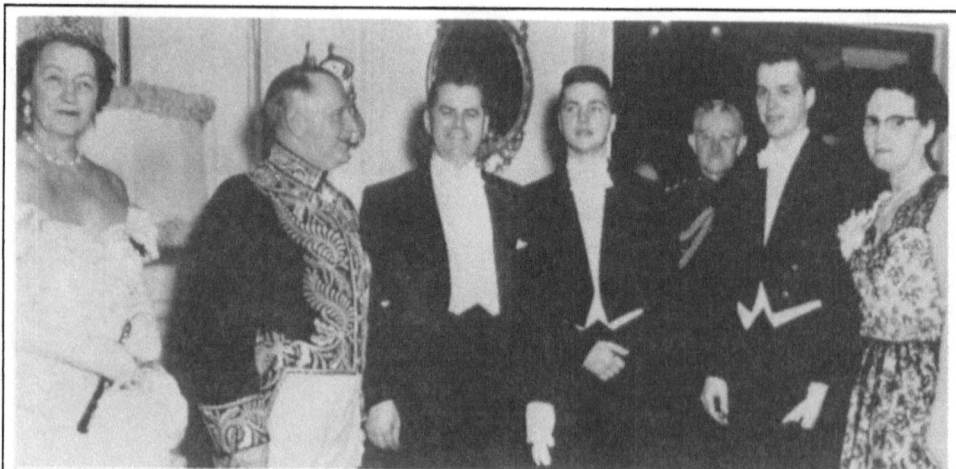

A FORMAL OCCASION at Government House: Lieutenant Governor and Mrs. Wallace, the premier, Bill Bennett, Jr., R.J. Bennett and May Bennett.

PABC

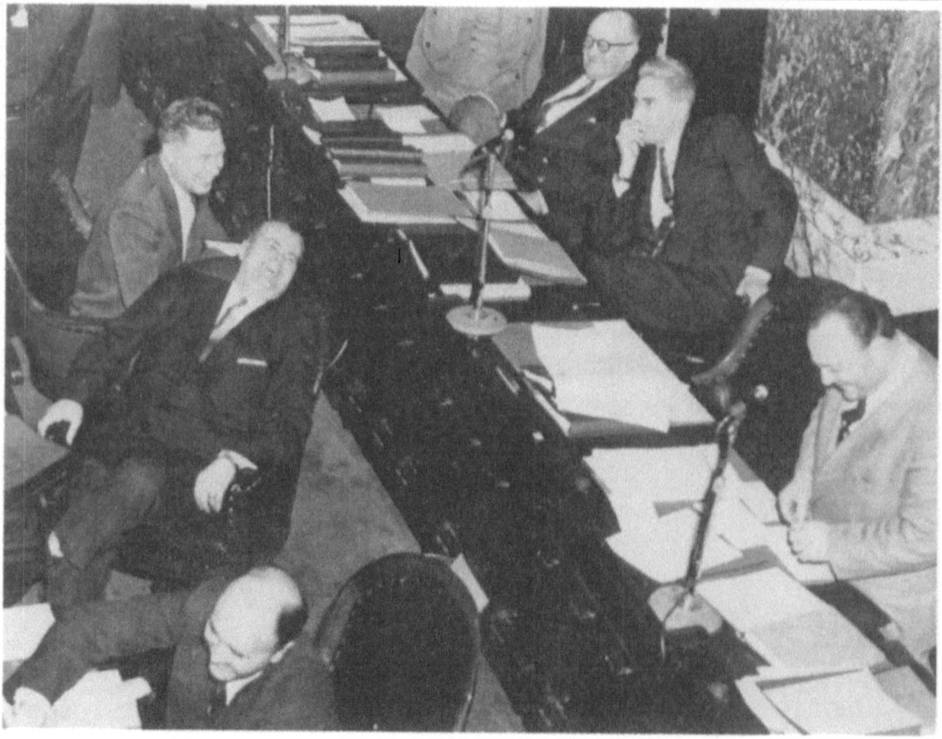

THE SOCRED GOVERNMENT front benches. On Bennett's right is lands and forests minister Ray Williston, on his left, mines minister Ken Kiernan, (*far right*) highways minister Phil Gaglardi, (*second from right*) Attorney General Robert Bonner.

Ryan Collection, PABC

PREMIER BENNETT, President Lyndon Johnson and Prime Minister Lester Pearson attend the historic signing of the Columbia River Treaty at the B.C.-Washington border in 1964.

LEN NORRIS cartoon

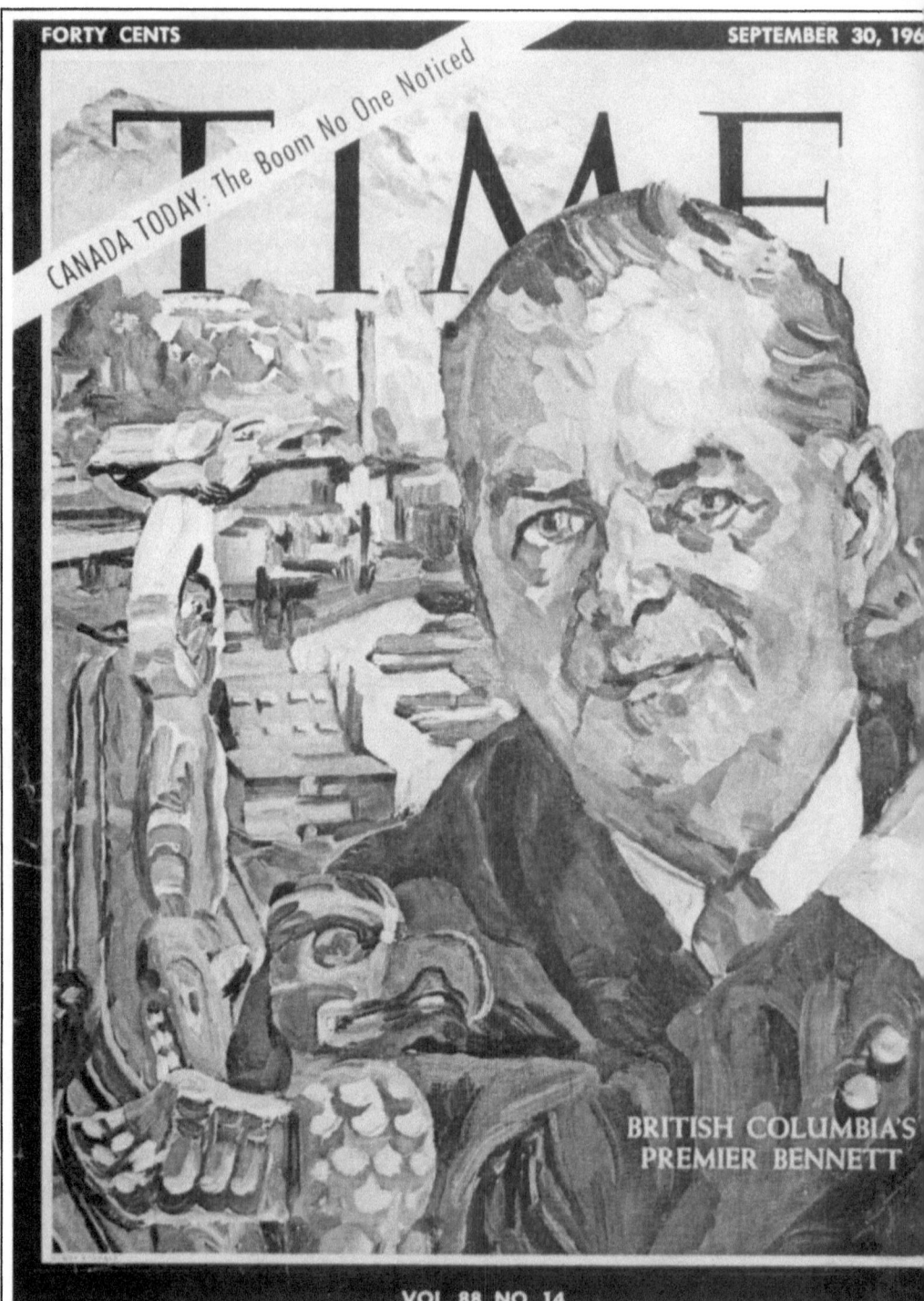

COMMENTED one wag: "This way to the bank."

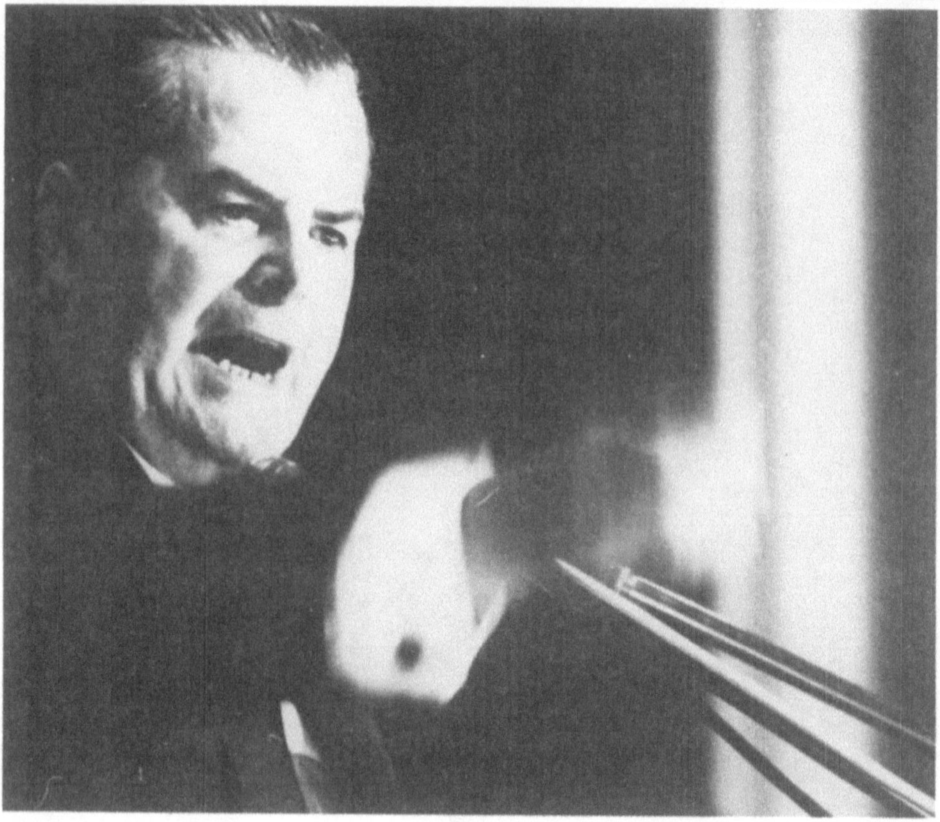

BENNETT campaigning.

Ryan Collection, PABC

MAY AND W. A. C. BENNETT exiting the legislature.

Ryan Collection, PABC

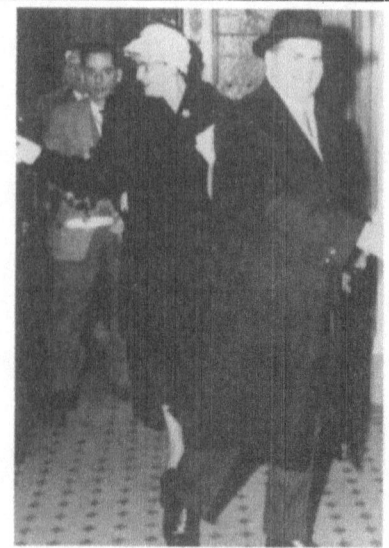

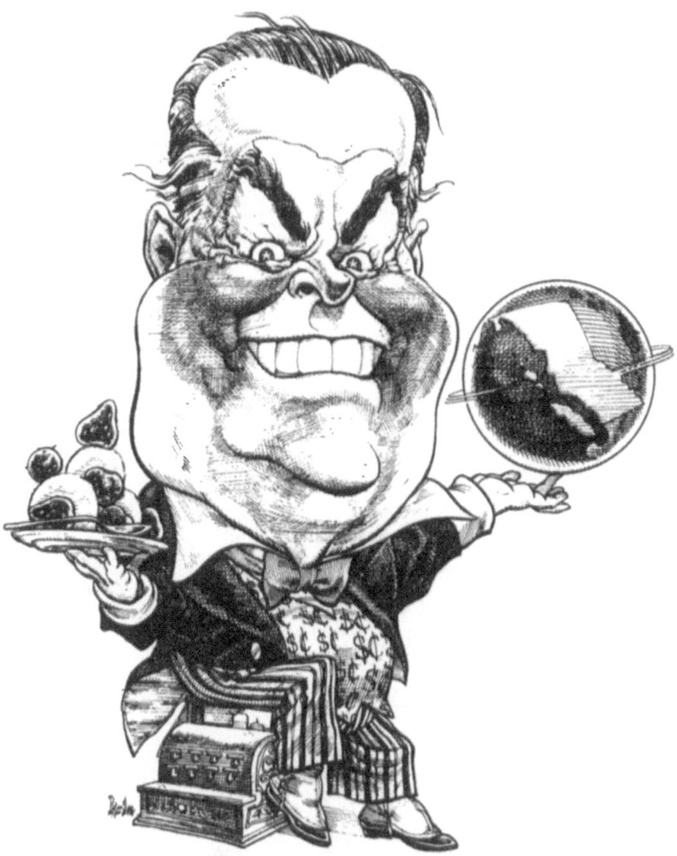

ROY PETERSON
cartoon

Courtesy Allan Fotheringham

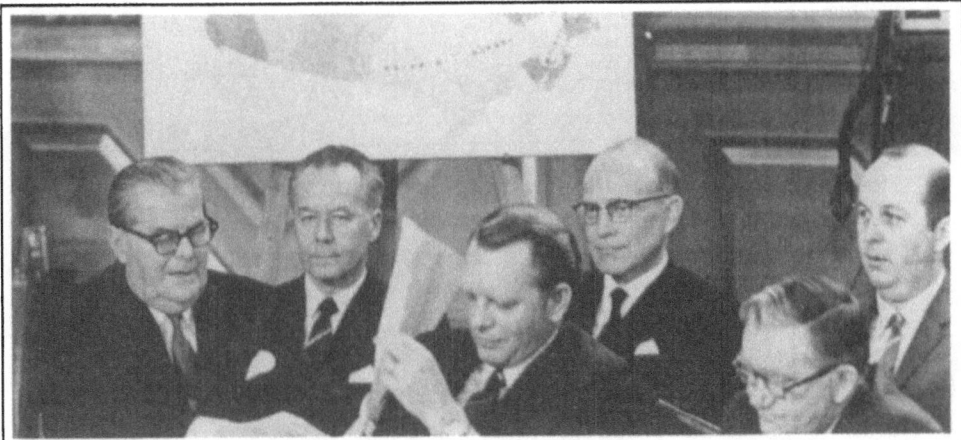

AT THE 1969 federal-provincial conference, Premier Bennett outlines his controversial five-region plan for Canada, assisted by Attorney General Leslie Peterson. The surprise map in question is displayed in background.

PABC

PRIME MINISTER Pierre Trudeau aboard a B.C. ferry during British Columbia's 1971 centennial celebrations.

OPPOSITION LEADER Dave Barrett and Bennett shake hands as the legislature is prorogued before the 1972 election.

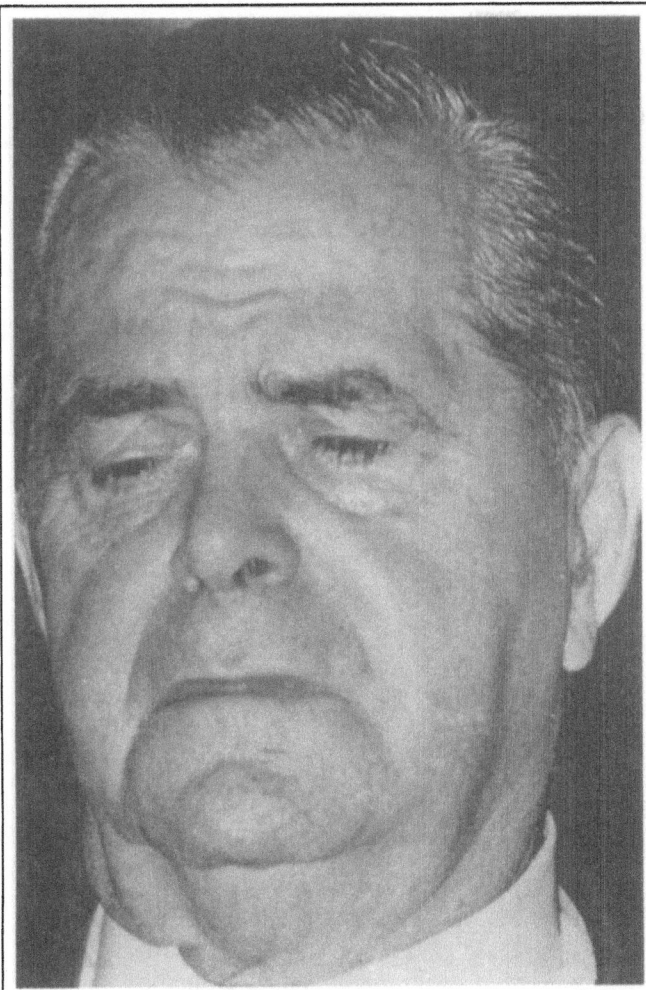

DEFEAT IN 1972, his government's first in eight consecutive elections.

MAY AND W. A. C. BENNETT listen to the Speech from the Throne at the opening legislative session of the reinstated Social Credit government under Bill Bennett, Jr., in 1976.

CHAPTER EIGHT

THE RISE OF BRITISH COLUMBIA

*All history—as well as all current experience—
points to the fact that it is man, not nature,
who provides the primary resource:
that the key factor of all economic development
comes out of the mind of man.*
E. F. Schumacher

The finest music in the land is the ringing of cash registers.
W. A. C. Bennett

The English poet, T. S. Eliot, once wrote that "history is a pattern of timeless moments." For British Columbia, one such moment occurred not long after W. A. C. Bennett became premier. He was on a summer tour of northern B.C., driving along the newly paved highway for which his government cheerfully and rightly took full credit, just outside Fort St. John. He ordered his driver to pull over to the side of the road, stepped out of the car and marched up a small hill from where he was afforded a grand view of the desolate and empty valley of the Peace River. He stood there for several minutes, transfixed, almost motionless. Suddenly an old trapper appeared, a man who had lived in the territory most of his life, and curiously asked, "Mister, what are you staring at?"

Slightly surprised, the premier turned to the old fellow and replied pointing towards the river, "Look down there. What do you see?"

"I see a small, winding, muddy river," said the trapper.

"Well, my friend," said Bennett, "I see dams. And I see power. And I see development. I see roads, highways, bridges and growing communities. I see cities—prosperous cities with schools, hospitals and universities. I see beautiful homes with housewives baking bread and . . ."

The old trapper, seeing only mud, interrupted, "Mister, I don't know who you are or where you come from, but we've had some pretty crazy people up in these parts in my time and as far as I'm concerned, you're the craziest of them all!"

From that timeless moment, from that vision, began a long series of dynamic and controversial developments on Canada's west coast: the rise of British Columbia. Bennett had come to power when the province was ripe for development, a rich frontier ready for experimentation and innovation. Bennett ignited the imagination of British Columbians with his own—and he did not have to impose it upon them unwillingly, for they proved eager to accept his ideas. In that context, B.C. was not so much his stage, rather he set the stage for B.C. Taking into consideration his background—the struggling and the ambition—perhaps it was no coincidence that the rise of W. A. C. Bennett practically coincided with the rise of modern British Columbia.

Bennett was fond of saying that his government raised B.C. from the number one "have-not" province to number one "have" province in Canada. Not simply an exaggeration, this statement is untrue. Moulded by the successive stages of exploitation of its natural resources, B.C.'s economy had been highly susceptible to fluctuations in the world demand for its products; nevertheless, the province's real per capita income since Confederation has been persistently higher than the rest of Canada's. The province has always been seen as a desirable place to live, with a quality of life superior to other parts of the country, evidenced by the fact that it usually has positive net immigration from other provinces. It is therefore difficult to substantiate any claim that British Columbia was ever a "have-not." However, if one looks at Bennett's statement from the perspective of unrealized potential, then it is certainly possible to make the case that B.C., as an economic region, had lacked the eagerness and willpower to develop its economy to the limits of human imagination.

The rise of British Columbia actually began well before Social Credit came to power in 1952. The Second World War had stimulated the provincial economy to new heights; the forest, mining, fishing, agriculture and manufacturing industries were operating at their full capacity. Population swelled and housing shortages were critical in some parts of the province. It is not difficult to see that Bennett became premier at a time when it was good to be government. Public revenues were increasing annually at rates twenty to thirty times those of the Depression era, and these hugely expanded revenues offered the provincial government the opportunity to undertake major public works. Moreover, the era of Big Government had dawned: the war had accustomed most Canadians to accept high levels of government spending and economic intervention as proper areas of public activity. These factors conspired to give Bennett, who had very definite ideas on the subject of how B.C. should develop, a special kind of *carte blanche*.

During the 1950s, the Western industrial world embarked upon a period of economic expansion and material prosperity that, in retrospect, we realize was exceptional. That decade in particular has come to be perceived as a time of social, political and economic innocence which later generations both long for and deride. It was a world without tranquillizers, jet travel, computers or shopping malls. It was a world not yet dominated by television. On the surface, the 1950s was for Canada a time of peace and prosperity, but it also brought important changes that were transforming society. In British Columbia, no less than elsewhere in North America, people were learning to live with bigness and record-breaking statistics. The new confidence on Canada's west coast was exemplified in the new political symbols of Social Credit, but it had its roots in the incontestible fact of economic growth and industrial expansion. During the decade, B.C. led the nation in population growth with almost half a million new residents, an increase of approximately 40 per cent. Its inflation was negligible, unemployment minimal and, despite a few temporary setbacks, output was continually breaking new records. Growth in the older established resource industries like lumber, mining and fishing was impressive; but the rapid economic upswing was in large part attributable to the huge Alcan aluminum smelting plant at Kitimat, the exploration for oil and opening of gas fields in the north, the steps towards tapping the province's tremendous hydroelectric energy potential, and the genesis of B.C.'s formidable tourist industry. No frontier has ever experienced a more concerted push towards economic expansion; this was British Columbia's Great Leap Forward. The ferocity of the drive towards prosperity and development signalled a new direction in Canada's national economy as well: the country's far west, the new west, now represented the chief hope and future locus of economic power.

Public policy was crucial to the path that B.C. followed during this era, and to an amazing degree that policy was centralized in the person of W.A.C. Bennett. The premier promoted a particular type of economy which emphasized the province's traditional and natural strength: resource development. Critics of Social Credit have suggested that he would have done better to encourage the growth of secondary industries, but federal tariff walls and the lack of a sizeable population for a local market or labour force worked against that approach. Bennett strongly felt that the province should concentrate on its obvious comparative advantages over lesser-endowed regions. He subscribed wholeheartedly to the economic ethos of the era, that resources and markets were inexhaustible. The idea that there could ever be an end to boom and expansion was unthinkable. The Socreds' secular faith in never-ending material progress was, of course, a weakness in Bennett's vision—but the strengths of his vision overshadowed the weaknesses. He gave priority to rapid and concentrated economic development because of his profound conviction that to hesitate would be to lose the golden opportunity. Of course, B.C. alone could not generate sufficient capital for the rapid development that he dreamed of, nor would the federal government help to subsidize his dreams. The imperative need to attract foreign investment had always been felt, but under Bennett's government it became an *idée fixe*, an ambition that, through careful promotion, was impressively fulfilled. Investment, particularly American, flowed into the province at a rate that will probably never again be equalled. While corporate earnings from such investment were undoubtedly great, the effect upon the province was more significant — unprecedented prosperity manifest in expansion, new communities and a rising standard of living.

In the best sense, Bennett was a "confidence man": he understood the psychological basis of economic development and saw his role as building up confidence in his province, since its material progress depended on people's faith in the future and on opportunity. Bennett himself possessed a deep, unquestioning faith and he worked assiduously towards expanding the economic opportunities of all British Columbians. His attitude became the key ingredient in the development formula for the province and, in many respects, he combined the ideal leadership traits: he was practical and a realist, yet he spoke the language of the visionary and idealist. He seemed to subscribe to the biblical invocation: "Where there is no vision, the people perish."

If Bennett supplied vision, his plans were certainly not the kind that had seen great deliberation over principles or objectives; they were characteristically simple and straightforward. Political opponents often complained that he and the Socreds lacked a refined philosophy. Certainly it can be argued that Social Credit in B.C. had no urge to remake society, but it does not follow that Bennett had no plan to develop that society, to build upon its foundations. Essentially, his goal was to improve the material well-being of his constituents; he planned to do it by promoting large-scale industrial developments which would have the effect of making the province an integrated economic region. Any historical evaluation of his efforts would have to conclude that this vision transformed British Columbia: Bennett's imagination and drive had as much impact there as did the efforts of any other twentieth-century policy maker in any other region of North America. With vigour and determination, he renovated the province as another person would a house.

At first glance, it might appear odd that a self-made small town businessman and conservative politician should have assumed such a leading role as a public policy maker. After all, Bennett was a firm believer in free enterprise and despised mindless government intervention in the marketplace; but as premier he defined the role of government as a dynamic agent of development. He took a consciously activist approach to government, applying the same principles to B.C. as had been applied to national development during an earlier period of Canadian history. From John A. Macdonald's "National Policy" onwards, a tradition of aggressive government involvement in the country's economic life was strongly in evidence—despite an equally strong drive to maintain private control over industry. These two seemingly contradictory attitudes are at the heart of modern Canadian history, and on the west coast became best exemplified in W. A. C. Bennett. His administration's primary operating principle was that the task of government is to manage the economy in a way that will achieve larger social goals established by the political process: improved transportation networks, full employment, a good health care system, better access to higher education and an increased standard of living. Bennett's perception of the relationship between private enterprise and provincial development was highly pragmatic. When private interests failed to co-operate with his vision, he never hesitated to fill an economic void through public-sector participation. Apparently he did not push public enterprise for its own sake, for he steadfastly acknowledged and approved private enterprise as the foundation of the B.C. economy. But neither did he shrink from taking direct government action if he felt that private industry would not act. While he was premier, Bennett, and Bennett alone, decided what was in the public interest. A fitting working motto for his government and his era would be: *intervention if necessary, but not necessarily intervention.*

The fact that he and his government subscribed to these principles and were firmly entrenched in power during this exciting period was of great significance for British Columbia's future. Bennett was driven partly by a need to build—a need for tangible evidence of achievement. The image he cultivated was that of the man who Got Things Done, who produced for the public visible, dramatic results: highways, bridges, tunnels. In a sense, public works became the *raison d'être* for Social Credit—public works on a grand scale. Bennett knew he was on solid ground in promoting such construction; both economically and politically, it could only rebound in his favour. As Stephen Leacock once wrote: "Canadians 'fall' for public works as a farmer falls for peas under a thimble." Bennett also realized that public money used to build transportation networks or to develop the energy potential of a region adds to the economic structure upon which other productivity depends. This public spending can encourage a capitalist economy to grow and therefore ensure that those functioning within it will prosper. Neither in the short nor long term could Bennett lose by selectively using public funds for developmental goals.

Large-scale public works shape a region for generations; some public works projects, notably roads, railways and bridges opening new areas to development, shape a region for centuries, possibly forever. Central to the

Socreds' pioneering activity was the opening up of the interior of the province, especially the north. As an interior businessman, Bennett had a good sense of the opportunities for development there, and by pushing at those resource frontiers he was now tapping the long-standing Canadian romanticism about the north. Far in advance of John Diefenbaker, Bennett espoused a "northern vision" which excited isolated northerners and romantic-minded southerners alike. Typical of his pronouncements on the subject was a keynote address to the Canadian Chamber of Commerce in Victoria in the fall of 1957 entitled "North America Looks North." To the assembled businessmen from across the country, he said: "The modern north is a land of people and communities, a land of agricultural riches, great storehouses of minerals, huge forest stands, uranium, coal, oil, natural gas, hydro-electric power. This is a land of the future.... The Government and the people of British Columbia have started a revolution in this province. No longer will our economy rest upon the development of a few basic industries in the southernmost sections of our land—a situation which unfortunately still exists in many other parts of Canada."

It would be difficult to dispute with Bennett that B.C. was advancing on all fronts at once. But if there was one area of government activity most responsible for opening up the province during the 1950s, it was highway construction, and the other individual who epitomized the ambitious provincial cast of mind and the collective Socred personality was the flamboyant, controversial minister of highways, Phil Gaglardi. Although in the eye of the press he always played Sancho Panza to Bennett's Don Quixote, Gaglardi became a symbol of the impatience and busyness of the period; he was always "talking and fighting and heating the air" wherever he went. Gaglardi took his job seriously—some would say too seriously—and was arguably the best available person to serve as highways minister in a "blacktop government." Certainly he seemed to fit nicely into Bennett's scheme of things, and perhaps only a premier from Kelowna and a minister of highways from Kamloops could have immediately grasped the necessity of opening up the hinterland as the first step towards large-scale resource development.

The province was seized by construction crews and littered with hard hats and bulldozers. For a time, Gaglardi became known as "Sorry Phil" after the "Sorry for the Inconvenience" signs that marked highway construction projects throughout B.C. During the first six years of Social Credit rule, more money was spent on roads and highways than during the entire history of the province. By 1960, thousands of miles of new roads had been built, often through extremely rugged terrain, and virtually all existing roads and highways were paved or repaved. Bennett declared it "the greatest highway building program, not just in British Columbia's history, but per capita in the entire Western world." Gaglardi described the program's importance:

The road up the Fraser Canyon was a goat trail. The pavement ended at 100 Mile House, so travel in the province of British Columbia was an adventure, a real excursion, and you usually carried about five spare tires. Every year in the wintertime in the interior, people used to jack their cars up off their wheels and block them up and leave them there for the winter, because they didn't maintain the highways in the wintertime. I said to the licensing department, "Do you sell a licence for half a year? You sell them for the whole year; therefore from now on the highways remain open all year"—and I saw to it that they did. . . . We didn't have the proper foundation for development without a transportation system. When we became government the province of British Columbia stopped at the Pattullo Bridge; the city of Vancouver had the parochial idea that they were the sum total of everything. Jumping Jehoshaphat, we made the province of British Columbia! We wanted highways in places where there was absolutely nobody because we knew that they would be the arteries that would carry the wheels of industry to all of the four corners of the province. And that's what they did.

Although the highway building program was a keystone in the Socreds' planned infrastructure for industrial development, the new roads were politically important, too: British Columbians took pride in the accomplishment, and that rebounded strongly in the government's favour. The quickly constructed, well-made highways were also symbolically important, for the automobile exemplified the tremendous economic and social changes of midcentury North America. The provincial government's heavy emphasis on roads was an assertion of B.C.'s own prosperity.

Highways were, in themselves, a growth industry of the 1950s. Full employment in the construction industry meant that virtually an entire generation of B.C. contractors devoted themselves to building the monumental road network. One operator who consistently cut his bids as close to the bone as possible in order to receive contracts from Gaglardi's highways department was interior entrepreneur Ben Ginter. He completed several contracts satisfactorily and almost single-handedly broke up the cozy fraternity of contractors who for years had been arranging bids among themselves. For helping the Socreds to reduce the high overhead cost of public works patronage, Ginter was awarded so many contracts that he became a wealthy man. Political opponents of Social Credit spread the rumour that the construction business in the interior was ruled by the triumvirate of Gaglardi, Ginter and God.

Phil Gaglardi soon became a legendary figure in B.C. Not only was he a minister of the crown but he was also a minister of the church; each weekend he flew home to Kamloops to preach to his congregation and to tape five fifteen-minute religious broadcasts carried weekday mornings by radio stations throughout the interior. Usually he mixed religion with politics and vice versa—which had a certain folksy appeal to the traditional Social Credit constituency. He gained a reputation as a man in a hurry. His frequent use of government aircraft often got him into hot water and helped to change his nickname from "Sorry Phil" to "Flying Phil." He also had a penchant for large American cars, and found his notoriety for fast driving not unpleasant. As minister of highways he was continually test-driving his product. He had several customized cars stationed at key points throughout the province and reserved for his exclusive use. These large late models were maintained by highways department staff; their custom air-conditioning was so powerful that in the summertime, in the absence of the peripatetic minister, the staff used the cars to keep their beer cold. Gaglardi also had a special multichannel radio system built into his various vehicles and aircraft so that he could keep in constant touch with every part of the province.

No doubt, "Flying Phil" Gaglardi's aggressive style had much to do with the public image of Social Credit as a government that Got Things Done. During the 1950s he was generally a positive political asset; Bennett used him on the hustings where he was an entertaining and effective government speaker. In the legislature, he was pure bombast. Leader of the opposition, Robert Strachan, said that: "Gaglardi in full voice was like a thundering herd of buffalo galloping across the prairie with about as much sense of direction." Nevertheless, the popular minister was doing his job and, for the first few years, did not cause any major political headaches. Soon, however, he became a favourite target for political opponents of Social Credit. He was accused of establishing new forms of patronage in highway administration and came under increasing fire for his constant use of government aircraft, which he claimed actually saved the government millions of dollars. On half a dozen occasions he was convicted of traffic violations and his driving licence was suspended several times; once he referred to the arresting RCMP officer as a "young punk." In spite of his personal popularity, Gaglardi became an embarrassment and potential liability for Social Credit. In 1958, for example, the opening of his Calvary Temple in Kamloops, attended by the premier and a variety of dignitaries and businessmen, was followed by the revelation in the *Vancouver Sun* that a portion of the construction labour had been paid for by contractors who were closely connected with the minister and employed on public highways. Bennett was forced to come to Gaglardi's defence, labelling the attack an attempt to "smear one of the finest men British Columbia has produced." But as the 1950s came to a close, Gaglardi was increasingly on the defensive—and convinced that a huge conspiracy which had destroyed Robert Sommers was out to get him. His ranting and his sanctimonious fist-shaking kept alive for several more years many of the questions raised by the Sommers affair. Gaglardi contributed to the rise of British Columbia, but as the first stage of development ended, he contributed as well to the decline of Social Credit.

Bennett's plans for a consistent and comprehensive policy of provincial development ran into surprisingly few snags during the 1950s; one of them arose over the Doukhobor settlements in the southeast interior. The manner in which the government dealt with the problem offers a useful illustration of the style and approach of Social Credit during this era.

The Doukhobors were a Russian sect who emigrated to Canada early in this century. Their pacifism and refusal to enter into any form of state activity placed them at odds with Russian authorities. They believed that every person has the capacity to know the spirit of God and a duty to follow the guidance of that spirit. From this simple belief evolved a communal lifestyle, resistance to leadership and a Christian theology based upon intuition and various forms of mysticism. Doukhobors, or "Spirit Wrestlers," have regarded themselves as free from responsibility or participation in the larger community; they are responsible only to the spirit of Christ. Their faith brought them into conflict with government over their refusal to perform ordinary acts of citizenship, including swearing allegiance, bearing arms in times of war, filling out census forms, paying property taxes and sending their children to public schools. Their lifestyle may have been appropriate to the social conditions of sixteenth-century Russia, but not to those of nineteenth-century czarist Russia, let alone twentieth-century Canada. Through the efforts of Count Leo Tolstoy, who helped them to secure permission to emigrate, several thousand Doukhobors moved to the Canadian prairies in the first decade of this century. They were welcomed by the Canadian government, intent on settling the west, but a crisis arose when they resisted individual registration of their land, claiming it ran counter to their belief in community property. When the government insisted, the Doukhobors looked elsewhere for a haven; in 1908, about two-thirds of them moved to the mountain valleys of the Kootenay region of British Columbia.

At first they lived austerely in the areas around Grand Forks and Castlegar, and cleared hundreds of hectares of forest. They planted fruit trees and grapevines, built roads and irrigation systems, sawmills, a furniture plant and a jam factory. Soon they prospered; many left the communes and acquired commercial skills working in larger communities. As the Kootenays became more populated, the Doukhobors again ran into problems with government over sending their children to public schools, recognition of their marriages and registration of births and deaths. In 1915 their passive resistance effected a compromise with the provincial government which relaxed its efforts to integrate them into the community at large. In the 1920s, serious problems arose when a small militant splinter group, the Sons of Freedom, began to fight against the prosperity, materialism and growing secular trends among their fellow Doukhobors. These zealots burned schools and community property to protest irreligious trends. After the Second World War, increasing numbers of Doukhobors abandoned their traditions and joined the mainstream of British Columbia society, while the militant Sons stepped up their acts of violence—"terror in the name of God"—and became a threat to society and themselves.

By the time Social Credit came to power in B.C. in 1952, the Sons of Freedom were very active: they demonstrated by parading nude; arson became more and more frequent, and they began experimenting with explosives. In 1953 the entire community of Krestova was burned to the ground and injury to property and human life became a growing threat. Although Bennett and the Socreds had no great urge to remake society, they did have a will to resolve all outstanding problems, and therefore embarked on an aggressive course of action for dealing with the militants.

On July 18, 1953, Premier Bennett made a major policy speech to the legislature on the Doukhobor problem. He carefully distinguished between the violent Sons of Freedom and the Doukhobors in general, whom he described as "law abiding people who are making distinctive and valuable contributions to the development and culture of this Country and Province." He estimated that in 1952 the damage attributable to the Sons by arson alone amounted to over $200,000, and in the 1952–53 fiscal year special security and police costs to the province for protection of the communities of the Kootenays was almost a quarter of a million dollars. He declared that the situation could not and would not continue: "One thing must now be said—that is, if procrastination were a proper charge to level at previous administrations, certainly such a charge cannot be made against this Government. . . . All citizens of British Columbia must obey the laws or otherwise a state of anarchy would exist. This Government will not shirk its responsibility no matter how difficult the situation becomes."

The cabinet, after a thorough discussion of the issue, decided to bring in legislation that would recognize Doukhobor marriages, legitimize their children and give them all the other normal rights and responsibilities under the law. In turn, the government would demand that all Doukhobors obey the laws or suffer the same penalties as other Canadian citizens. The person responsible for enforcing this new policy was Attorney General Robert Bonner, and he dealt with the Sons of Freedom in a decisive and effective manner, his view being:

The approach of the previous administration was entirely mistaken. They tried to negotiate a settlement through Doukhobor leadership. It never occurred to me as either practical or desirable that you could negotiate support for the law; people are either in conformity or violation. I soon discovered, when I read deeply into the origins of their movement and their history in Russia and their tactics in Canada, that one reason they had been able to persist for such a length of time was that they would involve officials in endless discussion, always with a view of finding the key to the "Doukhobor problem." Officials would be chasing their official tails looking for a solution to a problem that had never been defined. The definition of the problem was very simple: these people didn't want to obey certain laws. There was a campaign of terrorism in the Kootenays which consisted of bombing the railway and burning of buildings. That was certainly an urgent problem and we were anxious to solve it, and we were aggressive about it. But that was not a Doukhobor problem; there were Doukhobors *involved* in the problem. It was a problem of criminal law transgression. So we were anxious to put an end to it, and it was not a matter for anyone to broker. It was a straight matter of law enforcement, and that was a sharp break with the past. People tried to deal with it as a social issue. It wasn't a social issue; it was an issue of criminal law and criminal law enforcement.

Perhaps the most controversial and emotional side of the Socreds' policy with regard to the Sons of Freedom was the way in which they handled the enforcement of public education for Doukhobor children. Some leaders of the Doukhobor community decided to challenge the government's new policy and announced that they would not send their children to school as required. This mass truancy was a deliberate act of defiance, and Bonner treated it as a grave civil disorder: all of the children were picked up and placed in a special school camp; they became wards of child welfare. The parents were individually advised that their children would be returned if they were sent to school. Some parents persisted for several years in refusing to comply with the law, and the school at New Denver became a sensational media attraction. Photographs appearing in eastern Canadian publications showed Doukhobor women speaking to their children through a wire fence; the photographs did not reveal the wide-open gate a few yards away through which they were allowed to pass at any time. The government-operated school became a focus for commentary and the Socreds suffered a great deal of political criticism, as well as censure in the media, for being "cruel" and "heartless." Eventually, the Doukhobors came to realize that the government was not going to back down and, one by one, they agreed to send their children to school; the children were returned to their homes and the school camp at New Denver was closed.

In retrospect, it must be admitted that the Social Credit administration dealt with this unusually thorny issue in a highly effective fashion. The Doukhobors have been allowed to maintain the same rights and freedoms as any other ethnic group in a democratic society, and have been integrated at least to the point where they no longer enjoy immunity from the law. Doukhobor marriages were recognized, a new Election Act restored their franchise and the government assisted in the agricultural development of their land. By the 1960s, most of the economic and social difficulties had been resolved for the greater part of the Doukhobor population. Sporadic arsons, bombings and nude parades have continued among tiny remnants of the Sons of Freedom sect, but most Doukhobors have been integrated into the B.C. mainstream and are making valuable contributions in virtually all walks of life. Although it was initially the increased prosperity and affluence of the early Socred era that brought the conflicts to a head, in the end the Doukhobors have not been a casualty but are one of the many beneficiaries of the rise of British Columbia.

As the development of the province progressed under the early direction of Social Credit, the leadership of B.C.'s trade unions became increasingly at odds with the government. Canada's west coast province had always nurtured a tradition of labour activism and radicalism, and during W. A. C. Bennett's tenure as premier it became the most unionized jurisdiction on the continent. As the economy grew and with it the labour force, unions gained a growing might. At the leadership level, at least, labour unions became vocally aligned with the political opponents of Social Credit, the CCF. In one of the classic ironies of the province's history, the Socreds worked towards prosperity and development, and yet those very forces of progress helped to breed a powerful contingent of political opposition.

The Social Credit government undoubtedly had good intentions and viewed itself as a friend of the working man, but its labour policies became politically misconstrued. One of the problems was that policy making during a time of rapid development is generally more concerned with the large picture than with details. Labour was not a high-profile concern; certainly it was not the glamour area of government. B.C.'s first Social Credit minister of labour, Lyle Wicks, a former union man, described the labour portfolio as "difficult" and "negative." Few other Socreds were interested in labour problems or had direct experience with the trade union movement. The prevailing opinion within government ranks was that unions were fine so long as they did not get in the way of industry or deter the surge of development.

As an arbiter in the poisonous world of a labour-management relations in B.C., the Social Credit government tried to be fair and consistent. W. A. C. Bennett described his view of government's role:

> The economy should give labour the wage scales that the economy can afford—no less, no more. That was our policy.... The government's job is to be fair—fair to labour. Sometimes I was awfully tough on labour, and oftentimes I was awfully tough on business, especially big business. I always looked at the difference between the management of industry and the people who own the industry; and the management of unions—the labour bosses—and the workers. There is a difference, and I always saw that clearly. I had to be fair to the workers—not always to what the labour bosses wanted. I had to be fair to business, but not necessarily to what the business magnates wanted. They wanted the moon and the sky and everything else—no way! The government's role should be like that of a referee in a hockey game; the government should have the whistle, and when I was premier I blew the whistle a few times. The referee makes the decision on what he thinks is fair. At one time one side will think the decision is unfair, and another time the other side. If one side thinks he's unfair all the time, then perhaps the referee's a little biased. But if they're both mad at him, then he is a pretty good referee.

From time to time, both sides were mad at the Social Credit government—but they had decidedly different methods of expressing it. Big business interests would lobby informally, while quietly encouraging the rebirth of either of the old-line parties, Liberals or Conservatives. Organized labour, on the other hand, reacted with loud denunciations and open expressions of support for the CCF. During the 1954 session of the legislature, the government passed a contentious Labour Relations Act, better known as Bill 28. The act gave the minister of labour wide discretionary powers to handle labour disputes and gave supreme court justices the power to revoke a union's certification, its dues checkoff and collective agreements in cases of illegal strikes. Labour leaders reacted with a long and bitter campaign against the government, and the immediate effect of the act seems to have been to increase the politicization of the west coast labour movement. A committee of union leaders rushed to Victoria to fight Bill 28; they called the government a "dictatorship" and declared the act an attempt "to destroy trade unionism" and "vicious class legislation." One Vancouver labour leader stated that "if it had been drafted by Peron in Argentina or Hitler's Labour Front, it couldn't be worse." The labour leadership had adopted the paranoid style which seems so necessary a part of B.C. politics. Seen from today's vantage point, their militant stance was perhaps an overreaction; since unions have grown and prospered in British Columbia under Social Credit legislation, the old battle cries of labour sometimes ring hollow.

As the 1950s progressed, the number of labour disputes increased significantly. The trade union movement was prospering and flexing its muscles along with B.C.'s expanding economy. Nationwide, this new aggressiveness was marked by the founding of the Canadian Labour Congress in 1956. At the annual convention of the British Columbia Federation of Labour in 1957, the option of independent political action was rejected in favour of official endorsation of the CCF. Trade union leaders and representatives of the socialist party announced a "working relationship" for the purpose of fighting the next provincial election. This declaration of war seriously alarmed the Socreds and set the scene for the 1959 legislative session, the so-called "labour session." The government brought in Bill 43, a new Trade Union Act, which allowed unions to picket a plant where there was a legal strike, but precious little else. Sympathy or information picket lines were declared illegal. Both unions and management were defined as legal entities having the right to sue or be sued in civil court if they stepped out of line.

Bill 43 was generally viewed as a curb on the power of labour unions. The CCF stood on the side of their organized labour allies and branded Social Credit as an antilabour government. The B.C. secretary of the International Woodworkers of America, the province's largest union, said: "This brings us the closest we have ever been to Fascism." Attorney General Bonner told his constituents: "If you don't like a management boss why should you like a labour boss? A labour boss who goes wrong is worse than a management boss who hasn't the interests of his employees at heart." Phil Gaglardi described labour leaders as "agitators" and told the legislature: "We don't need any Hoffas or gangsterism in this province." Minister of Public Works William Chant echoed Gaglardi: "Union leaders in some quarters have replaced [i.e., preempted] bootlegging, gambling and the rackets as the recognized domain of the hoodlum and gangster."

The Socreds were always careful to draw a sharp distinction between trade union members and trade union leaders, believing that the average worker could identify with the government's development programs and see himself in the picture of a growing economy. Their appeal was therefore directed over the heads of union leaders, who invariably were opposed to the government's policies, to the rank and file. This was sound political strategy, and Premier Bennett was wary of becoming personally embroiled in the heated rhetoric over the issue. He usually attempted to play the statesman and never willingly placed himself in the direct line of fire. In the autumn of 1959, he addressed the Vancouver Board of Trade and, speaking of "The Golden Future" of B.C., turned his comments to the labour problem:

Naturally, when you have growth, you have a few growing pains. This year in British Columbia we've had some labour trouble, and I am glad to say that it now appears to be all behind us. I believe, as Premier, that the major cause of our labour trouble has been those very growing pains I mentioned. I believe that both labour and management need to approach their problems from now on with a new responsibility, a new maturity. And it was for that reason that our Government at the last session of the Legislature passed a new Trade Union Act, better known as Bill 43. When we brought this new legislation in, it was attacked in some quarters as being restrictive. It is no such thing. . . . But it does impose on both *labour* and *management* a new legal responsibility; and I think all of you gentlemen here today will agree with me that what we need in labour relations from here in is a reasonable attitude, a willingness to bargain in good faith—so that we can buckle down without interruption to the business of building British Columbia.

Bennett the "boomer" was being optimistic as usual. If the labour difficulties were caused by B.C.'s growing pains, the problems endured long after the growth had subsided. In fact, the trenches were dug and the battle lines were drawn for many years to come. When both the CCF and organized labour began discussing the formation of a new socialist-labour party in Canada, W. A. C. Bennett saw an opportunity to forge a sharply polarized political culture in B.C. which would be to the great benefit of Social Credit.

A labour dispute propelled Bennett's Socreds into an unlikely but highly successful public enterprise: the ferry business. It was 1958 and British Columbia was celebrating its centenary; a host of visitors and the first wave of summertime tourists were beginning to stream into the bustling province. The Seafarers International Union struck the CPR ferry connection between Vancouver and Victoria and sympathetic work stoppages threatened the Black Ball Line, the only other ferry service between Vancouver Island and the mainland. By today's standards, these ferry systems were tenuous and somewhat primitive, but at the time they were the only means of vehicle transport between B.C.'s two most populous centres. The labour dispute, therefore, threatened to seriously disrupt the coastal economy—if it continued for any considerable time its effect could have been crippling. Bennett appealed in vain for federal intercession to settle the problem. In an attempt to break the stalemate, he personally consulted with both the management of the ferry systems and the unions involved. When he realized that his efforts were for naught, he shocked most observers by proclaiming the Civil Defence Act and taking over the Black Ball Line. Few could remember a provincial government acting so quickly or so effectively; the Socreds would reap tremendous political benefit from the move. As it turned out, the government needed to operate the ferry line for only a few days before both sides in the conflict decided to lay down their arms and return to work, but much was learned during the course of those few days when the landlubberly Socreds operated the ferry boats. In particular, Bennett, quick to make inferences and to see possibilities, was determined to force events his way.

With transportation a crucial element in its plan for economic development, the government was busy building roads, highways and bridges throughout the province, and the ferry strike drove home the important fact that existing ferry operations were an essential if weak extension of the coastal highway system. Bennett's version of the events that followed the 1958 ferry workers' strike was:

> I got in touch with Black Ball; I wanted them to expand their services. Captain Peabody, who was in charge of Black Ball at Seattle, was for it—but his bankers weren't. Captain Peabody had a group of directors in New York and I had him bring his directors out to meet our administration, but I couldn't convince them. Then I sent Worley, my assistant, to see the president of the CPR in Montreal, twice, and I phoned them as well, but they wouldn't spend any money to develop and rebuild it into a modern ferry fleet. The last time Worley went down, the president of the CPR called in his expert who looked after the division of steamship lines. He told the president, in front of Worley, that the CPR had lots of experience in running ferries and they didn't need to take any advice from W. A. C. Bennett of British Columbia who knew nothing about ferries. Therefore, he recommended the CPR do not spend an extra nickel. But that was just the eastern approach to British Columbia.

In retrospect, it seems almost incredible that the CPR was so completely immune to the breezes blowing on the west coast; however, Capt. Alexander Peabody of the Black Ball Line had a good idea of what was to come:

> Every time W. A. C. Bennett made a speech anywhere he would say, "Listen, it is up to Black Ball and CPR to create an integrated ferry service." It made me so damn mad I couldn't see straight, and I would go to the CPR and say, "What are you going to do about this? Come on, let's get off our duff and get something done here." And they would say, "Uh-huh." [But] I couldn't get the CPR to budge. So I finally went up to Vancouver and I said, "Look, for God's sake, don't you guys get the message here? If we don't do something, the government is going to come in here and just take everything over. Are you going to do something about this or not?" The head of CPR said, "Don't you worry about it. I've got the ball. I'll let you know." Well, I haven't heard from him since! And neither has anybody else!

For Bennett, government's role was to regulate, referee, encourage, prompt and, occasionally, to intervene. He believed that government involvement in large projects necessary for the well-being and development of B.C. would naturally come about when private interests had either no interest or no business in them. He was not hesitant to involve the hand of government, but did so only after giving the private sector a reasonable chance to act. His administration did not stumble into government enterprises, all the while protesting distrust of state intervention—as did other "free enterprise" governments of the era. On the contrary, the Socreds plunged ahead in confidence. And Bennett, it must be noted, was a politician in a hurry.

Since nothing was developing on the ferry front, he decided to proceed with his contingency plan. He summoned Captain Peabody to his office in Victoria, requested copies of the Black Ball Line's books, balance sheets and other information, and asked him to come back in one week. According to Peabody, Bennett then said: "Here's the deal. Add up all your assets, deduct all your liabilities, cut your depreciation in half and that's the price. I don't want to hear another word about it." The price turned out to be about $7.8 million. Peabody immediately agreed to the deal, and the Social Credit government, through the Toll Highways and Bridges Authority, purchased the shares of the Black Ball Line and plunged into a completely new area of economic activity.

Reaction to the move was mixed at first. The CCF hailed it as consistent with their philosophy of public ownership. The editorial page of the *Vancouver Sun* was not impressed: "Normally a project of this magnitude would be explained and debated first in the legislature, MLAs' approval would be sought if only in the limited form of authorizing the Toll Authority to finance the ferry service. But the Premier . . . seems to have no time for these formalities. All this speed and high pressure call for something more substantial than Mr. Bennett has yet offered." The Socreds fought an uphill battle: economists, planners and academics almost all said that Bennett's plans to expand the ferry system could not succeed because of a lack of demand for the service. Naturally, they were basing their estimations on the existing traffic. Bennett, on the other hand, possessed an intuitive spirit not an analytical mind, and government, for all its apparatus of political "science" and cost-effectiveness studies, is still chiefly an intuitive art. Whereas academics and bureaucrats praise carefully tested methods and long-range planning, Bennett ably demonstrated that successful policy can be formulated as an on-the-spot response to unexpected circumstances.

The British Columbia Ferry Corporation, as it would eventually be called, had a modest beginning with only two ships and two terminals. The government rapidly expanded the service, in competition with the CPR, and developed it into a "water highway" system servicing the coastal regions. Employing the technique, "If you want a job done, give it to a busy person," Bennett assigned his highways minister, Phil Gaglardi, the task of putting the new ferry service in place. Gaglardi, who knew virtually nothing about life on the seas, said that he "built the entire system around my own impatience." Within six weeks, he called the first contract for the construction of more ships, and in the first year of operation the public-owned ferry system had depopulated the airlines, which were forced to drastically cut back their daily flights between Vancouver and Victoria.

The B.C. ferry system grew rapidly, as did the pace of economic activity along the coast. Within two decades it maintained a fleet of more than two dozen ships with hourly sailings from its many busy terminals. It created employment for thousands of British Columbians and carries millions of passengers and vehicles each year—and in the process turns over a tidy operating profit. The doomsayers of 1958 could only shake their heads in disbelief as "Bennett's Navy" thrived and developed into the world's largest and best-run ferry service. Its only consistent problem has been keeping enough vessels in operation to meet the constantly growing demand for what has become a popular and essential service. Robert Bonner said with relish: "Years later Ian Sinclair, the head of Canadian Pacific, was on board one of our ferries and we met on the deck. He turned to me and said, 'We certainly missed the boat on this one.'"

Not long after they came to power, the Socreds were accused of being a "one-man government"—and this was close to the truth. One of the important factors enabling W. A. C. Bennett to concentrate tremendous power in his own hands was that in addition to being government leader, he was also minister of finance. Since for him, money determined everything, finance was the foundation of his administration; ways and means needed to be found for the things the Socreds wanted to accomplish, and Bennett was the man who decided both what would be accomplished, and how. This point is crucial to understanding the *modus operandi* of his administration. He was often criticized for what he was doing; his critics would have been the wiser to explore how he was doing it. His approach to the business of government was relatively simple, but unconventional. In spite of his lack of university training, perhaps because of it, he had an eager, thrusting, creative mind. He was always seeking new political devices, and he viewed social and economic problems with a fresh mind, unclouded by the narrow skepticism with which some of his colleagues, most of his political opponents and virtually all bureaucrats and planners were plagued. Bennett looked on public works projects with a visionary's eye and he discerned ways to finance them with a banker's mind.

Accustomed to doing business in a certain way, he brought those methods with him to his tasks as premier and minister of finance. Although there is no comparison between guiding a government and operating a hardware store, and Bennett had not been directly involved in the day-to-day operation of his firms for years, he was inclined to employ techniques and formulas that had proven useful in the past. Problems of scale aside, it would not be too great an exaggeration to say that British Columbia's government was effectively run with the simplicity and practicality of a well-managed hardware store—and for Bennett it was the grandest hardware store imaginable.

Initially, he had some difficulty persuading officials in the Department of Finance to cater to his needs and wants. His first deputy minister of finance, J.V. Fisher, who had served the government for many years, remarked that Bennett was by far the most astute minister of finance he had ever worked under. Other ministers would approve virtually anything put before them; not Bennett, who went over everything with a fine-tooth comb. If the government's monthly financial statement was not on his desk by the second day of the new month, Bennett would be on the phone to his deputy wondering where it was. When it did arrive, he poured over it thoroughly sometimes discovering minute errors to the great embarrassment of his officials. The implementation of *daily* financial statements harked back to the careful hardware merchant checking his daily sales and inventory depletion. His government functioned on a strict pay-as-you-go system of balanced budgets and these various financial audits enabled him to keep a firm grip on the day-to-day, month-to-month operating expenses of government. He thereby had the power, and often used it, to reverse a trend of overspending by means of a phone call. A simple phone call could stop all the highway construction in the province, and another could start it up again.

Such detailed accounting measures gave Bennett tremendous power and manoeuvrability, especially since these financial statements were for his eyes only. He was fond of saying: "Information is power." As premier and minister of finance he possessed monopoly control over the financial information relating to his various government departments and agencies. He never made the information public, nor did he share it with his colleagues. Consequently, he usually knew far more about the finances of individual government departments than the ministers in charge.

Bennett's single-handed control over the provincial purse strings was his greatest source of power. It allowed him extreme flexibility in policy making, which proved to be to the government's advantage in this expansionary period. He could cut back if he had to, but he could signal the go-ahead as well, and more often than not during these days of buoyant revenues he played Santa Claus, not the Grinch. Because he alone was making those decisions, seemingly on whim, the Socred government had a reputation of "ad hoc-ery," but Bennett made his decisions carefully and deliberately. Countless examples of the improvisational nature of the power he wielded could be cited. For example, in the spring 1957 legislative session, "Benevolent Bennett" received credit for saving an historic stern-wheeler operating on Kootenay Lake. One day when the government caucus went along the corridor towards the chamber, Eric Martin found himself alongside CCF member Randolph Harding. "Eric, you were a Nelsonite weren't you? You used to live in Nelson?"

"Yes," said Martin.

"Do you remember the old paddle-wheeler *Moyie*?"

"Yes."

"Well, the CPR is selling it next week to a junk dealer. We mustn't let that happen."

"I'm horrified to think it will go that way," said Martin. The *Moyie* was the last such steamer in the province to carry passengers. He asked, "What do you propose should be done about it?"

"Well," said Harding, "the Kaslo Board of Trade would like to put it up on the beach and use it as a museum. Do you think the government would give them a grant?"

"I'll see," said Martin, as they filed into their seats in the House. Martin's seat was directly behind the premier's, and he was able to tell Bennett the details of the *Moyie*.

Meanwhile, Randolph Harding, CCF member for Kaslo-Slocan, made a plea for the preservation of the historic ship.

Bennett shouted across the floor of the House, "How much will it cost?"

Harding replied, "About $7,500."

Bennett then calmly said, "You can have the money."

Eric Martin described Harding's reaction as one of incredulity: "It was just as if you had struck him with something across the face, he was so startled and astonished. He didn't expect anything like that; at least he didn't expect such rapid action."

Another instance, which involved the expenditure of millions of dollars, occurred the day after Bennett came from the interior in his limousine and noticed that only two lanes of the four-lane highway through the Fraser Valley were being paved. When he got to his office in Victoria he phoned Gaglardi and said, "Phil, I notice you are only paving two lanes. What's the matter with the other two?"

Gaglardi said, "You didn't give me enough money in my budget to be able to look after those other two."

Bennett replied, "Well, you've got it now. Get them paved."

These examples demonstrate the kind of power Bennett exercised. His system of financial controls allowed him to act decisively when the situation demanded it. This was not so much a haphazard policy of incremental expansion as a consistent policy of development sprinkled with occasional indulgence. Bennett delighted in his personal views about the financial affairs of government:

> I had the conservative approach to government. The best conservative is he who cuts the smouldering branches away and doesn't let a burning branch destroy the whole tree. In my period of public life I cut away a lot of smouldering branches. A lot of my critics thought I was destroying the tree, but what I was doing was protecting it. My idea of conservatism is that you can conserve your resources so well that you can provide more money and services for the poor than any system of socialism. From the first day I became premier we had a policy of balanced budgets, and it built great confidence—people started to expand their businesses and buy property and the province started to grow. We built on that confidence. . . . Very few people really understand basic economics, that's the trouble. That's what confounded our friends and our enemies alike: we always had more money available. And it was sound economics. I told one minister about the value of tax money and he said, "Mr. Premier, I'll treat it just the same as if it was my own." I said, "No, you won't. With your own you can throw it away any place you want. But these are trust monies. You've got to get two dollars [of value] for every dollar's worth. . . ."

He showed a definite spirit of innovation in many of his government's financial policies but, essentially, he was a fiscal conservative with an exceptionally careful attitude towards the management of taxpayers' dollars. This approach is well illustrated by the budgetary process of the Social Credit administration. Each year Bennett's ministers and their departments went through a rigorous process of review and analysis culminating in the single most important statement of Social Credit policy: the budget. Bennett described the process:

> Before my administration in 1952, budgeting was very complicated. I developed a system of budgeting so simple that it worked like a charm. The government was divided up into departments, and as premier and minister of finance, I was also chairman of the Treasury Board. Before a department got to Treasury Board to determine their budget, a lot of preliminary work had to be done. So starting in late October, the estimates from all the departments came in from all over the province; they were assembled, and totalled. The amounts that we got in would make your head swim, because there wasn't that kind of money then available, and no way could it be secured. But we had to advance on all

fronts, and we had to be able to finance all fronts at the same time. . . . My deputy minister with his staff and the comptroller general would go through the estimates with every department separately in great detail. This was what I called "little treasury board." They would prepare a bare-bones estimate of the programs that were then operating and should be continued: the bare-bones budget. Then they made note of the things that the departments would like to have included in the next budget in addition, and they would place them in order of preference, and the reason why the preference should be given. That bare-bones budget would be really very tough: for argument's sake, $200 million less than I would be prepared to budget for the coming year. Because my finance department officials had already made a study of what the economic conditions were likely to be in the next fiscal year—the rate of expansion we could expect and so forth—I would have a certain amount to allocate over the existing programs of these departments.

Then we would have regular Treasury Board; I was in the chair and we had three ministers there. We'd sit around the table and each person would have the prepared estimates of the department we were dealing with in front of him. The minister in charge of the department and his deputy would appear before us, and we were dealing then with new policies and expansion of present ones. It didn't get into a debating society, but they were now arguing why they needed more money and for what reasons—not only for the good of the department, but for the good of the province—and they'd advocate the reasons. If they could convince us, they would get it, because I had my maximum budget I could allow before me at all times, which I didn't disclose. Over a week's time we'd hear from all the departments and I would prepare my budget. That budget was an instrument of government policy to get the province moving and increase the standard of living.

In comparison with today's increasingly complex, jargon-riddled public expenditure systems, the Social Credit Treasury Board was a simple and clean process—its only flaw being the margin for error inherent in its subjectivity. However, when one tries to assess the convoluted operations of many modern treasury boards, the inevitable conclusion is that objective tests of financial judgement are very difficult, if not impossible, to develop and apply. Bennett's system was probably superior to any that followed it in terms of its capability for producing results and rendering quick judgements on policies and priorities. In that sense, his Treasury Board was probably right for the time and place.

Bennett's cabinet ministers appeared before Treasury Board with a variety of attitudes: some played at overestimating their budgets in the expectation of being cut, while others asked for precisely what they needed. Bennett was hard on the former and more accommodating towards the later. The only minister with whom he and his finance officials had problems year after year was Phil Gaglardi, and special auditing controls were developed in order to keep him within his budget. These controls strengthened the entire Treasury Board process.

Bennett once stated that anyone who wished to study the history of his government should simply read his budgets. Although they do not tell the whole story, as a collection of official documents they are most revealing. Bennett's revenue and expenditure policies were both innovative and pragmatic. From 1952, when the Socreds came to power, to the end of the decade, the government's total annual expenditure doubled—and, naturally, revenues kept pace. Balanced budgets became Bennett's trademark, and well into the age of the so-called "stimulative deficit" he would never hear of budgeting for anything other than a surplus. "Deficit" became a dirty word in Victoria while he served as minister of finance; it was a heresy, synonymous with irresponsibility and socialism. Each year, no matter what economic conditions prevailed, Bennett was able to announce a "surprise surplus" in the provincial budget. Political opponents denounced his budgeting practices, claiming he deliberately underestimated revenues in order to achieve his impressive surpluses, but his answer was always a variation of the one he gave in January 1955: "My policy is to have enough money to tide us over the leaner times. I do not believe in being Saturday night rich and Monday morning poor."

During the 1950s, Bennett used his accumulated budgetary surpluses to reduce the public debt. Debt reduction was the prime economic objective of the Social Credit government during this period; it was a virtual obsession of the premier. In 1952, the public debt of the province stood at $190 million; by August 1, 1959, exactly seven years after he assumed office, Bennett proudly announced that B.C. was debt free. This was a remarkable achievement, especially when the government was preaching growth and accelerating economic development. Its debt reduction policies became a source of controversy and wide public discussion, with critics charging that Social Credit was playing a shell game with public funds. Bennett, however, was very serious in his aversion to debt, especially public debt:

> You must utilize the benefits and the forces of capitalism for the good of the ordinary people. If you get behind the eight ball in our system of government and get badly in debt and have to pay heavy interest rates, then the people have no chance to grow and prosper: they're under a burden just as if they're under a yoke, and a yoke of debt is the worst kind of yoke. If you can't pay for it today, how can you pay for it tomorrow—

plus additional services, plus the old interest and the other interest? How can you pay for the dead horse all the time? But if you have a government that doesn't create more tax-paying debt and pays off all the old debt so that you have a debt-free government, then you have all the taxes that you get from the people and industry, not to pay for deadweight debt, but to give services to the people so you can always give greater services every year. There are dividends everywhere because of that kind of policy. That was my philosophy. Instead of the government being a deficit business, we made it a successful business. We took a little corner grocery store and made it into a great market for the benefit of the people.

In 1959, the deputy minister of finance and comptroller general signed a declaration stating: "In our opinion, effective July 31, 1959, the public debt of the Province . . . is fully provided for by sinking funds so as to ensure the full payment of all principal and interest." The direct legal debt of British Columbia was thereby officially dissolved. Naturally, it was impossible to recall all long-term bonds that were due in twenty to thirty years' time, but sinking funds were secured to cover all direct outstanding debt. Bennett declared: "It took seventy years to build up the debt; it took seven years to wipe it out!"

Why the emphasis on *seven* years? Though no one examined why, Bennett always placed special stress on the fact that his signal accomplishment took *exactly seven years* to fulfill, and he had made a tremendous effort to see that it was accomplished within this specific timetable. Perhaps it was nothing more than one of his old-fashioned superstitions about the number seven; he often remarked that he believed in "lucky seven" and in cycles of seven in human affairs. Then again, maybe it had an obscure connection with Social Credit doctrine. The British Israelites, for instance, who were an integral part of the early Social Credit movement in the province, had developed elaborate teachings on the significance of the number seven and the importance of wiping out all personal debt every seven years. Bennett never spoke of any British Israelite influence, but he would probably have read some of their literature as part of his Social Credit immersion course several years earlier. In any event, on August 1, 1959, the "seven-year miracle" of eliminating B.C.'s direct debt was celebrated by a day of public festivities in the premier's home town of Kelowna, culminating in a massive "bond-fire" on Okanagan Lake.

The bond-fire celebration was a landmark event in the history of Social Credit in B.C. About $70-million worth of cancelled bonds were transported to Kelowna via armoured truck and piled on a barge floating on the lake. All day long, hoopla and festivities surrounded the exuberant cabinet ministers who were also celebrating the seventh anniversary of the initial Socred election victory. Hundreds of guests poured into Kelowna, and Phil Gaglardi organized a choir of several thousand children who sang "Happy Birthday" to the premier. A swimming race was staged with four young contestants representing the leaders of each of the provincial parties and, thanks to a hidden towrope, the boy representing Bennett won easily. As evening fell, the premier and his adoring cabinet ministers boarded a launch and approached the barge with its mountain of cancelled bonds. The premier fired a lighted arrow at the barge which had been generously dowsed with gasoline. The flaming arrow hit the chicken wire that was holding the bonds in place and deflected into the lake; but an RCMP officer out of sight behind the barge set the bonds afire and thereby helped to light a B.C. political legend.

The idea of burning the bonds was Bennett's. Today it may seem like a crass public relations stunt, or perhaps a bizarre pagan ritual, but at the time it was joyous festivity; thousands of people happily took part in the event. It was akin to an old-fashioned mortgage-burning after the final payment—a family celebration. It also reminded Bennett of his maritime relatives burning effigies of their political opponents after successful electoral battles. Those fires lodged in his memory came to the fore when he was reaching for a symbol that would have a similar effect on British Columbians. The Kelowna bond-fire was given wide media attention, and announcements of the government's freedom from debt were advertised in the daily newspapers. Then to reinforce in the public's mind that provincial finances would continue to be administered on a pay-as-you-go basis, Bennett produced a more important symbol: at the following legislative session, a bill cancelling the borrowing power of the province was passed. Barring rescinding this act, B.C.'s government was now legally obliged to practise economy and efficiency in the style of W. A. C. Bennett.

Naturally, the Kelowna bond-fire and Social Credit claims to freedom from debt became the subject of intense political debate. The leader of the opposition, Robert Strachan, said: "Bennett's so called bond burning to celebrate our debt-free status is a delusion and a show, a hoax, a cheap political fraud. . . . That bond-fire will be the funeral pyre of the Social Credit government." Others charged false bookkeeping and legerdemain. A frequent suggestion was that Bennett was keeping two sets of books, one for the public's eyes and another that told the real story. It was difficult for many to believe that the province's huge public debt could have been eliminated by a government that was spending far more than any previous administration. Nevertheless, the Socreds' claims were quite correct: through strict economies in public administration, pay-as-you-go financial policies, increased revenues from resource development and the achievement of considerable budgetary surpluses, the government had in fact legally paid off the direct debt of the province. The crux of the controversy, however, was the indirect debt. Bennett had devised a new improved system of bookkeeping that removed from the provincial budget large capital expenditures which were the specific responsibilities of authorities or agencies that were wholly or partially self-supporting. In the past, the government borrowed money for the PGE railway, thereby incurring a direct debt; now, after the Socreds had written off the railway's debt, the PGE would have to borrow its own money for capital construction and expansion, though the government would guarantee its loans to ensure a preferred rate of interest; these loans would not show as a direct debt on the public books. This system applied also to the construction of highways, bridges and ferries which now came under a new crown corporation, the Toll Highways and Bridges Authority, created in 1953. In 1954, when the government passed the Public Schools Construction Act, the same system was applied, on a cost-sharing basis with school districts, to the construction of new schools throughout the province. For Bennett's purposes, these public agencies would now assume their own direct debts and the government would regard them as contingent liabilities.

Was Bennett hoodwinking the public by making this new distinction between direct and indirect debt, direct versus contingent liabilities? Time has vindicated his system of bookkeeping, for his administration was simply the first in a wave of Canadian provincial governments that began to borrow indirectly in the name of crown corporations or other public authorities. Yet British Columbia's government was one of the few in the world to take direct action in wiping out its public debt and instituting a pay-as-you-go approach to public finance. When one examines the Social Credit system of indirect borrowing, the reasons for Bennett's goal of debt reduction become obvious. First, debt-servicing costs were eliminated or transferred: Bennett claimed that freedom from paying interest and other financial service charges saved B.C. about $25 million a year. Second, the credit position of the province was improved and that represented a saving which could be passed on to provincial crown corporations in the form of loan guarantees. Third, insofar as public approval was concerned, the government cultivated a "takeoff" atmosphere for economic development: the policy created a mood of optimism, energy and limitless economic possibilities. Bennett expressed this spirit when, after introducing his record-breaking 1959 budget of $300 million, he told reporters that it was a "happy budget, because everyone is happy when he is free of debt."

Bennett's new bookkeeping system was not only much more convenient administratively, but politically it was also far easier for the government to defend guaranteeing a loan than incurring more direct debt. This is an important key to understanding the rise of British Columbia under Bennett in the 1950s. Certainly the province was free of direct debt by 1959, but its guaranteed debt had grown to several hundred million dollars by then, and on a per capita basis it represented a larger debt than that of any other Canadian province. Building up such massive "contingent liabilities" could have been dangerous, but the province was fortunate to have both rapidly increasing revenues and a wily finance minister who personally kept its finances in order. The hundreds of millions of dollars of provincial guarantees were going towards public works projects administered largely by crown corporations. As minister of finance, Bennett was fiscal agent for all crown corporations; this served to further concentrate the important powers he possessed over the province's growing economy. His was one of the first Canadian provincial governments to make substantial use of crown corporations as quasi-independent agents of development. These instruments appealed to Bennett because, while publicly owned, they are capable of direct action and are free from some of the red tape that encumbers most government activity. However, these independent characteristics of crown corporations also create political difficulties in that they are not directly accountable to the legislature or to the public for their operations. This did not disturb Bennett; while he was minister of finance he considered himself to be the only necessary watchdog on the public purse—and, of course, he was the only person who had a complete view of the province's financial picture.

Bennett's use of crown corporations as aggressive instruments of government policy and his new system of bookkeeping were a source of controversy for several years and, on at least one occasion, caused serious political embarrassment. H. Lee Briggs was the general manager of the B.C. Power Commission, a public utility created in 1945 which provided electricity to a small but growing portion of the province. Briggs ran headlong into the premier's plans for a debt-free British Columbia, having developed a kind of paranoia over the government's new financial policies which he felt were being used to undermine the Power Commission. As fiscal agent for the Power Commission, Bennett wished to refinance some of its borrowings, making them a direct obligation of the power utility. The premier also informed the commission that its proposed rate increases would not be approved. On November 12, 1958, Briggs issued a 3,000-word statement in which he declared that he would not stand idly by "while those charged with the administration of the fiscal affairs of this province prostitute the 80,000 customers of the B.C. Power Commission to fulfill election promises." Over the next couple of days Briggs issued further public statements denouncing the government's stewardship of the province, attacking W. A. C. Bennett's integrity and suggesting that something was not right with Einar Gunderson's ambiguous relationship to the government and the Social Credit Party. On November 14, Briggs was fired; responding to the clamour for an investigation into his charges, on November 17 Bennett announced the appointment of a royal commission: "We are going to end once and for all this smear. The government is going to meet it head on. We intend to fight these forces of evil in the press and elsewhere." The royal commission, chaired by Dr. Gordon Shrum, a prominent Canadian physicist and dean of graduate studies at the University of British Columbia, reported the following year that Briggs's charges were largely unfounded. It said that he was probably right in his basic charge that the primary reason Bennett wanted to refinance the Power Commission's debt was so that he could declare B.C. debt free, but it decided that there was nothing improper about such government policy and that Briggs's other accusations of political interference were indefensible. Bennett made public reference to the findings of the Shrum Commission in advance of the release of the report to the public; his comments were directed at Briggs and constituted a vicious broadside against what he considered to have been essentially a political attack. As it turned out, Bennett had stretched the Shrum Commission's findings to suit his own interpretation, and he was severely criticized by opposition parties for doing so. But when the press suggested that Briggs had been partially vindicated, Bennett responded: "The former general manager may have been a good engineer, but he knew nothing of finances."

Briggs did not come out of the affair too badly; he became a kind of folk hero to political opponents of Social Credit and he subsequently received a federal government appointment to the National Energy Board. Bennett also came out of the affair all right—once more he had got his way—but his reputation for fairness was tarnished by the comments he had made about Briggs. Nevertheless, the significance of the Briggs affair far transcends the immediate issue, for it brought some important questions to the fore regarding the role of the provincial government in power development, and equally important, a new set of personalities now came forward who were to have a lasting impact on the future course of provincial development. One was Dr. Gordon Shrum who had impressed Bennett with his straightforward investigation and ability to break down problems to their bare essentials; Shrum became the first chairman of the British Columbia Energy Board created in August 1959 pursuant to a recommendation of his own commission into the Briggs affair. Another fresh face was Dr. Hugh Keenleyside who became the new chairman of the B.C. Power Commission and who would play an important part in the continuing rise of British Columbia.

Before leaving this discussion of the financial policies of the Social Credit government and their consequences, a couple of other innovations during this period should be mentioned; one was the homeowner grant, introduced as a result of one of Bennett's 1956 election promises. The homeowner grant was an innovative form of tax relief administered in an ingenious fashion and which Bennett described as an attempt to help "the little people" of the province. He recalled the reaction of his deputy minister of finance, J. V. Fisher, to the surprise announcement: "Jack Fisher couldn't wait to see me in my office in Victoria. He said, 'You were misquoted weren't you? Mr. Premier, tell me it's not true; you're not going to give our treasury away, are you? It's impossible.' I said, 'Jack, you might find it impossible, but it's not impossible for me. It's not impossible for Social Credit. I've just got one job for you to do this morning. I want you to find out what it would cost on an average in the province, in dollars, to give back to the people $1,000 of their tax from their assessment.' He figured it out to be $28, and that was our first grant."

The homeowner grant, which proved to be immensely popular, was unique in many ways: it was a tax exemption applied to a property tax; it was applied to a tax collected by other authorities, namely, municipalities; administration costs for distributing the grants were borne by the municipalities; and since the grants involved formal application on the part of the homeowner, they also contained a built-in reminder of the source of the benefit—the Social Credit government. The homeowner grant was a brilliant, even revolutionary, form of tax reduction and, while originally denounced as a "political sales gimmick," it became increasingly accepted by British Columbia's opposition parties and, in modified form, has been introduced in several other provinces. At the time of its inception on the west coast, there was no overt attempt to tie in the homeowner grant with the proverbial Social Credit dividend, but one cabinet minister exuberantly proclaimed: "We can see here the basis of Social Credit and the payment of the dividend." Over the years, Bennett himself increasingly referred to the grant as "Social Credit in action." Of course, there was no fundamental connection between the "dividends" proposed by Major Douglas and the tax remissions of the B.C. government. However, this was Social Credit according to W. A. C. Bennett: instead of giving the money in lump grants to municipalities, small payments were made to individuals. In that sense, at least, an analogy can be drawn between his policies and those of Douglas, for they were both preoccupied with expanding the purchasing power of people by placing money in their hands.

Another of Bennett's popular financial innovations bears a distant resemblance to classical Social Credit theory: parity bonds. Parity Development Bonds, as they were called, were a bold unique experiment for a provincial government; as it turned out, they were a surprisingly successful method of raising development capital for public works. The bond market in Canada, which had been seriously set back during the Depression of the 1930s, had been rejuvenated by the issue of government wartime bonds; that impetus pushed forward into the 1950s when the capital requirements of corporations and governments led to a heavy increase in the volume of new bond issues. Bennett was searching for methods of financing his vision for massive public works in B.C. but was reluctant to raise taxes and was totally averse to any kind of borrowing that would create a direct debt for the province. The day following the famous bond-fire in Kelowna, he flew to Vancouver for a meeting with representatives of the chartered banks; he told them of his plan to issue a provincial development bond. He enthusiastically described his idea to print a piece of paper that would do everything that money could do, and bear interest as well, and unlike any other bond issue, could be cashed at par, or face value, at any time. Apparently the bankers were unimpressed. Not surprisingly, so were his finance officials in Victoria. Bennett suggested that such a bond issue might raise as much as $10 million for the PGE railway, but his officials opined that it might raise $1.5 million and would not be worth the administrative hassle. But Bennett persisted and bulldozed his bureaucrats, the banks and bond dealers into co-operating with his radical proposal which was quickly put into action. The first issue of the world's first "parity bond" was offered for sale to the public on September 15, 1959; intended to raise $10 million, the parity bonds were so successfully promoted by the excited premier that orders reached $35 million before the sale was cut off. Demand for the bonds among individuals and small investors was especially great. Their popularity was probably at the expense of bank savings deposits and, as one authority has suggested, "they may also have absorbed some of the currency normally kept in boxes or mattresses."

The parity bonds—a precursor of the federal government's Canada Savings Bonds—were undeniably a huge success, a truly creative form of taxation that produced huge pools of capital for the provincial government and its crown corporations to draw upon for large-scale development projects. Other provinces experimented with such bonds, but B.C. remained the largest issuer; within a few years there were hundreds of millions of dollars of these bonds in issue, all guaranteed by the government, all oversubscribed, and soundly accepted in the money markets. While the success of the idea may have blinded Bennett to an unforeseen vulnerability that went with it, for the time being he exploited the concept for what it was worth. Like many of his successful ideas, he had to overcome tremendous resistance from orthodox thinkers, unimaginative bureaucrats and other defenders of the status quo. Bennett was obviously much brighter than he was given credit for and, in many ways, was an original thinker, especially when it came to questions of finance.

As the 1950s progressed, W. A. C. Bennett began to grope for a massive hydroelectric power development to complement and give impetus to industrial expansion. The Socreds had made the construction of modern transportation networks throughout the province their priority; it became equally incumbent upon them to develop sources of energy to fuel development, especially since B.C. is probably endowed with more potential sources of hydroelectric energy than any other single jurisdiction in the world. One source had been talked about for decades: the Columbia River, one of North America's great rivers, which traverses the Canada-U.S. border. The American side had been developed to control flooding and to produce energy. Huge dams like the Grand Coulee were familiar sights to tourists from all over the world. The Canadian portion of the Columbia, flowing in roundabout direction through southeastern B.C., had not yet been developed—but the Americans were anxious to exploit the entire potential of the river, and in 1944 the Canadian and United States governments asked the International Joint Commission to study the further harnessing of the river with a view to a possible large-scale international development. The IJC established the International Columbia River Engineering Board which spent years in study and debate. When Bennett became premier, no end to the Columbia discussions was in sight, but realizing the important role that hydro power would play in his plans, he was eager to press for a resolution to the issue, or else for an altogether different alternative.

Early in 1954, the Social Credit administration received an independent proposal that promised to allow them to achieve their goals and circumvent the international deadlock on the Columbia. The huge Kaiser Corporation of the United States proposed a private development which would focus on the construction of a large storage dam at Mica Creek, a site north of Revelstoke on the upper reaches of the Columbia. Discussions proceeded over the next several months between Kaiser representatives and the provincial government; the eventual agreement between the two parties included construction of the dam at no cost to the province and the issue of a fifty-year water licence to the corporation. Fundamental to the proposed project was the requirement that Kaiser pay provincial taxes and water licence fees and that 20 per cent of the tremendous power generated downstream in the United States be returned to B.C. Bennett and his ministers found the agreement appealing and began to paint a fantastic picture of an industrial empire emerging in the Kootenay region of the province. But when the details of the plan were made public, the Socreds were strongly attacked by the press and by the opposition parties who claimed that they were selling the province's birthright to the Americans. The CCF regretted the departure from a pattern of proposed public power development on the Columbia and called the Kaiser deal a "giveaway" and a "power grab." The Liberal government in Ottawa also reacted hostilely, calling it a "cock-eyed and improvident deal." Bennett personally entered into the fray: stating that all the "communists and socialists" were against the proposed Kaiser dam, he classified the federal Liberals as "only socialists in low gear." But the federal administration was seriously disturbed that the Kaiser deal would completely undermine years of painstaking international negotiation over the proposed joint development of the Columbia River. Provincial governments control the resources of their province, but the federal government wanted to dictate terms to B.C. on this issue because potentially it affected international relations. The fight was on.

In January 1955, the federal government introduced the International Rivers Improvement Act in parliament; the bill proposed that no party could build any improvements on an international river without federal licence. Bennett angrily refused to attend the committee hearings held in Ottawa to discuss the bill. "Committees deal with committees," he said, "ministers with ministers, and premiers with premiers." However, Attorney General Bonner did appear before the committee protesting that the bill represented "the most blatant piece of aggression against a provincial government that has ever been devised." Nevertheless, the bill became law in the summer of 1955, effectively quashing the Kaiser proposal. Although the Socreds appeared to have lost an important battle, the consequences of the Kaiser plan would be far-reaching and generally in their favour. The B.C. government strongly resented the treatment it had received from Ottawa and Bennett would not forget that his administration had been branded as both hasty and improvident. Years later, he and several of his ministers confided that they never seriously expected that Kaiser could have delivered on all its promises, but in the process of promoting the plan they were able to test the waters, find out what they were up against and establish important developmental principles such as downstream benefits. Equally important, Bennett became determined that Ottawa would never again be able to assert a fiat over provincial development.

In the autumn of 1956, a massive private development scheme emerged which not only conjured fresh visions of tremendous industrial expansion in British Columbia but also armed Bennett with a strategic new weapon in the continuing war over power development. It seems that the premier's bold assertions of the limitless possibilities for development were being heard far and wide. Through a contact made at B.C. House in London, England, a representative of Swedish millionaire Axel Wenner-Gren came to the Canadian west coast in 1956 to investigate the prospects for large-scale investment. Reports filtered back to Wenner-Gren's people that a huge area in north-central B.C., the Rocky Mountain Trench, which stretched right up into the Peace River district, was a vast storehouse of mineral wealth possessing fantastic opportunities for development. Wenner-Gren became keenly interested in these reports and in November 1956 sent his two key financial men, Bernard Gore and Birger Strid, from Stockholm to see W. A. C. Bennett. Gore and Strid impressed the premier with their knowledge of the interior terrain; they likened the Peace to parts of Sweden's northland. They proposed the construction of a railway through the Rocky

Mountain Trench and further detailed surveys of its resource wealth. On November 16, Bennett signed a memorandum of intent with Gore and Strid whereby the newly incorporated Wenner-Gren B.C. Development Company undertook to develop 40,000 square miles of the northern portion of the province—almost a tenth of the total land mass of British Columbia, an area as large as Nova Scotia. The memorandum stated that the Wenner-Gren interests would build a railway to the Yukon border and seek forest rights to support a projected pulp mill. The agreement also called for a reserve to be placed on the lands and timber within the proposed development area and for a general survey of the resources of the region, including the possibilities for hydroelectric generation. Witnesses to the document, which was sealed with a $500,000 deposit, were Lands and Forests Minister Ray Williston and Bennett confidant Einar Gunderson.

This agreement was conceived in strict privacy; the first inkling the public had of the Wenner-Gren scheme was when Bennett presented it to the legislature in the spring of 1957. Bennett and his colleagues were optimistic about the announcement, but pointed out that caution should be observed. The plan was greeted with skepticism and derision; it seemed too big, too grandiose and too, too good to be true. When Ray Williston told the legislature that it included a futuristic 160-mile-per-hour monorail that would zoom along a beam-like track mounted on pillars, and that this railway's cost would be $1 billion, he only added to the general incredulity of the Socreds' various opponents. The press and partisan observers labelled the huge land reserve a "giveaway" to a foreign interest; however, they ignored the fact that the memorandum of intent was simply a letter of assurance which might lead to a more concrete agreement for development in the north. A general reserve was placed on the land in the name of the crown, and the Wenner-Gren people travelled throughout the region conducting surveys and planning for development. As Bennett would say: "It is the free enterpriser's right to make money, and it's his right to go broke."

The Wenner-Gren proposal was subject to almost continuous skepticism, and contributing to the controversy was the mysterious, seemingly shady character of Axel Wenner-Gren himself. The enterprising Swede, apparently a millionaire since his early twenties, had built an international industrial empire based on his Electrolux vacuum cleaners and Servel refrigerators. Some of his proposed developments had not panned out, but his successful projects included pulp and paper and banking holdings in Sweden, canneries in the Bahamas, haciendas in Mexico and mines in South America. British Columbia in the booming 1950s was a natural target for his visionary approach to economic development. However, almost as soon as he entered the B.C. picture, a debate arose over the presence of his name on an Allied blacklist during the Second World War. As a Swedish neutral, he had apparently profited from both sides as a member of an international armaments cartel during the early stages of the war; some alleged that he was a personal friend of Hermann Goering. Years later, most observers felt that he had been unfairly blacklisted by the U.S. State Department; his neutrality had been unfortunately misconstrued. That a terrible mistake had been made was corroborated when the Chaim Weizmann Institute of Science in Israel made him an honorary fellow. Abba Eban, then minister of education and culture, praised Wenner-Gren: "In an earlier century he would have been one of the discoverers of new continents, but unfortunately all the five continents had been found already before his birth." Young Israel was hardly noted for loving Nazi sympathizers and collaborators and there can be little doubt that Wenner-Gren's background was thoroughly researched before he received this honour. But in British Columbia he had no supporters on the opposition side of the legislature and mostly detractors in the urban press.

Another target of criticism was the direct involvement of Einar Gunderson in the Wenner-Gren plan. Bennett's former finance minister was closely associated with the Socred government, serving as vice-president of the PGE railway, a director of the Toll Highways and Bridges Authority and ubiquitous financial adviser and Social Credit Party bagman. Now it was announced that he had been made a director of the Wenner-Gren B.C. Development Company. The opposition and the press charged a blatant conflict of interest. The premier rallied to his friend's defence, referring to him as "that great Canadian. . . . There is no finer man in British Columbia tonight," and dismissed opposition attacks as "smear, carping criticism, snide remarks and McCarthyism." For W. A. C. Bennett, having Gunderson as a director of the Wenner-Gren company was simply a way of keeping in close touch with the progress of events. Bennett was not discouraged by the criticisms levelled at the Wenner-Gren scheme. In 1957, when Axel Wenner-Gren visited B.C., the Victoria *Times*, a leading opponent of the proposed development, ran a front-page editorial addressed to the Swede; "We intend to watch you," it concluded. Stuart Keate, the editor of the *Times*, was surprised by the reaction of the premier. "Keep it up," Bennett told him, "the more you protest, the better deal I can make with these people. Now I can go to them and say, 'See, the people of B.C. really don't want you.' "

As it turned out, Wenner-Gren's British Columbia vision became clouded and events would soon rapidly overtake him. His original interest, which had been primarily in studying the feasibility of extracting resources from the Rocky Mountain Trench by rail, was soon scrapped, in spite of an opening ceremony staged for the Wenner-Gren railway, but one aspect of the exploratory surveys proved to be more significant than all of his dreams combined. Wenner-Gren surveys showed that the Peace River canyon possessed the basic requirements for a huge hydroelectric dam that would create the largest man-made reservoir in the world. The power from the Peace would be much greater than the potential from the Columbia and could be developed at less expense. On October 7, 1957, the Wenner-Gren people signed a new agreement which paved the way for a new company to construct a huge hydroelectric project. The following day, Bennett called a news conference, which he opened with the words: "This is the most momentous announcement I have ever made." The studies being conducted in the north, he said, "indicate the feasibility of establishing in the Rocky Mountain Trench the greatest hydro-electric power project in the world," a project that would be "entirely within the control of the government of British Columbia." He said it would produce 4 million horsepower and create a lake 260 miles long—so big that it would probably alter the climate of the north country. Bennett was gurgling with excitement and enthusiam; he told the incredulous reporters that this day was "the most important that B.C. has experienced in its whole history." Further, he said he did not think that this new plan would interfere with the Columbia negotiations. However, in typical fashion, he added: "Surely now both Ottawa and the U.S. will realize we mean business. This means the development of B.C. won't be held back while the U.S. and Ottawa hold pink teas."

The discovery and confirmation of the power potential of the Peace River quickened Bennett's thinking. After all, he always had a special soft spot for the Peace River, and now he could focus the world's attention on a spectacular plan of development. This was the genesis of what would become his famous "Two River Policy." He began talking about developing both the Peace and Columbia rivers simultaneously—and he was probably the only person capable of arousing what seemed at the time an extravagant hope. In spite of tremendous obstacles in his path, Bennett would be able to use the Peace River plan as leverage in getting all parties to agree to his plan for the development of the Columbia River.

International discussion over the Columbia continued, with very little success, while plans to develop the Peace progressed with greater speed. The new company was called the Peace River Power Development Company. W.C. Mainwaring retired as vice-president of the B.C. Electric Company and became president of the new company. An imposing board of directors attended the first meeting on November 12, 1957. They included Sir Andrew McTaggart, Bernard Gore, Lord Tweedsmuir, Senator S.S. McKeen, Einar Gunderson, A.F. MacAlpine, A. Bruce Robertson, Ralph Chantrill, William Murphy, George T. Cunningham and Birger Strid. Unable to be present at the first board meeting were Viscount Chandos and Lord Alexander of Tunis. A budget was presented, reports were made and, as jockeying for position and power within the new company proceeded, it became clear that the Wenner-Gren people would represent only a minor shareholding position in the Peace project. Over the next couple of years the pace of activity quickened. Suddenly, the Columbia project seemed close to resolution; both the Canadian government and the United States government appeared ready to come to terms in the face of competition from the British Columbia Peace River plan. Draft treaties were now being discussed and the crucial financing of the various Columbia alternatives was being calculated. In B.C., political opponents of Social Credit scoffed at Bennett's Two River Policy, claiming it was impractical and unnecessary to develop both rivers simultaneously, but for Bennett the two projects became increasingly intertwined. He told reporters in February 1960: "If the Peace dies today, the Columbia will die tomorrow. The Peace is the only reason why after all these years of talk there has been some real action on the Columbia. The Peace is an empire crying out for development. Its hydro, coal, gas and oil make it the greatest potential energy resource area in North America."

Bennett's biggest problem during these initial stages of his Two River Policy was finding immediate customers for the tremendous power potential of the Peace and Columbia rivers. His whole plan hinged on the assumption of future development; in the meantime, much more energy was being discussed than could be consumed in B.C. He wanted an agreement whereby the Columbia power would be sold initially to the United States, while the power of the Peace would stoke the furnaces of development and expansion at home. The stumbling block was the B.C. Electric Company, a private, federally chartered utility which provided almost 90 per cent of the electrical energy service to British Columbians. B.C. Electric consistently refused to commit itself to purchase Peace power and this caused delays in Peace River Power Development's plans. After recovering from a kidney operation in the spring of 1960, W. A. C. Bennett travelled to London, England, determined to see what could be done about the obstinacy of B.C. Electric. He has described that trip:

> Sir Andrew McTaggart was the former chancellor of the exchequer of the British government, and now he was chairman of the board of the Peace River [Power] Development Company. I cabled Sir Andrew in London that I was coming to Europe and I'd want to see him. . . . When I met with [him] I said that I was very pleased with the early stages of the company, but was very displeased now—six months, no action. He said, "Mr. Bennett, I must tell you that our company has lots of credit, there is no difficulty there; but you can't build great power dams unless you have some bond money. And you can't float bonds on a power development unless you have anticipated contracts. You have to get a market for this power. Is there really going to be lots of market in British

Columbia?" I said, "Yes." He then said, "The B.C. Electric Company has sole right over ninety per cent of British Columbia for distribution of power. While they are partners with us, they're not allowed to give us any contracts at any price. Ottawa won't let them do it." Ottawa was afraid that if we built the Peace, they would never be able to get the Columbia off the ground and the B.C. Electric, being a federal corporation, [was told by] Ottawa . . . that they didn't want any assistance from B.C. Electric on the Peace. The Peace River company was stymied; they couldn't move. I said to Sir Andrew, "Where is the president of B.C. Electric, Dal Grauer? Isn't he over here somewhere?" He said, "I was just talking to him this morning; he's in Paris." I said, "Have him over for breakfast tomorrow morning at my suite." The next morning I said to Dr. Grauer, "I want you to hear what Sir Andrew has told me. I want you to listen carefully, and be careful what you say. I'm talking to you now, not as your friend, which I am, but as premier of British Columbia; and you're the head of B.C. Electric." So Sir Andrew once more outlined the company's needs, and Grauer said he did not intend to buy Peace power. I said, "Never forget one thing in this world; in nature, what you don't use, you lose. We're not going to stand idly by in British Columbia and not have that Peace River power development go ahead!" This was one of the most important meetings I had while I was premier. Perhaps this was *the* most important.

Bennett returned home from that London breakfast meeting scheming, plotting and, as always, developing audacious contingency plans. He knew full well that the timing was not right for any drastic course of action which might risk a disintegration of everything he had worked for, including his Two River Policy. He did decide that the timing was right for a trip to the polls; on August 3, an election writ was issued for September 12, 1960. In announcing the election, he explained that the Social Credit government required a renewed mandate from the people so that the rise of British Columbia could continue.

In many ways, the last provincial election in 1956 seemed long in the past. B.C. had really started to grow, its economy was expanding rapidly and, despite the ubiquitous bulldozers and construction crews, the quality of life on Canada's west coast seemed materially better. So much had happened since the last time British Columbians had voted: a former cabinet minister had gone to jail, the province had celebrated a centenary, gone into the ferry business, paved ribbons of new roads and highways, celebrated the elimination of the public debt with a huge Okanagan bond-fire and entertained the dreams of Wenner-Gren. The province's life pulse was quicker than it had been before and, in that sense, it was probably a good time to call an election.

The Social Credit campaign slogan in 1960 was "Vote for the Government That Gets Things Done." It was a perfect example of Bennett's political salesmanship: simple and to the point. Critics of the government clearly missed the boat when they complained that the Socred political style was misleading and lacking any discernible ideological basis. Political style has much more to do with the way in which ideas are advocated than with the validity of their content; the Social Credit style which included simplistic slogans like "Progress not Politics," "Social Credit or Chaos," and "Pay-as-you-go" was in tune with the mood and thinking of British Columbia.

This is not to suggest that the electoral prospects were reassuring for the incumbent Socreds. The 1960 B.C. election was the closest and hardest fought political campaign in many years. As a government, Social Credit could run on an impressive, even staggering, record; as a party, however, its base appeared to be less stable. Bennett had become so preoccupied with huge development projects that he had not expended much effort on political fence-mending. He had not bothered to keep in contact with individual members of the legislature, and this caused resentment. One Socred MLA, Orr Newton of Columbia, wrote to Bennett in the spring of 1960 complaining that he had been trying for several weeks to obtain an appointment with the premier but with no success: "I have never bothered you as I realize how busy you are. I believe the last time I was in your office was four or five years ago. Also, I could often criticize the government but for the sake of the party I keep my mouth shut. . . . I am still awaiting word to go to your office." Out of necessity the premier would now find time for such meetings, but the populist foundations of Social Credit had developed visible cracks, and whether or not they were in serious need of repair could only be decided by the voters. At the 1959 annual party convention, vocal government backbencher Cyril Shelford warned delegates that they were slipping away from their grassroots and becoming too dominated by chambers of commerce. Whether the danger signals were evident to the premier or not, he hustled and bustled his way through the 1960 campaign battle doing his best to reacquaint himself with the ordinary citizens of the province, attempting to revitalize the Social Credit movement, and all the while boldly preaching "bigness" for the little people.

After Bennett's overwhelming 1956 election victory, he proclaimed: "The CCF Socialist party and the Social Credit genuine Free Enterprise movement are the intact political alternatives in the Province today." By 1960, the polarization had progressed further. The CCF, for over two decades the party of opposition in B.C., mobilized its forces as never before for the 1960 fight. The provincial election became a kind of trial run for the labour and socialist forces in Canada who were discussing the creation of a new political alternative. Unprecedented labour support gave new impetus to the

CCF campaign which spent more than three times as much money as in 1956. The B.C. Federation of Labour raised a campaign fund of $150,000 and ran large newspaper advertisements on behalf of its 126,000 members. Saskatchewan's Premier T.C. Douglas drew 5,500 people to a single meeting. Other CCFers from across the country paraded into the province hoping to create a previously unimagined socialist victory in B.C. Robert Strachan, likely the most honest and hard-working person ever to serve as B.C. CCF leader, ran a diligent campaign. He made public ownership of B.C. Electric the issue of the 1960 election: "Governments win and governments lose, but the B.C. Electric has never lost an election in its life." The Vancouver *Province* in its first election editorial said: "Robert Strachan, the Fidel Castro of British Columbia, breathing fire and smoke like the furnaces of Trail, proposes to nationalize the B.C. Electric as a starter...."

Although they ran spirited campaigns, neither the Liberals nor the Conservatives could be so optimistic. The new leader of the Grits, Ray Perrault, sought to prevent the polarization of opinion in the province and paved a safe middle road: "The CCF is going to save us from the octopus arms of the capitalists, Social Credit is going to save us from the cigar-chomping union bosses. I say a plague on both your houses. This is a phony class war of briefcases against lunchbuckets." Deane Finlayson somehow managed to mobilize yet another Tory campaign, and with the federal and provincial wings of the party reunified, a strong nucleus of British Columbia MPs, and considerable financial improvement, the Conservatives were praying for a breakthrough.

The CCF were unsuccessful in their attempt to make nationalization of B.C. Electric a major election issue. Although Bennett steered conspicuously clear of the issue, most Socred candidates simply ridiculed Strachan's attack on the private utility. Bennett, still recovering from his kidney operation, refused to publicly debate with any of his opponents; he appeared confident at Socred rallies, presenting a party program that included a new billion-dollar, ten-year highway construction program and an increase in the popular homeowner grant from $28 to $50. He proposed significant new social programs as well, including an increase in education grants of $10 million and augmenting social welfare payments by 20 per cent. For an election issue, Bennett decided on "a battle to the death with big labour bosses"—and he managed to effectively promote it in high-paranoid fashion. The CCF characterized the Socreds as an "antilabour" government and proclaimed their intention to repeal Bill 43, the new labour policy passed into law the previous year. Bennett responded: "Because this little government had the nerve to put this Bill through, all these labour bosses are moving into B.C. in an invasion now.... The issue is this: whether a government with the courage to protect not big business or big labour, but ordinary people, can last, or whether these pressure groups are going to run the country. If there is anything the working man fears more than industry bosses it is labour bosses. If they had control of the government as well as the unions the men will have to jump every time these big labour bosses with their cigars and their hotel rooms snap their fingers."

Bennett successfully stirred up the labour issue as the election campaign neared its conclusion. The CCF was not helped by the arrival on the west coast of Tim Buck, the national leader of the Communist Party, who claimed that sixty Communist Party workers were active in the local labour movement and were anxiously awaiting the approaching merger between the CCF and organized labour. Robert Strachan declared that Buck was "mentally incompetent" and speculated that he was "in the pay of the premier and the Socreds." A significant announcement was made on the Saturday before the Monday election at a luncheon meeting in the Peace River district where Bennett fittingly concluded his campaign. Frank McMahon, the president of Westcoast Transmission and chairman of Pacific Petroleum Ltd., was a mythic home-grown B.C. industrialist and a pioneer in the province's oil and gas industry. A Liberal by tradition, he was scheduled to say a few words after the premier, but instead of reading his prepared remarks—which he tore up and tossed aside—he rose and applauded Bennett and the Socred government, and closed his seemingly spontaneous burst of enthusiasm by predicting that if the Social Credit government was defeated and the socialists came to power, 10,000 jobs would be lost in British Columbia and a $450-million oil and gas development in the north would be wiped out. Although Bennett and the Socreds were a little uncomfortable with this well-known industrialist jumping so wholeheartedly on their bandwagon, coming when it did at the climax of the campaign, McMahon's statement, which received wide coverage in the press, probably had an important impact on voting behaviour.

As was his usual practice, Bennett returned home to Kelowna for polling day to await the people's decision. In public, the premier always exuded unruffled confidence; but privately he was worried about this election. Gathered around in their Kelowna living room on the evening of September 12 were the Bennett family and a few close friends. As the early returns came in it looked like a CCF victory—could it be? Bennett's son Bill was prepared to throw in the towel, and he offered to drive his father down to their local election headquarters to make a statement conceding defeat. Bennett told him to be patient, and patience paid off: as the evening wore on the Socreds grabbed a convincing victory from what earlier appeared to be the jaws of defeat. The Social Credit legislative majority, however, was reduced from thirty-nine to thirty-two seats. Robert Strachan would now lead a bolstered opposition contingent: the CCF won sixteen seats to their previous ten and garnered over 32 per cent of the vote, an increase of five points. The Liberals surprised many by doubling their representation to four seats and holding a steady 20 per cent of the vote, but the desultory Tories were again completely shut out; despite an energetic effort they acquired less than seven per cent of the vote. Missing from the provincial legislature for the first time in decades would be Tom Uphill who had at last retired from his Fernie seat—though his mischievous ghost would haunt the House for many years to come.

For Bennett, the election results could have been more agreeable. His large legislative majority had been reduced and he had lost two cabinet ministers in battle, including Social Credit veteran Lyle Wicks; but a sufficient portion of the record turnout of almost a million voters decided to sustain his government. As B.C. entered the 1960s, Bennett promised himself that he would keep closer contact with the ordinary folk he had fought so hard to represent and, most important, he would never relinquish his dreams of a spectacular provincial empire.

CHAPTER
NINE
THE POLITICS OF POWER

*Politics was at first the art of preventing
people from minding their own business.
A later age added the art of forcing people
to decide things they did not understand.*
Paul Valery

Nothing is freer than free, my friend.
W. A. C. Bennett

The 1960 provincial election was an appropriate climax to a decade of swift and significant change in British Columbia. In re-electing W. A. C. Bennett's Social Credit government, voters were saying clearly that they wanted more of the same. The 1950s had been a decade of almost uncontainable growth during which the Socreds provided the essential means for rapid economic development: roads, highways, bridges, tunnels, ferries and a railway to the north. Building upon this foundation, the 1960s would become a decade of even more spectacular development—probably more spectacular than Bennett himself could have envisaged.

If transportation seemed the keystone of growth in the fifties, then hydroelectric power would dominate the sixties. The harnessing of B.C.'s mighty rivers and production of immense amounts of electric power helped to focus attention as never before on Canada's west coast. Power became the resource around which all other questions revolved, much the way oil dominated the politics of Texas. Although huge personal fortunes were neither won nor lost over hydro energy to the extent they were in oil, political careers were, and Bennett was one of the few politicians in North America to seize this fact.

During the 1960s, hydroelectric power became Bennett's most important symbol, and as a public issue it took on a kind of mystic importance. This was a time of rival politicians struggling against the flow of mighty river systems, of governments locked in combat, of big money, big dreams and big debates. The controversies swirled around two rivers which rise in opposite corners of B.C. The Columbia River, the fourth largest river in North

America, and probably the greatest in potential for electrical power, was the cause of the initial conflict. The Columbia is born in the southeast corner of the province where it winds and twists through the Canadian Rockies before gushing across the border into the United States gathering tributaries for hundreds of miles on its way to the Pacific. As noted earlier, the Americans had dammed sections of the river on their side of the border for flood control and power, and in 1944 the International Joint Commission was assigned the task of studying the potential costs and advantages of a massive Canadian-American development of the northern Columbia watershed. After a decade and a half of study, the IJC paved the way for an agreement on a joint international development, and a draft treaty between the two countries was now approaching final discussion. British Columbia was mainly affected by the proposed treaty and Bennett was keeping a sharp eye on events, largely because of the other side of his Two River Policy—the Peace River. Rising in the province's northwest in mostly uninhabited land, the waters of the Peace flow back and forth through the Rocky Mountains then turn sharply north into the Mackenzie River before emptying into the Arctic Ocean. For several reasons, the Peace had always been important to Bennett, but when the dreams of Axel Wenner-Gren suggested the possibility of a huge Peace River dam, he became positively fixed on the idea; it fitted his plans for northern development and gave him leverage on the Columbia negotiations.

When he spoke of the power potential of the Peace and Columbia rivers he was speaking of potency on a grand scale. The Two River Policy appealed to all the elements in his indomitable personality. He enjoyed huge undertakings; he liked vigorous action and making quick decisions; he was psychologically prepared to take large risks. Many doubted that he really wanted to develop both rivers simultaneously, but Bennett rarely bluffed. Some of his motives may have been sentimental, he may have been ignorant of political and jurisdictional limitations, but he certainly was not awed by the gamble. Once his Two River Policy was defined, he rushed ahead with it as if he was personally fuelled by the millions of kilowatts of energy that the two powerful rivers possessed. For several years the politics of power development would be the dominant issue in British Columbia, and Bennett's personal will would test the resolve and deflect the goals of two national governments. This was achieved by a labyrinthine process of negotiation and policy making, and much of the political debate was couched in technical language that only an engineer could understand. However, Bennett would win this, his greatest battle, because of his political skills and stubborn nature. Although his opponents continually reminded him that B.C. could not consume all the energy he proposed to develop, he looked firmly to the future, convinced that his grandiose plans assured British Columbians a place of importance, if not greatness. Other Socreds helped to influence the public's mood with statements like the following made in 1960 by Phil Gaglardi: "By 1970 we will be walking around with candles in our hats to see our way if the Peace as well as the Columbia doesn't go ahead. I would like to know how we are going to get power if we are going to sit around quibbling about it. We are not interested in the politics of power. We want to be able to turn on a switch and see the lights go on."

Shortly after the 1960 election two facts became abundantly clear: the original Wenner-Gren plan for the transformation of the province's northern interior into an industrial empire was rapidly fading, and both the Canadian and American governments saw political advantage in associating themselves with the Columbia project and were pushing hard for an early treaty agreement. Bennett and a few others had privately recognized the difficulties facing the Wenner-Gren project. One was access. The Pacific Northern Railway, designed to provide a rail link with the Yukon and Alaska and hailed by Bennett as "the longest railway of the century," had been incorporated, and six weeks before the election it was officially inaugurated in the bush thirty-five miles north of Prince George. Bennett cut the ribbon, raised a flag and before a small group of dignitaries exclaimed: "Where are the critics now? They are never about when there is work to be done." However, not much work would be done. The impressive consortium of international firms involved in the venture failed to obtain any commitment or co-operation from the Americans who, it was hoped, would realize the benefits of a rail connection with Alaska. The project quickly became mired in legal problems and, two weeks after the provincial election, construction was halted, never to resume. In the end, the Wenner-Gren scheme was nothing more than a fantasy—the Wizard of Oz approach to economic development. Nevertheless, one feature proved significant and far-reaching in its impact on British Columbia—the Peace River power project. It now exerted enormous influence on the Columbia River negotiations.

The IJC had studied a variety of proposed methods for developing the Columbia River. Gen. A. G. L. McNaughton, the Canadian chairman of the IJC, advocated a wholly Canadian development of its portion of the Columbia watershed. The McNaughton Plan appealed to Canadian nationalists as well as avid anti-Americans, but it involved extensive flooding in the East Kootenay valleys, permanent loss of valuable B.C. farmland and, through a suggested diversion into the Fraser-Thompson river system, posibly disastrous effects on the province's annual salmon run. Another proposal, the "American Plan," gave as much benefit as possible to U.S. power authorities. A third proposal effected a compromise, and professed that "many more advantages and much less cost would flow from joint development and control than from two competing and often conflicting operations." This third proposal formed the basis of a draft treaty in the fall of 1960: it involved the construction of three huge storage dams on the Canadian portion of the Columbia, gave the Americans the option of a fourth storage dam on their side of the border, and provided that one half of the power generated in the U.S. as a result of Canadian storage would be returned to British Columbia. The draft treaty had the support of the Americans, was agreed to with some reluctance by Canadian federal negotiators, and was accepted in principle by the B.C. government. However, disagreements between Ottawa and Victoria over how the project was to be financed and how the downstream benefits were to be enjoyed threatened to destroy the agreement.

Victoria, of course, was simply a synonym for W. A. C. Bennett. With the assistance of two cabinet colleagues, Lands and Forests Minister Ray Williston and Attorney General Robert Bonner, Bennett made all the important decisions regarding the politics of power development during this period. Ottawa, on the other hand, had undergone a significant change since the Socreds first came to power in B.C. In 1957, for the first time since the Depression, a Conservative national government was elected under the fiery leadership of John Diefenbaker. After a brief stint with a parliamentary minority, the Conservatives swept the country in 1958 in the now legendary Diefenbaker Sweep. One might imagine that Bennett would be on good terms with the Conservatives; after all, he had once worked closely with many Diefenbaker Tories. But political and personal jealousies combined with the controversies of the day made relations with the federal Conservatives more bitter than would be expected of the normal stresses of Canadian federalism. Bonner believed that "they felt a certain resentment about Bennett and myself being Tories before and having displaced them provincially."

The pivotal factor in the lengthy negotiations over the Columbia was Bennett's Two River Policy. For both the Americans and Canadians it was an unknown quantity, possibly a red herring, whereas for Bennett and the B.C. negotiators it became an article of faith. Bennett's position was:

> The Columbia River had been a controversy with the United States and Canada for fifty years and getting nowhere. As governments do, they just appointed committees, made reports, surveys, and did nothing. I wanted to get the Columbia River developed as an international river, and to do that we needed an agreement between the federal government of Canada and the United States federal government. To bring that about, we needed a lever, because the United States said, "Canada is going to build it sometime anyway; we'll wait. We don't have to give downstream benefits. They've got to put power developments in, and when they put the dams in, we're going to get the benefits. It might not be as much as if it were controlled by a treaty, but once they start, then

we can enter into some discussions with them." I knew very well the way to get the Columbia was to get the Peace, then they'd know that British Columbia had lots of power and we wouldn't have to develop the Columbia. Everywhere I went and had meetings, people would show up in the audience, strangers. I did not know then, but I know now that they were CIA. They were there to see whether I was just using propaganda or whether I was genuine. As we went on, called tenders and let contracts, and they could see that we were beyond the point of no return, then the Americans talked business.

Bennett was especially anxious about major unresolved questions concerning the financing of the Columbia River agreement; his concerns did not relate to the international agreement per se, but centred on the degree of co-operation needed between the federal government and his administration. In particular, he wanted an assurance that Ottawa would help to finance the Columbia. In October 1960, Bennett wrote to the federal finance minister, Donald Fleming, demanding to know how much money his government would provide for construction of storage dams in B.C. Subsequent discussions with Prime Minister Diefenbaker and public statements by other Tory ministers plainly indicated that Ottawa would not give British Columbia any outright grant of money, but wanted a major hand in controlling the Columbia project in return for any financial assistance. The government's position infuriated Bennett, who felt that Ottawa was intruding on a provincial resource and denying B.C. compensation which had been offered to other provinces in similar situations. He was also worried about the huge amounts of electrical power that would be coming back to the province as downstream benefits; B.C. could not absorb that power and still justify the Peace River development. In order to pursue his Two River Policy, he explored the possibility of selling the downstream benefits to the Americans for cash, which could be used to construct the storage dams on the Canadian portion of the Columbia. The proposed sale of the downstream benefits would soon become a major controversy.

Further complicating matters was the clash of personalities. As premier and minister of finance, Bennett preferred to deal directly with Prime Minister Diefenbaker and federal Finance Minister Fleming, but the federal minister of justice, Davie Fulton, became Ottawa's chief spokesman and negotiator on the Columbia. Although he and Bennett were once west coast Tory colleagues, they now rubbed each other the wrong way. Fulton had been an early supporter of the McNaughton Plan for Columbia development and was an open critic of the proposed Two River Policy. During the course of well-publicized differences of opinion, Bennett repeatedly snubbed Fulton, refusing to meet with him publicly or privately.

In December 1960 the suave Davie Fulton went to Victoria for a meeting of the federal-provincial liaison committee which was looking at the details of a draft Columbia River treaty. At the same time, Bennett issued a statement to reporters which strongly reiterated his position that there would be no federal control of the Columbia project; he also rejected the proposed formation of a new separate agency to administer the development: "Under our constitution property and civil rights are the sole prerogative of the province. There is going to be only one agency, the B.C. Power Commission. We want no fifth wheel. I am protecting the rights of the people of British Columbia." When Fulton heard of the premier's comments he flamed with anger; he felt that Bennett was out to scuttle the treaty. Responding with a press conference of his own, Fulton attacked the premier's statements which he claimed were misleading and inaccurate. He defended the federal government's position and concluded his remarks with a broadside against Bennett's proposed sale of downstream benefits to the Americans: "We are not prepared to allow benefits under this treaty to be sold for cash into the provincial revenue, to be used for financing other pet projects of the Premier of B.C." Bennett became angry—unusually so. The next day, a Friday, Fulton tried to see him, but the premier was "busy." Fulton stayed on an extra day in Victoria in the hope that Bennett would meet with him, but Bennett was nowhere to be found. Before returning to Ottawa, Fulton noted to the press: "I understand they have not been able to locate the Premier anywhere in B.C." When reporters met Bennett Monday morning and asked him where he had been, he answered that on Saturday he was visiting a sick friend and on Sunday, "I was in church, my friend. Where were you?"

On the surface, it appears that Bennett was playing a childish game, but he was seriously worried about the federal government's ambitions with regard to the Columbia project. To this point, the discussions over financing had revealed only that British Columbia could not alone cover the costs and that Ottawa wanted to share in any possible credit for the prospective treaty. Bennett's fear that the federal administration was planning an outright takeover of the Columbia plan caused untold concern in Victoria and one of his most trusted cabinet colleagues, Ray Williston, almost resigned. The possibility that Ottawa might assume complete control of the Columbia River treaty and go it alone without B.C. was so real for Bennett that he instructed Williston to stop all large financial expenditures then in progress on the project: he did not want to spend any more money if it was going to be taken over. For Williston, the situation posed a serious dilemma. The actual engineering of dam sites on the Columbia was under way and the B.C. Power Commission had hired an expert team of engineers who were at an advanced stage in determining site feasibility and cost estimates. Williston felt that if he stopped all funding, thereby dissolving the engineering study and disbanding his international team, he would be losing too much and that the parties to the treaty would be heading towards an agreement that was only imperfectly understood. Yet Williston was loath to contradict Bennett, saying: "I knew better than to argue with him. If he made a decision and you started arguing, you'd likely get slapped down."

After struggling with his conscience, Ray Williston decided not to carry out the premier's instructions, in the hope that the awkward situation would soon be clarified. Through the fall of 1960 the unpaid engineering bills continued to mount, since they could not be paid without the premier's approval, and by Christmas they totalled about half a million dollars. At that point Williston was distraught and was prepared to acknowledge his failure to act as instructed; he consulted with his colleague Robert Bonner and told him that he intended to resign from the cabinet. However, right at this time, a public controversy regarding the comparative power costs of the Peace River and Columbia projects came to a head and Bennett referred the matter to the B.C. Energy Board for study. The engineering on the Peace had been completed, but the only available work on the Columbia had been done on the sly and was not yet paid for. Williston offered it to the chairman of the Energy Board, Gordon Shrum, at cost. The price was paid and important time had been saved, for long political battles were ahead on the horizon. Perhaps most important, Ray Williston was saved. He said of the incident: "I've never spoken with Bennett about it, but it was pretty obvious that he must have known. When the bill came through, he knew. And that's the closest I ever came to walking the plank politically."

The report of the B.C. Energy Board would take several more months to complete but, in the meantime, more important events were taking place. The federal Tories were well aware that Bennett was opposed to any form of federal control over provincial hydroelectric resources; they had failed to come close to a financial agreement with the province on the construction costs of the proposed Columbia dams; they also knew that, for all practical purposes, any agreement with the Americans was subject to the approval of British Columbia. In spite of all these serious problems, Ottawa decided to go ahead and sign the treaty with the United States. President Dwight Eisenhower was anxious to put his name to the document as one of the last acts of his term—John F. Kennedy had been elected president and was to assume office on January 20, 1961—and Prime Minister Diefenbaker was willing to gamble that an agreement on the Columbia might help to shore up the lagging popularity of his Conservative administration. For Diefenbaker, it was a profound miscalculation.

Bennett made no public protest when the imminent signing was announced, but he sent a private double-registered letter to Diefenbaker which said that B.C. was still committed to the Columbia project—but only upon conditions that had not been agreed to as yet. The formal signing of the Columbia River Treaty took place in Washington, D.C. on January 17, 1961.

At the first session of B.C.'s twenty-sixth parliament, which opened on January 16, 1961, Premier Bennett's disenchantment with the Columbia River Treaty was immediately evident. In an exchange with opposition MLAs, he intimated that the treaty, which would be ratified by the American Congress that spring but would wait much longer for Canadian approval, was not as favourable to B.C. as he would have liked. Then, on February 17, during a discussion of new federal-provincial tax-sharing proposals, Bennett criticized the way in which federal corporation taxes on private companies were siphoned off to Ottawa; he shocked the legislature when he said that his administration might have to take over B.C. Electric Company "unless we get fair treatment." The premier's statement caused the stock of B.C. Power Corporation, the parent body of B.C. Electric, to drop sharply the next morning. But Victoria politicians and the general public quickly recovered from Bennett's "off-the-cuff" suggestion, and officials of B.C. Electric believed he was simply exerting subtle pressure to persuade the company to purchase power from the Peace River project. On the final day of the spring session, March 27, the leader of the opposition Robert Strachan moved a resolution that the government consider placing B.C. Electric and other private utilities under public ownership. On Bennett's instruction, the motion was agreed to without debate.

Surprisingly, very few observers seemed to realize the direction in which Bennett was heading. For that matter, direct participants in the politics of power refused to believe the obvious. Clearly, Bennett had decided to take over the giant electrical utility, B.C. Electric—but he confided this intention to no one. In retrospect, it seems strange that such a move was not widely expected, for the premier was dropping hints at carefully chosen moments, and his motives are also revealed by studying his public record. Almost from the time that Bennett became active in B.C. politics he was particularly favourable to public power. Many of his ideas regarding the development of the province were shaped by his experience as a member of the Post-War Rehabilitation Council, which in 1943 recommended the establishment of a public-owned hydroelectric authority to provide cheap electricity to all of British Columbia. In 1944 the feisty South Okanagan backbencher had urged the coalition government to act on the council's recommendation; he even offered advice on how to expropriate the B.C. Electric Company. Bennett took a special interest in the work of the International Joint Commission on the Columbia River; his personal papers contain a variety of communications with the IJC dating back to 1944 and its original terms of reference on the Columbia investigation. In 1945, after the public-owned B.C. Power Commission was established, Bennett congratulated the government and, speaking in the legislature, stated: "After once stepping out on this path, there must be no turning back." Ironically, it would be Bennett himself who would take the next audacious step.

It is difficult to pinpoint the moment when Bennett decided that taking over B.C. Electric was a necessity. His public skirmish with H. Lee Briggs in 1958 seemed to spark the idea that the B.C. Power Commission could play a more active role in the politics of power. Certainly his meeting with Sir Andrew McTaggart and Dal Grauer in London prior to the 1960 election laid the groundwork for the expropriation of the privately owned utility — especially if it meant the success of his Two River Policy. The intense battle with the federal government over which specific agency would be responsible for administering the treaty obligations now forced his hand. As late as May 17, 1961, federal Finance Minister Donald Fleming wrote to Bennett regarding ratification of the treaty and, in addition to raising objections to Bennett's proposal to sell the treaty's negotiated downstream benefits to the United States, he proposed a "joint federal-provincial entity" to construct and operate the Columbia treaty projects. Bennett was appalled; he was adamantly opposed to any federal government participation in the development of provincial resources. This, after all, was British Columbia. He was in charge. He would provide the "entity" to do the job.

During the late spring and early summer of 1961 there was much jockeying for position and public posturing in the politics of power. The federal and provincial governments seemed to be making very little headway towards ratification of the Columbia River Treaty; the west coast socialist opposition went so far as to appeal to Prime Minister Diefenbaker to take control of the Columbia project in order to prevent Bennett from dictating events; and B.C. Electric Company, while waiting for the outcome of the controversy, scoffed at rumours of expropriation. Late in June, Bennett announced a special session of the legislature for August 1. The stated reason was to deal with Ottawa fiscal arrangements, but the real reason was the takeover of both the B.C. Electric and Peace River Power Development Companies. For weeks there was speculation about the government's intention in calling a summer session, but few guessed the premier's purpose. Only six men knew with certainty the basic outline of the script that was about to unfold. Bennett, his executive assistant Dan Ekman, Robert Bonner and his legislative counsel Gerald Cross, Deputy Minister of Finance Gerald Bryson, and Comptroller General Charles Ferber. These individuals — "the secret six" — were a kind of undercover special committee preparing draft after draft of legislation that would empower the Social Credit government to perform what seemed to many an unthinkable act.

Prevailing political assumptions usually set limits to the kinds of action an individual politician or government can take. The Socreds were a free enterprise party. The nationalization or "provincialization" of the privately owned power utility was therefore bound to invite serious questioning of the Socred's motives and philosophy. For years, Bennett had struggled with this ideological predicament and privately had arrived at what he considered an unavoidable conclusion. Now he wanted his cabinet and party backbenchers to instantaneously accept his own conclusion, less than a year after a general election in which they had all ridiculed the socialists for proposing the very act they were now contemplating. Social Crediters generally had an intense distrust of the socialization of enterprise. Bennett, of course, shared that distrust, but realized that the control he needed to exercise over power development in the province could not be achieved if he left matters in the hands of private enterprise. It seems incredible that he did not have a party revolt on his hands but, waiting until the last possible moment, he explained his position to his cabinet and caucus—and they acquiesced. The fact that this deeply controversial policy was accepted without dissent is testimony to the mastery Bennett had attained as leader of Social Credit and premier of the province.

Attorney General Robert Bonner was placed in direct charge of the sensitive, confidential task of devising legislation to carry out expropriation; in his view:

> We felt we had no alternative but to nationalize the B.C. Electric to make it a vehicle for electrical energy policy. It was with great reluctance, but nevertheless with steadfast purpose, that we finally took that step. We were never really very anxious to get involved but we felt that noninvolvement was worse than seeing an opportunity go by. I think there was a growing realization that the Two River Policy was probably beyond the capacity of private interests to deal with, and when we started to become more heavily involved with the Columbia, there was no way that we could control the pressure on negotiations without having the Peace development under our control as well. It was an evolution of analysis which gradually brought us into the picture: we had to have both the Peace and Columbia and it became apparent after a while that if we were going to deal ourselves a card, we had to hold it. I think we all had a good deal of hesitation about reaching such a conclusion, but we had a very easy and informal way of exchanging views. Once views had been exchanged and the decision was reached, we simply launched in another direction—which in this case involved nationalization. There was no great debate about it. Development of that particular policy had a logic of its own which at that time was quite unassailable. You know the French have an expression, "gouverner

c'est choisir," "to govern is to choose." We had to choose between doing nothing and looking stupid, or doing something and succeeding. So it was a simple choice.

The first public indication of what Bennett was up to came in the very brief Speech from the Throne read by Lieutenant Governor George Pearkes on August 1, 1961. The speech listed five bills to be placed before the House for consideration; the last one was referred to as "a bill concerning the development of electrical power resources." A few minutes later, the bombshell exploded when Bennett formally introduced Bill 5, the Power Development Act, 1961. This bill was the obvious focus for the drama-packed legislative session which would last only three days. In a tragic twist of irony, as the special session opened in Victoria, funeral services were being held in Vancouver for Dal Grauer, the head of B.C. Electric, one of the few persons who might have prevented the Social Credit government's last-ditch manoeuvre. Bill 5 made B.C. Electric a crown corporation and provided for its acquisition of all the assets of the Peace River Power Development Company. It allowed for total compensation of $180 million to B.C. Power Corporation, the B.C. Electric's federally chartered parent corporation, and replacement of $104 million in preferred shares by the new crown corporation which would in turn assume responsibility for some $400 million in company debts. In what was to become a very controversial section of the act, lawsuits by aggrieved shareholders were disallowed without the express consent of the provincial cabinet. In all of this there would be no direct financial burden on the government; the giant public-owned "entity" would raise what new money it required by issuing parity bonds. However, the cost of the takeover and the assumption of responsibility for B.C. Electric's financial obligations and indebtedness increased the province's contingent liabilities in one fell swoop by almost $700 million.

Almost immediately upon introducing Bill 5 for first reading in the House, Bennett tabled the *Report of the British Columbia Energy Board on the Columbia and Peace Power Projects*. Although he had obviously made up his mind about the takeover of B.C. Electric well before the report was available, Dr. Shrum's Energy Board study provided almost letter-perfect justification for his action. First, contrary to the claims of various opponents who criticized the Two River Policy as uneconomic because of the supposed expense of Peace River power, the report found that if the Peace was developed under public ownership, it would produce power at practically the same cost as the Columbia. The report calculated the combined costs of both projects at a startling $2,228 billion — but such numbers did not discourage Bennett. In general terms, the Energy Board report was favourable to the development of both the Peace and Columbia rivers more or less simultaneously. Nevertheless, it noted that they would generate far more power than the province could absorb in the immediate years ahead and recommended selling excess power to American markets. In particular, it suggested that the Columbia River Treaty downstream benefits would be the logical first choice for such a sale and recommended that: "Control over the disposition of downstream power benefits should be vested in the province before ratification."

For W. A. C. Bennett, events were proceeding according to plan and he was now suddenly in a much strengthened position to face the future, but first he had a few major hurdles to jump. As expected, Bill 5 did not take long to pass through the legislature. The premier justified the takeover as a response to the federal government's continued policy of taxing privately owned power utilities in monopoly situations in the provinces: "Because the federal government has refused to act in giving B.C. a fair return of the taxes paid by power corporations, it is this government's policy to have basically all electric power and energy that is supplied to the general public under public auspices." This was clearly more a rationalization than an explanation. Bennett also promised a quick start on the Peace, and it is worth remembering something often forgotten by commentators: Bill 5 also expropriated Peace River Power Development. All of the plans and studies that the company had conducted were paid for at cost, approximately $8 million. When the debate in the House was concluded, Bennett would proudly proclaim: "It answers, once and for all, charges that the Social Credit government had been controlled by the Wenner-Gren organization and that the B.C. Electric had never lost an election."

While Bennett explained the legislation to the stunned House, most Socreds sat silently. The opposition seemed to require twenty-four hours to regain its wits, but on August 2, CCF leader Robert Strachan launched a lengthy diatribe charging that the government was not only adopting a major socialist policy, but was doing so after winning an election in which it had campaigned against that specific policy. Strachan and other socialist MLAs joined together in chronicling what they considered the hypocrisy of the Socreds' new position. They dragged out quotes from several cabinet ministers during the 1960 campaign. Ken Kiernan, for instance, was reminded of this statement: "Government should stick to the business of government and not take over resource developments unless it is necessary to provide essential services." Ray Williston had criticized the CCF plan to take over B.C. Electric: "It would not create additional electricity and would not create a single job." And Robert Bonner had blasted the socialist platform as irresponsible, claiming that it "would set B.C. back 30 years" and "would not provide one new job except perhaps some for politicians." Somewhat embarrassed, the Socreds uneasily swallowed the crow served up by the opposition. Randolph Harding criticized the attorney general for having altered his position, to which Bonner replied: "If the Honourable Member wishes to make a speech based on my discarded opinions, he is welcome." On the evening of August 2, Bill 5 was agreed to in principle: the vote in favour on second reading was recorded as fifty to zero—making a rare and surprising moment of unanimity in the west coast legislature. One CCF member quipped: "Can't we at least record a whisper for free enterprise?" The next day, the bill received royal assent and was passed into law. The session was then prorogued amid shouts of "Well done, comrade" and "Hail Castro."

Some observers suggested that the expropriation of B.C. Electric Company, which was the largest remaining privately owned power company in Canada, was an attempt by the provincial government to bolster political support and steal the socialists' thunder. These comments were based upon a profound misunderstanding of the politics of power. The takeover of B.C. Electric was not the result of "contagion from the left," nor was it an effort on Bennett's part to co-opt the opposition in the manner of the federal Liberals, who had successfully undermined socialist support over the years. The CCF had advocated the takeover of the huge power utility as a seeming end in itself; Bennett, on the other hand, saw it as an unavoidable means to an end. The Socreds could easily live with the jeers and taunts of their local political opponents; in fact, they would have gladly preferred to eat that crow and even cough up an occasional feather rather than face the far more severe reaction of the national and international business communities.

In Ottawa, there was consternation and confusion. The only person immediately available for comment to reporters was H. Lee Briggs, now of the National Energy Board; his response to the news from the coast was: "Oh my goodness!" But within the next few weeks the reaction was deeper and more disturbing. B.C. Chamber of Commerce officials insisted that the Social Credit government had "repudiated its election position and violated its election mandate." Howard T. Mitchell, vice-president of the Canadian Chamber of Commerce, stated that British Columbia was becoming "the most highly socialized society in Canada, clearly well in the lead of socialistically back-slid Saskatchewan." Alarm was expressed far beyond the province's borders, for stock in B.C. Power Corporation was held around the world, a quarter of the shares being owned in Great Britain. The president of the Investment Dealers' Association of Canada stated that Bennett had badly shaken the confidence of the investing public in Canada and abroad. Canada's leading business journal, the *Financial Post,* called Bennett "Moses On A Mountaintop." The *Portland Oregonian* was extremely excited: "British Columbia's dictator-Premier, W. A. C. Bennett, is driving ahead with provincial development of the Peace River hydro-electric project and entombment of the U.S.-Canadian Treaty for a joint development of the Columbia with scarcely a ripple of opposition from an apathetic B.C. public. . . . Fidel Castro is no more dictatorial than Premier Bennett in the expropriation field. Both call it expropriation as a courtesy, for confiscation is a better word." The London *Sunday Telegraph* asserted that thanks to Bennett's move, "Canada is rapidly acquiring the financial reputation of one of the most unstable South American republics." The leading American financial weekly, *Barron's*, devoted an entire front page to a special editorial entitled "Lust for Power"; it strongly denounced the B.C. government, noting: "With a unanimity and speed of which a so-called people's republic might be proud, the lawmakers of British Columbia, at the behest of the Premier, voted to expropriate the B.C. Electric. . . ."

Did any of this bother W.A.C. Bennett? The answer is an unqualified "yes." The virulent reaction of the business world could have had disastrous effects on the rise of B.C., whose continuation was still largely dependent on foreign investment and business confidence. These attacks on Bennett were the most bitter and violent he would endure during his entire political career. Although in retrospect the business community was seen to have overreacted, the Socreds had to spend many months in tireless explanation and raucous public relations work to prove that the government's action was, in fact, in the best interests of all concerned. Meanwhile, buoyed by the hostility to the takeover, B.C. Power Corporation asked the provincial supreme court to rule on the constitutionality of the Power Development Act, arguing that it overstepped the powers of the provincial legislature and that the company ought to have received significantly more money than it was paid. A classic example of the inherent conflict between political and economic elites was shaping up.

If Bennett was concerned over all this, he also had reason to be smug. Taking control of all hydroelectric power in British Columbia would ensure his position as chief actor in the politics of power. The takeover of B.C. Electric earned him more prominence, both nationally and internationally, than any other active Canadian provincial politician enjoyed. He secretly revelled in his sudden notoriety abroad, for it did him no political harm at home. While opponents and big business interests attacked him, the B.C. public seemed strongly in favour of the takeover. B.C. Electric was, after all, a corporate giant with a reputation for overcharging its customers, and the public, never fond of the private monopoly, seemed relieved and happy that it was now under public ownership. Social Crediters were genuinely surprised at this positive reaction, and in the months to come Bennett could confidently proclaim: "No one seems to like us but the people." At a public meeting that Bonner attended a few days after the session in his Vancouver constituency of Point Grey, the only question that arose on the subject was: "We see you've taken over the B.C. Electric; when are you going to take over B.C. Telephone?"

The premier's big battle for his Two River Policy was still ahead. He indicated that the Peace River project was now all systems go, but the necessary ratification of the Columbia River Treaty was becoming mired in the bog of federal-provincial disagreement. Canada's unique brand of competitive federalism was especially manifest in the increasingly sulphurous exchanges between Bennett and Davie Fulton. Using the recommendations of the B.C. Energy Board report as ammunition, Bennett shot out public statements favouring the sale of Canada's share of Columbia downstream benefits to the power-hungry U.S.; he explained his plan to finance the Columbia River storage dams from the sale. This would mean, he claimed, that future power generation from those dams for B.C. consumption would be free and—his now famous aside—"nothing is freer than free, my friend." Fulton, however, absolutely rejected such a sale. Speaking in the House of Commons, he also suggested that Ottawa might prevent the damming of the Peace because it could interfere with navigation on the Mackenzie River. On September 16, 1961, Bennett furiously responded to Fulton by pointing out that regulation of the flow of the Peace River could only improve Mackenzie navigation. He said "to everybody in Canada in all seriousness that this may rank as the most frivolous, destructive statement ever made in Canada's long political history." Fulton next hinted that the federal government was still considering taking complete control of the Columbia, but Bennett knew he held the upper hand in negotiations with Ottawa and simply refused to ratify the Columbia River Treaty until the amendments he wanted were made. The degeneration of relations between Bennett and Fulton was destined to reach even lower levels, but in the meantime the treaty seemed dead. On October 28, the Vancouver *Province* moaned: "The most shocking thing is that there is no apparent effort by the two governments to get together to work out a compromise. Ottawa and Victoria are as far apart on the Columbia as Washington and Moscow on Berlin."

Events of the next twenty-four months would break the stalemate in the politics of power—and both make and break political careers. One interesting event occurred on November 16, when W. A. C. Bennett was invited to attend a testimonial banquet in Seattle for Washington senator Warren Magnuson. The dinner was plush and well publicized and when the premier was introduced by Senator Mike Mansfield as "William Andrew Cecil Bennett, the Prime Minister of the province of British Columbia," he could not suppress his million-watt smile as all guests joined in a rousing standing ovation. Significantly, the banquet was also attended by the new president, John F. Kennedy, and it afforded him and the premier the opportunity to meet privately over matters of mutual interest. Bennett gave this account of their discussion:

> I received an invitation to attend the banquet. I think it would have been very discourteous to a foreign but friendly power, our only land neighbor, the greatest customer of British Columbia—more so than the rest of Canada—if I didn't accept the invitation. . . . There were five different banquet rooms that night with closed-circuit TV, but I was in the main dining room, at the head table, three or four spaces from the president who later gave his officials "Hail Columbia" that I wasn't on his right hand. During the dinner, he came down to my place at the head table three or four times to chat with me. We got along very well. President Kennedy knew that British Columbia was a great customer of the United States and that there were great benefits both ways. He knew from my budget speeches and my statements that I was for Canada, but I was not anti-American. He said that he had studied all my budget speeches. Whether he did or not, I'm sure his advisers did, because he asked me point blank about one or two. He said he agreed with everything I advocated except the ninety-cent Canadian dollar versus the hundred-cent American dollar. So after we had some discussion, I said, "Of course, if I was president of the United States, I wouldn't be in favour of a ninety-cent Canadian dollar either, but with half a continent and a small percentage of the population on the continent, we need a little advantage on export markets around the world; we need that ten-per-cent advantage." He said, "Thank you, Mr. Premier, it hadn't been explained to me that clearly before."

Bennett would never say whether he broached the subject of the Columbia River Treaty with Kennedy, but it seems evident that this was his ulterior motive for seizing the opportunity to meet the president. His garrulous public relations man, Bill Clancey, who during the 1960s became something of a personal sidekick and court jester to the premier, has given his version of how Bennett managed to be invited to the gala American dinner. Clancey apparently took a call from Governor Rosellini of Washington, whom Bennett knew, asking him to pay a visit. Bennett was away on holiday at the time and could not be reached. Rosellini asked Clancey if he thought the premier would be interested in attending the Seattle dinner celebrating Senator Magnuson's twenty-fifth anniversary in public life, and mentioned that the president would be attending. Clancey immediately got in touch with Bennett, who was in Phoenix, and relayed the invitation to him: "You'll be the only outside guest," he said. "You're representing British Columbia and Canada." Bennett replied, "I can't do that— Are you drinking? You go sober up and call me back in a couple of hours." When he was called again,

Bennett agreed to attend the dinner and asked Clancey to tell no one of his plan but to meet him in Seattle with his tuxedo. Clancey accompanied him to the dinner, after which the premier and Kennedy had their private meeting in the president's hotel suite. According to Clancey, the only reason Bennett attended the dinner was that he wanted to discuss the Columbia River Treaty with Kennedy.

The U.S. ambassador in Ottawa later described the conference between the premier and the president as "purely social," but Canadian journalists had a veritable field day over the apparent violation of diplomatic protocol, for a provincial premier is formally obliged to deal through Ottawa when conducting business with national heads of state. The federal government was upset, because it appeared the premier had outflanked them on more than simply protocol: a few days later Secretary of the Interior Stewart Udall, of Kennedy's cabinet, called the Canadian claim that power sold to the U.S. could never be recaptured "stuff and nonsense." Shortly thereafter, Bennett wrote to Canadian Finance Minister Fleming urging an immediate agreement on Columbia financing, and he offered public assurance that B.C. could sell its power to the Americans. All of this failed to break the federal-provincial deadlock; if anything, it strengthened the resistance of Davie Fulton, still the chief federal spokesman on the Columbia. Speaking in Prince George on November 28, Fulton bitterly attacked Bennett: "The Americans haven't been offered such a windfall since they purchased Manhattan Island. . . . Of course Mr. Bennett is using this as a squeeze play. But Canadian government policy is still made in Ottawa, not in Washington and Victoria as Mr. Bennett would like to see it." Fulton concluded that Bennett's plan was "sheer madness. It would be an act of such reckless and improvident philanthropy as would make this country the laughing stock of the world." Bennett reacted strongly to these statements and declared that Fulton would regret his personal attacks to the end of his political career.

The premier and federal justice minister continued to hurl invective at one another, and the basic issues in this increasingly complex problem became obscured. Whether by design or not, the politics of power were being replaced by the politics of personality. Meanwhile, W. A. C. Bennett's comfortable perch was about to be rocked by an unexpected financial crisis. The Victoria legislative session that opened on January 25, 1962, produced more heated debate over the provincial government's energy policies. Two bills sparked one of the wildest episodes in the legislature's history. Bill 84 provided for the merger of B.C. Electric and the province's Power Commission, creating the B.C. Hydro and Power Authority. This not only established the "entity" that Bennett wanted to take charge of the Columbia project, but it so entangled the assets of B.C. Electric with an existing public agency that any legal action against the government for the takeover would be almost impossible. Bill 85 set a price tag of $171 million on B.C. Electric, declaring that this was a final offer and not open to question in any court. Playing to the people, Bennett justified these moves by promising major cuts in utility bills, but opposition MLAs were outraged, and the strange spectacle of socialist politicians defending the rights of B.C. Electric shareholders was the feature of an eight-hour debate on March 23. Opposition leader Robert Strachan exclaimed: "This is the end of the road. This can't go on. An election must be called." Liberal leader Ray Perrault declared: "This is one of the most blatant attempts to shackle the courts and deny justice that has ever been attempted in any free country in the world." After a great free-for-all, the two bills passed second reading. The next day, one reporter recorded the event:

> It might have come straight from the Reichstag of the early thirties, and left one with the feeling of not knowing whether to laugh, cry or throw a bomb. There was Premier Bennett, red-faced, shouting at full throttle, gesticulating so wildly he must have the shoulder muscles of a wrestler. Yet not a word could be heard for the shouting of almost everybody in the House. There were chants of "Sieg Heil" from the opposition benches. The Premier kept up his outburst about Social Credit being for the common people for maybe a couple of minutes before he suddenly realized that even his nearest neighbor couldn't hear a word he said. He sat down abruptly. . . .

The House endured only a few more days of similar bedlam before proroguing on March 29, but reaction to Bennett's latest legislative manoeuvres prompted an organized run on B.C. parity bonds which, at least for a short while, threatened the provincial government's solvency.

The standing of all British Columbia bonds had been adversely affected by the takeover of B.C. Electric, but now it seemed that some eastern Canadian investment firms in collusion with certain media interests were attempting a reprisal. The number of outstanding parity bonds was very large and included a $100-million issue raised practically within hours of the takeover. All of these bonds were payable on demand, and suddenly they were being cashed in by the millions—and then the tens of millions. Bennett was worried, and it did not take long for him to realize what was happening. On April 5 the Vancouver *Province*, a newspaper that had staunchly supported Social Credit in the last election, came out with a front-page editorial: "Time to End One-Man Rule." The newspaper demanded the premier's resignation, referring to him as a "dictator" with a "messianic complex," and for several months lashed out at him on a regular basis, hinting that the provincial government's finances were out of control. Bennett discovered that the *Province* had hired John DeWolfe, a Toronto economist, who he believed was working full time on the destruction of the Social Credit administration's financial reputation. He said: "John DeWolfe phoned all the financial capitals of the world and said British Columbia was going haywire, going broke, so we didn't have any friends anywhere. Then they got a run going on our parity bonds; they did everything they could to damage us. And the banks opposed us something terrible."

Although Bennett later brushed aside any suggestions that his government faced serious financial difficulty, the organized run on provincial bonds came closer to destroying his dreams than anyone suspected. As minister of finance, he kept a close watch on the daily stream of inflowing parity bonds. The government redeemed every one, but as the amounts grew without any hint that the run was slowing, the picture turned ominous. Bennett sold off blocks of federal securities held by various provincial accounts and used the funds to pay for the returning bonds. He ordered an almost complete halt on government spending, slowed down the payment of government bills and practised severe economies in personnel administration. Still, the tide continued. In July 1962, at the peak of this financial scare, the premier returned home to Kelowna, accompanied only by Bill Clancey, who described their sojourn:

> We drove up to Kelowna to the chief's home; there was nobody there but he and I. They were phoning from all over the world—London, New York, newspapers, financiers—wanting to know what was going on. I looked out the window and he was lying on the swing on the front lawn, and I'm inside answering the damn phone. Later I said, "Chief, what am I gonna do with all these phone calls?" He was the kind of man who couldn't tell a lie—lying was real sin—but his home was in the Guisachan district, not really in Kelowna, and he said, "You tell them Mr. Bennett is not in Kelowna." I said, "Chief, what were you thinking about when you were in the swing looking up at the sky?" He said, "Well, you know when we went to Las Vegas, Bill, and you saw all that money they were gambling with—thousands and thousands of dollars—what was going through my head was that it was petty cash. . . ." He was lying there thinking, "How am I going to get out of this?"

Bennett outlasted the concerted drive to wreck his administration—but only by a combination of creativity, resourcefulness and a little timely help from an unexpected source. According to Ray Williston:

> When John DeWolfe and the Vancouver *Province* took off on their campaign for the resignation of the premier, they were attempting to get people to dump their parity bonds and put the government into a straitjacket financially. In the middle of this campaign, we needed

funds for our development program. The president of the Bank of Nova Scotia, [F. William] Nicks, phoned the premier up one night and said, "I know what they are trying to do to you. I know what the whole financial community is trying to do, and I don't agree with them. I have $40 million"—I think that was the figure—"lying unused in New York. If you want it, you can have it tomorrow morning." We weren't even doing business with that bank. The money was made available and the impasse was broken immediately. We were told not to say where the money came from.

Coming at a cruicial moment, this action of the Bank of Nova Scotia enabled Bennett to turn the situation around. He issued new parity bonds at a rate higher than the going market and they were quickly sold out. To fill the gap, he flew to New York where he was able to secure $45 million in short-term loans at rates well below the going Canadian rates. Gradually the bond run subsided and, while it took time for a complete restoration of public confidence, Bennett actually emerged from the crisis stronger than ever: because of the harsh cutbacks on government spending he had ordered, he was able to complete the 1962–63 fiscal year with a budgetary surplus of $41 million. The wily finance minister was always loath to admit it, but his pet financial innovation—provincial parity development bonds—had almost proved a fatal Achilles' heel. He did, however, address the problem directly in his 1963 budget speech. Speaking of the larger national financial picture, he did his best to lay the scare tactics of his opponents to rest and put the whole affair into perspective: "Coincident with the dislocation of national money markets, a few political publicists and politically motivated financial groups circulated rumours implying that individual crown corporations might not be able to redeem parity bonds if presented for payment. . . . These 'axe to grind' groups presented blocks of parities for payment, and a number of small holders were stampeded into similar steps by press distortions. However, the vast majority of individuals and business groups with parity bonds retained them and demonstrated their confidence in our crown corporations and the unfettered credit of the province."

Bennett survived this near financial catastrophe and as the year 1962 unfolded, events outside his control played into his hands. The federal election of June 18 crippled John Diefenbaker's mighty Tory administration; the Conservatives survived, but as a minority government with a slim hold on power. In August, Davie Fulton was demoted from the federal justice portfolio to the post of public works, and the once fiery nationalism of the Diefenbaker government seemed considerably subdued; the Speech from the Throne read in Ottawa on September 27, 1962, stated: "Large-scale, long-term contracts for export of power surpluses . . . should now be encouraged."

On the Pacific coast, Bennett smiled approvingly and began to talk of an early ratification of the Columbia River Treaty. Nevertheless, sensing the instability of the federal political situation, he wisely decided to cover all his bases. He wrote to Diefenbaker informing him that he was coming to Ottawa for further discussion on the treaty and that he intended to speak also with the federal opposition leader, Liberal Lester Pearson. Diefenbaker apparently expressed no objection and Bennett saw Pearson, who agreed to most of the treaty changes that the premier wanted.

On the home front, there was an interesting development. Almost immediately after Davie Fulton's humiliation in the federal cabinet shuffle, rumours began to circulate that he might leave national politics and seek the leadership of B.C.'s moribund Conservative Party. John Diefenbaker wrote in his memoirs: "Davie Fulton was one of those whose ambition would not let him be. . . . He now broached the suggestion that he move to provincial politics. When he first brought this to my attention in October 1962, I was maladroit enough to tell him that I did not believe him capable of beating the old master, W. A. C. Bennett. Fulton replied that his roots were in B.C. politics. His place, he said, was provincial." On another occasion, Diefenbaker said: "I didn't want him to go. I wanted him to stay. I think that would be in December 1962. I said, 'You go out there, and you'll be done. You can't win against him.' He said he felt otherwise; everything pointed to the reverse. 'Well,' I said, 'that's my view. I could be wrong, but I wouldn't think you'd have a snowball's chance." Ignoring his leader's warning, Fulton charged ahead. At a hastily called press conference in his Ottawa office, in a voice husky with emotion, he said: "The call of my native province cannot be disregarded. . . . I have been pressed to return." Fulton then issued the following public declaration: "My objective is to form the next government of British Columbia." On January 24, 1963, he officially became leader of the west coast Tories who, thanks to Bennett, had been seatless in the provincial legislature for years.

There is a chance that Fulton knew what he was doing, for if he had remained in Ottawa he would have been further humbled. In February the minority Conservative administration fell, and the election on April 8, 1963, produced a new prime minister, Lester Pearson, heading a minority Liberal government. This change augured well for Bennett, who had established a rapport with Pearson. On May 10, the prime minister met with President Kennedy and proposed some modifications to the Columbia River Treaty; the following week he wrote to Bennett suggesting the changes might take the form of a protocol to the treaty which would be negotiated subsequent to a federal-provincial agreement on costs. On June 3, Bennett and Pearson met in Ottawa to discuss the terms of the protocol and it quickly became clear that more had been accomplished in a matter of weeks than in the previous two and a half years of squabbling with Fulton and Diefenbaker. Pearson assigned his minister of external affairs, Paul Martin, to take charge of negotiations with the United States and agreed that British Columbia should negotiate the sale of downstream benefits with the Americans. To the surprise of many observers, the long-sought federal-provincial agreement on the Columbia was rapidly hammered out and signed in Ottawa on July 8, 1963.

The way was now paved for a final resolution of all the hard problems associated with the politics of power—though a couple of important snags still lay in Bennett's path. The first was "Black Monday"—July 29, 1963. On that day, Chief Justice Sherwood Lett brought down his decision on the almost forgotten B.C. Electric case, and it caused shock waves in the corridors of Victoria. Lett ruled that the legislation to expropriate B.C. Electric and create the B.C. Hydro and Power Authority was beyond the power of the provincial government because the company's interconnecting operations went beyond the province. The Socreds, therefore, had acted illegally and unconstitutionally. This was one of the most stunning upsets Bennett had ever experienced. The chief justice had wiped out the entire basis for Social Credit's hydroelectric empire. B.C. Hydro had no legal existence; the Peace and Columbia projects were put into doubt and confusion. In addition, Lett decided that if the takeover had been constitutional, Bennett should have paid some $21 million more for the company. Since the judge did not order the return of B.C. Electric to the parent company, this left control of the utility in a confused state. Immediately, warring words were exchanged between executives of the B.C. Power Corporation and Premier Bennett, who bravely but blindly declared that the judgement would not affect his government's Two River Policy. He announced that an appeal would be taken to the Supreme Court of Canada and, leaving Attorney General Bonner to work out the details, departed the province for a premiers' conference in Halifax.

Bonner and the B.C. Power Corporation, each aided by a battalion of lawyers, launched into intense negotiations centring on the question of a more appropriate purchase price for the two-year-old takeover. Sensing that things were tough at home, Bennett unexpectedly flew from Halifax to London, England, where he relaxed and thought his way through this most recent perplexing development. He returned home on August 20 firmly decided on a bold gamble. Previously, he had ruled out a 1963 election, but now he called a special cabinet meeting to announce that a general election was the best way out of the the Sodreds' assorted problems. It was an instinctive, populist reaction to an unfavourable court verdict; the people, he thought, would be a final judge.

Perhaps as important in helping him to make up his mind was the Fulton challenge. Bennett knew that the provincial Tories needed a lot of time to get their constituency organizations in shape—and he decided not to give it to them. A three-way split in the free enterprise vote among Socreds, Liberals and Conservatives was the perfect recipe for a socialist victory in B.C., so it was a dangerous time to be examining the province's political mood, and the last two by-elections would have to be factors in the premier's decision. In December 1962, a by-election was held in Vancouver-Point Grey as a result of the death of Socred MLA Buda Brown. The Liberal candidate, Dr. Patrick McGeer, won a shattering, unexpected victory, the first by-election defeat for Bennett since his old friend Einar Gunderson had lost in Victoria nine years earlier. On July 15, 1963, another by-election was held in the riding of Columbia after the death of Orr Newton, one of the original Social Credit class of 1952. Columbia was close to the centre of the discussions over the Columbia River Treaty and the contest represented a local referendum in the politics of power. Strangely, Davie Fulton, the new Tory leader, refused to personally contest the by-election, but his party's candidate made a strong showing. Nevertheless, and much to Bennett's surprise, the Social Credit candidate handily won an interesting four-way battle. Coming just prior to "Black Monday," the Columbia by-election likely helped to persuade Bennett that he stood a good chance of renewing his government's hold on power. There was, however, virtually universal astonishment when the premier told a press conference on August 22 that a provincial election would be held on September 30.

The election call caught all other parties unaware and unprepared, but during the month-long campaign, which focussed on the public power development, all parties pushed hard and made their presence felt. For the first and probably last time in the province's history, voters would have a choice from among four political alternatives. Ray Perrault, leader of the Liberal Party, asked: "Is a provincial election necessary?" He was honeymooning in Hawaii when the election announcement came. Davie Fulton, leading a hopefully revitalized Conservative Party, aimed his attack at Bennett personally and at the Two River Policy generally. One of his advertisements proclaimed: "I couldn't sit by and watch Mr. Bennett use my province as his plaything. I have come back to stand up to Mr. Bennett." Robert Strachan, leading the new CCF-labour alliance, which in 1961 was provincially christened the New Democratic Party, hoped to take advantage of the split among nonsocialist parties. When Fulton had first entered the provincial fray, Strachan stated: "I don't think there is much doubt now that the New Democratic Party will form the next government of B.C." Groomed and brought along by the pseudo-intelligentsia in his new party, Strachan, formerly nicknamed the "wild man" by Bennett, was presented as a responsible, almost businesslike alternative. Social Crediters joked about Strachan's new "Bond Street" look, but were seriously concerned about the uncertainty in the air during this most fluid B.C. election campaign since 1952.

The Socreds themselves were not exactly ready for an election, but as the party of government they were in reasonably good shape to do battle. During the spring 1963 legislative session they had introduced a variety of popular initiatives including the removal of tolls from all bridges, an increase in the homeowner grant from $50 to $70 per year, an increase in municipal aid, sundry tax reductions, and a University Act which established two new universities and provided for the creation of a network of regional colleges. Bennett's 1963 budget, the printed version of which "put the glossy annual reports of the giant corporations in the shade" and was distributed to every household in the province, forecast record expenditures of over $372 million and predicted that "the greatest period of economic and social progress in our history" was on the horizon. Social Credit candidates promoted the glories of their premier's Two River Policy and the imminent billion-dollar construction projects on the Peace and Columbia. On top of all this, they came out with a large sixteen-page brochure, "Time-Table for Progress," an elaborate campaign manifesto announcing carefully documented spending programs for each government department. Voters were urged, "Keep B.C. Moving" and "Forward With Social Credit."

Never for a moment did Bennett forget that the government's primary enemy was the NDP, or as he dubbed it, the "New Depression Party," but the highlight of the 1963 election campaign was clearly the Fulton challenge. In realistic terms, Davie Fulton could not have hoped to achieve power in 1963; Conservatives were caught so completely off guard by the call to the polls that they failed to field a full slate of candidates. Privately, the best Fulton could hope for was a strong enough assault on fortress Social Credit to assist in the victory of a socialist government, and from that position later launch a campaign for provincial power under his own auspices. Of all the factors blocking Fulton's aspirations, three stand out: first, he lacked a strong party organization; second, he made the mistake of personally contesting his home constituency of Kamloops which was held by Socred heavyweight Phil Gaglardi; third, the most masterful parish pump politician in the province's history, W.A.C. Bennett, was determined to shut him out.

Davie Fulton was destined to become one of the tragic figures of Canadian political history. He had been groomed for the top. His grandfather was British Columbia's eighth premier; his great-uncle was the tenth premier and chief justice. Another uncle was Speaker of the legislature. His father was attorney general of B.C. and later served as an MP in the Borden government. Fulton himself was a Rhodes scholar and had served in Italy with the Seaforth Highlanders during World War Two. His career in federal politics was so full of promise that he had been frequently touted as a future prime minister. He persuaded himself that he could lead the provincial Tories, like Moses led his followers, to the promised land, but he based his campaign on a fundamental misunderstanding of the psychology of his home province; he did not see that British Columbians enjoyed the politics of grandeur as preached by Bennett. They did not enjoy hearing that the visions of the Two River Policy were impractical or "not feasible at present." An interesting footnote to his 1963 challenge was that a young Conservative law student who wrote terse but effective daily newspaper advertisements for him was a young Albertan by the name of Joe Clark. The future prime minister could have learned some valuable political lessons from Fulton's mistakes, one of which was his going toe to toe with the likes of W. A. C. Bennett. "British Columbia is my province," Fulton said, "my place, the province of my destiny. . . . I looked at B.C. . . . I became angry . . . I became determined to dislodge this stupid and short-sighted government, to dislodge this arrogant man from his seat of power and to give back security and confidence to the people." But Bennett turned his attack around by castigating Fulton as an "outsider," an "interloper" trying to parachute his way to power from Ottawa where he had helped to wreck one government and who now wanted to destroy another. Compared to Fulton, it was Bennett who was clearly the outsider. The native of Albert County, New Brunswick, could never aspire to the blue-blooded west coast pedigree of Davie Fulton — but he could, and would, teach him a few facts about practical politics.

On the Friday before the Monday election, Bennett arrived in Kamloops for his final big election rally in what had been an exciting and vigorous campaign. As the election reached its climax, Kamloops became the focal point for the whole province. As a federal Conservative, Fulton had for years enjoyed the support of the same Kamloops voters who marked their provincial ballots for Phil Gaglardi. Now they were faced with a difficult choice. Earlier in the day, Bonner called Bennett from Vancouver and ecstatically informed him that the B.C. Electric case had been closed: dramatic last-minute negotiations had produced a settlement in which the government agreed to pay B.C. Power Corporation just over $197 million. This was $4,286,233 over the amount recommended by Chief Justice Lett, representing interest for the time that had elapsed since his judgement. Bennett's gamble had paid off: the election had forced a settlement of the messy B.C. Electric controversy, since B.C. Power Corporation was more than a little apprehensive about the election outcome. Now, coming when it did, the settlement would play a significant role in the voting on Monday. That Friday evening in Kamloops, Bennett announced: "You can say the B.C. flag is flying over the B.C. Hydro building tonight." Speaking directly to Kamloops voters, he claimed he would not want to be premier without Phil Gaglardi at his side.

Most commentators expected a close finish to the wild political race on September 30. Their predictions favoured a minority government presided over by either the Socreds or the NDP. Of course, a good deal hinged on the respective showings of the Grits and Tories. Davie Fulton described his impression of election day in Kamloops: "It was always my custom on voting day to go into the polling station in Kamloops just about the time the polls would close and thank our workers and try to get some feel for what had been going on. I remember that it was so different from the federal elections which I'd run and won and everybody was looking happy, including voters who were just leaving having cast their ballots. But this time I noticed that people would recognize me and turn their faces away and hurry by. I knew they weren't very happy with what they had to do; and I knew perfectly well that they were voting against me or voting for Gaglardi." On this occasion, at least, Fulton was correct. The flamboyant Socred highways minister beat Fulton by over 1,200 votes; and as Kamloops went, so went the province. Social Credit increased its share of the popular vote to 41 per cent and gained an extra seat for a total of thirty-three. The NDP, under the new, force-fed image of their old leader, Robert Strachan, lost five per cent of their popular vote and finished with two less seats, fourteen. The Liberals held steady at 20 per cent and, surprisingly, gained an extra, fifth seat. The Conservatives managed to win 11 per cent of British Columbians' votes but were once again completely locked out of the legislature.

For W. A. C. Bennett and the Socreds it was a convincing, satisfying and somewhat surprising victory. Contrary to popular belief, the Tories, rather than stealing votes from Social Credit, apparently siphoned off support from the NDP. The socialists were hurting from their poor showing, which was quite unpredicted; the new provincial left-wing alliance would undergo some serious soul-searching and bitter internal divisions in the months to come. But, for the moment, no one hurt more than Davie Fulton. For all intents and purposes, his political career was ruined. He resigned as provincial Tory leader and would flirt again with federal politics before eventually receiving an appointment to the B.C. judiciary, where his last days of public service became mired in pathetic petty controversies and scandal. The man who had it all—the genes, the training, the grooming—was given the tragic epitaph in the press: "The Magnificent Failure."

If Fulton was the greatest Canadian casualty of the politics of power, then Bennett would be the greatest beneficiary. With a strongly renewed mandate from the people of British Columbia and the entente on the Columbia recently signed with the federal Liberal administration, the way seemed clear for the realization of Bennett's Two River dream. Contracts were let for construction of the Peace River dam. The final series of negotiations with the Americans over the protocol to the Columbia River Treaty commenced in Ottawa early in December 1963; they centred on the problem of how much the U.S. should pay for the previously negotiated downstream power benefits. This last round of bargaining produced some tense moments and tough decision making. Presided over by Paul Martin, the Canadian team was actually led by British Columbians: Ray Williston, Robert Bonner and Hugh Keenleyside who, with Dr. Gordon Shrum, had become a co-chairman of the B.C. Hydro and Power Authority. Of course, Bennett quarterbacked the negotiations by long distance. He had a secret bottom-line dollar figure that he was prepared to settle for and which he shared only with Paul Martin, with whom he had developed a great personal rapport.

After a day and a half of negotiation, the two sides were still about $28 million apart on a final price for the downstream benefits. Ray Williston was not given any parameters by Premier Bennett, but was simply told to get the best deal possible; he therefore refused to budge any further, causing the Americans to threaten to go home. Paul Martin, through Hugh Keenleyside, advised that it was time to let up a bit, but Williston was uncertain. Finally, when the meeting was on the verge of dissolution, Williston turned to the American negotiators and said: "Let's split the $28 million in half, $14 million apiece." The Americans agreed, though Charles Luce, the administrator of the Bonneville Power Administration, which was ultimately responsible for coming up with the money, turned red with anger. Of this interesting bit of negotiation, Williston said: "I remember standing up when it was finished and Paul Martin kind of sidling up and saying, 'You know, the chief will be pleased about this. You're well over the basic minimum.' That was the first time I ever realized that the two of them had established a basic minimum. Naturally, I was quite relieved. Of course, some people say we never secured enough, but I'm absolutely sure that if we'd gone for any more at that particular moment, the whole Columbia River development would have disappeared."

With a price fixed for the downstream benefits, in the manner that Bennett had insisted on for so long, the story of the Columbia agreement should have been concluded. But it was not quite, for the question of how that money was to be paid seriously threatened to destroy the entire treaty. If not for some last-minute long-distance diplomacy, decades of effort could have been lost forever. Ottawa proposed to retain the advance benefit payment from the U.S. and forward amounts to B.C. according to actual capital expenditures on treaty projects. Williston said that this proposal almost scuttled the whole agreement: "Premier Bennett was not going to allow any federal official to handle sums of money on his behalf at any point in the future. He was absolutely adamant about this. Nobody was going to handle it but himself. Even the inference that anybody else would handle it better than him was viewed as an insult to his financial ability—and he really stuck with this." Ottawa next proposed to withhold from B.C. money owing on the international agreement should the province ever be in default on the terms of the treaty. Bennett was infuriated since it gave the federal government power over the provincial government without recourse to arbitration. The premier left for a holiday in Hawaii telling his negotiating team that they were to get the money with no strings attached as far as B.C. was concerned—and he warned them not to try to reach him, that he would not be answering his telephone. Negotiations with the federal government continued, but with no solution in sight. It was Christmas Eve 1963, and everyone wanted to go home; the situation had become desperate. Williston and Keenleyside drafted a press release indicating, in bitterness, that the talks over treaty implementation had completely broken down. Williston tried several times to phone the premier in Hawaii but there was no answer. At last, late in the afternoon, Bennett called; curiosity had got the better of him. Paul Martin, Robert Bonner and Ray Williston spoke with him on a multiparty line and, among them, arrived at what Bennett could call an honourable settlement. They agreed that if B.C. was in default for a specified period of time and if the Exchequer Court found the province to be in default, the federal government would be within its right to withdraw the money from the next federal transfer payment to the province.

Finally. The infuriatingly complicated Columbia River Treaty puzzle was solved. After years of exhaustive study and exhausting negotiation, all parties to the treaty appeared happy. Through sheer staying power, W. A. C. Bennett had forced the national governments of Canada and the United States to face the fact that if any agreement was to be reached, it would be on his conditions, and only his conditions. As one Canadian authority, Neil Swainson, has written: "Seldom if ever before in Canadian experience had the final resolution of what was a major foreign as well as a major domestic policy issue been marked by so little direction from the national government." On January 22, 1964, the revised treaty and sale agreement were signed in Washington, D.C. by Prime Minister Pearson and President Lyndon Johnson; present at the ceremony was the ubiquitous B.C. representative Ray Williston. In Victoria, Bennett called it the happiest day of his premiership and added: "The fact that B.C. did not agree to the original treaty will save us hundreds of millions of dollars." The final agreement provided for a lump sum payment of $274.8 million to purchase Canada's share of downstream power for the first thirty years of the sixty-year treaty. To this would be added $69.6 million in flood control payments between 1968 and 1973. Bennett estimated that by investing the funds at five-per-cent interest, they would come to over a half a billion dollars by 1973 and so would cover the estimated capital costs of the three storage dams to be constructed on the B.C. portion of the Columbia watershed. Thus, he would reiterate his earlier statement that Columbia power would be free—"And nothing is freer than free, my friend."

After the new Columbia River Treaty had been ratified by both the Canadian parliament and the American congress, arrangements were made for formal proclamation. On September 16, 1964, a large public ceremony was staged at the Peace Arch at Blaine on the border of British Columbia and Washington State. President Lyndon Johnson and Prime Minister Lester Pearson attended the ceremony to symbolically seal the agreement, yet these heads of state both seemed like stagehands compared to the obvious star of the show, W. A. C. Bennett. Pearson would write: "While I was the head of the Canadian government and Mr. Johnson was the head of the American government, in British Columbia Mr. Bennett was the head of all he surveyed." In the pouring rain, the president and the prime minister abbreviated their prepared speeches, but not the proud premier who was only too happy to wallow in the glory of the moment. Bennett read his entire speech, which included the following self-congratulatory remark: "We would perhaps be less than human if we did not take real satisfaction in the knowledge that the financing formula put forward by the British Columbia government was accepted by both national governments as the means of implementing the treaty's terms." Then, Johnson handed Bennett a cheque in the amount of $273,291,661.25, commenting wryly that "the Canadians even went for the last twenty-five cents." The sum represented a small discount for prepayment and the cheque was a facsimile. Actually, Bennett had carefully invested the money before this ceremony and had already earned several thousand dollars in interest.

So ended an important and controversial chapter in the rise of British Columbia. But the politics of power would continue to thrive on Canada's west coast, and one of the more enduring disputes would centre on the relative merit of the Columbia River Treaty. Was it a good deal for Canada, or was it a resource giveaway to the Americans? Who benefited more from the treaty, Canada or the United States?

These are difficult questions to answer, particularly when debate over them is emotional or partisan. The treaty has been hailed as an example *par excellence* of the friendly relations between two nations co-operating in the joint development of a natural resource to their mutual advantage. But it has also been labelled a naive sellout of Canada's birthright. It would be impossible to sum up all the arguments for and against the treaty. Millions of words have been written on the subject, having become a landmark case for international lawyers, political scientists, historians, engineers—perhaps eventually for psychologists. It is agreed that the treaty provided for the development of something approaching the optimum potential of the Columbia River in terms of flood control and electrical power benefits. And it is instructive to point out that the treaty is criticized on both sides of the border as representing a net loss to each country. Unfortunately, most of the loud criticisms levelled from the Canadian side fail to take into account the negotiating achievement of the time; any evaluation of the treaty results must take hindsight into account. For example, W. A. C. Bennett has been castigated for the massive price increases that resulted from unexpected rates of inflation which, strictly speaking, rendered the cost of the Columbia project not quite "freer than free." But all major long-term construction projects of the era have been hit by the same unanticipated and unwelcome inflationary spiral, and public policy makers can hardly be faulted for lack of prescience. Another usually overlooked aspect of the treaty is that downstream benefits were sold to the Americans for only the first half of the sixty-year treaty, so that depending on conditions in the Pacific Northwest in the 1990s, the Columbia River agreement could turn out to be an extremely favourable deal from the Canadian standpoint. However, since the future, as ever, cannot be predicted, it is safer to record the retrospective assessment of three of the important participants.

W. A. C. Bennett, who often referred to his Two River Policy and particularly the Columbia River Treaty as his greatest achievement, said:

> We were able to make the best deal internationally on water power ever made in the world. There's no place else that I know of where one country [Canada] gets downstream benefits from another country, keeps all their own power and gets half of the new power generated in a foreign country—no place else. The whole idea of the treaty was that we would put in certain dams, use all the power that we could develop on our side of the boundary and keep that one hundred per cent for ourselves. And the Americans, because of our control of the releasing of water from the dams and knowing what was coming on a regulated basis, could use this water instead of it going wasting to the ocean. They could get a lot more power from it through their different installations—and that's called the downstream benefits. People did not understand, don't understand, still don't understand that these downstream benefits are American-developed power. The idea was that, [of this] power the United States would develop on their own side, they'd keep half and half belonged to British Columbia. Now, if we brought back all our [share of the] power, we couldn't develop the Peace, because the policy in Canada then was no export of power. Anyway, it would be foolish to bring American power back and then export it back to them again—it

would be stupid. So the best thing was to leave it there and take cash payments in advance, and with that money earning interest and so forth, develop our power while costs were still low, before wild inflation, and develop the Peace at the same time. We drove the toughest bargain we could. We got the last cent we could possibly get out of the treaty from the Yankees. Ottawa would have settled for way less. When that treaty is over, the sixty-year treaty, and the last half of the treaty which the Americans haven't paid for yet [has been paid], with the high costs of energy now, this will prove to be a terrific treaty for Canada.

Paul Martin said:

I know there are those who say we sold water—valuable water—to the United States. Of course we did. But that water was on its way to the sea. Canada lost nothing. British Columbia lost nothing by making an agreement, a limited agreement, for a period with the United States. As a result it was able to build dams that are going to give British Columbia a preferred position in the market for the sale of electric energy. I know the NDP particularly complained about the sale of a resource. Of course it was the sale of a resource. But it was a resource that had been for years flowing into the sea lost to anyone, and I don't think the mighty Columbia is servicing Canada or British Columbia any less today because of that agreement. I think it was a good agreement.

And Robert Bonner responded to criticism of the treaty:

We in effect sold our entitlement to benefits for thirty years. And at that point we have the option to take our benefits in cash or kind. . . . If inflation keeps on, God knows how much those benefits might be worth. If we had listened to the critics and not entered into the Columbia River Treaty, just think what inflation would do to us if we now tried to crank it up when our need is evident. I think generally speaking we have reason to be satisfied with the way it turned out. . . . Did we sell our birthright to the United States, as has been charged by some critics? These are rhetorical expressions which defy definition. What could possibly be called our birthright in these circumstances? We had no particular birthright to flood the United States. We had no particular birthright to waste the energy of an uncontrolled river. And these were the two things which were affected by the treaty. We had no birthright to participate in improved downstream benefits; that was a negotiating achievement. So semantically, "selling your birthright" really does not conjure up anything of fact. What we *did* do was stop flooding ourselves and stop flooding the Americans at unseasonable times. What we *did* do was create the benefit which nature did not provide by storing flood waters. And what we *did* do was achieve participation in the improved generation of power in another country, which could never have been conceived as a birthright to anybody. And for all that, we got paid a heck of a lot of money, which enabled us to put major works in our province which have since been machined to produce some of the cheapest electricity in North America. That doesn't sound like a bad deal to me.

The Columbia River Treaty episode demonstrated both the best and worst sides of Canadian federalism. During his tenure in office, W. A. C. Bennett's associations with Ottawa were usually competitive rather than co-operative. He was quite capable of striking up close, sometimes warm, one-to-one relationships with individual federal personalities—for example, Paul Martin—but he steadfastly maintained a healthy distrust of the central government's designs to share in B.C.'s new found affluence. This stance is well illustrated by his promotion of a provincial bank for British Columbia.

It is probably not possible to pinpoint the precise moment when Bennett was seized by the plan to establish a Bank of British Columbia, but its genesis was clearly his overall frustration with the eastern-dominated Canadian financial establishment, and likely goes right back to his failure to win election to the board of directors of the new Bank of Canada in 1935. At the same time, the battles in the politics of power had not exactly endeared him to the country's chartered banks. True, one bank president had helped him out of a near ruinous financial catastrophe, but the others had turned a blind eye to him. At one point in 1963, the Royal Bank of Canada had even refused to cash provincially guaranteed parity bonds at their face value. Bennett had long been upset over the Canadian chartered banks' unsympathetic approach to financing private development in B.C. and was convinced it was because all major lending decisions were made in head offices in Toronto or Montreal. He tried, without success, to lure one of the big chartered banks to move its head office to Vancouver. Then in 1964 he dabbled with the idea of having the provincial government purchase a large percentage of shares in one of the national banks. The problem, however, was that these were federally chartered institutions: under the Canadian constitution, banking and control of most money matters rests exclusively with the federal government. Nevertheless, Bennett next plunged ahead with a radical proposal to establish a new bank, a Bank of British Columbia, with 25 per cent of the shares owned by the provincial government. The idea was a popular one and Bennett had little difficulty in securing the legislature's approval for the plan; Robert Strachan and the NDP, for instance, said they supported the concept of public ownership of financial institutions. Next, Bennett appointed a provincial board of directors for the proposed bank, which included his close friend and adviser Einar Gunderson, and prepared to make a submission to the Senate banking committee in Ottawa.

The Senate committee began hearings on July 22, 1964, into the proposal to incorporate a Bank of British Columbia. It was almost unprecedented for a provincial premier to appear before a parliamentary committee—which itself attests to the importance of the proposed bank in Bennett's mind. Other witnesses appearing with the premier were cabinet ministers Robert Bonner and Leslie Peterson and, of course, Einar Gunderson. The committee was on the defensive from the start, for it was common knowledge that several senators held directorships with existing Canadian chartered banks. For two hot but entertaining summer days they debated the various B.C. briefs and expressed widely divergent views on the relative merits of the proposed new bank. In his brief, Bennett did his utmost to alleviate concern that the bank might be used for political purposes, and he offered to reduce the provincial government's portion of share capital from 25 to 10 per cent. He testified:

> Perhaps you are all wondering why the Premier of the province is appearing before you in support of a Bill to incorporate a private bank. I do so wholeheartedly on behalf of the people of British Columbia to assist them in setting up a large financial institution with its head office in the province of British Columbia. . . . Vancouver is further away from the head office of a chartered bank than any other city of comparable size in the whole free world. . . . The government of British Columbia believes that the national strength and conscience of a federal nation must flow from the sum of all its regions. . . . Does the present level of economic activity and its more recent growth in the Pacific region, as compared with the progress of the nation, support a charter for the Bank of British Columbia? The answer appears strongly in the affirmative. . . . I want to make it very clear that any government would be very stupid indeed to run a partisan bank or try to influence its operations or loans or anything else. . . . Our support for the bank is non-partisan. . . . The only partisan thing about this bank is the criticism, the political criticism, of the government's position.

After the briefs of the other witnesses were heard, the senators opened fire with pointed questions concerning the B.C. government and its motive in wanting to be so directly involved in a private banking operation. Bennett and several of the senators had sharp exchanges. One member of the committee asked why it was the premier who had made an announcement concerning the location of the prospective bank's Vancouver headquarters. Bennett replied: "Well, the Premier is the life of the British Columbia government, you know." Said the senator: "I have known that for a long time." Another senator suggested that Bennett had delivered quite a homily on constitutional law, to which he quickly answered: "No, I am not a lawyer. I am just a blunt businessman." When Einar Gunderson assured the committee, "The Board of Directors are not going to pay too much attention to what politicians say," one senator asked: "How do you think you got there?" This brought Bennett back into the fray to defend his old friend: "I want to tell you this, the best profession in the world is not a chartered accountant, nor a lawyer, nor a businessman. The best men are those who give their life to public service; and politicians represent policies. All this talk in the country about people and politics—they mean partisan, a dirty type of politics; but there is nothing better for the youth of our land than to have a proper respect for politics; and to me it is the best word in the dictionary."

Not all of the senators were opposed to the proposal for a Bank of British Columbia; however, on December 14, 1965, the committee rejected the plan by a vote of nineteen to seven. All of their views are available in the many hundreds of pages of transcript of the Senate banking committee's deliberations; but perhaps the reflections of a few members of the committee fifteen years later are more revealing. Senator Hartland de M. Molson said he considered it "very unusual for a provincial Premier to make the presentation of a brief on behalf of what was described as a private group applying for a bank charter. . . . The major obstacles in the path of approval by the Senate committee were first, that it was a political move heretofore not present in our banking system, and second the very serious danger of a provincial government owning a substantial interest in a chartered bank and using the bank to further its own power." Senator D. A. Lang recalled: "During the committee hearings Mr. Bennett took it upon himself to answer all questions, no matter to whom among the delegation they had been specifically directed. . . . Mr. Bennett's replies were largely irrelevant to the points at which the questions were directed. They sounded like a Chamber of Commerce promotion for British Columbia." In contrast, Senator Jacques Flynn believed that the B.C. delegation "was knowledgeable, articulate and very well-prepared." Senator David Croll, who likely knew Bennett better than any other member of the committee, said: "I was for it, right from the minute that Bennett opened his mouth on the thing. I was in his corner right from the beginning. But, look, he wasn't riding out of the west; he was flying out of the west. And people were suspicious."

Bennett had put tremendous effort into the proposal for the Bank of British Columbia and was sadly disillusioned when he realized that the Senate banking committee hearings had been an exercise in futility. His view was that:

Those senators had great connections with the other chartered banks. They were our enemies, not our friends. However, at these Senate hearings I had a friend, Senator Croll. And so I discussed it with him and I said, "Why are we not making headway here, Senator?" He said, "I'll tell you why. It's the East Block." That's the prime minister's office. I said, "They've agreed with everything." "Oh, no," he said. "[But] if they just phoned over and told us—we have the majority there in the Senate to pass it—we'd pass it in ten minutes."

So I went over and saw Paul Martin. I said, "You're my friend, Paul. I've trusted you on the Columbia and found you to be an honourable man. We're not getting a fair deal on this Bank of British Columbia." "Oh yes," said Paul, very persuasively. "Oh, yes, Mr. Premier, you've just got to fight hard. No bank has ever been set up like this in all the history of Canada; it's something new." I said, "One of the senators tells me that if the East Block okayed it, it would be passed in ten minutes." A funny expression came over Paul's face, and he said, "He shouldn't have said that!" I said, "Paul, you know it's true."

The prime minister and minister of finance at first had agreed with me, but once they found out what I was after, to build Vancouver into a rival for Montreal and Toronto as far as finance was concerned, they said, "No, no, no." They reneged on that. They came back to me when they had a survey done about it; the survey said, if you let Bennett have this strong bank he wants in British Columbia, with the government in their financial shape, owning ten or twenty-five per cent of the shares, it will become such a strong force that the central bank of Canada won't be able to control Bennett and the B.C. government. Why would they want to control us anyway? If we strengthened British Columbia, who gets the lion's share of the taxation anyway? The federal government. Stupid people!

Senator Croll later confirmed Bennett's reason for exasperation:

There was influence being brought to bear. They weren't completely sold on it. Bennett wasn't the most welcome politician when he came down here to Ottawa. He was a political threat. He built up something from nothing in British Columbia and suddenly he was in charge. He could have made it very uncomfortable for the government here, but he didn't choose to do that. You see, the influence by the banks was being used on the government. They didn't want any new banks; they didn't want this fellow in the banking business; they didn't want any province in the banking business. It wasn't with the Senate so much—we were of a different view—but the East Block was doing what they could to hold him back.

When the committee's rejection came, Bennett said that "it appears that they are anxious to keep financial control in Canada in the hands of the Eastern Establishment. That Establishment is opposed to a large rival being established with headquarters in Vancouver." During the 1965 session of the B.C. legislature he threatened the federal government by indicating that he intended to continue his assault on the Canadian banking world. In Ottawa, federal Finance Minister Walter Gordon announced plans to amend the Bank Act to block provincial shareholding. Asked if this altered his plans, Bennett snapped: "B.C. does not back up. It only goes further ahead." He pressed on against the eastern Canadian financial establishment, but eventually gave up the direct challenge.

In March 1966, the Senate banking committee gave approval to a new, completely private proposal for a "Bank of British Columbia." The bank's charter received royal assent on December 14, 1966, and it started operation in 1968 without any direct or official government assistance and with a modest asset base of $34 million. A little over a decade later, the Bank of British Columbia had climbed to the billion-dollar club in terms of net assets and, though it has not yet challenged the "big five" Canadian corporate banks, it has been successful in making west coast banking more competitive and more responsive to local needs. The Bank of British Columbia certainly differs from W. A. C. Bennett's original vision, but in a real sense it is a product of his initiative. He retained a strong personal interest in the bank, and it is significant that his eldest son, R. J., became a member of the board of directors.

As the Senate banking committee had correctly perceived, Bennett was the life of the B.C. government, and in February 1965 he had been the life of the government longer than any previous premier—almost thirteen years. The small-town hardware merchant from the poor, broken New Brunswick family had worked and schemed his way to power and pushed and plotted to maintain firm control over Canada's burgeoning west coast empire. Indeed, some people claimed the initials B.C. stood for "Bennett Country." If he had relinquished power at this point in his career, he would have already achieved a record in office noted for more than sheer longevity. Although his greatest challenges were probably behind him, he gave no thought to stepping down. Well into his seventh decade of life Bennett was setting personal goals and public ambitions that would require years, if not decades to achieve. One wonders if he was not beginning to flirt with notions of immortality.

On February 16, 1965, politics were placed aside for a few minutes in the legislature as both sides of the House congratulated the premier—who sat quietly choking back tears—for his record-breaking years of service to the province. Shortly afterwards, the Vancouver establishment held a lavish testimonial banquet for Bennett, where many offered eloquent praise for the political rebel who had done so much to reshape public life in British Columbia. Many others attending this special dinner may have wished that it marked the retirement or even the funeral of the man who sat at the head table beaming his infuriating smile. Perhaps the most prescient tribute of the evening came from H. H. Stevens, a former federal Conservative cabinet minister: "You are now at a crisis of your life. We meet here tonight to honour you for great, dedicated public service to this province and to this country. We do it gladly. We do it feeling that we are only doing what is fair and right and what is deserving. But may I suggest to you, sir, that from now on in your great life you will pass through years that will determine in the historic sense how great a man you are or will be."

CHAPTER
TEN
THE POWER OF POLITICS

History demonstrates without exception
That successful sovereign power seizers
And successfully self-perpetuating
Supreme physical power holders in general
Will always attempt to divide the opposition
In order to conquer them
And thereafter keep the conquered divided
To keep them conquered.
R. Buckminster Fuller

Politics—to me it's the best word in the dictionary.
W. A. C. Bennett

Power means control over other people's lives. The desire to control both human and material resources and exercise personal prerogatives is the motivating force behind many great ambitions. Power is the backdrop against which most confrontation scenes occurred between Premier W. A. C. Bennett and his political adversaries. Bennett's whole public career was based on the dramatic interplay among power, politics and personalities.

In everything he did, Bennett was always "engaged." He was eternally manipulating, manoeuvring, always with his fingers in the many pies he coveted. He was not happy unless he was involved in some form of human exchange or collision of ambitions. He was not content just to savour his power; he had to exercise it and continually extend its base. Bennett practised the power of politics as an art—a truly creative, all-consuming art—yet he was fond of describing it as a science: "Politics is the only real science. All other sciences are subject to politics. It's the one that affects them all; it's the number one science. But, unfortunately, too many chaps who are able to make a speech, able to write an article, able to make an argument, think they should be in politics. . . . Unless they have some vision for the country, for improvement, and have some talent in that respect, they shouldn't be there."

Did Bennett ever seriously consider extending his personal power by seeking national office? After all, there seemed little left for him to accomplish on the provincial scene and, as a younger man, he had once professed a passionate interest in national politics. His only real flirtation with federal politics had occurred in 1948 when he ran as the Tory standard-bearer in a by-election in Yale. After joining Social Credit and becoming premier of B.C., probably he did not again long for far-off Ottawa. Apparently he made a commitment to his wife, who had objected to his federal election attempt, that he would remain in provincial politics, later saying: "I think if you are going to be successful in your business life and your political life, it must be based on confidence at home."

Not to deny the influence of May, there were other reasons Bennett did not reach for federal office after he became premier of B.C. Foremost was the nature of Canadian federalism. As Bennett grew into office in Victoria he came to resemble something very close to a head of state in his own right—a kind of provincial warlord—and, like most other premiers, he was satisfied with that status. Within a few years of realizing provincial power he would not have relinquished it for anything. Unlike his west coast domain, the field of federal politics involved too much uncertainty, too many compromises— not to mention the chance of personal failure or defeat. The Canadian federal system pressured Bennett to work tenaciously towards increasing the power of his politics within B.C. rather than extending it beyond the province's boundaries. He was the single most powerful figure in his provincial bailiwick and he did not want to jeopardize that position, even it it sometimes meant weakening the larger federal structure.

All of this is not to say that as a Social Crediter Bennett was uninterested in Canadian politics. For several years during the late 1950s and early 1960s he was one of the most active of the federal Socreds' power brokers. He has said: "When I joined Social Credit I made it very clear that I joined the Social Credit movement in British Columbia, the Social Credit movement in Canada and the Social Credit movement throughout the world—that I was a genuine Social Crediter." Ever since the days of Aberhart, the Socreds had been active at the federal level, but had never managed to elect more than a handful of MPs from Alberta and, after 1952, a few from B.C. Under the leadership of Solon Low, an Albertan, Social Credit had established itself as a kind of regional third party, a voice of western protest, but hardly a political force to be reckoned with. Bennett felt that Low was a good pioneer leader for Social Credit but that he became too engrossed in parliamentary skirmishes in Ottawa where the party was constantly derided for its "funny money," "Bible-punching" background. As the granddads of the Social Credit movement, the Albertans naturally guided and controlled most of the party's federal effort, but with the arrival of W. A. C. Bennett and a strong B.C. party new vitality was injected into that effort. Bennett and his cabinet ministers campaigned for Social Credit during federal elections and did their utmost to spread the faith eastward.

In the federal election of 1957, Social Credit won nineteen seats, all in Alberta and B.C., momentarily raising the sights of the far westerners.

However, in the election a year later the Socreds were trampled by the Diefenbaker juggernaut and elected not a single member of parliament. This led to a period of reappraisal by Social Crediters in the two westernmost provinces. The Albertans, headed by the earnest premier Ernest Manning, seemed willing to fight another day, particularly since Social Credit monetary policies could only be effected by a national government. In British Columbia, Bennett decided that a fresh approach was required; he developed an interesting kind of domino theory cum federal battle plan, which he described:

> As a boy, did you ever split wood? When you split wood you don't have to cut the block of wood straight through; you hit it here and there—and the block flies open; it splits. That's exactly what you do in the political war. Unless you organize a strong movement and base in the provinces, you wouldn't last federally. That's why I said, "Alberta first, then B.C., then Saskatchewan, Manitoba and so on." I wanted our party to be more active provincially than federally at that stage. If we had more provincial governments with us, from coast to coast, the federal party would come along in time, when they saw Socred strength in the rest of Canada. We couldn't do it with one province, we couldn't do it with two, but if we had three or four we'd be on the way. Our strategy was to take another province. . . . That's the reason I put a lot of effort in Saskatchewan; I took my whole cabinet there and we campaigned in every area. I was very disappointed that Alberta didn't support us in the campaign, because if we could have taken Saskatchewan, then we would have taken Manitoba; I'm sure of that.

If Bennett's assessment of their chances was correct, then also crucial was the decision of a maverick Saskatchewan politician during this period. For the Social Credit Party to make significant headway in the province of Saskatchewan, where it had elected only a few provincial members, a leader was needed to light the way, a bona fide statesman. Saskatchewan Socreds were keenly aware of this fact, as was Bennett, and they separately attempted to persuade Ross Thatcher to take the job. A former CCF member of parliament, Thatcher had abandoned the socialists and in the late 1950s was searching for an outlet for the abilities and energies that made him one of the most forceful prairie politicians of his day. Bennett, who had met Thatcher and was acquainted with his mother who lived on the coast, tried to persuade him to embrace Social Credit, but to no avail. According to Bennett: "Liberals like Jimmy Sinclair and others were buddies of his in Ottawa and they convinced him that he could make a better contribution as a Liberal. I said, 'No way, Ross. If you join Social Credit, become our leader in Saskatchewan, we'll sweep the province—you'll last at least twenty years. You won't be tied down and always fighting against federal Liberalism. You made one mistake before by joining the CCF; don't make a second mistake. . . .' " Martin Kelln, longtime Social Credit national president and leader of the Saskatchewan party, also made an overture to Thatcher, who asked: "What have you got to offer me?" Kelln apparently replied: "Nothing but hard work and sacrifice." That was the end of the conversation.

Unwilling to take the gamble that Bennett had taken in 1951, Ross Thatcher made the "mistake" and in 1959 converted to Liberalism, eventually becoming premier of Saskatchewan for two eventful but ill-fated terms. His controversial Liberal administration suffered a crushing defeat in 1971 at the hands of the NDP and Thatcher tragically passed away only days after. Martin Kelln speculated: "If Ross Thatcher had taken the leadership of the Social Credit Party he'd still be in office today, because he wouldn't have had people that destroyed him from within: the Liberals never did forgive him for having been a CCFer—and Ross never was a socialist at any given time. And of course the CCFers hadn't forgiven him either. But there, unfortunately, was a man who was raised in politics all his life and he didn't want to be part of a force that he wasn't assured of being successful with."

Bennett was convinced that the primary reason Social Credit failed to catch fire in Saskatchewan and Manitoba was the lack of strong leadership in those provinces. Ross Thatcher's decision set back Bennett's west-to-east domino plan, but did not dash his hopes for a greater Canadian Social Credit movement. That ambition was kept alive by a dramatic development in Quebec, where a singular version of Social Credit arose under the fiery leadership of Réal Caouette, a car dealer by trade. Bennett became unusually excited about this intriguing development in the east and discerned in it an opportunity for Social Credit to break out of its western mould; and he saw the chance for national statesmanship in a movement long dominated by his Alberta colleague, Premier Manning. Late in 1960, Bennett travelled to Quebec to meet with Caouette:

> When I arrived on a Sunday in the little town of Rouyn, they called a special council meeting in my honour, and I spoke to them; they gave me a very warm welcome. Then they had a big meeting down in the basement of a big church, a Roman Catholic church. They had a band that paraded me down to this meeting with all the warmth of the real French Canadian; it was wonderful! . . . I said, "I cannot speak French, and so I appreciate your coming to listen to me speaking English." And I never saw such a reception; they stood and cheered. . . . I wanted to check into Caouette in his own home town to see how he lived, to see his home, his family life—it was sound, and I knew he was genuine.

The local Rouyn press recorded that Bennett held an audience of more than

1,000 "completely captivated for more than two hours" telling of Social Credit's achievements in British Columbia. "The ovation for Mr. Bennett lasted more than five minutes while the audience sang 'Alouette' and 'Il a gagné ses épaulettes.'... The audience stamped and cheered more than ever when Mr. Bennett said the foundations of Social Credit were laid in Alberta and British Columbia and 'You in Quebec will lay the cornerstone for the movement to cover all Canada.'"

Thus started an alliance between two strikingly dissimilar but equally flamboyant Canadian politicians. Especially touched by the mood of Quebec and the tremendous fervour that Caouette elicited from the growing ranks of his followers, Bennett became convinced that Caouette was capable of building a strong base for Social Credit in Quebec which, in turn, would help to give the party a truly national character. In support of Caouette, the B.C. premier made several ventures into French Canada preaching the western Canadian creed of Social Credit. At one enormous meeting in Montreal, he received a thunderous ovation when he told the crowd that he was pleased to be in "la belle province," the most French part of all Canada, "because I come from the most English part of the country, *British* Columbia." Years later when Bennett first met Pierre Trudeau, the prime minister said that he first saw him at that Montreal meeting. Always alert to the transformational nature of political power, Bennett quipped, "Mr. Prime Minister, you weren't a Liberal then, were you?"

The intense organizational and promotional activity reached a great climax for the federal Socreds during their national leadership convention on July 4–6, 1961, in Ottawa. The Socred heavyweights were all present, including Manning and his Alberta troops, Bennett and the B.C. delegation, which included several of his cabinet ministers, and an impressive entourage from Quebec. The two most prominent leadership aspirants, who would replace the retiring Solon Low, were Robert Thompson and Réal Caouette. Bob Thompson, a protégé of Ernest Manning, was a teacher, missionary and chiropractor with strong Alberta roots and overseas experience that included teaching and administrative services for the government of Haile Selassie in Ethiopia. Thompson was a decent, hard-working fellow, not quite made for the cut-and-thrust world of politics. He did not consider himself qualified to assume the leadership of a national political party: "My motive was to pave the way and to provide an organization that might result in Mr. Manning transferring to the federal field." Of course, at the time this was not widely known, but the delegates to the convention were keenly aware that Manning was in Thompson's corner and they soon learned that Bennett was supporting Caouette. One observer suggested that the B.C. premier was simply attempting to add some excitement to the leadership contest, but for Bennett politics was serious business; his support for Caouette was both determined and sincere. Bob Thompson's view was that "Mr. Bennett was a master politician who believed in the old theory of divide and rule. Whether he ever saw himself running as leader and becoming prime minister of the country or not, I don't know. But if he could divide any major support from me and hold the loyalty of Quebec, it would give him a much stronger voice in the management of the party."

The Ottawa convention was a novel experience for the federal Socreds who had never before attracted such interest from the media or general public. During the first two days the lobbying in the jam-packed Ottawa Coliseum was fierce. Both Manning and Bennett made statesmanlike speeches. Bennett said it was the "most important hour in the political history of Canada." The Albertans, who had always controlled the national party, seemed concerned about Bennett's position and were determined to prevent the election of Caouette. Their disaffection with the latter seemed based partly on his mercurial personality and partly on dissimilarities of religion and culture. Manning reminded the convention that being a French Canadian and a Roman Catholic would prove to be a serious handicap to any leader campaigning in the west.

As the time for nominations drew near, the convention atmosphere heated up. The Albertans had nominated Thompson, and a couple of other half-serious western candidates threw their hats into the ring, but there appeared to be some confusion over who was going to put forth the name of Réal Caouette. Said Bennett: "My minister of highways, Phil Gaglardi, agreed that he would nominate Réal Caouette as national leader. Then he came to me and he said, 'Mr. Premier, anything you ask me to do, of course, I would do, but please let me out of this commitment, because my church groups won't forgive me.' So I released Mr. Gaglardi and asked another of my ministers, Leslie Peterson, to nominate Mr. Caouette." As Peterson said: "The premier had a quick word with me and I went up to the platform and nominated Caouette. I gave a little speech in French, and the audience was very good—after every sentence, they applauded so long I was able to think of another one. I have to confess that I was hesitant. I don't like to nominate people I don't know . . . and you like to have a little more notice than that, but it looked as though nobody else was going to nominate him."

The actual voting, which was more confused than anyone at the time realized, produced a remarkably close victory for Robert Thompson by a margin of only four or five ballots—no one knows precisely since Alberta organizer Orvis Kennedy had all the ballots burned after the convention. Bennett, who was certain that Caouette would be elected, said that he was defeated because some Quebec delegates did not arrive at the convention until after the vote. A more interesting account suggests that Caouette had in fact narrowly won the ballot, but during the count it was discovered that five of the Quebec delegates had voted twice—perhaps on behalf of their tardy *frères!* Apparently a secret meeting was hurriedly arranged between Caouette, Thompson and the Albertans in order to prevent this information from being made public and forcing the embarrassment of a new election; in typically impulsive fashion, Caouette conceded defeat to Robert Thompson, who therefore became national leader of the Social Credit Party.

W. A. C. Bennett was very disappointed about the outcome of the convention, and it meant for him both a personal failure and the beginning of his withdrawal from direct involvement in federal Social Credit politics. He believed that Caouette could have become a new Laurier for Canada and that the Socreds made a tragic mistake in not making him national leader. Certainly, if the power of Bennett's politics had prevailed, the Canadian federal scene would have evolved in a markedly different manner and, to some extent, history bears out his fears. The federal election of June 1962 saw the remarkable resurgence of Social Credit, which won thirty seats, eleven more than the new socialist alliance, the NDP. The Socreds had become the third largest group in what Robert Thompson referred to as the "parliament of minorities." Thompson, however, was hardly the man to lead Social Credit in Ottawa, for twenty-six of his thirty members came from Quebec and owed their election to the colourful and dynamic Réal Caouette. The Albertans may have won the federal party leadership, but the west failed at the hustings. The western wing of the federal party now seemed a spent force and, as far as Ottawa was concerned, Social Credit was becoming a Quebec phenomenon, Le Ralliement des Créditistes. This is not to say that hopes were not high after the 1962 election: many considered this the golden opportunity for Social Credit in Canada. But with two divisive and lopsided camps in Ottawa and two jealous provincial premiers in the west, the chemistry was all wrong. W. A. C. Bennett refused to co-operate with Robert Thompson; he referred to him as "what's-his-name." Holding the crucial balance of power in the parliament of minorities, Thompson became best known in debate for mixing his metaphors: "If this thing starts to snowball, it will catch fire right across the country."

In the 1963 election the federal Socreds failed to make any gains, and by the mid-1960s the Quebec wing had separated from the party and the western Socreds completely lost their narrow foothold in Ottawa. Robert Thompson failed in his attempt to play John the Baptist for Ernest Manning; he stayed on as leader of the party until 1967, at which time he flirted unsuccessfully with Conservatism. One could argue that Réal Caouette would not have significantly altered the national impact of Social Credit; but the mettlesome Bennett firmly believed that the federal Socreds had missed their main chance. Should he have pushed harder and promoted Caouette more effectively? Bennett's answer to that question is typically folksy: "I never tried to force anything. I don't believe in forcing issues. I believe in letting things happen in their natural way. It was all right when I was a boy in New Brunswick sliding in the winter on sleds and going fast; certainly we used our toes a little to steer the sled. And perhaps in politics I'd steer a little if I could. But I wouldn't force the issue."

The dream of Social Credit forming a federal government in Canada may have momentarily caught Bennett's fancy, but it did not engage his interest long enough to distract him from more pressing and practical concerns. It almost goes without saying that he practised political power in British Columbia by the seat of his pants. Although his home was and always would be in the interior of the province, he was becoming increasingly at ease in Victoria where he spent most of the year, governing comfortably and confidently from his headquarters in the ostentatious provincial legislature overlooking the harbour.

Bennett's attitude towards the legislature led to charges that he was a dictator who disregarded the niceties and principles of parliamentary government. Certainly, he was not a great parliamentarian, but neither was he made of the stuff of a dictator. During his years as government leader he was one of the deans of the legislature and was the only government member to have served in opposition. His own personal career had included a series of dramatic and critical moments in the Assembly and, for that reason alone, he possessed a special appreciation of the role of parliament. He held a traditional view of the House and its proceedings and stuck to the formula of short annual spring sessions of eight to ten weeks' duration. He developed the natural, and perhaps inevitable, attitude of the leader of the executive branch in combat with the legislative branch, and undoubtedly would have concurred with John A. Macdonald that it would be wrong "to waste the time of the legislature and the money of the people in fruitless discussions on abstract and theoretical questions of government." The self-described "blunt businessman" resisted what he considered unnecessary chatter and presided over the House with an iron fist—but, at the same time, he had a good sense of the House; he loved to talk, to beguile, to play to his troops and the public galleries, to taunt and outrage the beleaguered opposition. He thrived on heckling, and repartee became a well-established part of his political repertoire. On other occasions, he could be so bored and impatient with the windy pace of the legislative session that he would be disturbed from a cat nap or a game of gin rummy with a crony in his office only for an especially important recorded vote.

During these years in B.C., politicians were not full-time members of the legislature. MLAs' modest salaries reflected that fact, and most of them of necessity held part-time or regular jobs at home. A year in the life of a provincial member was punctuated by sporadic party activity, continuous foot-slogging constituency work, and a short, usually controversial spring session in Victoria. Bennett believed that MLAs should spend most of their time in their constituencies where they could be close to the people, helping them with their problems: "Then, when they came back to the House, they came back fresh, with new ideas. You get them in there with these long sessions, month after month after month—they hardly know what year they're going to end in really!—with the result that they're all tired and they've lost their zip and they've lost their drive. Not being home amongst their constituents, they're out of touch. That's the worst thing that can happen in a democracy, in a parliamentary system of government. That didn't happen under my system."

Not everyone agreed with Bennett's system, and one of its most reviled aspects was "legislation by exhaustion." The B.C. House developed a reputation as one of Canada's liveliest and most entertaining legislatures, but never were sittings more infused with raucous and absurd behaviour than when the premier decided to break the back of an opposition filibuster by letting the members speak until they could speak no more—all night long if necessary. Bennett insisted that legislation be passed by a certain date and, if members were still raising objections or asking questions about the business before the House, he would make them sit right through. When a marathon debate ensued, it often turned out, in the long run, largely insignificant; as Randolph Harding of the NDP said: "After you've been sitting for long periods of time you get tired and a lot of things get by that shouldn't. It's no way, really, of intelligently legislating important pieces of business." Bennett defended "legislation by exhaustion" by placing it within the context of his system:

> There's two ways that you can curtail the length of a session and its debates. One way used in other parliaments is closure, which I never applied and never would have. That cuts the debate right off. I wanted to give people every chance to talk. So in any of the debates there was never any containment, and the hours were always reasonable, unless the opposition was putting on a very determined filibuster, just killing time, wasting the people's money and getting nowhere. I wouldn't have a night sitting the first night, or the second night, or the third night. But if they filibustered day after day with repetition, then I just let them talk all night if they wanted to, with no control on time. In all the time I was premier we only had five really late or all-night sittings. That's all we needed. It made for great efficiency in the House, because the government members knew that the premier meant business and the

opposition knew that he meant business, too. If you have filibusters, then you do the same thing that nature does—you let the storm blow itself out.

W. A. C. Bennett always had an adept House leader like Attorney General Robert Bonner to rescue him from the treacherous shoals of parliamentary procedure, but the premier was generally in command in the legislative chamber. He had a great sense of the House: he could be dramatic, or he could alter the mood of the House simply by going into it. He could usually be counted upon for an effective performance, but he was no great orator. He rarely completed a sentence; his vocabulary was amazingly restricted; he massacred rules of grammar. His agile mind raced ahead of his ability to speak and his words often sputtered out in a confusing, excited stream. In fact, it has been suggested that Bennett suffered from a slight speech impediment. This is not to say that he was a poor public speaker; on the contrary, the art of oratory is the art of influencing people and, in that sense at least, Bennett was compelling. The manner of his presentation was always fascinating. The mumbo jumbo of the delivery along with his indelible grin and chopping hand gestures, which were used to full effect, were set characteristics of his ritualistic speeches. Opposition leader Robert Strachan described the premier's performance:

> Bennett was a pretty formidable character in the House. It was very frightening at times, especially when he gave what we called his "flying fish act." He gave it about four times a session; he had it letter-perfect and word-perfect and gesture-perfect. The backbenchers knew all the cues and they would applaud and cheer and hurrah. He had all these phrases that rolled off and he was great. . . . He'd go on for about an hour and the place would be in an uproar. He would talk about the PGE railway as "the brightest jewel in our crown"; and "this little government . . ." and he'd go right through their history about all that they'd done. He'd go on about this awful opposition, that was "throwing sand in the gears." He'd have all the Socreds pounding their desks and their eyes would be sparkling and they'd be grinning from ear to ear. It was quite a show. He hadn't talked about the particular piece of legislation we were on, but that was all right. . . . It wasn't great debate, but it was a good circus.

Relatively speaking, these were genteel days when the power of politics in B.C. could be exercised in an atmosphere free from excessive partisanship and polarization. During legislative sessions Bennett and Strachan, or as they addressed one another, "Mr. Premier" and "Mr. Leader of the Opposition," would have a weekly cup of tea together. But like all successful politicians, back in the chamber Bennett subscribed wholly to the dictum of Dr. Samuel Johnson: "Treating your adversary with respect is giving him an advantage to which he is not entitled." When Social Credit cabinet minister Dan Campbell, in his early days in the legislature, said to Bennett that he was too hard on Strachan and could be a little more generous with him, Bennett cut him off: "Young man if you think this is a Sunday school picnic, you'd better go back to Sunday school. Don't stay around here!"

In spite of Bennett's traditional view of the limited role of the Legislative Assembly, possibly because of it, the B.C. legislature was more vital during the years he served as premier than it has been since. Legislative sessions were short, snappy events—the media was provided a regular, if seasonal, feast of some fine and some bizarre performances. Bennett's administrations were always successful in completing their legislative agenda, but the opposition parties also did a commendable job in their role as watchdog on the executive: both sides of the House understood the rules and limits of the game. One of the reasons for the vitality of west coast parliamentary democracy was the character of the members who populated the legislature. In the government front benches there was the striking contrast between Attorney General Robert Bonner—articulate, urbane, always well prepared, air of superiority and a ready laugh (though few laughed with him)—and Highways Minister Phil Gaglardi—the proven master of spurious bombast who frequently lifted the dome off the House with his booming voice and stentorian inanities. Until 1960, Tom Uphill sat in the opposition benches as an independent labour member. A legendary folk figure in west coast politics, Uphill was responsible for daily practical jokes; he once distributed copies of a Parisian "girly magazine" to his dozing fellow members. If a member was bent over in stitches, it was usually because he had just deciphered a handwritten message from old Tom. There was Robert Strachan, with his beautiful Scottish brogue and hard-working sense of outrage. In most other political cultures Strachan would have eventually become premier, but Bennett ensured his unenviable record of nearly a decade and a half as leader of the opposition. There were old-time Socreds like William Chant who each session could be relied on to make a major address on Social Credit monetary theory—during which the opposition ranks could be depended on to shout in unison: "A plus B! A plus B! . . ." And there was Bennett's old crony, Waldo Skillings, who finally made it to the House in 1960 and served as an amiable but quick-tempered government whip. Skillings, who had a reputation for fisticuffs, repeatedly challenged opposition members to "step outside." On one occasion, when the opposition was filibustering on the premier's estimates, Skillings and Bennett decided to have a cup of tea in the legislative dining room. An NDP member, upon discovering them, began to berate the premier for shirking his duties and relaxing when he should have been in the House. Skillings quickly rose, slugged the offensive member and shoved him down a flight of stairs. Surprisingly unharmed, the opposition member climbed back up the stairs and, after kicking Skillings with great force in the shins, rapidly retreated from the dining room. Waldo Skillings pursued at a limp but could not catch up. There was also the uncelebrated Agnes Kripps, Social Credit member for Vancouver-South, who aroused the House one day by proposing to eliminate the offensive word "sex" from west coast vocabulary and offered for substitution "BOLT"—"Biology of Living for Today." Her astonished fellow members could hardly believe their ears. "I'm bolt upright just listening to you," cried one NDP backbencher. Poor Mrs. Kripps floundered on, but a government member shouted: "It's okay for the bolts but what about the nuts?" Flustered and off stride, Kripps vainly tried to silence the wildly amused House by pleading to the Chair: "Mr. Speaker, Mr. Speaker, won't you please bang that thing of yours on the table?"

The various Speakers who served the legislature while Bennett was premier were accorded the independence and respect necessary to fulfill the duties of their office, though at the same time, one area that the premier was adamantly against was legislative reform. Procedures in the House had not been altered since 1930. Changes that were being adopted or experimented with in other legislatures were simply not considered. The premier liked things the way they were and made his point of view well known. He was opposed to instituting a daily oral question period and could not see the benefit of a regular *Hansard* service. Legislative committees met infrequently during legislative sessions, and rarely were matters of substance referred to them. Bennett could not see—or did not want to see—why the House should have the services of an independent auditor general when his own comptroller general was already inspecting the government's books. Nor could he appreciate the argument for improving members' services and facilities or increasing their pay—they were representatives of the people and should live like ordinary people. The opposition hammered in vain on the need for House reform. Bennett defended his stand on this issue:

> The questions that are asked in a question period are not the questions of the day; they are partisan, political questions asked for political advantage. The answers are withheld or, when they are given, are political answers—just trying to score points. They don't get down to brass tacks. Our system was way better than that. We would have a session of seven or eight weeks. The first part of the session is the Speech from the Throne and in the debate which follows every member can get up and speak as long as he likes and say what he likes. Following that we have the budget and the budget debate—again, freedom to say anything they like on the budget or anything else. This was a great avenue for new

ideas into the legislature forum. Following that you get into the meat of the session which is the estimates where every minister has to defend his own salary and department's budget and the premier had to defend the whole government. When I was there, the opposition would quiz me back and forth; they could get up and speak twenty times, not just ask one question but ask a hundred questions, pointed questions, which are the best. So it wasn't just a few little questions politically asked and politically answered at the opening of each day, killing a quarter of the session when we could be getting work done. Instead, most of the session was devoted to real questions and answers between ministers and the legislature. I wanted a system in British Columbia where we'd have good attendance every day, every member in his seat, every member afraid that he would miss something if he was not in his seat. I think that made for a better parliamentary system. I think independent minds would say that the legislature was more dynamic in those years than it has been since . . . we had a very efficient House.

We had the *Votes and Proceedings*, which are the records of the House . . . made every day by the staff set up for that purpose. There were no secrets in the House; it was all done openly; everything was recorded. The reason I was opposed to *Hansard* is because parliament must be a debating society and people must be on the floor of that House to hear the debate—bang, bang across the floor; that's parliament. The best parliament is the debating parliament, where everybody's in their chairs wondering what the next guy's going to say, making notes. The worst parliament you can have is one where a chap says, "I don't have to be there today, I can be playing cards somewhere, be anywhere, because I'm going to read it all in *Hansard.*" So the members don't go into the House at all; they just keep a few in there for a quorum, they pay no attention. So you've killed your thrust of debate; you've destroyed parliament. *Hansard* is destroying the legislature.

Of course, he did not allude to his own extracurricular gin games. Curiously, although his view of the legislature was a static one, and things like the lack of *Hansard* can be considered shortcomings, the House he was master of was a dynamic place. There are those who argue that since Bennett's day, the B.C. legislature has become a less relevant forum for government and opposition.

During the 1950s and 1960s Canada underwent a political and economic transformation which later generations are only beginning to understand. As a consequence of initiatives taken during the Second World War, the federal government acquired increased responsibilities resulting in an explosion of bureaucracy. Meanwhile, provincial governments flexed their muscles, guarded their prerogatives and competed with Ottawa's huge expenditures and public-sector growth. The country became less a confederation than a loose federation of semisovereign states. B.C. departed from this trend in one respect: W. A. C. Bennett competed by setting himself firmly against the new style of Canadian public administration. While his fellow premiers were institutionalizing their powers in bureaucracies, Bennett consolidated his power through personal control over the elected Assembly; he actually trimmed the provincial civil service and boasted that he ran a tight ship.

The rapid rise of British Columbia under Social Credit allowed Bennett to adopt his independent stance. The province may have lacked the comprehensive jurisdictional powers of a unitary state, but through controlling and developing its natural resources, it enjoyed governmental resources more appropriate to an autonomous nation-state: a provincially owned railway, steadily pushing into the northern interior; "Bennett's Navy," consisting of a modern fleet of gleaming white ferries; a miniature air force employed by the highways department, including a Lear jet used by the minister in charge; a giant public-owned power utility engaged in some of the world's largest construction projects; and a new provincial bank, though a scaled-down, privately owned version of Bennett's plan. While debate in central Canada raged over the neo-nationalism of Quebec's "révolution tranquille" the country seemed almost oblivious to the "quiet revolution" in the far west. The rise of French Canada had largely a cultural and linguistic foundation, whereas British Columbia surged ahead on the impetus of its expanding economy. But politically, the transformations in these provinces would produce a similar effect. The 1960s witnessed the further balkanization of a country at war with itself; provincial leaders were becoming powers in their own right, battling with the Ottawa mandarinate, determined not to be dismissed again as "hopeless provincials." In the long run, the separatism of the west would be at least as important a national force as the discontent of Quebec.

As premier, Bennett's relations with Ottawa were usually antagonistic, always controversial. He had inherited the long list of B.C.'s historic grievances which included: high freight rates, high protective tariffs, immigration policy, revenue-sharing policy, and so on. In particular, Bennett castigated Ottawa for shortsighted expenditures, failure to assist in west coast resource development, and "tight money" policies. At federal-provincial conferences in the 1960s, he argued that Ottawa should get out of the direct taxation field and leave it to the provinces, and he complained loudly about significant losses to B.C. as a result of transfer payments to other regions of the country. Canada's Pacific coast province has seldom been a beneficiary of federal policies but, at the same time, Bennett's cries of discrimination and neglect were always compromised by the fact that the "promised land" he so frequently boasted of was the product of a burgeoning economy. Nevertheless, Bennett flamed with righteous anger and criticized successive federal administrations for their narrow obsession with redistributing wealth rather than concentrating on creating wealth.

Another barrier between Victoria and Ottawa was the process of Canada's federal system. Federalism is largely finance; this necessary aspect of relations with Ottawa involved Bennett deeply and was the subject of his greatest battles. B.C.'s historic disenchantment with the east had a strong economic basis and, to that extent, B.C.'s separatism was the separatism of the cash register. On the other hand, federalism is legalism; this side of federal-provincial relations, with its intricate and time-consuming machinery of negotiation, was foreign to Bennett's personality and made him dislike the evolving diplomatic process. Normally, he left "federalism as legalism" up to Attorney General Bonner, while he hotly pursued the matter of his heart: money.

For all his deep differences on matters of important policy and his public hostility to the "feds," on the personal level Bennett was always capable of treating federal personalities to his smile. He has described each of the prime ministers with whom he dealt as "great men," and he built up trusting relationships with several federal cabinet ministers including Paul Martin, Don Jamieson and his favourite, C. D. Howe, the manager-mastermind of successive Liberal regimes. Louis St. Laurent, was "the easiest prime minister to deal with." John Diefenbaker "meant exceedingly well and he was a great Canadian, but he had terrible trouble in his own party."

> He took the Conservative Party from opposition into the largest majority in parliament that any party has ever had in Canada. But he didn't agree with his colleagues and his colleagues didn't agree with him; they would make plans and moves in cabinet to get rid of him. And Diefenbaker had brought them to government! Without Diefenbaker none of them would have had positions as ministers—but they couldn't see it.
>
> Diefenbaker was great on attack, attack, attack; he was great as opposition leader. But his training and background, in my opinion, didn't train him to be head of a country like Canada. That's the trouble with politics in Canada: there's nothing wrong with lawyers, they've got to be trained in a certain way, but they're not trained to administer. If you get one good lawyer that administers, you'd only get one out of a thousand. The average lawyer is trained not to make decisions, but to give advice. He'll say, "Well, this might happen, or this might happen,

but you—the client—have got to make the decision." We've had too many lawyers [dominating] public life in Canada. People think they can talk and make speeches, but they don't realize that that's only a small part of public life.

Bennett felt that Lester Pearson was a better minister of external affairs than prime minister. Bennett claimed that at one federal-provincial meeting, when he tried to persuade Pearson to assist with some B.C. development projects, Pearson said: "Mr. Premier, you've convinced me. You *are* getting the worst deal in Canada." But at the conference the next morning, he said he had been shown figures by his officials: "You don't really need the money. You're in the best financial shape of any place in Canada so, I'm sorry, you've got to just give more help to the rest of Canada." For his part, Pearson wrote in his memoirs: "While the British Columbia Premier always greeted me with the widest smile of anyone around the federal-provincial table, and was always the most cordial when it came to slapping me on the back and telling me what a fine boy I was, I cannot flatter myself that our warm personal relationship had much effect on Mr. Bennett's attitude toward the federal government when he got back to Victoria."

Pearson was correct. Bennett was, and always would be, strongly opposed to federal policies that penalized B.C.'s thrifty style of public administration and various wealth-producing activities. Bennett's reaction to Pearson's view was:

> When I went to Ottawa, certainly I would smile, because I was their friend, their genuine friend. I never fought with any Canadian prime minister, because my politics have not been based on personalities at any time. I made it a rule of my life never to fight people, only to fight principles and policies, and to advocate principles and policies, but never to get tied up to any hatred of any individual. We were fighting Ottawa's policies but not Ottawa. Irrespective of whether it was Conservatives or Liberals in Ottawa, they were very jealous of the Social Credit government in British Columbia, because we'd made such great strides. We were opening up a great empire in British Columbia and we couldn't afford to be stopped by petty argument or petty differences of opinion because some person was a temporary prime minister of Canada. Ottawa couldn't see the great development that was necessary in this province, which was different from other provinces. This mountainous province . . . had development only around the coastal areas. The interior of our great province, 360,000 square miles, was never properly opened up with communications. So I struggled to get proper highways and a railroad. My idea was that if we could get

co-operation from Ottawa on these kinds of projects, out of the development Ottawa would get the lion's share of the revenue; they'd get their money back many times. That was always my philosophy. I never tried to get money from them for money's sake. Other provinces wanted to drain the federal goblet; that's the reason they were afraid Canada might break up, because Ottawa wouldn't be able to funnel the money into the maritimes and into Quebec. I didn't try to get any money from Ottawa for that kind of reason, but only for constructive things, to build the province—not only to create jobs but to bring back revenue to the federal government and the province, but mostly to the federal government over the years to come. It was all on a good, sound business basis. Ottawa just wouldn't participate. They would always participate in the results, in the income tax, corporation tax, the federal sales tax, but they put none of the seed money in. That was the unfair part.

Robert Bonner, who as attorney general carried the B.C. end at countless federal-provincial get-togethers, summed up the Socreds' attitude towards Ottawa:

It was our impression that federal policy was not altogether sympathetic to British Columbia. We felt, in tax-sharing arrangements for example, as did Ontario, that we were considerably put upon, and specifically in British Columbia we were considerably penalized in the revenues which we derived from natural resources. I challenged Lester Pearson on one occasion about this, but the general reaction from the federal side was a shrug and their saying that this in effect was the way it was going to be. Most of the dominion-provincial relationships, as evidenced in the federal-provincial conferences, amounted to a scheme whereby the federal government would transfer wealth earned by Ontario and British Columbia—which was well above the national average—and just casually transfer it to other provinces. Not to people of other provinces, where it might have done some good, but to governments of other provinces where it bolstered bad revenue policies. For example, Quebec at no time got from their natural resources the type of revenue that we earned in British Columbia. But nevertheless we were expected to make up Quebec's shortfall per capita income by sharing our positive resource policy revenues with their negative policy revenues. It never struck me that that was a particularly equitable arrangement, although it might have been very neat from a federal point of view. So I think our attitude to the feds was, "Just stay out of our way and we'll run our own show." I'm pretty sure that the federal people were exasperated with what they viewed as a brash point of view.

That brash viewpoint was often seen as a latent—sometimes blatant—form of west coast separatism. In 1962 when the last section of the Trans-Canada Highway was finally completed through the Rockies, Bennett rushed in before the federal government to conduct an "official" opening and renamed the B.C. portion of the jointly financed highway "B.C. No. 1." John Diefenbaker wrote: "In British Columbia the Honourable W. A. C. Bennett, the Premier, a remarkable man, never gave us credit for completing the Trans-Canada at tremendous cost through the Rogers Pass. Indeed, knowing that we were going to have an official opening, he had his own opening for the province of British Columbia a couple of weeks in advance. I did not regard this as abnormal. This is politics." On a later occasion, however, Diefenbaker was less gracious: "There was one of the most peculiar, self-centered actions that I've ever known. For years the completion of that highway was a matter of national importance, and particularly to B.C. We paid; we set the date. . . . And he rushed in to celebrate something to which he had contributed little or nothing, except vociferous support."

Bennett, who was a master of the art of shifting the blame and accepting the credit, justified his action:

> These federal politicians, and I think Diefenbaker was one of the greatest of them, they'd collect the money from British Columbia, more per capita than any province in Canada—our money, our people's money—and then they'd come back and give you a little bit to share, fifty per cent of one road, and say, "Here, we are opening up your country for you." I could never follow that argument. Back in Prince Edward Island at election time if a chap was going away he would put a sign on his lawn: "Don't pave my lawn." Ottawa was spending so much money in these other provinces—no comparison, no comparison at all. It was only our fight for a better deal. In the United States on all the main highways the federal government spends ninety per cent. In British Columbia and Canada the federal government only paid fifty per cent, and then on certain short parts of the highway they paid a little extra, but it didn't pay one cent toward any other highway. We in British Columbia didn't want just one trans-Canada highway. We wanted a southern trans-Canada highway, the Southern Transprovincial Highway, right through Trail and through Cranbrook to Alberta—Ottawa didn't pay one nickel; a northern trans-Canada highway which was Highway 16 going from Prince Rupert right through to Jasper—which we built and Ottawa didn't pay one nickel. All the north and south highways—Ottawa paid nothing. The great Second Narrows Bridge, which is part of the Trans-Canada Highway—Ottawa paid not one nickel towards it. So we were negotiating for them to

either pay something towards other main highways, like they do in the United States, or have a share-cost on upkeep, because it's one thing to build a highway, but who is going to pay the millions every year for upkeep of the highway? Ottawa wouldn't pay one nickel. Why should it be called the Trans-Canada Highway if Ottawa wasn't paying one nickel towards [maintenance]? . . . So we just called it "No. 1."

This was politics. Bennett would often appear to be more a B.C. nationalist than a Canadian statesman. Liberal critics decried his "indifference to the problems of Canadian nationhood." In 1965 when he made the decision to formally identify himself as "Prime Minister," it only served to reinforce the image of the Dominion of British Columbia. Earlier that year, when one of his junior ministers revealed that the subject of separating from Canada had been discussed in cabinet, the province's urban newspapers rebuked the government with bold headlines and fervently nationalistic editorials. The minister in question, Ralph Loffmark, later said: "When they asked the premier whether I was telling the truth when I said the question of separation had been discussed in the British Columbia cabinet, he said, 'He's a minister of the crown.' And that's all he'd say. In other words, he didn't say that I had said anything wrong, or that he didn't agree with me or anything. As a matter of fact, he went even further and said, 'The gap is widening every day.' "

Was Bennett a kind of proto-separatist? Or was he just giving expression to the peculiar form of isolationism which was part of the Pacific coast heritage? It seems clear that he was simply exploiting a traditional western Canadian streak of independence and resentment towards central Canada, enhanced now by B.C.'s new economic vitality. Certainly, Bennett challenged many established assumptions about Confederation, but he was always talking about improving the country, making Canada a better place to live, and he often painted himself as a kind of supernationalist. In 1964 when he received the huge Columbia River Treaty down payment from the United States, he lent $100 million to Quebec on the basis of a handshake with Premier Jean Lesage. After making the loan, Bennett stated: "Where your treasury is, there your heart is also."

In Canada's centennial year, 1967, Bennett said in an interview with journalist Peter Newman: "Even though it doesn't pay us, we're great Canadians. The dollar sign isn't everything. We believe in the Canadian dream. Ocean to Ocean. Greater than the men who first dreamed it. When I land in Canada after coming back from Europe, I feel something different. It does something to you. . . . I give thanks daily that we're part of the Commonwealth, and if we ever did separate from Canada, we would become the Dominion of British Columbia and stay in the Commonwealth. . . . We're the only part of Canada that really could go it alone. We have year-round ice-free ports, favourable balance in world trade, and the necessary resources."

"If we ever did separate . . ." Even in the context of describing his feelings as a Canadian, these were the kinds of words that Bennett would utter to the despair of the various nationalist groups preoccupied with the identity crisis of the 1960s. But Bennett would always return to his basic position of faith in Canada; B.C. might be Confederation's chief victim but that would not deter him from deftly assuming the role of Canada's number one patriot. He enjoyed recounting this incident:

Mr. René Lévesque, whom I met at a number of conferences, was minister in charge of natural resources in the Lesage government of Quebec. He said to me one day, "Look, W. A. C., when you took over the British Columbia Electric, you showed us in Quebec how to take over our Hydro. You notice we did it, and we followed your pattern."

I said, "I didn't take over the B.C. Electric because of socialism or anything, because I'm the opposite. I took it over so we could have more development, energy. I'm not against private enterprise. It created energy for thousands and thousands of small private enterprises, on which my whole philosophy is built."

"Oh," he said, "I've taken it over for another reason. But that isn't the point I'm getting at, Mr. Bennett. I've heard you at these conferences, and I know that we in Quebec are getting a bad deal, but I know that you in British Columbia are getting ten times the worse deal in Confederation than Quebec. Ten times! So you leave first and show us the way."

I said, "Mr. Lévesque, no way! You don't leave your family because you have a disagreement. We will stay with Canada. Canada needs British Columbia, and it needs Quebec. If we left Canada we would be ten times better off as far as dollars and cents are concerned, I'll agree, but we would lose something. We have a great faith in the destiny of Canada and we think that all Canada would be poorer without British Columbia. As long as I'm premier, I would never do that to my nation. I'm out to build a stronger Canada, never to weaken it. No matter how I argue at these conferences, my arguments are always on policies to strengthen Canada. None of these arguments are personal."

It is interesting that the same kind of metropolitan-hinterland relationship that was behind western-versus-central Canadian political antagonisms also existed on a smaller scale inside British Columbia, between Vancouver and the interior. During Bennett's era, however, the age-old tension took on a decidedly different twist; for the first time, it was charged that the hinterland was too dominant over the metropolis. As B.C.'s largest city and head-office centre, Vancouver had held a commanding position over the vast interior of the province—though northward-looking politicians like Premier Pattullo had occasionally sought a new balance. With the arrival of a Social Credit government which drew its electoral strength from the interior and which concentrated its energies on developing regions well beyond Vancouver's sphere, the traditional relationship between metropolis and hinterland appeared to be reversed.

Responding to complaints that he discriminated against the populous urban centres in favour of the rural heartland of the province, he could be subtly mischievous. For years, many Vancouverites had suggested that B.C.'s capital should be in the province's chief city rather than inconveniently located on the southern tip of Vancouver Island. Bennett came up with his own proposal which caused Victoria dowagers to become faint, civil servants to shudder and Vancouver's business establishment to choke on their whiskey sours: he casually allowed that the provincial capital might be more appropriately situated nearer to the geographical centre of the province, Prince George. Bennett was simply playing the devilish advocate—one of his favourite political games—but during the wild course of his premiership he did succeed in opening everyone's eyes to the fact that British Columbia was much more than Vancouver and environs. That will likely stand the test of time as one of his most significant accomplishments.

Vancouver always maintained a special love-hate relationship with Bennett. Residents honoured him, cheered him, many voted for him and his party, and in 1965 he was made a Freeman of the city. At the same time, he was reviled for his government's supposed "antiurban policy." Vancouver City Council continually complained about lack of provincial financial assistance, and the business community grumbled that it was being ignored. A *Vancouver Sun* columnist referred to the city as the "unknowing silent partner in the economic surge." Naturally, the belief that the good fortune of others is also one's own does not come easily to the human breast, but Bennett did his utmost to show Vancouverites that the Socreds' province-wide development projects would ultimately benefit their metropolis. During an address to the Vancouver Board of Trade in 1962, Bennett said:

> Perhaps the best illustration I can give is to draw a parallel between Vancouver and the great river which reaches the sea here, the Fraser. Some of you may have seen the Fraser at its headwaters. If so, you will remember that where it rises 700 miles away, it is barely more than a creek. Left to fend for itself, so to speak, the Fraser might grow a bit, but it would still be quite a small stream when it reached the ocean. It is the tributaries of the river which make the river great. And so it is, I suggest,

with the great city of Vancouver. Undoubtedly, you would have grown in a modest way without a vast hinterland to support your growth. But because of your key position geographically, almost all the commerce of this great hinterland flows *through* Vancouver and *to* Vancouver. And therefore I want to urge you to think of development wherever it takes place in British Columbia as development which surely must benefit Vancouver, not just in the long haul, but immediately.

Many Vancouver-related complaints were political, the most heated emanating from Vancouver MLAs representing the opposition parties, and from Vancouver City Council where a succession of strong, popular personalities occupied the mayor's chair. Bennett and his ministers were never completely successful in persuading them that the city was the beneficiary of policies which seemed to favour the interior, and relations between Victoria and Vancouver were sometimes as strained as those between Victoria and Ottawa. Mayor Bill Rathie, elected in 1963, muttered after a trade trip to Europe that it was easier to get through the Berlin Wall than it was to meet with Premier Bennett. But the Socreds did not actually sacrifice the provincial-municipal relationship, as Robert Bonner, a Vancouver-area MLA, remarked:

> It really became a question of whether governments are elected to help other governments, or whether they are elected to help people. We were pretty satisfied in our own minds that the development policy that we were promoting in the province, and the opening up of the interior, the development of power and major investment which was being attracted, was securing a much more rapid improvement in the lot of people than would otherwise have been the case. I used to say that there was no money earned in the province that didn't eventually find its way to Vancouver, because Vancouver was the head of the place. People were getting jobs and opportunities in Vancouver and salary improvements; and we were witnessing an expansion of the city not because of what was going on in Vancouver, but what was going on everywhere else. Vancouver flourished in that period.

Perhaps another reason the Social Credit government received the anti-Vancouver label was precisely that the city was the most vibrant and rapidly growing conurbation in the province—if not the country: it became the most demanding region of British Columbia. Social problems, transportation difficulties and industrial disputes were endemic, and frequently blamed on the Socreds. The 1960s had brought the welfare state in Canada to full bloom; public-sponsored social programs were ubiquitous. Even as the different levels of government bickered over who was to pay, irresponsible politicians practically climbed over each other in the race to spend money for voter support. The prosperity of the period combined with the general reformist orientation of the media seemed to fuel an ever-increasing demand for new social programs. Governments generally responded by throwing money at problems—even imagined ones. This statist approach, which became fashionable in most parts of Canada during the sixties, was largely absent in Bennett's British Columbia. The Social Credit administration was branded by opponents as "behind the times" and "unable or unwilling to cope with the social needs of a growing population."

Certainly, Bennett's public expenditures were out of step with those in most other Canadian jurisdictions. He was not interested in building up a sclerotic provincial bureaucracy with legions of social planners; for Bennett, these were counterproductive activities which could only serve to stifle creativity and prosperity, or "throw sand in the gears." Yet by the mid-1960s, the priorities of the provincial government had shifted decisively. Throughout the 1950s the highways and public works departments were consistently the biggest spenders in government. Early in the 1960s, for the first time, education surpassed highways in total government expenditures. By 1965, when Bennett introduced another record budget of $446 million and declared his "Dynamic Society," the three largest departmental spending envelopes were education, with 34 per cent of the provincial budget, health and welfare, 26 per cent, and highways down to 18 per cent. The Socreds had moved considerably away from their initial emphasis on raw physical growth; in their own way, they were coming to terms with the fundamental needs of B.C.'s booming populace. Bennett proclaimed that 1965 would be "the beginning of British Columbia's dynamic society," built upon "the two greatest victories of all time, the victory of the Peace and the victory of the Columbia against reactionary forces on both the right and the left."

Social Credit had gone from a Blacktop Government to a Big Dam Government to sponsor of a Dynamic Society—but had anyone noticed the change? B.C. was obviously one of the richest provinces in Canada and received a comparatively high yield from its various tax sources, but, as observers would frequently point out, the provincial government still tended to spend less on its social welfare functions than did other jurisdictions. And despite significant changes in provincial spending priorities, many British Columbians were still likely to see the Socreds in their original incarnation as the government that Got Things Done, headed by an unapologetic "Boomer." Bennett would never manage to shake that image; it was reinforced daily in the local press and interpreted coldly, sometimes cruelly, by opposition politicians. Yet in spite of his stern, uncaring media-face, Bennett saw himself as a sort of political Robin Hood, compromising the rich, helping out the poor and, with the assistance of his merry band of Socred followers, building a Dynamic Society. Where was the truth in these discrepant public and private perceptions?

The power of politics is normally expressed in government policy. What, then, was the social policy of Bennett's Social Credit administration? From critics of the government, the facile answer is that it had none. The attitude of the premier and cabinet gave some credence to this impression. When asked to formulate the Socreds' social welfare philosophy, Wesley Black, who for many years held the social welfare portfolio, responded: "We are against the establishment of a Welfare State." This meagre guideline was translated into government policy whose overriding goal was "economy with efficiency." As a result, the average caseload of government social workers was ridiculously large, and in 1959–60 one out of every four social workers resigned. At the same time, welfare costs were rapidly escalating and the province's population was growing faster than that of any other North American jurisdiction. Wesley Black said of his experience as minister of social welfare:

> We were in changing times, a period of affluence. . . . But the lame and the blind will be with us forever, and the indigent will be with us. From somewhere had to come some common sense as to what welfare was really for. I had to take a tough but compassionate attitude. Taxpayers were complaining that we were giving welfare away and we had to have investigations. While the public was critical of welfare spending, so were my colleagues in the cabinet and in Treasury Board. Some ministers would make the crack, "Why don't we give welfare all the money and we'll take what's left." . . . You're not a producing department and you have to understand the taxation system and what the revenue system brings in, and balance that against the needs of the broad community.

Social Credit welfare policy was not made through some kind of legislative or financial oversight; it was deliberately designed by Bennett to both keep costs down and discourage waste and indigence. The premier was hardly the heartless man he was made out to be by opposition politicians; he was, however, self-made, and believed that others were capable of his success. At the same time, he came from a poor family and was determined that people would not go without the essentials of life or even middle-class comforts. Bennett was convinced that the rise of British Columbia would carry people to whatever prosperity they were willing to reach for, but he believed in the merit of personal initiative and steadfastly resisted a system whereby individuals who required temporary assistance became permanent wards of the state. Operating on a strict system of balanced budgets, the Social Credit government provided the basic services for a relatively enlightened social policy, but the financial controls Bennett exercised as minister of finance ensured that frills and government-sponsored social experiments were almost nonexistent.

Evidently, the Socreds' approach to social matters was strongly shaped by the premier's domineering will, and though it seems unlikely that the cabinet was ever seriously split on such issues, some prominent ministers did question the wisdom of their policies. For instance, according to Ray Williston:

> As a government we were far too conservative. I think that Premier Bennett really had to see the ability to pay for every program he initiated. Before he initiated a program he had to see exactly how that program was financed, not only for next year, but into the future. No program that he ever initiated had any trouble continuing, and he left a substantial surplus to be able to do this. . . . I honestly think as a member of the government that he was too conservative. He should have had a little more generous wage policy; he should have had a more generous social policy. I think we were wrong, and seriously wrong, when we had the money with which to carry out certain programs which should have been carried out. This is particularly true of some welfare programs, certainly treatment homes for elderly citizens—several things of this kind that we could well have paid for and didn't.

Health was one consistently controversial area of social policy in British Columbia. The Socreds had been elected in 1952 partly as a result of the previous administration's mishandling of the new hospital insurance plan. Bennett's government put hospital insurance on a sound financial footing, but the squeeze of population growth began to choke existing facilities, and overcrowded hospitals became a common complaint of British Columbians in the 1960s. Conditions were not helped by the fact that Bennett kept his old Socred supporter, Eric Martin, in the health portfolio until 1966. Martin was a likeable fellow but completely over his head in the complex field of health administration. It would not be too cruel to suggest that his single greatest achievement as minister of health was having his name in every public washroom in the province: it was attached to a health department poster, "FOUR OUT OF FIVE PICKUPS HAVE VD." Even here Martin received complaint; the poster was protested by a Vancouver Island family of five whose surname was "Pickup."

As with so many other government departments, Bennett unofficially carried the health portfolio. In 1965, a provincial medicare scheme was established which offered medical coverage for low-income groups. The plan, which was approved by B.C. doctors as "a very sane and sensible" approach, provided some impetus for national coverage. Bennett the nationalist promoted Canadian medicare, but with the ulterior motive of relieving some of the financial burden on his provincial plan:

> I give credit to the socialist government in Saskatchewan for establishing the first medicare plan, but it was opened up with great controversy with the doctors there—an awful mess. We were the second province, and we started medicare in a small way for those in need. The NDP called it "tin-cup medicare"—they held it up to ridicule. The federal government passed an act in parliament permitting them [the federal government] to come in on a combined basis with the provinces on medicare. What province was pushing stronger than all other provinces combined? British Columbia. Saskatchewan wasn't pushing it, because they had theirs; all they wanted was the federal government to pay a share. British Columbia wanted it not only for British Columbia, we wanted medicare for all Canadians. And we fought it out in the conference in Ottawa.

In 1968 nationwide medicare began.

Because of the tremendous population growth in B.C. during Bennett's years in power, education became another major public concern—and the needs were aggravated by the postwar baby boom children, now attaining school age. The Socreds seemed to recognize a top priority in education and from 1960 onward spent approximately a third of the provincial budget on it. The increase in education expenditures during the rise of British Columbia was astonishing: in 1952 less than $18 million was spent by that department, but by 1965 the government was projecting over $152 million for education—a whopping 850-per-cent increase; the entire provincial budget amounted to less when the Socreds first arrived on the scene in Victoria. Yet Bennett's administration was hard pressed to keep up with the demand for school construction, teacher shortages reached critical proportions in the 1960s, and the government was criticized for a "penny-pinching attitude towards education."

One of the important concerns was postsecondary education, and the Socreds were castigated as a bunch of country hicks unaware of the place of university education. Given his well-known disdain for "experts" and "technocrats," Bennett was regarded as an anti-intellectual, but to some he became a kind of primitivist hero. He secretly admired the most practical-minded graduates of the universities and, like most parents, he encouraged his children to pursue the education he had never obtained:

> A lot of people thought I was opposed to universities. I'm in favour of good, clean minds that come from universities. What I was opposed to was all the people in universities that just waste their time cross-piling

sawdust through a knothole, having no original ideas themselves on anything—just part of the establishment. . . . Where I differ with some of the so-called professionals is that they think that because they've got a little diploma, they're educated. No person is educated, really. From the time you are born till the time you die you are in a progressive system of seeking more knowledge, always more knowledge. And knowledge is education, not a few facts in a book: all life is an educational force. I think universities are a great force for good in our country. I'm only critical to this extent: they've trained too many people to be looking for jobs, for being employees, where they should be training a certain percentage of people who will be leaders, who know how to form businesses and create jobs.

In my own family, my daughter went to university; my two sons, Russell and William, by their own choice, chose not to go to university—but not at my suggestion; my suggestion was just the opposite. I did everything possible to encourage them to go to university. I arranged, from time to time, for different people in the university field to visit us in our home. One night at dinner, when I was strongly trying to influence Bill to go to university, I had this president talk to him specially. He said, "Now, Bill, in this period which we are in, in any line of endeavour, to compete you'll need to have a degree from a university. It's vitally important to you, because after you are out of school and into the workaday world, what are you going to do when these other people all have the special qualifications and you haven't got them?" I'll never forget Bill's answer. It was clear and crisp, and it wasn't a smart-aleck answer either—a very sincere answer: "These people will all be specialists. I intend to be a generalist. They'll all be specialists and I'm going to employ them." And the university president had no answer.

The Social Credit government was criticized for spending less money per capita for postsecondary education than other Canadian provinces, but it introduced many new options for postsecondary education. Trade and vocational schools were established; regional colleges blossomed; and two new universities—one in Victoria and one in Burnaby—challenged the monopoly of the stodgy University of British Columbia. The new Burnaby university, a cross-town rival for UBC, was the product of Bennett's imagination. Over lunch one day in 1963 with Dr. Gordon Shrum, co-chairman of B.C. Hydro, the premier expressed a desire to build a new university to serve the fast-growing Fraser Valley area; he asked Dr. Shrum to take on the task. The doctor could never say no to Bennett, and he became a one-man committee with the mandate to build an "instant university." Shrum located an appropriate site atop Burnaby Mountain and set to work on construction without a fixed budget, although he "knew how far I could go before Bennett would put his foot down." It was decided to name the university "Fraser University" after the great explorer who had first navigated the Fraser River, but Minister of Education Leslie Peterson thought that "Simon Fraser University" was a better name, especially for the acronym! Incredibly, just two years later, in 1965, the architecturally stunning Simon Fraser University offered its first classes.

Another still more controversial area was the government's labour policy. Branded in the 1950s as "antilabour," the Socreds continued into the next decade their practice of appealing directly to B.C. workers instead of through the trade union leadership. To a certain extent, the government had been forced into that approach, for the NDP had an alliance with organized labour, and labour relations became a major political concern. In 1961, the Social Credit government introduced Bill 42, an amendment to the Labour Relations Act, which prohibited union payroll deductions from being used for political purposes. Naturally, opposition MLAs and labour leaders howled in protest. The head of the B.C. Federation of Labour suggested a general strike would bring the government to heel. But the Socreds plunged ahead, passed the amendment into law and worried aloud about irresponsible union leaders threatening to sabotage the continued rise of British Columbia. Leslie Peterson, who held the difficult labour portfolio simultaneously with his onerous responsibility as minister of education, said of the political problems associated with labour relations in the 1960s:

> If we had never appealed directly to the workers, and had only appealed through the union bosses, we would never have been elected government, because the affiliation with our political opponents was at that level, and not with the ordinary rank-and-file union members. Their union leader was probably a prominent member of the NDP, and was in a formal affiliation with the NDP, and their major objective was to get us out of office. . . . The formation of the NDP made my job more difficult. You would wonder whether you could rely on [the union leaders'] sincerity or whether they were attempting to pull the rug out from under you politically. It made the job of minister of labour much more difficult to have either segment [i.e., labour or management] tied to a particular party. I remember I became very exercised when I phoned the head of the labour movement and found the number he'd left was the NDP headquarters. . . . Bill 42 was certainly a response to the action of the NDP and labour. Our existing law allowed them to negotiate into collective agreements a compulsory checkoff. That is, the dues were paid to the union on a regular basis regardless of the wishes

of the individual member. He had no choice: he had to pay. It was one thing to have to pay it to a union, another thing to have to pay it to a political party which he did not support—and that was what was happening. The union dues paid to the union were given to the NDP to support their political work. We had a tremendous number of complaints from union members saying, "We need our union, we want our union, they're doing a good job for us in collective bargaining, but we're not going to support these socialists, the NDP. What can we do about it?" They could do nothing as individuals; they wouldn't be able to work without their union membership. So that was why Bill 42 was born.

Bennett was always interested in labour-related problems—not only as premier, but as minister of finance. The economy of the province could be seriously hurt by work stoppages, especially in B.C.'s major industry, forestry. Labour peace was definitely in the best interest of the province, and Bennett was occasionally called on to intervene in a deadlock between union and management. Political opponents promoted the view that the Socreds were "antilabour," but in corporate board rooms the government was often denounced as "antimanagement." Indeed, the interests of government never strictly coincide with those of big business, and the point was never better demonstrated than during a labour dispute in the sixties involving the woodworkers union and the entire coastal forest industry. The premier and his minister of labour decided to quietly intervene, since the government could not afford the substantial loss of crown revenue from the industry-wide shutdown. After meeting privately with union negotiators in a downtown Vancouver hotel, Bennett and Peterson paid a late-night visit to the Shaughnessy residence of J. V. Clyne, head of MacMillan Bloedel Ltd., B.C.'s giant forest corporation. This secret mediation meeting was apparently brief but fiery. Bennett was convinced that the management side was dragging its feet; he called Clyne "public enemy number one" and threatened to make a statement the next day indicting the company as unreasonable and irresponsible if a settlement were not reached. Bennett's intervention was completely behind the scenes, but the records show that the labour dispute was suddenly resolved early the following morning.

Political power as practised by Bennett was used sparingly in the tense and dramatic atmosphere of labour-management relations in B.C.; however, it was a power that both labour and management were forced to respect. Peterson said: "I think that would not be the only occasion that we were regarded as antimanagement. The fact is that a government cannot be antimanagement or antilabour, and you can't be promanagement or prolabour either. You have to put the public interest first. That's where I feel one political party in the province and in the country is making a serious error. It can't work in the long run. It might have its short-term successes but in the long run that approach cannot be successful."

Bennett's social and labour policies seemed to be continually at the forefront of public controversy but, contrary to the assertions of opposition parties, they could never be justifiably labelled "scandalous." There were other areas to which one could look for scandal during this period, and these were usually well mongered, too. For example, there was the case of George E. P. Jones, who in 1965 was fired from his position as the provincial purchasing commission agent for allegedly taking benefits. If there was one thing that could turn Bennett white with anger, it was the suggestion that old-style political patronage had crept into his government's operations. In a speech in Victoria, the premier referred to the dismissal of the "Jones Boy" and, in remarks intended to be humorous, he said he could "tell more stories about him" but would not. Jones objected to the hint of wrongdoing and sued Bennett for slander. He won the first round in the B.C. supreme court and was awarded $15,000 in damages. Bennett appealed and was victorious; the award was dismissed. Jones instructed his attorney, Thomas Berger, a prominent labour lawyer, to proceed to the Supreme Court of Canada where in 1965 the $15,000-award was reinstated. Bennett paid the damages and preferred never again to discuss the matter.

A more bizarre and widely publicized case involved Al Williamson, a public relations flack who handled the government's lucrative PGE railway account. This was the celebrated "Dear Hal" affair. It seems that Williamson became indiscreetly involved with an international wheeler-dealer by the name of Harry S. Stonehill, "a blunt, beefy Chicagoan" who had made a postwar fortune out of shady dealings in the Philippines. For his efforts, Stonehill was deported from there; the deportation order, signed on August 3, 1962, by the Philippine president, stated that he had "defrauded the government," "committed acts inimical to the interest and security of the State effected through influence peddling and or corruption of public officials," and charged him with "economic sabotage and blackmail." Following his expulsion, Stonehill went briefly to Mexico but after being declared *persona non grata*, he decided to settle in Canada, setting up headquarters in Vancouver. Stonehill had a lot of money, but not much influence; he wanted to avoid being deported from Canada and therefore single-mindedly pursued his Canadian citizenship. After meeting the gullible Al Williamson, a plot was quickly hatched. An old friend of Williamson's, Hal Dornan, was working as an assistant to Prime Minister Lester Pearson. Meetings were arranged in Ottawa where an executive assistant to the minister of immigration wondered aloud about the possibility of Stonehill investing $25,000 or $30,000 in the Liberal Party.

An inquiry into alleged corruption in the federal government's immigration department involving the minister, René Tremblay, uncovered the Stonehill caper and with it a letter from W. A. C. Bennett to Hal Dornan lobbying on behalf of "our friend" Stonehill—who had quietly fled the country in January 1965. This was the infamous "Dear Hal" letter which Bennett denied signing. Apparently Williamson, who had access to the premier's stationery while conducting public relations campaigns, had cooked up the scheme with Stonehill and forged the letter to Dornan. On June 10, 1965, Al Williamson was sentenced to six months in jail for his activities on behalf of Stonehill. The Vancouver *Province* referred to the affair as "one of the most squalid and contemptible episodes in B.C.'s political history."

No government exists without scandal, and the independent manner in which Bennett exercised power made him susceptible to influence from external forces. Yet the most destructive scandals always worked at the Social Credit administration from the inside, almost as if to prove Bennett's cherished maxim, "Governments are destroyed not from the outside, but from within." The Sommers affair had hardened the Socreds of the 1950s to the depressing facts of political life. Throughout the 1960s, smaller controversies erupted from time to time, but the most enduring target of disparagement and political backbiting was the hard-nosed minister of highways, Phil Gaglardi.

From the time Gaglardi arrived on the Victoria scene, controversy had buzzed around his head like flies around a fresh cow-pie. Several opposition MLAs seemed to make legislative careers out of attacking Gaglardi—and certainly he offered them an enticing if fast-moving mark. In 1963, after a bitter debate in the House, charges that the highways minister was involved in a series of political kickbacks with various contracting firms were referred to the legislature's public accounts committee. Following six weeks of testimony the committee, dominated by government MLAs, found no substance to the charges, but NDP members referred to the hearings as "a farce and a whitewash." The peripatetic minister was also criticized for his sons' involvement with a number of companies which were allegedly buying up large areas of real estate along proposed highway routes. In addition, he gained widespread notoriety—and fines—for fast and reckless driving, and even had his driver's licence suspended. Bit by bit, those charges and his carelessness had a wearing effect on Gaglardi—a proud little man who adorned his office desk with an oversized leather-bound Bible and a replica of his controversial Lear jet. As time passed, he became a heavier and heavier albatross around the government's neck.

W. A. C. Bennett's relationship with the Social Credit Party was one of the few areas where he demonstrated ambivalence. Throughout his years in power he remained almost aloof from the Social Credit League. Aside from attending the annual convention and participating in the occasional party function, he never delved too deeply into internal or local party politics. He was a great booster of the various Socred women's auxilliaries and during the 1960s helped to promote a Young Socreds organization, but when it came to the league's inner workings, Bennett separated himself, as if they were church and he was state. In like manner, he insisted that government policy would not necessarily be influenced by the League, nor would he be committed to acting upon resolutions passed at its conventions. In 1960, he outlined his views on this subject in a letter to J. A. Reid, an interior Socred MLA: "I consider my position with respect to the Social Credit League to be an advisory one, because I believe that the strength of our movement is due, in great measure, to the autonomy of the League." Bennett did not, however, shy away from taking every possible opportunity to promote Social Credit in B.C. — the holy crusade would never end; he attempted to keep the flickering spirit of 1952 alive. Even after a decade and a half of power, he regularly signed official letters over the title: Premier and Leader of the Social Credit Movement.

Another area that Bennett steered clear of was party fund raising and election financing. Of course, each constituency had its own party machinery for gathering money, mainly individual donations, but a special problem for Vancouver-area riding organizations was the oft-heard: "Sorry, I gave at the office." This was a reference to the British Columbia Free Enterprise Educational Fund presided over by Socred party bagman Einar Gunderson. The educational fund was the central treasury for Social Credit election campaigns; it was a completely separate operation from either the government or the League and was funnelled through Gunderson's private accounting firm. The fact that Bennett's old friend and former finance minister administered the fund while serving in several government-related positions brought frequent suggestions that all was not right in the cloudy world of Social Credit election financing. Gunderson attempted to clear away the mist, saying:

> We called it the Free Enterprise Educational Fund for the simple reason that the government was all for free enterprise, and we had to educate the public to vote the right way. As a matter of fact, I think I thought up the name. Every political party has to have money for an election. You don't get elected if you can't spend money sending speakers around, putting up ads, advertising on radio. This was a fund which was established so people knew where to make their donations. The people who would make donations were the ones who felt the government was doing a good job, and wanted them back again. Some firms gave us $500 a year and others gave us $1,000 a year, just automatically. We'd

establish some arrangement with the firm, then they'd continue with their donation. We only approached people who were doing business on a province-wide basis.

Now, a minister or some member running in a certain constituency would have his manager collect from hotels, and maybe filling stations, and the general stores, and so on; we never touched those. We only touched the bigger firms... Then we'd use those funds for our purposes and also to assist some of those constituencies that needed money and didn't have it. The fund was looked on as providing money for the propaganda arm. We had PR men who did all the propaganda; all we did was pay their expenses. They'd have to submit their plans for an election campaign and we'd go over it, and if it looked reasonable we'd okay it, and then we'd pay for it. When you are starting an election campaign, you can't do it off the cuff: the newspapers and the radio stations require money in advance, so you had to have a fund ready. Otherwise, you'd never get TV time or radio time or newspaper advertising.

A funny thing happened whenever the papers would criticize us and bring in my name and mention this fund and so on. The minute they put an article in the paper about me being the head of the fund, I'd immediately get more donations from people. They said, "Gee, we didn't know where to give it before." So, trying to hurt us, they'd help us!

Einar Gunderson and the Free Enterprise Educational Fund were an integral part of a tightly administered, behind-the-scenes team which, under the personal direction of W. A. C. Bennett, set the election agenda. Although a variety of individuals worked for the Socred election team over the years, only three men consistently shaped public relations. Bill Clancey was responsible for old-fashioned hoopla and crowd control; Dan Ekman was the premier's speech writer and image-worker; Cam Kenmuir took care of the technical side of campaign advertising, most of which was funnelled through the Vancouver firm for which he worked, James Lovick and Associates. On a month to month, year to year basis, these three men had better access to the premier than most cabinet ministers, and they each became trusted friends of Bennett. Together, they were in almost complete charge of the extragovernmental side of the power of politics.

Bill Clancey was an outrageous kind of circus master, the man who organized bond-burnings and drum-beatings and ensured that Bennett never experienced what the poet Robert Frost once called the hell of a half-filled auditorium. Initially, Bennett was attracted to Clancey simply because he was so very unlike anyone he had previously met. Clancey was good at getting the crowds out, the bands playing, loudspeakers blaring and all the old-time political hype that Bennett thrived on. The premier had rejected a 1957 proposal by William Clancey and Associates to establish a more professional approach to government political relations, including an official press secretariat; however, he maintained a long-lasting relationship with Clancey, who became one of his favourite cronies. He usually accompanied the premier on the interminable safari of an election campaign, and could be counted on to do things like buy up dozens of Bennett-burgers in B.C.'s famous hamburger polls, wherein the comparative sales of burgers named for the leading candidates were used as an election forecast. He got into the occasional tight spot too. Late in 1962, an important Vancouver-Point Grey by-election sent the Liberal candidate, UBC medical researcher Pat McGeer, to the legislature for the first time. It was a hard-fought by-election, and on the final night of campaigning McGeer and Liberal leader Ray Perrault appeared on a popular Vancouver radio open-line show. The program went smoothly enough until the very end. Then a caller phoned in to ask, "Dr. McGeer, are you still putting needles in monkeys' heads out there at the university?" McGeer groaned, for he knew the harder he denied a story like that, the more people would think there was something to it. However, Ray Perrault smiled, for he recognized the voice of the questioner. "Folks," he said, "I would like you to meet one of Premier Bennett's public relations men, Bill Clancey. Bill, it was nice of you to call. Be sure and vote for Pat McGeer on Monday."

Dan Ekman was the first—and perhaps only—truly professional communicator in whom Bennett would place any trust. A former journalist and Liberal supporter who moved into the ranks of corporate public relations before his stint as the premier's executive assistant, Ekman provided the substance for many successful Socred political battles. He wrote the election manifestos and the copy for brochures and pamphlets and often travelled with Bennett in order to get a feel for his mood. Ekman generally counselled against saturation election advertising: "The old man, if he could, would have had in a forty-eight-page newspaper twenty-four full-page ads!" He also tried to make Bennett more available to the press and more congenial to the business community.

Cam Kenmuir, who took care of the mechanical aspects of election advertising, said of his relationship with the premier:

> I really got to know W. A. C. Bennett when he first decided to bring out parity bonds.... Through that, we became friends. I handled pretty well all the advertising campaigns from then on, in conjunction with Danny Ekman, who was the real brain in PR and advertising. I did get

the bulk and the cream of the government business, because Bennett trusted me. We travelled together. I was a gin rummy partner. We went to New York, to Europe a couple of times, to the Orient. I always paid my own way. I never received [trip] fees from the government. He didn't believe in that. He was a very tough man with the public purse. . . .

He had the team: Einar, Clancey, Danny—and I had the agency and all the facilities to carry out the creative end. We were Bennett's boys and we worked as a team when it came to an election. He'd tell you what he wanted, then he'd take a look at it and say, "Yes, my friend," or "No, my friend." He never nit-picked. He didn't interfere once a campaign was set. That's what makes good advertising: when you work for a man who knows what he wants, and you don't have a committee nit-picking. Headlines were what he wanted. You must remember that Mr. Bennett was first of all a merchandiser. He was a superb buyer, but he was a superb seller as well.

Bennett never travelled a full four years of his five-year mandate without calling an election. In fact, he established a B.C. political tradition of holding provincial elections every three years or so. Of course, the timing of the next trip to the polls was the most carefully guarded of the premier's secrets, but as his government approached the third year of a term, his PR men would automatically move into gear. This was the case as British Columbia entered the year 1966, and the spring legislative session offered many hints that a trip to the polls was not far distant.

One of the highlights of the session was the introduction of a bill to redistribute the province's electoral boundaries. Unlike the 1955 redistribution, this time Bennett had appointed a royal commission under the chairmanship of Henry Angus, a retired political scientist, to study the question. The Angus Commission reported in January 1966, recommending a reapportionment of the existing fifty-two legislative seats—additional representation for the greater Vancouver area at the expense of the rural north and Kootenay regions. The report also recommended the abolition of multiple-member constituencies. But the redistribution bill that the government brought to the legislature on February 15 ignored several of the Angus Commission's key recommendations: the number of seats was increased to fifty-four by retaining two of the northern constituencies; six dual-member ridings were proposed for Vancouver instead of the recommended twelve single-member ridings; and one dual-member constituency was retained in Victoria. Bennett explained: "My belief is that a government appoints a commission to investigate something and bring all the information out. But you don't have to accept that report one hundred per cent, fifty per cent, or ten per cent. You hold that judgement in the government. It must be that way. If not, these commissions would be the government instead of the government."

Bennett was especially opposed to recommendations that would allow the balance of power in the Legislative Assembly to tilt too heavily in favour of the populous urban centres at the expense of the resource-rich, solidly Socred rural interior. He defended the apportionment on three grounds:

> The rural parts of the province of British Columbia have always had more members in the legislature than the urban parts—and always should have. Suppose the citizens of Victoria have you as their member. The province has jurisdiction and [so do] the municipalities, where they have certain powers from the legislature; so your constituents have representation as well in their mayor and council. If you're an MLA in the city of Victoria you can get on a streetcar and go around your riding in an hour or so. In a rural area, it might take two or three days to get to parts of your riding. It's more awkward to represent it, more difficult. I'm opposed to dividing the province up into such small constituencies that somebody is representing a few blocks in the city: that's parish pump stuff, and it makes for Tammany Hall type of politics.

Needless to say, the 1966 redistribution bill was fiercely opposed in the legislature. Opposition leader Strachan charged that it had been written by two people—Gerry and Mander. Liberal leader Ray Perrault called it "political bossism of the worst kind." But perhaps the most significant protests were heard from within government ranks. On second reading of the bill, two Socred members whose seats were to be obliterated and a third whose riding was to be merged with opposition-held areas voted against the proposed redistribution. Under pressure from his own back bench, Bennett relented and moved an amendment to the bill which added another seat in the Kootenays, increasing the total seats to fifty-five. The Socred backbenchers were happy with the change, and the amended bill passed third reading without further internal dissent. While one student has concluded that the bill "brought the province considerably closer to a semblance of representation by population" than it was during the previous quarter century, it is clear that the 1966 redistribution was advancing a different approach to electoral representation—an approach later labelled "one mountain, one vote."

Aside from the highly charged redistribution issue, the 1966 legislative session featured classic paranoid flourishes, election threats and a goody-filled budget. On one occasion when the government and opposition clashed over a proposed re-enumeration for the provincial voters' lists, an NDP member pointed across the floor at the premier and said: "Look at him sitting there like a little Hitler." Bennett jumped to his feet to protest: "I'm not having any of these Communists calling me a Hitler." The newspapers were quick to label Bennett's budget presented on February 11 an "election budget." Total expenditures of more than $657 million were forecast, a whopping gain of 21 per cent over the previous year. The budget offered no spectacular revelations, but increased the annual homeowners' grant to $110, augmented medicare subsidies, raised civil service salaries, offered significantly more education spending, and slashed or eliminated a few nuisance taxes. The session ended on April Fools' Day amid predictions that an election was imminent. In early August, the premier announced an election for September 12, 1966.

Compared with the past few strident and costly provincial elections, the 1966 contest was a nonelection. The obtuse campaign lacked an issue and the Socred government seemed to lack a serious challenge. Bennett plainly wanted a solid majority of the seats in the new fifty-five-seat legislature; indeed, it almost seemed as if he wanted them all. He called on the voters to completely reject the opposition parties on the grounds that they were obstructionist. If the premier were to have his way, British Columbia would have been on its way to a one-party state. Of course, the Conservatives were already virtually extinct. Without the fire or promise of a leader like Davie Fulton, they managed to field only three half-hearted candidates. The Liberals, under the energetic leadership of Ray Perrault, were much livelier: with almost a full slate of candidates, they bashed away in their old-fashioned style. But Perrault seemed to be pleading more for survival than victory when he exclaimed of the premier: "He wants to create one great movement under an all-powerful leader. . . . A heavy-handed totalitarian system. Make no mistake." The NDP was the established alternate government in the province, yet they handled their opportunity clumsily. Robert Strachan, despite the schisms and bitter personal differences in his party, once again hit the campaign trail as leader of a mismatched but fervent crew of party workers. Their biggest problem was being so caught up in their ideological crusade and so steeped in W. A. C. Bennett's rhetoric that they undoubtedly believed they made a better opposition than government. Strachan was aided by the socialist party's federal leader, T. C. Douglas, who described the Socreds as "the most ruthless, arrogant, well-oiled, wealthiest political machine that ever existed in British Columbia."

By far the most interesting campaign was waged by the incumbents. In the past, Social Credit supporters had always been difficult to find between elections, yet on voting day the Socreds seemed to receive a great boost from their underdog status. By 1966, the change of mood was evident: Social Credit had been in power long enough to become accepted, and with a recognizable, popular premier who presided over a stable government and a flourishing economy, the Socreds could presume for the first time to be heavy favourites. This new position and altered political mood was reflected in the quality of candidates fielded by Social Credit in 1966. The government party standard-bearers were no longer old-guard monetarists, retiring tradesmen and "little old ladies in tennis shoes"; rather, there was a surge of new, formally educated young bloods—almost an "embarrassment of good candidates"—including five women, four doctors and several leading professionals and businessmen. Social Credit had finally come of age in British Columbia, but in addition, the premier made a conscious effort to revitalize and modernize the party. The Social Credit nomination process resulted in an unprecedented 20-per-cent turnover, with several weaker members and party mavericks being defeated in their bid for renomination. This led to opposition charges that Bennett was purging his party of deviationists and undesirables, but he was not engaged in that kind of housecleaning. He did actively encourage the infusion of fresh talent into the party but he also valued his independent-minded members whose rough edges and outspokenness were proof of Social Credit's populism and tolerance. As Bennett informed an enquiring reporter: "When everybody thinks alike, my friend, nobody thinks at all."

September 12 brought another impressive election victory for W. A. C. Bennett. Social Credit held steady with thirty-three seats and increased its share of the popular vote to 46 per cent; the NDP gained two seats for a total of sixteen and garnered 34 per cent; the Liberals elected six and received 20 per cent of the ballots cast. Bennett did not mourn that there were still opposition parties in the legislature; he declared that the election represented "the sixth great victory of Social Credit over socialism." He must have been heartened by the sight of several new faces in government ranks, including Robert Wenman, a Delta schoolteacher, Herb Capozzi, a businessman, sportsman and son of his old Kelowna friend Cap, and Grace McCarthy, a Vancouver businesswoman with a flair for political organizing—but much of the joy of victory was qualified by the unexpected defeat of Attorney General Robert Bonner in the redistributed riding of Vancouver-Point Grey. The Liberal tag team of Pat McGeer and Garde Gardom swept the new dual-member constituency and, in doing so, created a serious dilemma for Bennett.

Bonner's reaction to the Point Grey defeat was: "I had begun to feel that I had been there too long, and my suggestion to the premier was that I would really prefer to leave the government at that point. He was very keen that I should stay. I had received a number of offers from industry to go into private business, and they were sort of attractive to me. After fourteen years in politics you don't find it financially the best long-term occupation on earth. So I was getting a little concerned about what I was going to do for the rest of my life." Bennett was shaken by the defeat of his first lieutenant and persuaded him, as only he could, to stay on. He called for a government backbencher to step down so that a by-election could be held for Bonner. On October 27, William Speare resigned his Cariboo seat and the premier announced a by-election for November 18. Like so many years earlier when Bennett was forced to employ a similar manoeuvre, the city-slicker lawyer was being parachuted into the legislature via a rural stronghold. In the hotly contested by-election, Bonner won the Cariboo seat against a determined attempt by the NDP strongly supported by the B.C. Federation of Labour and party workers from across Canada. This election marked a new direction in campaigning in B.C.: intense party organization at the grassroots level. Following his victory Bonner warned Bennett that, in future, elections would be street fights.

With his renewed mandate and his attorney general reinstated, W. A. C. Bennett was again free to turn his attention back to the rise of British Columbia which proceeded at a terrific pace throughout the late 1960s; the high growth predictions advanced by Bennett in the 1950s, which were widely discounted at the time, were now proven out. His Two River Policy was already being justified by huge annual increases in demand for electrical power from B.C. Hydro, and investment in all major west coast industries reached, and annually exceeded, multibillion-dollar record levels.

A few weeks following the 1966 election, the premier's portrait graced a special fold-out cover of *Time* magazine's international edition. The "rare gatefold cover" was a reproduction of an oil painting by Henry Koerner which showed a pudgy-faced Bennett pointing over his shoulder to British Columbia's snow-capped mountains, totem poles, fresh water, lumbering and petroleum industries. The gesticulating pose was most appropriate; one *Time* reporter suggested a caption for the portrait: "This way to the bank." The American news magazine devoted special detailed coverage to "Canada Today: The Boom No One Noticed" and used Bennett as the focus. "No man exemplifies the spirit of machine-tooled pioneering better than British Columbia's Premier William Andrew Cecil Bennett, 66, full-time politician and part-time prophet," said *Time*. The premier was referred to as a man who "typifies the questing confidence" of the newly emerging class of provincial leaders, and western Canadian prosperity was labelled: "Bennett's Boom." The special edition of *Time* hit the newsstands just as the premier was departing for a European tour; at the airport he confessed his glee at this international recognition to a reporter: "I don't know how to express myself. It's extremely flattering for a humble little chap from New Brunswick to get in *Time*, not only in Canadian and U.S. editions, but world editions as well, it's almost embarrassing to go abroad. . . . This will bring tremendous results in British Columbia and western Canada. It will show the country to people who want to come and share in it. It will get millions and millions of new investment and new industries and it's all bound to be on the plus side."

The "humble little chap" gave no indication in the months after the election that his appetite for power had been satisfied. Both in his travels abroad and at home, Bennett continued to preach the faith of Social Credit and to glorify British Columbia. Despite a temporary setback in international markets in 1967 and 1968, the province was alive and growing like no place else in North America. The new oil and natural gas industries in the northern interior were drilling and building pipelines and the long-term construction projects on the Peace and Columbia rivers were providing employment for legions of construction and engineering firms. In August 1967, Bennett happily dedicated the 130-foot Duncan Lake Dam, the first of the three Columbia River Treaty dams to be completed. On September 12, the week following the premier's sixty-seventh birthday, he travelled up to the Peace River country to open the huge $750-million power project which was christened the "W. A. C. Bennett Dam." Normally, Canadians have waited until public figures leave office or die before monuments are dedicated to them, but Lieutenant Governor Pearkes and local Peace River enthusiasts pressed for the province's largest-ever construction project to bear the imprimatur of B.C.'s greatest builder. "For years, some people have been saying 'damn Bennett,'" remarked the premier. "It's nice to see it reversed for a change." Six hundred feet above the Peace River canyon, Bennett hopped aboard a giant belly-dump Caterpillar to release the final eighty tons of earth fill on the dam which stretched a mile and a quarter across the river. The dam contained 57 million cubic yards of fill—enough to build a nine-foot by twelve-foot wall from Vancouver to Halifax. Early the following year, when the diversion tunnels were closed, the Bennett Dam created Williston Lake, British Columbia's largest, covering 640 square miles. It was named after the premier's trusted cabinet colleague who had championed the province during the prolonged negotiations for power development. Bennett predicted that the dam, which was hooked up to a 574-mile transmission line to Vancouver, would bring "the greatest prosperity this province has ever known—*la dolce vita* for all our people." Gordon Shrum, B.C. Hydro chairman, exuberantly compared the premier to King Khufu and the dam to the pyramid of Gizeh, but, he added: "The Pharaoh went broke building the pyramid. We intend to make it pay."

Ever since 1952, the Socred government had been undergoing a slow but steady evolution. Changes in the players and occasional cabinet realignments had given Social Credit a new face which was often obscured by the overwhelming presence of W. A. C. Bennett. Especially after the 1966 election, a changed image was discernible to observers who cared to look past the premier's smile. The B.C. Executive Council was usually a small group, and because of Bennett's proclivity for doubling portfolios onto a single minister, the cabinet always numbered less than the total of government departments. The premier continued this controversial practice when instead of giving the health portfolio to a new member following Eric Martin's retirement in 1966, the department was added to the duties of Provincial Secretary Wesley Black. On the other hand, Bennett surpassed his promise to appoint a woman to the cabinet when in December 1966 he made all three Social Credit female members—Pat Jordan, Isabel Dawson and Grace McCarthy—ministers without portfolio. The premier imagined himself to be somehow anticipating the women's movement by the blanket appointment. In truth, he was being unnecessarily paternal, and thereby diminished the currency of Grace McCarthy, the only one of the three with actual cabinet potential or genuine political savvy.

In 1968 the cabinet experienced a much more serious change which saw the old guard clearly in retreat. First, there was the continuing saga of Phil Gaglardi. During the 1968 session of the legislature, the opposition hammered hard at the feisty highways minister with charges of land speculation involving highway access granted by the department to a company in which Gaglardi's sons were involved; and that the company's signs were apparently painted in the Department of Highways' sign shop; and that an ornamental wall had been constructed around a Department of Highways yard across the street from a motel owned by Gaglardi's sons; and that emergency work was done on Gaglardi's ranch by the department. The minister responded with a loud, emotional speech that brought tears to Bennett's eyes. He claimed that the charges were part of a sinister gangland-type plot to embarrass him and destroy the government, and spoke of a $25,000-bribe that was offered to someone to give evidence against him. The stream of accusations reached a high point on March 20 with revelations that Gaglardi's daughter-in-law had flown to Dallas, Texas, in the government's Lear jet. The following day the minister of highways tendered his resignation, but remained in cabinet as a minister without portfolio. Loyal to the end, the premier paid Gaglardi a tribute in the House: "British Columbia's highways will always be Gaglardi highways, even if we have twenty-two highways ministers. They talk about Roman roads in Europe but they don't compare to Gaglardi highways in British Columbia." Bennett, who temporarily assumed the highways portfolio, later revealed that Gaglardi did not resign but was sacked. When he heard reports that the minister's daughter had flown in the Lear jet to Dallas, "I questioned him about it," said Bennett. "He told me, no, his daughter was not on the plane, but he didn't tell me his daughter-in-law was. I took a dim view of that." It seems clear that the public scandal was only one facet of the Gaglardi affair. For several months prior to his removal there were a series of internal Treasury Board investigations into his administration, or perhaps maladministration, as highways minister. These studies were highly confidential and were never released but they undoubtedly contributed to Gaglardi's fall from grace.

On April 16, 1968, Bennett announced another cabinet shuffle. He surrendered the highways post to government workhorse Wesley Black who, in turn, gave up health to Ralph Loffmark; and Bennett's old bridge partner, Waldo Skillings, finally made it into the cabinet as minister of industrial development, trade and commerce. At the swearing-in ceremony, Bennett's "lips were quivering and he was blinking back tears as Skillings was sworn in." He admitted to reporters that bringing his crony into the Executive Council really represented no change, "because Skillings has been an ex-officio member of cabinet for some time as a close personal friend of the premier."

In the evolution of the Social Credit cabinet during these years, Bennett's ministers fell into essentially three categories. First, there were the large majority who handled their portfolios in a marginally competent manner. These were the quiet administrative and political figureheads who contributed to the image of one-man government in B.C., handling the small day-to-day problems, but rarely developing new policy initiatives; for all intents and purposes, the premier was *de facto* minister of their departments. This category included such long-familiar, now long-forgotten Victoria faces as Lyle Wicks, Eric Martin, W. N. Chant, Ralph Loffmark, Waldo Skillings, Donald Brothers, Frank Richter, Earle Westwood and a host of others. Secondly, there were the few ministers who were actually given considerable leeway in departmental authority and over the years had significantly influenced the direction of Social Credit policy. These were the ministers whom Bennett, because of proven competence, sincerely trusted and they often served as government spokesmen. This category included people like Ray Williston, Ken Kiernan and, latterly, Leslie Peterson. The third category was Robert Bonner.

Only Bonner was accorded the premier's complete confidence. Bennett knew that he was both cautious and intelligent; he could be closely trusted and he rarely committed even a slight blunder. Bonner was widely recognized as the heir apparent to Bennett's throne, but after more than a decade and a half there was no sign of an imminent or even an eventual vacancy. The question of succession was a touchy one. According to Bonner:

> We never discussed it once. I would have been interested in succeeding him, but at the time it wasn't something that was prospective or apparent. One of the difficulties was something I thought was an Anthony Eden-type problem. If you serve alongside a very well-recognized and successful leader, it's very difficult to think of succeeding him and being equally successful. That was Anthony Eden's difficulty. He was the longtime foreign minister associated with Churchill, a man

of very considerable talent. He eventually succeeded to office, but never quite got out from under Churchill's shadow. I recognized that as a problem and was never really too keen to try it.

Perhaps Bennett erred in never having forthrightly discussed the question of succession with his attorney general, but Bonner's 1966 defeat in Point Grey and further opportunities in the flourishing world of west coast industry prompted him to resign from the cabinet on May 17, 1968, to take an appointment as a senior vice-president with MacMillan Bloedel Ltd., the giant forest products company. Although he stayed on as an MLA, his decision stunned most political observers; even his Social Credit colleagues were shocked at the loss of the premier's right-hand man and certain successor. It caused another immediate cabinet shakeup: Leslie Peterson took Bonner's post as attorney general and retained the labour portfolio; Donald Brothers moved from mines to education; Frank Richter shuffled along from agriculture to mines; and outspoken backbencher Cyril Shelford broke into the cabinet via the agriculture department.

With Gaglardi's demotion and Bonner's resignation, the face of Social Credit was considerably transformed. Only a few of the original class of 1952 were left in Victoria and Bennett was the main source of continuity. Critics of the government predicted that it was slowly breaking apart, but inside the party there was a certain amount of relief over the signs of Social Credit regeneration. Gaglardi, for instance, may have been a continuing embarrassment for the government but his political popularity, especially in the province's interior, was still high. The loss of Robert Bonner, which was far more serious, was a devastating blow for the premier. Bennett had been able to exercise his power in such an easy and accomplished manner for so long in part because he could always count on the cool competence of his "bright young attorney general" to rectify errors when they were made. Bonner had never been a "yes-man" and Bennett would regularly discuss policy options with him before deciding on a course of action or announcing a new program. Without a Bonner to lean on, the aging premier might rely too much on his own judgement and be tempted to take unnecessary risks.

For his part, Robert Bonner experienced a kind of liberation when he stepped down. "It's like being out of school," he said at the time. The day following his resignation he made a Cassandra-like statement to the press regarding the fantastic rise of British Columbia he had assisted in and the attendant political problems and increasing expectations that the Socreds now faced: "We may have oversold it. Now there is a feeling there is no limit to what can be done. Everything has to be done at once. . . . There is a failure to relate our expectations with our capacities. We have deluded ourselves into believing that there is some sort of magic in government financing."

CHAPTER ELEVEN
THE GOOD LIFE

Everyone has his day and some days last longer than others.
Winston Churchill

The socialist hordes are at the gates.
W. A. C. Bennett

Premier W. A. C. Bennett loved his job. He was the undisputed boss of what he believed to be the best of all provinces in the best of all countries in the best of all possible worlds. He had achieved and maintained power by a great capacity for hard work and quick decisions. He slept well at night and developed the ability, not uncommon among hard-pressed administrators, to fall asleep for short intervals during the day. Most men wither with age, but in his sixth, seventh and well into his eighth decade of life, Bennett's output seemed only to increase. He appeared as tireless at seventy as he had been at thirty—still driven by a furious but controlled urge to Get Things Done. His working life span defied comparison with those of most other men.

Bennett described a typical day as premier in the provincial capital:

I would get up about 7:30 in the morning and have a quiet, relaxed breakfast in our apartment with my wife. We'd chat about our family mostly. We would not talk about the legislature. My wife never asked me what happened yesterday or the day before; we kept politics out of our home lives. We had our own group of friends which we visited, with whom we didn't talk of partisan politics. Our life was protected, away from the crowd. . . . That's the only way to last, I think. At about twenty to nine, my driver would arrive and I'd drive to the Parliament Buildings; everybody knew what time I'd arrive. Outside my office, outside the buildings, there would be the news media. They fired their questions, and I answered them. I chose these occasions, mainly, to get messages out. It was my belief that you can turn out press releases and they're not a dime a dozen, they're a dime a million! The media pays no attention to a prepared release. So when they asked me questions, I turned their questions around and got my statements out on other questions as well.

Ironically, Bennett's informal approach made it easier for him to manipulate the news media than it would be for latter-day governments with all their costly apparatus of communications advisers and press secretariats. In his office:

First thing, I'd read the press. Second, I'd get a report from my executive assistant and my secretary on things that were happening that I should know about and any special letters. The only letters I didn't want to know anything about were the crazy letters. I said, "Don't acknowledge them; just give them the treatment they deserve, right in the wastepaper basket! But proper letters you are to acknowledge only and then send to the departments with which they are involved. We're not going to answer their questions, and I don't want you to ask the ministers what the answers are. They must answer them themselves, on their own." So up grew the myth that the premier didn't answer his letters. My office acknowledged them; if I had answered them, I'd destroy my ministers. I'd be answering for the whole government, which would be very improper. After a few minutes of that, my deputy minister of finance would be ushered in, and he'd have all the figures of the day before, from all over the province, on all departments, on revenue and expenditures. So we knew what the cash balance was that day and how it compared to the same day last year. Are we running ahead in revenue? If so, what per cent are we running ahead on budget expenditures? Then I discussed with my deputy what correspondence he had, what representations had been made and if any acts should be changed at the next session, and so forth—general discussions on finance and how the economy of the province was going. Then I would see, perhaps, one or two ministers. I'd meet one or two or three delegations—it might be one person or ten people; some foreign company or an ambassador. It would have been arranged ahead of time, and would be all on my schedule....

I had very efficient staff, a hard-working staff. I had my executive assistant and my secretary to the premier. I had no secretary as the minister of finance—just the one secretary and the one executive assistant for both of my jobs. Then I had a stenographer as well, and a receptionist: everybody had to go through her office first. My driver acted as a messenger as well. That was the total staff.

Most days in Victoria, the premier would walk to the Union Club for lunch, just a few blocks from the legislature. Until Robert Bonner's resignation from government, he was Bennett's invariable luncheon partner, and the premier continued his noon ritual with a variety of companions. Like clockwork, he would leave his office at 12:10; the press would again be waiting outside his office with questions of the day, and Bennett enjoyed this impromptu bantering with reporters. After lunch, he would return to his office and pursue an afternoon routine similar to his morning. His office set an example for the provincial civil service to follow. It was busy, perennially understaffed, but an exciting place; it operated on strict business hours which were applied to all government offices in B.C.

The premier always left his office at 5:30 P.M. and made sure that his staff also left on time. He discouraged them from working late, arguing that they would be of no use to him in the morning if they failed to get a proper rest. Bennett would relax at his Oak Bay apartment where, most evenings, May would prepare a quiet dinner for them between 7:30 and 8:00. Together, they sometimes went out to visit close friends in Victoria for a game of bridge, but more often they would stay home and discuss family matters, perhaps phoning Kelowna to hear of their young grandchildren's progress. Each evening Bennett would follow up on the news of the day with the radio, television and newspapers and, before going to bed at about midnight:

> I'd devote at least one hour to thinking of things that happened that day, things I wanted to happen tomorrow and new policies. That's when I'd think up new things that I wanted to get out in the news the next day. I do my best work late at night, when my mind is clear; it isn't in the morning. . . . I always thought the premier's position in the province of British Columbia was the best job in the world. I never had pressure on me that we've got to do this, we've got to do that. I always said, you must not do anything ever in a hurry. You must have time to think things out. There must be no rush, or any appearance of being rushed, because it isn't how hard you work, it's how effective your work is. An executive is supposed to delegate. It wouldn't be the proper thing to do but a person could be a premier and minister of all departments, because an executive is never overrushed. He's not adding up columns; he's not doing the detailed work. While I was premier I was minister of finance, president of the railroad, fiscal agent for all crown corporations; I had a hundred jobs. I was never busy at any time. I had time to see my ministers and see other people. I was never overworked. If any person says he is overworked, he should be fired, because he's not equipped to handle the job. So it's a very simple job being premier, but you must not get rushed. You must obey three rules: you must never get

yourself tired—you can never make a decision if you're tired; you must make no decisions when you're angry or mad at people or provoked—walk away from the situation and come back with a clearer mind; and make no decisions when you're hungry. These are basic.

Bennett did not always have the services of an executive assistant. Ron Worley served in that position during the early years of Socred rule; Dan Ekman filled the post for a few years in the early 1960s; later on, the premier hired an old buddy from his Edmonton days, Clarence Budd, but more often than not he did without the services of an executive assistant, as did most of his ministers. Dan Ekman said Bennett's office "was run on the proverbial smell of an oil rag." But Ekman described his years there as happy ones, and said he never had a harsh word with the premier. Many of Bennett's colleagues and subordinates feared him, but they also respected and admired him—those few with whom he worked closely seemed to love him.

In an era before executive, administrative and special assistants ran rampant in government, the most powerful people in the Victoria Parliament Buildings were the secretaries, for they controlled access to the premier and his ministers and, with the best of intentions, could shield them from reality. For most of Bennett's years in office, his secretary was the indefatigable Katherine Mylrea, who said that working in the premier's office was "like working in the eye of a hurricane." But she enjoyed her job, admired her boss and gained a telling insight into his personality:

> The first time I took dictation from the premier was a harrowing experience for me. He spoke very rapidly and was inclined to change his mind in midsentence; it was quite a while before I lost my feeling of trepidation when the intercom buzzed and he'd say, "Will you bring in your book please, Mrs. Mylrea!" . . . He had such a sense of humour. He just loved, when he was away, to phone us, and I would answer and say, "Premier's Office." He'd say, "Oh, I'm glad to see you're working today," disguising his voice. One time I thought it was some wag trying to get a rise out of me and I said, "Oh, go and take a jump in the lake." And this voice says, "Yes my dear, I will." It was the premier!

W. A. C. Bennett was a parsimonious premier whose attitude towards the public purse would be considered quaint and old-fashioned by today's profligate standards. His only indulgence was the chauffeur-driven Cadillac which carried him about during working hours. Otherwise, Bennett was a constant scrooge. The $26,000 annual salary he collected hardly covered the cost of his property taxes and living expenses. One of Katherine Mylrea's duties was to prepare the vouchers covering his travelling expenses:

The premier would only claim the bare necessities of the government allowance, and of course in his position he had to do a certain amount of entertaining. He wouldn't charge for taxis or gratuities when he was entitled to do so. Sometimes the cheque we got back from the audit office wouldn't even cover his hotel bill, and at first I really hated to tell him about it because I didn't think he should have to be spending his own money while on government business. But then it became a game with us. I would say, "Mr. Premier, I'm afraid this cheque isn't enough to cover . . ." And he would look at me plaintively and say, "What? Again?" Then he would pretend to be reluctant about taking out his wallet, but as he passed the cash over he always did so with a big smile and a twinkle in his eyes. Another example of his attitude concerned the furnishings: it was an office befitting a premier, that is, handsome, plain, dignified, but getting a little shabby withal as to the leather chairs, but more especially the draperies which had been up there since time began. Several times I suggested that perhaps we might do something about it, but he'd always say, "No, no, my dear, we can't spend money on such fripperies!"

Bennett's forthright and folksy approach to government was at odds with the best contemporary models of public administration. Few agreed with his system, but even fewer could deny that it worked. He succeeded in centralizing to a remarkable extent in his person all the forces that play decisive roles in public policy making, and he carried it off in an easy and accomplished manner. Curiously, the small-town hardware merchant had the knack of a great executive when it came to delegating authority. His subordinates quickly learned that once the premier had established a policy in their area of authority, the details of implementing it were strictly up to them. All he was concerned with was that it get done. His one-time executive assistant, Dan Ekman, observed: "He ran a very simplistic government, but simplistic only with respect to numbers. He wouldn't spend a nickel of public money on any of what are now considered to be essential trappings or depth of staff. By the same token, it did not follow that he did it all himself; he delegated like mad. . . . He was very good at delegating; too damn good."

Bennett managed by objectives before business consultants or public administration theorists understood that concept. But he also ruled in an era when a comfortable margin for error existed in areas of public policy; he took advantage of this flexibility and often made immediate decisions with little or no consultation. He developed his famous "second look" approach to most matters of government activity, being willing to change horses in midstream since admission of error was to him a lesser evil than failure to adapt to the changing circumstance or public mood. Above all, Bennett was a political leader with a special genius for conjuring visions that the individual citizen could share. He painted a large picture of B.C. which had room for everyone's hopes and ambitions. As premier, he never portrayed himself as a delegate of the people; rather, he presented himself as their trustee. In the best Burkean tradition he wielded the powers of government in pursuit of his entrusted mission, and his success as a politician can be judged by the number of times his trusteeship was re-endorsed by the voters. In defining his mission as theirs, he came close to achieving the ultimate illusion of democratic personification.

In retrospect, W. A. C. Bennett's means would become as controversial as his ends. Political scientists will long debate the relative merits of his day-to-day microadministration. As premier and minister of finance his control was so complete that civil servants required his signature before they could travel outside the province; when he wanted to temporarily tighten the screws on government spending, long-distance phone calls needed his approval in advance! Paper flow in Victoria was kept to an absolute minimum while he was in office. Others might write and distribute memos; he made decisions. He preferred to obtain information from people rather than from briefs or voluminous reports, and if he wanted to persuade someone to see things his way, he would not send a letter but believed in the efficacy of nose-to-nose contact. In person, Bennett could be very persuasive, possessing an uncanny ability to inspire confidence and transmit his sense of purpose. The most determined resistance would usually break down in face of the premier's enthusiasm. The cleverer the individual, the sharper the tool he became in Bennett's hands.

The Social Credit government did not evolve much in organization or style during the long course of Bennett's stewardship. The basic system he had established in the early 1950s continued with little modification, save for the different faces appearing around the cabinet table. Bennett would never seriously consider introducing elaborate planning, programming or budgeting systems for the provincial government; he had no desire to modify or diminish the power he had so carefully accumulated. The cabinet remained a very simple structure which revolved around the premier. Control of money was very tight but policy control did not exist in any formal sense, and ministers were actually given great leeway to both determine and carry out policies, so long as they stayed within their budgets and did not get into trouble. The system worked because it was based upon specific and limited goals which required no sophisticated bureaucratic processes or interdepartmental communication, and it all hinged on Bennett's authority and his ability to delegate.

The persons whom Bennett relied upon, who acquired the power of decision making under his system, shared certain qualities: they had a capacity for hard work, for subservience and for complete loyalty. They were dedicated, often faceless and yet possessed considerable power. Not all of them were members of cabinet. Bennett's system was to simply appoint a reliable and sympathetic manager and watch the project come to completion. The government succeeded in achieving most of its large goals because of the few outstanding individuals who made it succeed and the many mediocre persons who did not get in the way. In a 1967 interview, the premier elucidated: "I believe in picking the right man for the job and then letting him get on with it. . . . My cabinet ministers and the heads of the crown corporations are all chosen so that they can get on with developing the business of their department or corporation. . . . That means I get the right men and they can follow the agreed general policy, but it leaves me free to take the long look."

Certain key bureaucrats and heads of crown corporations possessed considerably more authority than most Social Credit cabinet ministers, but generally speaking this was a time when elected politicians were in control and a healthy distrust of bureaucracy prevailed. Bennett may have relied on his deputy minister of finance, and some of his ministers worked very closely with and depended on their top officials, but senior B.C. civil servants always knew who was in charge. Minister of Municipal Affairs Dan Campbell said inelegantly of his relationship with his deputy minister: "He knew if he goofed he was gonna get his tits in the wringer." Minister of Agriculture Cyril Shelford commented: "I certainly would never exchange the loyalty or services of my secretary for my deputy minister."

With Bennett at its head, the tightly administered British Columbia government resembled more a monarchic than a democratic state. But if Bennett possessed a certain easy, spontaneous imperiousness, he worked harder to maintain his power than any monarch ever did. He had a tremendous capacity for concentration; his underlings were frequently amazed at how much he knew about the details of departmental budgets. Although he maintained a sweeping overview of the government's operations and objectives, he could also recite detailed facts and statistics which he had lived with and absorbed. On issues he deemed important, he had a memory like an elephant. His was not, however, an analytic mind; rather, he saw intuitively into personalities and politics and reached conclusions by a short cut. For his ministers and senior officials, this made him often extremely difficult to deal with. He was keen, clever and very quick, but had no great power of reasoning to conclusions or of explaining them to others: he would circle among random facts to swoop down on the essentials of a problem while his associates had yet to postulate it. Many of his cabinet colleagues never felt comfortable with the premier's intuitive faculties — nor did he want them to be comfortable.

Bennett worked constantly at keeping his cabinet ministers in what he considered to be their proper places. He inspired them and made them feel that what they were doing was vitally important for the welfare of British Columbia, but he reinforced that he, and only he, was the boss. He could be caustic, too, and would regularly catch his ministers off guard with blunt questions about their department operations or even details of their personal lives. Ray Williston commented on the premier's approach to cabinet meetings: "I've never seen in my life a man who could pick out the weak point of your argument or the weak point of your presentation and stick a needle in it immediately and make you squirm. If you started to argue and you were on weak ground, he could get pretty sharp, pretty fast, and some people used to react negatively."

Why was Bennett so tough on his cabinet? He could afford to relax a little; his position was secure, his government machine was purring smoothly, and the power of his politics was unquestioned. Perhaps he felt it was a matter of discipline, or possibly it was just an element of his political style, but he kept on top of things and made sure his Social Credit teammates did not emerge from his shadow. One reason behind Bennett's continued strong-man approach was also the favourite subject of political conversation in British Columbia: "the succession." He had been in power longer than any other premier in the province's history and was getting on in years. Surely he would soon step down? Quietly, ever so quietly, the jockeying for position in a prospective leadership race had commenced within the ranks of Social Credit. Bennett's toughness was, at least in part, an effort to keep a lid on the struggle to succeed him.

The final proof that Bennett's was a one-man administration is the absence of any timely effort to prepare a successor. Robert Bonner had been the premier-in-waiting for years, but with his resignation from the cabinet in 1968 the field was left open to a variety of contenders and pretenders to the throne. The problem for Social Credit was that, after Bonner, those touted as potential leaders were second-stringers. From the ranks of cabinet there were Attorney General Leslie Peterson, Dan Campbell of municipal affairs, Ray Williston of lands and forests, Ralph Loffmark of health, and the incorrigible Phil Gaglardi. In addition, there were young, ambitious Socred backbenchers like Herb Capozzi and Robert Wenman. No doubt, the opposition parties wanted to see Gaglardi as Social Credit leader; he would have been easily the most abrasive and vulnerable choice. Bennett knew that a "Premier Gaglardi" would have spelled the end of Social Credit in B.C. and, realizing that his former highways minister was itching to fill his shoes, he did his best to block him. Bennett indicated his new attorney general, Leslie Peterson, as his first choice for a successor and even left confidential instructions to that effect in the vault of his Victoria office in the event that something unexpected happened to him. Unfortunately, Peterson would never emerge as an obvious front-runner; health problems and the continuing dominance of the premier prevented the new attorney general from establishing leadership credentials.

A wealthy man, with a spectacular career behind him, Bennett could have easily retired to enjoy his later years in the peace of the Okanagan Valley, but apparently he did not want that, and even if he had, Bennett could not let go, for how could he ensure what and who would follow? After the 1966 election he began to consider the question of his retirement, but he gave not the slightest hint, public or private, that he was planning to step down. In the autumn of 1968 when the matter of setting up the machinery for a potential leadership review was raised at the Social Credit annual convention, it was embarrassingly laughed off the agenda. Privately, Bennett had decided to run one more time; he was convinced that he alone could keep Social Credit in power in British Columbia. He had learned of an elaborate, confidential Liberal public opinion poll conducted in the summer of 1968 to assess John Turner's chances as leader of the B.C. Liberal Party. The survey showed that Turner would be a better choice than any known B.C. Liberal, but that he would not have a chance against a Social Credit Party led by Bennett: "The public rates W. A. C. Bennett as their first choice for Premier. Turner, however, rates strongly in this respect. When W. A. C. Bennett is not in the running, Turner is preferred over Peterson who is the other Social Credit member balloted. . . ."

Bolstered by this intelligence, the premier persuaded himself that it was his duty to stay on. He publicly dismissed the suggestion that he would retire ever. In the spring of 1969 he admitted: "Yes, I'm 68. But when I was a boy I was too poor to smoke, so knock off ten years. That makes me 58. And since I have never developed a drinking habit, you can knock off ten more years. So I'm 48 — in the prime of my life. Retire? Retire to what?" In November of that year, after he had turned sixty-nine — or was it forty-nine? — when he seemed to be actively promoting Leslie Peterson, "the brilliant young member of my cabinet," as his successor, a reporter told Bennett that his action was the "clearest indication yet" of his retirement. The premier answered with a smile: "My friend, I have no intention of retiring. Like a brook I am going to go on and on forever. . . ."

In the late 1960s British Columbia prospered, enjoying what Bennett liked to call the Good Life. Riding the crest of a huge wave of international economic expansion, it was the envy of other Canadian provinces and boasted the highest growth rates in all North America. Unemployment fluctuated, but at consistently low levels; personal income rose annually by ten-per-cent leaps; retail trade levels soared; housing starts climbed rapidly and still could not keep up with the influx of middle-class newcomers. The economic surge showed no signs of ending, for there were several new megaprojects afoot: a $50-million railway extension into the north; a $150-million pipeline expansion by Westcoast Transmission Company; a multimillion-dollar expansion program by Alberta Natural Gas; new investments in the forest industry estimated at $200 million; and the huge Roberts Bank deep-sea superport under construction just outside Vancouver to handle hundreds of millions of dollars of Kootenay coal being sold to Japan. One of the most important features of this period was British Columbia's developing Pacific presence; Canada was only beginning to realize that it was a Pacific as well as an Atlantic nation. Bennett promoted his province throughout the Pacific Rim and made special overtures to the resource-hungry Japanese who often showed a keener understanding of B.C.'s development potential than did central Canadians. Always the publicist, Bennett declared: "There are great mountains separating British Columbia from Ottawa, but between us and Japan there is only the peaceful sea."

External economic conditions and the growing demand for B.C.'s resources made for happy times and booming budgets. On February 7, 1969, Bennett brought down what he called "The Social Credit Miracle Dividend Budget" which forecast provincial expenditures for the first time exceeding $1 billion. The budget, which of course was balanced, showed an anticipated 18-per-cent increase in overall spending with not a penny increase in taxes. By far the largest spending area was education, with 32 per cent of the total budget; health and welfare expenditures were increased by 33 per cent over the previous year; special perpetual funds were established for the province's native peoples and for natural disaster relief, and a fifty-storey government office tower was planned for Vancouver. Perhaps the most innovative scheme was an attempt to beat the housing pinch with a $5,000 government-sponsored second mortgage at cut-rates for anyone building a new home. Boasted the premier: "This is the only place in Canada, maybe in all North America, where everybody will now be able to buy a home if they have any income at all."

The billion-dollar budget of 1969 must have been mind-boggling to those who could recall the first Social Credit budget speech of 1953 which waxed enthusiastic about total government expenditures of $174 million. The province's growth under Bennett was truly remarkable, and his long line of ever-increasing but carefully balanced budgets was the primary obstacle to political opponents of Social Credit. The fact that by 1969 B.C.'s contingent liabilities totalled more than $2 billion did not deter a population only too eager to believe in Bennett's boosterism. After seventeen years in power, Canada's senior premier declared: "Today, British Columbia is the No. 1 *have* province in the nation. . . . No other government with only 2 million people can do what we are doing." In the spring of 1969, in what was widely believed to be the kickoff for a provincial election, the premier embarked on a 10,000-mile grandstanding tour of the province showing audiences of all sizes a controversial government-commissioned film, a glossy review of the rise of British Columbia. Its title was— what else—"The Good Life."

Bennett's Good Life defied contemporary mainstream economic thought and ran counter to the practice of elected politicians in other jurisdictions. At a time when deficits were rising in virtually all other Canadian provinces, Bennett managed balanced budgets. Most postwar western governments accepted a misinterpretation of the economic theory of J. M. Keynes which abused his concept of the "stimulative deficit." Bennett was commonly seen as an old-fashioned fiscal purist, but he described himself as a "true Keynesian"—he believed that governments should build up surpluses in the good years and, if necessary, spend on a deficit basis in lean times; he did not believe in deficit spending in boom times and severely castigated the common policy of other governments to stimulate even the booming economies of the 1960s. Bennett claimed that this profligate misuse of public funds could only bring dangerous overstimulation and an inability to deal with an eventual serious economic downturn.

Bennett's Good Life was founded upon a lean and waste-conscious approach to government; he never altered the spare style he initiated in the early 1950s. He had called for restraint as early as the mid-1960s and constantly argued that Ottawa's fiscal policies were irresponsible and, if unchecked, would lead to runaway inflation. His outbursts were viewed as simplistic reactions to an increasingly complex world; he was so unlike the new generation of political leaders who spoke righteously against inflation and excessive government spending but in practice steered the opposite course. Bennett's calls for restraint during the booming sixties would be echoed by helpless politicians in the decades to come, when it became a fairly accepted economic tenet that government deficits were a major contributor to inflation.

Many British Columbians, in particular, the highly politicized labour movement, were not certain that they shared the Good Life. The continuing war between the provincial government and the west coast union leadership was intensified in 1968 with the passage of the Mediation Commission Act. Known as Bill 33, the act ignored some of the key recommendations of a major report on industrial relations by Justice Nathan Nemetz and established a new kind of mediation machinery, a modified form of compulsory arbitration to be applied at the discretion of cabinet, a virtual ban on strikes in the public service, and heavy penalties for contravention of the act. Bill 33 met with fierce opposition from the NDP and labour leaders who referred to it as the death knell of free collective bargaining. The B.C. Federation of Labour launched a vitriolic campaign against the measure; there was talk of a general strike and a boycott of the new mediation commission. However, the government had shrewdly staffed the new commission with prominent unionists, a move that gave it some credibility and made the screams of the left-wing labour leadership appear paranoid.

The biggest problem for the B.C. Federation of Labour was its domination by reactionary pork-choppers who, because of their constant complaints of persecution and hardship, were simply no longer believable. The historic struggle between labour and capital in British Columbia was not the emotion-stirring mismatch it had once been. Labour was now a powerful, well-informed and well-financed force, allied with an established political party which had a good chance of becoming government.

The biggest problem for the NDP was that it was seen increasingly as a labour-dominated socialist party with a radically different vision of the Good Life. This not inaccurate image was strongly reinforced when in the spring of 1969 the NDP selected a new leader, Thomas Berger, a prominent young labour lawyer. In shedding the experienced but unsuccessful Robert Strachan, the socialists were hoping to achieve not only a new face but a new approach against Social Credit. Berger had challenged Strachan once before, in 1967, but had been beaten by long, bitter infighting. When Strachan finally resigned, the contest came down to a close race between Berger and David Barrett, a folksy, young former social worker. At the April 1969 leadership convention, Berger edged out Barrett by a handful of votes on the second ballot, and his victory was seen as a triumph for the outspoken labour wing of the socialist party. At the same time, Berger projected a youthful, moderate look which was felt to be in tune with the era.

Were Bennett and the Socreds worried about a new challenge from the left? Many government members were extremely uneasy about Berger's unknown effect, but Bennett told British Columbians that his selection marked a distinct turn to the left for the NDP and he predicted that in the next election voters would have to decide whether they wanted to be guided by "the heavy hand of state socialism." The Socreds were fighting another, more insidious enemy, their own complacence; they had been in office so long and had been so successful with the same leader that it was difficult to get the troops fired up for another electoral battle. In August 1968, the premier wrote to all Social Credit MLAs: "The latest survey shows the Government in most districts now riding very high, but we must not take anything for granted, and I would ask you to have meetings with your local organization and have a drive for membership. The aim should be ten per cent of the voters' list." In January 1969, Ken Kiernan presented a confidential report to cabinet on policy matters which listed alarming deficiencies in the government's operations: "Our public information machinery is in poor shape.... Our distribution is inadequate and we are continually being attacked, often over little points that we could eliminate. . . . We lack proper coordination. . . . We are not devoting enough time as a Cabinet to policy matters. . . ." But the premier made no great effort to alter their course before the next election. Never afraid to gamble, he believed he could win one more time. Speaking to his political opponents, who were all a generation younger than he, Bennett said: "You and I can both be successful hardware merchants, my friend. You and I can both be successful lawyers. You and I can both be successful surgeons. But you and I can't both be successful politicians. In politics, only one of us can win." With these challenging words, the most successful politician in B.C.'s history announced an election for August 27, 1969.

The provincial election of 1969 was a curious contest. Social Credit was generally believed to be in serious trouble. On the face of it, this was true: the province was blasé about the Good Life, and tempted by the rise of national "flower power"; the urge to experiment was strong. The New Politics of the 1960s had brought sweeping changes throughout North American public life and there was no reason to believe that B.C. would remain immune—no reason other than W. A. C. Bennett. The Socreds were aided and abetted by the Tories, who, on the basis of a deal made with Bennett, ran only one candidate, their leader John DeWolfe. The Liberals, whose leader Ray Perrault had stepped down, waged a vigorous campaign under new leader Patrick McGeer, the lively MLA from Vancouver-Point Grey who, in pursuit of the elusive New Politics mystique, traded in his professorial spectacles for contact lenses. McGeer sped across the province advocating various reforms and a middle-of-the-road government. In Victoria, he enthused to party workers: "We're going to win! Our campaign in the interior is snowballing!" When told of McGeer's optimism, Bennett casually joked: "That's a great selling point, but everyone knows what happens to a snowball in July!"

The real battle, naturally, was between the Socreds and the socialists. The NDP waged a professional media campaign built around their youthful new leader; the press responded by touting Berger as the almost certain premier. The organizers were essentially the same elite party activists who had designed the poorly calculated gray flannel effort of Robert Strachan in 1963. This time it was Berger who was promoted as a "moderate" and "responsible" alternative to Social Credit. A bevy of paid NDP organizers were airlifted from Ontario, Saskatchewan and Manitoba and placed in priority constituencies. Berger played down the previously high-profile nationalization planks and instead stressed the need for tougher pollution control, changes in the educational system and parliamentary reform. Bennett did his best to puncture the supposed new image of moderation, referring to Berger as a "city-slicker labour lawyer" and describing the major issue of the election as "strike pay with Berger or take-home pay with Bennett." In classic west coast paranoid style, he spoke of the challenge of "Marxian Socialism"—he warned the electors that the NDP spokesmen were not honest working people but "paid professional organizers whose entire livelihood is derived directly from the people." "The barbarians," he exclaimed to a throng of excited partisans, "are at the gates!"

As the campaign heated up, most candidates agreed that it was the toughest election in many years. Thomas Berger, who found it difficult to adapt to B.C.'s populist style of politics, came across as a bit of a cold fish, and he made the mistake of responding to the premier's purple prose by calling him "a pathetic old man clinging desperately to power." Not only did this make the NDP leader seem the desperate one, but it represented an ugly personal attack on a venerable B.C. institution.

Bennett, of course, took it all in his stride; driving in his prime ministerial black limousine, he was greeted everywhere like a rich, eccentric uncle. The Socreds may have been weak and ill organized but their leader's confidence and exuberance seemed all that mattered. On the verge of his sixty-ninth birthday, the premier looked at least ten years younger. With his round beefy face bursting with health and happiness, his indelible smile and flashing teeth, he was his own best advertisement for the Good Life. At the peak of his personal popularity, Bennett eschewed the New Politics and ran an old-fashioned, glad-handing, baby-kissing campaign. It was vintage W.A.C. Bennett. "Now I don't make promises," he told a large gathering at Port Alberni. "I've only made one promise in my life. That was to my wife." The crowd, like so many others, roared with approval. At another meeting, a heckler interrupted, "Mr. Premier, what about our schools?" "My friend," he said, "my brother was a teacher. My sister was a teacher. I married a teacher. My daughter is a teacher. No one can say I'm not for education!" Throughout the campaign, Bennett seemed to be having a good time—too good. One of the horde of reporters who travelled with him asked if he was serious; the premier responded: "I'm always serious about politics. Politics is serious business. I love it. It's my life. You keep asking me if I find this dull, if I'm not bored shaking hands and saying nice things to people. You don't believe me when I say I'm not. I *like* to shake hands. I *like* to talk to people. It's the way I've spent my life."

As election day drew near, an air of uncertainty hung over the province. Staunch Socreds were asking themselves: "Has the old man got a chance?" The urban press said the best Bennett could hope for was a minority government, and the socialists were quietly predicting a major upset. The premier seemed to be the only person in B.C. confident of the government's position. "I smell a big win," he told reporters on his way to vote in Kelowna on August 27. That evening the Social Credit Party chalked up its greatest-ever electoral victory. The government increased its majority in the fifty-five-seat legislature from thirty-one to thirty-eight and gained almost 47 per cent of the popular vote; the NDP, polling almost 34 per cent, was reduced to twelve seats, and Thomas Berger was one of the many unexpected casualties; the Liberals held almost steady, electing five members and acquiring 20 per cent of the ballots cast.

The relieved Socreds were in joyous celebration. "My cup runneth over," exclaimed the premier. "The people of British Columbia have stopped the socialists in their tracks. . . . They have saved Canada from socialism." On election night in his Kelowna committee rooms, with excited party supporters and disbelieving media representatives, Bennett wallowed in the pandemonium of victory. Looking up at a television set which showed two successful Socred candidates pouring champagne over each other in the lobby of the Bayshore Inn in Vancouver, the premier proclaimed: "Alright, this one has been the sweetest of them all. So let us celebrate . . . My place. Tea and chocolate chip cookies."

The 1969 election victory was amazing in that it confounded the best attempts at political analysis and sophisticated forecasting, entered another prominent name into the long honour roll of opposition leaders retired by Social Credit, and, especially, was won almost completely on the basis of Bennett's personal stature. The NDP and the Liberals had cleverly changed their leadership and approach to suit the reformist tenor of the times. This was the election the Socreds were supposed to lose. Instead, it became W. A. C. Bennett's great hurrah. The size of the victory, however, created a dangerous illusion: to his fellow Socreds, the premier was now more a god than a leader; he seemed infallible. How could anyone question his judgement? Who would have the temerity to say that the 1969 election, his seventh consecutive mandate to govern, may have been a sympathy vote, a retirement party writ large, a crowning tribute to an old man who had brought British Columbia the Good Life?

The election was also important for reinforcing the populist tradition in B.C. politics. It has been argued that the province's politics are naturally divided along class lines reflected in the different bases of support for the Socreds and NDP. W. A. C. Bennett always rejected attempts at class analysis and his successive electoral victories, the result of support from all socioeconomic groups, were his best argument. Social Credit was first successful as a form of institutionalized protest against established social elites. During the long course of Bennett's premiership, Social Credit had become a kind of establishment in its own right, but Bennett did his best to maintain his populist roots. He established himself as an antipolitician, often standing alone against the big guys on behalf of the taxpayers. In their efforts to look respectable and urbane, the NDP had badly miscalculated. They would have probably fared better with the rough-hewn Robert Strachan. In any event, all parties now agreed that a strong element of populism was an indispensable part of political success in British Columbia. Meanwhile, W. A. C. Bennett remained unassailable, impossible to analyse, easy to misunderstand. The federal leader of the NDP, Tommy Douglas, observed: "He was the only man I ever knew who could get money from the rich and votes from the poor with the promise to protect them from each other."

With the question of his retirement on hold, the period following the 1969 election became one of the most controversial chapters in the history of Bennett's administration. Many of the large questions of those years involved the difficult process of federal-provincial negotiation. Bennett had definite views on federalism and strongly resented what he considered to be the centralizing tendencies of Ottawa politicians, particularly of the fourth Canadian prime minister with whom his premiership coincided, Pierre Elliot Trudeau. Naturally, Bennett was agitated most about the financial arrangements so integral to federal-provincial relations. He had long advocated that the national government withdraw from the field of direct taxation, and he wrote:

> The main revenue that any government must use for the raising of the standard of living of ordinary people is the income tax. Under our constitution such direct taxation belongs to the provinces. In 1917 when we were under a wartime government, and everyone wanted to win the war, Sir Thomas White, then the Minister of Finance in the Conservative Government, brought in the Federal Income Tax under the War Measures Act. He made it very clear in the House of Commons that this would only be in duration to apply for the war. When the war was over the federal government would be barred from that field because the field was provincial. But after the war they occupied it more and after the second war they occupied it more again until they thought they owned that field. In that sense, it's been a long war.

Bennett viewed himself in the context of that long war as fighting against creeping centralization, trying to promote a different view of Canadian federalism. He stated: "Our trouble is that we have a central government duplicating what should be regional or provincial services. There is duplication everywhere, and only because Ottawa has so much of the revenue that belongs to the provinces that they've got to look for places to spend it. Of course, when these centralists spend all that money, and they print all the currency they can print as well, then they borrow all they can as well. They're so anxious to hold control!"

Bennett had under constant review virtually every area in which British Columbia was tied to Ottawa by a financial formula. One could not argue that he was indifferent to Canadian nationhood if one were to chronicle the persistent efforts he made to alter existing intergovernmental arrangements. He argued that federal fiscal policy was inequitable, advocated a devalued Canadian dollar so that B.C.'s exports could be sold more competitively, and harangued federal finance ministers about the need to keep down the interest rates on Canadian Savings Bonds. He urged restraint in public spending and worried loudly about inflation; in 1969 he wrote to Trudeau: "I must reiterate, Mr. Prime Minister, that the finanacial policies of your Government are one of the chief causes of inflation in the country." No reply seems to have been preserved for posterity.

Because Bennett headed an administration having no direct tie to a federal governing party, he could take a forthright, independent stance on issues without fear of party conflict. Aside from fiscal and monetary issues, Bennett was also involved in several disputes over resource policy, including the question of who had jurisdiction over offshore mineral rights, a very important issue for British Columbia. Perhaps the only visible accomplishment of the era was the modicum of co-operation between B.C. and Ottawa on the Roberts Bank superport which was officially opened on June 15, 1970. At the time of the opening, Bennett stood on the same platform as Prime Minister Trudeau and said some kind words about the federal government's contribution to the project. Yet a few months later, in answer to a question about Ottawa's role in establishing the superport, Bennett said curtly: "Well, you always must give thanks, for even a crumb."

Bennett belonged to an older generation of Canadian politicians and especially after 1968 did not feel at home sitting at federal-provincial conference tables surrounded by the new faces of the bland, university-educated technocrats who had come to dominate Canada's politics. The Social Credit premier had always been unenthusiastic about the never-ending rounds of discussion, negotiation and debate with other Canadian governments, and in his later years he was just as likely to boycott meetings which he deemed either a waste of time or an excuse to socialize. It was not so much that Bennett was indifferent to federal-provincial diplomacy; rather, he simply had little expectation about the outcome — and he was seldom disappointed. British Columbia became known as "the empty chair" at federal-provincial conferences. Bennett was the only Canadian premier absent from the Confederation of Tomorrow conference in 1967, convened to discuss constitutional issues. On other occasions when he did attend, he would invariably leave early, but as he pointed out years later, he was the only one to leave these conferences with a smile on his face: "They never knew if I was smiling with them or at them, but they at least knew I was smiling."

There were also the myriad meetings of ministers and department officials at at provincial and federal levels. The premier was very tough on his cabinet members and senior bureaucrats who wanted to attend these conferences, apparently regarding them as excuses to waste time and money. Through the Treasury Board process, Bennett maintained firm control over representatives of his government who travelled outside the province. Unless a conference had a specific objective which he considered important, permission to attend was not likely to be granted. When B.C. did participate at a federal-provincial meeting, its delegation was invariably smaller than the others; even the maritime provinces generally sent twice as many delegates.

In addition, there were the annual summer premiers' conferences; again, Bennett felt they were a waste of time—too many parties, picnics and balls and not enough work. The little that was accomplished, he believed, could have been done by telephone or letter. Typical was the premiers' conference hosted by Saskatchewan in the summer of 1968. When Bennett announced he would be unable to attend, the host, Premier Ross Thatcher, wrote to him: "Why not weaken and come out to Saskatchewan. . . ?" Bennett resisted, sending instead a junior cabinet member, minister without portfolio Grace McCarthy.

Bennett's attitude here was shaped by his general disapproval of wasting taxpayers' money on what he considered frivolities, and the recognition that he had little chance of playing an important role in Canadian federalism. He had accepted that fact early in his premiership and resolved to spend his energies in British Columbia, not Ottawa. When he did attend federal-provincial meetings he often aroused the resentment of his fellow premiers when, at the inevitable news conference that followed, he upstaged them with his folksy wit, bombastic exhortations or exotic ideas. No one was certain if Bennett was serious or if he was intentionally satirizing the futility of these conferences.

It has been argued that B.C.'s halfhearted participation and lack of preparedness may have resulted in the loss of benefits or rights which might have been attained from a fuller participation at federal-provincial conferences. Bennett naturally disagreed. During the early years of Social Credit rule, he had argued forcibly on behalf of his province and had gotten nowhere; he and his British Columbia delegates were treated as remittance men at those early federal-provincial meetings. By the late 1960s, Bennett's lengthening list of grievances had not been resolved or addressed, and his dissatisfaction and inability to affect the course of Canadian federalism forced him to take what was seen as a perverse, even frivolous approach. Never did there seem to be more madness in his method than at the Canadian constitutional conference of February 1969 in Ottawa where, in his opening statement, he stole all the limelight with another of his "wacky" ideas. As he came to the section of his statement entitled "Correlation of Economic and

Political Units," a map of Canada was unveiled directly behind his chair. At first glance, the map seemed quite normal—but as Bennett read on, the conference delegates realized that it depicted a Canada with not ten provinces but five regions: Atlantic—consisting of the four easternmost provinces; Quebec; Ontario; Prairies—comprising the three prairie provinces; and British Columbia. Bennett continued with his opening statement: "I believe the time has come to recognize that in the interest of economic realities the boundaries of some of the provinces will have to be altered so as to provide five viable and effective political units consonant and in conformity with the five economic regions of Canada. Imagine the increased efficiency and resultant substantial savings to the Canadian taxpayer. . . ."

Neither Prime Minister Trudeau nor Bennett's fellow premiers knew exactly how to react to the proposal. Such a radical scheme had never before been put forward at a federal-provincial gathering. How was the idea received? "Shock!" Bennett said. "The prime minister nearly had a fit when he saw this map." Incredulous delegates and the press stood gawking at the smiling west coast premier and studied his map. The Prairie region was by far the largest of the proposed political divisions, since the provincial boundaries had been extended northward to include most of the Northwest Territories. British Columbia, emblazoned in green on the map, also had its northern boundary extended to include Yukon Territory. This prompted one official at the conference to refer to Bennett as the "Jolly Green Giant."

Bennett was completely serious in his advocacy of a five-region Canada. Although he was the eldest of the assembled leaders at the 1969 conference, almost a generation older than most of them, he was regarded as a kind of radical. His wholehearted endorsement of a plan that suggested a massive realignment of the country's political structure was at odds with too many vested interests, but Bennett proposed his five regions as a natural evolution of Canada's political boundaries. He emphasized that those boundaries had been continually changing since 1867, and suggested that there was no reason why they could not continue to adapt to changing reality, to regional economic interests. The premier anticipated that his daring proposal would be received less than enthusiastically by his counterparts from across the country, if only because it represented an extreme alteration of the status quo, but the subtext was one of Bennett's favourite themes: Canada was suffering from too much government. The five-region concept has to be understood as coming from a practical-minded ex-hardware merchant concerned that the overhead expenses were excessive. There was altogether too much duplication—no way to run a successful enterprise! As he was fond of saying, "Government in this country is our biggest business and should be run on sound business principles."

Bennett departed from the 1969 constitutional conference, as always, smiling. He had received a tremendous amount of press coverage for his five-region concept and, if other political leaders seemed cool to the idea, interest was piqued across the country. He said: "You must plant seeds. All my political life I've been a planter of seeds, of ideas. The only trouble with the five regions idea is that it's too logical." Whether or not this particular seed will ever sprout, one repercussion is that a new word suddenly crept into the lexicon of Canadian politics. In subsequent years, politicians no longer spoke simply of their *provinces*, they talked of their *regions*. Canada had always been a country shaped by regionalism, but perhaps the greatest effect of Bennett's five-region plan was that it prompted Canadians to think about themselves in terms of their regions. That will likely stand as one of W. A. C. Bennett's most lasting contributions to the debate over the future of Canada.

One subject that consumed a great deal of the diplomatic energies of federal-provincial delegates during this era was constitutional review, in particular, the protracted effort to patriate Canada's constitution and find an agreement on an amending formula. Bennett and the B.C. Socreds never maintained a lasting interest in the constitutional gymnastics of Liberal Prime Minister Pierre Trudeau. However, Bennett did play a role, if only as host, in the June 1971 constitutional conference in Victoria, which was billed as the finale in the long search for a Canadian constitution. The subject was neither dear to Bennett's heart nor was it on his list of priorities, but he and his administration did have a clear position on the salient issues and helped to shape the generally agreed upon amending formula which became known as the Victoria Charter. In the past, Quebec had always been a stumbling block to agreement on important constitutional issues, but Trudeau felt that he was the person who could bring his native province in line. According to Bennett, in discussing the issue with Trudeau he had said: "Are you sure, Mr. Prime Minister, that Quebec is going to go for it?" Trudeau replied: "Yes, they want it badly. They want some changes in it, but we can compromise and we'll come to a formula at Victoria."

The Victoria conference was orchestrated to fit into British Columbia's grand centennial celebrations of that year. Bennett staged an impressive open-air cavalcade through the capital—Trudeau in the vanguard in a big Cadillac, Premier Alex Campbell of Prince Edward Island bringing up the rear in a Mustang. Aside from the parades and hoopla there was a minimum of fun and games for the visiting Canadian heads of state, though Bennett did host a midconference moonlight cruise aboard one of his impressive new government ferries. Those who knew their host well thought to bring their own bottles aboard for the alcohol-free evening. Back at the conference, which was held in B.C.'s legislative chamber, an agreement seemed to be at hand, and on the final day of the meeting it only remained for the Victoria Charter to be agreed to by the various Canadian legislatures. Bennett's version of the event was:

> We thrashed everything out and agreed to the Victoria formula. I said, "Mr. Prime Minister, before we break up, let's have a little meeting in our cabinet room so we can just say good-bye to each other. It's been a great conference." He said, "That would be a good idea." So we all went up there, and I said, "Mr. Prime Minister, we are all agreed and it's a great day for Canada. But let's be clear that we understand each other before we go. I'm sure we do, but let's just be double sure." Trudeau said, "Well, Mr. Bennett, it's not necessary." I said, "Since the conference is here in British Columbia, I want to be the first to say that as the premier of the province I will not only recommend to my cabinet and to my legislature that we endorse it, but to the people of British Columbia, without any restraints at all." So the prime minister said, "Then let's have everybody else say something." We went around the room and we got to Quebec; Robert Bourassa said, "Very sorry. I can't give that assurance." You could have knocked Trudeau off with a feather. I said, "Mr. Prime Minister, what have you been telling us all these months?" And, gee, he was mad!

Premier Bourassa, the only leader to travel to the constitutional conference with a personal hairdresser as part of his large entourage, not only failed to give an assurance that he would recommend adoption of the Victoria Charter, but within two days of his return to Quebec flatly announced that his province would not accept the package. Despite tremendous progress and hard work, these were the days when unanimity was considered the *sine qua non* for constitutional change. So near, yet so far, the entire question was set aside for another decade.

Bennett was strongly opposed to the preferred treatment that Quebec received from the federal government, particularly when Pierre Trudeau became prime minister. He also disagreed with the official policy of bilingualism and biculturalism, arguing that it was both too costly and nonsensical, particularly in western Canada. On his way home from a federal-provincial constitutional conference in February 1968 where Trudeau was pushing the idea of national language and education rights for French Canadians, the premier told a scrum of newspaper reporters who met him at the Vancouver airport: "We in B.C. don't believe there are any special Canadians or hyphenated Canadians. We stand for fair treatment in B.C. for the British, the French, the Irish or any others. I find myself at conferences like this, the champion of that 40 percent of British Columbians who are neither British nor French. We'll never stand for putting some Canadians ahead of others. All Canadians should be proud of their heritage, but when people come to live in this country of B.C., they're just Canadians." For Bennett, symbolism was always more important than rational argument, so to bolster his point about B.C.'s opposition to the federal government's bilingual policies, he brought with him to the 1968 constitutional conference the newly elected president of the Union of British Columbia Municipalities, Mayor Peter Wing of Kamloops, the first Chinese Canadian to be elected mayor of a Canadian city. Bennett brought him along to reinforce for Ottawans that the Chinese language would benefit more British Columbians than would French.

Some federal politicians were exasperated with the west coast premier's reluctance to embrace the central Canadian obsession with the French fact, and in return Bennett continually expressed his dissatisfaction with the policies of a federal government increasingly dominated, as he saw it, by French Canadians with little or no knowledge of western Canadian needs and a maniacal preoccupation with placating the never-defined desires of Quebec. In the summer of 1971, when he was making an announcement regarding the opening of the Yellowhead Highway, Bennett criticized the failure of the federal government to assist in construction of the highway. "They are a negative little group down there," he pronounced. "We haven't got a Canadian government—it's a Quebec government." That autumn, when told that Prime Minister Trudeau had made a statement warning the provincial government not to hold its breath in the hope of receiving more federal funds, Bennett replied: "Those French Canadian nationalists who operate the government of Canada ought to have something more to hold than their breath, my friend."

There was little respect or admiration lost between W. A. C. Bennett and Pierre Trudeau. The premier regarded the prime minister as a socialist masquerading as a Liberal, a dilettante playing games with political power. For his part, Trudeau showed a bit of his famous arrogance when, in February 1972, speaking of British Columbia, he referred to "the bigot who happens to run the government there." It was a typical Trudeauism, a characteristically non-prime ministerial statement which produced near-violent reaction in some quarters. Asked for a response by reporters in Victoria, Bennett said: "Just say I smiled and smiled and smiled." Later, he said: "In what way did Trudeau think I was a bigot? Something must have been bothering him. There is more than one road to any place, and if you only believe there is one road, and somebody believes there are other roads, tell me, which one is the bigot?" At the time of the incident, other Socreds were more vocal than the premier. In the legislature the day following Trudeau's gaffe, Attorney General Leslie Peterson referred to the insult as "the most unprecedented and unwarranted attack by a prime minister of this country since Confederation."

In a stirring defence of his chief, Peterson pleaded: "Listen to the West, Mr. Prime Minister—just for once. We've had enough sneers, we've had enough shrugs, we've had enough profanity from the present prime minister. B.C. has had enough."

To demonstrate that British Columbia was fed up with the centralist edicts of the federal government, the Socred administration launched a court action in the spring of 1972 challenging the constitutional validity of equalization payments, of which Bennett was a longtime critic. His argument was:

> The money was collected by the federal government and the provinces and they poured it out into provincial governments. I'd go to visit these provincial governments and I'd see in their offices the enormous staffs they had, all with our money. I would see at these conferences in Ottawa or elsewhere that British Columbia wouldn't have a quarter as many of the delegates there as the poorer provinces of Canada who were getting these equalization payments. I only opposed these equalization payments because they were going to the wrong people. They were going to the provincial governments so they could let political contracts—a lot of patronage for their party. I wanted this money, all of it, to raise the standard of the poor and to help the working poor. I was a populist leader of a populist party—fair treatment to everyone, special privileges to none.

Even during these later years, B.C.'s septuagenarian premier was espousing ideas which he described as "too advanced for others." In the fall of 1971 he became the first Canadian politician and one of the first public figures in the world to advocate a negative income tax. He argued that such a system could be used to replace the dreaded equalization payments; instead of large cash payments being paid to provincial governments, cheques would be issued to individuals whose incomes fell below a certain level. Bennett felt that the idea, which was consistent with classical Social Credit theory in that it proposed to increase the purchasing power of individuals, was being resisted largely because provincial governments feared to give up revenues. At this same time, the premier advocated a common market with the United States, believing that free trade between the two neighbours would ultimately benefit all regions of Canada. "The important thing to remember in Canada," he said, "is that we must have political union east and west but trade should flow north and south." Bennett was confident that, like his five-region plan, these ideas would be accepted in time. Returning from a federal-provincial conference where he had advanced both the negative income tax and free trade with the U.S., he told reporters: "We planted our seeds and now we must have patience, cultivate them and reap the harvest."

Bennett spent much more time travelling and meeting people than at federal-provincial get-togethers in his later years as premier. His administration established a record for celebrating anniversaries, jubilees and centennials, the largest of which was British Columbia's one-hundreth birthday as a Canadian province in 1971. He spent New Year's Day 1971 atop a magnificent award-winning B.C. float in the annual Tournament of Roses parade in Pasadena, California. He could have welcomed in the province's centennial year at home with a traditional fireworks display on the lawns of the legislature, but chose instead to steal a show hundreds of miles away with his eye fixed on winning a half minute of television exposure in front of an American audience estimated at more than 100 million. Under sunny skies and palm trees, Bennett seemed in his element in the brash razzle-dazzle of the parade, his unabashed motive to reap the enormous potential returns of American tourist dollars. In that sense, B.C.'s super salesman was in the right place to kick off the province's birthday festivities. The following day, he attended the Rose Bowl game where, at intermission, he went up to California Governor Ronald Reagan and shoved into his hand a B.C. flag and other centennial trinkets. Momentarily irked, Reagan quickly recovered and assured the smiling premier that he welcomed British Columbia's use of the Rose Bowl as a means of publicizing its centenary because "we think California is a place people can come to to celebrate almost anything." Of course, Bennett liked to think the same of British Columbia.

Back at home, the premier set a frantic pace during 1971, travelling throughout the province on a specially appointed centennial train, stopping at every town, speaking to every possible group, shaking every possible hand. Nearly as old as the century, he was the ultimate politician; he could not stop campaigning. It was like a compulsive form of entertainment for him. It was in his blood.

The only time Bennett managed to really relax was when he journeyed outside British Columbia. He always enjoyed travel and particularly during his later years in office became a bona fide world citizen. Annual trips to New York to meet with financiers and bond market representatives were *de rigueur*, and he loved to spend time in Japan and Europe as a kindly ambassador of the Good Life. He was well known in London business and political circles, met with most major European public figures, and even managed a private audience with the Pope. Following one of his European jaunts he received a postmarked letter from a continental admirer; the envelope found its way to him in Victoria despite bearing the abbreviated address: "W. A. C."

Winters in Victoria were too wet and in Kelowna too cold for the premier; he and May took regular holidays in Phoenix or Palm Springs, but most of all he loved to travel with his cronies—his few close friends with whom he could unwind and play gin rummy. Always shy and completely deferential in the company of women, Bennett was undeniably an old-fashioned man's man. Nevertheless, he could be a frustrating travelling companion. Einar Gunderson, for example, complained that he always—*always*—wanted to talk politics. But he could be fun, too, and usually managed to attract a lot of pleasant fuss and attention. Bill Clancey described their visit to Las Vegas: "He didn't gamble, but I gambled a little bit. He was a lovely country boy, sweet and innocent. We went into the Folies Bergère and had four or five drinks, because you had to buy so many. He'd have four or five orange juices or apple juices in front of him. Then the girls came on stage and he turned around and said, 'I wonder how we can get out of here in case of a fire?' He wouldn't even look at the girls!"

Cam Kenmuir also became a frequent travelling partner of the premier, and thereby learned a good deal about him:

> I remember going through Toledo. We were in a magnificent cathedral and I was going on about how marvellous it was. This is a measure of the man: he wasn't really interested in the cathedral; he was interested in the man who caused it to be built—not the magnificent structure or how it was finished. Nor in the exterior of the House of Commons in London: it was the people inside the House of Commons who turned him on. It was the same when we were in Greece viewing the Acropolis. The guide pointed out the recently uncovered spot, below the Parthenon, where they believed the old town had been, where St. Paul had spoken to the Athenians. This really excited him. Those were the things that turned him on: people who did things.

After Bennett's extraordinary 1969 electoral victory, the question of his retirement was rarely raised. Not only did he seem convinced of his own infallibility but those close to him were also convinced. For different reasons, those who were not as close did little to discourage the idea. The premier seldom asked for advice and was offered none; consequently, he suffered by suppression of information. These days, cabinet members, party officials and close acquaintances told him what he wanted to hear. Hardly ever did they speak their minds; few would dare to, and none had the fortitude to suggest he might be wrong. More than ever, Bennett seemed secretly convinced that he had an arrangement with fate.

After 1969, B.C. politics took a more strident and venomous turn. The opponents of the aging political master had no illusions that he was infallible or invincible. By far the most outspoken opponent was the new leader of the opposition, David Barrett, who had succeeded Thomas Berger as leader of the NDP following his disastrous defeat at the polls. Barrett was a young ambitious, jovial, self-styled man of the people. Before being elected to the legislature in 1960, he had been fired from his government job as a social worker for engaging in political activity. A compelling public speaker, Barrett approached his role as opposition leader in a decidedly different manner than his predecessors. This was evident almost from the start when, in January 1970, at the first meeting of the legislature following the 1969 election, the NDP opposed the Socreds' nomination for Speaker of the House. In years past, former socialist leader Robert Strachan had normally seconded the premier's choice. After a bitter procedural wrangle, which certainly damaged the dignity of the Chair, the government's nominee, W. H. Murray, was elected. But the new found acrimony and ill feeling evident in the legislative chamber would remain for a long, long time.

Dave Barrett loved to play the good-natured clown in public, but in his relations with the government he seemed to be saying: "No more Mr. Nice Guy." He had received his political education from W. A. C. Bennett, and in a very personal way regarded the premier as a kind of model. He said of him: "He was my opponent, and I learned, as Sun-tzu, the famous Chinese military philosopher said, 'You must respect your opponent if you wish to defeat him.' I learned a great deal about Bennett in terms of the political wars that we were in. After all, it was he who defined the clash of politics as war, and I accepted that definition because he was the one that called the shots. In that sense, I learned from him and respected him."

The legislative sessions of 1970 and 1971 were lively affairs, full of controversy, innuendo and political speculation. The Socreds brought in increases for old-age pension and welfare recipients, a civil service pay hike ranging from six to eight per cent, and a new age of majority lowered from twenty-one to nineteen. These were the same kinds of methodical increases and reforms that the Social Credit administration had sponsored for almost two decades—but now, the Good Life somehow did not seem to be enough. Stable government and steady advancement appeared only to frustrate rapidly rising expectations, and the opposition parties were yelling loud and hard about misplaced priorities and the need for more social programs, more educational spending, more health services, more pollution control. More. And the more the government gave, the more they wanted. Of course, those difficult-to-satisfy expectations were the legacy of Bennett's never-ending promotional blitzes, and he was only pouring oil on the flames when he announced in February 1970: "We've got the structure built, and now we're going to build the super structure. . . . The Social Credit government will give the people of British Columbia the highest and best standard of living in the whole world."

During these years Bennett appeared to be deliberately addressing the long-standing contention of his critics that Social Credit was more concerned with physical and economic development than with individuals, social services or the environment. In his 1970 budget speech he stated: "The Government's first policy for this new decade is for people—to provide continuing improvement in government services and to increase social and economic benefits." He also strove to refine a middle-of-the-road political philosophy. The underlying purpose of his career had been to promote capitalism, purge its defects, and so ensure that socialism would never become a viable political alternative. But his brand of state capitalism in British Columbia may have actually encouraged a greater public reliance on government than he had once approved, and his personal style of governing produced a paternalistic approach to public affairs. If, for instance, he was met at an airport by a crowd of demonstrating strikers or placard-carrying unemployed he never cringed or complained; rather, he felt it entirely proper for people to aim their complaints in his direction, for he regarded himself as responsible for their well-being. This was not necessarily the view of his party or cabinet, but it was the prevailing view. Despite the increasingly self-righteous rhetoric of political opponents and the editorial views of the urban press, which regularly castigated the Socreds as a party dominated by big business interests, Bennett truly considered himself a moderate populist, guarding the interests of the people from the evils of both the left and right. In the summer of 1970, for example, he disarmed an interviewer by saying: "We can't live in the world of the old liberal philosophy of *laissez-faire*. It's now out of date. It can't work in this period. You can't have either pure capitalism or pure socialism."

In one sense, Bennett was old-fashioned and out of date. In another, he was too modern to be in fashion. A good example was the legislation he shepherded through the House in 1971 which outlawed all tobacco and liquor advertising in the province. The legislation was controversial not only because it enraged liquor and tobacco interests, whom Bennett referred to as "pushers," but also because it proved almost impossible to enforce — incoming newspapers, magazines and television signals were in violation of Bennett's effort to legislate a new morality. The premier was far ahead of his time; a decade later, so-called "progressive" jurisdictions brought in similar legislation. Meantime, reaction to the measures in 1971 was heated and often hostile. The public perceived him as heavy-handed and politicians saw him leaping dangerously ahead of the crowd. He turned the ad ban into a moral crusade; as he told the Socred annual convention in November 1971: "Our government is entitled to take a stand that we don't want the pushing of these things, and if anyone wants to challenge that stand, we'll have an election tomorrow, my friends."

The liquor and tobacco ad ban again demonstrated the premier's complete dominance over his party. Years later, it was nearly impossible to find a former cabinet minister who would admit to feeling comfortable with the legislation when it was passed. Yet none of them dared to challenge Bennett at the time. They feared he was wrong, whispered to each other that it was political suicide, but knew better than to argue with him, especially on a question of morality. Bennett simply informed them that it was time to stand on a matter of high principle. "If you don't stand for something," he remarked, "you'll fall for anything, my friend."

Despite the premier's unyielding stranglehold on political power—maybe because of it—there were some telling instances of internal dissent during these years of the Good Life. Dr. Scott Wallace, the independent-minded Social Credit gadfly from Oak Bay, had been a persistent critic of the government's medicare policies; in August 1971, in a move that surprised many, Wallace left the ranks of government to become an independent MLA. Bennett, who had made just such a move twenty years earlier, dismissed Wallace as an "extreme rightest" who "represented only one group—doctors." However, in following months, the premier was given reason for concern. First of all, Derril Warren, a tall, young, well-spoken lawyer, was elected leader of the moribund B.C. Conservative Party. Warren, who assisted his Tory friend Peter Lougheed in toppling Alberta's thirty-six-year-old Social Credit government, began to speak of a possible replay on the west coast. Warren persuaded Scott Wallace to join the Conservative Party and began working on several other disaffected Socred backbenchers. A few months later he succeeded in luring away Don Marshall, the soft-spoken government member from South Peace River. With two born-again Tory MLAs in the legislature—the first Conservatives in the House in many years—and an ambitious party leader who cultivated an effective media presence, Bennett began to worry about the possibility of being undermined from the right.

To an extent, it was this concern that prompted him to give Phil Gaglardi a full cabinet post following the 1969 election. Gaglardi was popular among the ultraconservative fundamentalists who formed the traditional but weakening backbone of the Social Credit Party. Recognizing he had to do something with Gaglardi, Bennett gave him the social welfare portfolio, a post that would both keep him busy and ensure he would never win a popularity contest. Gaglardi, who renamed the department "Rehabilitation and Social Improvement," snarled that he was sure to be "the roughest, toughest, most effective welfare minister the world has ever known." He began talking about kicking "deadbeats" off the welfare rolls and cutting down on bureaucracy; he enlisted the help of a specially created agency, the Provincial Alliance of Businessmen, to secure jobs for the indigent. Just when the Socreds were shifting in public estimation from a no-holds-barred growth party to a new kind of welfare party, Gaglardi changed that image and bred new antagonisms.

It was frequently suggested that Bennett had given in to a dangerous though admirable loyalty when he reinstated his controversial former highways minister. But the premier was motivated by practical, not emotional reasons—not the least was the much talked about, if not imminent, succession to the Socred leadership. Incredibly, Gaglardi was still being touted as a possible successor and he made occasional noises that confirmed his interest. In that sense, Bennett was clasping Gaglardi to his breast in order to avoid having him clasped to his back. The idea of a "Premier Gaglardi" was so horrendous to Bennett and many others that it may have been one of the most important factors in the premier's refusal to consider retirement. He probably overrated Gaglardi's chances of winning a leadership contest but, at the same time, his own preference, Attorney General Leslie Peterson, "the white hope of the anti-Gaglardi forces," was laid up with ulcer complications and was not emerging as an obvious leader.

Gaglardi was extremely unpopular in cabinet. Frequently the insults had to be checked lest they become public. To keep him in his place, the premier pitted one rival against another. Dan Campbell, the ambitious and effective minister of municipal affairs who had developed the concept of regional districts in British Columbia, promoted the decentralization of social services which would be administered at the regional district level. This policy proposal was in direct opposition to the "Czar of Rehabilitation's" efforts to centralize all such services in his department in Victoria. The premier did little to discourage this policy difference and allowed his two ministers to slug it out in public; Campbell thereby took some of the hot air out of Gaglardi's swollen sails and the press began to promote the tough minister of municipal affairs as a possible future leader.

Dan Campbell saw his differences with Gaglardi as being more than a disagreement over public policy, and he also talked about the question of leadership of the party:

> I never discussed the question of running for the leadership with W. A. C. The only people I ever discussed it with were the members of caucus who came to me and said, "What's your attitude going to be, Dan, if this comes about?" I told them if that came about I would value their support; that's all, but I told them quite distinctly that I would not entertain taking on the old man as long as he wanted to stay there. I'd be prepared to go down with the ship or stand on the deck or whatever. ... I don't believe the judgement that the old man had at that time about Gaglardi was the correct one. I don't believe that Gaglardi would have been anything more than a factor. ... I did have some run-ins with Gaglardi on matters of policy. At one stage I caught him tape recording a conversation which I insisted he give me back, but he never did. I never deliberately went out to drive a wedge. I just didn't like the guy. It's that simple. I thought he was a phony. I think he was overrated.

I could see Gaglardi's usefulness to the party sometimes—he was an entertaining little bastard. But he was a little bastard.

When Bennett resuscitated Phil Gaglardi it not only opened old wounds but also alienated many of the brighter and more ambitious Socreds who were hoping for advancement within a party that seemed gripped by inertia. The premier was closing himself off from collegial consultation, and it is amazing that he was able to maintain a convincing united front when the Socreds were in fact seething with frustration. A good example is Grace McCarthy who, despite demonstrating ability and successfully implementing a variety of government pilot projects, was never promoted from minister without portfolio. She believed: "W. A. C. Bennett was surrounded by people who protected him from the world. That happens to people in public life, but I made no effort to penetrate it. People who were well-meaning would shield W. A. C. Bennett from the telephone and from visits. It would be impossible to say he didn't know what was going on. He did know. But if people were going to get into the office to see him, it was only because it was very well known what they were going to see him for. If anybody was going to be any problem, he was shielded from it."

Dissension was also rife in the Social Credit back bench. Vancouver MLA Herb Capozzi, a well-known and outspoken business and sports figure, never made it close to the cabinet door. Perhaps Bennett discriminated against Capozzi because he was the son of his old friend Cap; or possibly it was because of Capozzi's involvement in the wine industry, now in confrontation with government over the advertising ban legislation; or maybe it was simply because there was a virtual halt to promotion from the back bench during this period. Capozzi's frustration took the form of open opposition to a variety of government policies: he spoke out against the proposed government skyscraper for Vancouver; he fought the premier over the lack of funding for independent schools; he criticized Gaglardi's description of welfare recipients as "deadbeats"; he voted against the government's liquor and tobacco ad ban. Capozzi's actions were not so much those of a maverick as symptomatic of a general but never fully expressed dissatisfaction with the continuation of one-man rule.

Capozzi had no illusions on that score, for when he first went into the House in 1966 he had said to Bennett, "It's great to be on your team, sir. A team is only as strong as its weakest link and we've got a great team."

The premier replied, "That may apply to teams and it may apply to chains, but it doesn't apply to political parties or governments. A government is not as strong as its weakest link, it's only as strong as its most brilliant mind."

Even doggedly loyal Social Credit backbenchers were beginning to wilt.

Robert Wenman, the young member for Delta who looked up to Bennett as a father figure and developed a strong admiration, even love, for the man, described their working relationship:

> When I would have some constituency problem and I would go to his office, the first question he would ask me was, "How is your wife, and how is your family?" He was always interested and had a tremendous concern for family. After that was cleared out of the way, . . . he wanted you to present your case quickly, efficiently, in a businesslike way: "Let's not waste time. Let's just get to the facts. You don't have to try and convince me, just give me the outline." The fewer words you could say, I'm sure the happier he was. Then he'd tell me why it could or could not be done, and that was it. . . He punches the button on his phone and gets someone on the line and says, "All right, hear this now!" And he'd say to me, "Repeat that." So I'd repeat it to whoever was on the phone, and he'd say, "Now I want that done." It was done. You knew it was done.

After 1969, however, Wenman and his fellow members in the sprawling Socred outfield grew baffled and disenchanted as their access to the premier became more and more restricted. Without any other outlet for their ideas, some frustrated party members began to attack the government with them. As Robert Wenman said: "The government was becoming deaf to new ideas. W. A. C. didn't, but he couldn't hear any more because his channels were being closed to him. There were cries of frustration, cries of not being heard, cries for change."

The internal disaffection was only a small problem for the Socreds when compared with the amorphous external forces working against the government, eroding its foundation of popular support. At the start of the 1970s, significant social, economic and political changes were occuring throughout North Amerca. In Canada, the transformation of popular attitudes was most evident on the west coast. The long period of sustained innocence that had characterized most of Bennett's tenure was apparently over. The warm, comfortable postwar feeling of the people being in control of destiny was suddenly gone. In a political sense, so was the margin for error: there was much less scope for policy misjudgements, not as much time to take a second look. A kind of siege mentality in government accompanied the rise of myriad pressure groups, and the overall effect was a new antidevelopment sentiment—a counterpressure to the rapid rise of British Columbia during the fifties and sixties and a reaction to the achievement of the Good Life.

At a time when pressure groups and special interests were increasing their hold on society, W. A. C. Bennett vainly tried to speak for everyone. He was the last successful Canadian politician to believe in the possibility of representing the people in the broadest democratic sense, but he had entered a new era dominated by single-issue politics, economic instability and watchdog media. No matter what government action was taken, there was bound to be a negative reaction; no policy could satisfy business, labour, doctors, teachers, cultural organizations, pensioners, university students, welfare recipients, developers, environmentalists, farmers—all the various groups who were organizing as never before, looking to government for help, demanding that government finance their projects, and pouncing on each statement of public policy as an infringement of their rights.

The environmental lobby is a good example of the vocal and powerful pressure groups that emerged during these years. Before the late 1960s, the word "environment" had never appeared in the lexicon of B.C. politics. Suddenly, numerous groups were agitating for pollution control and improved conservation of natural resources; the media and opposition parties lent support to their causes. The Socreds were accused of encouraging the rape of the province's wilderness and of spoiling the environment for all time. The government responded rather simplistically that the people had to choose between jobs and the landscape or, as Phil Gaglardi used to say: "How can you make an omelette without breaking a few eggs?" The Socred cabinet established the Environment and Land Use Committee in 1969, imposed stringent penalties for industrial pollution, established provincial parks and wildlife preserves and promoted tourism as the new, clean industry of the 1970s. Their actions were severely criticized as being too little too late.

W. A. C. Bennett understood that the questions being raised by the various environmental lobbies were motherhood issues and that his government's efforts were falling short; nevertheless, he promoted himself as British Columbia's number one environmentalist and declared that care for the environment was his top policy priority. Actually, as early as 1966 he had campaigned on a program of "pure water, clean air and fertile soil," but by the early 1970s the environment issue had taken on very serious political overtones; it was nearly impossible to fight the loudly promulgated notion that there was no room for conservationists in the premier's Good Life.

One of the interesting features of this period was that most major public issues seemed to be generated by special interest groups through the media rather than by political parties. Of course, other serious issues were taken up by the House, such as the multimillion-dollar government bail-out of a suspicious financial institution called Commonwealth Trust, and the proposed construction of a $95-million natural gas pipeline to Vancouver Island by a private group, Malaspina Gas, which included the premier's friend, Dan Ekman, and which was opposed by B.C. Hydro. But this was the dawning of the media age, and future B.C. governments would be opposed most fiercely by these traditional guardians of the public interest, which now to a large extent defined that interest. Television, which had come of age as electronic chronicler and commentator on public affairs, changed the rules of politics. The development of mobile video TV cameras meant that government policies and personalities were constantly in the public eye—and W. A. C. Bennett did not project well on television.

Opposition parties sat back and watched, sometimes riding the coattails of popular issues or media attacks on the government, but rarely initiating or defining substantive issues themselves. Instead, they developed a special west coast penchant for muckraking. In particular, the NDP under the aggressive leadership of Dave Barrett established a new B.C. opposition tradition of ignoring major issues for the minor flaws; instead of offering a rational critique of government policy, they appeared more interested in peeping through keyholes in the hope of finding a Socred in a compromising position. An example of the new kind of vindictive and personal attack that now regularly took place in the legislature was the harsh criticism of Bennett's sons. In February 1971, NDP member Bob Williams referred to Bill and R. J. Bennett as "rip-off artists" and "millionaires on the make," charging that they were capitalizing on land deals along highway routes. Later that month, during a shouting exchange among members of the legislature's public accounts committee, NDP member Gordon Dowding alleged that Bennett's boys were profiting by selling hardware materials to B.C. Hydro at twice the market price. After these incidents were reported in the *Vancouver Sun*, the two younger Bennetts launched a libel suit, eventually winning $16,000 in damages and the joy of seeing two irresponsible MLAs look very bad. In the legislature, before the issue had been settled, a heckling opposition member asked the premier where his sons were. Bennett quickly—prophetically—shot back: "They'll be here! They'll be here!"

Not only did this ugly style in B.C. politics belie the Good Life but sometimes it also took on a dangerous twist of violence. This was an era of mass demonstrations—well-organized protests sponsored by a host of organizations. In January 1971, the B.C. Federation of Labour staged a monster rally on the lawns of the legislature coinciding with the opening of the second session of B.C.'s twenty-ninth parliament. Thousands of demonstrators, including "a raft of branch plant yippies" according to one source, were bussed to Victoria from the mainland ostensibly to protest unemployment. They chanted obscenities and made rude gestures to the assembling MLAs and guests; they invaded the legislative public galleries and disrupted the reading of the Speech from the Throne by Lieutenant Governor John Nicholson; those who did not manage to make their way into the Parliament Buildings pounded on the doors and broke windows. Although no one was hurt, it was a new and frightening experience for the government. Attorney General Leslie Peterson demanded that the NDP "forthwith and without equivocation divorce themselves officially from an unholy wedlock, once and for all, with the B.C. Federation of Labour who financed the demonstration today." But Bennett viewed the incident philosophically: "These people hadn't been able to defeat Social Credit all these years; they were getting bitter."

Under seemingly constant seige, the Socred regime carried on. Premier Bennett continued to promote the idea that the province was best and getting better all the time. In February 1972, he introduced a staggering $1.4-billion budget, which he said would increase the beauty of and raise the quality of life in B.C. When asked if it was an election budget, he replied: "All my budgets are election budgets, my friend." In an interview later that year, he said: "We'll now build the finer things in British Columbia. . . . We will have more time for leisure, more time to be spent on making sure that we protect our ecology and protect against pollution of all types. . . . There will be more green belts, and more programs to stop sprawls from the cities, to encourage secondary industries, but only clean industries." However, one man's vision of the Good Life could not satisfy the various and conflicting demands of an increasingly fragmented society—and those demands were considerable. Several west coast unions in 1972 were demanding huge wage increases while Bennett was talking restraint. In a period when inflation was only just beginning to show its potential destructive power, the Socred premier became the first Canadian political leader to advocate wage controls.

Going on seventy-two years old, W.A.C. Bennett had been in power longer than any other head of government then in office in North America. Afraid to let go of that power, lest it mean the end of Social Credit in British Columbia, the premier gave every indication that he intended to stay on and fight another election. In the late spring of 1972, he took his entire cabinet on a province-wide travelling roadshow which was widely seen as a pre-election testing of the waters. The "Magical Mystery Tour" lasted for almost two weeks and took them to nearly every corner of the province; in each community the Socred cabinet met with concerned groups, heard briefs from local politicians, attended school and park openings, and dispensed grants and promises to the citizenry. And at almost every stop along the tour there were protests as well as greetings, placard-wielding demonstrators as well as welcome delegations. In Kamloops the welcoming committee included 200 government employees' union members demanding overdue collective bargaining rights and burning the minister of labour in effigy. Their jeers and taunts interrupted a speech by the premier during opening ceremonies for a new vocational school. Following the ruckus a reporter asked Bennett if he would take another look at bargaining rights for civil servants. "The answer is no," he replied.

One of the unusual features of the cabinet tour was the media coverage it generated. Unlike earlier efforts aimed at "bringing the government to the people," the official activities and movements of the cabinet received less attention than the backstage details. There were reports identifying which cabinet ministers went to local bars for a "cool one" after a long day of public meetings and business sessions, and bold front-page newspaper headlines quoted an RCMP officer who claimed that "Gaglardi Drove Like a Bloody Maniac" travelling from one meeting to the next.

The tour culminated with a major reception at the Royal Towers Hotel in New Westminster on June 8, a reception marred by an organized labour demonstration that turned ugly, violent and potentially disastrous. By the time the Socred cabinet began to arrive at the hotel, a rowdy mob of 500 protesters had been milling about for several hours, waiting for a chance to demonstrate their dissatisfaction with the government's threatened use of the Mediation Commission Act to settle a construction workers' dispute. With assistance from the local police, the premier and a few of the first cabinet ministers to arrive slipped into the hotel, running a gauntlet of people kicking and hammering on their cars and chanting obscenities. Other Socreds weren't so fortunate: Attorney General Peterson was hit on the head with a placard, Wesley Black received a blow to the stomach, Pat Jordan had her shoulder wrenched. Altogether, eight ministers incurred bumps and bruises, but the worst treatment was reserved for the last group who arrived after the mob had been whipped up into a frenzy. Agriculture Minister Cyril Shelford described the scene:

> We parked way out at the far end of the parking lot along with Gaglardi. These fellows immediately recognized Gaglardi; someone said, "There's Gaglardi! Let's get him!" So Gaglardi started talking, like he usually did: "Now listen fellas . . ." The police, one on either side of him, just picked him up by one arm apiece and said, "C'mon Phil, this is no place for your b.s." They hustled Phil into the hotel. That left Frank Richter, myself, Ray Williston, Isabel Dawson and Grace McCarthy out in the lot. Everyone tried to get through and the crowd of 500 were trying to get into the hall. The police were lined up along the driveway to escort us in and the demonstrators were spitting on these policemen until it was running down their jackets. I don't know how they stood it. They were linking arms to hold them back. Time went on, we were still trying to get in and the chanting changed; they started to chant: "Kill them! Kill them!" It was a pretty frightening experience. Then they started to swing two-by-fours, and Ray Williston pulled his collar up and some big fellow said, "We'll get those bastards, won't we?" And Williston said, "We sure will." He just kept going into the hotel; they didn't recognize him. Then Isabel Dawson was right in front of me, and I looked over backwards and saw this club coming down; I put up my arm, and it

would have hit Isabel on top of the head if it hadn't been for my arm. That's where I got my arm cracked. On the way in I got hit on my collarbone and got that broken.

The New Westminster labour demonstration was the most violent political protest in modern B.C. history; with less police protection, it could have easily resulted in tragedy. When Premier Bennett returned to Victoria with his war-torn cabinet colleagues, he commented on the incident: "I think it was a black day for labour in this province when they decided to use violence and they were badly advised to do so. . . . This government will never yield to force from violent pressure groups and any government worth its salt must stand up to these groups to protect the people as a whole as it was elected to do. . . . If pressure groups are allowed to rule a country, you've got the rule of the mob, you've got anarchy, you've got chaos. That is the issue in this province today and I think the people understand that full well." The stage seemed ready for a provincial election on a good old-fashioned law and order issue. Several days later, Bennett tied the New Westminster incident to opposition leader Dave Barrett, whom he called a member of the "extremist Waffle group" and "the most radical leader of the NDP since I've been Premier in 20 years." Referring to the New Westminster troublemakers, Bennett said: "Certainly they're his friends . . . the NDP arranged it. It was straight party, NDP socialist politics. I consider this the price British Columbia is paying for the unholy alliance between the NDP socialist party and the labour bosses of this province. . . . They're responsible for the anarchy that was shown at New Westminster." When Barrett launched a libel and slander suit against the premier for his comments, Bennett called him "a cry-baby trying to muzzle the premier."

As the weeks passed by, the prospective election call failed to materialize. Several cabinet members urged the premier not to let the opportunity pass. Bennett may simply have been not accustomed to dealing with political violence in the province, but he seemed uncertain. For perhaps the first time in his public career he hesitated, and as the weeks progressed things turned sour for the government. The terrible New Westminster incident seemed to fade into the past and the political scene rapidly degenerated as the special interest groups which Bennett had spoken against renewed their attacks and the opposition parties sharpened their axes for battle. Finally, by midsummer 1972, Bennett decided not to wait any longer—but the revealing manner in which he made the election announcement would influence the upcoming campaign.

The political decisions of public men are often determined by their adversaries. One of the factors worrying the premier in 1972 was what appeared to be a resurgence in west coast Conservatism under the vital leadership of Derril Warren. Ironically, the new Tory leader played a part in the election call on July 25, which he described:

> Deane Finlayson, the former leader of the Conservative Party in the province in the fifties, said to me, "Everyone who has come up against W. A. C. Bennett has come up head to head, toe to toe, swinging—and everyone has lost. I think you should consider, if you can find it within yourself, loving him to death." In other words: give him credit, be friendly with him, and don't try to take him on because he'll whip you.
>
> I had some friends in the media and we were waiting for the announcement from W. A. C. as to when the election was going to be. One day I got a call from a radio reporter who said, "W. A. C. has quickly announced a press conference in the Hotel Vancouver. Speculation is he is going to announce the election. Why don't you come over?" So I phoned some friends of mine and we went over to the hotel. Robin Leckie was with us—he was with a public relations firm—and he strolled in and, sure enough, W. A. C. was announcing the election. Leckie sat down beside Clancey, confirmed what was happening and then he strolled out. They had me hiding behind the pillars outside the mezzanine floor. There were about seven of us forming a chain, and we'd pass information up and down this chain. I was behind the pillar, not knowing what we were going to do, except the basic thought was that I would rush in after W. A. C. left and I'd use his press conference to get some coverage. Well, one of our guys got a brainwave. The *Province* photographer, whom we knew, came out for a smoke and one of the guys said, "Would you like to get a picture of W. A. C. and Warren shaking hands?" He said, "Oh, that would be great." So he hid me outside the door and we had it all lined up. W. A. C. got up and, of course, he was shaking hands with the reporters as he walked out. There was a sort of channel on each side of him of people saying hello, how are you. Clancey saw me coming—he could see what was coming—Robin Leckie gave him a shoulder and knocked him down into a chair. I walked up, six feet five and three-eighths inches thin and, of course, W. A. C. was quite short and rotund, and I grabbed his hand and he thought it was another reporter or something. I said, "Hello, Mr. Premier." I had hold of his hand, and he looked up. All of a sudden he realized, as quick as a flash, that he was being had. Well the *Province* guy was standing right there and—bang!—got the picture. W. A. C. started to pull his hand away and I wouldn't let him because I thought there might be other pictures. I was smiling, and he was looking at me like he could just kill me. Then he turned and walked away.

It was a flawed start to an unusual Socred campaign. The front page of the Vancouver *Province* carried a large photo of the two political leaders: a tall, young, handsome, smiling Derril Warren shaking the hand of a scowling old W. A. C. Bennett. The premier was not true to his usual form. In earlier elections he would have chewed Warren up and spit him out; he would have outsmiled and outflanked his opponent and told the press that he was a nice young fellow who needed a little more experience but would someday make it to the House; not this time though. Instead, Bennett seemed tired and worried. Following the incident with Warren, he warned his cabinet colleagues not to publicize their speaking events during the campaign because political opponents were bound to crash them. Thus began a strange cloak and dagger affair for Social Credit candidates who puzzled over the problem of how to stage election rallies without the benefit of advertising. Bennett refused all interviews, would not release his itinerary to the press and turned his provincial tour into a game of hide-and-seek.

Going into the political race which would end on August 30, 1972, the Socreds held 70 per cent of the seats in the legislature and an impressive, if recently battered, record of service. Bennett issued an election manifesto called the Kelowna Charter, which had been announced from his Okanagan home during the recent cabinet tour. The Socred platform called for further increases to senior citizen allowances, social assistance benefits for the handicapped, an increase in the homeowner grant, established in 1957 at $28 a year, to $185, and a new crown corporation—the British Columbia Development Corporation—to assist small business with low-interest loans. Perhaps the most contentious aspect of the Social Credit program was Bennett's call for public-sector wage controls. Here again, the premier was ahead of his time; predicting that inflation was a major problem on the national horizon, he placed an annual ceiling of 6.5 per cent on public-sector salary increases. Naturally, civil servants, who were still fighting for collective bargaining rights, were opposed to this policy, and the province's teachers' federation worked aggressively towards the government's defeat. Nevertheless, Bennett's campaign was directed against special interests, who he believed were attempting to impose their will on society. As a perpetual office seeker he had always been on trial for his political life, always required to court his restless constituents—now, in his pointed style, he reminded voters that his were: "Policies for people . . . *All* the people."

The opposition parties, all with new leaders, waged lively campaigns with an array of new policy proposals. Derril Warren and the Conservatives modelled their campaign on that used so successfully by Peter Lougheed in Alberta. Warren politicked in high style, with a heavy emphasis on media events and television advertising; his policy proposals, however, were not unlike the Socreds'. Pat McGeer stepped down as leader of the Liberals and was replaced by David Anderson, who had served a term in the House of Commons and had become a mouthpiece for several environmental groups. The Liberals attempted to pursue their traditional middle route through the polarized west coast minefield and advocated such nonemotional issues as parliamentary reform and the extension of the right to sue the crown. The NDP, with Dave Barrett at the helm for the first time in electoral battle, steered a very different course than in previous elections. Barrett neither launched into a socialist crusade for expropriation and state ownership, nor vainly tried to present himself as a moderate premier. Instead, he spoke about "people" issues like urban transit, day-care centres, government auto insurance, increased pension allowances and increased natural resource royalties. Barrett smiled a lot, and with his warm, friendly, pudgy demeanour seemed less than threatening. When Bennett pointed out that Barrett had signed the radical socialist document known as the Waffle Manifesto, the opposition leader replied: "If he calls me a waffle, I'll call him a pancake. If he calls me a double waffle, I'll call him a stack of pancakes. And if he keeps on calling me a waffle, knowing his attitude toward Quebec, I'll call him a crêpe suzette."

The Social Credit campaign was a low key effort centred around the premier, who was the only real issue in the province. Political observers conceded that the Socreds could not maintain their overwhelming majority in the House, but no one was writing them off. Some pundits were predicting a minority government, but Bennett had pulled so many irons out of political fires in the past that the suspicion of a repeat performance lingered. However, the demons of havoc pursued the elderly premier throughout the campaign. At first, there were small foul-ups, scheduling problems caused by the Social Credit peekaboo campaign. Then, a week before the election, Phil Gaglardi committed a major indiscretion. Speaking to a Toronto newspaper reporter, Gaglardi said: "Bennett will win next Wednesday's provincial election and step down soon afterwards." He accused the premier of being "an old man who doesn't understand what is happening with the young people of this province." Further, Gaglardi claimed that the Socred cabinet was "filled with square pegs in round holes." And, resolving the question of succession to the Social Credit leadership, he stated: "I'm the only real choice for the job."

Gaglardi's comments created a huge leadership controversy during the final days of the election campaign. He denied making the remarks which were attributed to him; but none of his cabinet colleagues believed his denials, and the premier, who ordered him to sue the offending newspaper, said that his rehabilitation minister "must—m-u-s-t win the case" if he wanted to remain in cabinet. In an effort to counterbalance the repugnance of Gaglardi's reported assertions, other cabinet ministers like Ray Williston and Dan Campbell announced that they, too, might be willing to place their names before a future Socred leadership convention. However, the damage was done, the press was having a field day and the opposition parties spoke of a Social Credit leadership race in the middle of an election.

How was W. A. C. Bennett going to pull this one off? Few things are as immutable as the addiction of politicians to the ideas by which they have once won power. When there is no time for thinking or for bold moves, the tendency is to repeat formulas that have proven successful in the past. Election after election, B.C. voters had surged to the polls and, as faithfully as spawning salmon returning to their natal streams, re-elected Bennett and his Social Credit government. He had won seven in a row—lucky seven—and now was furiously trying for an eighth. He reached deeper and more dramatically for the paranoid style that he had come to master, but was somehow less effective, like the boy who had called wolf once too often. Whenever he called Barrett a Marxist, the NDP leader jocularly referred to Harpo and Groucho. For perhaps the first time as premier, Bennett sounded desperate when he told one of his final large rallies of the 1972 campaign: "I want to tell you tonight, that the socialist hordes are at the gates of British Columbia!"

In the final days of the campaign, did Bennett believe in the possibility of losing? The number one devotee of the power of positive thinking would never admit it at the time, but his instincts were never wrong, and they told him he was in trouble—serious trouble. Even while riding around the province in the isolation of his chauffeur-driven limousine, he sensed the changing mood of the people. He was worried, and strangely helpless. Dan Ekman, who spent a good deal of time with the premier during the campaign, said: "He was trying to persuade himself that he had a good chance of winnng, but he knew there was a damn good chance that he might barely squeak through or be in a minority. I don't think he ever allowed himself to even consider that he could outright lose." In his hotel room in Vancouver on the Saturday before the election, with his son Bill, Dan Ekman, Cam Kenmuir and a couple of others, Bennett asked what their predictions were. One said what he thought the old man would want to hear, that everything was fine. Ekman said it could be as low as twenty-four out of fifty-five seats, and Bill Bennett said he thought it could be as low as seventeen. The premier just nodded. He knew how bad it was.

On election night, August 30, 1972, W. A. C. Bennett was at his Kelowna home with his family and a few cronies waiting apprehensively for the election results to appear on the television screen. Early returns indicated a whopping socialist victory. Bennett wiped his tears and decided to head down to his campaign headquarters to concede defeat. But unlike a similar night a dozen years earlier when a younger Bill Bennett had been unnecessarily prepared to say die, this time the roles were reversed: the father was ready and the son wanted to wait—just a little longer. But to no avail. All was lost.

Before the night was over, the standings in the B.C. legislature were dramatically reversed. Social Credit received over 31 per cent of the popular vote but elected only ten members; eleven senior cabinet ministers went down in defeat. Bennett, however, was handily re-elected in South Okanagan. The giddy new NDP administration would base its strength on almost 40 per cent of the vote and a surprising thirty-eight-member majority government. The Liberals polled 16 per cent of the vote and elected five members, while the Tories received 12 per cent and elected two candidates; Conservative leader Derril Warren was defeated in North Vancouver-Seymour.

British Columbia was in a state of shock. No one could quite believe what was happening. W. A. C. Bennett's sirloin face appeared before the television cameras to wish the new administration well, then he slowly made his way home through the quiet mob of stunned well-wishers. The Good Life was over.

CHAPTER TWELVE
THAT GOOD NIGHT

Do not go gentle into that good night,
Old age should burn and rage at close of day;
Rage, rage against the dying of the light.
   Dylan Thomas

One must wait until the evening
To see how splendid the day has been.
   Sophocles

Many British Columbians awoke pinching themselves on August 31, 1972, the day following the provincial election. It was, of course, true: W. A. C. Bennett and the Social Credit government had been defeated; in fact, they defeated themselves. The gates having been left open, the surprised socialists simply let themselves in.

The surprise was not just the defeat, but its magnitude. Aside from the premier and a couple of junior members, the Social Credit cabinet had been decimated; Leslie Peterson, Ray Williston, Dan Campbell, Phil Gaglardi, Wesley Black, Cyril Shelford, Waldo Skillings, Ralph Loffmark and Grace McCarthy led the long list of overthrown Socreds. The government's demise had not been foreseen by any political commentator.

After a single, tearful night, in the morning W. A. C. Bennett called his office in Victoria to calm his distressed staff. Secretaries were seen crying, wandering aimlessly through the corridors of the Parliament Buildings. Never having known another government, many civil servants feared for their jobs. The premier advised the employees of his office to clean up whatever work was on their desks and said he would be back to the capital in a few days. Exhausted from a month on the campaign trail and without the customary boost of adrenalin that winning an election brought, Bennett spent a few numb days with his family in Kelowna before facing the task of closing up the shop in Victoria.

During the first week of September, when Bennett quietly celebrated his seventy-second birthday, defeated Socreds licked their wounds, election post-mortems filled the air, and eulogies poured in from across the country and around the world. *Le Monde* of Paris headlined its analysis of Bennett's defeat "The Last of the Mohicans." In Britain, the *Guardian* expressed surprise at the British Columbia election results, saying, "The world is changing even in that picture-book province." In Canada, as elsewhere, it would take time to adjust to the fact that W. A. C. Bennett no longer represented the province which, to a great extent, he had defined.

For two weeks, the new NDP administration waited anxious and excited in the wings while the Socreds finished up their business and cleared out their offices. At the final cabinet meeting on September 13, 1972, in the presence of all Social Credit ministers, Bennett passed an order-in-council outlining the state of B.C.'s finances after twenty years of Socred rule. The cabinet document declared that "the economy of British Columbia is in excellent condition with more persons employed than ever in its history, and the gross provincial product growing at an annual rate of 11 per cent, on provincial government tax rates among the lowest in Canada. . . ." It listed perpetual capital funds of $85 million, special capital funds of over $126 million, $200 million in temporary investments, almost $100 million invested on behalf of B.C. Hydro, which was in an advance cash position, and $66 million invested temporarily on behalf of the provincial railway, which Bennett had renamed the British Columbia Railway. The order-in-council further boasted that pension and trust funds were fully invested in government guaranteed securities, and that the province had no direct borrowings or debt.

Bennett wanted to emphasize that the incoming administration would be inheriting a healthy state of affairs with bulging provincial coffers. It was also a final attempt to justify his fiscal policies and financial wizardry. In his last press conference as premier, he referred to the special order-in-council: "It is a matter of great personal satisfaction to me as steward of the provincial treasury for the past 20 years to report current reserves of $374.8 million. . . ." The figures and the millions and the endless zeros rolled out for the eager tape recorders and TV cameras. It was a fitting farewell; Bennett's final accounting to the people of the province was in the books. But there was more than a little irony in the fact that he had lived by the financial figures and now died by them. Some said that he had been defeated finally because of his blind adherence to figures, to the detriment of social concerns. Nevertheless, Bennett delivered no jeremiads, only a dry recitation of incomprehensible figures. Following that press conference on his 7,350th day as premier, he stepped into his big black chauffeur-driven Cadillac for one last ride — to Government House where he tendered his resignation to Lieutenant Governor John Nicholson. A few hours later, forty-one-year-old Dave Barrett, with his family in their little Volvo, arrived at the residence of the Queen's representative to be sworn in as the province's new premier.

The British Columbia leadership had leaped a full generation. How and why did it happen? The 1972 election has been much discussed and subjected to much analysis—none of which offers a more profound conclusion than that the government failed to receive enough votes to maintain power. Clearly, the socialist victory was not the result of a simple splitting of the vote among the free enterprise alternatives; indeed, the NDP would have won even had the Tories' 12 per cent and the Liberals' 16 per cent of the vote been tacked onto the Social Credit total. The election results were astonishing in that the dissatisfaction among the electorate—the urge to accept the NDP slogan "It's Time for a Change"—was inchoate until the day of balloting. Many have suggested that if voters could have been asked for a second opinion the day following the election, they would have immediately placed W. A. C. Bennett and the Socreds back in office, that there was never any real intention to defeat the government, simply a desire to trim it down to size. But by 1972 the premier was over two generations removed from the province's youngest voters and the British Columbia population had changed considerably from the early days of Socred rule. Never having experienced the alternative, the electorate exercised their democratic freedom to gamble.

Moreover, in 1972 almost every organized pressure group in B.C. was advocating the defeat of the government. As Dan Campbell put it: "The old man coalesced everybody and his dog against him." Bennett's crony, Waldo Skillings, believed that the fantastic 1969 election victory had gone to the premier's head a bit: "I hate to say it, but I really think it did. But we're all human, and when you are right as many times as he was, you don't listen to too many critics."

No doubt, leadership was a crucial question in the 1972 election; the desire for change was a desire for new, younger leadership. Cyril Shelford thought: "There were so many people around the province by that time that had never seen any other government but W. A. C. Bennett's and they felt that all governments were equally as good—which, of course, is far from the truth. And there is no doubt that he was wearing thin, he wasn't as aggressive as he had been." Ray Williston went further: "I think that Bennett was one of the real issues. I think he should have stepped down halfway in the term before and let somebody become established as leader for a brief period and then let the people decide whether they wanted that person for leader or not. The way it was working it was coming up the other way. He was going again as leader but people didn't have confidence that he was going to be there for any period of time. I think they thought that in voting for him they really weren't voting for the person who was going to be leading and that he was taking them on a bit of a wild goose chase."

Dave Barrett explained the leadership factor his way:

A lot of credit is given to me as the guy who defeated W. A. C. Bennett. It's incorrect. I came in and took on W. A. C. Bennett when he was past his gianthood in terms of leadership; I never tackled him in his prime. I happened to be there . . . the right person at the right time. The process of decline had nothing to do with age in my opinion. He was just as tough a bird in politics when I ran against him in 1972 as when I first came in the House in 1960. The decline took place to a large part, in my opinion, in the people around him. Bonner was gone, and also other people were gone, people who had been around early on in the fights in Social Credit and the development of it. He had not prepared a successor. He had not seen a need to prepare a successor. So the decline was not on the basis of age, but the decline was in the nature of the strength of his colleagues and the party. And that strength had waned considerably from '69 to '72.

Shakespeare wrote truly when he noted: "Politics is a thieves' game/those who stay in it long enough are invariably robbed." In 1972 W. A. C. Bennett may have been a liability for Social Credit, but he saw himself as an indispensable liability and was fully prepared to take a deep breath and set sail for the eye of the gathering storm. Following his government's devastation he offered no excuses; he apologized to his fallen colleagues, stating that the defeat was his fault, suggesting his timing was wrong. He did not engage in the expected political post-mortems; he wove no self-justifying cloak of rationalizations; rather, he admitted an error and began looking for ways in which it could be remedied.

Several years later, Bennett gave his view of his government's defeat:

> In nature you have two laws, both opposites—a law of growth and a law of decay. The older a tree gets, the sooner it starts to decay. The older the government gets, it gets into some problems. That's been true of all democratic governments; in time they have been removed from office. We'd been in office longer than any other government in the history of the province. People thought it was time for a change. And it was a combination of things, really. The government's policy of restraint, to protect against the onset of inflation—I established a policy of 6.5 per cent increases for public servants, when they wanted double that or more. The teachers raised a fund of $1 million for the purpose of defeating the Socreds because of the 6.5 per cent. The doctors and the civil servants opposed us as well. The powerful liquor and tobacco interest opposed us because of the bills we had passed in the legislature outlawing these pushers from advertising their products—I know the value of advertising. The newspapers and magazines and other media were all opposed to us; I was hitting their pocketbooks, their advertising

budgets. Plus we had all the other political parties and everybody attacking us. You'd wonder if we had anyone supporting us at all in 1972. The opposition was smart too; they said [to the electorate], "There's no question of beating W. A. C. Bennett and the Socreds, but they're too powerful; they've got to be cut down to size. So last time, maybe you voted Socred; this time you should vote for one of the opposition parties, just to give them some opposition in the House." The people fell for that; they fell for that in the last two weeks of the campaign, and that's where our vote went out from under us. But looking back at '72 now, I glory in that defeat. Either you steer the ship, or why be captain? My belief was—and that's why we'd have an election every three years—if the people didn't want me to be the captain, they had the right to choose somebody else. I never ducked from elections. I was never afraid of the cold water. I was elected and never defeated personally in my riding in eleven different provincial elections. When they defeated my administration, I didn't resent it. That's the right of choice. Nobody has heard me being critical of it. I've been critical of what's happened since, but I'm not critical of the defeat of my government. It's the best thing that ever happened. How could people find out the difference between the populist party called Social Credit—middle-of-the-road, private enterprise—and the leftist socialist policies of the NDP? They had the right to have a chance, so they got the chance.

W. A. C. Bennett was the victim of his own success. His economic achievement—the rise of British Columbia—and his political achievement—a polarization of mainstream factions—both contributed in a very direct way to his eventual overthrow. In that sense, he sowed the seeds of his own destruction.

Bennett's economic achievement had been made possible in part by the bullish conditions of the 1950s and 1960s: assured markets; cheap energy sources; plenty of investment capital, and international buoyancy. During the period that Bennett served as premier, productivity of workers increased steadily, technological innovations rapidly boosted the process of industrialization, and the demand for British Columbia's natural resources was voracious. Without a doubt, W. A. C. Bennett benefited from the coincidence of running a pioneering government in a resource-rich frontier during the greatest prosperity in western industrial history. While he was in office the population of the province doubled, the real income of British Columbians more than doubled and provincial government expenditures increased tenfold. The standard of living went up and up. The exuberance of B.C.'s prosperity was an important indicator of the shifting balance of economic power in Canada, from the central provinces to the New West. When Bennett became premier in 1952, B.C. was just emerging as an economic power in postwar Canada. By 1972, when he left Victoria, the province was a well-managed, loosely regulated jurisdiction with seemingly free-flowing public revenues and a wide reputation for the Good Life: it was Canada's most blessed and well-endowed province, commonly referred to as a "lotus land." But within the Pacific province the wild prosperity tended to make things look simpler than they really were; west coast society was becoming more urbanized, producing new, young, rising classes of restive individuals who did not embrace their aging premier's world view. Thus, the social forces produced by the new affluence were largely responsible for the demise of Social Credit. Change and progress, the dominant themes of W. A. C. Bennett's stewardship, left him behind.

Bennett always advocated an economic system based upon free enterprise and private initiative; therefore it is ironical that he, more than any other B.C premier, encouraged the citizenry to rely upon the government to promote their economic well-being. In truth, Bennett was a practising interventionist who taught British Columbians to look to Victoria as the miracle mechanic of the economic machine; and, of course, the main structural changes in the provincial economy from 1952 had been engineered in his office. Bennett also promoted the idea of unlimited horizons and forever-increasing material wealth—a boom-or-bust mentality that never busted while he was on the scene. The problem with his visionary outlook was that economic expectations, once raised, are not easily lowered— governments which followed in Bennett's footsteps would be forced to grapple with this uneasy inheritance.

The rapid rise and industrialization of British Columbia between 1952 and 1972 also had the effect of encouraging support among both private and public employees for the NDP through the concomitant growth of the power of organized labour. Union membership tended to insulate individuals from conservative political influences at the same time as connecting them with a province-wide network favouring the policies of the socialist opposition. As B.C. became more geographically integrated and economically homogeneous, it also developed the most heavily organized labour force of all the provinces. W. A. C. Bennett, therefore, can be thanked for the steady increases in support which the NDP accumulated, particularly during his latter years in office.

This was no accident: Bennett's economic and political achievements were tightly intertwined. The system he fathered, which allowed him to maintain power for two decades, involved a deliberate promotion of the NDP as *the* alternative to Social Credit. Bennett encouraged the development of a rigidly polarized two-party system as a means of preventing a resurgence of the old-line parties. Only by ensuring that the Grits and Tories would never come back to life could Bennett consolidate power behind Social Credit. He was successful in this goal: to be a provincial Liberal or Conservative in B.C. since his time has been little more than quixotic adventurism. His achievement of a polarized political culture may have allowed him to become a Methuselah of a premier but it also ensured the eventual defeat of his government. In a democratic two-party system it is likely—and probably desirable—that the alternative government will eventually come to power. No matter how skilled or proficient, a politician and his party will sooner or later be traded in for a different model. Even the paranoid style of Bennett's politics, which in years past had worked by painting the NDP as wild-eyed, fire-breathing extremists, had worn thin on an electorate gorged with the Good Life.

W. A. C. Bennett's economic and political achievements became an important part of his legacy, for they still influence the province. In retrospect, the defeat of the Socreds in 1972 is not all that amazing; the wonder is that they survived for as long as they did. Twenty years at the top suggests a stranglehold on power which Bennett never actually possessed. He had established a virtually brand new party, which was at first tenuous, and which was always faced by a vocal and strong opposition; furthermore, he had fought endless political battles and conquered legions of formidable opponents along the way to 1972. Political longevity is not the best measure of success in government—but in a fiercely partisan province like British Columbia, where one-party dominance will likely always exist, W. A. C. Bennett's record will stand alone. In that sense, at least, his career can be regarded as a triumphant one. It was his tremendous willpower that enabled him to prevail over circumstances, over enemies and over his allies and subordinates. The will to power would never be admitted by Bennett, but it was nevertheless the dominant influence on his career. So it is remarkable that he was able to conceal the crushing effect that the 1972 electoral defeat must have had on him.

Longevity aside, W. A. C. Bennett's administration is more noteworthy for its bold practice of the power of politics. Curiously, critics of his government used to argue that Social Credit represented power divorced from purpose—a claim which seems incredible when his administration is compared with the floundering west coast power-holders who have followed the perdition of 1972. Indeed, W. A. C. Bennett's was the last B.C. government to have a clear idea of where it was going and how to get there, all of which was based upon the premier's master plan for provincial development—a vision which preoccupied his administration for the greater part of its long tenure. Many successful politicians hold power without exercising it, but if one is to subscribe to Bertrand Russell's famous definition of power as the production of intended effects, then Bennett was surely one of the most powerful premiers in Canada's history. With his power, for twenty years he shaped a province and its developing hinterland: he shaped British Columbia.

Bennett was a seminal force in the modern development of the province; second only to the ice age, he was the force that did the most to sculpt the face of British Columbia. He left his record not so much in the statute books but in miles and tons of asphalt, concrete and steel. His priorities for the development of the province have inexorably affected the west coast social fabric, the quality of life there, and the polarity of its politics. It may be difficult to say that B.C. would today be either a better or worse place if W. A. C. Bennett had never become premier. But there is no question that it would be a very different place.

But what was the essence of W. A. C. Bennett the man? He did not lack compassion or social reach in his quest for power, but he was always seen as a flamboyant boomer who epitomized the virtues of hard work, perseverance and self-confidence. He came from a different era, when politics was serious business, not the sour and demeaning contest it has become. Lost in a kind of political time-warp, during his final years in power W. A. C. Bennett was as famous for his personality as for his achievements. He was a larger-than-life character, a walking-talking aphorism, a time-honoured conversation piece, revered but no longer taken altogether seriously. He had a monolithic quality about him which in the new age of media politics was widely misunderstood. Political colleagues, opponents and the press viewed him as a sly old Machiavelli, a consummate strategist, forever conniving, forever smiling, full of old-fashioned gimmickry. However, Bennett was simpler than most of his contemporaries ever imagined; his public face was usually his real face—deep down inside, he abhorred deceit.

Bennett suffered from being misunderstood, but perhaps he would have suffered more and earlier in his career if he had been understood. He was neither the political and economic wizard that Socreds believed him to be, nor the ogre and tyrant his opponents saw. Would he have been sustained in power if people had seen him for what he was: a very clever, extraordinarily sincere, emotional old man with an abundance of energy and a desire to convert it into political and economic accomplishments? Would British Columbians have been satisfied?

People invariably expect too much of their leaders. As premier, W. A. C. Bennett fulfilled the wants of British Columbians after first defining them as needs, and he thereby conjured a series of goals which seemed to largely satisfy a growing populace for two rambunctious decades. When his government was defeated, a phase of provincial self-expression went with him and a time of self-evaluation began.

W. A. C. Bennett became B.C.'s leader of the official opposition—a position he held in unspectacular fashion for only ten months. Behind the scenes, however, those ten months produced some startling twists and new commitments which allowed the former premier to continue playing a decisive role in the province's affairs.

The new NDP government announced a special session of the legislature for October 17, 1972, but opposition leader Bennett issued a statement saying he did not plan to attend the session as he had already made arrangements to take his "first real vacation in 20 years." The statement also referred to his intention to step down as leader of the Social Credit Party and included words which many have now forgotten: "It is my strong conviction that Mr. Leslie R. Peterson, former Attorney General, whose lengthy legislative experience includes service as Government House Leader, has a further outstanding contribution to make to the public life of the Province. . . . I would hope, therefore, that at an appropriate time Mr. Peterson will seek nomination and election to the Legislature when a by-election is held in my own constituency of South Okanagan." Then, accompanied by a few friends, Bennett and his wife left for a European holiday.

As leader of the opposition, Bennett was entitled to only a few staff appointments. He asked two former cabinet ministers, Dan Campbell and Grace McCarthy, to take on the large task of remoulding Social Credit. Campbell accepted the offer without hesitation; Grace McCarthy, whom Bennett thought of as glamourous, took some time before eventually saying yes. Both of them plunged into the job and, along with the former premier's personal secretary, Katherine Mylrea, formed the entire staff of the province's official opposition. While in Great Britain, Bennett announced the staff appointments to his travelling campanions. One of them, Ron Worley, had served as the premier's executive assistant in the early Socred years and Bennett, in a moment of weakness, had later appointed him deputy minister of travel industry. While serving in that senior position Worley had published an embarrassing panegyric, *The Wonderful World of W. A. C. Bennett*, which, in retrospect, was simply another nail in the Social Credit coffin. Incredibly, Worley had expected his boss to keep him on the payroll after the 1972 election and, when he learned of Campbell's and McCarthy's appointments, he packed his cases and left London in a fury. Of course, Worley was ill-suited for the job whereas Campbell and McCarthy were hard workers, not slow to attack political opponents and were doggedly loyal to both Bennet and the Social Credit Party.

Unexpectedly, W. A. C. Bennett returned from his European vacation in time for the special session in Victoria, but left on a round-the-world cruise shortly afterwards. He was not, however, giving up or becoming resigned to his fate; rather, he needed time to think and freedom to develop a plan of action. While he was away, two important decisions were made by other key players. Bennett's former attorney general, Leslie Peterson, after many sleepless nights, simply turned down the invitation to succeed his former boss whereas Bennett's younger son, Bill, decided that he would like to succeed his father at the helm of the Social Credit Party.

Bill Bennett decided on his own to leap into the fray. This is an important point, for it would be assumed by many that his father pushed him into politics or that the family was intriguing to create a dynasty. In fact, nothing could be farther from the truth. W. A. C. Bennett was a proud father and certainly hoped that one of his offspring would follow in his footsteps, but he neither prodded nor directly encouraged. The family felt, however, that if any of them were to pursue a public career, it would be Bill who, in so many ways, was his father's son. Having worked in his father's hardware store from the time of his high-school graduation, Bill and his brother R. J. had built up their own impressive businesses in real estate and development in the Okanagan Valley. Bill was clearly the most competitive of the younger Bennetts, and the most keenly interested in politics; speculation was that he would have run in South Okanagan if his father had stepped down prior to the 1972 election — but no one seriously believed that he could attain the Socred leadership. Even while his father was still premier there was an effort to get him into the House; apparently he was secretly prepared to run in 1969 but the Socred MLA who had agreed to step down decided at the last moment not to move aside. Closer to 1972, Bill Bennett was toying with the idea of federal politics and had made a tentative commitment to run as a Progressive Conservative at the next federal election. On the night of the 1972 election one of the more persistent callers who managed eventually to get through on the busy telephone line at the senior Bennett's home in Kelowna was the Conservative leader of the opposition in Ottawa, Robert Stanfield. Like others, he was conveying his sympathy, but he was also wanting to know if the Socred defeat would change Bill's unannounced intention of running federally, for it was almost a guaranteed seat in British Columbia for the Tories. Stanfield did not find out what he wanted to on that fateful evening — but he would know soon enough.

While W. A. C. Bennett and wife were away on their world cruise and the NDP administration was settling into office, Bill Bennett was quietly assessing his future and that of the Social Credit Party. He found that the Socred opposition was listless and floundering and that opposition House leader, former mines minister Frank Richter, was uninspiring and virtually useless. Dan Campbell and Grace McCarthy were frazzled with frustration and deeply worried about the growing rumours of well-moneyed efforts to build a new political party. Together with Campbell and McCarthy, the younger Bennett sent a telegram to his father, who was in South Africa: "If you're going to save the party, you must come home now." W. A. C. Bennett and May immediately left their cruise ship in Durban and spent the next thirty-six hours in transit. When they arrived at Vancouver airport they were greeted by a mob of well-wishers, all the Social Credit MLAs and a throng of reporters. Also present to greet them were Dan Campbell, Grace McCarthy and Bill Bennett. The former premier, exhausted and rumpled, came alive in front of a barrage of microphones and television cameras; he launched into an emotional attack on the province's new socialist administration and exclaimed: "I'm home now. I'm back—for a purpose!"

Without stopping to catch his breath, Bennett began an arduous series of breakfast, luncheon and dinner meetings and a round of speaking engagements, at which he railed against the policies of British Columbia's NDP government and called for a rebirth of Social Credit, a "great holy crusade against socialism." With Dan Campbell and Grace McCarthy, he toured the province in an evangelistic effort to boost membership and to light a fire similar to that of 1952. The rhetoric was all aimed at the NDP, but the undeclared targets were the various free-enterprise political alternatives which, on the presumption that Social Credit was dead, were looking for ways to form a new B.C. party, a new antisocialist alternative.

With W. A. C. Bennett back, the Socreds had a rallying point—a potent symbol upon which confidence and strength could be restored. For his part, the former premier was psychologically prepared for the task. He could never willingly purge himself of all lust for power; he was a man in whom ambition never ceased to agitate. Now, after an emotional homecoming, a reunion with the remnants of his party and a brief but excited chat with his son Bill, he was more eager than ever before. W. A. C. Bennett was determined not to go gentle into that good night.

To live forever is a human hunger. When Bennett learned in the spring of 1973 that his son Bill was interested in running provincially, his appetite became more than just healthy: he could taste the future. Although somewhat surprised by his son's private declaration, he became freshly and furiously motivated by the possibility of starting a political dynasty. Bill Bennett, however, wanted to do it on his own. He therefore asked his father to remain quiet, not to interfere, and to let him make his own announcements when the proper time came. W. A. C. Bennett agreed that he would need to be his own man, but behind the scenes he was already plotting to help win for him the power that was once his own.

Several years later when asked about his son's intentions and how his decision to run was made, Bennett pointed to a confidential meeting at his home in Kelowna with Conservative leader Derril Warren. The rendezvous took place at Warren's request, subsequent to the former premier's early return from his world cruise but well in advance of any public knowledge that

Bill Bennett was interested in pursuing a provincial political career. Warren intended the meeting to be a private tête-à-tête but W. A. C. Bennett invited Bill to attend. Warren described the meeting:

> I said, "Our parties should join forces. I don't think we can both afford to go on hurting each other, to the benefit of the NDP and to the detriment of the province. I'm not here to promote myself; I will resign as leader if the two parties come together. And I don't care who is leader; I'll give you a promise I won't even run; if you want my promise that I won't run, I'll give it to you. Let's have a leadership contest; I think we should have a joint convention. I don't even care what we call the party, but it can't be Social Credit, and if you say to me it can't be Conservative, I'll accept that. But the Social Credit Party was you; it's over. It has no place to go. You are its leader. You are the party. It has no new leader, and it isn't going to have anyone from the ranks. . . ." It was a very confidential meeting and it was all off the record. Bill stood up beside the fireplace during the whole thing. The phone rang, and May Bennett answered it and said, "Bill, it's for you." Bill went and took the phone and had his back to us in the other room, and W. A. C. Bennett turned to me and pointed to Bill and said, "There's the new leader of the party." I said, "What?" He said, "That's what the people want. They want a young W. A. C. Bennett!" I was floored. I said, "Really?" He said, "He'll be the new leader." And I couldn't believe it. Bill had never said a word during the whole meeting, never said a word about leadership aspirations. W. A. C. said, "You have only one choice, and that is to join the Social Credit Party." I said, "I expected you to say that, but I'm not going to and I have no intention of doing that." We left on the basis that it wasn't going to work.

Late in March of 1973 in New Westminster, the Socreds held their first large provincial get-together since the disastrous election. Originally intended as a leadership convention, it instead became the preliminary to the election of a new leader, which was rescheduled for November. The New Westminster meeting saw a great deal of public wound-licking and low-keyed lobbying for position in the future leadership sweepstakes. Les Peterson hinted publicly for the first time that he would not seek the post; Dan Campbell also stated that he would not be a candidate, but refused to say why. However, many other names were bandied about by the press as potential contenders for the party leadership including Phil Gaglardi, Grace McCarthy, Herb Capozzi, Robert Bonner and several sitting Socred MLAs; even Bill Bennett was mentioned, though not seriously. W. A. C. Bennett, who was the centrepiece of attention at the convention, made an emotional keynote speech to the 700 assembled Social Credit delegates. In his address, he rejected the idea of an alliance with the provincial Liberals or Conservatives and charged that Tory leader Derril Warren was "as responsible as much as any person in B.C. for putting the socialists in." He said that the Conservatives had succeeded only in splitting the vote and stealing "two eggs out of our nest"—a reference to the two Tory MLAs who had been elected. "The only movement that can beat the socialists is the same movement that beat them 7 times in a row," said the former premier. "There is only one way to stop these socialist hordes and that is to join the Social Credit movement now, now, now!" And, referring to the upcoming leadership convention, Bennett said: "I know you will elect a brilliant young person to lead you for another 20 years of continuous victory in government." Several times he referred to the next leader, conspicuously refraining from naming a personal choice, but placing a steady emphasis on the word "young." Asked later what he meant by "young," Bennett smiled, paused and said, "younger than me."

In the spring of 1973 W. A. C. Bennett gladly finished off his days in Victoria as leader of the opposition. Many years earlier he had relished sitting in the opposition benches and assaulting the old Liberal-coalition government. His performance more than two decades later, however, was lacklustre. The NDP administration had introduced several House reforms, including a daily oral question period. The first-ever oral question in the west coast legislature was put by Bennett on March 5, 1973, and, in a move which one commentator has described as "suffused with poetic justice," the Speaker ruled it out of order. In mid-April, during debate on proposed amendments to the Revenue Act, the aging opposition leader delivered a broadside against the Conservatives and said he would never tolerate a coalition between the Socreds and the party he had first represented in politics. At one point, new Tory MLA Hugh Curtis called out: "Who's going to lead you? Is Phil going to lead you?" Bennett paused briefly, turned to his heckler and said with a smile: "No, I think he's too old," drawing desk-thumping applause from NDP members.

W. A. C. Bennett constantly reiterated the need for a young, new Social Credit leader. He never once mentioned the name of his son; but in due course it became obvious that he was thinking in very specific terms—"young" meant a generation younger. On April 26, 1972, he wrote to his elder brother, Russell, in New Brunswick: "I seem to be busier than ever building up our Socred Party before I retire as Leader of the Party on November 15. Funny how years catch up with one, isn't it? But it's time a younger person is elected as Leader of our Party. I would be pleased if our son Bill would follow in my footsteps, but of course I would not make the suggestion, and I know that you wouldn't either, because one must make these difficult decisions on their own." Gauging events as closely as possible and considering the crucial factor of timing as the Socred leadership convention drew nearer, Bennett decided to resign his seat shortly after the spring legislative session in the hope and expectation that a by-election would be called forthwith. His letter of resignation of June 5, 1973, to the Speaker of the legislature stated: "While I have been a Member for so many years representing South Okanagan, it is with great regret that I tender this resignation, but I feel it is the time for a younger person to represent the Constituency."

A week following W. A. C. Bennett's resignation, Bill Bennett announced he would seek his father's seat; it then became abundantly clear to everyone that the young person that the former premier had been touting was his son. Premier Barrett called a by-election for September 7 and the various parties lined up their candidates for what would be one of the pivotal by-elections in modern B.C. history. In August, Bennett junior was successful in attaining the Social Credit nomination after his father had laid on hands in late July at the annual Socred nonalcoholic tea party at the senior Bennett's Kelowna home which was attended by more than 7,000 people. Five other candidates were nominated, including a Liberal, an independent and a communist. The NDP government candidate could hardly hope for victory in this interior Socred bastion, but the Progressive Conservative nominee was party leader Derril Warren, and he threatened to make the contest interesting. Warren decided that he had to try to prevent the Social Credit Party from winning the by-election:

> I think we looked at each other the same way: so long as they came up, we went down; and if we went up, they came down. I was going to be forced into resigning the leadership very shortly anyway, because I was not prepared financially to carry the party. I knew Kelowna; I was married there; my wife's parents lived there. And I really wanted to be the MLA from there. . . . The choice almost came down to getting out of politics or taking one last try and maybe doing it in South Okanagan. I thought we had a chance because I thought Barrett had sent out the word to vote for us. I'm told he said, "Look, let's have Warren, not Bennett—because if a Bennett comes back, here we go again."

For Bill Bennett, a neophyte who had never before sought elective office, the by-election was an awesome challenge. So desperately did he want to be his own man that he prevented his father from openly campaigning for him. Burdened as much as aided by his family name, dismissed contemptuously by NDP spokesmen as "daddy's little boy," he also had to contend with Derril Warren's strong appeal to the constituents of South Okanagan. Warren considered this episode as crucial in the by-election:

Hugh Harris was Bill Bennett's campaign manager. He told me later that a group of twenty-five businessmen, who were very influential in Kelowna, got together after W. A. C. Bennett decided to resign and said, "We're going to have to support Warren or Bill, because we've got to get free enterprise back in there." They had a vote; twenty-one supported me, three supported Bennett, and one abstained. So they said, "Okay, we'll call Warren and we'll tell him that we'll go to work for him." One of the three Bennett supporters went over to Bill and said, "It's curtains for you if that's the way they go, and you'd better get in there and do something." So, Bill Bennett called them and said, "Look, at least give me an opportunity to talk to you." So he came over, and they reversed their vote—because, you know, "Sammy, I went to school with you," and "John . . ." that sort of thing. It was something I didn't know anything about at the time. But you come so close sometimes without even knowing.

Despite dropping ten per cent of his father's 1972 vote total, Bill Bennett managed to beat off his opponents and win the South Okanagan by-election. It was a joyous victory for the Bennett family with important consequences for the future of British Columbia's politics. Derril Warren, who made a strong showing in the race, resigned as Conservative leader shortly thereafter. On the night of the by-election the tall young Tory had an interesting encounter with an excited seventy-three-year-old W. A. C. Bennett who was always fond of saying that revenge is best eaten cold. Warren recalled:

> I was very sad because I knew it was over, but I felt an obligation to go to Bill's campaign headquarters and offer congratulations. Bill was very gracious. He had a packed place and, as you would expect, W. A. C. and his wife May were there. I went up to the front with Bill and he asked me, "Would you like to say something?" I said, "No, it's your evening, Bill. I'd like to hold your hand up, then I'm going to leave." So I held his hand up and there was a big cheer for him. I came down, walking through the crowd; I knew a lot of people there—who I thought were voting for me. The reporters wanted, obviously, some statement on what was going to happen to me, and so on. So they were huddled around me with their cameramen and W. A. C. was standing over in the corner. I waved to him and, quick as a shot, he came over, grabbed my hand, pulled me back to the wall and said, "Let's have a picture! Let's have a picture!" I knew right there: I was being had. He was all smiles, and I was gloomy. I pulled my hand away from his; he didn't get a picture. I just didn't want it. I was feeling low enough. I said congratulations to him. But he came within a hair of getting it all back. If they

had got the picture, it would have been just the reverse of the one taken at the start of the '72 campaign. He came so close, and he was so quick to do it that way.

It is probably safe to say that Bill Bennett never realized how much his father helped him in his first electoral victory. Behind the scenes, W. A. C. Bennett called in favours from a generation of Okanagan supporters. In the months ahead, the former premier did more to ensure his son's future than Bill Bennett would want to know. The South Okanagan by-election served as an obvious springboard for Bill Bennett to contest the Social Credit leadership; suddenly he became the top contender for that position. The new MLA for South Okanagan could thank his father for so carefully timing his resignation and for safely delivering the seat—thereby almost assuring his son the party leadership. Of course, the 1972 electoral devastation made the whole thing a lot simpler for the Bennetts. Among the ten re-elected Social Crediters there was no obvious or credible leader; every single serious leadership aspirant had been defeated. Former cabinet ministers Peterson, Campbell, Williston, Gaglardi, Loffmark and others were without legislative seats—and with an anticipated three years until the next election, that was a serious liability. Among the defeated Socred backbenchers with potential and ambition was the frustrated Herb Capozzi, who believed:

> W. A. C. Bennett made it impossible, not just for me, but for anybody but basically Bill to become the leader. It was in how and when he resigned.... Normally, what should have been done would have been for the party to have a leadership convention and select a new leader. Then Bennett should have stepped down and given that leader the opportunity to run in his seat, because it's been proven a thousand times that you cannot be a leader of a party if you're not a member of the House. It was tried with Derril Warren and the Conservatives. You cannot do it; you cannot function; you have no voice; you cannot speak. So what Bennett did basically was limit the opportunity for a new leader to come only out of the MLAs that were elected at the time of the convention. It was a very interesting example of the shrewd political moves of W. A. C. Bennett.

The Social Credit leadership convention which took place in Vancouver on November 24, 1973, was an intriguing exercise in political organization and family influence. Bill Bennett had worked hard to prepare for the contest and was riding high as the newest Socred MLA, but unbeknownst to him his father's forces had been busy behind the ramparts ensuring that the party would make no mistake. Many of the convention's 1,500 delegates were hand-picked Bennett supporters; several hundred were bussed to the convention from Vancouver Island and the province's interior, their transportation, accommodation and meals heavily subsidized or paid for outright. Many old-guard Socreds seemed leery of Bill Bennett's leadership potential and were noncommital when asked if they were supporting him. On the sidelines was Phil Gaglardi who muttered: "I could win!"—but, in the crunch, he declined to let his name stand. In spite of all the tension and extra effort on the part of Bennett supporters, the forty-one-year-old son of the ex-premier was easily elected leader on the first ballot, tallying 883 votes to 269 for Langley MLA Bob McClelland, his nearest opponent. Of equal significance for the Socreds was the election of Grace McCarthy as the new party president. Challenged for the position by former cabinet minister Ken Kiernan, her victory by a mere twenty votes can be attributed to last-minute strong-arming and gladhanding by W. A. C. Bennett, who admitted that it was the only time he had ever interfered with the internal organization of the Social Credit Party. Grace McCarthy's presidency would prove to be a crucial factor for the Socreds in the months ahead.

Perhaps heredity enables apprenticeship, but Bill Bennett was determined to live up to the challenge of leadership by virtue of hard work, not whispers of nepotism. In his victory speech to the Socred delegates, he went out of his way to emphasize: "I am my own man." But his apprenticeship in political life was more trying than he could have imagined, as he was forced to grapple concurrently with the problems of consolidating his position as leader and reinvigorating a battered old party amid increasing calls for a new unity party divorced from Social Credit.

Bill Bennett may have been his own man but, lucky for him, his father was W. A. C. Bennett. The former premier conspicuously steered clear of his son in his position as new Socred leader, but continued his travelling roadshow with Grace McCarthy and Dan Campbell. He toured the province with the hauteur of a fallen monarch, and drew huge crowds wherever he appeared. He dubbed Grace McCarthy "British Columbia's number one freedom fighter" and called Dan Campbell "Dangerous Dan." The trio took turns bashing the NDP government, preaching against the "foreign" philosophy of socialism and selling Socred memberships like bubble-gum cards. The party's enlisted ranks had fallen to less than 4,000 prior to the 1972 election, but while W. A. C. Bennett was on his world cruise he dreamed up the idea of selling four-year memberships for five dollars apiece—thereby avoiding the awkward problem of annually renewing pledges. The gimmick worked and, largely through Grace McCarthy's unflagging zeal, Social Credit memberships swelled to the point where the party became the largest provincial political organization in Canadian history. She peddled

32,000 memberships in 1974 alone and by the time of the next election the flame-headed freedom fighter could boast of 75,000 signed-up born-again Socreds.

With his father travelling throughout the province beefing up the troops and promoting a holy crusade against socialism, Bill Bennett was able to concentrate on the important legislative battle in Victoria where the splintered opposition forces were gnawing on each other as eagerly as they were keeping the NDP administration in check. For Socreds, Liberals and Conservatives, the main sources of controversy and intrigue following the 1972 election were the persistent and loud calls for a union of the nonsocialist parties. Ever since 1952, Social Credit had been B.C.'s party of antisocialist unity, but with its defeat and the subsequent retirement of its one-and-only leader, it was widely assumed that the party was doomed to extinction. Jockeying for position was intense among the ten Socreds, five Grits and two Tories on the opposition side of the legislature; talk of unity was sporadic but popular, with stalwarts like Socred House leader Frank Richter stating early in 1973: "I certainly feel there has to be a new approach to getting back to the two-party system with free enterprise on one side and the socialistic philosophy on the other."

Prior to his resignation from the House, W. A. C. Bennett had played a crucial role in keeping the surviving Socreds in line. Several of them were quietly flirting with the idea of a new party and were taking active part in secret discussions with the Liberals and Conservatives. On the former premier's express order, Dan Campbell had each Social Credit MLA sign a till-death-do-us-part pledge of loyalty to the party. Not all of the Socreds were eager to sign, but with W. A. C. Bennett's authority behind the request, Campbell recalled that it was not a difficult task: "I just told them what to do—right now!"

By the time Bill Bennett became leader of Social Credit late in 1973, the main impetus behind the movement to form a new free-enterprise omnibus party was coming from extralegislative forces. A variety of people were looking for a simple and effective way to prevent a repetition of the events of 1972. Businessmen and chamber of commerce types frequently pointed out that the NDP's huge majority was based on less than 40 per cent of the popular vote, while the three nonsocialist opposition parties received the remaining 60 per cent. This seeming paradox, however, ignored the fact that in two decades of majority rule the Social Credit Party of W. A. C. Bennett never achieved 50 per cent of the vote. Nevertheless, in 1973, a self-made millionaire from Kamloops by the name of Jarl Whist and a Burnaby lawyer, Arnold Hean, formed the Majority Movement for Freedom and Private Enterprise. The Majority Movement soon became the dominant vehicle for the various interested groups and individuals in search of a new provincial unity party—a modern non-Socred version of the kind of political party W. A. C. Bennett had once advocated in the pre-1952 days of coalition government in British Columbia.

The Majority Movement did not play a role in the South Okanagan by-election which sent Bill Bennett to the House, but when Liberal D. M. Brousson resigned his seat, causing a by-election in North Vancouver-Capilano in February of 1974, the "nonpartisan" movers and shakers promoted the idea of a single nonsocialist candidate. The political parties, however, vividly demonstrated the obstacles to the creation of a united front by each running strong candidates. Liberal candidate Gordon Gibson, Jr., son of the "Bull of the Woods" of Sommers affair fame, won by a mere sixty votes over the Social Credit candidate. Undeterred by the lack of co-operation from the party machines, the Majority Movement pushed ahead with public meetings and media advertising; their cause was buoyed by the interest of sitting MLAs such as Liberals Allan Williams and Pat McGeer, Tories Scott Wallace and Hugh Curtis, and former Socred MLAs like Herb Capozzi.

Perhaps of greater significance was the fact that moneyed interests were becoming attracted to the option of the Majority Movement. Several leading B.C. businessmen saw the prospective launching of a new nonaligned free enterprise party as the surest and easiest way of defeating the NDP and preventing its return to power. Not unexpectedly, they purposefully ignored the possibility that the Social Credit Party could be revived, though it was the single greatest threat to the Majority Movement. In that respect, the defeat of Social Credit was a first step for the unity movement: only with the complete elimination of Social Credit could a new antisocialist force emerge.

Every party has an instinct for self-preservation, and after 1972 it was W. A. C. Bennett playing the quietest but one of the most important and effective roles of his career who personally guarded the Socred party's life. In fact, it was through his considerable influence that the Majority Movement was eventually quashed and Social Credit preserved. In retrospect, it is easy to laugh at the naive businessmen and grasping opportunists who advocated a new political party—but there was a period between W. A. C. Bennett's resignation and Bill Bennett's first tentative year as Socred leader when the Majority Movement almost succeeded in reshaping the face of B.C.'s politics and adding a new wrinkle to its paranoid style. Indeed, the temptation to succumb to the logic of the new party concept was very great and if not for the elder Bennett's direct intervention might have proved irresistible.

W. A. C. Bennett believed that a group of wealthy businessmen had each put up several thousand dollars to help the Majority Movement on its way, and that J. V. Clyne, the west coast establishment figure, was head of this group. During a short respite in the former premier's gallivanting crusade against the NDP, a meeting was arranged with one of these men at the Vancouver home of Grace McCarthy. Bennett verbally pummelled him with an awesome combination of common sense and outrage and by the end of the evening had convinced him to ask for his money back from the Majority Movement fund. Shortly thereafter a couple of other members of the group were persuaded to withdraw their substantial monetary contributions.

Financial backing was an important consideration for the Majority Movement, but even more crucial was the question of leadership. Before a new antisocialist alliance could be formed, it needed a leader who could unite all the free enterprise factions and simultaneously win the respect of British Columbians. Several public figures were considered—even tentatively courted—but none of the active B.C. politicians of the day had the necessary diplomatic abilities or stature. The backers of the Majority Movement, however, seized on the good idea of encouraging a former political star who was probably tailor-made for the job: Robert Bonner. The former attorney general had all the qualities needed for leadership and had not been active in Social Credit politics for over five years. Since his resignation from the government in 1968, Bonner had busied himself in business and had risen to the top management post with MacMillan Bloedel Limited. Now, the crucial question was whether or not he was prepared to leave the corporate boardroom to lead a new unity party to Victoria.

It is difficult to say what the effect would have been had Bonner openly declared an interest in the leadership of the Majority Movement; certainly the prospect became a powerful motivating force for many behind-the-scenes power brokers who lobbied the former attorney general, promoting him as a certain premier if he accepted the challenge. The Bennetts, however, were seriously worried about rumours of Bonner's intentions. Before Bill Bennett had won the Socred leadership, there was talk of a "draft Bonner" movement within the Social Credit camp. At that time, W. A. C. Bennett did his best to steer his former colleague away; when asked if Bonner could win the Socred leadership, the elder Bennett said: "I wouldn't think he would have a chance. He made his decision when he went into big business, and I told him so at the time. If it had been small business, it would have been different. But big business—no. We are not a party of big business, but a party of all economic groups."

However, Bonner's corporate connections were not seen as a liability to the businessmen and budding politicos who actively beseeched him to take the helm of the Majority Movement for the good of British Columbia. One night early in 1974, W. A. C. Bennett received an urgent phone call from his son Bill who expressed grave concern that Robert Bonner was about to announce his intention to head a new political force in the province. He asked his father to phone Bonner, who was then in Toronto, and to talk him out of making such an announcement. It was late at night back east, so Bennett left a message for Bonner to call him first thing in the morning. When Bonner called, the former premier assured him that the Socreds were surging ahead and that they were making a strong revival; Bonner said that he had heard differently. Bennett made Bonner promise that he would meet with him in Vancouver the next day, before taking any precipitous action. The two men met, talked things over, and Bennett somehow dissuaded his former colleague from making what seems to have been an imminent public declaration of support for a new coalition party.

W. A. C. Bennett's clandestine efforts to scuttle the Majority Movement were key factors in the rebirth of Social Credit and the slow emergence of his son as the only possible person who could lead a united antisocialist opposition. Together with Dan Campbell, who was tutoring Bill Bennett on the intricacies of politics in the legislature, and Grace McCarthy, whose fantastic membership drive was ensuring Social Credit's place as the only alternative government, W. A. C. Bennett served as the rudder of a good but battered old vessel undergoing a major overhaul.

By midsummer of 1974, Social Credit was attracting both money and new members at a steadily increasing pace and it was becoming evident that a new party was not going to be formed. Tory MLA Hugh Curtis joined the Socreds as did Conservative Party president Peter Hyndman and former Liberal and mayor of Surrey, Bill Vander Zalm. Soon the stampede was on. The logic of joining the Socreds proved irresistible in the face of the obvious failure of the Majority Movement. Bill Bennett, who was steadily obtaining control of the reins of a Social Credit Party becoming dynamically transformed, was probably stating the obvious when in 1975 he said: "In business when you want to expand, you use one company as a vehicle. You naturally choose the one with the broadest base and the best-known name." That point became patently clear when, in September of 1975, after lengthy negotiations, three Liberal MLAs, Allan Williams, Pat McGeer and Garde Gardom, announced at a press conference in the Hotel Vancouver that they, too, had pledged support to Bill Bennett.

In spite of being completely written off in the aftermath of the 1972 election defeat, Social Credit had become the new sought-after unity party—or, as it was derided in the press, the "united vegetable party." British Columbia history is full of surprises and Bill Bennett's rise to the top of a rejuvenated Socred party is one of the greatest surprises in the province's recent past. Of course, none of it would have been possible without the steady determination and uncanny manoeuvring of W. A. C. Bennett, one of the most surprising politicians in Canada's history. It was largely through his efforts that the born-again party managed to co-opt the movement whose goal was to swallow Social Credit as well as nonassociated political fish. In a shrewdly engineered political merger, the Socreds became the Majority Movement without changing the name of their old family firm.

All of this strategic planning, fancy dancing and hasty amalgamation would seem ludicrous if not placed into the context of the time. The motivating force behind the various attempts to create a unity party of nonsocialist factions was the election in 1972 of an NDP government, for fear is always a great motivator. B.C. history shows us how fear of socialism had helped fuse an uneasy but highly successful coalition of Liberals and Conservatives in the 1940s. An exploitation of that same fear had helped W. A. C. Bennett consolidate power behind his triumphant Social Credit machine. Now, in post-1972 B.C., the fear had been realized, not imagined—and the motivation to dislodge the NDP from Victoria was almost frantic. Socialism in power was an abysmal failure when it came to representation of working class concerns or fulfillment of proletarian expectations, but it proved remarkably successful in solidly uniting British Columbia's bourgeoisie. Canada's west coast province was unwittingly entering a strange, new world with a sharply polarized style of politics.

Far from allaying the generations-old nightmares of antisocialists, the NDP administration of Dave Barrett not only justified them but elicited new ones almost daily. The new premier, who was given to occasional fits of temper and public bad language, was critical and suspicious of the press; both he and his colleagues believed that they were being subjected to unfair attacks and excessively harsh judgements by the news media. Barrett screamed with rage and pain when, in the spring of 1973, *Barrons's*, the leading American business and financial weekly, described the NDP regime as "the Chile of the North," but the premier's reaction was a typical overreaction. There was not much truth in his cries of persecution; rather, he and other New Democrats ignored the all-important fact that the election of a socialist government in one of the wealthiest jurisdictions in the world, enjoying one of the highest standards of living in the world, was a dramatic, newsworthy political development and therefore practically demanded saturation coverage by the media. The critical coverage had more to do with the substance of NDP politics and the miscalculated effects of the government's programs than the supposed biases of a capitalist press.

What did the NDP do to deserve the obloquy heaped upon it? The pugnacious Barrett administration engaged in a continuous process of what has been referred to as "legislation by thunderbolt." During the first year of socialist government in B.C. the legislature sat 140 days, double the average under W. A. C. Bennett's government. The NDP administration brought 400 bills to the House in its first full year in office, 300 of which were bills of substance; under the elder Bennett's auspices, the legislature had received forty or fifty bills per session, a half dozen of which were deemed important.

The abruptness and magnitude of these various legislative initiatives were matched only by their often controversial nature: by virtue of the Land Commission Act of 1973, all agricultural land was "frozen" for other uses; that same year the Insurance Corporation of British Columbia (ICBC) was also established, to the explicit chagrin of private companies operating in the field of automobile insurance; the Mineral Royalties Act of 1974 imposed heavy new taxes and royalty structures on the province's mining industries; the Timber Products Stabilization Act of 1974 brought about a new centralized means of control for British Columbia's forest industry; the Public Service Labour Relations Act of 1974 granted full bargaining rights to provincial government employees. The NDP government also established several new crown corporations, including the B.C. Development Corporation, several resource companies, including Canadian Cellulose Co. and Ocean Falls Corp., companies active in real estate and public transport, and even a poultry operation in the Fraser Valley. Reaction to these various and ambitious government initiatives was generally hostile. Farmers complained that they were being made serfs on their own land; developers and development capital fled the province; the mining industry came to a virtual halt in protest against the new mineral royalty legislation; the province's forest industry underwent a period of serious re-evaluation. The Barrett administration was exceptionally weak in the area of public relations, but the opposition parties, particularly Social Credit, never hesitated to let British Columbians know that they were being led down a dangerous socialist path. The aging godfather of B.C. politics, W.A.C. Bennett, explained in the summer of 1975 that socialism would simply not work: "This province depends on individual initiative. The North—all those resources—depend on someone taking a gamble: opening it up. Schools, hospitals, services—they all follow later. But somebody has to take a chance first. Socialism may work here 200, 300 years from now when British Columbia is developed. Won't work now."

Nevertheless, it was not so much *what* the NDP administration was doing as *how* they were doing it that caused their most serious difficulties. As many NDP admit, they tried to do "too much too fast"; and they did too much without explanation, for the Barrett regime's biggest mistake was their belief that they had been given a mandate to implement socialism in B.C. The NDP never came to terms with what in retrospect is so startlingly obvious: they had not been so much elected as W.A.C. Bennett had been defeated. In addition, their unco-ordinated socialist rhetoric far outstripped their fairly moderate policy initiatives. British Columbians felt ill at ease with this new, aggressive, sometimes foreign-sounding kind of populism. In 1972 residents of the province had much and expected more; with the NDP, they did not get what they had bargained for.

Although the socialists' victory in 1972 had been a surprise, it still seems strange that the NDP came to power with no clear policy priorities or conception of how to exercise the power they had rightfully won; in many respects they governed with an opposition mentality. This had much to do with the fact that Dave Barrett and each of his ministers had been schooled in W. A. C. Bennett's politics. For a party that had been in opposition for almost forty years, the last twenty of them spent in frustrated, near-violent attack on Social Credit, it is amazing how few structural changes they made to the actual machinery of government. Of course, they brought about substantial reforms in the procedures of the legislature, but these worked to the distinct advantage of the opposition and, along with the dramatic increase in sitting time and session length, helped bring about a feeling of crisis and lack of confidence in the NDP administration. When it came to the day-to-day operation of government, the formulation and implementation of policy, there was an informal kind of acceptance of the system which they had inherited. NDP caucus meetings were "rap sessions" with little effort at policy direction; the cabinet was an unorganized body of old-style socialist politicians, excited about being in possession of the power to fulfill the many promises made in days gone by.

Dave Barrett and his resources minister, Bob Williams, were practically the entire decision-making apparatus of the NDP government, and this was unfortunate in a political sense because Barrett did not possess the requisite administrative skills and Williams, who did, had over the years earned the almost pathological hatred of political opponents. With callow executive assistants and in a peculiar kind of delirium, the NDP cabinet stumbled from problem to problem like a ball in an arcade game. Although individual ministers made many innovations at the departmental level, the NDP government retained the previous administration's simplistic organization which lacked any kind of planning or integrated system of policy control or co-ordination. W. A. C. Bennett had been able to pull it all off because of his special financial and administrative genius and because his government's goals lay in ecomonic development; co-ordination among the various projects which he initiated was a relatively straightforward technical matter. With the vast power which the old Socred premier had carefully accumulated, he could set priorities, authorize construction, evaluate progress and maintain an overall vision of provincial development without the assistance of planning committees and policy units. NDP goals, however, were quite different — especially in that they were not parts of a holistic vision like Bennett's. Without taking time to identify their goals, the more forceful NDP ministers flew off on policy tangents of their own without setting program priorities or attempting any kind of interdepartmental co-ordination. Many of these programs were aimed at social change and individual betterment, but without ongoing evaluation or central control over expenditure they were experiments marked for disaster. It is, therefore, no wonder that the NDP administration has been characterized as incompetent, spendthrift and out of control. According to political scientist Paul Tennant, Barrett and his ministers were "unaided politicians in unaided cabinet" who never came to terms with the exhilaration of power.

One of the primary reasons for the NDP's problems was the obstinance and ambition of their leader, Dave Barrett. One of the best orators in Canadian history, Barrett provides irrefutable evidence that the qualities necessary to achieve power are often diametrically opposed to those necessary to consolidate and exercise power. In opposition, he had led the attack on W. A. C. Bennett's practice of doubling huge portfolios on the backs of individual ministers. In government, he was as guilty of this particular sin as Bennett had been and, in a surprise move, he retained the finance portfolio for himself despite having strongly criticized the former premier for having done so.

Once in power Barrett was obviously impressed with the reasons Bennett had retained control over the provincial purse strings, but the social worker as finance minister proved more than simply deficient; lacking even informal training in the fields of economics and finance, Barrett had neither the background nor the ability to use the positions of finance minister and head of Treasury Board for the purposes of fiscal control or economic planning. Small problems occurred which were due largely to carelessness. For instance, in 1967 the Socred government had signed an agreement which allowed the United States to flood the Skagit Valley for a ridiculously low yearly payment. The NDP opposed the scheme and argued that the agreement was invalid. However, when the Americans sent a payment cheque to Victoria which went through normal channels, it was carelessly cashed, thereby weakening the government's legal position. Larger problems also plagued the socialist government and added to the pervasive air of money mismanagement in Victoria. When in 1974 it was revealed that the Human Resources Department had overspent by a startling $100 million, Barrett tried to dismiss the whole episode as a "clerical error." Opposition politicians expressed a more popular view when they described the socialists as drunken sailors shovelling money out of the back doors of the provincial treasury.

In many ways, Dave Barrett was a caricature of W. A. C. Bennett: like Bennett, he carried on about how his "little government" was being challenged by hostile forces; like Bennett, he ranted and raved against the insensitivity of far-off federal politicians; and like Bennett, he cultivated a paranoid kind of populism centred around the image of a single strong leader. Many civil servants and government members referred to him as "W. A. C. Barrett." However, unlike Bennett, Barrett could not fully comprehend the power of politics from a government standpoint. Unlike Bennett, he was forced from the start to contend with the new roller-coaster economy of the 1970s which was clearly on a downhill run. Barrett tried to play state capitalist at a time when the international capitalist system was beginning to suffer a severe economic recession. After 1970 the era of high growth and annual five-per-cent jumps in economic indicators was over. This slowdown was probably one of the many reasons for the defeat of Social Credit in 1972, but it would play far more havoc with Dave Barrett's attempts to expand the Good Life.

This is not to say that the Barrett regime was a victim of international recession. The socialists' fiscal problems were in large part of their own making. If W. A. C. Bennett had conservatively underestimated revenues, Dave Barrett went to the opposite extreme of underestimating expenditures. Salaries for MLAs were increased to recognize their new full-time status and Barrett doubled the premier's salary to $52,000 per year. The civil service grew by more than 28 per cent under NDP auspices and public-sector salaries were raised up to 56 per cent. With these various increases went a concomitant surge in prices; the NDP aaopted an attitude which worsened an already dangerous inflationary spiral. The problem of rising expectations, which was such an important ingredient in the Socred downfall, was clearly getting out of hand. In addition to all of this was the fact that NDP policies had frightened developers and venture capital from British Columbia and brought the province's major resource industries to a virtual standstill. Recognizing his inability to deal with the deepening fiscal quagmire, Barrett relinquished the finance portfolio late in 1975 after first bringing in an astonishing $3.2-billion budget, fully $1.1 billion larger than the preceding year's and $2 billion more than the 1972 budget of W. A. C. Bennett. The incredible dollar sums soon became meaningless as problem piled upon problem for the hapless socialists, whose tenure in office by 1975 resembled a hangover following a wild binge on the Good Life.

The NDP administration voiced a strong egalitarian spirit at a time when British Columbians wanted more prosperity not equality. One of the government's most difficult problems was an inability to satisfy one of their prime constituencies: labour. Because organized labour's expectations from the NDP were higher, their level of satisfaction with the policies emanating from Victoria was lower. Labour made great strides in areas such as collective bargaining and the right to strike, but labour disputes increased and often made the government look spineless and inept. Dave Barrett struggled valiantly with the paradox of socialism in power; several times, to the chagrin of many of his colleagues, he stated that: "We are not a labour party." In October 1975, after a summer of crippling strikes, he confronted B.C.'s militant labour union leadership by ordering some 15,000 workers in the province's pulp and paper industry back to work. In an emergency session of the legislature he passed legislation ordering striking workers in major food retail chains to return to their jobs. The unions cried "betrayal" and "treachery" but Barrett had to play tough. The provincial treasury was dangerously depleted and heading for an obvious deficit, which in British Columbia's political vocabulary, W. A. C. Bennett had decreed, was a dirty word. The Socreds were on the march, gaining strength with every passing week, with new defections from the ranks of Liberals, Conservatives and other disaffected groups. Barrett, meanwhile, was basking in the imaginary glory of strong and decisive leadership following his showdown with the labour unions; impulsively, without consulting any colleagues, he decided to follow W. A. C. Bennett's pattern of three-year electoral terms. On November 3, 1975, he startled nearly everyone by announcing an election for December 11.

British Columbia's 1975 election was a tense and dramatic contest between two belligerent factions with generally opposed but sometimes overlapping views of how the province should be managed. The Liberals and Conservatives ran meagre slates of half-hearted contenders, but the big battle was between Barrett's socialists and the new Socreds under Bill Bennett. Barrett fought a strange kind of campaign which emphasized his leadership and little else. At meeting after meeting he delivered bravura performances; it seemed as if he believed that the election was some kind of a vaudeville contest which could be won by personal showmanship. It was equally clear that the NDP premier thought he could win—otherwise, why would he have called the election with twenty-one months remaining in his mandate? But as the election battle progressed, laughter and derision turned into unease and fear; the paranoid style of B.C. politics seized hold of the campaign. The NDP, the party that prided itself on its intellectual substance and moral righteousness, appeared exhausted after only a little more than three years in power. "Fat little Dave" Barrett was dished out to the voters as a strong leader; barely another cabinet minister was heard from during the entire campaign. The socialists were reduced to a leader and the leader to a slogan: "Don't let them take it away!"

The Social Credit campaign got off to a shaky start with Bill Bennett cold and wooden by comparison with the flamboyant Barrett. Bennett, who was derided as "daddy's boy" by NDPers, was in a make-or-break situation, a Canadian west coast version of a classical Greek tragedy. W. A. C. Bennett, because of his son's insecurity and ardent striving to be his own man, was placed "on hold" in Kelowna throughout the campaign. Unable to participate or to finish the job that he had made possible, the old man was forced into an invisible role and was almost cruelly neglected. His stubborn son, who refused to ask for advice from his politically wise father, made the best out of a very good situation and seemed to gain confidence as the campaign neared its conclusion; he promised British Columbians a big pre-Christmas present—a Socred victory. He refused to appear in a televised debate with Barrett, who would have easily mopped the floor with him; instead, he travelled the province promoting Social Credit as the party of unity and focussing his attack on ICBC losses, welfare overruns and socialist mismanagement. With the benefit of hindsight it is easy to see that Bill Bennett had won the election before it was called. But B.C. elections are always full of surprises and, as December 11 got closer, no one was willing to make any definite predictions; some felt that Barrett, playing a variation on a theme established by W. A. C. Bennett as the persecuted loner, might squeak back in on a tide of sympathy.

It was not to be. British Columbia's first socialist government went down to ignominious defeat. Not only were the province's voters unsympathetic, they were absolutely eager to get rid of the NDP. Dave Barrett suffered a personal, humiliating defeat at the hands of an unknown car dealer in Coquitlam. In Kelowna, Bill Bennett smiled so hard he nearly broke his face as the nouveau Socreds racked up almost 50 per cent of the popular vote and reversed the standings in the legislature which now consisted of thirty-five Social Crediters, eighteen New Democrats, one Liberal and one Conservative. The NDP was defeated not through loss of popular support, which remained almost exactly the same as the 1975 level, but through the success of Social Credit in winning new support in marginal ridings. On election night at the Socred campaign headquarters the loudest—and most hysterical—applause was for W. A. C. Bennett who was simultaneously laughing and crying as he mounted the podium to tell the crowd: "Now a people's government is back in power and everybody can breathe easier tonight. There have been three and a half years in the wilderness for the people and that's too long. I said in the past people need to put their finger on the hot stove of socialism. They felt it. Now they've taken their finger away."

There is no humorist like history. If it had not been for the NDP interregnum, the Bennett dynasty would not have been possible. It was W. A. C. Bennett's 1972 defeat that paved the way for his son and a kind of personal revenge in 1975.

W. A. C. Bennett had helped engineer the rebirth of the Social Credit Party and with his invisible hand guided his son to power in Victoria. However, with a rebelliousness more commonly associated with teen-age years, and believing that his father's political influence might have a negative effect, Bill Bennett did not permit his father to become involved in his practice of power in post-1975 British Columbia. This is unfortunate, for W. A. C. Bennett was by far the most respected and revered public figure in the province; in any other context he would have been an asset, not a liability. But Bill Bennett was determined to govern on his own; he shunned his father's advice and was extremely sensitive to the frequent suggestions that he was not his own man. Despite this, his cold, nervous personality did not project well, especially on television, and many British Columbians saw him as a wooden man controlled by his ventriloquist father in Kelowna. It was imagined that he ran home on the weekends for advice. In fact, Bill Bennett ran from his father, not to him. Every son has to fight to free himself from his father, but with Bill Bennett that struggle sometimes seemed the equivalent of a kind of psychic patricide. In his attempt to build a new, liberal kind of Social Credit Party, he shunned most of the old Socreds and studiously ignored his father's cronies. The only debts or acknowledgements he made to paternal influence were practical decisions rather than gestures of gratitude. One of Bennett, Jr.'s first appointments as premier put Robert Bonner into the chairmanship of the B.C. Hydro and Power Authority, the massive and most important crown corporation in the province, to which Bonner had served as a midwife during its birth in 1961; Dan Campbell, who worked indefatigably throughout the election campaign, received a senior civil service position in intergovernmental affairs; and Grace McCarthy, who was elected in Vancouver-Little Mountain, was given the cabinet portfolios of provincial secretary, travel industry and, significantly, was also appointed deputy premier.

The 1975 election marked the practical end of W.A.C. Bennett's public career. After that date he was expected to retire as the grand old squire of the Okanagan. It was, however, an expectation he could not willingly fulfill. He was, of course, elated with the outcome of the election and was proud of his son; he enjoyed recalling that this was the very same person he used to haul down to the woodpile for disciplining many years before. But W.A.C. Bennett was frustrated that he could no longer speak out on public issues in B.C. He did not wish to offend or embarrass his oversensitive son, but neither was he a man who could accept being muzzled. The only influence the former premier could now exert in Victoria was through Grace McCarthy who, in a political sense, was more a daughter to W.A.C. Bennett than Bill Bennett was a son.

The new Social Credit government was a very different sort of administration than the pre-1972 Socreds. In fact, Bill Bennett is the person who brought "modern" government to B.C. with planning and co-ordination capability at the cabinet level and all the expected committees, commissions and agencies necessary to lock horns with other provincial and federal bureaucracies. Ironically, Bill Bennett was referred to derisively as "Mini-Wac" when it was his government that was the first to break away from the simple and crude governmental machinery that it inherited. In terms of policy, style and decision making, it was Dave Barrett who had actually played the role of "Mini-Wac." Now, Bill Bennett's administration was building up a large new government machine which spouted the dull public administration language of other colourless Canadian governments. It seemed that the era of flamboyant populist leadership was over in British Columbia. Just as in physics antimatter behaves opposite to matter, Bill Bennett, Jr., became anti–W. A. C. Bennett. Of course, the inevitable comparisons would often be made between the new premier and his father, but the two men were as different as their generations and as contrary as their public images. Herb Capozzi said of them: "The difference between Bill Bennett and W. A. C. Bennett is that when Bill Bennett goes to Victoria he takes the ferry but when W. A. C. goes he walks."

The elder Bennett was extremely critical of the new Social Credit government, but kept his criticisms to himself. He sometimes tried to feed the new power-holders in Victoria helpful ideas, but they were rarely accepted. He thought that his son had surrounded himself with too many yes-men and he was very severe on the Liberal element in the new unity party; however, in private conversation he would always stop himself from raking them too vigorously with his contempt by reminding his listeners that, after all, he had put them there. He laughed at the assertion that his son was establishing a "modern" government in Victoria and sincerely believed that the elaborate machinery being implemented was unnecessary. "Government is not complicated," he would say, "only people make it complicated." Referring to the new Socreds, he stated only half-jokingly: "The trouble with that bunch of reactionaries is that they won't accept any progressive ideas."

Many old-line Socreds—or as W. A. C. Bennett preferred to call them, "genuine" Socreds—lobbied for the province's elder statesman to take some kind of public appointment during his twilight years. Some suggested he would make a good senator; however, no offer of appointment was imminent and it is doubtful that he would have accepted one. Others asked his son to appoint him to some kind of a special commission or as a goodwill ambassador for the province, but without success. It was even suggested that W. A. C. Bennett become British Columbia's next lieutenant governor, an idea that Prime Minister Trudeau would never have accepted and that the former premier laughed off: "I know how powerless that position is." Nevertheless, his ostracization from Victoria and his inability to speak out was difficult for him to accept, even if he could understand the reasons. His last years should have been a glorious release and peaceful retirement; instead, they were a painful experience. His former sidekick, Bill Clancey, believed that the old man was dying of a broken heart.

Without a doubt, W. A. C. Bennett was unhappy and frustrated with his lot in life during his last years. He felt that the new Socreds were making serious blunders in Victoria but that after helping put them in office, he was prevented from advising them how to consolidate their power. His contact with his son was minimal after Bill became premier, but he took advantage of every opportunity to ensure that he got good advice and stiff criticism. W. A. C. Bennett told this story of the Bennett holiday get-together in 1976:

> Every Christmas morning our family all assemble at our place in Kelowna and we have a great time and a great Christmas breakfast before anyone opens their presents. So on this Christmas morning the breakfast was well launched and R.J., my eldest son, got up in a quiet and relaxed way and started to tell a story which he had told me the day before. So I said, "Louder, R.J.!" I got Bill's attention, all the grandchildren's attention, everybody's attention. R.J. told his story about this great company that had selected a new president, and the old president was making a few remarks to the new president at a banquet. He said, "There are a lot of things that I could tell you today. I could tell you about how great this company is that you've taken over. I could point out all the great things we have done and how we have served not only ourselves, but the community. I could tell you about what we are doing now as you take over the great challenge that faces you. And I could go into some detail about all the great plans that you should be able to carry out with this company in the interest of its shareholders, its customers and the general public. But," he said, "I'm not going to tell you any of that today. I'm not going to present you with any gift either. The only thing I'm going to give you are three envelopes, and these three envelopes"—and he took them out of his pocket—"are numbered and sealed: number one, number two, and number three. Mr. President-elect, in your first year of running the company, if you run into difficulties, and only then, open up letter number one. Then, if you're still running into difficulties in the second year and you find it absolutely necessary, open letter number two. I hope you don't run into difficulties the third year, but should things be tough and you're still in great difficulties, open letter number three." So, the first year, the president did run into some troubles. "Gee," he said, "I'd better open that letter." So he opened letter number one and it said: "Blame all your troubles on your predecessor." So he went out and that's what he did. Then, the second year he was still in trouble. So at last he said, "I'd better open letter number two." He opened it and it said: "If you still have problems, Mr. President, blame all your problems on the economy." So, then he got into the third year and he thought he'd have everything solved. But the third year no matter what he did there were more problems. He hesitated a long time but at last said, "Well, the old

president must have had something in mind when he wrote letter number three, so I'd better open it." He opened up letter number three and all it said was: "Mr. President, prepare three envelopes."

W. A. C. Bennett did his best to fill the role of a retired provincial statesman. In his last years he lived and breathed for the opportunity to talk politics, to reminisce with former colleagues and adversaries about battles long gone and to speculate about the future of British Columbia. He travelled with his wife and a few select acquaintances to warmer climates during the winter months and loved journeying through his home province the rest of the year in a quiet, unadvertised reminder of election campaigns past. Having spent much of his time during his years as premier keeping people from getting close to him, he had no close friends; indeed, he had no yen for intimacy. He once offered this sound but sad advice for those interested in achieving political success: "Make lots of friends, but don't get to know any of them too closely." Nevertheless, he did not consider himself to be lonely, and there were always his cronies and a variety of hangers-on whom he could count on for company.

To most British Columbians W. A. C. Bennett was a folk hero; even those who had opposed his government or never voted for him loved to approach him in public, shake his hand and wish him well. He was a reminder of the good old days of prosperity and comparative stability; he was a nostalgic symbol of the Good Life. He loved praise and recognition and was extremely susceptible to flattery—therefore, he enjoyed being seen in public where he was the cynosure of all eyes. He was probably the only public figure in B.C. who was universally recognized and greeted wherever he appeared. Dressed forever in his standard dark suit with a plain dark tie, immaculate white linen and polished black shoes, he loved to walk down a busy street in Vancouver or Victoria where he would often take a half hour to cover a single city block shaking hands, signing autographs and responding to compliments. He had a naive sense of his own personal safety and yet was never threatened in public. When in Victoria, he regularly lunched at the exclusive Union Club where he was always greeted as "Mr. Premier" and ushered to his specially reserved table. Throughout his meal he scattered pithy comments to members of the club, scions of the Victoria establishment, who passed by his table. These were no mere exchanges of pleasantries, however, but were more akin to the bestowal of benedictions.

W. A. C. Bennett now had much more time for his family than ever before: he and May spent long enjoyable hours together and delighted in the company of their burgeoning kin. Several of their grandchildren became close to them during these years and the former premier playfully quizzed and searched each of them for hints of future abilities or a latent interest in politics and public life. In July of 1977 W. A. C and May Bennett celebrated their fiftieth wedding anniversary. Their special golden day was marked at home in Kelowna in a quiet fashion, for the elderly couple would have been exhausted by extravagant festivities. Bright and early on the morning of the anniversary, the first of an apparently endless stream of bouquets of flowers arrived: it was an elaborate arrangement of beautiful red roses sent by Dave Barrett!

W. A. C. Bennett did not, indeed could not, steer completely clear of the political scene, for British Columbia politics was too absorbing, too all-consuming. With the return of Dave Barrett to the legislature in 1976 after he won the by-election caused by the resignation of former NDP minister Bob Williams, the tensions and conflicts between personalities in Victoria had become intense. As the well-known west coast anarchist, George Woodcock, remarked, the roll call of B.C. premiers sounded like the members of an old-fashioned attorneys' firm: Bennett, Barrett & Bennett—and looking ahead to the 1980s there was no sign that the firm was about to article any new talent.

In November of 1977 W. A. C. Bennett appeared at what would be his last Social Credit convention. During the course of the large and festive get-together which took place in Vancouver's Hyatt Regency hotel, the former premier made only one major address: to the party's women's auxiliary. It was an emotional speech. He told the matronly crowd that they were the Socred shock troops; the government had to maintain power at all costs; the socialist hordes must remain dispersed. At the conclusion of his forty-minute harangue both he and the large group of sympathetic women broke into tears. For the remainder of the convention Bennett senior was careful not to upstage his son. He remained high above the convention floor in a special suite which, in his honour, the hotel designated the "Premier's Suite," and received party leaders past and present. They came in a steady stream to offer tribute and pay allegiance to the patriarch of the party. The variety of individuals who waltzed through the suite was an interesting testimony to the changing nature of Social Credit: everyone from "genuine" Social Crediters with Albertan roots to Liberal *cum* Socred cabinet ministers; from elderly charter members of his first government to brash deputy ministers with wholly academic backgrounds, to young, pimple-faced executive assistants. All came to offer best wishes and to shake the hand of the Socreds' political godfather.

One of the few occasions when father and son shared a public platform was when Bill Bennett dedicated the Mica Dam project in October 1977. Mica was the third and final dam project required by the controversial Columbia River Treaty and W. A. C. Bennett sat beaming as his son paid tribute to the "vision and courage" of those who had established the scheme.

The only major public intervention on the part of W. A. C. Bennett came in the spring of 1978 when controversy swirled around one of the former premier's pet projects, the British Columbia Railway. A royal commission had been appointed to look into the operations of the BCR and was highly critical of the previous management of the railway and the methods used for northern expansion. When the ambitious but deficit-ridden Fort Nelson extension of the BCR seemed threatened to be closed down, the former premier sent a Churchillian telegram to the Fort Nelson chamber of commerce: "Have faith in your dark hour. Your best years lie ahead. Build a better and stronger Fort Nelson." Of course, W. A. C. Bennett was only defending his northern dream and thereby indirectly encouraging his son's government not to abandon it.

Another more private intervention by the old man took place in the spring of 1978 when, after Tory Scott Wallace resigned his seat in Oak Bay, a by-election was announced for March 20. W. A. C. Bennett saw the by-election as a major test for the new government, and a struggle for the party nomination emerged within Socred ranks between the old and new guards. Frank Carson, a Victoria car dealer, represented the old-line Socreds in the battle for the Oak Bay nomination and Brian Smith, the mayor of Oak Bay, represented the new Socreds. W. A. C. Bennett privately backed Carson and helped him organize an easy victory over Smith at the nominating convention in February. The morning after the intraparty battle the former premier collected several small wagers from friends and former colleagues, including $100 from his son Bill. However, in the by-election which ensued, the stubborn Conservatives held on for a victory over the elder Bennett's nominee. Not long after, the former premier made a surprise appearance as a guest on the floor of the B.C. legislature. Bill Bennett was shocked when he entered the legislative chamber at the commencement of the daily proceedings to see his father's broad smile from behind the government benches. Members from all parties paid tribute to the man who had for so long dominated that House; and the young Bennett coughed up: "I would like to add my welcome to the former premier and to tell him that no matter what he's heard in the last few days, the job isn't open."

W. A. C. Bennett never made it to the autumn 1978 Socred convention; it was the first time in more than twenty-five years that he was absent from the party's annual meeting. The old gentleman displayed an undeniable vigour of mind and was more vital than his body would permit. He had recovered well from a heart attack in 1976, but in the spring of 1978 he contracted viral pneumonia that he could not completely throw off and his health deteriorated throughout the year. Resting at home in Kelowna he would slip into a decline but his will to live would bring him back time after time. He hoped to make it to Victoria early in 1979, but over the holiday season he suffered a stroke and went into hospital in serious condition. He never managed to get fully back on his feet before an accumulation of ailments, best summed up as old age, felled him on the evening of February 23, 1979, with his dedicated wife, daughter Anita, and eldest son R.J. at his side. With his death came the conclusion of the most amazing personal saga in British Columbia's history.

Tributes and praise poured in from all political parties, from all corners of the country and from several foreign capitals. His last rites, the closest the province has ever come to a full state funeral, were marked by simultaneous ceremonies in Victoria, Vancouver and Kelowna. Thousands of British Columbians, mostly the "ordinary people" whom Bennett strived to represent, paid their respects at the various services. In Victoria the eulogy was delivered to a large congregation, including Governor General Edward Schreyer and Lieutenant Governor Henry Bell-Irving, by former cabinet colleague, Ray Williston; in Vancouver, where the memorial service took place against the backdrop of quiet weeping, Robert Bonner offered words of tribute to his late political boss; and in Kelowna, where many could not contain their unabashed grief, Grace McCarthy delivered a stirring eulogy in front of the Bennett family, assembled dignitaries and a huge crowd which spilled out of the local United Church and lined the streets. His coffin was draped in the sun-emblazoned provincial flag that he, as premier, had introduced.

W. A. C. Bennett's death was an event of symbolic as well as of personal significance for British Columbians—and especially for its premier. With his father gone, Bill Bennett would finally be free to prove himself and his ultimate worth. Of course, he would never escape his father's long shadow; and, for that matter, neither would other west coast politicians who, consciously or not, would be forced to grapple with the manifold legacies of the province's late populist master.

But, now, Bill Bennett was on his own. And for the first time in more than a quarter of a century, so was British Columbia.

AFTERWORD

*The vanity and presumption of governing
beyond the grave is the most ridiculous
and insolent of all tyrannies. Man has no property
in the generations which are to follow.*
Thomas Paine

On one of the last occasions I spoke with W. A. C. Bennett shortly before his death, he urged me to tell the story of the "*real* W. A. C. Bennett."

It was an emotional moment. The old man was in a state of severe physical decline. In fact, he knew he was dying. Surprising to me at the time, his request contained a rare hint of self-doubt, of human weakness, of mortality. During the heights of political campaigns, W. A. C. Bennett had harboured little, if any, uncertainty. Few individuals possessed his special abilities to inspire optimism or proffer uplifting advice. Yet, in the very twilight of his life, he questioned himself. No matter how glorious were the battles of the past, they would now be left open to the interpretation and judgement of future generations.

In retrospect, I believe W. A. C. Bennett was asking me to do two things. First, to write a true account of his life and political career. (He was dissatisfied with the literature that had been published up to that time and realized he would not live to see this book completed.) Second, he wanted me to not only give expression to his most unlikely of careers but to make sense of it and ensure his place in history.

Now, many years after his death, and nearly a quarter of a century after the defeat of his government, it is clear that his influence lives on. In fact, the new generation of voters and politicians, with no direct memory or experience of W. A. C. Bennett, might be surprised to learn the extent to which public discourse in British Columbia continues to be shaped by the various legacies of the province's longest-serving premier.

It is instructive to compare the British Columbia of today with the wonderful world of W. A. C. Bennett. In the postwar era when Bennett became premier, B.C.'s rapidly growing population had proudly surpassed the one million mark. Twenty years later, when his government was defeated, there were more than two million British Columbians. Today, almost four million residents call Canada's fastest-growing province home.

The province has also grown by leaps and bounds in economic terms, with a few stumbles along the way. Since 1972 the gross domestic product of B.C. has increased fivefold, and its economy, which remains export-based, has diversified into offshore markets, with less reliance on American trade than any other Canadian province. Although the number of jobs in natural resource industries has declined, manufacturing and resource industries continue to drive the economy. In the 1990s, when B.C. is described both at home and abroad as the "Brazil of the north" and when talk continues of diverting interior rivers to generate electricity or to irrigate Californian farmlands, British Columbians cannot pretend to have yet outgrown the epithet: "hewers of wood, drawers of water."

Bennett's final provincial budgets were notable for the fact that they had surpassed the then-magical billion-dollar mark. Today, the provincial government spends about $20 billion per annum. As both premier and minister of finance, he ran an extraordinarily tight ship and encouraged British Columbians to regard his government as the miracle mechanic of the economic machine, driving the province to ever-greater prosperity. He presented himself as a wily old financial wizard working wonders on behalf of the people. Each and every year he spent more and borrowed more, yet boasted of a debt-free province with forever-balanced budgets. Indeed, deficit spending became anathema to B.C. during these years, and balanced budgets became one of the province's trademarks. As a result, even in the mid-1990s, Premier Harcourt could not conceive of calling a general election until his government was able to balance the provincial budget.

When W. A. C. Bennett left Victoria in 1972, the province had no direct debt, although the government's books showed $2.7 billion in indirect or crown corporation borrowing. Today, the total provincial debt is in excess of $27 billion. The provincial governments that followed Bennett faced extremely volatile economic conditions in the 1970s and '80s and could not practically come to terms with new fiscal realities. British Columbians eventually lost confidence in the fiscal credibility of all political parties and began to demand legislation that would prevent deficit-spending and halt the growing public debt.

Of course, statistics can never tell the whole story. To truly measure W. A. C. Bennett's impact, it is necessary to go well beyond facts and figures and to assess the continuing influence of his political legacies on public life.

The polarization of politics, one of Bennett's principal legacies, has become one of the great myths about B.C. Although the province's political left seemed further left and the right further right than in other parts of Canada even before the advent of Social Credit, this extremism existed only around the edges; the fact was that most British Columbians viewed themselves more moderately, toward the centre of the political spectrum. Bennett sought to change this: first, by crushing the two traditional parties, the Liberals and the Conservatives, then by presenting Social Credit as the only viable alternative to the socialism of the NDP. Bennett was surprisingly successful in his advocacy of a polarized political culture, ensuring the dominance of Social Credit for more than a generation.

But polarization was never complete. During his two decades as premier, W. A. C. Bennett always faced Liberal and Conservative opponents both on the hustings and in the House. In fact, it was not until 1979, during his son Bill Bennett's second term in office as premier, that the provincial legislature was completely "polarized," with only two parties electing MLAs. This was the first such occurrence in B.C. since the introduction of party politics at the turn of the century. That the multiparty system is actually the norm in British Columbia is often lost on observers or commentators who do not understand that the poisonous polarization of the 1980s was but an aberration in the larger sweep of B.C. history.

Hand in hand with polarization came the paranoid style of B.C. politics: good guys versus bad guys; fear and loathing; class conflict. When Social Credit came to power in B.C. in the 1950s, McCarthyism and red-baiting were at their peak in the United States. W. A. C. Bennett perfected a local version of that paranoid style when he regularly warned against the disastrous results of a socialist political victory in the province. "The socialist hordes are at the gates!" he would exclaim during election campaigns, suggesting an urgent need to cast the right vote lest the future of the province and the livelihood of its workers and their children be ruined, perhaps for all time. His extremist style was easily adopted by the NDP, who were also given to preaching, in their case about the evils of capitalism and the exploitation of B.C workers by the captains of industry. True believers on both sides often got caught up in the wild rhetoric, and British Columbians gained a reputation for an exaggerated emphasis on political ideology.

When the NDP was elected to office in the province for the first time in 1972, this paranoid style was instrumental in galvanizing anti-socialist support and reviving the Social Credit Party. A concerted province-wide effort, sustained by virulent political fear-mongering, helped drive the hapless administration of Premier Dave Barrett from office in 1975. A generation later, there are still traces of the paranoid style in B.C. politics, but with much less intensity.

The province's second NDP government, elected under the leadership of Mike Harcourt in 1991, certainly never won the favour of the business community, but neither did it ever face the same kind of mordant apprehension or political abuse which confronted Barrett. No longer were British

Columbians encouraged to guard against reds under their beds. Instead, a convergence to the political centre resulted in all parties toning down their rhetoric; moderation became the order of the day. The paranoid style of politics, practised and perfected by W. A. C. Bennett, outlasted him by many years but now seems more a relic of the past than an enduring B.C. tradition.

Another important Bennett legacy worth questioning is the politics of personality. In a time before the electronic news media dominated coverage of public affairs, W. A. C. Bennett succeeded in focussing a disproportionate amount of attention on the personalities of leaders. He cultivated a folksy, strident image as he expounded his views and elaborated upon his vision of a growing, resource-rich economy. He became as famous for his personality as for his achievements and won seven consecutive general elections as premier. And because his unusual style dominated public life for so long, it seemed as if the politics of personality would remain a dominant force in British Columbia long after his exit from Victoria. Today, however, it is sobering to reflect upon the political leaders who have followed in his formidable steps: Premiers Barrett, another Bennett, Vander Zalm, Johnston, and Harcourt. This sometimes colourful but generally cheerless catalogue of political personalities brings to mind the famous lines from the great poet W. B. Yeats:

> The best lack all conviction, while the worst
> Are full of passionate intensity

W. A. C. Bennett tried to lead public opinion; today's leaders follow it. They are specialists in the cultivation of popularity, willing to do or say anything that public opinion research suggests might be in accord with the majority of British Columbians. In politics, the influence of television and public opinion polls is now overwhelming. And instead of being a clash of values or ideas, the democratic process has increasingly come to resemble a series of popularity contests. In British Columbia, the effect has been a decided shift from the politics of personality to the politics of popularity.

Perhaps the strongest and most durable legacy that took hold during W. A. C. Bennett's years in office was his unique brand of populism. Under his leadership, Social Credit was an anti-establishment party, and he did his utmost to represent the concerns of ordinary citizens rather than elites or moneyed interests. He fought for all British Columbians—the "little people," as he liked to call them. He carefully adopted the stance of the battling outsider, the leader who spoke not for one group or class but, with a certain deep conviction and heavy emphasis, for the people. This populist attitude has helped produce in British Columbia a tradition of distrust towards large powerful organizations such as big business, big labour or big government—

particularly the federal government in far-off Ottawa.

As part of his populist approach, W. A. C. Bennett was anxious to supplant the big-city corporate and professional interests that had long supported the old-line parties. The rise of Social Credit and its consolidation of influence saw the centre of political power shift from Vancouver to the hinterland, or "heartland" as W.A.C. called it. Social Credit grew into an aggressive, populist party with a bias towards small towns, small businesses and main street politics.

This tradition lives on in British Columbia. Who can forget Dave Barrett's efforts to mimic W. A. C. Bennett with populist flourishes and political rhetoric, culminating in his desperate 1975 election campaign appeal: "Don't let them take it away!" Bill Bennett was much less flamboyant, but no less affected by his father's dominating influence. Perhaps this was best demonstrated in 1978 when he threatened eastern-based Canadian Pacific during their attempted takeover of MacMillan Bloedel, the province's largest forestry firm, with his public admonishment: "B.C. is not for sale!" Certainly, Bill Vander Zalm was at heart a populist leader who took great delight in ignoring the advice of professional public servants, preferring instead to govern by gut instinct and on the basis of advice from taxi-drivers or glad-handers on street corners. Even Mike Harcourt succumbed to the populist tradition. Early in 1995, for instance, when he announced that the NDP government was cancelling Alcan's massive Kemano project in the province's northwest, he did so by attacking the large corporation and suggesting that any compensation owing for his decision was the responsibility of the federal government.

Where, one might ask, does Social Credit itself fit as part of W. A. C. Bennett's political legacy? As an independent party, not aligned with any federal counterpart, the Socreds were left in tatters following the defeat of W. A. C. Bennett's government in 1972. Most observers felt sure it was the end. However, efforts to form a new unity party were stymied by the unexpected rise of another Bennett. Bill Bennett served as Socred leader for almost 13 years, close to 11 of them as premier. It was an unlikely political dynasty, unprecedented in Canadian political history.

The younger Bennett sought to modernize the tired old party bequeathed to him by his father by actively recruiting prominent Liberals and Conservatives and by moderating the party's rough-hewn image. After a near-defeat in the 1979 general election, Bill Bennett began to construct a formidable machine, importing political professionals, primarily from Ontario. His objective was to institutionalize Social Credit by building a party structure that would outlive his own leadership. There can be no doubt that this impressive party organization was decisive in winning the Socreds another mandate in the 1983 provincial election, following which

Bill Bennett launched his controversial restraint program.

Three years later, when Bill Bennett announced his resignation as leader of the party and premier of the province, he was able to take much of the controversy and ill-will towards the Social Credit government with him. During three terms in office, he achieved something that had eluded his father: in spite of all the acrimony generated by his bureaucracy-slashing restraint program, it had now become somewhat respectable to be a Social Credit supporter. Under W. A. C. Bennett it always seemed difficult to find a British Columbian who would admit to even voting Socred. Bill Bennett transformed his father's old party into a modern electoral machine, openly supported by business and professional groups. And he left office both undefeated and unloved.

In 1986 the challenge for Social Credit was to elect a new leader, the party's first who was not a Bennett. Bill Bennett had given a great deal of thought to the process of leadership succession and he left the party in much better shape than his father had in 1972.

A strong field of a dozen candidates vied for the position of Socred leader; with the job came the premiership of the province. Bill Bennett never anointed a successor, but it is safe to say that he would have been pleased had his former principal secretary, Bud Smith, been victorious. Other contenders were Attorney General Brian Smith, who seemed to command the respect and support of a sizable portion of the party's establishment, and Grace McCarthy, who certainly inspired fierce loyalty and likely represented the traditions of the Social Credit Party better than any other candidate. But these three possibilities were ultimately swept aside by the force of personality of an outsider, a maverick, an individual whose appeal was strictly to the party's grassroots, not its elite: Bill Vander Zalm.

The Social Credit leadership convention staged at Whistler at the end of July 1986 was an intense weekend of intrigue and machinations. In the end, there was no stopping Bill Vander Zalm from reinforcing the party's populist heritage. And while there was no question that his personal appeal and charm would be tremendous assets for Social Credit heading into the next general election, there were serious doubts about his ability to run a government. Nevertheless, Social Credit delegates wanted a change, some fun and adventure. Their smiling new leader would, however, provide more than they ever bargained for.

Bill Vander Zalm never clawed his way to power; rather, he seemed to stumble toward his personal destiny, always surprising himself along the way. He was a former mayor of the Vancouver suburb of Surrey and the first former mayor to become a B.C. premier (municipal politics not being a very effective training ground for the partisan fray at the provincial level). After running for the leadership of the B.C. Liberal Party and losing, he joined

Social Credit and served as a colourful cabinet minister in Bill Bennett's government. During the summer of 1982, in the single most significant breach of solidarity during the younger Bennett's premiership, Vander Zalm publicly referred to his cabinet colleagues as "gutless" when they refused to endorse one of his legislative initiatives. He seriously contemplated resigning at that time. At a crucial moment, however, Grace McCarthy attempted to change his mind and left him with these fateful words: "Remember what W. A. C. Bennett used to say: 'Don't get mad. Get even.'"

Vander Zalm stayed on but did not seek re-election in 1983. He returned to his family business, ran for mayor of Vancouver and was soundly beaten by Mike Harcourt. He was generally regarded as a spent political force until he won the Social Credit leadership at Whistler. The morning after his victory, Grace McCarthy felt compelled to remind him: "Well, you certainly did get even, didn't you Bill?"

Shortly after his Whistler triumph and being sworn in as premier, Vander Zalm called a provincial election. The 1986 campaign was run on the fuel of Vander Zalm's supercharged personality against that of a new, weak-kneed NDP leader, Bob Skelly. Although his campaign floundered during the final phases of the election, Vander Zalm still won a comfortable victory. However, what should have been a Social Credit landslide amounted to less than a seven per cent margin over the lacklustre NDP campaign. Even more surprising was the fact that the Socred percentage of the popular vote actually declined slightly.

Expectations for the Vander Zalm government were very high, perhaps unrealistic, but regularly raised by the new premier's willingness to publicly entertain almost any idea or policy option. In the early days of the new administration, cabinet minister Rita Johnston summed up the Social Credit Party's nervousness about dealing with these public expectations: "Heaven help us if we let the people down."

As it turned out, Bill Vander Zalm became living proof that the qualities and abilities required to obtain power are very different from those needed to exercise it competently or responsibly. While he enjoyed an extended honeymoon as premier, he failed to consolidate his power within the Social Credit Party or in his government. Wounds created by the bitter leadership race never completely healed and, as a result, Vander Zalm commanded loyalty from only certain elements of his cabinet, caucus and party.

To make matters worse, Premier Vander Zalm, a devout Catholic with a strong appeal to fundamentalist Christians, decided that his personal mission was to provide moral—not necessarily political—leadership for his fellow citizens. He railed against sex education, birth control and advertisements for contraceptives. And he used his standing in the legislature as a kind of bully pulpit against abortion rights advocates. Many British Columbians were perplexed, confused and disappointed with their premier's inability to separate church from state.

Two years into his mandate, Bill Vander Zalm's status had changed from that of a provincial folk hero to the most despised man in British Columbia. The news media turned on him with a viciousness rarely, if ever, seen before. After losing a series of by-elections and suffering the resignations of a string of high-profile cabinet ministers, it seemed inevitable that Vander Zalm would have to go. But how? The Social Credit Party bears a special responsibility for its inability to rid itself of an unpopular leader who had become an embarrassment. However, this failure serves to highlight the challenge for any governing party: there are few checks and balances to maintain leadership accountability. Opportunities for autocracy abound within our so-called modern democratic party system.

Vander Zalm stubbornly and tenaciously clung to power, surrounding himself with a diminishing band of sycophants and influence-pedlars. Ultimately, however, he stumbled into a massive conflict of interest scandal that forced him from office. In the fall of 1990, it was announced that he had sold his Fantasy Gardens biblical theme park to a Taiwanese billionaire. Then it was revealed that he might have used his influence as premier to arrange business access to cabinet ministers and government officials for the Taiwanese firm. A series of high-profile investigations took place exposing, amongst other things, that Vander Zalm and his wife had attended a suspicious late-night meeting in a Vancouver hotel, where the premier had pocketed an envelope containing $20,000 in American $100 bills.

A political crisis gripped British Columbia. Finally, on 30 March 1991, Vander Zalm stepped down, first as Social Credit leader and then, following a damning report by the province's conflict of interest commissioner, as premier. He later became the first current or former government leader in the history of the British Commonwealth to be formally charged with a breach of trust.

W. A. C. Bennett must have been rolling in his grave. Could the Social Credit Party possibly survive? To add to the party's woes, Vander Zalm had violated W.A.C.'s tradition of calling elections every three years or so; in desperation, he had waited until close to the end of his five-year mandate before leaving in disgrace, allowing his successor very little room to manoeuvre. By a vote of the Socred caucus, Vander Zalm loyalist Rita Johnston was elected interim leader, thereby becoming Canada's first female premier—hardly a proud day for the women of the nation. A leadership convention was called for the summer of 1991.

Rita Johnston served as premier of B.C. for seven months, as Socred leader for less than a year. In spite of all his foibles and the shame he brought to his province, Bill Vander Zalm still retained a hard core of support among true believers and religious fundamentalists within Social Credit. This support was now transferred to Johnston, who had long been a devout follower of Vander Zalm's. In fact, British Columbia's new premier characterized herself as more of a follower than a leader. To this base of "Vander Zombie" supporters was added the "back-room boys" of B.C. politics. These were the fixers, fundraisers, consultants, public relations flaks and political hacks who hoped to sustain Johnston in office and even beat the NDP in the next election. Why did these political mercenaries back Johnston? First of all because, as interim leader, she held an inside track in the race to be confirmed as party leader and, second, because they felt they could control her. As it turned out, they were right on both counts.

The Socred leadership convention held in Vancouver late in July 1991 was a tense and dramatic affair. Although there were five candidates in the contest, Rita Johnston's only competition came from the party's other matriarch, Grace McCarthy. Entering the race late, but rallying the more moderate elements of the old populist party, McCarthy very nearly won the day. On the second ballot she lost to Johnston by the narrowest of margins. Of more than 1,800 votes cast, a mere 31 would have reversed the decision in McCarthy's favour. As one bitter McCarthy delegate left the convention centre in dejection, he was confronted by a Johnston supporter urging him to "Come and join us. God will forgive you."

Johnston's confirmation as leader resulted in a serious split in the party; there were now two separate and irreconcilable factions at war with each other. As the 1990s unfolded, British Columbia saw the eclipse of Social Credit and the emergence of two very different parties from its former base of support: Liberal and Reform.

Rita Johnston's victory was short-lived. An election was soon required, and on voting day, 17 October 1991, the Socreds were devastated. Under Mike Harcourt's stewardship, the NDP formed a strong majority government; the Liberals, who had not elected an MLA for more than a decade, became the official opposition under Gordon Wilson; and Social Credit was reduced to third party status, electing only seven MLAs. Rita Johnston was humiliated, losing her own seat in Surrey.

Although the 1991 election proved to be the death knell of Social Credit, political parties do not die easily. Another leadership race in the fall of 1993 finally saw Grace McCarthy emerge as Socred leader—but it was too late. Her loss in a by-election in Matsqui early in 1994 confirmed that both she and the great party of W. A. C. Bennett were now a spent force. Through a process of resignations and defections to the provincial Reform Party, Social Credit even lost its official party status in the legislature and was reduced to a single seat in the House. McCarthy stepped down and yet another leadership contest in the fall of 1994 saw a little-known businessman from North Vancouver, Larry Gillanders, become the sixth leader of the B.C. Social Credit Party. Will he be the last? If Social Credit has a future in British Columbia, it almost certainly is not as a political party. It could conceivably survive by returning to its roots as an educational society interested in policy rather than in running candidates in elections.

Who killed Social Credit? It would be too easy to lay the blame at the feet of Bill Vander Zalm. After all, up until his time Social Credit in B.C. had been one of the most successful political parties in Canadian history and should have been strong enough to withstand a single bad leader, even one as destructive as Vander Zalm. In order to explain Social Credit's demise, which was certainly not inevitable, it is necessary to look deeper. The inescapable conclusion is that the Social Credit Party has itself to blame for its fall. Perhaps W. A. C. Bennett's primary rule for governments also applies to political parties: they are never defeated, but are destroyed from within. For almost five years, the Socreds had meekly endured Vander Zalm, never mustering the strength to seriously censure him or to use the opportunity for leadership reviews to take their party back from the precipice. They had vainly hoped he would simply go away and naively dreamed that, once he departed, they would be able to regain their lost public trust. A large part of the blame for this delusion must be accepted by the hangers-on, the influence-pedlars and political advisers who assured the Socreds that everything would be all right. These mercenaries were much more interested in their own short-term futures than the long-term survival of a political institution. Another major factor preventing the Socreds from pulling themselves out of their tailspin was a repressive party discipline, which infects most modern Canadian parties. Of course, it must be exceedingly difficult for a governing political party to admit an error so grievous as embracing a politician the likes of Bill Vander Zalm. Yet, the fortitude was lacking to deal with the issue in a forthright manner. The cabinet, caucus and entire party structure must collectively bear the guilt for not acting sooner to preserve the health of Social Credit.

It is instructive to consider what might have happened in the aftermath of the 1991 leadership race had Grace McCarthy been successful—with 31 more votes—in toppling this grasping group of political mercenaries within the Socreds. She probably would have attempted to rejuvenate the party by distancing herself from the Vander Zalm record, a task to which she could bring a modicum of credibility, having been the first to resign from his cabinet in 1988. Mike Harcourt and the NDP would probably still have been elected, but the Socreds under McCarthy would almost certainly have been the official opposition. A few years later, instead of facing extinction, Social Credit would probably have been once again rallying the free enterprise forces to do battle with the socialists. But it was not to be.

In the spring of 1995 as I write this, it is more than a little ironic to note that as a single, independent MLA, I hold as much voting power in the B.C. legislature as the powerful and proud party W. A. C. Bennett once led. When I ran in the 1991 provincial election as a Liberal candidate in the new riding of West Vancouver-Garibaldi, I expected to be one of a handful of independent voices in the House, but I wound up being part of a Grit tide led by Gordon Wilson. As Liberal leader, Wilson effectively placed himself within the B.C. populist tradition, fighting his way into a televised election campaign debate with Harcourt and Johnston. There can be no doubt that it was on the strength of Wilson's performance alone that most of the surprised group of 17 Liberal MLAs was elected. A college instructor and great admirer of Pierre Trudeau, Wilson became leader of the opposition and I took my place alongside him in the House.

A brilliant orator, with a near-photographic memory, Gordon Wilson was also elusive and appeared constantly threatened. Following the election, during one of the first meetings of the Liberal caucus, he predicted that his leadership would be challenged. Whether it was prescience or a self-fulfilling prophecy, it was not long before he became both isolated and embattled. However, the threat to his leadership did not come from within his rookie caucus, but from the Liberal establishment and Vancouver business interests. Sensing the historic opportunity created by the unexpected provincial election results, they could not reconcile themselves to Wilson as their leader. They distrusted him, resented his independence and wondered about how to replace him.

Of course, in politics, rumours run rampant. Shortly after the election, former prime minister John Turner cautioned me to keep an eye on the mayor of Vancouver, Gordon Campbell, as he was after Wilson's job. Not long after that, a prominent Vancouver businessman and federal Liberal confided to me that he and others were attempting to persuade Campbell to seek Wilson's position. All of this seemed improbable, especially since the Vancouver mayor was not even a member of the Liberal Party. Gordon Wilson, who apparently heard the same stories, met with Campbell to confront the rumours, but the mayor flatly denied them.

The rubicon in my journey through provincial Liberalism was the Charlottetown Accord. Canada's agreement on constitutional reform was put to a national referendum in the fall of 1992. This was an historic political event that saw rare cross-party alliances and intense national debate.

Gordon Wilson was firmly opposed to the accord and most polling data indicated he was on the right side of public opinion. I decided to support the accord and was in a minority position within the Liberal caucus. I was in favour of allowing MLAs to go their own way on the issue, believing there was no need for party discipline on such a matter. However, emotions were running high and my position was regarded by some as a challenge to Wilson's leadership; I resigned as Liberal house leader over the issue. Shortly after the rejection of the accord in the referendum of 26 October 1992, I left the Liberal caucus to sit as an independent in the House.

When I stepped down as Liberal house leader, Gordon Wilson replaced me with Judi Tyabji, the youngest member of caucus, the first woman ever to become a mother while serving as a B.C. MLA, and a voluble supporter of his. Apparently this decision was not popular with the Liberal caucus and several MLAs and staff began murmuring about the perceived special relationship between Wilson and Tyabji. There was rumour upon rumour, denial upon denial and, finally, an admission that the party leader and his house leader—although both married to others at the time—were indeed a couple. The nadir of Wilson's public esteem likely came when a Vancouver morning newspaper, in a screaming headline story, quoted his disbelieving wife saying she still did his laundry.

On 19 February 1993 Gordon Wilson resigned as Liberal leader, called for a leadership convention and announced that he would run for re-election. The Liberal MLAs who had earlier been devoutly loyal to Wilson—who, after all, was responsible for electing virtually every one of them—now turned on him. These same Liberals soon emerged as the staunchest supporters of the leading candidate to succeed Wilson: Gordon Campbell. All is fair in love and war—and politics!

The race for the Liberal leadership, and with it the opposition leadership in the legislature, was dominated by three Gordons: Wilson, Campbell and Gibson. Before signing up as a party member and throwing his hat into the ring, Mayor Campbell had to decide whether he should run for the top job with the Liberals or the Socreds, who were also in the throes of a leadership campaign at the time. Campbell apparently concluded that the Liberal Party was a preferable vehicle to travel in and, interestingly, a number of long-time B.C. Grits supported this instant Liberal's candidacy. Gordon Gibson possessed a far superior pedigree. Not only had he served as a Liberal MLA, he was a former party leader and the son of Gordon Gibson senior, the "Bull of the Woods," who as a Liberal MLA in the 1950s had brought down W. A. C. Bennett's infamous cabinet minister Robert Sommers.

Nevertheless, in politics like sports, the most deserving player does not always win. On 11 September 1993, the provincial Liberals elected the suave Gordon Campbell as their new leader on the first ballot.

Campbell's relatively easy victory reinforced a few important lessons about modern party politics. Banished to the political wilderness for so many years, Liberals were willing to anoint a newcomer who showed the appearance of being a winner. It mattered little that he could not enunciate a recognizable Liberal philosophy; in fact, it was very difficult to discern what he stood for. This was most aptly pointed out by *Vancouver Sun* columnist Denny Boyd, who wrote that "you could wade through the deepest part of Campbell's political philosophy without getting your cuffs wet."

However, there was dark humour mixed with hypocrisy on the part of some long-time Liberals, who had barely survived the lean years under the Bennetts. Now, by supporting Campbell, they had surrendered even any pretence to the flame of Liberalism that they had fought to keep flickering for more than a generation. By opting for Campbell, B.C. Liberals demonstrated that their party had become simply a holding company for one individual's personal ambition. It should not have come as such a great surprise when, instead of the expected rewards for loyal Liberals, Campbell began appointing a number of former Vander Zalm-Johnston Socreds to key positions within the party organization.

Like most other organizations, political parties can be judged by how they treat their leaders, particularly former leaders. The Social Credit Party, unable to come to terms with its ill-fated love affair with Bill Vander Zalm, entered a bleak period of denial from which it never re-emerged. The provincial Liberals, instead of being gracious and thanking Gordon Wilson for his contribution to the party, continued kicking their former leader even after he was down—and out.

Campbell eventually completed his term in the Vancouver mayor's office and found his way into the legislature via a by-election. Gordon Wilson and Judi Tyabji left the Liberal caucus and formed the Progressive Democratic Alliance Party, ironically becoming my seat-mates in the legislature. And a provincial Reform Party—comprised of former Social Credit MLAs—became the "third party" in the House, hoping to capitalize on the 1993 federal election breakthrough of the Reform Party of Canada. Indeed the federal Reformers' largest contingent of MPs came from B.C., demonstrating once again the populist nature of Canada's westernmost province.

Those who suggest that the provincial Reformers are simply an offshoot of Social Credit or an attempt to rehabilitate the Socreds under a new name ignore the fact that Campbell's Liberals also contain remnants of the discredited Socred regime. Even Rita Johnston was sometimes seen at Gordon Campbell fundraising dinners, although organizers were careful to seat her at the back of the hall, where she would not be too easily noticed. In the mixed-up political world of the mid-1990s, there were two offspring of Social Credit vying for position: Campbell Liberals versus B.C. Reform. Although they tried different ways to disguise it, neither of them could truthfully deny their family lineage.

There was another new political twist for populist British Columbia, however, and it was caused by the fact that two former Vancouver mayors now faced off in the legislature: Harcourt versus Campbell. Would W. A. C.

Bennett's anti-establishment legacy continue to prevail under the influence of big-city mayors in provincial office? In fact, consciously or not, politicians are still grappling with a variety of themes established by the late populist master, even as some of them attempt to re-establish the powerful urban political machines he had worked so hard to smash.

It is both entertaining and perplexing to observe the frequency with which W.A.C.'s name is invoked in political debate. Not only is he still often mentioned in the news media but references to W. A. C. Bennett in the B.C. legislature are a regular, even daily, occurrence. Indeed, since his death in 1979, the Hansard index lists more than 700 entries under his name!

To be sure, the late premier is often misquoted, misunderstood or misinterpreted. But most remarkable is the penchant for singing his praise and virtues on the part of those who were once his most bitter opponents or mortal enemies. Of course, it is never polite to speak ill of the dead, but New Democrats such as Mike Harcourt and a few of his ministers have often verged on shamelessness in either claiming to be W. A. C. Bennett's political heirs, or in attempting to justify NDP policies by suggesting they might be consistent with Wacky's record or spirit.

For example, a revealing incident occurred in the summer of 1994 when the provincial government commenced negotiations with the Americans for the downstream benefits of the Columbia River Treaty. There is no humorist like history. When the treaty was negotiated in 1964 by W. A. C. Bennett as part of his famous Two River Policy, the NDP led the opposition to it, castigating the agreement as a massive sellout of the birthright of British Columbians. Now, they happened to be in government at the crucial moment of deciding on B.C.'s position for the last half of the 60-year treaty. W.A.C. had always argued that the second half of the treaty was potentially more important than the first 30 years, predicting that hydro power would be an even more valuable commodity by the time the downstream benefits were required to be returned to British Columbia. The NDP were now rubbing their hands in glee as they would decide how these benefits—estimated at more than $5 billion over the next 30 years—would be returned to the province. W. A. C. Bennett was finally, if posthumously, receiving fulsome praise for his astute negotiating.

W. A. C. Bennett had been adamant that these downstream benefits were a provincial resource and should one day be used for the improvement of all British Columbians. He was concerned about the possibility of a future government using them to fund pet political projects. As it turned out, his concern was well justified.

The NDP government announced that revenue generated from the downstream benefits would go towards a variety of uses but would be primarily invested in the region of the Kootenays that had been flooded by the dams. Presumably, this would be a kind of *ex post facto* apology to those whose property had been legally expropriated or for environmental damage caused by the flooding a generation ago.

While there may be a case for a symbolic gesture in this regard, it ignores the fact that the Columbia River Treaty was part of the Two River Policy and would not likely have proceeded without the simultaneous development of hydro power on the northern Peace River. Using the same logic, the Peace region should be eligible for receiving a share of Columbia downstream benefits as well. However, not to be outdone by the NDP government of Mike Harcourt, opposition leader Gordon Campbell suggested that much more needed to be done for the Kootenays, including direct payments to residents. As the two Vancouver political bosses duelled with one another over who would pay more for the votes of rural residents of the Kootenays, W.A.C.'s fears came true.

In Bennett's time, politics was the art of managing government. Today it has become a performing art, with politicians spending more time manufacturing news and attempting to attract the attention of the media than daring to dream of their province's or country's future greatness. As we approach the new millennium, British Columbians are suffering from a lack of political leaders with either a knowledge of history or a breadth of vision. W. A. C. Bennett possessed both. He was acutely aware of his own historic role, as well as the larger context of his various policy initiatives. And despite his frequent bombast and fierce partisanship, he had a boyish idealism about him which was captivated by the magnificent province he so boldly governed.

W. A. C. Bennett is dead; long live W. A. C. Bennett.

NOTE ON SOURCES

The chief source for this book is its subject: W. A. C. Bennett. The late premier was generous with both his time and influence, spending many hours in formal taped interview sessions with me, even more hours in informal discussions, and opening doors to other sources which would have otherwise remained closed—perhaps forever. Bennett also allowed me exclusive access to his personal papers in Kelowna which have helped to shape this biography.

Oral history—first-person reminiscence tape recorded many years after the event—is one of the primary documentary sources for this book and, indeed, for this period of B.C. history. For a variety of reasons ranging from the marginal biographical value of much of the massive volume of official source materials to the secretive nature of W. A. C. Bennett's practice of political power, the book could not have been written from conventional sources. Oral history therefore became not only an indispensable tool for chronicling the life of Bennett but also a way to cut through the documentary maze. I conducted hundreds of hours of recorded interviews with Bennett's family, colleagues and political opponents. In addition, wide use was made of oral history produced by other interviewers. The interviews include over thirty hours on tape between Bennett and myself accumulated during the course of almost three years, as well as highly specific interviews of less than an hour in length with selected subjects.

Following is a list of the interviews that helped to mould this book; reminiscences directly quoted in the text are derived from these sources, some of which have been transcribed into print but most are preserved in tape form.

APP   Author's Personal Papers
PAA   Provincial Archives of Alberta, Edmonton, Alberta
PABC Provincial Archives of British Columbia, Victoria, B.C.
SAB   Saskatchewan Archives Board, Regina, Saskatchewan
PAC   Public Archives of Canada, Ottawa, Ontario

AUTHOR'S INTERVIEWS

Barrett, David, 1980, PABC #1704
Bennett, May, 1977, PABC #2703
Bennett, R.J., 1977, PABC #2703
Bennett, W.A.C., 1976-1978, PABC #1675
Bennett, W.R. (Bill), 1978, PABC #1707

NOTE ON SOURCES · 469

Bonner, Robert, 1980, PABC #244
Browne-Clayton, Robert, 1979, PABC #3555
Bryson, Gerald, 1980, PABC #3724
Campbell, Dan, 1980, PABC #3717
Capozzi, Herb, 1977, PABC #2741
Clancey, William, 1980, PABC #3681
Croll, David, 1978, PABC #3346
Detwiller, Lloyd, 1977, PABC #2601 (co-interviewer W.J. Langlois)
Diefenbaker, John G., 1978, PABC #996
Earl, Winnifred, 1978, PABC #3344
Ekman, Daniel, 1978, PABC #3341
Ferber, Charles, 1978, PABC #3332
Gaglardi, Philip A., 1978, PABC #1644
Gow, Dorothy, 1978, PABC #3199
Green, Howard, 1979, PABC #525
Gunderson, Einar, 1977, PABC #2639
Hecht, John, 1977, APP
Helps, Arthur, 1977, PABC #2641
Kelln, Martin, 1981, SAB #R7755
Kenmuir, Cam, 1980, PABC #3682
Kennedy, Gilbert, 1978,, PABC #3229
Kennedy, Orvis, 1977, PABC #2701
Landry, Henry, 1978, PABC #3336
Lillico, Richard, 1978, APP
McCarthy, Grace, 1980, PABC #995
MacDonald, R.C., 1977, PABC #2638
McInnes, Dermott, 1978, PABC #3343
Manning, Ernest, 1977, PABC #2702
Orchard, Ray, 1978, PABC #3197
Peabody, Alexander, 1978, PABC #3092 (technician Michael P. Mitchell)
Peterson, Leslie, 1978, PABC #3330
Shelford, Cyril, 1980, PABC #3683
Skillings, Waldo, 1977, PABC #2705
Smith, Melvin, 1977, PABC #3091
Snowsell, Frank, 1978, PABC #3094
Strachan, Robert, 1978, PABC #528 (co-interviewer D. Reimer)
Tames, John, 1978, PABC #3342
Thompson, Robert, 1977,, PABC #2704
Tozer, Anita (Bennett), 1977, PABC #2706
Tozer, Tony, 1978, PABC #3358
Wallace, Clarence, 1977, PABC #3333
Warren, Derril, 1978, PABC #3095
Wenman, Robert, 1978, PABC #3331
Westwood, Earle, 1978, PABC #2662 (co-interviewer C. Nikitiuk)
Young, Walter, 1978, PABC #3203 (co-interviewer D. Reimer)

OTHER INTERVIEWS

Anscomb, Herbert, interviewed by Martin Robin, 1967, PABC #1967
Black, Wesley, interviewed by W. J. Langlois, 1975, PABC #1410
Brothers, Donald, interviewed by C. Nikitiuk, 1978, PABC #3235
Capozzi, Pasquale (Cap), interviewed by D. Bowers, 1973, PABC #194
Chant, William, interviewed by D. Reimer, 1976, PABC #1378
Collison, Doris (Patullo), interviewed by T. Eastwood and D. Reimer, 1977, PABC #1249
English, J. F. K., interviewed by A. Specht, 1974, PABC #1364
Eyres, Leslie, interviewed by D. Reimer, 1978, PABC #2887
Fulton, E. Davie, interviewed by P. Stursberg, 1972, PAC #1972-62
George, Percy, interviewed by A. Specht, 1974,, PABC #1365
Gibson, J. Gordon, interviewed by C. D. Orchard, 1960, PABC #1856
Gibson, J. Gordon and Jack, interviewed by D. Reimer, 1977, PABC #2719
Haggen, Lois, interviewed by W. J. Langlois, 1974, PABC #288
Harding, Randolph, interviewed by A. Petter, 1978, PABC #3228
Kiernan, Kenneth, interviewed by D. Reimer, 1977, PABC #2665
Loffmark, Ralph, interviewed by C. Nikitiuk, 1978, PABC #Martin, Eric, interviewed by R. H. Roy, 1970, PABC #1440
Nimsick, Leo, interviewed by A. Petter and D. Reimer, 1978, PABC #3224
Orchard, C. D., self-interview, 1960, PABC #1860
Paynter, Peer, interviewed by D. Reimer, 1977, PABC #1175
Richards, Percy, interviewed by D. Reimer, 1977, PABC #1203
Sommers, Robert, interviewed by S. Dixon, 1976, PABC #1133
Torey, Gordon, interviewed by D. Reimer, 1977, PABC #1293
Trusswell, H. A., interviewed by P. Sherman, 1965, PABC #3586
Turnbull, Douglas, interviewed by W. J. Langlois, 1974,, PABC #270
Turner, Arthur, interviewed by M. Karnouk, 1973, PABC #251
Wicks, Lyle, interviewed by W. J. Langlois, 1976,, PABC #2348
Williston, Ray, interviewed by D. Reimer, 1975, PABC #1375
Wilson, J. O., interviewed by R. B. Hutchison and W. B. Hutchison, 1979, PABC #3542
Winch, Harold, interviewed by G. Jenkinson, 1973,, PABC #148
Wurtele, Alfred, interviewed by D. Reimer, 1977, PABC #1093

As sources for this biography, the interviews were corroborated by research in other primary sources and in all available secondary materials. Since the full bibliography would be of borderline use or convenience to the readers, instead the following short selected list of the most frequently used sources is provided for the enquiring reader; and specific references to other primary and secondary sources for particular portions of W. A. C. are found in the Chapter References which follow this Note on Sources.

PRIMARY SOURCES

W. A. C. Bennett Papers, Kelowna, B.C.
Budget Speeches, Province of British Columbia
Journals, Legislative Assembly of British Columbia
Statement of Votes, Province of British Columbia

SECONDARY SOURCES

BOOKS
Diefenbaker, John G. *One Canada*. Toronto: Macmillan of Canada, 1977.
McGeer, Patrick L. *Politics in Paradise*. Toronto: Peter Martin Associates, 1972.
Munro, John A., and Inglis, Alex I., eds. *Mike: The Memoirs of the Right Honourable Lester B. Pearson*. Toronto: University of Toronto Press, 1975.
Ormsby, Margaret A. *British Columbia: A History*. Toronto: Macmillan of Canada, 1958.
Robin, Martin. *Pillars of Profit: The Company Province, 1934–1972*. Toronto: McClelland & Stewart, 1973.
Sherman, Paddy. *Bennett*. Toronto: McClelland & Stewart, 1966.
Swainson, Neil A. *Conflict over the Columbia: The Canadian Background to an Historic Treaty*. Montreal: McGill-Queen's University Press, 1979.
Walker, Russell R. *Politicians of a Pioneering Province*. Vancouver: Mitchell Press, 1969.
Worley, Ronald B. *The Wonderful World of W. A. C. Bennett*. Toronto: McClelland & Stewart, 1972.

PERIODICALS
Canadian Annual Review. Toronto: University of Toronto Press, 1960–76.
Kelowna *Courier*
Maclean's
Time
Vancouver *Province*
Vancouver *Sun*
Victoria *Colonist*
Victoria *Times*

THESES
Alper, Donald Keith. "From Rule to Ruin: The Conservative Party in British Columbia, 1928–1954." Ph.D. thesis, University of British Columbia, 1975.
Bentley, Byron David, *et al.* "The Social Welfare Philosophy of the Social Credit Party of British Columbia." M.S.W. thesis, University of British Columbia, 1965.
Carlsen, A. E. "Major Developments in Public Finance in British Columbia, 1920–1960." Ph.D. thesis, University of Toronto, 1961.
Horsfield, Barbara. "The Social Credit Movement in British Columbia." B.A. essay, University of British Columbia, 1953.
Sanford, T. "The Politics of Protest: The CCF and Social Credit League in British Columbia." Ph.D. thesis, University of California, 1961.

CHAPTER REFERENCES

1 · HIS FATHER'S SON

W. A. C. Bennett's school and attendance records were obtained from his alma mater, now Hampton Junior High School, and from the New Brunswick Department of Education. Andrew Bennett's military records were obtained from the Public Archives of Canada, Ottawa.

Author's correspondence with Mr. Ted Evers, 1980. APP.
Author's correspondence with Mrs. Cora (Bennett) Macaulay, 1980. APP.
Author's correspondence with Mrs. Iris MacGillvray, Albert County Historical Society, 1980. APP.
Doyle, Arthur T. *Front Benches and Back Rooms*. Toronto: Green Tree Publishing Ltd., 1976.
Macaulay, Cora (Bennett). "Our Burns Story" (unpublished history of W. A. C. Bennett's mother's family). 1978. APP.
Marden, Orison S. *Pushing to the Front*. New York: The Success Company, 1911.
Morris, Zaslow. "The Struggle for the Peace River Outlet: A Chapter in the Politics of Canadian Development." In *The West and the Nation: Essays in Honour of W. L. Morton*, edited by Carl Berger and Ramsay Cook. Toronto: McClelland & Stewart, 1976.
Torrance, Robert. Papers (material on the Tuxis movement). PAA.

2 · "IT COULDN'T BE DONE"

Author's correspondence with Mr. Ted Evers, 1980. APP.
Leckie, David Russell. "David Leckie." *Okanagan Historical Society Report* 38 (1974).
Ormsby, Margaret A. "T. Dufferin Pattullo and the Little New Deal." *Canadian Historical Review* 43, no. 4 (December 1962).
Parker, Ian D. "Simon Fraser Tolmie: The Last Conservative Premier of British Columbia." *B.C. Studies* 11 (1971).
Pattullo, Thomas Dufferin. Radio broadcast, June 17, 1935 (on federal-provincial relations). PABC #1672.
Stokes, M. L. *The Bank of Canada*. Toronto: Macmillan of Canada, 1939.

3 · THE PARANOID STYLE

Maitland, R.L. Papers. PABC.
Post-War Rehabilitation Council. *Interim Report*. Victoria: King's Printer, 1947.

4 · A STAB IN THE DARK

Anderson, Alan. "A Passion on the Prairies." In *Flamboyant Canadians*, edited by E. Stafford. Toronto: Baxter, 1964.
Barr, John J. *The Dynasty: The Rise and Fall of Social Credit in Alberta*. Toronto: McClelland & Stewart, 1974.

Douglas, C. H. *The Alberta Experiment*. London: Eyre and Spottiswoode, 1937.
Douglas, C. H. *The Policy of a Philosophy*. Liverpool: K.R.P. Publications, 1948.
Finlay, J. L. *Social Credit: The English Origins*. Montreal and London: McGill-Queen's University Press, 1972.
Johnson, L. P. V., and Ola J. MacNutt. *Aberhart of Alberta*. Edmonton: Institute of Applied Art, 1970.
Leacock, Stephen. *Canada: The Foundations of Its Future*. Montreal: House of Seagrams, 1941.
Mallory, J. R. *Social Credit and the Federal Power in Canada*. Toronto: University of Toronto Press, 1954.

5 · THE WHIRL OF CIRCUMSTANCE

Alper, Donald Keith. "The Effects of Coalition Government on Party Structure: The Case of the Conservative Party in B.C." *B.C. Studies* 33 (Spring 1977).
Angus, H. F. "The British Columbia Election, June 1952." *Canadian Journal of Economics and Political Science* 18 (1952).
Jamieson, Stuart. "Hospital Insurance in British Columbia." *Canadian Forum*, September 1952.
Johnson, Byron. Papers. Special Collections, University of Victoria, Victoria, B.C.
Paynter, Peer. Papers. PABC.
Social Credit convention proceedings, New Westminster, B.C., April 26, 1952. PABC #3651.
Taylor, Malcolm G. *Health Insurance and Canadian Public Policy*. Montreal and London: McGill-Queen's University Press, 1978.

6 · AN EXPERIMENT IN DEMOCRACY

Chetwynd, R., and N. Burris. *Heifer Dust Inn*. Lillooet, B.C.: Lillooet Publishers Ltd., 1941.
Edmonton *Journal*, 1952–1953.
Keate, Stuart. "Political Hypnotism on the Coast." *Saturday Night*, February 18, 1956.
West Coast Advocate, 1952.

7 · DEFINITE INDICATION OF WRONGDOING

Baptie, Sue. *First Growth*. Vancouver: British Columbia Forest Products, 1975.
Bernsohn, Ken. *Cutting Up the North*. North Vancouver: Hancock House, 1981.
Brooks, Jack. "The Sommers Affair." *Vancouver Sun*, November 6, 1971.
Butler Report and accompanying letter of transmittal. APP.
Collins, Doug. "The Sommers Affair: Our Very Own Watergate." Victoria *Times*, December 7, 1976.
Gibson, Gordon. *Bull of the Woods*. Vancouver: Douglas & McIntyre, 1980.
Lord Commission. "Report of Inquiry Pursuant to the 'Public Inquiries Act' into Allegations of Impropriety in Connection with the Issuance of Forest Management Licences." March 12, 1955.

Moore, Vincent. *Angelo Branca: Gladiator of the Courts.* Vancouver: Douglas & McIntyre, 1981.
Turnbull, Elsie Grant. "Reminiscences." 1952. PABC.

8 · THE RISE OF BRITISH COLUMBIA

Bagnell, Kenneth. "Breathe a Prayer Fella, It's the Second Coming of Flyin' Phil." *Globe Magazine*, July 25, 1970.
Fullerton, D. H. *The Bond Market in Canada.* Toronto: Carswell, 1962.
Holt, Simma. *Terror in the Name of God: The Story of the Sons of Freedom Doukhobors.* Toronto: McClelland & Stewart, 1964.
Keate, Stuart. *Paper Boy.* Toronto: Clarke Irwin & Co., 1980.
Woodcock, George, and Ivan Avakumovic. *The Doukhobors.* Toronto: Oxford, University Press, 1968.

9 · THE POLITICS OF POWER

Author's correspondence with Senators J. Flynn, D. A. Lang, and H. de M. Molson, January 1979. APP.
Bohrs, Glenn. "When Dreams Were All of Wenner-Gren." *Vancouver Sun*, August 26, 1977.
Canada. Departments of External Affairs and Northern Affairs and National Resources. *The Columbia River Treaty, Protocol and Related Documents*, February 1964.
Canada. Senate. *Proceedings of the Standing Committee on Banking and Commerce*, July 22, 1964.
Fotheringham, Allan. "Has It Come to This Davie?" *Maclean's*, March 1, 1982.
Johansen, D. O., and C. M. Gates. *Empire of the Columbia.* New York: Harper & Row, 1967.
Keenleyside, Hugh L. *On the Bridge of Time.* Toronto: McClelland & Stewart, 1982.
Krutilla, John V. *The Columbia River Treaty: The Economics of an International River Basin Development.* Baltimore: Johns Hopkins University Press, 1967.
LeMarquand, David G. *International Rivers: The Politics of Co-operation.* Vancouver: UBC Westwater, 1977.
Newman, Peter C. *Renegade in Power: The Diefenbaker Years.* Toronto: McClelland & Stewart, 1963.
Stursberg, Peter. *Lester Pearson and the American Dilemma.* Toronto: Doubleday Canada, 1980.

10 · THE POWER OF POLITICS

Burns, R. M. "British Columbia: Perceptions of a Split Personality." In *Must Canada Fail?* edited by Richard Simeon. Montreal: McGill-Queen's University Press, 1977.
Fotheringham, Allan. "Never Mind Who's Going to Lead B.C. Who's Going to Make It Laugh?" *Maclean's*, December 1, 1975.

Greer, David M. "Redistribution of Seats in the British Columbia Legislature, 1952–1978." *B.C. Studies* 38 (Summer 1978).
Newman, Peter C. *The Distemper of Our Times*. Toronto: McClelland & Stewart, 1968.
Scott, A. D. "Introduction: Notes on a Western Viewpoint." *B.C. Studies* 13 (Spring 1972).
Stein, Michael B. *The Dynamics of Right-Wing Protest: A Political Analysis of Social Credit in Quebec*. Toronto: University of Toronto Press, 1973.

11 · THE GOOD LIFE

Alderman, Tom. "The Mysterious Charmer Called 'Wacky'." *The Canadian Magazine*, October 25, 1969.
British Columbia. Opening Statement of the Province of British Columbia to the Constitutional Conference, Ottawa, February 10–12, 1969.
Brown, Brian A. *The New Confederation*. Saanichton, B.C.: Hancock House, 1977.
Galbraith, Gordon S. "British Columbia." In *The Provincial Political Systems*, edited by D. J. Bellamy et al. Toronto: Methuen Publications, 1976.
Gwyn, Richard. *The Northern Magus*. Toronto: McClelland & Stewart, 1980.
McLean, Bruce. *A Union amongst Government Employees*. Vancouver: B.C. Government Employees Union, 1979.
Robin, Martin. "The Social Basis of Party Politics in British Columbia." *Queen's Quarterly* 72 (1966).
Toronto *Telegram* Canada 70 Team. *British Columbia: The Great Divide*. Toronto: McClelland & Stewart, 1969.

12 · THAT GOOD NIGHT

Blake, Donald E., et al. "Sources of Change in the B.C. Party System." *B.C. Studies* 50 (Summer 1981).
Cairns, Alan C. Review of *The 1200 Days: A Shattered Dream*, by Lorne J. Kavic and Garry Brian Nixon; and *Son of Socred*, by Stan Persky. *B.C. Studies* 49 (Spring 1981).
Kavic, Lorne J., and Gary Brian Nixon. *The 1200 Days: A Shatterd Dream. Dave Barrett and the NDP in B.C., 1972–75*. Vancouver: Kaen Publishers, 1978.
Kristianson, G. L. "The Non-Partisan Approach to B.C. Politics: The Search for a Unity Party, 1972–1973." *B.C. Studies* 33 (Spring 1977).
Persky, Stan. *Son of Socred: Has Bill Bennett's Government Gotten B.C. Moving Again?* Vancouver: New Star Books, 1979.
Tennant, Paul. "The NDP Government of British Columbia: Unaided Politicians in an Unaided Cabinet." *Canadian Public Policy*, Autumn 1977.
Wilson, R. Jeremy. "Continuity Despite Change: Reform of the British Columbia Legislature." *The Parliamentarian* 62, no. 1 (January 1981).
Woodcock, George. "Playing to the People." *The Canadian*, January 8, 1977.

INDEX

Aberhart, William, 63, 109-12, 114, 115-16, 118, 119, 120
Adams, Theo, 93
Alberta Natural Gas, 385
Alberta Older Boys' Parliament, 27
Alberta Social Credit League, 149
Aluminum Company of Canada (Alcan), 133, 257
Anderson, David, 414
Angus, Henry, 367
Angus Commission, 367
Anscomb, Herb, 61, 69, 70, 73, 80, 84-101 passim, 140-41, 146, 148, 149, 151, 154, 158, 159, 160, 162
Argus Corporation, 216

Bank of B.C., 331
Bank of B.C., proposed provincial, 327-31, 346
Bank of Canada, 47-48
Bank of Nova Scotia, 315
Barker, Frank, 128
Barrett, David, 387, 400-401, 408, 411, 414, 415, 418, 419-20, 430, 438, 440, 441-42, 443, 444, 445, 449
Barron's, 309, 438
Bell-Irving, Henry, 451
Bennett, Andrew Havelock (father), 13-15, 20, 22-24, 37
Bennett, Annie Elizabeth May (née Richards) (wife), 32, 34, 42-43, 58-59, 81, 179, 334, 376, 448-49, 451
Bennett, Bernice (sister), 24
Bennett, Catherine Jane Foster (grandmother), 13
Bennett, Cora (sister), 16, 20, 24, 25
Bennett, John G. (grandfather), 13
Bennett (Tozer), Mary Anita (daughter), 35, 59, 60, 81, 359, 451
Bennett, Mary Emma (née Burns) (mother), 13-14, 16, 24-25
Bennett, Olivia (sister), 24, 25, 30
Bennett, R.B., 12, 46-47, 53
Bennett, Russell (brother), 16, 20, 24, 25, 429
Bennett, Russell James (R.J.) (son), 36, 60, 81, 179, 331, 359, 408, 426, 447, 451
Bennett, W.A.C.: birth, 12; education, 16, 28; religious influence, 16-18, 26-28; marriage, 34; elected MLA, 64; joins B.C. Social Credit League, 135; becomes leader of B.C. Social Credit League, 165; becomes premier, 174; defeat, 416; retirement, 384, 430; death, 451
Bennett, W.R. (Bill) (son), 43, 59, 81, 179, 294, 359, 408, 415, 426-27, 428, 429, 430, 431-32, 434, 435, 436, 437, 443, 444, 445, 446, 447, 449, 450, 451
Bennett Hardware, 39, 58, 82, 179, 273
Berger, Thomas, 362, 387, 388, 389, 390, 400
Bewley, Les, 86, 97
Black, Wesley, 144, 155, 174, 177, 211, 249, 356, 373, 374, 410, 417
Black Ball Line, 269, 270
Bonner, Robert, 97, 99, 167-68, 173, 174, 178, 180, 182, 186-93 passim, 203, 204, 218-53 passim, 264-65, 268, 272, 286, 299, 302, 304, 305-306, 307, 308, 317, 320, 322, 323, 326, 328, 342, 343, 347, 349, 354, 370-71, 374-75, 378, 383, 420, 428, 436-37, 445, 451
Bourassa, Robert, 396
Bracken, John, 84, 91, 92
Branca, Angelo, 246
Briggs, H. Lee, 281-82, 304, 308
B.C. Development Corporation, 413, 439
B.C. Electric Company, 290, 291, 293, 303, 304, 305, 308, 309, 312, 313, 320, 352
B.C. Energy Board, 282, 302, 310
B.C. Federation of Labour, 268, 293, 386-87, 408, 409
B.C. Ferry Corporation, 271-72, 346, 395
B.C. Forest Products Ltd., 216, 217, 220, 221, 231, 242, 246, 247, 248, 250
B.C. Free Enterprise Educational Fund, 364-65
B.C. Fruit Growers' Association, 82
B.C. Government Employees' Association, 181, 409
B.C. Hospital Insurance Service (BCHIS), 89-90, 95, 96-97, 100-101, 102, 126, 146, 157-60, 163-64, 183, 184, 206-207, 357
B.C. Hydro and Power Authority, 312, 317, 322, 346, 371, 407, 418, 445
B.C. Medical Services Plan, 357-58
B.C. Power Commission, 74, 77, 281, 282, 301, 304, 312
B.C. Power Corporation, 77, 303, 306, 308, 309, 317, 320
B.C. Railway, 418, 450
B.C. Teachers' Federation, 413
British Israelites, 119, 278
Brothers, Donald, 249-50, 374, 375
Brousson, D.M., 435
Brown, Bruce, 228
Brown, Buda, 318
Brown, Roy, 198
Browne-Clayton, Robert, 92, 93
Brownlee, John, 109
Bruhn, Rolf, 70, 73, 78
Bryan, Mel, 243-44
Bryson, Gerald, 304
Buck, Tim, 294
Budd, Clarence, 34, 379
Bull, Alfred, 232, 235, 242, 247
Bull, Capt. Cecil, 55, 63
Burns, Henry (grandfather), 13
Burns, Mary Spence Murray (grandmother), 13
Butler, W.J., 228
Butler Report, 228, 231-32, 237, 238, 241, 250
By-elections, federal: Yale, 1948, 90-91, 92
By-elections, provincial: Salmon Arm, 1942, 78; Revelstoke, 1943, 78; South Okanagan, 1948, 92; Esquimalt, 1951, 127-31; Similkameen, 1952, 187-88; Columbia, 1952, 187-88; Victoria, 1953, 204; Lillooet, 1955, 221-23; Vancouver-Centre, 1956, 227; Rossland-Trail, 1958, 249-50; Vancouver-Point Grey, 1962, 318; Columbia, 1963, 318; Cariboo, 1966, 371; South Okanagan, 1972, 430; North Vancouver-Capilano, 1974, 435; Oak Bay, 1978, 450

Calder, Frank, 161

INDEX · 477

Calona Wines Ltd., 44-45, 82
Campbell, Alex, 395
Campbell, Dan, 343, 382, 383, 404, 414, 417, 419, 425, 426, 427, 428, 432, 433, 434, 437, 445
Canadian Cellulose Company, 439
Canadian Labour Congress, 268
Canadian Pacific Railway (CPR), 270, 271, 272
Caouette, Réal, 336, 337, 338-39
Capozzi, Pasquale ("Cap"), 42, 44, 45, 64, 82
Capozzi, Herb, 370, 383, 405, 428, 432, 435, 446
Carnell, Stan, 243
Carson, Ernie, 73, 86, 99
Carson, Frank, 450
Carvell, Frank, 19
CCF News, 154
C.D. Schultz and Co., 242
Chambers, Edward John, 91
Chandos, Viscount, 289
Chant, W.N., 130, 150, 153, 268, 343, 374
Chantrill, Ralph, 289
Chetwynd, Ralph, 161, 174, 177
Church Young People's Movement, 28
Civil Defence Act (1958), 269
Clancey, Bill, 311-12, 314, 365-66, 367, 400, 412, 446
Clark, Joe, 320
Clarke, George, 19
Clyne, J.V., 361, 435
Coalition government, 65-71, 75, 77, 78, 80, 84-85, 87, 92, 93-95, 96, 100-102, 125-26, 130, 131, 140-42
Colpets, Dean, 29
Columbia-Peace power projects, 289, 302, 355, 372; Columbia River project, 285, 300, 302-303, 304, 312; Columbia River Treaty, 300, 301, 303, 304, 307, 310, 311-12, 316, 317, 321-27, 351, 449; Duncan Lake Dam, 372; Mica Creek Dam, 285, 449; Peace River project, 298, 322; Two River Policy, 289, 290, 297-98, 299-300, 304, 305, 306, 310, 317, 320, 325, 371; W.A.C. Bennett Dam, 372
Columbia River Treaty. *See* Columbia-Peace power projects
Connell, Rev. Robert, 56
Conservative Action Club, 97
Conservative Party, 46, 47
Conservative Party of B.C., 49-50, 53, 56, 61, 62, 63-64, 65, 69-70, 85-100 passim, 116, 141, 146, 148, 160-63, 195, 197, 200, 202, 203, 223, 234, 237, 250, 295, 315, 316, 321, 403, 411, 413, 416, 430, 434, 443, 444
Co-operative Commonwealth Federation (CCF), 51, 52, 56, 61, 62, 64, 65, 69, 77-78, 79, 80, 89, 90-91, 94-95, 116, 130, 131, 146, 149, 159, 160-63, 187, 188, 195, 197, 200, 201, 202, 203, 207, 223, 233, 237, 250, 266, 267, 268, 269, 271, 292-95, 308. *See also* New Democratic Party
Corbett, Irvine, 243, 244, 249, 251
Croll, David, 329, 330
Cromie, Don, 224
Cross, Gerald, 304
Cruikshank, George, 158
Cunningham, George T., 289
Curtis, Hugh, 429, 435, 437

Dawson, Isabel, 373, 410
Detwiller, Lloyd, 159, 160, 164
DeWolfe, John, 313-14, 388

Diefenbaker, John, 91, 178, 299, 300, 302, 304, 315, 316, 347, 350
Dornan, Hal, 362-63
Douglas, Maj. Clifford Hugh, 104-113 passim, 119, 183, 283
Douglas, Tommy C., 293, 369, 391
Doukhobors, 263-66
Dowding, Gordon, 408
Dryer, Victor, 247

Earl, Winnifred, 43, 81
Eisenhower, Dwight D., 302
Ekman, Dan, 304, 365, 366, 367, 379, 380, 407, 415
Election Act amendment (single transferable ballot) (1951), 88, 97, 126-27, 154, 160-61, 163, 202, 203, 204
Elections, federal general: 1935, 53, 114-15; 1945, 78; 1949, 95; 1957, 299, 334; 1958, 335; 1962, 315, 339; 1963, 316, 339
Elections, provincial general: Alberta, 135, 110-11, 114; 1940, 112; B.C., 1928, 49-50, 1933, 50, 51, 53; 1937, 55, 56, 116; 1941, 63-64, 65, 118; 1945, 79-80, 120; 1949, 93-95, 121-22; 1952, 148-49, 153-57, 160-63, 182-83; 1953, 200-203; 1956, 233-34, 235-37, 292; 1960, 291-95, 296; 1963, 318-21; 1966, 369-70; 1969, 388-90; 1972, 412-16, 417, 419; 1975, 443-45; Saskatchewan, 1944, 78; 1971, 336
Environment and Land Use Committee, 407
Evergreen Lumber Sales, 242
Evers, Ted, 25, 26, 33-34, 36, 38, 39, 40
Eversfield, Charles W., 224, 225, 229, 231, 247, 250
Eyres, L.H., 85

Farris, John, 80
Ferber, Charles, 304
Fielding, William Stevens, 19
Financial Post, 308
Finlayson, Deane, 200, 202, 203, 204, 234, 235, 237, 293, 412
Fisher, J.V., 184-85, 273, 283
Fleming, Donald, 300, 304, 312
Fleming, James Kidd, 19
Flynn, Jacques, 329
Forest management licences (FMLs), 215-33 passim, 245, 246, 247, 248, 250, 251
Foster, Walter, 19, 21
Francis, Rev. Harry, 156, 187
Fraser, Blair, 142
Freemasons, 44
Fulton, Davie, 91, 97, 300-301, 310, 312, 315, 316, 318, 319-20, 321

Gaglardi, Rev. Phil, 165, 171, 174, 177, 194, 208, 212, 249, 260-63, 268, 272, 274, 277, 279, 319, 321, 338, 343, 363, 373-74, 383, 403-405, 407, 410, 414, 417, 428, 432, 433
Gardom, Garde, 370, 437
Gargrave, Tony, 227
Garland, F.M., 83
George, Percy, 130, 131
Gibbs, Archie, 203
Gibson, Gordon, 210, 217-29 passim, 235, 253
Gibson, Gordon, Jr., 435
Gillis, R.J., 27, 37, 64
Ginter, Ben, 261
Gordon, Walter, 331
Gore, Bernard, 286, 287, 289

Grauer, Dal, 291, 304, 306
Gray, H. Wilson ("Wick"), 214, 223-24, 225, 231, 235, 238, 242, 246, 247-48
Gray, Arthur W., 69
Green, Howard, 84, 85, 90, 91
Gregory, George, 204, 227-28, 230, 238
Guardian, 418
Guest, Edgar A. *(It Couldn't Be Done)*, 21, 59
Gunderson, Einar, 29, 168-69, 174, 177-78, 182, 185, 186, 187-88, 189, 193, 195, 203-204, 209, 216, 287, 288, 289, 318, 328, 329, 364-65, 367, 400

Hansell, Rev. Ernest, 144, 145, 150, 151, 152, 154, 156, 164
Harding, Randolph, 188, 200, 228, 250, 274, 308, 341
Harris, Hugh, 431
Hart, John, 67-78 passim, 84, 86, 87, 88, 101
Hart Formula, 78-79, 94
Hazen, John Douglas, 19
Hean, Arnold, 434
Hepburn, Mitchell F., 63
Hodges, Nancy, 192
Howe, C.D., 347
Hyndman, Peter, 437

Insurance Corporation of B.C. (ICBC), 439, 444
International Joint Commission (IJC), 285, 297, 298, 303
International Rivers Improvement Act (1955), 286
Irwin, Thomas, 165, 186, 191, 218

James Lovick and Associates, 365
Jamieson, Don, 347
Johnson, Byron ("Boss"), 89, 93, 94, 101, 133, 140, 141, 145, 146, 148, 159, 160, 162, 163, 167, 171
Johnson, Rev. Hewlett, 111
Johnson, Lyndon B., 323, 324
Jones, George E.P., 362
Jones, Owen, 91, 93
Jordan, Pat, 373, 410
Jukes, Maj. A.H., 120-21

Kaiser Corporation, 285
Keate, Stuart, 208, 224, 229, 288
Keenleyside, Hugh, 282, 322, 323
Kelln, Martin, 336
Kelowna Charter, 413
Kelowna *Courier*, 83
Kenmuir, Cam, 365, 366-67, 400, 415
Kennedy, Gilbert, 231, 242
Kennedy, John F., 310, 311, 312, 316
Kennedy, Orvis, 144, 145, 152
Kenney, E.T., 195, 200
Keynes, John Maynard, 106
Kiernan, Kenneth, 161, 174, 176, 191, 192, 228, 249, 307, 374, 387, 433
King, Lew, 201
King, Mackenzie, 31, 46, 67, 80, 88
Koerner, Henry, 371
Kripps, Agnes, 344

Labour Relations Act (1954), 267
Labour Relations Act amendment (1961), 360-61
Laing, Arthur, 200, 201-202, 203, 221, 234, 235, 237
Land Commission Act (1973), 439

Lang, D.A., 329
Leacock, Stephen, 111, 259
Leckie, David, 39
Leckie, Robin, 412
Lesage, Jean, 351
Lett, Sherwood, 317, 320
Lévesque, René, 352
Liberal Party, 50, 55, 56, 63-64, 69, 89, 90-91, 94-95, 96, 116, 148, 159, 160-63, 187, 195, 197, 200, 203, 219, 221, 223, 229, 234, 237, 250, 252, 295, 321, 369, 370, 390, 414, 416, 434, 443, 444
Liquor Act (1953), 206
Liquor Act amendment (1971), 402-403, 420-21
Loffmark, Ralph, 351, 374, 383, 417, 432
London *Sunday Telegraph*, 309
Lord, Arthur, 219, 220
Lord Commission, 219, 220, 224, 225, 250
Lougheed, Peter, 403, 413
Low, Solon, 121, 137, 150, 334, 337
Luce, Charles, 322

MacAlpine, A.F., 289
McCarthy, Grace, 373, 393, 405, 410, 417, 425, 426, 427, 428, 433, 437, 445, 451
McClelland, Bob, 433
McCutcheon, Wallace, 216
MacDonald, K.C., 69
MacDonald, R.C., 85, 141
McGeer, Patrick, 318, 366, 370, 388, 414, 435, 437
McInnes, Dermott, 26
McKeen, S.S., 289
MacLean, H.A., 231
McMahon, Frank, 294
MacMillan Bloedel Ltd., 361, 375
McNaughton, Gen. A.G.L., 298
McTaggart, Andrew, 289, 290-91, 304
Magnuson, Warren, 310, 311
Mainwaring, W.C., 289
Maitland, R.L. ("Pat"), 61, 62, 65-76 passim, 84
Majority Movement for Freedom and Private Enterprise, 434-38
Manning, E.C., 109-110, 112, 137, 145, 150, 152, 156, 160, 186, 189, 336, 337
Mansfield, Mike, 310
Marden, Orison Swett *(Pushing to the Front)*, 28-29, 102
Marshall, Don, 403
Marshall-Wells Ltd., 24, 25-26, 178
Martin, Eric, 120, 121, 127, 132, 134, 138, 147, 151, 152, 153, 162, 165, 167, 174, 176, 183, 211, 237, 249, 274, 357, 373, 374
Martin, Paul, 317, 322, 323, 326, 327, 330, 347
Mediation Commission Act (1968), 386-87, 410
Meighen, Arthur, 30, 31
Mineral Royalties Act (1974), 439
Mitchell, Frank, 130, 131
Mitchell, Howard T., 308
Molson, Hartland de M., 329
Mulholland, Ellen, 30
Munro, Hector, 246
Murphy, William, 289
Murray, W.H., 401
Mylrea, Katherine, 379-80, 425

National Energy Board, 282
Nemetz, Nathan, 386
New Democratic Party (NDP), 318, 319, 321, 327, 336, 339, 358, 360, 369, 370, 386, 387, 388, 390,

400, 408, 411, 414-16, 418, 422, 425, 429, 430, 438-41, 442-43, 444. *See also* Co-operative Commonwealth Federation
Newton, Orr, 187, 292, 318
Nicholson, John, 408, 418
Nimsick, Leo, 124
Norris, Tom, 54-55, 86, 99
Northwest Digest, 127

Ocean Falls Corporation, 439
Orchard, C.D., 216, 219, 220

Pacific Coast Services Ltd., 214, 231, 242
Pacific Great Eastern (PGE) railway, 74, 97, 177, 189, 208-209, 236, 280, 284, 288, 346, 385
Pacific Northern Railway, 298
Paris *Le Monde*, 418
Patterson, F.P., 53, 61
Pattullo, Thomas Dufferin, 51-53, 56-58, 61-63, 66-68, 71-72, 80, 113, 114, 116, 189
Paynter, Peer, 116, 117, 120, 121, 122, 135, 136-37, 144, 153, 160, 165, 183
Peabody, Capt. Alexander, 270, 271
Peace River Power Development Company, 289, 290, 291, 304, 306, 307
Peace River project. *See* Columbia-Peace power projects
Pearkes, Maj.-Gen. George, 91, 306
Pearson, George, 67, 69
Pearson, Lester B., 316-17, 323, 324, 348-49
Perdue, John, 183
Perrault, Ray, 293, 313, 318, 366, 368, 369, 388
Perry, Harry, 69, 72, 74, 75, 76, 80
Peterson, Leslie, 227, 328, 338, 360-62, 374, 375, 383, 384, 397, 404, 408-409, 410, 417, 425, 426, 428, 432
Portland Oregonian, 308-309
Post-War Rehabilitation Council, 72-73, 74, 76, 102, 303
Pound, Ezra, 106
Power Development Act (1961), 306, 307, 308, 309
Price, Bert, 162
Progressive Conservative Party. *See* Conservative Party
Provincial Alliance of Businessmen, 403
Public Schools Act amendment. *See* Rolston Formula
Public Schools Construction Act (1954), 280
Public Service Labour Relations Act (1974), 439

Ralliement des Créditistes, 339
Rathie, Bill, 354
Reagan, Ronald, 399
Redistribution bill (1966), 367, 368
Reid, J.A., 165, 364
Renaud, Joe, 33, 35, 37
Richards, Percy, 78, 87, 172
Richter, Frank, 374, 375, 410, 426, 434
Roberts Bank coal port, 385, 392
Robertson, Mrs., 30
Robertson, A. Bruce, 289
Robertson, Foster & Smith's, 20
Robin, Martin, 119
Robinson, Donald, 222, 223
Rolston, Tilly, 75, 86, 99, 125, 129, 130, 146, 149, 153, 156, 166, 171, 174, 176, 191, 192, 197, 203
Rolston Formula (1953), 196, 197, 200
Rose, William, 112
Rosellini, Albert D., 311

Rowell-Sirois Commission. *See* Royal Commission on Dominion-Provincial Relations
Royal Bank of Canada, 327
Royal Commission on Dominion-Provincial Relations (Rowell-Sirois Commission), 62-63

St. Laurent, Louis, 347
Schreyer, Edward, 451
Schultz, C.D., 231, 242
Seafarers International Union, 269
Shantz, Hugh, 243
Shantz, L.H., 152
Sharpe, Fred, 244
Shelford, Cyril, 133-34, 153, 157, 243, 244, 251, 292, 375, 382, 410, 417, 419
Sherman, Paddy, 246
Shrum, Gordon, 282, 302, 322, 359-60, 372
Shrum Commission, 282, 306-307
Simon Fraser University, 359-60
Sinclair, Ian, 272
Skillings, Waldo, 99, 131, 135, 239-41, 252, 343, 374, 417, 419
Sloan, Gordon, 170, 173, 214, 216, 225, 242, 245
Sloan Commission, 214-15, 221, 225, 226, 242, 245
Smith, Brian, 450
Snowsell, Frank, 91
Social Credit Association of Canada, 120, 149; B.C. wing, 120, 121
Social Credit doctrine, 104-108, 139, 169
Social Credit Party, 334-35, 339
Social Credit Party of Alberta, 108-112, 116, 120, 123, 144, 149, 152, 189, 291-94, 334, 335, 338, 339
Social Credit Party of B.C., 121, 160, 182-83, 204-205, 207, 222, 223, 227, 237, 249-50, 253-54, 258, 259, 260, 263, 319, 320-21, 337-39, 356-57, 363, 369-70, 372-73, 389-90, 415-16, 422, 428-29, 432-33, 434, 437, 443-44, 445; B.C. Social Credit League, 103, 119, 121, 122-23, 127, 130-31, 132, 134, 138, 139, 143-44, 149-51, 155-57, 159, 160-63, 164-65, 182; B.C. Social Credit Union, 115; Douglas Social Credit Group, B.C. Section, 112-14, 122; Perfect Circle, 117-18; Social Credit League of B.C., 114-21 passim, 200-203, 204, 207, 363-64
Social Security and Municipal Aid Tax, 89
Sommers, Robert, 174, 177, 196, 212-52 passim, 263, 363
Sons of Freedom. *See* Doukhobors
South Okanagan Coalition Association, 79, 83, 92
Speare, William, 371
Stanfield, Robert, 426
Stevens, H.H., 332
Stirling, Grote, 49, 90
Stonehill, Harry S., 362-63
Strachan, Robert, 233-34, 237, 243, 244, 253, 262, 279, 293, 294, 303, 307, 313, 318, 327, 342, 343, 368, 369, 387, 401
Strid, Birger, 286, 287, 289
Sturdy, David, 224, 225, 226, 227, 229, 233, 234, 238, 241, 250
Swainson, Neil, 323

Tames, John, 27, 30
Taylor, E.P., 216
Tennant, Paul, 441
Thatcher, Ross, 335-36, 393
Thompson, Robert, 337, 338, 339

Timber Products Stabilization Act (1974), 439
Time magazine, 371
Tisdalle, John, 244
Tobacco Advertising Restraint Act (1971), 402–403, 420-21
Toll Highways and Bridges Authority, 193, 208, 271, 280, 288
Tolmie, Simon Fraser, 50
Torey, Gordon, 113
Torey, Henry, 112
Tozer, Tony, 40–41, 60
Trade Union Act (1959), 268, 269, 293
Trans-Canada Highway, 350–51
Treasury Board, 208, 275–77, 356, 373, 393, 418, 441
Tremblay, René, 363
Trudeau, Pierre Elliot, 337, 391, 392, 394, 395, 396, 397, 446
Trusswell, H.A., 45, 47–48, 54, 55, 56, 86, 93, 99
Tunis, Lord Alexander of, 289
Turnbull, Douglas, 100, 213
Turner, Arthur, 192, 197
Turner, John, 384
Tutte, William, 112
Tuxis movement, 26, 27
Tweedsmuir, Lord, 289
Two River Policy. *See* Columbia-Peace power projects

Udall, Stewart, 312
United Farmers of Alberta (UFA), 108, 110
United Progressive Party, 75–76, 77, 79, 127
University Act (1963), 319
Uphill, Tom, 64, 72, 155, 161, 162, 170, 172, 199, 202, 237, 295, 343

Vancouver *Province*, 78, 83, 88, 114, 158, 160, 195, 219, 293, 310, 313, 314, 363, 412, 413
Vancouver Sun, 76, 100, 114, 146, 147, 159, 219, 237, 262, 271, 408
Vander Zalm, Bill, 437
Victoria Charter, 395, 396
Victoria *Colonist*, 114, 129, 136, 142

Victoria *Times*, 88, 115, 136, 173, 187, 207, 229, 288

Waffle Manifesto, 414
Walker, Russell, 80, 85, 98
Wallace, Clarence, 170, 171, 172, 173, 191, 197
Wallace, Scott, 403, 435, 450
Warren, Derril, 403, 412, 413, 416, 427, 429, 430–31, 432
Webster, Arnold, 200, 201, 221, 227, 233
Wenman, Robert, 370, 383, 406
Wenner-Gren, Axel, 286, 287–88, 297
Wenner-Gren B.C. Development Company, 287, 288, 298
Westcoast Transmission Company, 385
Westlock Hardware and Furniture, 33, 34, 35, 37
Westwood, Earle, 374
Whist, Jarl, 434
Wicks, Lyle, 118, 121, 124, 127, 130, 137, 145, 149, 150, 151, 153, 155, 165, 170, 174, 176, 266, 295, 374
Williams, Allan, 435, 437
Williams, Bob, 408, 440, 449
Williamson, Al, 362, 363
Williston, Ray, 201, 228, 230, 251, 287, 299, 300–302, 307, 314, 322, 323, 357, 374, 383, 410, 414, 417, 419, 432, 451
Wilson, J.O., 235, 245, 247, 248
Winch, Harold, 61, 62, 65, 66, 68–69, 73, 79, 124, 133, 146, 154, 160, 161, 170, 194–200 passim
Wing, Peter, 397
Wismer, Gordon, 85, 89, 94, 95, 103, 159, 167, 219, 239
Woodcock, George, 449
Woodward, W.C., 189–90
Worley, Ron, 135, 138, 142, 160, 164, 171, 211, 270, 379, 425
Wright, Percy, 204
Wurtele, Comdr. Alfred, 128–29, 130, 131

Yale Conservatives, 92
Yellowhead Highway, 397
Young Progressive Conservatives, 86

www.ingramcontent.com/pod-product-compliance
Lightning Source LLC
Chambersburg PA
CBHW032126010526
44111CB00033B/118